EXPLORING MUSIC

fifth edition

EXPLORING MUSIC

Robert Hickok
University of California-Irvine

WCB Brown &
Benchmark
PUBLISHERS

Madison, Wisconsin • Dubuque, Iowa • Indianapolis, Indiana
Melbourne, Australia • Oxford, England

Book Team

Editor *Kathleen Nietzke*
Developmental Editor *Deborah D. Reinbold*
Production Editor *Kennie Harris*
Designer *Kristyn A. Kalnes*
Art Editor *Kathleen M. Huinker*
Permissions Editor *Vicki Krug*

Brown &
Benchmark

A Division of Wm. C. Brown Communications, Inc.

Vice President and General Manager *Thomas E. Doran*
Editor in Chief *Edgar J. Laube*
Executive Managing Editor *Ed Bartell*
National Sales Manager *Eric Ziegler*
Director of CourseResource/Developmental Services
  Kathy Law Laube
Director of CourseSystems *Chris Rogers*
Director of Marketing *Sue Simon*

Director of Production *Vickie Putman Caughron*
Marketing Manager *Carla J. Aspelmeier*
Advertising Manager *Jodi Rymer*
Manager of Visuals and Design *Faye M. Schilling*
Design Manager *Jac Tilton*
Art Manager *Janice Roerig*
Publishing Services Manager *Karen J. Slaght*
Permissions/Records Manager *Connie Allendorf*

Wm. C. Brown Communications, Inc.

Chairman Emeritus *Wm. C. Brown*
Chairman and Chief Executive Officer *Mark C. Falb*
President and Chief Operating Officer *G. Franklin Lewis*
Corporate Vice President, President of WCB Manufacturing *Roger Meyer*

Consulting Editor *Frederick Westphal*

Photo Editor *Kathy Husemann*

The credits section for this book begins on page 549 and is considered an extension of the copyright page.

Library of Congress Catalog Card Number: 91-76901

ISBN 0-697-12534-3

Printed in the United States of America by Wm. C. Brown Communications, Inc., 2460 Kerper Boulevard, Dubuque, IA 52001

10 9 8 7 6 5 4 3 2 1

For Roanne, Paul, and Laura

CONTENTS

Part 5
Music of the Classical Era

PRELUDE III THE CLASSICAL ERA: REASON AND REVOLUTION 164

9
MOZART AND HAYDN

10
CLASSICAL VOCAL MUSIC

11
THE MUSIC OF BEETHOVEN

Part 6
Music of the Romantic Era

PRELUDE IV THE ARTS OF THE ROMANTIC ERA 242

Part 7
Music of the Early
Twentieth Century

PRELUDE V THE GENESIS
OF THE MODERN ERA 364

17

BRIDGING THE GAP
BETWEEN CENTURIES

18

TOWARD THE
MODERN PERIOD

19

SERIALISM

Part 10
Pop Culture in
American Music

22

JAZZ AND ROCK

RECORDINGS

The following recordings are on the CD and cassette packages that are available from the publisher. Page numbers indicate where text discussions of the pieces may be found.

CD 1

Cassette 1/A

Britten: *Young Person's Guide to the Orchestra,* pp. 31, 45
Contractus: "Salve Regina" (chant), pp. 24, 90
De Machaut: *Nostre Dame Mass, Agnus Dei,* p. 94
Josquin: *Ave Maria Gratia Plena,* pp. 25, 47, 96
Palestrina: *Missa Salve Regina,* Kyrie, p. 98
Morley: *Now Is the Month of Maying,* p. 100
Jannequin: *Chant des oiseaux,* p. 101

Cassette 1/B

Praetorius: *Terpsichore,* Passameze and Galliarde, p. 103
Monteverdi, *La favola d'Orfeo,* p. 119
Handel: *Messiah* ("Comfort Ye," "Ev'ry Valley," "And the Glory of the Lord"), pp. 13, 14, 26, 128
Bach: Cantata no. 4, *Christ lag in Todesbanden* (verses 1, 5, & 7), p. 135
Bach: Fugue in G Minor ("The Little"), pp. 25, 43, 148

CD 2

Cassette 2/A

Bach: Brandenburg Concerto no. 5, I, pp. 42, 152 (Listening Guide, p. 158)
Vivaldi: *The Four Seasons: Spring,* I, p. 154 (Listening Guide, p. 159)
Mozart: Symphony no. 40 in G Minor, I & III, pp. 26, 45, 178, 182 (Listening Guide, p. 196)
Mozart: Piano Concerto no. 27 in B-flat Major, II, p. 193 (Listening Guide, p. 199)

Cassette 2/B

Haydn: *Lord Nelson Mass (Gloria, Qui Tollis, Quoniam Tu Solus),* pp. 47, 202
Haydn: String Quartet, op. 33, no. 3, in C Major ("The Bird"), IV, pp. 45, 190 (Listening Guide, p. 198)
Beethoven: Symphony no. 5 in C Minor, op. 67, I & III, p. 224 (Listening Guide, p. 235)
Beethoven, Piano Sonata no. 23 in F Minor, op. 57 ("Appassionata"), pp. 42, 231 (Listening Guide, p. 238)

CD 3

Cassette 3/A

Mozart: *The Marriage of Figaro,* excerpt from Act III, p. 208
Schubert: "Erlkönig," pp. 30, 256
Chopin: Ballade no. 1 in G Minor, op. 23, p. 264 (Listening Guide, p. 266)
Mendelssohn: Violin Concerto in E Minor, op. 64, III, p. 281 (Listening Guide, p. 290)

Cassette 3/B

Brahms: Symphony no. 2 in D Major, I, p. 272 (Listening Guide, p. 288)
Berlioz: *Symphonie fantastique,* IV, pp. 45, 296 (Listening Guide, p. 304)
Liszt: *Les Préludes,* p. 300 (Listening Guide, p. 305)

CD 4

Cassette 4/A

Tchaikovsky: *Romeo and Juliet* (fantasy overture), p. 286 (Listening Guide, p. 291)
Mussorgsky: *Boris Godunov,* Coronation Scene, p. 311
Dvořák: Symphony no. 9 in E Minor ("From the New World"), IV, p. 322 (Listening Guide, p. 326)

PREFACE

The goal of *Exploring Music,* fifth edition, is to help the student acquire informed and sensitive listening skills that promote the development of a curiosity about, an enthusiasm for, and an enjoyment of many types and styles of music. In its organization, its contents, and its supplemental materials, the fifth edition is calculated to enhance the pursuit of this goal.

Exploring Music is intended for introductory music literature courses at the college level. The book is structured to accommodate a variety of course lengths. It affords ample flexibility to allow instructors teaching a semester, a one-quarter, or a two-quarter course to use the book selectively to fit the length of time at her or his disposal.

ORGANIZATION

Part 1 presents the fundamental elements of music, along with appropriate vocabulary, in three concise chapters. Musical examples and recorded excerpts from works to be covered in more detail later in the text are used to illustrate concepts. Part 1 concludes with a chapter on musical instruments, including the human voice, and outlines combinations of instruments and voices in small and large musical ensembles.

Part 2 provides an introduction to the music of non-Western cultures, offering the student a broad perspective before moving on to an examination of Western music in the remainder of the book. Using the foundation put forth in part 1, parts 3 through 9 explore in chronological order the major stylistic periods of music history from the Middle Ages through the twentieth century, concluding with part 10, which focuses on jazz and rock music.

To provide a general cultural context for stylistic musical periods, seven prelude sections, accompanied by full-color as well as black-and-white photographs, provide introductory historical, philosophical, and artistic background. In these sections, particular emphasis is given to the visual arts—painting, sculpture, and architecture.

LISTENING

The major emphasis of this text and the course of study it presents is on listening to music. Its chief objective is the development of sensitive and perceptive listening. To this end the fifth edition includes as an important tool succinct listening guides relating to the works that receive major coverage in the text as well as a significantly expanded selection of recordings that supplement the book. The listening guides, located at the end of the chapters, are designed to clarify the form of the piece and to actively involve the student, step by step, in the musical processes taking place. They are not intended as complete descriptions of the works to which they relate; rather, they pinpoint "cues"—easily heard points to help the student follow the musical process. The best way to use these guides is to review the text description of the music before listening, then listen several times while following the listening guide, and finally listen to the music alone, with the greater sensitivity and awareness the text description and the listening guide have helped to foster. Locations of the pieces on the accompanying CDs and cassette tapes are given with each listening guide. CD track numbers are enclosed in squares; CD index points are enclosed in ovals.

THE FIFTH EDITION

This new edition of *Exploring Music* includes new material and expanded treatment of significant areas of music literature in the text itself and in its supplementary materials, principally the recordings.

The chapter on baroque instrumental music includes a new section on Antonio Vivaldi, with emphasis on *The Four Seasons*. The field of opera has been expanded to cover Monteverdi's *La favola d'Orfeo*, Verdi's *La Traviata*, and Alban Berg's *Wozzeck*. The chapters in part 7, devoted to music of the early twentieth century, include new sections on Schoenberg's *A Survivor from Warsaw*, Bartók's *Music for Strings, Percussion, and Celesta*, and Anton von Webern's *Symphonie*, op. 21, in addition to Stravinsky's *The Rite of Spring* and Britten's *Serenade for Tenor, Horn, and Strings*, opus 31. An enlarged section on music by African-American composers features William Grant Still's *Afro-American Symphony*. The influence of jazz on concert music is treated via George Gershwin's *Rhapsody in Blue*, and the recognition of the contributions by women to musical literature, begun in the fourth edition of this text, is enriched by the inclusion of a major section on Ellen Taaffe Zwilich and her *Symphony No I*. Leonard Bernstein's versatile capabilities as a composer are explored, with emphasis on a portion of his *Chichester Psalms*, and the final chapter on jazz and rock is thoroughly updated with substantial representation in the recordings. In addition to these changes, the fifth edition offers a more attractive visual presentation by integrating full-color photos throughout the text.

STUDY AIDS

The fifth edition of *Exploring Music* maintains several features that both instructors and students have found particularly valuable. Musical terms are printed in boldface and defined when they first appear; they are also listed at the close of each chapter as well as in the comprehensive glossary at the end of the text. Also included at the end of each chapter is a list of suggested listening pieces intended to enrich and broaden the student's listening experience.

Summaries at the end of each chapter offer a concise review of the material covered. Many students like to read the summary before beginning the chapter in order to get a quick overview of its major points.

As in previous editions, this new edition includes the texts of almost all the vocal works discussed in the book to enable the student to follow the music by paying attention to the words. For works in foreign languages, both the original and English translations are given.

In addition to the glossary, an updated list of suggested readings is included at the back of the book.

SUPPLEMENTS

Three supplements have been prepared for use with the fifth edition. The increased number of recordings prepared by Sony Music Special Products Division contain many of the pieces discussed in the text. The locations of these pieces on the accompanying CDs and cassette tapes are noted in the margins alongside the text to which they apply. These recordings provide the basic listening experiences, which may be expanded and enriched by the additional listening suggested at the end of each chapter.

The *Instructor's Manual* includes detailed charts showing how the text can be adapted to a one-quarter and a one-semester course. The *Student Workbook and Listening Guide* offers exercises aimed at improving listening skills and questions that test mastery of text material.

ACKNOWLEDGMENTS

It is my happy privilege to acknowledge and express my thanks for the advice and help extended to me in the process of preparing the fifth edition of *Exploring Music.*

Dr. Michael Saffle provided Prelude VII introducing music of the late twentieth century. R. John Specht of Queensborough Community College prepared the listening guides and provided valuable advice on many aspects of this edition. The work of the staff of Brown & Benchmark, under the leadership of Kathleen Nietzke and Deborah Reinbold, was (as usual) of a high professional standard from beginning to end in matters great and small.

Great thanks are due to my research assistant, Danny Thom, and to Leigh Wood-Ingram for their contributions to this new edition.

I am also grateful for the thoughtful criticisms and suggestions of the following reviewers who read all or portions of the manuscript: Jane P. Ambrose, University of Vermont; Howard Brahmstedt, Tennessee Technological University; Ricard C. Cole, Virginia Polytechnic Institute and State University; Janet E. Griffith, University of Wyoming; Harold E. Griswold, Towson State University; William Hinkle, Seminole Community College; Thomas King, Austin Peay State University; Jerome Laszloffy, University of Connecticut; William L. Kellogg, University of Southern Colorado; Roy V. Magers, Winthrop College; DeWayne Pigg, Middle Tennessee State University; and Johannes Tall, University of Michigan.

Robert Hickok
Irvine, California

EXPLORING MUSIC

Fundamentals of Music

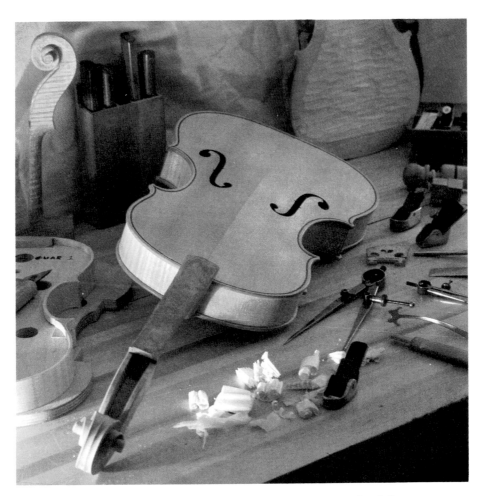

© 1992, Michael Krasowitz, FPG International Corp.

MUSICAL SOUND

We are a people surrounded by sounds. The roar of airplanes, the rumble of automobiles, the blare of horns, the screech of sirens, and many other types of sounds constitute an ever-present aspect of the day-to-day environment in which most of us live. In addition to these random sounds, the average American is subjected to a constant flow of music. We experience music almost continuously—the phonograph as we chat, the radio while driving, Muzak in the supermarket, the restaurant, and place of employment. What student lounge is without music? Indeed, from playpen to funeral parlor, we are bombarded by the sounds of music. Although we hear these sounds, we often hear them only as a background against which more immediate activity takes place. Most of us do not consciously respond to such music; it is merely part of the atmosphere. To be fully alive to music, we must learn to listen with curiosity and care, with attention to the flow of musical sound. An important aid in developing skill at this kind of listening is some understanding of the nature of the materials out of which music is made.

Music is built from particular elements and described by a particular vocabulary. In these first chapters, then, we will introduce the elements of music and establish the vocabulary used to discuss them.

Musical sound is not like the random noise we experience. Rather, it is highly organized and displays four general characteristics—**pitch,** its highness or lowness; **duration,** its longness or shortness; **volume,** its loudness or softness; and **timbre,** its tone quality.

PITCH

A sound, any sound, is the result of vibrations set in motion by the activation of a sounding body—the slamming of a door, the ringing of a bell. In the case of a *musical* sound, the rate of vibrations is definite and steady, producing a **tone.** The precise pitch, the exact highness or lowness of the tone, is determined by the *frequency* of its vibration—the *faster* the frequency, the *higher* the pitch and, conversely, the *slower* the frequency, the *lower* the pitch.

For instance, if we pluck a string, it vibrates at a certain rate of frequency and produces a tone of a certain pitch. If we *shorten* the string, the tone it produces will be *higher;* if we *lengthen* the string, the pitch of the tone will be *lower.*

Other things, such as volume, duration, and timbre, being equal, two tones sound different because they have different pitches. The *distance* between two pitches is called an **interval.** Intervals can be small or large depending upon the pitches involved.

Example 1.1

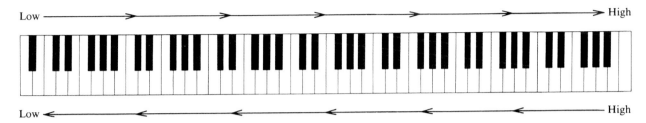

Each key of the piano represents a specific pitch that is sounded when the key is pressed. If you begin with any key and press successive keys to your *right,* each tone produced is slightly *higher* than the one before it—the interval between the two tones is small. If you skip a few keys, the interval between the two is larger. Beginning on any *white* key (such as key 1 in example 1.2) and moving upward (to your right) on the white keys, you will discover that the tone produced by the eighth key sounds very much like the tone produced by key number 1. These two tones are so much alike that the upper tone is heard as a higher *duplicate* of the lower tone and vice versa, and the tones are referred to by the same name (see pitch notation on pages 6–9). The interval formed by these two tones is called an **octave.** If we continue the process, starting with the eighth key, we come to the same result— another tone that sounds the same on a higher pitch level—an octave higher.

Example 1.2

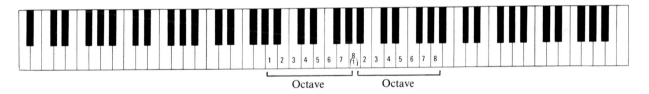

Each and every pitch has its upper and lower octave duplicates—a fact that makes the interval of the octave very important.

Returning to the piano keyboard, we find that *within* the octave there are other pitches represented by the black and white keys. The tones produced by the succession of white and black keys fills the octave with twelve different pitches, the thirteenth being an octave duplicate of the first.

The distance between each pair of tones in example 1.3 is the interval of the **half step (semi-tone),** the smallest interval used in most music in Western society. These twelve pitches and their upper and lower octave duplicates constitute the total pitch resource out of which composers select their materials and fashion them into melody and harmony, which we will examine in the next chapter.

Example 1.3

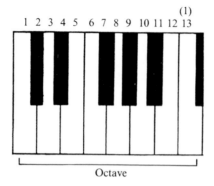

Octave

NOTATION OF PITCH

Example 1.4

Pitches are named using the first seven letters of the alphabet—ABCDEFG—this sequence being repeated over and over through upper and lower octaves. These letter names apply to the white keys of the piano as shown in example 1.4. (The key labeled **"middle C"** is located approximately in the middle of the keyboard as a point of reference.)

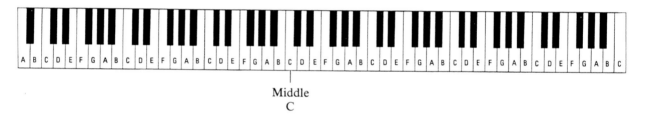

Middle
C

In musical **notation,** the pitch of a tone is indicated by the position of a symbol (○ or ♩ or ♪, for example) called a **note** on a graphlike structure called a **staff,** consisting of five lines and four spaces. Each line and each space represents a different pitch.

Example 1.5

The higher the position of the note on the staff, the higher the pitch of the tone:

Example 1.6

Higher

Lower

Pitches that are too high or too low to be written on the staff are notated by using **ledger lines** above or below the staff:

Example 1.7

The staff location of specific pitches is indicated by a **clef** sign placed at the beginning of the staff. The G clef or **treble clef** (♩) is used for higher pitches and designates the second line of the staff as the pitch "G."

Example 1.8

The F clef or **bass clef** (𝄢) is used for lower pitches and designates the fourth line as the pitch "F":

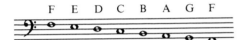

Example 1.9

The treble clef is used to notate music for the violin, flute, and other instruments that play in the higher pitch-ranges; the bass clef is used for instruments that play in lower ranges such as the violoncello and bassoon.

For keyboard music, *both* clefs are used on what is called the **grand staff:**

Example 1.10

The notes written in the treble clef are usually played by the right hand, the notes in the bass clef by the left hand.

Example 1.11 shows notes on the grand staff correlated with the white keys of the piano:

Example 1.11

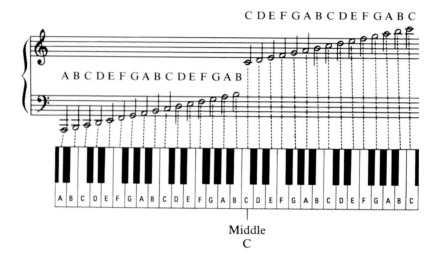

Pitches represented by the *black* keys of the piano are notated by the use of two symbols: the **sharp** (♯), which *raises* the pitch of the note to which it is applied, and the **flat** (♭), which *lowers* the pitch.

For instance, the black key between the white keys C and D is regarded as either a raised C (C♯) or a lowered D (D♭). C♯ and D♭, therefore, are two ways of designating the *same pitch:*

Example 1.12

The same is true of the other black keys and the pitches they represent: D sharp or E flat; F sharp or G flat; and A sharp or B flat (example 1.13).

Example 1.13

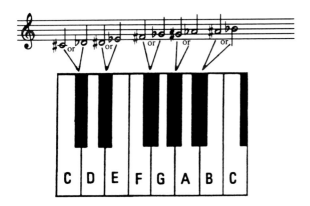

The symbol called a **natural** (♮) is employed to cancel the effect of a sharp or a flat.

DURATION

The element of *time* is extremely important in the art of music. The flow of music creates the illusion of the passage of time—a very special kind of time that exists on many levels, as we shall discover when we consider *rhythm* in the next chapter.

On its most fundamental level, musical time has to do with the relative longness or shortness of individual sounds.

NOTATION OF DURATION

The principle underlying duration and its notation is fairly simple. Time values are expressed in *relative* terms. A **whole note** (○) lasts twice as long as a **half note** (♩). A half note lasts twice as long as a **quarter note** (♩), which lasts twice as long as an **eighth note** (♪) and so on:

Example 1.14

1 whole note

2 half notes

4 quarter notes

8 eighth notes

16 sixteenth notes

Notice that eighth notes that look like quarter notes with single **flags** attached may be written separately (♪♪) or may be grouped together by a connecting **beam** (♫). The same is true of sixteenth notes (♬♬), which have two flags when written separately and are grouped by a double beam (♬). Further subdivision is used such as thirty-second (♪) and sixty-fourth (♪) notes.

So far we have considered the division of each successive "long" note by two: a whole note = two half notes; a half note = two quarter notes; and so on. Divisions by three are indicated by adding a "3" above the *shorter* notes, producing a **triplet:**

Example 1.15

The length of a note can be extended by the use of a **tie** (⌣)

Example 1.16

or by placing a **dot** (•) to the right of the note. The dot extends the note by half its original length.

Example 1.17

The duration of *silence* is just as important as the duration of sound and is indicated by the use of a symbol called a **rest:**

Example 1.18

Whole rest   Half rest   Quarter rest   Eighth rest   Sixteenth rest

These rests are equivalent to the note values discussed previously.

VOLUME (DYNAMICS)

Musical dynamics have to do with the relative degree of loudness or softness in the flow of music. Along with pitch and duration, the relative shades of volume (loudness and softness) are important in determining the character of music.

NOTATION OF VOLUME (DYNAMICS)

Written indication of the dynamic aspect of music is less precise than that relating to pitch and duration because there is no absolute standard for degrees of loudness and softness. The *performer* has a great deal of latitude in the interpretation and execution of dynamic indications provided by the composer.

These dynamic indications consist of a set of words and signs placed below or above the staff. By tradition, most dynamic instructions are indicated by the use of terms in Italian.

pianissimo (*pp*) very soft
piano (*p*) soft
mezzo piano (*mp*) moderately soft
mezzo forte (*mf*) moderately loud
forte (*f*) loud
fortissimo (*ff*) very loud

Intensified extremes of dynamic levels are indicated by *ppp* or *pppp* and *fff* or *ffff*.

To indicate *gradual* change from one dynamic level to another, the following signs and terms are used:

crescendo (cresc.)   ◁———————   gradually louder

decrescendo (decresc.)
diminuendo (dim.)   ———————▷   gradually softer

TIMBRE (TONE COLOR)

Each type of musical instrument has its own distinct kind of sound. A melody played on the oboe sounds different from the same melody played on the clarinet because the sound quality of the clarinet is clearly different from that of the oboe. As we mentioned earlier, the distinctive sound quality of an instrument is called tone color or **timbre**. The elements that contribute to the tone color of an instrument are various and include the nature of the material out of which the instrument is constructed and the method by which it is made to sound (such as a plucked instrument as opposed to one into which air is blown).

Instruments differ from each other in tone color on several levels. The most obvious difference is between families of instruments. As a group, brass instruments (trumpet, horn, trombone, and tuba) sound quite unlike the woodwinds (flute, oboe, clarinet, and bassoon), and both these instrument groups contrast sharply in sound with the string family (violin, viola, cello, and string bass). Within each instrument family there is a certain similarity of sound that distinguishes that family as a whole.

While the difference between the tone color of one instrument family and that of another is fairly obvious, there is a more subtle contrast in timbre among instruments in a single family. For instance, the flute and the oboe, both of which are woodwinds, sound quite distinct from each other; similarly, the violin and cello each sound unique. On a still more subtle level, a considerable variety of tone colors can be produced on a single instrument. For example, the flute can be manipulated to produce shades of tone color ranging from "bright" to "velvety" and from "piercing" to "warm."

Nineteenth-century composers were especially intrigued by the uses of tone color. It was during the Romantic era that color came to be regarded for the first time as an element as important as melody, harmony, and rhythm. Many modern composers share this view and continue to explore the expressive possibilities of tone color, using not only conventional instruments, but also electronic media and nonmusical sounds as well.

SUMMARY

In the preceding pages we described the qualities of musical sound—those properties that distinguish musical sounds from simple, random noises. Musical sounds have pitch, the quality of being high or low; they exist in durations of varying lengths; they can be produced at varying levels of intensity, or volume; and they are imbued with distinctive tone colors. The desired pitch, duration, and intensity of musical sound can be expressed, though not always with precision, in a system of written notation.

Thus far we have been dealing with the raw material of music, not music itself. Individual sounds achieve musical significance only when one tone relates to another and groups of tones relate to other groups, organized in the time flow they create. The next two chapters will consider musical relationships and musical organization.

NEW TERMS

pitch
duration
volume
timbre
   tone
   interval
   octave
   half step (semi-tone)
   middle C
notation of pitch
   note
   staff
   ledger lines
   clef (bass; treble)
   grand staff
   sharp
   flat
   natural
notation of duration
   whole note
   half note
   quarter note

eighth note
sixteenth note
flag
beam
triplet
tie
dot
whole rest
half rest
quarter rest
eighth rest
sixteenth rest
volume (dynamics)
   pianissimo
   piano
   mezzo piano
   mezzo forte
   forte
   fortissimo
   crescendo
   decrescendo (diminuendo)
timbre (tone color)

MUSICAL ELEMENTS

I n chapter 1 we concentrated upon the characteristics of musical sounds. This chapter deals with the various kinds of relationships *among* sounds and the resulting musical elements known as **melody, harmony, tonality,** and **rhythm.** These elements are the primary ingredients out of which music is fashioned.

MELODY

When we listen to music, we are usually drawn first to a melody. We tend to follow the melodic flow with the greatest interest and ease, and in general, it is the melody that lingers with us. When we think of a piece of music, we tend to recall the melody or melodies that represent the piece for us.

We can define a melodic line, or **melody**, as a series of pitches and time values that sound one after another. Melody gives music a sense of movement up and down through space as it moves forward in time. Different melodies follow different patterns of movement. For example, the melodic line in example 2.1 gives the impression of moving upward.

Example 2.1 Handel, *Messiah,* "Ev'ry Valley." Cassette 1/B, Track 3 CD 1, Track 11

On the other hand, a melody—even one with some upward skips—can give a sense of moving downward:

Example 2.2 Handel, *Messiah,* "And the Glory of the Lord." Cassette 1/B, Track 3 CD 1, Track 12

In comparison, the following melody seems anchored. Its movement is evenly distributed around a particular tone:

Example 2.3 Handel, *Messiah,* "And the Glory of the Lord."

for   the   mouth   of   the   Lord hath   spo - ken   it.

Melodic movement can be smooth and even, as the preceding examples show. It can also be jerky and angular, leaping over a wide span of pitches:

Example 2.4 Handel, *Messiah,* "Ev'ry Valley."

the   crook - ed straight,   the   crook - ed   straight and rough pla-ces   plain

A melody consists of two inseparable, interacting elements: a succession of *pitches* and a succession of *time values* (durations). The "highs and lows" of pitch and the "longs and shorts" of duration combine to give a melody its particular shape and form, its "personality."

The character of melody is an extremely important aspect of any piece of music. In a long piece of music some melodies assume greater importance than other melodies. Those that constitute central musical ideas are called **themes.** In the course of a musical composition, important themes may be stated and restated in many different forms. Later in this text we will see how themes are developed in a variety of musical works.

HARMONY

While a piece of music consisting of a single melodic line can be complete in and of itself (see Gregorian chant, pages 89 and 90), most Western music depends heavily on **harmony** to help give it structure and to enhance its expressiveness. We speak of melody as the horizontal aspect of music, because it consists of pitches sounding one after another, in a linear fashion. Harmony, on the other hand, involves the vertical aspect of music, the tones that sound together. A harmony is a composite sound made up of two or more tones of different pitch that sound simultaneously. The smallest harmonic unit is one consisting of two tones. A harmony of three or more tones is called a **chord.**

The tones that make up a chord are heard not only individually; they also blend together into a composite sound that has its own distinctive qualities.

Chords can appear in "solid" form (example 2.5) or in "broken" form, with the notes played in rapid succession (example 2.6).

Example 2.5

Example 2.6

A broken chord (example 2.6) is called an **arpeggio.**

As a musical element, harmony functions in a variety of ways. Harmonies are often used to support and enrich melodies. A particularly distinctive series of harmonies, or *harmonic progression,* often becomes an important element in its own right. In addition, the harmonic qualities of **consonance** and **dissonance** contribute to the energy and interest of a piece of music.

CONSONANCE AND DISSONANCE

An important quality of a given harmony is its degree of consonance or dissonance. A consonant harmony imparts a sense of stability, simplicity, and repose. In contrast, a dissonant harmony creates a feeling of complexity, instability, and the necessity for movement.

Dissonance is important in creating a feeling of tension in the musical flow. Without points of tension the music would quickly become boring and lifeless. Dissonance usually occurs as a transient tension in a harmonic progression. This tension is immediately relieved by the resolution of the dissonant harmony into a consonant harmony. Thus, the movement from dissonance to consonance contributes to the balance between movement and rest that makes music vital and coherent.

The general character of some pieces is consonant, even though some dissonance may be employed. Haydn's String Quartet in C, op. 33, no. 3 (cassette 2/B, track 2; CD 2, track 9) is a good example. Other works are predominantly dissonant, such as Schoenberg's *A Survivor from Warsaw,* op. 46 (cassette 5/B, track 3; CD 5, track 6). As we move through music history from century to century, we find that the relationship of consonance and dissonance begins to change, with a gradual increase in the importance or prevalence of dissonance as we approach the twentieth century. Indeed, much of the serious concert music written today is predominantly dissonant.

TONALITY (KEY)

One of the fundamental characteristics of Western music is its reliance on **tonality** as an organizing element. *Tonal music* is characterized by the presence of a central tone called the **tonic** and the chord built on that tone, called the **tonic chord.** The tonic chord acts as the musical center of gravity, a kind of "home base" in a piece of music. It is the point of rest from which the musical flow departs and to which it returns, creating a sense of convincing conclusion.

Although there are several ways of establishing a tonal center, the most familiar method is embodied in the **major-minor system** of scales.

A **scale** (sometimes called a *mode*) is a series of ascending or descending pitches in a certain pattern. What is called the **major scale** consists of eight notes filling the octave with the following pattern between notes:

whole step, whole step, half step, whole step, whole step, whole step, half step

as illustrated using only the white keys of the piano in example 2.7.

Example 2.7

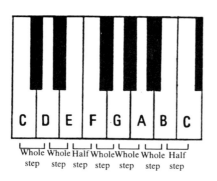

The C major scale begins and ends on the note C, its tonic. The tonic chord of a major scale is a *major chord.* A stretch of music written on the basis of this scale is said to be in the tonality, or **key,** of C major.

The major scale can be built on any one of the twelve pitches (white and black keys) using the fixed pattern of whole steps and half steps previously described.

The **minor scale** also consists of eight tones filling an octave but in a different arrangement of whole steps and half steps, producing a quality that is quite different from that of the major scale. The third tone in the minor scale is a *half step* rather than a whole step above the second tone, making the tonic chord a *minor chord* and imparting a distinctive character. The upper part of the minor scale assumes different forms depending upon the musical context.

Example 2.8 shows the C minor scale. It begins and ends on the note C, which is its tonic. The tonic chord of a minor scale is a *minor chord*. A section of music written on the basis of this scale is in the tonality, or key, of C minor. The minor scale can be constructed beginning with any one of the twelve tones contained in the octave.

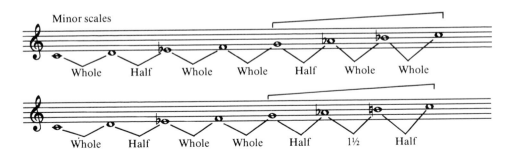

Example 2.8

Major and minor scales and the music constructed from them differ considerably in character, but they have in common the strong sense of tonality—a clearly felt tonal center. The tonic note and the chord built upon it are supported by the other tones and chords in the scale. Melodically, the seventh tone in the scale, called the **leading tone,** has a strong "pull" into the tonic: it *leads* to the tonic. If we play the scale of C major and stop on the seventh tone,

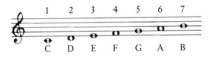

Example 2.9

the listener is left with an unsettling feeling of incompleteness. The ear expects to hear the tonic tone. Without it, no sense of finality is achieved. Once the C is played, however, "home base" has been reached and there is a convincing sense of completeness.

While the leading tone is the strongest *melodic* force supporting the tonic, the **dominant chord** (the chord built on the fifth note in the scale) performs the same function in the realm of *harmony*. The dominant chord demands *resolution* to the tonic chord in the same way the leading tone creates the need for the tonic tone. The dominant to tonic harmonic progression is an important force in most of the musical styles we will deal with later.

MODULATION

In addition to the relationships among tones and chords *within* a key, tonality also refers to the relationship *among keys*. A piece of music of any appreciable length seldom stays in one key. When we say that a piece of music is "in C major," we actually mean that the piece *begins* and *ends* in that key. Within the piece, different keys are introduced, thereby providing an important aspect of variety. The process of shifting from one key to another is known as **modulation.** The diagram below illustrates one of the most frequent modulations found in Western music, that growing out of the tonic-dominant relationship.

Section A	**Section B**	**Return of Section A**
C major (tonic key)	G major (key of the dominant)	C major

RHYTHM

All the elements discussed thus far come together and interact to create the sense of movement in time. Everyone has had the experience of being so caught up in an enjoyable activity that time seems to fly by. Similarly, the same amount of time spent doing something we dislike can seem interminable. Thus the way we experience time is on the basis of the events that occur during the course of an hour or a day. Without these events there would be less sense of the passage of time. Musical time is similar to this kind of "personal" time. It is perceived and experienced on the basis of musical events that occur. If we play a single tone over and over again for two minutes, it may seem as though a long period of time has elapsed. However, if we fill that two minutes with a cheerful and interesting melody, the same length of time will seem quite short. Although the length of time is the same by the clock, the *experiences* differ because the quality and character of the time are structured differently by the musical events that take place.

Like "personal" time, the passage of musical time is created by change. One tone leading to another in a melody, the progression from one harmony to another, the movement from one key to another—these and many other musical "incidents" work together to create the sense of musical time. The element that encompasses all aspects of musical time is called **rhythm.** Musical time consists of two different aspects: *regularity* and *diversity.*

BEAT

If you clap along while singing or listening to the familiar patriotic song "America the Beautiful," it is probable that you would clap as follows (X = clap):

Example 2.10

X X X X X X X X X X X X X X X X

Oh beau - ti-ful for spa - cious skies, for am - ber waves of grain,

In doing so, you are instinctively responding to the **beat** of the music. Beats are the most basic units of musical time. Instead of measuring the duration of individual tones in seconds or fractions of seconds by the clock, we use the beat as a measuring device. Each tone is judged as lasting one beat, several beats, or a fraction of a beat. Once we select the beat at the beginning of the composition, we become accustomed to it and expect that it will continue. The regular beat is fundamental to our response to music.

Against this background of regularly occurring beats or pulsations, notes of varying lengths make some beats more prominent than others.

METER

As you sing or listen to the beginning of "America the Beautiful," you will find that certain beats have more "weight" than others:

Example 2.11

Oh beau - ti - ful for spa - cious skies for am - ber waves of grain

Because of their longer duration and placement, the notes marked (X) stand out. The fact that these prominent notes happen at *regular intervals* creates a new kind of regular pulsation that groups the beats into equal units of four beats each.

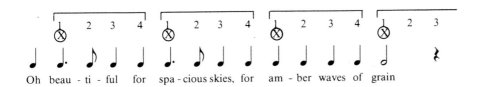

Example 2.12

Oh beau - ti - ful for spa - cious skies, for am - ber waves of grain

This grouping of beats into equal units is called **meter,** and the units themselves are called **measures.** There are several types of meter defined by the number of beats in the measure. The most common are:

Two beats to the measure (12,12) *duple meter* ("Yankee Doodle")
Four beats to the measure (1234,1234) *quadruple meter* ("America the Beautiful")
Three beats to the measure (123,123) *triple meter* ("The Star Spangled Banner")

More complicated meters with more beats to the measure are also used. Inherent in all meters is the fact that the first beat in the measure is stressed or **accented.**

Notation of Meter

Two notation devices are used to indicate meter: the **time signature** and the **bar line.**

The time signature consists of two numbers, one above the other. The top number indicates the number of beats per measure; the bottom number indicates the kind of note getting the beat. For instance:

3 ——— Three beats to the measure
4 ——— Quarter note (♩) equals one beat

4 ——— Four beats to the measure
2 ——— Half note (♩) equals one beat

6 ——— Six beats to the measure
8 ——— Eighth note (♪) equals one beat

The bar line is a vertical line drawn through the staff separating one measure from the next, as shown in example 2.13. (Note: The beat *before* the bar line is called the **up-beat;** the beat after the bar line is called the **down-beat.**)

Example 2.13

Oh   beau - ti - ful   for   spa-cious skies, for   am - ber waves of   grain

SYNCOPATION

Ordinarily the first beat of a measure is stressed or *accented*. A piece in triple meter, for example, has a *one*-two-three accentual character. When the accent falls somewhere other than on the first beat—on another beat or in between beats where it is *unexpected*—the rhythm is **syncopated.** Syncopation is a favorite device in jazz.

TEMPO

All aspects of musical time are very much affected by the **tempo** of the music. The tempo is determined by the rate of speed of the beat. If the beat is quick, the tempo is *fast;* a long beat results in a *slow* tempo.

Tempo Indications

Indications concerning tempo are usually given in Italian at the beginning of the piece or in another section of the piece:

Very slow:	*Largo* (broad)
	Grave (grave, solemn)
Slow:	*Lento*
	Adagio (leisurely; literally, at ease)
Moderate:	*Andante* (at a walking pace)
	Moderato
Fast:	*Allegretto*
	Allegro (faster than allegretto; literally, cheerful)
Very fast:	*Vivace* (vivacious)
	Presto (very quick)
	Prestissimo (as fast as possible)

These basic terms can be modified by adding such words as *molto* (very), *meno* (less), *poco* (a little), and *ma non troppo* (not too much). For example, *allegro molto* is very fast; *poco adagio* is somewhat slow; and *allegro non troppo* is fast but not too fast. Gradual changes in tempo are indicated by such words as *accelerando* (getting faster) and *ritardando* (becoming slower). To reestablish the original tempo, the term *a tempo* is used.

Tempo can be altered in other ways. The term **rubato** indicates freedom to move ahead and fall behind the tempo, and the symbol ⌢ (**fermata**) tells the performer to hold the note longer than its normal time value—suspending the meter and tempo for the moment.

As was the case with dynamic indications, tempo indications are approximate and relative, leaving a great deal of discretion to the performer.

LEVELS OF TIME

As we have seen, musical time exists on different levels—on the most fundamental level, the *beat;* on a higher level, the grouping of beats into longer units of equality, the *measure.* On yet still a higher level are longer segments of musical time consisting of groups of measures. These larger units are called **phrases.** If we examine the entire melody of "America the Beautiful," we find that it consists of four phrases, each consisting of four measures:

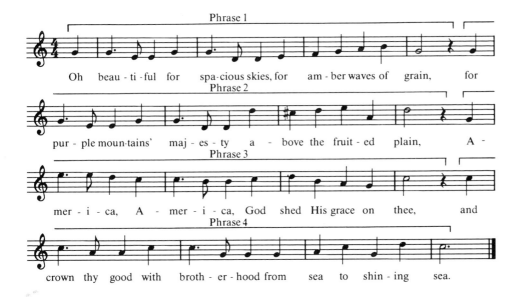

Example 2.14

With the concept of the musical phrase, we enter the realm of musical form, a major subject in our next chapter.

SUMMARY

Melody is the element of music we tend to follow with the greatest ease. A melody consists of two inseparable, interacting elements: a succession of pitches and a succession of time values. Moving in a linear fashion through space and forward in time, melody represents the horizontal aspect of music.

Harmony is an expressive and structural element, representing the vertical aspect of music. The tones of a harmony are heard not only individually, but as a composite sound. The smallest harmony consists of two tones; chords are harmonies of three or more tones. Harmonies are usually described as consonant (in repose) or dissonant (in a state of tension).

Tonal music is characterized by the affirmation of a central tone, the *tonic,* which is the first degree of the scale. The principle of tonality involves relationships among tones and chords *within* a key and also relationships *among* keys. Modulations, or shifts from one key to another, are usually employed in larger works of music as one means of providing musical interest and variety.

Rhythm encompasses all aspects of musical time. It includes, but is not confined to, meter—the grouping of beats into regular units. Meter imposes regularity by providing the basic groupings within which the listener organizes sound. Rhythmic variation lends diversity and inequality.

NEW TERMS

melody (melodic)
  theme
harmony (harmonic)
  chord
  arpeggio
  consonance
  dissonance
tonality (tonal)
  tonic
  tonic chord
  major-minor system
  scale (mode, major, minor)
  key
  leading tone
  dominant chord
  modulation

rhythm
  beat
  meter (metrical)
  measure
  accent
  time signature
  bar line
  up-beat
  down-beat
  syncopation
  tempo
  rubato
  fermata
  phrase

MUSICAL ORGANIZATION

We have seen that combinations of individual sounds produce the basic elements of music: melody, harmony, tonality, and rhythm. In this chapter we explore the ways these elements are combined to create musical texture, musical form, and musical style.

MUSICAL TEXTURE

Like cloth, music is woven of horizontal and vertical strands. We think of melody as moving horizontally, because one tone follows the next along the flow of time. We describe harmony as vertical because it is based upon sounds that happen simultaneously—in combination with one another.

Musical **texture** is created by the ways that these vertical and horizontal strands are interwoven. There are three basic musical textures: **monophony, polyphony,** and **homophony.**

MONOPHONY

Monophonic music (monophony literally means "one sound") consists of a single melodic line with no accompaniment. If you sing or hum by yourself, you are creating monophonic music.

Example 3.1 Monophony, single voice.

Similarly, when many people sing exactly the same notes at the same time (in unison) or the same notes an octave apart, the texture is also monophonic (example 3.2).

Example 3.2 Monophony, two voices an octave apart.

CONTRACTUS:
"Salve Regina"
Cassette 1/A, Track 2
CD 1, Track 2

A good example of monophony is the chant "Salve Regina," discussed in chapter 6.

POLYPHONY

Music consisting of two or more "independent" melodic lines that are roughly equal in their melodic and rhythmic activity and interest creates a texture known as **polyphony.**

In example 3.3, both voices sing the same melody. But because the lower voice begins later than the first, we hear two independent lines of music. It can be said that the second voice *imitates* the first—it sings exactly the same melody immediately after the first voice. Music that uses this device is known as **imitative polyphony.**

Example 3.3 Polyphony.

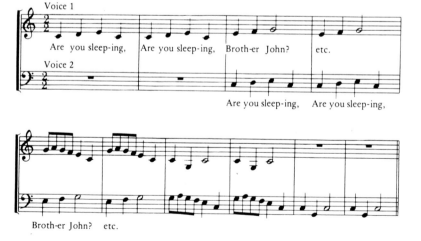

Examples of imitative polyphony are the motet *Ave Maria* by Josquin des Prez, discussed in chapter 6, and Fugue in G Minor by J. S. Bach, discussed in chapter 8.

Independence and equality of voices are the defining characteristics of polyphony. A **voice** is a single line of music; independence is its ability to compete with other melodic strands for the attention of the listener.

In polyphonic music we are interested in the relationship among the independent, simultaneous melodies. Our attention will shift from one melodic line to another, depending on which is most important at any given moment. The melodic lines thus enhance and enrich each other, contributing to the expressiveness of the overall sound. The interplay of melodies that characterizes polyphonic music is known as **counterpoint,** and polyphonic music is also termed **contrapuntal.**

JOSQUIN:
Ave Maria
Cassette 1/A, Track 4
CD 1, Track 4

BACH:
Fugue in G Minor
Cassette 1/B, Track 5
CD 1, Track 16

HOMOPHONY

In **homophonic** music, a *single* melodic line predominates, while the other voices or instruments provide harmonic **accompaniment.** The listener's attention is focused on the melody; the harmonic accompaniment is heard as a kind of musical background.

In example 3.4 the voices sing the melodic line while the piano provides harmonic accompaniment.

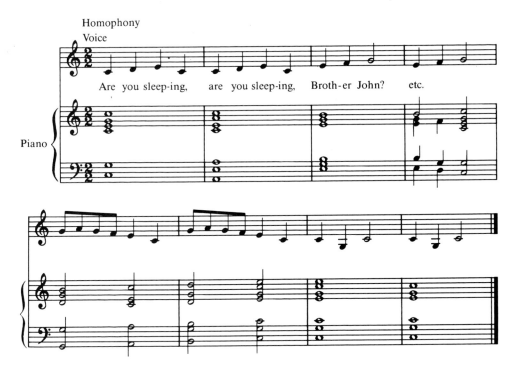

Example 3.4 Homophony.

MOZART:
Symphony no. 40,
Movement I
Cassette 2/A, Track 3
CD 2, Track 3

HANDEL:
"And the Glory of
the Lord"
Cassette 1/B, Track 3
CD 1, Track 12

A more elaborate example of homophonic texture is the first movement of Symphony no. 40 by W. A. Mozart, outlined in chapter 9.

TEXTURAL VARIETY

Actually, much music employs both polyphonic and homophonic textures, and frequently the texture of a piece of music alternates between the two. An essentially homophonic stretch, for example, may be followed by a polyphonic section. But even in these stretches, the distinction may not be clear-cut. One voice may dominate the polyphonic section, or in a homophonic section, the accompaniment may assume enough interest to compete with the main melodic line. A good illustration of textural variety is the choral movement "And the Glory of the Lord" from Handel's *Messiah,* discussed on pages 131–134.

MUSICAL FORM

Musical **form** involves the overall structuring and organization of the flow of musical time. Sustaining the listener's interest in music depends on the presence of two essential factors: **unity** and **variety.** Unity satisfies the listener's need for coherence, sameness, and familiarity. Variety sustains interest and appeals to the human enjoyment of the new, different, and unexpected. Musical variety is the result of *change;* musical unity is achieved by *repetition.* From the balance between unity and variety (repetition and change) are derived the distinguishing characteristics of the many different types of musical form.

The most obvious type of musical change is inherent in the contrast between two different musical ideas. Proceeding from one melody to a different one, or from one key to another, or from one dynamic level to another—all can contribute to change and thus to musical variety.

The most obvious form of repetition is the immediate restatement of the same musical idea in the same way, without any change.

Actually, both change and repetition vary greatly in the ways they are applied, but both are present in all types of musical form.

BINARY FORM

Binary form consists of two contrasting musical sections, A and B. Each section is usually repeated, resulting in the pattern AABB. Usually the A section begins in the tonic key and modulates to the dominant. The B section begins in the dominant and modulates back to the tonic. In this structure, variety results from the melodic contrasts between A and B and the modulation to a new key. Unity is ensured by returning to and ending in the key in which the piece began. This form is subject to various refinements, but the basic melodic contrast and return to the original key are frequent principles of organization.

TERNARY FORM

Ternary form also utilizes the principles of contrasting thematic material and return to the original key. However, it includes the added unifying element of returning to the original thematic material as well as the original key after the contrast. Ternary form consists of three sections: ABA. In practice, the first section is usually repeated, resulting in the pattern AABA. The final A section is a repetition of the first. In binary form, A ends in the dominant; in ternary form, by contrast, it ends in the tonic key in which it began. Then, all of the B section is in a contrasting key. With its contrasting melodic material *and* key, B supplies the element of variety. Finally, the return or *reappearance* of A in the tonic provides the unifying component.

ALTERNATING FORMS

Ternary form (ABA) is the simplest example of the principle of **alternation.** Music built on this principle consists of a main section (A) alternating with contrasting sections (B,C,D, etc.):

ABA	three-part form
ABACA	five-part form
ABACABA	seven-part form

The contrasting sections and their different keys provide the element of variety, while the reappearing A section with its "home key" ensures unity. Section A may appear in a shortened or modified form (particularly in longer pieces), but it nevertheless has the unifying effect that comes from the return and recognition of familiar material.

The baroque *aria,* the classical *minuet and trio,* and the **rondo,** each of which we shall encounter in subsequent chapters, are forms that employ this principle of alternation.

THEME AND VARIATION

While alternation is based upon the contrasts among *different* musical materials, other formal procedures are based on the statement of a *single* idea and its subsequent change. *Variation* and *development* are the two principal homophonic techniques used in this type of formal structure. **Development** technique is best seen in the sonata-allegro form, which we will study in detail in chapter 9. **Variation** is most clearly demonstrated in the procedure known as **theme and variations.** A theme is stated and then is repeated several times, each time changed or varied in some particular way:

Statement	Variation[1]	Variation[2]	Variation[3]	
Theme (A)	A^1	A^2	A^3	etc.

In this procedure the restatement of the same basic thematic material is the unifying factor; the successive changes provide variety. Charles Ives's *Variations on "America"* is a good example of theme and variations (see chapter 20). The techniques and devices by which thematic material may be varied are numerous. However, regardless of the devices employed, each variation usually utilizes the *entire theme.*

IVES:
Variations on "America"
Cassette 6/B, Track 2
CD 6, Track 12

In addition to alternation, variation, and development, there are polyphonic techniques such as **canon** and **fugue.** In a canon, a melody is strictly imitated in its entirety by another voice or voices. A **round** like "Brother John" in example 3.3 is a simple type of canon. We will study fugue in connection with the music of the Baroque era (chapter 8).

Musical form and musical texture are the materials with which music is made. The specific way in which these materials are combined in any musical piece determines the style of that work.

MUSICAL STYLE

In any discussion of art the word *style* appears in many contexts and with seemingly endless applications. Broadly defined, **style** is a manner of expression characteristic of an individual, a historical period, an artistic "school," or some other identifiable group. In speaking of musical style, we are referring to the methods of using melody, harmony, rhythm, tone color, tonality, form, and texture.

In music, the term is applied in numerous ways. We speak of the style of Beethoven's Ninth Symphony as compared with that of his Second Symphony; or the style of Debussy as compared with that of Ravel; or operatic style as distinguished from oratorio style. We also speak of instrumental style, vocal style, keyboard style, German style, Italian style, or the style of Western music as contrasted with Oriental music.

In a larger sense, the word *style* is applied to periods of music history. Every age presents new problems, makes new demands, and offers new possibilities; and every artist responds in a unique way. Yet no matter how varied the stylistic traits of the individual artists of a particular era, when they are seen in historical perspective common manners of expression bind them together. Thus we are able to identify the common practices of a specific period and talk in general terms about its style. Although scholars never completely agree on the boundary lines separating one period of style from another, the following outline of the major periods of music history provides approximate dates. Each period had a unique means of expression.

600–1430	Medieval
1430–1600	Renaissance
1600–1750	Baroque
1750–1825	Classical
1820–1900	Romantic
1900–present	Twentieth Century

Style periods overlap; the new exists side by side with the old. Elements from an older style may be combined with new procedures to create what is sometimes called a neoclassical (or neobaroque and so on) style. Although Italy was the very heart of the Renaissance spirit in literature and the visual arts, Renaissance *music* originated and developed in northern France and Belgium. The baroque style appeared earlier in Italy than in Germany or England. Nevertheless, the style periods listed are a useful guide in exploring developments in Western music.

SUMMARY

The relationship between the vertical and horizontal aspects of a piece of music is known as its texture. Monophonic music consists of a single melodic line with no accompaniment. Polyphonic music consists of two or more "independent" melodic lines that are roughly equal in their melodic and rhythmic interest. Homophonic music is dominated by a single melodic strand, with the other voices providing harmonic support.

Musical form refers to the structuring and organization of the musical time-flow. Forms are derived from the elements of unity and variety and the balance between them. Variety is the result of change; unity is achieved through repetition.

Alternating forms are based upon the contrasts among different musical materials, while variation and development procedures are based on the statement of a single musical idea and its subsequent alteration.

The specific way in which musical elements are combined in a piece of music determines its style. Music has evolved through a series of style periods, each with general distinguishing characteristics. In the subsequent chapters of this book, we shall trace the development of Western music from the Middle Ages to the twentieth century.

NEW TERMS

texture

monophony (monophonic)

polyphony (polyphonic)

   imitation (imitative)

   voice

   counterpoint (contrapuntal)

   canon

   fugue

   round

homophony (homophonic)

   accompaniment

form

   unity

   variety

   binary form

   ternary form

   alternation

   rondo

   development

   theme and variation

style

SUGGESTED LISTENING

Bizet, Georges

L'Arlesienne, Suite 2, "Farandole." This is a good example of the various kinds of musical texture.

MUSICAL INSTRUMENTS AND ENSEMBLES

CHAPTER

4

T he musical instruments available to the composer offer a wide variety of pitch ranges, modes of articulation, and tone colors. They are traditionally grouped into seven categories or families: **voices, strings, woodwinds, brasses, percussion, keyboard,** and **electronic.**

VOICES

SCHUBERT:
"Erlkönig"
Cassette 3/A, Track 2
CD 3, Track 2

BRITTEN: *Serenade for Tenor, Horn, and Strings*
Cassette 6/A, Track 1
CD 6, Tracks 1–7

Because it is part of the human body, the voice is in many respects our most fundamental musical instrument. The expressive qualities of the voice are greatly enhanced by its ability to combine music and words.

Individual voices vary in pitch range, but male and female voice types are generally divided into high, middle, and low **registers.** Arranged from highest to lowest pitch register, the basic vocal categories are:

Female[1]
$\left\{ \begin{array}{l} \textit{Soprano} \\ \textit{Mezzo soprano} \\ \textit{Contralto (alto)} \end{array} \right.$

Male
$\left\{ \begin{array}{l} \textit{Tenor} \\ \textit{Baritone} \\ \textit{Bass} \end{array} \right.$

Luciano Pavarotti, world-famous operatic tenor.

1. The "female registers" are also sung by young boys with unchanged voices.

STRINGS

The string family has two branches—those that are *bowed* and those that are *plucked*.

BOWED INSTRUMENTS

From highest to lowest pitch register, the bowed instruments are as follows:

BRITTEN: *Young Person's Guide to the Orchestra*
Cassette 1/A, Track 1
CD 1, Track 1

Violin—noted for its lyric expressiveness. The neck is held with the left hand, and the tail rests beneath the player's chin.

Viola—produces a more sombre tone quality than the violin. Held in the same way as the violin.

Violoncello—usually referred to as simply *cello.* Because of its size, it rests on the floor and is held upright between the player's knees.

Double bass—also called *string bass,* the largest and lowest-voiced member of the family. Because of its size, the player sits on a stool or stands.

With the exception of size, these instruments are similar in construction, as illustrated by the violin in figure 4.1. Each of its four strings is stretched between two fixed points, with one end attached to a *peg* on the neck of the instrument and the other to the *tailpiece* at the base of the instrument's body. The strings pass over the *bridge,* which holds them away from the *fingerboard,* allowing them to vibrate. The strings are tuned to specific pitches when the player adjusts the tension by tightening or loosening the pegs to which the strings are attached.

The instrument is made to sound when the *bow* (fig. 4.2) is drawn across the string, causing it to vibrate.

The player determines the pitch produced by the string by using the fingers of the left hand to press the string against the fingerboard, thereby adjusting the length of the string. This is known as **stopping** the string.

A variety of musical effects can be achieved by using different bowing techniques:

Legato—smooth and connected up-and-down strokes of the bow

Staccato—short and detached strokes of the bow

Tremolo—very rapid strokes of the bow

The tone quality of the instrument can be made richer or warmer by the use of **vibrato,** rapid vibration of the left hand while pressing the string against the fingerboard. And a subdued, velvety tone is produced by the use of a **mute,** a device clamped onto the bridge.

Figure 4.1 First developed by early sixteenth-century Italians, violins have undergone little structural change since their invention.

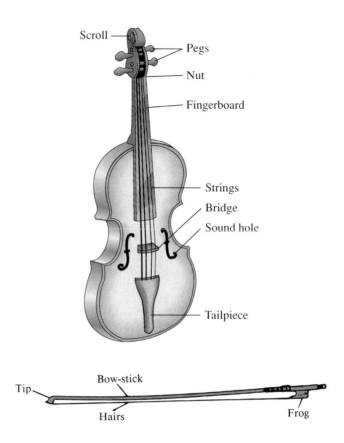

Scroll

Pegs

Nut

Fingerboard

Strings

Bridge

Sound hole

Tailpiece

Figure 4.2 Horsehair bows are used to vibrate the strings of instruments of the violin and viola da gamba families. The adjustable frog enables the artist to tighten the hair.

Bow-stick

Tip

Hairs

Frog

Itzhak Perlman, violinist.

When the player plucks the string, the result is short, crisp notes. Plucking is called **pizzicato.**

The violin, viola, cello, and string bass are among the most important instruments in the history of Western music. They constitute the backbone of the symphony orchestra and are used extensively in chamber music. All of them, particularly the violin, are used as solo instruments, and the double bass ("bass fiddle") is frequently used in jazz ensembles.

Yo Yo Ma, violoncellist.

Garry Karr, virtuoso bassist.

During the Renaissance and Baroque periods of music history, the five members of the *viola da gamba* family were the basic string instruments. They are similar to the violin family in appearance, but they produce a much lighter and more nasal tone quality. All of them are played in the cello position, between the player's knees.

Viola da gamba.

PLUCKED INSTRUMENTS

Today the prominent plucked instruments are the **guitar** and the **harp.**

The guitar has become popular as a solo instrument and is used widely in folk, jazz, rock, and country and western music. The harp is used as a solo instrument and is a member of the symphony orchestra. The modern harp has forty-seven strings stretched vertically in a triangular frame. Seven pedals at its base are used to adjust the pitch of the strings.

The late Andres Segovia popularized the classical guitar as a solo concert instrument.

A stringed instrument played by plucking, the harp has foot pedals that alter the pitch of the strings. Concert harpist, Nanette Felix.

WOODWINDS

Woodwind instruments produce sound when air is blown through the tubelike body of the instrument. The length of the vibrating air column is controlled by opening or closing small holes along the side of the instrument with fingers or pads activated by a key mechanism. In closing or opening the *finger holes,* the player lengthens or shortens the air column, thereby lowering or raising the pitch of the tones produced.

The most commonly used woodwind instruments from highest to lowest in pitch range are the **flute,**[2] **clarinet, oboe,** and **bassoon.** The difference in tone quality among these instruments is more pronounced than that among the members of the string family. Each has its own very distinctive sound caused, in part, by the different ways of blowing air into the instrument.

The flute is **edge blown.** The player activates the column of air inside the instrument by blowing across a hole called the embouchure hole. The other instruments use a vibrating **reed**—a small strip of cane—through which the player blows air into the instrument.

Clarinets use a *single reed.* Oboes and bassoons use a *double reed,* two pieces of cane fastened together. The flute, oboe, clarinet, and bassoon are used as solo instruments, in chamber music groups, and as members of larger performing groups such as wind ensembles, bands, and symphony orchestras.

In symphony orchestras and concert wind ensembles, this basic group of woodwinds is often expanded to include other instruments to provide a greater overall pitch range and an expanded variety of tone color. Often included in this expanded group are the **piccolo** (little flute), the **English horn** (a lower version of the oboe), the **bass clarinet,** and the **contrabassoon** (the lowest pitch range among woodwinds).

---

2. In the twentieth century, the flute came to be made of metal rather than wood.

James Galway, flutist and
conductor.

Richard Krauchak (*a*),
oboist. (*b*) An English horn.

(a)

(b)

Richard Stoltzman, concert clarinetist.

(a)

Dennis Williams (*a*), bassoonist. (*b*) A contrabassoon.

(b)

From highest pitch range to lowest, the expanded woodwind group is:

piccolo
flute
oboe
English horn
clarinet
bass clarinet
bassoon
contrabassoon

The **recorder,** in its various sizes and pitch ranges, was popular in the Renaissance and Baroque eras. It is **end blown** and produces a tone similar in quality to that of a flute.

The recorder is popular for folk music and as a concert instrument. Michala Petri playing the recorder.

The **saxophone,** invented in the mid-nineteenth century by Adolphe Sax of Brussels, is a single-reed instrument with a body made of brass. Although it is most commonly encountered as a jazz instrument, it is sometimes employed as a solo instrument in the symphony orchestra and as a member of bands and wind ensembles. In the twentieth century it has been developed as a solo concert instrument.

BRASSES

The most commonly used brass instruments, from highest to lowest in pitch range, are the **trumpet, horn, trombone,** and **tuba.**

Like the woodwinds, brass instruments produce sound by sending a vibrating column of air through tubing. (In brass instruments the tubing is coiled to facilitate handling of the instrument by reducing its overall length.) At one end of the tubing is a **mouthpiece;** at the other end the tube is flared to form a bell. Pitch adjustments are made by a combination of adjusting the tension of the lips of the player and manipulating a mechanism that extends or shortens the length of the tube.

The Canadian Brass Quintet, consisting of Ronald Romm (left) and Fred Mills, trumpets; David Ohanian, horn; Charles Deallenbach, tuba; and Gene Watts, trombone.

In the trumpet, horn, and tuba this mechanism is a set of **valves** operated by the fingers. In the trombone, the mechanism is a **slide,** a U-shaped piece of tubing operated by the player's right hand. The *tenor* and *bass trombone* are most frequently seen in the modern orchestra, while the *alto trombone* is encountered less often.

Other brass instruments such as the *cornet* (similar to the trumpet) and the *euphonium* (of the tuba family) are used in both concert and marching bands. Both the trumpet and trombone are popular jazz instruments.

PERCUSSION INSTRUMENTS

While the string, wind, and brass instruments we have discussed have become standard members of the modern symphony orchestra, percussion instruments—those whose sounds are produced by being struck, shaken, or scraped—vary greatly from ensemble to ensemble and from composition to composition. They cover a range of instruments—all the way from a single pair of timpani with one player to a large "battery" consisting of a wide variety of instruments and many players.

Essentially, percussion instruments fall into two categories: those that produce *definite* pitch and those that produce *indefinite* pitch.

DEFINITE PITCH

The most commonly employed instruments capable of producing different pitches are the *timpani, glockenspiel, celesta, vibraphone, xylophone, marimba,* and *chimes.*

Timpani, which come in various sizes, are also known as kettledrums. They are the most commonly used percussion instruments in concert music. Sound is produced by the vibration of a calfskin *head* stretched over a kettlelike base. The pitch of each drum is controlled by the player, who adjusts the degree of tension of the head by manipulating a set of screws around the rim of the drum or by employing foot pedals.

The *glockenspiel* consists of two rows of steel bars, each producing a definite pitch. A crisp bell-like sound is produced by striking the bar with a mallet.

The *celesta* is a keyboard glockenspiel that looks something like a small upright piano. Unlike the glockenspiel, the celesta is capable of producing many different pitches simultaneously and has a wider range of pitches.

The *vibraphone* (also referred to as a vibraharp), popular in jazz, consists of metal bars arranged similarly to the keyboard of a piano. An electrical mechanism produces the instrument's characteristic vibrato effect.

The *xylophone* has tuned wooden bars that produce a hollow sound when struck by a mallet.

The *marimba* is a xylophone with resonators under each bar of the instrument.

Chimes, also known as *tubular bells,* are a set of tuned metal tubes suspended vertically in a frame. They are played with one or two mallets, and their sound resembles that of church bells.

Figure 4.3 Percussion instruments. Back row (left to right): gong, assorted hand-held instruments (on stand), bass drum, drum (trap) kit (floor tom, ride cymbal, kick [bass] drum, snare drum, rack tom, hi-hat, crash cymbal), tam-tam, congas, timbales, bongos. Middle row: tom-toms (assorted sizes), snare drums (assorted sizes), tambourines (on stand), triangle (hanging from stand), cymbals (hand-held), ride cymbals, chimes. Front row: xylophone, glockenspiel, marimba, celesta, timpani, vibraphone, various hand-held instruments (on stand).

INDEFINITE PITCH

Percussion instruments of indefinite (or fixed) pitch include just about anything that can be struck or scraped or manipulated in some other fashion to produce a sound. Those used most commonly are the *bass drum, side* (or *snare*) *drum, tambourine* (shaken or struck), *triangle, cymbals, gong, tom-toms, bongos,* and *congas.* Add to these a host of hand-held instruments, such as the *cowbell,* the *ratchet, sleigh bells,* the *slapstick, castanets,* and many others, and you have an enormous resource for the production of musical sounds. Indeed, the multitude of percussion instruments has led to the formation of ensembles that consist only of percussion instruments. Most of these items, as well as others, are shown in figure 4.3.

KEYBOARD INSTRUMENTS

The most widely used **keyboard** instruments today are the **piano,** the **harpsichord,** and the **organ.** Unlike most of the instruments we have explained thus far, these instruments have in common the important capability of producing many different tones at the same time. They are, therefore, both *melodic* and *harmonic* instruments—capable of playing a melody and its harmonic accompaniment. In addition, all three have a very wide pitch range— wider than that of any other single instrument.

While the piano, harpsichord, and organ all operate from a set of keys, the precise manner in which the keys produce tones differs from instrument to instrument.

The plucked strings of the harpsichord produce much softer sounds than those of the piano.

HARPSICHORD

BACH: Brandenburg
Concerto no. 5
Cassette 2/A, Track 1
CD 2, Track 1

The harpsichord is a *string* instrument; its tone is produced by a vibrating string stretched over a sounding board that amplifies the sound. Each key of the harpsichord operates a *plectra* that *plucks* a specific string. This mechanism allows for very little sustaining power or variation in volume.

The harpsichord was the favored keyboard instrument in the Renaissance and Baroque eras and was finally replaced by the piano in the Classical era. It has been revived during the twentieth century as part of a renewed interest in preclassical music.

PIANO

BEETHOVEN:
Piano Sonata op. 57
Cassette 2/B, Track 4
CD 2, Track 12

The piano is also a string instrument. Each piano key operates a *hammer* that *strikes* the string. Unlike the harpsichord, the piano mechanism allows for a great range of dynamic variation; the greater the force pressing the key, the louder the sound of the resulting tone.

The ability to sustain tones is an important feature of the piano. This continuation of the sound is accomplished by using the *damper* pedal which, when pressed by the foot, sustains the sound even after the keys are released. The middle pedal of the piano (*sostenuto* pedal) makes it possible to sustain selected tones.

Since the end of the eighteenth century, the piano has been an extremely popular instrument in both concert halls and homes. Its lyric, harmonic, and dynamic qualities make the piano a favorite instrument for solos, for accompaniment, and as a member of chamber ensembles.

André Watts, pianist.

ORGAN

The **pipe organ** is a wind instrument. In its simplest and original form, it consists of a set of pipes controlled by a keyboard that sends air into the pipes from a blower.

Gradually, the instrument became more complicated and versatile as more sets of pipes, each with its own tone quality, were added to the instrument. Today, the organ consists of many sets of pipes that are controlled from multiple keyboards, including a *pedal board* played by the organist's feet. The various sets of pipes are put in or out of operation by a series of knobs called *stops*. A vast variety of tone colors and dynamic levels can be controlled by this combination of stops and keyboards.

The greatest period of development for this instrument took place in the Baroque era, particularly in Germany, culminating in the organ music of the great German composer J. S. Bach, whose G Minor Fugue for organ is discussed on pages 148–150.

BACH:
Fugue in G Minor
Cassette 1/B, Track 5
CD 1, Track 16

Pipe organ.

ELECTRONIC INSTRUMENTS

One of the most powerful and far-reaching forces in music in the twentieth century has been the application of electronics to the performance, reproduction, and creation of music. The radio, phonograph, electronic tape, and more recently, the compact disc revolutionized the dissemination of music of all kinds.

Many instruments such as the organ, the piano, and the guitar were transformed into electronic instruments, and the development of sophisticated and powerful amplification systems made it possible to increase the sound of a small instrumental ensemble and the human voice to great volume beyond their normal capacity.

In terms of the *creation* of music, the invention of the **synthesizer**, an electronic instrument that can duplicate almost any sound and can be used to create entirely new sounds, was extremely important. The combination of the synthesizer, electronic tape, and computer created new tools and methods of musical composition that had a profound effect on both the art and the business of music in the twentieth century. These methods and the music produced by their use will be discussed in detail in chapter 21.

ENSEMBLES

Throughout the history of music, composers have written works that call for the use of instruments and voices in a great variety of numbers, combinations, and groupings. These range from the unaccompanied solo instrument to the large orchestra consisting of more than a hundred players, often combined with a chorus and solo voices. Instrumental music falls into two broad categories: chamber music, in which one player executes each part, and orchestral music, which requires sections with more than one performer. Within the category of orchestral music are again two major divisions: the small chamber orchestra and the large symphony orchestra.

The Juilliard string quartet, featuring Robert Mann, violin; Joel Smirnoff, violin; Joel Krosnick, cello; and Samuel Rhodes, viola.

CHAMBER ENSEMBLES

Chamber music is classified by the number of instruments for which it is written. Thus, we have *duos* for two performers, *trios* for three, *quartets, quintets, sextets, octets,* and so on. The combinations may be for a single type of instrument (such as a flute trio), instruments of the same family (such as a brass quintet consisting of trumpets, horn, trombone, and tuba), or assortments of instruments of different types.

The most important chamber combination, the **string quartet,** has been widely used by composers from the middle of the eighteenth century into the modern period. The string quartet consists of a first and a second violin, a viola, and a cello.

Frequently a fifth instrument is added to the string quartet to create a quintet; ensembles of this type are named after the added instrument. Thus, a *clarinet quintet* is a string quartet plus a clarinet; a *piano quintet* is a string quartet plus a piano. Clarinet quintets were written by Mozart and Brahms, and piano quintets by Schubert, Brahms, Dvořák, and Fauré. A quintet consisting of five strings is also common. Mozart, Beethoven, Mendelssohn, and Brahms wrote works of this type for ensembles consisting of two violins, two violas, and a cello. Chamber groupings, some for larger ensembles, have continued to the present day. Igor Stravinsky, for example, wrote his *Octet for Wind Instruments* for two bassoons, two trombones, two trumpets, a flute, and a clarinet.

HAYDN: String Quartet op. 33, no. 3
Cassette 2/B, Track 2
CD 2, Track 9

THE ORCHESTRA

Throughout its history, the **orchestra** has varied in size and composition. As determined by individual composers, it is an ever-changing unit, not only in size but also in makeup.

One of the earliest orchestral ensembles was established in Paris by Jean-Baptiste Lully in the mid-seventeenth century. His orchestra consisted mainly of strings. During the first quarter of the eighteenth century, wind instruments, trumpets, and kettledrums were added.

In the mid-eighteenth century, the orchestra became more standardized. The strings remained dominant, but the woodwinds took on an increasingly important role.

In the early decades of the nineteenth century, many woodwind and brass instruments underwent significant technical improvements. Composers were quick to take advantage of the greater versatility of these instruments. In the second half of the nineteenth century, the orchestra grew extensively in both size and makeup. Today's symphony orchestra consists of a nucleus of about one hundred players, with additions and subtractions made to suit the requirements of individual pieces. The players are distributed according to the plan shown in figure 4.4.

BRITTEN: *Young Person's Guide to the Orchestra*
Cassette 1/A, Track 1
CD 1, Track 1

MOZART: Symphony no. 40, Movement no. I
Cassette 2/A, Track 3
CD 2, Track 3

BERLIOZ: *Symphonie fantastique,* Movement no. IV
Cassette 3/B, Track 2
CD 3, Track 6

BANDS AND WIND ENSEMBLES

The word *band* has many applications. Marching band, military band, stage band, jazz band, hillbilly band, and the rhythm band that many of us played in as children give an idea of the variety of bands possible. For much of its history, the band has been associated with summer concerts in the park. Today the term is most often applied to two types of musical organizations: the marching band and the concert band.

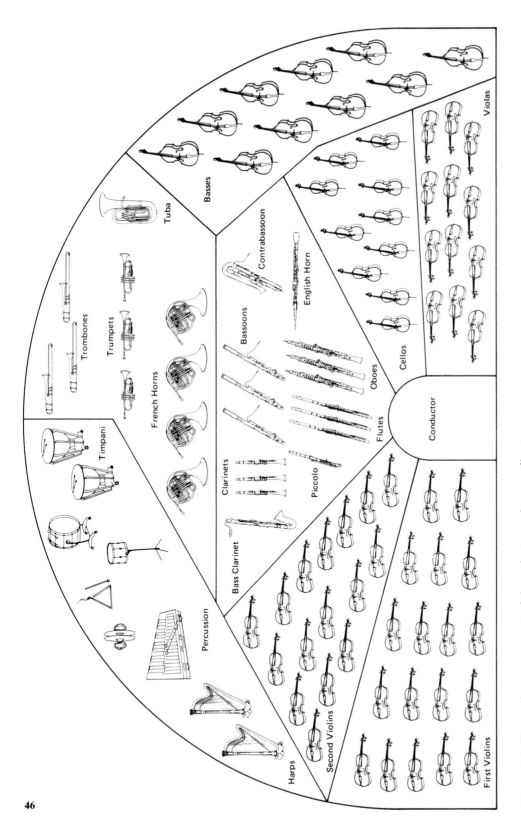

Figure 4.4 The seating arrangement of the orchestra varies according to the preferences of the conductor, but generally the strings are to the front, the woodwinds in the middle, and the brasses and percussion to the back. The numbers of each kind of instrument also vary slightly from orchestra to orchestra. (Reprinted courtesy of *The Boston Globe.*)

We are all familiar with the **marching bands** that play at high school and college sports events, march in military parades, and participate in municipal celebrations. The **concert band,** often referred to as a **symphonic band** or **wind ensemble,** is perhaps less familiar. It became an important musical force in the years following World War I. It differs from the marching band because of its smaller size, its emphasis on performing original compositions, and the fact that it was intended for indoor concerts. The wind ensemble, with its lighter sound, has attracted the attention of several serious modern composers: Darius Milhaud, Paul Hindemith, and Ralph Vaughan Williams are among those who have written original works for wind ensemble.

Whereas the members of the violin family form the mainstay of the symphony orchestra, concert bands rely primarily on woodwind, brass, and percussion instruments to produce their unique tone colors. Concert bands generally contain no violins, violas, or cellos but do employ the string bass.

VOCAL ENSEMBLES

Chamber vocal ensembles vary in size and makeup in much the same way that chamber instrumental ensembles do. There are vocal trios, quartets, quintets, sextets, and so on. The vocal quartet usually consists of soprano, alto, tenor, and bass. So long as only one or two singers sing each part, the ensemble is essentially of chamber music proportions. However, when there are four or five or more singers in each section, the ensemble is referred to as a **chorus** or **choir.** Several types of choruses are possible. A *women's chorus* usually consists of two soprano parts (first and second) and one or two alto sections: SSAA. A *men's chorus* is made up of two tenor sections (first and second), baritone, and bass: TTBB. The mixed chorus consists of both female and male voices, divided into soprano, alto, tenor, and bass: SATB. In church choirs before the nineteenth century, female voices were not generally used; soprano and alto parts were sung by boys whose voices had not yet changed.

Choral music is sometimes intended for voices alone, without instrumental accompaniment, a style of performance called **a cappella.** But choral music is also frequently performed with instruments—for example, piano, organ, or orchestra.

CONDUCTOR

Large ensembles usually require the leadership of a **conductor.** Standing in front of the orchestra or chorus, usually on a podium, the conductor directs the ensemble and is responsible for all aspects of the performance. The craft of conducting is a complex one, and conducting techniques and styles are highly individual and vary widely. In general, the conductor's right hand indicates the tempo and basic metrical structure of the music. With the left hand, the conductor cues the entrances of instruments, guides the shadings or dynamics, and indicates other nuances relating to the expressive character of the music.

JOSQUIN: *Ave Maria*
Cassette 1/A, Track 4
CD 1, Track 4

HAYDN:
Lord Nelson Mass
Cassette 2/B, Track 1
CD 2, Tracks 6–8

A page from the complete score of Dvořák's Symphony no. 9 in E Minor (to be discussed in chapter 15), illustrating how all the instrumental parts are combined for the conductor. The individual players normally use partial scores, showing only the music to be played by their particular instruments. Note that the trombones and viola use a special clef (called the C clef); the intersection of the two backward Cs in the clef sign locates the position of middle C.

The late American conductor Leonard Bernstein assembled an orchestra and choir from both East and West Germany and performed Beethoven's Ninth Symphony at the East Berlin Schauspielhaus in 1989.

SUMMARY

In this chapter we have examined, both individually and in groups, some of the most important instruments in Western music.

Musical instruments are classified into groups: voices, strings, woodwinds, brass, and percussion. Although they can be classified as wind, string, or percussion instruments, keyboard instruments are often considered separately. Operated by air under pressure, the human voice is technically a wind instrument. In recent times the computer and other electronic media have emerged as new means of producing music.

A great number of combinations and groupings are possible with both instrumental and vocal music. Chamber ensembles include trios, quartets, and a number of other small groups, with usually one voice or instrument assigned to a part. Larger groupings, such as the orchestra and chorus, have several voices or instruments performing a single part. Bands come in many varieties, the two principal types being the marching band and the concert band.

In the next chapter we will look at some instruments used in the performance of non-Western music.

NEW TERMS

voice
  register
string
  violin
  viola
  violoncello
  double bass
  harp
  guitar
  stopping
  legato
  staccato
  tremolo
  vibrato
  mute
  pizzicato
woodwind
  flute
  clarinet
  oboe
  bassoon
  piccolo
  English horn
  bass clarinet
  contrabassoon
  recorder
  saxophone
  edge blown
  end blown
  reed (single; double)
brass
  trumpet
  horn
  trombone
  tuba
  mouthpiece
  valves
  slide

percussion
  timpani
  glockenspiel
  celesta
  vibraphone
  xylophone
  marimba
  chimes
  side drum
  bass drum
  tambourine
  castanets
  triangle
  gong
  cymbals
  battery
keyboard
  piano
  harpsichord
  organ
electronic
  synthesizer
chamber music
string quartet
orchestra
marching band
concert band (symphonic band;
  wind ensemble)
chorus (choir)
  a cappella
conductor

The Music of World Cultures

© 1992, Keith Gunnar, FPG International Corp.

THE MUSIC OF WORLD CULTURES

CHAPTER

5

an introduction

E ach of us is, to some extent, a product of the culture into which we are born. Our physical, intellectual, and emotional lives are affected continuously by our surrounding social environment. The foods we consider most succulent, the art we enjoy, our patterns of friendship, family solidarity, and group identity are influenced by the cultural standards we absorb.

The same is true of music. A people's sense of their history, of their relationship to a deity, of their joy in life and sorrow in death are revealed by the use they make of musical materials. And ideas of what music should be—how it should sound, when it should be heard, and who should perform it—are related directly to cultural backgrounds. In short, the listener's "ear" is very much conditioned by his or her culture.

SOME PRELIMINARY COMMENTS

In this chapter we will consider examples of musical cultures outside the Western European tradition. Although there are many fundamental differences between Western and non-Western music, certain similarities appear to be a common heritage of all humanity. In every culture music plays an important role in rites and ceremonies, and for all people music has an emotional content that satisfies certain deeply felt needs. Yet the resulting sounds are often so diverse that the music of one group may not be recognized as music at all by other groups. A significant degree of contrast also exists between the relative positions of music in the social fabric of various cultures. For example, the traditional work music of some African tribes is so closely integrated into daily life that it is not even recognized by its members as basically the same phenomenon as the European-derived music they hear on transistor radios. Thus, any study of the music of non-Western cultures must include a description not only of its technical nature, but also of its role and function in society.

Let us begin by clarifying some terms. The music described in this chapter is variously called *ethnic, folk,* and *traditional.* Although these terms are not synonymous, the distinctions among them are sometimes unclear. *Ethnic* music usually refers to the music of a group of people who have shared a common cultural history over many generations. *Traditional* music, which can also be considered "classical" or "sophisticated," is classified by its use. In this category are included official music, such as the imperial court music of ancient China, Japan, and Vietnam, and ceremonial music used in all cultures for specific rites and festivals. Traditional (or classical) music is often formal, following more or less rigorous principles of content, style, and performance. It is usually performed by artists who have refined the music through continued use or disciplined training. *Folk* music is the music of everyday life—work songs, children's songs, lullabies, love songs, and ballad-story songs sung and played by ordinary people. In contrast to traditional music, folk music is available for all to learn, enjoy, and modify as occasion demands. In this chapter we will consider representative examples of both traditional and folk types of ethnic music.

WRITTEN AND ORAL TRADITIONS

The music we will spend most of our time exploring in this text—the concert music of Western Europe and the United States—is based on a tradition of written notation through which the artistic expression of individual composers is carefully preserved. This written music is usually recreated in performance by highly trained musicians at scheduled concerts and recitals. While the performer may take some liberties with the score, using a variety of musical techniques and resources to interpret and enrich the music, the final role of performance is to recreate sounds as intended by individual composers.

The musical heritages of many world cultures, by contrast, are usually transmitted orally. Young musicians learn by carefully listening to, observing, and imitating elder musicians. While music composition is treated with seriousness and reverence, in many cultures the name of an individual composer is not attached to the piece. In ancient cultures music was linked with supernatural beings and mythical gods, and was considered a reflection of universal order and spiritual purity.

MUSICAL ELEMENTS IN NON-WESTERN MUSIC

Part 1 discussed many of the elements common to all music, emphasizing how these elements are organized in the practice of Western music. Now we will look briefly at how some of these elements are organized in non-Western music.

PITCH AND SCALE SYSTEMS

The scales employed in many non-European cultures are unfamiliar and strange to Western ears. While certain cross-cultural similarities do occur, such as the significance applied by many cultures to the intervals of the octave and the fifth, octaves frequently have more, or fewer, than twelve subdivisions, and the smallest pitch differences found in non-European music may be larger or smaller than the European semi-tone (half step).

One of the most prevalent combinations of pitches is the **pentatonic scale**, a series of five tones. Pentatonic scales are found in the music of North and South American Indians and in African and Far Eastern cultures. If we play the pentatonic scale CDEGA(C) on the piano, we Westerners will quickly hear a characteristic "oriental" quality. It is the same scale structure as that produced by playing the five black keys of the piano. A subtle difference will be noted if we play instead the scale CDE♭GA♭. This scale is one of several pentatonic scales used commonly in Japanese music, while the first scale is typical of Chinese music.

African cultures south of the Sahara use, in addition to pentatonic scales, a variety of **tritonic** (three-tone) and **heptatonic** (seven-tone) scales, including patterns of whole and half steps that are common in Western music. Japanese music also employs heptatonic scales. In the classical music of India, sequences of pitches known as **ragas** are employed. The basic tones of a raga are modified by the use of **microtones,** intervals smaller than a half step. Microtones cannot be played on the piano, but can be produced on any stringed instrument such as a guitar, violin, or Indian sitar.

HARMONY

Most cultures use simultaneous sounds. As we shall see in succeeding chapters, Western music is governed by a long tradition of rules of harmonic organization. In non-Western music there is little use of harmony per se, particularly in countries such as India, where melodic intricacies are far more important. One prominent form of harmonic texture in Indian music is provided by a **drone,** a stationary tone or tones of constant pitch played throughout a piece. The four-stringed dulcimer used in performing Appalachian folk music also makes use of the drone, sustaining a continuous tone on one of its strings. Some cultures employ **heterophony:** Two or more individuals perform a single melody, adding their own rhythmic or melodic modifications. And in some non-Western cultures textural variety is provided by changes in tone quality and vocal inflection. Such vocal or instrumental variations as slides, trills, and vibrato are among the techniques through which the effect of varying textures is achieved.

RHYTHM

Much Western music is based on symmetrical rhythmic patterns and uniform time intervals. However, many world cultures use complex, irregular, and free rhythms. Many cultures use primarily vocal forms; in these cultures rhythms conform to the stress patterns of the words sung. In African music, **polyrhythms**—two or more contrasting and independent rhythms used at the same time—are common, and the sophistication of the use of rhythm in Africa is unmatched in any other culture. Polyrhythms have increasingly fascinated and influenced Western jazz and concert music composers. A good example of their adaptation in Western music is Stravinsky's *The Rite of Spring* (see pages 388–392).

EXAMPLES OF TRADITIONAL AND FOLK MUSIC

Rarely have any cultures lived in complete isolation for many centuries. As a result, the music of the dominant culture of a region has often been influenced by contacts through trade, exploration, and migration. Thus, the music in world cultures today has often been transformed to some degree from its original character. The examples we will survey here represent music of ancient origin in which many indigenous characteristics have been preserved.

THE MUSIC OF CHINA

Background

From its beginnings, Chinese music was conceived of as a system that would reflect the order of the universe. Musicians and philosophers in ancient China believed in the existence of one true "foundation tone" upon which the whole edifice of musical composition should be built. This foundation tone, or *huang chung,* was thought to have social, cosmological, and mystical significance. For many centuries, the disappearance of a dynasty was attributed to its inability to find the true *huang chung.* Several methods were used to discover the elusive tone. One method prescribed that the correct height of the pipe that would produce the true *huang chung* would be equal to ninety average-size grains of millet laid end to end. From this tone the pitches of the other tones in the Chinese musical system were derived. Small bamboo tubes, sized through an exact mathematical formula, were used to produce twelve tones, or *lu,* which were roughly comparable to the twelve months of the year, so that each month had its tone. Musicians selected five tones from these twelve to form a pentatonic scale based on the hours of day and night and the revolving cycle of months in the yearly calendar.

Because each tone was invested with mystical significance, Chinese music developed as a system in which the perfect performance of individual tones was regarded as the highest art. The philosopher Confucius (ca. 551–479 B.C.) played a stone slab on which only one note could be produced. Yet he is said to have played it with such a full heart that its sound was captivating. The sophistication needed to enjoy subtle colorations and inflections on only one tone was, of course, not a universal gift among the ancient Chinese. Popular discontent with "scholarly music" led to the development of more accessible forms that could be enjoyed by everyone. The most enduring secular form was Chinese opera.

Chinese Opera

Presented originally in teahouses or outdoor arenas, Chinese opera evolved in an atmosphere of noisy informality. Today, the uniform loudness with which the operas are performed is thought to be a stylistic holdover from the days when players had to compete with squalling babies and clattering rickshaws for audience attention. To involve the audiences emotionally, singers and musicians presented operas in which characterization was the overriding concern.

NGOH WAI HENG
KONG: Chinese Opera-
Songs and Music
Cassette 7/B, Track 12
CD 7, Track 17

Peking Opera: *The Monkey-King.*

To portray three basic emotional moods, three corresponding musical styles became customary. For scenes involving agitated emotions such as happiness, gaiety, or temporary distress, a quick, light style was employed. Music written in another style portrayed subdued, contemplative moods, whereas a character's despair or depression was conveyed through a third style of composition.

Similarly, various dramatic situations came to be associated with certain melodic patterns. These stereotyped melodic formulas are still available to any composer who wishes to communicate one of the standard dramatic incidents common to Chinese operatic plots. Consequently, in a number of operas the same melodic material forms the basis for any set aria (vocal piece) describing the anguish of the abandoned wife, a villain's intended vengeance, or the final triumph of good over evil.

The vocal quality and range in these arias also depends, to a large extent, on the type of character to be portrayed. Heroes are required to sing wth a tight, controlled rasp, whereas heroines often produce a high, nasal sound that originated with the male singers who, until recently, played the female roles.

The scenes of an opera generally begin with percussion overtures. Percussive devices are used to accompany the recitative (dialogue that is half spoken and half sung) and to mark off one character's words from another's. In melodic passages, instruments of the orchestra—bowed and plucked lutes, fiddles, and flutes—play the main melody either in unison or at various pitches. The crashing of cymbals emphasizes the end of a melody. As the Chinese opera form developed, energetic acrobatic displays and dances were introduced, adding greatly to audience enjoyment.

In modern China, the traditional music, which was associated with the old aristocratic society, has been systematically suppressed. Classical Chinese instruments are very rarely played today, and it is feared that much knowledge of the traditional performance styles used in Confucian rituals and imperial court music has been irretrievably lost. Yet the Chinese opera continues to thrive with the sanction of the Communist regime (although themes acceptable to the ideology of the revolutionary government have replaced traditional ones), because of its origin as the theater of common people.

Traditional Chinese Instruments

The musical instruments of China are classified according to the material from which they are made; metal, stone, silk, and bamboo are among the most common. Metal instruments include bells, gongs, chimes, and the carillon (a set of chromatically tuned bells). The stone chime, rarely used today, is constructed of small, L-shaped plates.

Of the silk instruments, the *ch'in,* or silk-stringed zither, is considered the most prestigious. Used as both a solo instrument and to accompany solo songs, the ch'in dates back to the Confucian period.

The transverse flute and the panpipe are bamboo instruments. The wood and skin instruments include a rich variety of percussive devices. The globular flute, an instrument similar to our ocarina (a simple wind instrument) is defined as a clay instrument, while the *sheng* mouth organ (fig. 5.1) fits into the category of gourd instruments. Important in the Chinese orchestra, the sheng consists of seventeen pipes set into a gourd wind chest. Its sound is said to imitate the cry of a phoenix bird, and its shape resembles a phoenix with folded wings. (The phoenix is a legendary bird that is said to have arisen from its own ashes to live again.)

Ancient Chinese orchestras were immense in size and diverse in instrumentation. The orchestra of the Temple of the Ancestors at Peking included over 150 players. Some musicologists have come to believe that the Chinese use of a variety of instrumental timbres represented an attempt to provide harmonic density (texture) to their music. The existence of such a variety of instruments also encouraged "programmatic" styles, in which the instruments were used to create realistic sound effects such as animal cries or roaring gales.

THE MUSIC OF INDIA

Background

The cultural heritage of India is divided between two basic traditions: the Moslem culture of the north and the Hindu tradition of the south. Indian music, too, reflects this cultural split; for example, the two systems use different instruments and different naming systems. Yet they also hold many things in common, including the philosophic premise that music is intimately connected with the spiritual world. In our discussion we will generally refer to the music of the southern, Hindu tradition.

The Hindu religion influences many forms of musical expression in India. The majority of Indian songs are devotional, expressing love for the deity. The religious spirit expresses itself throughout a wide range of subjects, from personal and familiar to esoteric, abstract philosophy. Even the songs of erotic love convey the bliss of union with the divine.

The basis for Indian melodies is the ancient religious music of the Aryan-speaking peoples of West Asia who migrated to India as early as the third or fourth century B.C. About 1500 B.C. the music began to be recorded in sacred books or *vedas* ("knowledge") containing prayers, chants, hymns, and other religious knowledge. Sung as incantations to the divinities or as sacred sacrificial formulas, the hymns were performed to ensure the order and stability of the universe. The oldest known treatise on classical Hindu musical theory, the *Natya Sastra,* dating from about 200 B.C., provides the bridge that connects the ancient musical heritage of India with forms still in use today.

The basic motive force of Indian music has remained constant: Music must reflect the inherent order and majesty of the universe and contribute to a performer's own spiritual development. This deep and sustaining motivation, which anchors Indian music to its mystical, philosophic framework, is reflected in the ordering of the melodic modes known as *ragas.* Each raga is related to a certain time of day or night. Indian historians tell of a musician at the court of the sixteenth-century emperor Akbar who sang a night raga at midday with such power and beauty that "darkness fell on the place where he stood." Each raga is associated also with a definite mood, a color, a festival, a deity, and certain specific natural events. Sexual differentiation of the ragas into male ragas and female *raginis* completes the unification of Indian music with the total surrounding cosmology.

A teacher of Indian music is considered a true guru, responsible not only for his students' musical progress but also for their spiritual development. The guru receives no money for his services. The knowledge and wisdom he imparts are thought to be priceless and far beyond any conceivable financial remuneration. Often, a student binds himself to one guru for a period of ten years or more. During that time he will be expected to memorize more than sixty ragas and rhythmic cycles called **talas.** The memorization is demanded not to ensure perfect reproduction of the ragas as such, but to promote the complete familiarity and understanding needed to master the pinnacle of Indian musical art—the art of improvisation.

Pitch, Scales, and Harmony

The Hindu scale consists of seven tones or *svars—sa, re, ga, ma, pa, dha,* and *ni*—each of which represents a basic mood. *Sa* and *ma* are associated with tranquility; *re* connotes harsh feelings; joy or gaiety is expressed in *pa;* sorrow is shown in *ni;* and solemn moods are expressed through *ga* and *dha.*

These seven tones, which correspond approximately to the Western diatonic scale, are modified through the use of microtones called *srutis.* Srutis alter the basic tones in much the same way that accidentals in Western music change tones. The srutis can prescribe that a tone be played in its natural state, flat, very flat, sharp, or very sharp. These srutis are very difficult for even the well-trained Western ear to distinguish.

The ragas have been developed from the seven basic tones and their modifications. Ragas are governed by a complex musical system in which certain tonal combinations are permitted while others are strongly prohibited. For example, some ragas do not allow the tones *re* and *dha* to be used in an ascending melodic progression but permit their use in descending melodic progressions. Occasionally, a tone that does not belong in the raga at all is sounded intentionally to heighten the tension and the poignancy of the melody.

To set off the melody of Indian ragas, a harmonic drone is played almost constantly throughout the piece. This drone consists of the key tone for the raga, the tone a fifth above, and the higher octave. For example, if the raga is played in C, the drone would include the tones C, G, and C. Or if the raga is constructed in E, the drone would be E, B, and E. This drone supplies the only harmonic element of Indian music. It serves an extremely important function by providing a harmonic frame of reference for both the audience and the performer.

Rhythm: The Tala

As the drone holds an Indian raga together harmonically, the rhythmic cycle, or **tala,** unifies it metrically. Talas comprise a fixed number of beats, or *matras,* which are grouped together in an orderly arrangement. The tala known as *tintal* refers to a cycle of sixteen beats grouped in four (4-4-4-4). Save for a rhythmically free prelude known as the *alapana,* this rhythmic arrangement is continued throughout the raga. Another popular tala is *jhaptal,* in which ten beats are divided into four bars (2-3-2-3). In *sultal,* the same ten beats are divided into five bars (2-2-2-2-2). Although there are twenty talas in common use, the most frequently employed tala is tintal.

While maintaining the strict division of the tala, the players are free to explore and improvise on their own rhythms, competing with each other in a contest of rhythmic skill. The rhythmic tension is increased only by the requirement that all players reach the *saman,* or first beat of the cycle, exactly together. As the players attempt more and more daring cross-rhythms, and yet still manage to come out together on the saman, the audience begins to assist the performers by clapping out the beats of the tala.

The tempo, or speed, at which a raga is performed does not vary within a section. Southern Indian music is played from beginning to end at a constant tempo and is generally performed in only one of three tempos: slow, moderate, and fast. The moderate tempo is exactly twice as fast as the slow tempo; the fast tempo is precisely twice as fast as the moderate tempo.

Performance

The ability of a performer to improvise and create his or her own music within the strict structure of the raga and tala is the standard by which Indian audiences judge the art of a musician. To leave room for the performer to improvise, the forms of Indian music have remained quite flexible. In a rhapsodic, rather free introduction to the raga, the performer gradually reveals the main notes of the raga. At some time during this introduction (the alapana), the drone softly begins to intone the raga's harmonic structure. Not until the rhythmic cycle, or tala, is set into motion does the main section of the raga get underway. Then, using an individual style of *gamaka,* or melodic ornamentation, the performer begins the raga, varying and elaborating it with a variety of technical resources.

The master performer is always bound by the rules of the raga, which govern not only the tones that may be used, but the relative importance of each tone and the way in which each tone is normally approached. The musician is usually expected to center the performance on one important tone at a time, presenting the tones in the prescribed ascending or descending order.

If the raga is being performed by more than one musician, the competitive, improvisational rhythmic exploration of the tala cycle often becomes predominant. For an Indian audience, these feats of rhythmic and musical daring are more than mere pyrotechnics. Each time the performers reach the saman, or first beat of the tala cycle, with exact precision, it is as though the reality of universal order has been reaffirmed.

Musical Instruments of India

Musical instruments of India fall into four general categories: *tata* ("taut"), stringed instruments; *avanaddha* ("covered"), drums; *susira* ("perforated"), wind instruments; and *ghana* ("fixed"), solids that are beaten.

The oldest of the Indian stringed instruments is the *vina,* which is associated with Saraswati, the Indian goddess of music and learning. Still used in southern India, it is a large lute constructed of jackwood, rosewood, or ebony. It is strung with seven strings (four playing strings and three drone strings) controlled by pegs and two sets of movable bridges. The

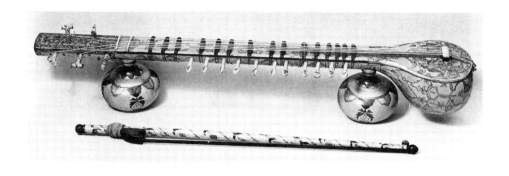

Figure 5.2 Vina, with two gourds added as resonators; movable threads. The vina is the oldest of the Indian stringed instruments. It is used today in southern India, but in the north it has been supplanted by the smaller sitar. (Courtesy The Metropolitan Museum of Art; gift of Alice E. Getty, 1946.) (46.34. 3ab)

Figure 5.3 A tabla of northern India. Drum; brown, with red, yellow, and green bands. Wood (body); skin (head); braced by strips of skin on sides. H. 10 in., Diam. 7½ in., 8 small cylinders L. 3 in. Diam. 1½ in. (Courtesy The Metropolitan Museum of Art; The Crosby Brown Collection of Musical Instruments, 1889.) (89.4.166)

main playing strings are pulled sideways on the frets to produce the characteristic ornamentation. Two hemispheric resonators fashioned from gourds amplify the sound. When played, the vina is either placed horizontally across the performer's knee or laid slanting against the left shoulder (fig. 5.2).

In the northern regions of India the vina has been supplanted by the *sitar,* which is smaller and simpler to play. The sitar has a track of twenty metal frets, above which are the seven main strings. Below the frets, a set of thirteen "sympathetic" strings can be tuned to the pitches that will most advantageously pick up the main notes of the raga to be performed.

The drums of India are fashioned so that they will reinforce the most important tonal pitches of the raga. In the south, the *mridanga,* a single-piece drum with two heads, is treated with tuning pastes so that various areas on the playing surface produce differing pitches. The *tabla* of the north (fig. 5.3) is a right-hand drum that is often tuned to the tonic. A single performer plays the tabla simultaneously with the *banya,* a left-hand bass drum.

THE MUSIC OF AFRICA

Background

In this discussion we shall be concerned only with those cultures found in the area south of the Sahara Desert (fig. 5.4). Many diverse cultures inhabit this vast area, representing a wide variety of musical styles. Nowhere in the world is music more a part of the very process of living than in Africa. Almost all communal activities are accompanied by singing, dancing, and drumming. These three activities are rarely separated; they are interdependent. As a whole, the music is characterized by sophisticated and complex rhythmic structures, a wide range of indigenous instruments, a strong oral tradition of songs, and a vast store of dances to accompany and celebrate all aspects of life.

Figure 5.4 Africa, showing countries whose music is discussed in the text.

Figure 5.5 African dancers.

These African cultures are based on the power of the spoken word, which is believed to be the "life force," called *nommo* in Bantu languages. The languages are often inflective, and common speech assumes musiclike qualities. Musical sounds produced most often are percussive, and players use bodily gestures to enhance a performance. Polyphonic textures are employed, and polyrhythms are common.

Uses of African Music

The abundance of songs may be classified into two broad categories: secular (nonreligious) and sacred (religious). Secular music is usually a common property of the people and may be performed for pure entertainment (fig. 5.5) or as an accompaniment to daily tasks. Religious music may be either ceremonial or *esoteric.* Ceremonial music is heard on such diverse occasions as the end of harvest or fishing season, at weddings and funerals, and at installations of heads of state or rulers. Esoteric music is played only by the particular religious group for which it is designed. These organizations have a repertoire of drummings, dances, and songs that are performed only by their members.

Much African music is meant to be heard by the deity. The Dogon of Mali believe that music, specifically that of the drums, is the vehicle through which the sacred word is brought to human beings. More commonly, music is used to lift up prayers to a divinity. To ensure the delivery of a healthy baby, special songs are sung during the hours of childbirth. After birth, the thankfulness of the family finds expression in chants and dancing. The naming of the baby, the loss of a first tooth, and other incidents in the life of the child from infancy through puberty are celebrated with music.

In addition to marking the stages of life, music also deepens and defines African existence. Through songs and dances young men and women are taught the language of the tribe, the traditions of family living, the obligations they will be expected to fulfill, even the "facts of life." Communal holidays and festivals are celebrated through seasonal musical offerings. In some West African cultures, political music is considered so important to the general welfare that select groups of musicians, known as *griots,* specialize in songs of governmental and social information. Each event has a consciously selected musical program, the use of which is strictly adhered to. For example, among the Banum people of the Cameroons, a specific piece of music is traditionally performed only at the hanging of a governmental minister.

To ease the strain of monotonous labor, people everywhere have sung work songs. Today in Africa, work songs coordinate communal efforts such as the closing of the fishnet after a day's harvest, counter the dreariness of repetitive agricultural tasks, and provide diversions from the dangers of gold and diamond mining.

Tonality and Styles of African Music

Africa's vocal and instrumental music exhibits a variety of styles and scale patterns. Much music is composed on a foundation of pentatonic (five-tone) or heptatonic (specially derived seven-tone) scales. In addition, a large body of African songs is based on the diatonic pattern found in Western music. A characteristic song style is based on the repetition of a short melodic phrase. This style, known as **call and response,** is found in much West African music. Repetitions of a phrase sung by a leader alternate with repetitions of the responding phrase of the chorus. Call and response singing is done in unison or with two and three parts sounded simultaneously in the chorus. The following example of call and response style is a song of exhilaration of the Akan people.

Example 5.1

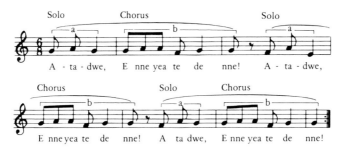

African harmony differs from Western harmony. Where it occurs, it exists mainly as a by-product of melodic elaboration. Some African folk songs carry over into an imitative type of polyphony or a simple harmonic structure in which one group of performers sustains the key tone of a melody while another group repeats the tune. At times, both groups will sing the same melody at different pitches in heterophonic style. While the interval of the third is common, harmonic intervals of a fourth, fifth, sixth, seventh, and octave may be heard in *kple* music of the Ga people (a music also based on the pentatonic scale).

Figure 5.6 A village boy sings and plays an mbira near Ibadan, Nigeria.

The unvarying pace with which Africans sing and play their music is both legendary and amazing. For long periods of time, even hours, African musicians are able to maintain an exact and constant beat. Within this framework of a steady, changeless tempo, groups of musicians drum, sing, and play in spontaneous patterns of "rhythmic polyphony." Drums beat out rhythms that are imitated and varied by voices. Instruments play in one meter, while a singer chants in another. This use of polyrhythm is customary in much African music.

Musical Instruments of Africa

The basic types of instruments found in all areas of Africa include *idiophones* (solid instruments that are beaten, such as gourds, and instruments combining both string and percussive qualities); *aerophones* (wind instruments); *membranophones* (drums); and *chordophones* (string instruments).[1]

The idiophones include some of the most common instruments found in West Africa. The most popular of these is the *mbira,* which also has many other African names, depending on the culture in which it is found. It is said to be second only to the drum in popularity. The soft and gentle sound of the *mbira* is produced when metal reeds, constructed of varying lengths and attached to a wooden sounding board, are plucked. Figure 5.6 shows an mbira from Nigeria.

1. The terms used here describe general types of instruments and thus are not unique to instruments of Africa.

A song of the Shona people of Rhodesia entitled "Gumbukumbu" uses the mbira and the *hosho,* a rattle made out of a gourd with a network of beads encircling it. The text, a proverb sung perhaps by a mother to a child, states simply:

Gumbukumbu, my mother's child, we are climbing a hill and must keep fit and strong to go on climbing. If you don't take it seriously, you will never make it, or you may, but your children will not make it as you did.

Another popular African instrument possessing both percussive and tonal qualities may be the xylophone. Used both in instrumental ensembles and alone as a solo instrument, the African xylophone may be constructed in one of many ways. In some xylophones, wooden planks or keys are set across banana trunks, while in others, wooden keys, each with its own gourd or calabash resonator, rest in a wooden frame (fig. 5.7).

The string instruments (chordophones) of Africa include lutes, zithers, harps, and lyres. Two of the most unique chordophones are the *musical mouth bow,* a single string attached to a bow that is resonated in the mouth, and the *gonje,* a small fiddle of which both bow and fiddle strings are made of animal hair.

The membranophones are the most important African musical instruments. The need for drums that can produce a variety of tones is nowhere felt more keenly than in Africa. Intricate and complex messages are relayed by drumbeat. Because many African languages are tonal, or inflected, languages in which the meanings of words are changed by delicate alterations of pitch, drums tuned to higher and lower tones can imitate the talking voice. The "talking drums" of the Ashanti people in Ghana are used to transmit various messages—from announcing emergencies to greeting the people at the opening of a ceremony

Chapter 5

or the heralding of the chief. The talking drums are also used as a vehicle for communicating literature and poetry. On state occasions, poems of honor are drummed and danced to the chief and to the community as a whole.

One of the most tonally flexible drums, the hourglass drum (called the *donno* in Ghana and the *dundun* in Nigeria) is a double-headed drum held in the player's left armpit. By applying pressure with the arm, the player alters the length of the strings that hold the two drum heads together, and is thus able to raise and lower the drum pitch.

The aerophones, or instruments whose sound is produced by blowing, include flutes, panpipes, horns, bugles, trumpets, trombones, and oboes (double and single reed). Most African aerophones, such as the flutes shown in figure 5.8, are end blown.

An Ewe Drum Orchestra

ATSIAGBEKOR: Music of the Ewe of Ghana
Cassette 7/B, Track 8
CD 7, Track 13

For ceremonial occasions it is often customary for large ensembles to be assembled. Traditional festivals may extend over several days, with different programs of music planned for each day. A festival drum orchestra of the Ewe (ay'-way), who inhabit southeastern Ghana, may consist of a drum section led by the master drummer, a percussion section (for timekeeping), singers, dancers, and a "master of ceremonies." The drum section consists of three to seven drums of various sizes and tones. The percussion section consists of two gongs—one made of metal with two bells that are tapered and joined together to form a

Figure 5.8 Two flutes and a small drum from Liberia. (Courtesy Peabody Museum, Harvard University. Photograph by F. P. Orchard. Photo No. N17211.)

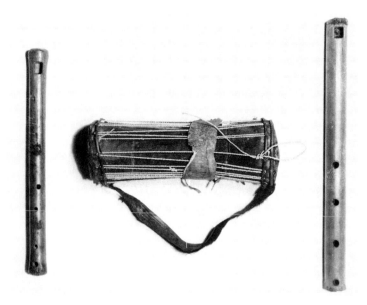

handle, the other shaped in the form of a canoe—and a rattle with a husklike shape, made from a dried gourd covered with nets of beads of tiny sections of bamboo. These instruments usually act as timekeepers and in almost every case play a standard, regular pattern, such as tap-rest-tap-rest while other members of the orchestra play contrasting rhythmic parts.

The third part of the orchestra consists of a trained chorus, headed by one or two cantors, which claps as it sings. The drum orchestra is completed by a group of costumed dancers, male and female. The "master of ceremonies" maintains decorum among the dancers and encourages the singers. All of these sections perform in a semicircle facing an open space reserved for dancing. Figure 5.9 shows orchestration for some of the drum and percussion sections of an Ewe drum orchestra.

Performance Styles

Africans are far more apt to play an instrument or sing *with* others than *for* them. It is this ease of coming together to make music that results in the characteristic group performance of African music. Although there is solo singing and playing in the music of Africa, the most typical musical expression involves any number of singers and players. The melodies that form the basis for ensemble singing or playing are generally quite short. This shortness of the melodic unit helps to keep the phrase easily workable and open to improvisation.

In every ensemble there is a master drummer. The master drum is capable of great range of expression and is most often played by true artists with a genius for improvisation. The master drummer signals the group to begin and end and is essentially the conductor

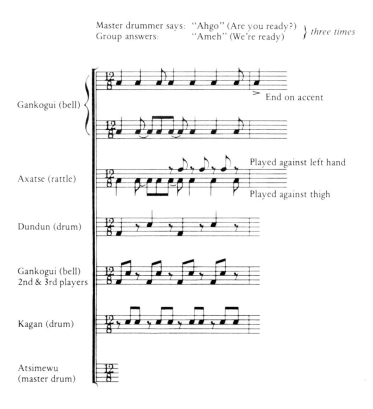

Master drummer says: "Ahgo" (Are you ready?) } *three times*
Group answers: "Ameh" (We're ready)

Gankogui (bell)

> End on accent

Axatse (rattle)

Played against left hand

Played against thigh

Dundun (drum)

Gankogui (bell)
2nd & 3rd players

Kagan (drum)

Atsimewu
(master drum)

Figure 5.9 Typical fragment of music performed by an Ewe drum orchestra, as transcribed into traditional staff notation. Note the varying rhythmic patterns assigned to the instruments. The master drummer plays all these parts as well as variations and improvisations. In addition, he is responsible for starting, stopping, and coordinating the performance of the entire ensemble.

of the orchestra. The master drummer's repertoire includes any number of standard phrases with which he improvises to enhance, articulate, accentuate, and modulate the music at appropriate points. The expression of mood and true feeling of the occasion is left to the dancers.

THE MUSIC OF NORTH AMERICAN NATIVE AMERICANS

Background

In the United States today, music is highly diversified. In addition to sophisticated concert music and many types of popular music, there are considerable repertoires of folk and ethnic music, including folk ballads, black spirituals, blues, and Native American tribal music. These latter types, which have their roots in the cultural identities of generations of large ethnic groups, form the core of what may be called traditional American music. They have three broad cultural sources: the folk music of Europe (especially the British Isles), the tribal music of the West Coast of Africa, and the music of aboriginal America. We will consider the African-American contribution to music in chapter 22. Our focus here will be on the music of the Native Americans.

The Character of Native American Music

The fact that there are approximately two hundred different Native American tribes in the United States today is evidence of the enormous variety and diversity of American Indian culture. The tribes were scattered over a vast geographic area, and each tribe had its own way of life, its own customs and traditions; yet a fundamental belief shared by the many Native American nations was the importance of song and ceremony to all aspects of life. Songs were part of every act of worship and every important ritual to mark the passing of time and the coming of death. Native American songs were also associated with the routines of daily life: hunting, praying for rain or successful harvest, coming of age, curing ills, preparing for war, or celebrating peace.

The Native Americans believed that every living thing had power—the buffalo, the eagle, the tree (fig. 5.10), even the ant. Power also resided in unseen things, in powerful spirits who could be called upon to help supply whatever was needed to sustain the life and health of the tribe. Songs were the means of invoking the aid of these seen and unseen beings; thus, songs were imbued with almost supernatural powers.

An important source of new songs was the "vision quest," a trancelike ritual in which a member of the tribe was "given" a new piece of music through supernatural means. He became, temporarily, a mouthpiece through which powerful beings spoke. A song revealed in a dream was always used to improve the life of the people in some way—for example, to heal the sick or achieve victory in war. An interesting aspect of these dream songs was that they became the personal property of the dreamer. Singing the song gave him power, power that would be lost if the song were sung by someone else, especially without the agreement of the owner.

Another type of individual expression was the song of praise sung to honor a powerful chieftain, a courageous warrior, or a loyal friend. A third type of song was associated with the rituals and ceremonies of the tribe. Such songs belonged to everyone and were sung during various kinds of ceremonies.

Since Native American songs had a specific function—to invoke the aid of powerful or supernatural beings in meeting the needs of the tribe—it was essential that they be performed correctly. For example, the chants and incantations that were used to heal the sick had to be performed accurately; if they were not, the whole ceremony would be invalidated and the sick person might not recover. Thus, much Indian music was practiced again and again until a perfect rendition was virtually ensured. An individual performer was not judged by the "beauty" of his voice; the "good" singer was one who could perform the song without error, thereby helping to ensure that the needs of the people would be met.

Technical Aspects

The music of Native Americans is for the most part vocal and accompanied by drumming. The range of tones used is small, frequently less than an octave. Various scales are employed, including diatonic, tritonic, pentatonic, and heptatonic. Vocal styles are generally emphatic and resonant, well suited for the out-of-doors. Multiple rhythms that change from duple to triple and back again are employed. The rhythm of the drum is strong, its heavy accent helping the singers to keep the beat. The melodies are usually short, simple, and repetitive.

MUSIC OF THE
SIOUX AND THE
NAVAJO:
Peyote Cult Song
Cassette 7/B, Track 9
CD 7, Track 14

Love Song
Cassette 7/B, Track 10
CD 7, Track 15

Squaw Dance
Cassette 7/B, Track 11
CD 7, Track 16

Figure 5.10 *Pine Tree Ceremonial,* by Jose Rey Toleda, Jemez Pueblo. Tempera, 1940, 19″ × 25″. (University of Oklahoma, Museum of Art, Norman, OK.)

Many Native American songs are set to poetic texts that are remarkable for their beauty and economy of expression. Often only a few words are used to convey an entire story or to trigger a whole series of associations. When words are set to music, it is not considered important that they conform to a regular meter or rhyme scheme. The words are simply small prose poems—mystical, melancholy, or frighteningly fierce.

An Arapaho vision song is set to these gentle words:

The star-child is here.
It is through him that
our people are living.

A Sioux warrior's song to his horse is intended to bring victory in battle:

My horse be swift in flight
Even like a bird;
My horse be swift in flight.
Bear me now in safety
Far from the enemy's arrows,
And you shall be rewarded
With streamers and ribbons red.

Native American songs also use meaningless syllables such as *hi ya ya ya* or *he ya ne.* Their function is to complete the rhythm of the song, much as the syllables *fa la la* do in the English carol "Deck the Halls." Although the syllables do not communicate specific meanings, they are arranged to create an abstract rhythmic pattern. For the most part, their order is intended to be strictly observed. A Shawnee Peyote text uses the following design:

He ne ne yo yo (five times)
He ya ne, he yo ca, he ya ne (twice)
Yo ho ho, yo ho ho, he ya na
He yo wa ne hi ya na, he ne yo we.

Musical instruments that accompanied the songs and dances of the Native Americans consisted of a variety of drums, rattles, and flutes. Drums were basic to rhythmic accompaniment, and like so many aspects of Indian life, certain drum rhythms had mystical significance. Three types of drums were most important: small, hand-held drums for single players; drums several feet in diameter that could be played by several people at once; and the water drum of ancient origin. While the first two types of drums were made by hollowing out both ends of a section of log, the water drum was hollowed out only on one end. Water was placed in the open end, and the drumhead was dampened as much as needed to produce the desired pitch. The water contributed to the unique resonance of the drum, which could be heard over a long distance. Drums were made from whatever materials were available to the particular tribe. Ash, cedar, and hickory were among many types of wood used.

Like the drums, the rattles also had supernatural meaning and were often used in ceremonies intended for the cure of the sick. Hand-held rattles were frequently made from gourds filled with loose materials such as seeds, pebbles, or corn. Other types of rattles, made from such materials as turtle shells and deer hoofs, were tied to a dancer's waist or below the knee.

Woodwind instruments played by the Native Americans included flutes, flageolets (a small flute resembling a recorder), and bone whistles. The young men used the flutes for courting and singing love songs; whistles played a role in certain ceremonies and in treating the sick.

SUMMARY

The distinct musical idioms of the world are virtually as numerous as the languages and social customs of the world's diverse cultures. In many non-Western societies, music is woven into the fabric of daily life. African folk music, for example, is not reserved for highly trained musicians, but may be composed and performed by all members of the community, who modify it as the occasion demands. By contrast, traditional or classical non-Western music is usually performed by artists who have refined the music through continued use or disciplined training. The Indian ragas, for example, require years of study before the performer is able to master the pinnacle of Indian musical art—the art of improvisation.

Much of the traditional music of the non-Western world is based on the belief that music is a reflection of universal order and spiritual purity. The Chinese belief in one true tone and the traditional association of Indian ragas with moods and times of day exemplify the ways in which music often becomes an integral part of belief systems in non-Western cultures.

Technically, the melodies and rhythms of ethnic music are its strongest features. There is little use of harmony per se, but a variety of instrumental and vocal timbres are employed. Stringed instruments, flutes, drums, bells, rattles, and xylophones are only a few of the many instruments crafted to enrich musical performance.

NEW TERMS

pentatonic scale
tritonic scale
heptatonic scale
raga
microtone
drone
heterophony
polyrhythm
tala
call and response

SUGGESTED LISTENING

China

The Chinese Opera. Lyrichord LLST 7212.

The Ruse of the Empty City (a Chinese opera). Folkways FW 8882.

Beating the Dragon Robe (a Chinese opera). Folkways FW 8883.

Chinese Classical Instrumental Music. Folkways FW 6812.

India

Music of India: Folk, Traditional and Classical. Ethnic Folkways Library FE 4409.

India. Columbia KL 215.

Classical Indian Music. London CM 9282.

Ragas from South India. Folkways FW 8854.

Africa

Anthology of the Music of Black Africa. Everest SDBR 3254 (3-record set).

Ewe Music of Ghana. Folkways FW 4222.

The Soul of Mbira. Nonesuch H 72054.

African Drums. Folkways 4502.

Africa—South of the Sahara. Folkways 4503.

Musique Du Burundi. Ocora OCR 40.

Music of Mali. Folkways 4338.

Native American

Authentic Music of the American Indian. Everest 3450 (3 volumes).

Indian Music of the Canadian Plains. Folkways FE 4464.

Dance and War Songs of the Kiowa Indians. Folkways FE 4393.

Healing Songs of the American Indians. Folkways FE 4251.

Indian Music of the Southwest. Folkways FW 8850.

Medieval and Renaissance Music

Pieter Brueghel the Elder, 1525/30–1569, *The Wedding Dance,* oil on panel, 119.38 cm × 157.48 cm. City of Detroit Purchase, Detroit Institute of Arts.

PRELUDE I

The Culture of the Middle Ages and Renaissance

I n 1907, a well-known art historian writing of the Middle Ages declared that art and society had ". . . degenerated into coarse decoration and vulgar copying. Learning was forgotten. The sun set in a somber sky, and civilization settled down to a millennium of sleep." Nothing could be further from the truth. Medieval Europe was a place of great artistic production, work later dismissed undeservedly as barbaric or "Gothic." Perhaps medieval design still suffers from being judged by classical standards of beauty—that is, by the values of Greek and Roman artists before and Renaissance artists after. And indeed, if we use realism as a criterion in assessing the quality of art, medieval work will look inferior. The symbolic nature of medieval art made the accurate representation of humanity and nature irrelevant.

THE MIDDLE AGES

The period of almost a thousand years known as the Middle Ages (A.D. 600–1430) grew out of the slow disintegration of the Roman Empire. The once-invincible empire was weakened by administrative disarray in its far-flung holdings, invasions from the north and east, the spread of Christian doctrine, and the removal of the imperial capital to Greek-speaking lands in the east at Constantinople. Problems began before A.D. 300; by the fifth century, Rome had faded into a town where cows grazed on the once-great forums and avenues, and a tiny fraction of its earlier population lived squalidly in the shadow of the past. In the seventh century, with the Islamic sweep of the Mediterranean, the last traces of Roman culture vanished in the west.

There is no easy explanation for a decline that took centuries. Clearly, however, the most threatening challenge to imperial values was Christianity. The Christian faith advanced its mystical Son of God as an object of faith. Christians maintained that all people were brothers and sisters in the eyes of God; they were drawn toward a Heavenly City where earthly matters were of no consequence.

It was the Church, though—one church, linked by common language and doctrine—that acted as the central agent of culture and knowledge in the Middle Ages. The monasteries, particularly before the revival of towns in the twelfth century, were the principal patrons of art and architecture. They were the vehicles for the preservation of literacy and of great literary works. In the monasteries, music in the form of liturgical chants that we call Gregorian was used in the recitation of the psalms. After the ninth century, monks composed new music for feast days.

Between the seventh and twelfth centuries, Europe turned into a mosaic of self-sufficient farms and manors that were controlled by secular lords or by the Church. Cities disappeared. Many areas that had been productive farmland became forest and wilderness. As written communication and road systems broke down, people (especially outside the Church) became less mobile. Peasants living in Burgundy had no concept of the ocean. They would all probably live their lives never traveling beyond their valley.

Europe remained on the whole rude, agrarian, and poor for hundreds of years. The arts could not flourish in an environment where survival and nourishment were daily preoccupations. Yet in spite of the small artistic output—illumination of sacred books, small sculptured reliefs, and jewelry—the quality of the art was sometimes miraculous (see page 80).

In the eleventh and twelfth centuries, however, interregional trade once again became common. Villages developed into towns and cities. Great universities were established at Paris and Bologna. Bishops, using cities as administrative centers for a wealthy and powerful Church, built great cathedrals that in the later Middle Ages replaced monasteries as the focal buildings of the Christian West. A small but important new class of merchants and artisans acted as the spearhead for economic recovery. After 1100, the economic foundations of the Renaissance began to set.

No artists of the Middle Ages thought that their abilities or achievements were anything more than a gift of God. But many artists in the later Middle Ages thought that these gifts could beautify God's universe. This attitude, along with the new money in towns and the Church, explains the building of fine churches in the twelfth century and later. We call the first phase of this new architecture Romanesque, a loose term that suggests a style closer to the Roman Empire than to the ninth-century empire of Charlemagne (see page 81). These solid, monumental churches were built mainly by rich monasteries. They were the first large-scale, stone-vaulted buildings in the West since the days of the Roman Empire; they were decorated by splendid, complicated sculpture of biblical subjects, often crowned by the awesome subject of the Last Judgment.

The second (and much longer lasting) phase of the later medieval architecture we call Gothic. By contemporaries it was called the "royal French style," because it was given its impetus by the brilliant Abbot Suger at the royal abbey of St. Denis in the 1140s. Gothic architecture borrowed from earlier buildings in the Romanesque style, but it used pointed rather than rounded arches, a change that allowed higher ceilings, and it used flying buttresses, which threw the weight of those ceilings outside the buildings. The combination of these techniques produced an entirely different appearance from that of the Romanesque. Thick, massive walls became unnecessary with the new arches and supports. Naves were built higher and higher.

The rich, translucent colors of stained glass replaced the solid wall surfaces of the Romanesque. The century after the 1140s was the time when the great French cathedrals were built—Laon, Paris, Chartres, Reims, and Amiens. In Sainte Chapelle, built in the 1240s (see page 82), the masonry became merely a skeleton for brilliant colored light.

In the thirteenth century the Gothic style radiated from the area around Paris to become the predominant style in European art for the next three hundred years. It became an "international" style with ingenious local variations. It was applied to secular (nonreligious) buildings in the great towns: In Flanders, France, and Germany excellent guild houses, town halls, and townhouses were constructed in the Gothic style.

The west facade of the Gothic cathedral (see page 83) often displayed an ambitious sculptural program with a wealth of carved designs.

In contrast to the sculpture of the previous eight hundred years, Gothic sculpture rapidly assumed a more realistic, ordered, and three-dimensional appearance, particularly in the representation of human figures (see page 84). Sculpture remained, however, a handmaiden of architecture and overwhelmingly religious in content.

THE RENAISSANCE

The raw materials of the Renaissance are visible in European culture from the twelfth century. But it was in the 1400s that the Renaissance flowered. New literary and design values, discontent in the Church, exploratory ventures in Asia and the Western Hemisphere, and the consolidation of nations under powerful monarchs—all this would completely reshape the nature of European life before 1600. The cultural future was being redefined, however, in Italian towns where artists and intellectuals were passionately admiring the achievements of ancient Rome.

These Italians, especially in Florence, were contemptuous of the recent past. They called the Gothic style "the merest travesty of art" and felt that only "in our own day . . . men dare to boast that they see the dawn of better things." Over a very short period of time—less than two generations—Florentine masters transformed the look of art. Masaccio developed systematic perspective in painting; Donatello sculpted bodies based on the proportions of Roman statues; Brunelleschi reintroduced an architecture of clear plan and classical forms.

Florentine discoveries and innovations were imitated, first by Italians and later by northern Europeans (see page 85). In the early sixteenth century, Italian artists were imported wholesale by the French king. In fact, Leonardo da Vinci died in a chateau in the Loire Valley. Italian principles became doctrine in the training of artists. The Gothic pinnacle and tower were replaced by the Renaissance capital and dome.

What captured the Italian mind of the early Renaissance was a sense of the tremendous power and beauty of the human being. While medieval Europe idealized meditative withdrawal, the Renaissance stressed activity and worldly excellence. In this climate, portraiture and the ideal nude—kinds of art that had vanished in Western art for a millennium—again became the fashion (see page 86). Humanistic literature examined the state of the world instead of heaven. Reason replaced faith as the intellectual norm.

Music, like the other art forms, developed in new directions. Composers of religious music drew on the Gregorian chants as source materials for longer, more complex polyphonic works. The more worldly outlook of the Renaissance was expressed in the composition and performance of secular vocal music, especially the English madrigals, French chansons, and German Lieder.

The northern Renaissance of the sixteenth century brought less change than the Italian Renaissance, being more a blend of the old and new. Yet it was two Germans who revolutionized the European conception of humanity's place in the cosmos. Copernicus advanced the thesis that the earth revolved around the sun and thus was not the center of the universe. Martin Luther broke with the Roman Church on the grounds of corruption in the Church and disagreement with doctrine, thus igniting a firestorm of conflict in which Protestants saw themselves as individually responsible for their spiritual destinies, not subject to papal authority. The Renaissance not only revised the look of European art, but with its emphasis on things secular, individual, and objectively observed, also transformed the assumptions of European society.

This Cross Page from the Lindisfarne Gospels (A.D. 700) was painted by
Irish monks and demonstrates the movement of Christianity into
northern Europe in the early Middle Ages. The interlace design shows
distinguished craftsmanship but no interest in representing
the visible world.

Baptistery of St. Giovanni, Florence. Eleventh century. A remarkable example of Romanesque architecture, consecrated in 1059.

Sainte Chapelle, the royal chapel in Paris, is a culmination of the Gothic
style of the thirteenth century. Between 1140 and 1240, French designers
developed a system of supports and pointed arches that made masonry
merely a skeleton for colored glass. The result was highly
spiritual and elegant.

Chartres Cathedral, France. West facade of a masterpiece
of Gothic architecture. The cathedral has very beautiful
stained glass windows.

The Culture of the Middle Ages and Renaissance

The sculpture on the west portals of Chartres Cathedral, done in the middle of the twelfth century, demonstrates the greater order and realism of Gothic design as compared with Romanesque work. The three-dimensionality of the figures suggests the growing independence of sculpture from architecture.

Garden of Delights, center panel of triptych by Hieronymus Bosch
(c. 1450–1516). Panel painting, 86⅝ in. × 76¾ in. The left panel depicts
the creation of Eve; the right panel represents the artist's vision of hell.
(Museo del Prado, Madrid/Photo Researchers, Inc.)

The Culture of the Middle Ages and Renaissance   85

Michelangelo dominated Italian art during the sixteenth century. His athletic figures, often in highly imaginative, complicated poses, were copied and paraphrased by later artists throughout Europe. *The Dying Slave* (1513–1516), shown here, was meant for a papal tomb that was never completed.

Crowning with Thorns, oil on canvas, 4'2" × 5'1½", c. 1570,
by the great Venetian painter Titian (c. 1490–1576). (Alte
Pinakothek, Munich.)

The Burial of Count Orgaz, by El Greco (1586). Oil on canvas. 16′ ×
11′10″. Created for the Church of Santo Tomé. El Greco's masterpiece
represents both terrestrial and celestial spheres, depicting Saints Stephen
and Augustine who, by legend, descended from heaven to lower the
count's body into its sepulchre.

MEDIEVAL AND RENAISSANCE MUSIC

The beginnings of our Western musical heritage are lost in the shadow of prehistoric times. But relics of musical instruments and drawings of musical activity indicate the important role music played in the earliest societies. The Bible makes frequent reference to music: David singing psalms while playing the harp, trumpets leveling the walls of Jericho. Ancient Greek philosophers wrote extensively about music, and Greek and Roman art abounds with musical scenes. Yet today we can know nothing about the sound of such early music, either because it was not preserved in any form of musical notation or because it was written in a form of notation we have not been able to decipher.

EARLY SACRED MUSIC

As the early Christian church grew, music played a major role in its ceremonies, and the body of music developed to accompany religious rites expanded enormously. At first, this music was not written down but was passed on by oral tradition to the monks, priests, and nuns of succeeding generations.

Pope Gregory I, who served as pope from 590 to 604 A.D., ordered the simplification and codification of music assigned to specific celebrations in the church calendar. This organization, combined with the development of a standardized system of musical notation, resulted in the preservation of one of the greatest bodies of musical literature in the history of Western civilization. This music is known as **Gregorian chant.**

GREGORIAN CHANT

The chants, also known as *plainsong* or *plainchant,* are monophonic, or single line melodies. Their texts are in Latin, and many are derived from the Bible, particularly the Book of Psalms.

The rhythm of the chants is unmeasured, and the tempos are flexible. The melodic material is based upon a system of scales now referred to as **church modes.** They are similar to the major and minor scales developed in the Baroque period (see page 117). However, they are different in that the church modes do not express as strong a tonal center (tonic) as do the scales that make up the later major-minor system.

Gregorian chants continue
to be a part of monastic
worship.

The melodies achieve their aesthetic beauty with the most modest means. They have an undulating, wavelike quality and a simplicity that is wholly in keeping with their religious intent as a functional part of worship. Generally, chant melodies follow the implied inflections of the text with its stressed and unstressed syllables.

"Salve Regina," a chant written by Hermannus Contractus, a Benedictine monk, is a hymn to the Virgin Mary. It was sung as part of evening worship (vespers) during a specified portion of the church year.

The chant (example 6.1) is made up of six sections. The first section (A) consists of a melodic phrase and its immediate repetition with different words. Each subsequent section (B through F) consists of a line of text with its own individual melody. Two types of phrases are employed: **syllabic,** in which each syllable is given one note, and **melismatic,** in which one syllable is spread over several notes. The concluding section (F) is of particular interest because of the expressiveness resulting from the extended phrases on "O," the last of which is the longest **melisma** in the entire piece.

Many chant melodies such as "Salve Regina" were used by composers in the Middle Ages and throughout the Renaissance as the basis for longer and more complex compositions such as the Mass and the motet. The *Missa* (Mass) *Salve Regina* by Palestrina (see pages 98–99) is a good example of the use of this melody in the construction of a longer and more elaborate musical work.

HILDEGARD OF BINGEN

Hildegard of Bingen (1091–1179) was a remarkable Benedictine abbess who composed chants for services that took place in the convent she headed. This mystic, composer, and poet collected these chants into a manuscript volume entitled *Symphonia Armonie Celestium Revelationum* (*Symphony of the Harmony of Heavenly Revelations*). This volume

Example 6.1 Hermannus Contractus, "Salve Regina."

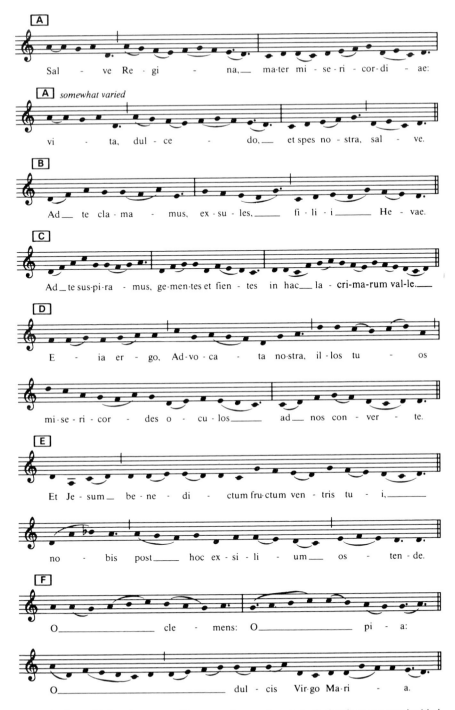

Hail, Holy Queen, Mother of mercy, our life, our sweetness, and our hope. To thee do we cry, poor banished children of Eve. To thee do we send up our sighs, mourning and weeping in this valley of tears. Turn then, most gracious advocate, thine eyes of mercy toward us; and after this our exile, show unto us the blessed fruit of thy womb, Jesus. O clement, O loving, O sweet Virgin Mary!

included the chants sung at special services in the convent for saints' feast days and other special ceremonies throughout the church year. The words of many of these chants are poems in praise of the Virgin Mary; others are descriptions of the accomplishments of saints.

Hildegard was the author of the earliest known morality play, *Ordo virtutum* (*Play of the Virtues*), a sung drama in which personified Virtues and the Devil fight for control over the soul.

THE MASS

The **Mass** is the most solemn service of the Roman Catholic church. It is the commemoration and symbolic reenactment of the Last Supper of Christ. The *liturgy* of the Mass, the prescribed ceremony, is divided into two parts: the *Ordinary* (using those texts that do not change from day to day) and the *Proper* (using those texts that vary according to the religious nature of the specific day in the church year). The Mass combines the items from the Ordinary and the Proper according to the plan shown in figure 6.1.

Over time, five of the texts from the Ordinary came to be favored for musical settings: Kyrie, Gloria, Credo, Sanctus and Benedictus, and Agnus Dei. These texts have been a source of inspiration for composers since the fourteenth century, including Machaut, Josquin des Prez, Palestrina, Bach, Mozart, Haydn, Beethoven, Berlioz, and Stravinsky.

MEDIEVAL SECULAR MUSIC

In addition to the music of the Church, the Middle Ages witnessed the growth of a rich tradition of nonreligious, or *secular,* music. Gregorian chants used only Latin, but secular texts came to be written in the vernacular (everyday) language of the country of origin. Like today's popular music, these texts often concerned the subject of love. Some texts were humorous or bawdy; others treated political subjects or told stories of vagabonds.

The most important early secular vocal music was created and performed by poet-musicians, called *trouvères* in northern France, *troubadours* in southern France, and *Minnesingers* in Germany. Their ranks included many members of the nobility who traversed the countryside as court musicians, poets, and sometimes even jugglers. The number of musical and poetic works created by these wanderers is enormous. The melodies of their songs, like the melodies of the chant, were monophonic and simple in design. But they were probably sung with some kind of instrumental accompaniment. The songs mainly consisted of one note of music to one syllable, with occasional ornamental melismas. In the case of the trouvères and troubadours, the form of their pieces was rather free, often including a refrain—a recurring line of words with its distinctive melody. The Minnesingers favored the AAB form.

Instruments not only accompanied songs, but also played an important role in the dance. Many types of instruments were employed, including the harp, the vielle (a precursor of the modern violin), the psaltery, a kind of zither played by striking or plucking its strings, lutes, horns, drums, trumpets, a variety of wind instruments and bells, and portable organs.

Figure 6.1 The liturgy of the Mass.

Proper	Ordinary
1. *Introit* (Processional)	
	2. *Kyrie eleison* "Lord have mercy on us"
	3. *Gloria in excelsis Deo* "Glory to God in the highest"
4. *Collect* (Prayer on behalf of the congregation)	
5. *Epistle* (From the Epistles of the New Testament)	
6. *Gradual* (a psalm verse)	
7. *Alleluia* (or *Tract*) (During times of penitence, such as Lent, the Alleluia is replaced by a psalm, called the Tract.)	
8. *Sequence* (A form of hymn)	
9. *Gospel* (From one of New Testament Gospels)	
	10. *Credo* (*in unum Deum*) "I believe in one God"
11. *Offertory*	
	12. *Sanctus* "Holy, holy, holy"
	13. *Benedictus qui venit* "Blessed is he that cometh"
	14. *Canon* (A series of prayers said by the priest in a low voice during the consecration of the bread and wine)
	15. *Agnus Dei* (*qui tollis peccata mundi*) "Lamb of God, who taketh away the sins of the world"
16. *Communion*	
17. *Post-Communion* (A prayer of prayers)	
	18. *Ite missa est* "Go" (The congregation is dismissed)

POLYPHONY AND MEASURED RHYTHM

Both sacred and secular music remained monophonic and unmeasured until the tenth century, when two or more voice parts began appearing in combination. This new method of composition went through a number of stages over a long period of time. The development of polyphonic music from the twelfth to the fourteenth century was centered in northern France and was dominated by the Notre Dame school under the leadership first of Leonin and then his successor, Perotin. At first, two melodic lines duplicated each other at different pitch levels. They moved in parallel motion—that is, at the same time and in the same melodic direction. Gradually, contrary motion was introduced—when one voice moved upward, the other moved in the opposite direction. In this way the two voice parts began to be melodically independent; they moved in different directions but at the same time. These early compositions were called **organa** (singular, organum).

The rhythm of early organa was unmeasured, and it remained so as long as the two melodies moved at the same time. Eventually, the voice parts assumed rhythmic independence. They not only moved in different melodic directions but in different time patterns, necessitating the development of a new type of notation in which the relative length of notes in the melody were indicated with precision, a technique called **mensural notation.**

The independence of simultaneous melodies that moved in different directions *melodically* and at different times *rhythmically* resulted in what became known as polyphony. Thus, two major developments in Western music took place: (1) the change from monophony to polyphony and (2) the change from unmeasured, relatively free rhythm to **measured rhythm,** in which precise time values were related to each other. Polyphony and measured rhythm were fully developed in the polyphonic setting of the Mass and the **motet.**

THE MOTET

Much as the organa had added an independent line of music to the chant, the **motet** added a second set of words (the name *motet* comes from the French word *mot,* meaning "word"). Originally a form of religious music, the motet grew out of the two-part organa in the thirteenth century. While the lower voice continued to sing the words and music of the chant, a second text was sung in the upper voice. The second text at first paraphrased the chant text being sung below.

The motet was soon also employed for secular occasions. As its form evolved, the upper voice began to sing in the vernacular. The subject matter was usually secular and sometimes bawdy. Gradually, composers added a third and even a fourth voice part.

By the fourteenth century, the motet had increased in length and had become more elaborate in its melodic and rhythmic structure. But even with the increased number of melodic lines and texts, the range of voices remained narrow, and the chant was almost always retained in some form in the lowest voice part. Without question, the most important composer of the fourteenth century was Guillaume de Machaut (ca. 1300–ca. 1377). In addition to large quantities of secular music and motets, he wrote the earliest polyphonic setting of the entire Ordinary of the Mass, *Messe de Nostre Dame (Mass of Our Lady),* probably the most famous piece of music from the fourteenth century:

DE MACHAUT:
Agnus Dei from *Messe de Nostre Dame*
Cassette 1/A, Track 3
CD 1, Track 3

Agnus Dei, qui tollis peccata mundi:	*Lamb of God, who takest away the sins of the world:*
miserere nobis.	*Have mercy upon us.*
Agnus Dei, qui tollis peccata mundi:	*Lamb of God, who takest away the sins of the world:*
dana nobis pacem.	*Grant us peace.*

By the fifteenth century, the motet had evolved full circle. Once again it became primarily a religious form, using one text for all voices. The text was almost always taken from the Bible. One of the leading motet composers of the fifteenth century was Guillaume Dufay (ca. 1400–1474).

Entwickelung der Notenschrift.

1. Codex 339 der Bibliothek zu St. Gallen (10. Jahrhundert).

2. Neumen und Buchstaben. — Antiphonar von Montpellier (11. Jahrhundert).

3. Neumen auf einer geritzten Linie ohne Farbe. → Graduale von Albi (11. Jahrhundert).

4. Neumen auf vier Linien. — Graduale aus dem 12. — 13. Jahrhundert.

5. Auf Linien gesetzte Neumen mit viereckigem Notenkörper [Nota quadriquarta] seit dem 12. Jahrhundert bis heute.

6. Schwarzrote Mensuralnote des 14.—15. Jahrhunderts. — Tenor einer 3 stimmigen Chanson von G. Binchois.

7. Weiß-schwarze Mensuralnote des 15.—17. Jahrhunderts. Dasselbe Stück.

8. Dasselbe Stück mit heutigen Noten ohne Verkürzung der Werte.

9. Dasselbe, die Werte auf den vierten Teil verkürzt.

Meyers Konv.-Lexikon, 5. Aufl.   Bibliogr. Institut in Leipzig   *Zum Artikel »Noten«.*

The evolution of the writing of musical notes has taken nearly a thousand years. Not only has the style changed, but the indications for durational values have become increasingly precise. Time periods for the examples shown are as follows: line 1, tenth century; lines 2 and 3, eleventh century; line 4, twelfth to thirteenth century; line 5, twelfth century onward; line 6, fourteenth to fifteenth century (mensural notation); line 7, fifteenth to seventeenth century (mensural notation); lines 8 and 9, modern notation.

RENAISSANCE SACRED MUSIC

The Renaissance in literature and the visual arts began in the fourteenth century and was centered in Italy. The Renaissance in music began in the fifteenth century in what is today northern France, Holland, and Belgium. The Franco-Flemish style developed in these countries and spread to all parts of the Continent.

In addition to Guillaume Dufay, the outstanding members of this early Flemish school were Johannes Ockeghem (ca. 1430–1495), Jacob Obrecht (1452–1505), and Josquin des Prez (ca. 1450–1521). In their Masses and motets, four-part writing became standard. An independent bass part was added beneath the chant for the first time, so that the chant was no longer the lowest voice part. In addition, the use and treatment of the chant as a basic material became much freer and at times was abandoned altogether. The practice of using secular tunes (rather than chant) as the musical raw material for sacred compositions became extremely popular. The polyphonic style emphasized the true independence of each of the four parts.

JOSQUIN DES PREZ

The greatest representative of the Franco-Flemish school was Josquin des Prez, who spent most of his creative life outside his native country, Belgium. In 1475, he was a member of the choir at the court of the Duke of Szorfa in Milan, and later he joined the Papal Choir in Rome. He was also active in the Italian cities of Florence, Ferrara, and Modena. In the last years of his life, he returned to northern Europe.

Josquin was acknowledged by his contemporaries as the greatest master of the time, and he developed the complex Franco-Flemish style to its highest point. In much of his secular music he employed a lighter, more homophonic style, then popular in Italy. His polyphonic style is distinguished by the use of *imitation,* wherein a melodic fragment stated in one voice is repeated or imitated by another voice a measure or two later. Examples of imitative polyphony appear earlier than Josquin, but he was the first to apply the principle consistently.

Josquin's motet *Ave Maria (Hail Mary)*, a portion of which is shown in example 6.2, is typical of his motet writing in the following ways:

1. The melodic material is freely based on a Gregorian chant, in this case *Ave Maria, gratia plena.*

2. It is a four-part composition in which the voices are often paired, the two upper voices pitted against or alternating with the two lower voices.

3. The music is **through-composed**—that is, each unit of text is given a different musical setting. (This contrasts to **strophic** music, in which each stanza of text is sung to the same melody.) A feeling of continuity is achieved through overlapping phrases: Before one phrase ends, another voice begins a new phrase, so that there is seldom a cadence when all four voices come to a stop. This continuous flow is characteristic of later Renaissance polyphony.

JOSQUIN:
Ave Maria
Cassette 1/A, Track 4
CD 1, Track 4

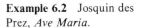

Example 6.2 Josquin des Prez, *Ave Maria*.

Hail Mary, full of grace, the Lord (is with thee).

4. Contrapuntal passages alternate with homophonic sections, another hallmark of Josquin's style. Despite the complexity of the contrapuntal writing, the text remains clear, for Josquin assigns to the homophonic sections the expressive parts of the text, particularly at the very end where Josquin adds an unusual personal note—*O Mater Dei, memento mei* (O Mother of God, remember me).

Josquin left many motets, many Masses, and a considerable amount of secular music. He was also a gifted teacher, and many of his pupils became outstanding figures in the next generation of composers.

Medieval and Renaissance Music

GIOVANNI PIERLUIGI DA PALESTRINA

One of the most distinguished of Josquin's successors was Giovanni Pierluigi da Palestrina (1524–1594), who spent the greater part of his life as choirmaster of St. Peter's in Rome. Palestrina's great contribution was to return church music to the simplicity and purity of earlier times. Although his motets are masterpieces of composition, his Masses constitute his most important work.

Palestrina lived and worked during the Counter-Reformation, the reaction by the Catholic church to the spread of Protestantism. Central to this reaction was the Council of Trent, which met from 1545 to 1563 to formulate and execute the means by which church reform could be accomplished. The Council investigated every aspect of religious discipline, including church music. It was the opinion of the Council that sacred music had become corrupted by complex polyphonic devices that obscured the text and diverted attention from the act of worship. To remedy this situation the Council called for a return to a simpler vocal style, one that would preserve the sanctity of the text and discourage frivolous displays of virtuosity by the singers.

Legend has it that Palestrina, in order to prevent the Council from abolishing the polyphonic style entirely, composed a Mass of such beauty and simplicity that he was able to dissuade the cardinals from taking this drastic step. Without abandoning polyphony, Palestrina created a style that was less intricate and more direct than that of his predecessors. A prolific composer, Palestrina wrote more than one hundred Mass settings. One of his relatively late Masses was based on the chant melody "Salve Regina." The *Missa Salve Regina,* which is an excellent example of late Renaissance polyphony, employs elements of the chant in each movement.

Notice in example 6.3 that the notes of the chant, marked with an X, are used as the basic melodic material. The Mass also exhibits the following characteristics:

1. All the voice parts (five in this case) are of equal importance. Each participates fully in singing the text.
2. The general style is imitative polyphony, with occasional homophonic sections.
3. Strong cadences set off sections from each other.

Palestrina's sacred music was performed *a cappella,* without instruments, but this was the exception rather than the rule. Although no instrumental parts were written, it is well known that instruments frequently played along with or substituted for a voice in one or more of the parts.

PALESTRINA:
Missa Salve Regina
Cassette 1/A, Track 5
CD 1, Track 5

Example 6.3 Palestrina, *Missa Salve Regina.*

Lord have mercy on us.
X = notes of chant incorporated into each vocal part.

RENAISSANCE SECULAR MUSIC

In addition to being a time of great piety, the sixteenth century was also a period of bawdy earthiness, irreverent humor, and celebration of sensual love. The same composers who created works "for the greater glory of God" also wrote compositions of an entirely different character. In Italy and England, the principal form of secular music was the *madrigal;* in France, it was the *chanson;* in Germany, the *Lied.*

THE MADRIGAL

The Renaissance **madrigal** is a poem set to music. It had its beginnings in the fourteenth century among the aristocrats of the small Italian courts. The texts, written in the vernacular, were often twelve-line poems whose subjects were sentimental or erotic. The early madrigal was written in a predominantly homophonic style. It was usually in three, but sometimes four parts, and its expressive qualities were subdued and restrained. The so-called *classical madrigal* of the mid-sixteenth century was written usually for five and sometimes for four or six voices. Its texture was more polyphonic than that of the early madrigal, and a greater attempt was made to capture in the music the expressive possibilities of the words.

The final flowering of the madrigal took place during the closing decades of the sixteenth century. The late madrigal was an elaborate composition, invariably nonstrophic, with a mixture of homophonic and polyphonic textures. It used notes from the chromatic scale (all twelve notes in the octave) for bold effects, often to express sadness. The compositions also used coloristic and dramatic effects. One of the most interesting elements of the madrigal style was **word painting,** which attempted to represent the literal meaning of the text through music. Thus, the melody would ascend for the word "heaven," and a wave-like melody would depict the word "water."

Around the middle of the sixteenth century, the Italian madrigal was brought to England. There it flourished under a variety of names: song, sonnet, canzonet, and ayre. William Byrd (1543–1623) and Thomas Morley (1557–1603) were the first English composers to cultivate the genre. Morley wrote simplified versions of the madrigal, known as *balletts.* Adapted from the Italian *balletti,* they were usually characterized by a *fa-la-la* refrain of the type that appears in the English carol "Deck the Halls." Enlivened by accents and a regular beat, the music was largely homophonic.

MORLEY:
*Now Is the Month
of Maying*
Cassette 1/A, Track 6
CD 1, Track 6

THE CHANSON

In the sixteenth century the **chanson** (the French word for "song") was to France what the madrigal was to Italy and England. Early chansons developed with the work of Clement Jannequin (ca. 1485–ca. 1560), Claudin de Sermisy (ca. 1490–1562), and Pierre Certon (ca. 1510–1572).

During the Renaissance, music became a popular leisure-time activity for both the educated middle class and the aristocracy. This detail of a fresco in the Este palace, Ferrara, Italy, depicts the musical and sensual delights of spring.

Chansons modified the motet style with strong accented rhythms, frequent repetitions, and short phrases ending simultaneously in all parts. They were usually sung by three, four, or five voices, and sections of simple imitation alternated with sections that were essentially homophonic.

Word painting occurred frequently in the early chansons. Jannequin wrote several *program chansons,* in which the music imitates a nonmusical idea. An example is his *Chant des oiseaux* (*Song of the Birds*), in which the singers' voices imitate the sounds of birds such as the cuckoo.

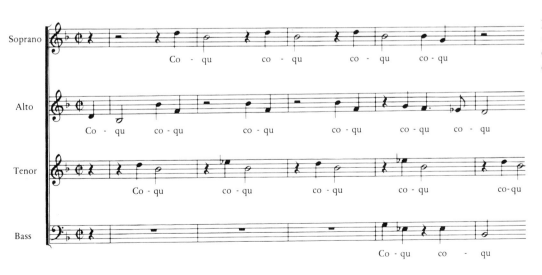

Example 6.4 Jannequin, *Chant des oiseaux.* Cassette 1/A, Track 7 CD 1, Track 7.

In Germany, the counterpart to the French chanson was the **Lied,** also meaning "song." The Lied (plural, **Lieder**) dates from the middle of the fifteenth century, when both monophonic melodies and three-part settings appeared. The early Lieder, which were heavily influenced by the Netherlands' polyphonic style, later provided the Lutheran church with many melodies for chorale tunes (see chapter 7). The first important Lied composer was Heinrich Isaac (ca. 1450–1517).

In the sixteenth century, Germany looked to Italy and France for musicians to staff her courts and municipalities. As a result, Lied composers turned from the Franco-Flemish styles to the chanson and madrigal as their new models. In these Lieder, the text was treated in the manner of the madrigals, and the various melodies were set in imitative counterpoint.

RENAISSANCE INSTRUMENTAL MUSIC

Although most of the music of the Renaissance was written for voices, the role of instrumental music should not be underestimated. Instruments were used in church, at many festive and social occasions, as part of theatrical productions, and in private homes.

The earliest music played on instruments was sacred or secular vocal music. During the Renaissance, some music was written specifically for instruments. Most of it was dance music, because dancing was an important part of Renaissance social life. A fairly large collection of this music has been preserved, but apparently much of it was improvised on well-known tunes or harmonic bass patterns, as jazz is today.

The most popular instrument of the fifteenth and sixteenth centuries was the lute. The earliest lute music consisted of transcriptions (a **transcription** is an arrangement of a composition for a medium other than that for which it was originally written) of vocal pieces and dance music, but in the sixteenth century, composers began to write original pieces for the lute. These **ricercari,** or **fantasias,** were elaborate polyphonic pieces that demonstrated the virtuosity of the performer, who was often also the composer. Beginning in the early sixteenth century, volumes of solo music for the lute were published in Italy, France, Germany, England, and Spain.

TERRA.

Humorum guttas mater cum Terra recepit ;
Fœta parie nitidas fruges, arbustaque læta,
Et genus humanum, parit omnia secla ferarum :
Pabula dum præbet, quibus omnes corpora pascunt,
Martin de Vos figuravit.

Et dulcem ducant vitam, sobriemque propagent :
Vnde etiam maternum nomen adepta es &
Luxuriem ergo caue partis quæ parcere nescit,
Donorumque Dei, quæ Terra hæc gignit, abutun .
Crispin de Passe sculpsit &c.

The lute was the most popular Renaissance stringed instrument. During the sixteenth century, volumes of solo music for the lute were published all over Europe.

Keyboard instruments, especially the clavichord, harpsichord, and organ, were also popular during the Renaissance. Keyboard music evolved through the same phases as lute music, from vocal music to dance music, and then to original compositions, which were increasingly complex.

Small chamber music ensembles, called consorts, were favored among those who performed music in their homes. One of the favorite groupings, especially in England, was a consort of several viole da gamba. Polyphonic pieces for such consorts of two to five or more were written by some of England's greatest composers, including William Byrd and Orlando Gibbons (1583–1625). Similar pieces were also played by consorts of recorders and other woodwinds. Music for brass and reed instruments was popular for outdoor occasions, for festive church ceremonies, and for dancing.

PRAETORIUS:
Dances from *Terpsichore*
Cassette 1/B, Track 1
CD 1, Track 8

Characteristics of Medieval and Renaissance Music

	MEDIEVAL	RENAISSANCE
Texture	Gregorian chants and troubadour songs were monophonic; medieval motet employed polyphony	Polyphonic
Tonality	Church modes	Church modes
Rhythm	Gregorian chant employed unmeasured rhythm; secular music employed measured rhythm	Measured
Singing Style	Sacred music: solemn, expressive, small voice range Secular music: simple, strophic, more rhythmic	Four-part singing common; some virtuoso singing Late madrigal used "word painting"
Large Vocal Works	None	Polyphonic Mass
Small Vocal Works	Gregorian chant, organum, medieval motet	Motet, madrigal, chanson, Lied
Musical Instruments	Instruments accompanied songs and dances. Lute, psaltery, pipes, and bells.	Lute, chamber consorts (especially viole da gamba), recorder, organ, clavichord, and harpsichord.
Instrumental Music	Sacred music: arrangements of vocal pieces Secular music: isolated dances	Ricercari, fantasias, dance forms

SUMMARY

Western music grew out of the religious music of the Middle Ages. The liturgy of the Mass is divided into the Ordinary and the Proper. The Kyrie, Gloria, Credo, Sanctus and Benedictus, and Agnus Dei became the parts of the Ordinary most favored for musical settings. Chants, closely allied with the Roman Catholic liturgy, were codified and compiled during the time of Pope Gregory. In the following centuries the simple, monophonic form of these chants evolved into the more complex, polyphonic forms of the organum and the motet. These forms, in turn, were further developed by Machaut and Dufay, and the sacred music of the Renaissance culminated in the words of Josquin des Prez and Palestrina.

Together with the sacred music, secular music was also developing. Early vocal music was performed by trouvères in northern France, troubadours in southern France, and Minnesingers in Germany. The vernacular and sometimes bawdy tradition of their songs was preserved in the madrigals, chansons, and Lieder of the Renaissance.

Instrumental music of the Renaissance evolved from vocal music to dance music, and then to more complex original compositions. The most popular Renaissance instrument was the lute, with keyboard music and chamber consorts also coming into use.

NEW TERMS

Gregorian chant (plainsong, plainchant)
   church modes
   syllabic
   melismatic (melisma)
Mass
   organum (organa)
   mensural notation
   measured rhythm
   motet

through-composed
strophic
madrigal
word painting
chanson
Lied (pl. Lieder)
transcription
ricercari (fantasias)

SUGGESTED LISTENING

Musical Organizations

Capella Antiqua (Munich). Directed by Konrad Ruhland, this group employs original instruments of the Renaissance or modern copies. Its performances are attempts at reconstructing the original musical practices of the times. (Telefunken Records, *Das Alte Werk* series.)

The Early Music Quartet (Munich). This vocal and instrumental ensemble of three Americans and one German specializes chiefly in medieval song literature. (Telefunken Records, *Das Alte Werk* series.)

New York Pro Musica Antiqua. Founded in 1952 by Noah Greenberg, this group (now, sadly, defunct) was for a number of years the most prominent of American early music groups. (Decca Records.)

The Waverly Consort (New York). This ensemble of ten men and women, directed by Michael Jaffe, is a leading American group specializing in the performance of medieval and Renaissance music. (Vanguard and Columbia Records.)

Choir of the Monks of the Abbey of Saint Pierre de Solesmes (Solesmes, France). The performances of chant by this Benedictine order are considered by many scholars to be among the best, historically as well as musically. (Deutsche Grammophon Gesellschaft, DGG, Archive series.)

Medieval Secular Music

John Dunstable, *O Rosa bella.* Though Dunstable was an English composer, he spent much of his life on the Continent; some of his vocal works employ French or Italian texts.

Medieval Sacred Music

Guillaume de Machaut, *Messe de Nostre Dame* (*Mass of Our Lady*). One of the earliest and best-known polyphonic settings of the Ordinary of the Mass. The five interrelated movements demonstrate most of the important compositional techniques of the late medieval period.

Renaissance Secular Music

Roland de Lassus, *Matona, mia cara* (*Matona, Lovely Maiden*). One of the best-known of Renaissance satirical pieces, this madrigal for four voices makes fun of the German soldiers occupying much of sixteenth-century Italy by—among other things—mocking their pronunciation of Italian ("Matona" for "Madonna").

Orlando Gibbons, *The Silver Swan*. One of the loveliest vocal compositions ever written, this melancholy work is an outstanding example of English madrigal style.

Thomas Morley, *My Bonnie Lass She Smileth*. Using both homophonic and polyphonic textures, swift changes from the major to minor, and a "*fa la la*" section, this song is typical of Morley's balletts.

Renaissance Sacred Music

Guillaume Dufay, *Missa Se la face ay pale* (*Mass on "If My Face Is Pale"*). A classic example of early Renaissance polyphonic style, this four-voice setting of the Ordinary takes its rather odd name from the title of the chanson melody upon which it is based.

Josquin des Prez, *Missa Pange lingua* (*Mass on "Sing, My Tongue"*). One of the great masterpieces of the Renaissance, this work is based on the plainsong hymn for the Feast of Corpus Christi.

Giovanni Pierluigi da Palestrina, *Sicut cervus desiderat* (*Like as the Hart Desireth*). One of Palestrina's most expressive and technically perfect works, this motet, its text taken from Psalm 42, is a classic example of Palestrina-style harmonic and melodic construction.

Hildegard of Bingen, *Ordo Virtutum*. Harmonia Munchic-20395/96. Hildegard's music represents the transition from chant to polyphony.

Music of the Baroque Era

The Lute Player; Orazio Gentileschi; National Gallery of Art, Washington, D.C.;
Ailsa Mellon Bruce Fund.

The Triumph of the Baroque Style

Baroque is a word that eludes easy definition. It refers to a special approach to the arts that dominated all of the European continent in the seventeenth and eighteenth centuries—an approach that sought consciously to move the emotions and arouse the feelings of an audience through spectacular displays of sight and sound.

The early Baroque is grounded in Italian art and reflects the recovery of the Roman Catholic church after the Protestant challenge of the sixteenth century. In 1517, Martin Luther had openly defied the authority of the pope and the legitimacy of church doctrine. He and his followers wanted to reform and "purify" the Christian religion; in doing so they set into motion a religious controversy that shattered European stability for more than a century. In the 1500s, large blocs of anti-Romanists threatened to bring about the utter collapse of Catholicism.

The Catholic response to the Protestant heresy is called the Counter-Reformation. It included a far-reaching "housecleaning" within the Church to stamp out clerical abuses and to shore up the faith where it was crumbling. Between 1545 and 1563, church leaders at the Council of Trent drew up a broad program that included tighter discipline for the clergy and a strong denial of the individual's right and ability to interpret the Bible. The Church reexamined its rituals. The Jesuit Order was established as an international force for teaching, missionary work, reconversion, and protection of the faith. By the seventeenth century, the Counter-Reformation had paid its dividends: Most of Europe remained bound to Catholicism and Rome.

After 1600, the arts were used by the Italians to celebrate the power and glory of the Church. The Italian artist became a narrator of the Christian spectacle. All over the peninsula, painters and sculptors reworked ceilings and chapels. Architects built new churches and palaces, and craftsmen decorated them with rich gilding and ornamentation. The energy of Italian design was imitated throughout the continent, and Rome became an unparalleled cultural center where artists from many different countries came to admire the classical ruins and modern wonders of the city. Pilgrims and noblemen returned to their lands with marvelous tales of "the first city of the world."

The baroque style grew out of renaissance forms that were employed in dynamic and grand ways to trumpet church prestige. The look was sparkling, exciting, and new: It is not surprising that the new Roman style was immediately and immensely popular and that it rapidly spread to the north and became an international style.

In the case of painting, the most radical of early baroque artists in Italy was Caravaggio, whose striking contrasts of light and shadow and vigorous realism in figures and settings redirected the course of all European painting (see page 111).

But the two greatest baroque painters who followed were Rubens, who was Flemish, and Poussin, who was French. In different ways these artists both depended on Italian sources. Rubens traveled in Italy as a young man and was influenced by Michelangelo's powerful figures and Venetian color, as well as by Caravaggio. Poussin lived for more than forty years in Rome.

The differences between Rubens and Poussin reveal the breadth of the baroque style in painting during the seventeenth century. Rubens's complicated compositions, full of rich color and straining movement and packed with gesturing figures and dramatic emotions, are one kind of baroque (see page 112).

Poussin, who had tremendous impact on his French contemporaries, was much more reserved, crisp, and logical in his design. He was deeply affected by classical sculpture and anxious to achieve a baroque that was balanced and elegant in its drama (see page 113).

Bernini, another of the great baroque artists, was aided by a large group of assistants. He produced, over a very long career, an extraordinary amount of sculpture whose appearance set the style of work in stone and metal in the seventeenth century. His most famous work is the exquisite *Ecstasy of St. Theresa* (shown on page 114).

To present this radiant moment, Bernini showed the instant when the saint was pierced by an angel's golden arrow. His cutting of the marble is delicate and fluid, the drapery sweeping in such magnificent folds that the saint appears to float in absolute exaltation in the clouds of heaven itself. The drama of the scene makes apathy or detachment on the part of the observer unlikely. Like so much baroque work, Bernini's sculpture meant to force the onlooker into active participation with the image.

Bernini was also a great architect. He finished the great Basilica of St. Peter's, begun 150 years earlier; his masterful colonnade in front of the facade is a monumental pair of arms that reach out toward the faithful and almost compel them to move toward the church itself.

The most inventive of baroque architects, however, was Borromini, a designer whose work was the culmination of baroque ingenuity. The most radical of his buildings was San Carlo alle Quattro Fontane (see page 114). Full of weirdly undulating surfaces, the walls of the church protrude and recede, creating a wavelike effect, and the contrasting planes of stone produce sculptural patterns of light and shade. The church seems built not of stone but of some pliable material.

Borromini had great influence on the building of the late baroque churches of Germany and Austria (a more delicate eighteenth-century style usually called rococo). The baroque fondness for ornate decoration reached its greatest emotional extremes here in gilded altars with carved scrolls and garlands, and in gold and white walls with pastel-painted ceilings—all calculated to awe and delight. Critics of these beautiful churches too easily disregard their sincerity and dismiss them unfairly as "gaudy" and "vulgar" interiors with "false fronts." To their builders they were magical syntheses of painting, sculpture, and architecture that mirrored the magnificence of the Roman Catholic church.

Music played an important role in the life of the churches. Sounds, perhaps more than the visual arts, could move, elevate, and involve a congregation and thus intensify the spiritual experience. While Protestants were skeptical of visual displays and the veneration of images, they warmed to the use of music in church services. In the seventeenth century, major Protestant churches began to form orchestras and choirs and to hire organists, soloists, and music masters. The greatest baroque church musician was Johann Sebastian Bach, who spent a major part of his career at Leipzig, leaving a vast treasure of sacred music, vocal and instrumental, at the time of his death in 1750.

It is wrong, however, to think of the baroque arts as exclusively religious. In France they were used to enhance the position of Louis XIV and his court. The efforts of architects, stonemasons, sculptors, painters, furniture makers, and gardeners were carefully coordinated to remake the royal palace at Versailles in the latter half of the seventeenth century. By 1700, the visitor to Paris would have been overwhelmed by French monuments to the power of the Crown, in a style codified and taught by the Royal Academy, a style increasingly fashionable throughout the continent. In the eighteenth century, Paris replaced Rome as the leader in European culture and design.

Because the seventeenth century was fascinated with the natural world, baroque art could also celebrate the ordinary and commonplace. In Dutch painting, a brilliant artist like Rembrandt might craft biblical scenes, such as *The Blinding of Samson,* page 115, but the predominant taste in baroque Holland leaned toward paintings of the familiar world of town and country. Walls were decorated with landscapes, still lifes, and scenes from everyday life. There was a rage for portraiture among bankers and businessmen, prominent civic leaders, and well-heeled families. Citizens, soldiers, and peasants, their daily occupations and amusements, their gardens and taverns, all became the subjects of works of art. This naturalism reminds us of the scientific investigation taking place during that century, when basic laws of the physical and biological sciences were uncovered. In 1702, a primitive steam engine was developed.

The best example of the worldly side of the baroque spirit is perhaps in opera, a medium developed to entertain royalty and aristocrats of highly discriminating taste in surroundings like the opera house at Versailles (see page 115). This kind of theater integrated scene painting, costuming, dancing and choreography, and vocal and instrumental music. Opera thus achieved the synthesis of many different arts in one grandiose spectacle to thrill its audience. It is this elevating exploitation of the senses that is the hallmark of the baroque style.

Caravaggio's *The Conversion of St. Paul* (1600–1601) not only demonstrates the theatrical lighting for which he is famous but also shows his rejection of the idealism of the High Renaissance. Caravaggio declared early in his career that nature—not tradition— would be his teacher.

The Rape of the Daughters of Leucippus (ca. 1618), by Peter Paul
Rubens. Rubens created a highly charged style full of color,
energy, voluptuous and powerful figures, and complex,
dynamic composition.

Nicholas Poussin's *Rape of the Sabine Women* (1636–1637) exemplifies
the classical style of the most influential of seventeenth-century French
artists. While Poussin exploited the drama of his subject, he presented
it with balance and restraint, with figures based on Roman statuary
rather than on Rubens's flashy nudes. Oil on canvas, 60⅞ in. × 82⅝ in.
(The Metropolitan Museum of Art; Harris Brisbane Dick Fund,
1946.) (46.160)

Bernini's *Ecstasy of St. Theresa* (1646) demonstrates the baroque attempt to involve the spectator in art through highly dramatic, emotional presentations. Here, the fluid interaction of space and stone belie the marble's hardness.

Despite its diminutive size, Borromini's San Carlo alle Quattro Fontane (1662–1667) is highly baroque in its undulating, sculptural facade, which engages the passerby with its complicated architectural detail.

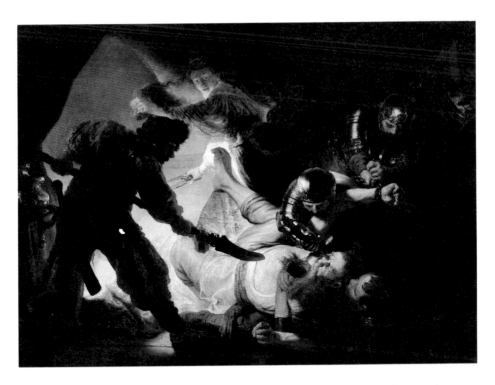

Rembrandt's *The Blinding of Samson,* completed in 1636, indicates the impact outside Italy of Caravaggio's modeling through light and shadow. Likewise, its passionate energy and violence are unmistakably Rubenesque. Later in his career, Rembrandt developed a more individual style. (© Städelsches Kunstinstitut, Frankfurt, West Germany.)

Baroque opera achieved a synthesis of many different arts in one grand spectacle to thrill its audience. The opera house at Versailles was built for Louis XIV (1638–1715), the most grandiose of the French kings and one of the chief patrons of the new art form.

BAROQUE VOCAL MUSIC

The Baroque era, spanning the century and a half between the composition of the first opera in 1600 and the death of Johann Sebastian Bach in 1750, is a period of vast significance in the history of Western music. This period witnessed fundamental changes in musical thinking and practice that resulted in new forms, including the opera, cantata, and oratorio in vocal music, and the concerto, the concerto grosso, and the sonata in instrumental music, which gradually achieved a place of importance equal to that of vocal music. The intensified interest in harmony and tonality that characterized the beginning of the period eventually led to the development of the major-minor system of musical organization that would dominate Western music for the next three hundred years. The Baroque period saw the emergence of the virtuoso performer in both vocal and instrumental music—a fact that had a profound effect on the course of music throughout the Baroque and subsequent historical periods.

THE NEW MUSIC

The fundamental change in attitude toward music that laid the foundation for baroque style occurred in Italy around 1600 and focused on the relationship between words and music in vocal compositions. In Florence a group of scholars and musicians calling themselves the *Camerata* rejected the polyphonic style of the late Renaissance on the grounds that its elaborate contrapuntal texture obscured the words and diluted their emotional impact.

The renaissance preoccupation with the polyphonic relationship between the voice parts often meant that the various voice parts sang different words at the same time, with the result that no words were heard distinctly. In a single voice part, a word frequently was stretched out over so many tones that its identity and meaning were lost to the listener.

The members of the *Camerata,* including the composers Giulio Cassini and Jacopo Peri, insisted that the words must be clear and that the music should serve the meaning and emotional content of the text. They sought to recapture the spirit of Greek drama as they understood it by creating a new kind of music capable of expressing emotional extremes with powerful impact. Their concepts led to the development of the **monodic style** in which a single-voice part was predominant and was supported by harmonies played by a combination of instruments called **basso continuo.**

BASSO CONTINUO

The monodic style consisted of a single vocal line accompanied by a bass instrument (cello or bassoon) and a keyboard instrument (harpsichord or organ). The composer wrote a two-part structure consisting of a melodic line for the singer and a simple bass. The bass was played by the cello or bassoon and the left hand of the keyboard player. Above this bass the keyboardist improvised chords according to a musical shorthand called **figured bass.** Figures (numbers) written below the notes of the bass line indicated the chord to be played. But the keyboard player had wide latitude as to the manner in which the chord was executed and was guided in doing so by the nature of the words being sung by the solo voice. Both the melodic line for the singer and the realization of the figured bass reflected and intensified the meaning and emotional quality of the words.

While the basso continuo (or simply **continuo**) originated in the vocal music of the early baroque, it came to be applied to virtually all music throughout the period, both vocal and instrumental. So prevalent was the continuo practice that the Baroque period was later nicknamed the "continuo period."

THE MAJOR-MINOR SYSTEM

The flow of music in the homophonic style of the early baroque depended upon a single predominant melodic line with strong harmonic support supplied by the basso continuo. The progression of one harmony to the next was of fundamental importance. The desire to make the harmonic aspect of music more effective led to the reduction in the number of modes (scales) from many in the Renaissance to just two—the *major* mode and the *minor* mode—in the Baroque period.

While these modes and the music based upon them differ in character, they share the important aspect of imparting the sense of a strong tonal center or *tonic*. The establishment of a clear tonic, movement away from it through the use of other chords, and the return to it, usually through the dominant chord, brought into being important new structural and expressive possibilities. And the device of *modulation,* the establishment of one or more secondary tonal centers within a composition, opened up a new way of organizing musical time flow. It permitted the development of larger structures, for the expectation of eventual return to the original tonic could support long excursions away from it. Also included in this new harmonic approach to music was an expanded use of *dissonance* as an expressive element.

BAROQUE VOCAL STYLES

The monodic style became the basis for the vocal forms of the Baroque period.

RECITATIVE

The **recitative** is a kind of singing speech in which the musical rhythm is dictated by the natural inflection of the words. In contrast to the Renaissance idea of an even flow of music, the recitative is sung in free, flexible rhythm with continuo accompaniment. The tempo is slowed down or speeded up according to the performer's interpretation of the text.

Within baroque opera and oratorio, the recitative primarily served to further the action of the story. As it evolved, the recitative acquired greater dramatic importance. The recitative with only continuo accompaniment, known as **secco recitative,** usually introduced an aria or appeared in the less dramatic moments of a piece. The **accompanied recitative,** in which the voice is accompanied by instruments in addition to continuo, produced a more powerful effect and was used for dramatic situations.

ARIOSO AND ARIA

While the general character of the recitative is declamatory, that of the **arioso** is essentially lyrical. The tempo in the arioso is steady. Unlike the recitative, which can portray swift dramatic change, the arioso is comparatively static and tends to dwell on a single emotional state. In the early baroque, it is not uncommon to find these two styles side by side within the same movement, depending upon the progression of dramatic events.

The arioso was later expanded into the **aria,** which is a three-part form, ABA. The first section (A) was followed by a contrasting section (B), at the end of which appeared the words **"da capo,"** instructing the performers to return to the beginning and repeat section A. It was intended that the A section differ in its repeated version. Singers would decorate, ornament, and embellish the original melody of the A section the second time around to further intensify the spirit of the words and to add excitement to the performance by a display of vocal virtuosity. This style of performance became an inherent part of the opera and, to a lesser extent, the oratorio.

The recitative (both secco and accompanied), the arioso, and the da capo aria were the principal ingredients for the important forms of baroque vocal music—the opera, the oratorio, and the cantata.

The early baroque **opera** was a dramatic form based on secular themes and written in Italian. Sung primarily by solo voices, operas were fully staged with costuming, scenery, acting, and instrumental ensembles.

The early **oratorio** was a dramatic work for chorus, solo voices, and orchestra. Unlike opera, it did not include scenery, costuming, or stage action. Texts were usually taken from the Old Testament and sung in Latin. A singing narrator helped to explain the dramatic action, which unfolded in a series of arias, recitatives, choral movements, and instrumental sections.

The **cantata** was shorter and used fewer performers than the opera and oratorio. Either sacred or secular, it was usually written in Italian rather than Latin and emphasized solo voices with continuo.

OPERA

The earliest surviving opera was written by a member of the Camerata named Jacopo Peri (1561–1633), whose *Eurydice* dates from the year 1600. Based on the Greek legend of Orpheus and Eurydice, it consists almost entirely of recitative with continuo. In accordance with the principles of the Camerata, Peri wrote in the foreword to his opera that its style was intended to "imitate speech in song."

CLAUDIO MONTEVERDI

The first master of operatic composition was the Italian, Claudio Monteverdi (1567–1643) (fig. 7.1), whose treatment of the Orpheus legend *La favola d'Orfeo,* marks the beginning of opera as a major art form. First performed in Mantua in 1607, *Orfeo* had elaborate costuming, staging, and lighting, an instrumental ensemble of forty players, and a chorus of singers and dancers.

One of the most powerful moments in the opera is the scene in act 2 in which Orpheus is informed that his beloved Eurydice has died and expresses his sorrowful reaction in the famous recitative "Tu se'morta, mia vita . . ." ("You are dead, my life . . ."). The scene is an excellent example of the monodic style and Monteverdi's masterful use of it for dramatic and expressive purposes, and it rivals any operatic scene written since his time in terms of emotional impact. The voice is prominent (accompanied only by continuo), and the singer has great freedom in terms of rhythm, vocal inflection, and melodic decoration to enhance the spirit of the dramatic situation and its emotional content.

MONTEVERDI:
La favola d'Orfeo
Cassette 1/B, Track 2
CD 1, Track 9

Figure 7.1 Claudio
Monteverdi.

SCENE FROM ACT 2[1]

Messenger

A te ne vengo, Orfeo,
Messagiera infelice
Di caso più infelice e più
    funesto!
La tua bella Euridice . . .

Orpheus

Ohimè, che odo?

Messenger

La tua diletta sposa è morta.

Orpheus

Ohimè!

Messenger

To you I come, Orpheus,
A woeful messenger
Of tidings yet more wretched and more
    tragic!
Your lovely Eurydice . . .

Orpheus

Alas, what do I hear?

Messenger

Your beloved wife is dead.

Orpheus

Woe is me!

Messenger

In un fiorito prato
Con l'altre sue compagne
Giva cogliendo fiori
Per farne una ghirlanda a le sue chiome,
Quand' angue insidioso
Ch'era fra l'erbe ascoso,
Le punse un piè con velenoso dente:
Ed ecco immantinente
Scolorirsi it bel viso e ne' suoi lumi
Sparir que' lampi, ond' ella al sol fea
    scorno.
Allor noi tutte sbigottite e meste
Le fummo intorno, richiamar tentando
Gli spirti i lei smarriti
Con l'onda fresca e con possenti
    carmi;
Ma nulla valse, ahi lassa!
Ch'ella i languidi lumi alquanto aprendo,
E te chiamando, Orfeo,
Dopo un grave sospiro
Spirò fra queste braccia, ed io rimasi
Piena il cor di pietade e di spavento.

First Shepherd

Ahi, caso acerbo! ahi fat'empio e
    crudele!
Ahi, stelle ingiuriose, ahi ciel
    avaro!

Third Shepherd

A l'amara novella
Rassembra l'infelice un muto
    sasso,
Che per troppo dolor non può dolersi.

First Shepherd

Ahi, ben avrebbe un cor di tigre o
    d'orsa
Chi non sentisse del tuo mal pietade,
Privi d'ogni tuo ben, misero amante!

Messenger

In a flower-decked meadow
She was walking with her companions
And gathering flowers
To make a garland for her tresses,
When a treacherous snake
Concealed in the grass
Pierced her with its poisonous fangs.
And lo! at once colour draining from
Her countenance, those lights in her eyes
Grew dim, lights which could outshine
    the sun.
Then we, all downcast and in tears
Stood about her, trying to revive
Those spirits now lacking in her
With cool water and with powerful
    charms;
But naught availed, alas,
For she, half opening her languid eyes
And calling upon you, Orpheus,
After a deep sigh
Expired in these arms, and I remained
With my heart full of pity and terror.

First Shepherd

Ah, bitter chance! ah, cruel and wicked
    fate!
Ah, stars of ill omen, ah heaven
    avaricious!

Third Shepherd

At this harsh news
He seemed, unlucky man, a speechless
    rock,
So heavily sad that it cannot lament.

First Shepherd

Ah, he would indeed have a bear's or
    tiger's heart
Who did not feel some pity for your ill,
Deprived of all your bliss, wretched
    lover!

Orpheus

Tu se' morta, mia vita, ed io respiro?
Tu se' da me partita
Per mai più, mai più non tornare, ed io
   rimango?
No, no, che se iversi alcuna cosa ponno
N'andrò sicuro a più profondi abissi,
E intenerito il cor del Re do
   l'ombre
Meco trarrotti a riveder le stelle:
O se ciò negherammi empio destino
Rimarrò teco in compagnia di
   morte.
Addio, terra; addio cielo, e sole, addio.

Orpheus

You are dead, my life, and I breathe?
You have left me,
Never, never more to return, and I
   remain?
No, no, for if my songs can take effect
I shall go surely to the deepest abysses,
And having softened the heart of the
   dreaded king
I'll bring you back again to see the stars:
Or if this is denied me by cruel destiny,
I shall stay with you in the company of
   death.
Farewell earth; farewell sun and heaven.

In addition to *Orfeo,* Monteverdi wrote several other operas. Among the most successful were *Il ritorno di Ulisse in patria (The Return of Ulysses to His Homeland,* 1641) and *L'Incoronazione di Poppea (The Coronation of Poppea,* 1642). Like those of his contemporaries, Monteverdi's operas were written in Italian. They drew mainly upon Greek and Roman legends for their plots, which were adapted by poets into **libretti,** or operatic texts.

Originally performed for aristocratic gatherings, opera gradually became a popular form of entertainment for the middle class. Public opera houses were built, and composers and librettists adapted their operas to a wider and more varied audience. The popularity of many opera singers was as intense as that of today's movie and TV celebrities.

Opera, with its concentration on secular subjects, greatly increased the professional opportunities for women, whose role in the music of the church had been and continued to be quite limited.

During the Baroque period, Italian opera spread throughout Europe, reaching its heights in the Italian operas of Handel in England. The Italian style had less influence in France, where the composer Jean-Baptiste Lully (1632–1687), ironically an Italian, headed the group that created and supported French opera.

SECULAR CANTATA

The secular cantata was a popular form of musical entertainment in baroque Italy. Prominent composers such as Luigi Rossi (1597–1653), Giacomo Carissimi (ca. 1605–1674), and Antonio Cesti (ca. 1623–1669) wrote numerous cantatas for performance at social gatherings in the homes of wealthy aristocrats. The earliest secular cantatas were comparatively short and consisted of contrasting sections of recitatives, ariosos, and arias.

One of the most prolific composers of secular cantatas was Barbara Strozzi (1619–ca. 1664). Between 1644 and 1664, Strozzi published eight volumes of vocal works containing about one hundred pieces, most of which were individual arias and secular cantatas for soprano and basso continuo. The texts of many of her cantatas center on unrequited love, a favorite theme among seventeenth-century composers. In all probability, Strozzi performed these pieces for the Accademic degli Unisoni, a Venetian fellowship of poets, philosophers, and historians who met in the home of her father.

ORATORIO

Early baroque oratorio appeared in two forms—the *Latin oratorio* and the *oratorio volgare,* which used Italian texts. The Latin oratorio included the roles of narrator and chorus in addition to the central characters. It reached its peak in the works of the Roman composer Giacomo Carissimi (1605–1674). The finest of his many oratorios, *Jepthe* (ca. 1649), was based on an Old Testament story from the Book of Judges.

Carissimi's pupil Alessandro Scarlatti (1660–1725) was one of the principal composers of the *oratorio volgare.* In the hands of Scarlatti, the oratorio became musically indistinct from opera. While the themes were still religious, the texts were in Italian, the role of the narrator was eliminated, and the chorus was abandoned. Actually, the oratorio was little more than a substitution for opera, theatrical performances of which were banned by the church during Lent.

The oratorio spread from Italy to the other countries of Europe. Henrich Schütz (1585–1672), who studied in Italy, introduced the oratorio to Germany, and Marc-Antoine Charpentier (1634–1704), a pupil of Carissimi, was the principal oratorio composer in France. But the oratorio rose to its height in England in the monumental works of George Frideric Handel.

HANDEL (1685–1759)

George Frideric Handel (fig. 7.2) was born in Halle, a trading center some eighty miles southwest of Berlin, the son of a prosperous barber-surgeon attached to the court of the duke of Saxony. His father had in mind a legal career for the boy, but did allow him to begin music study at age eight with the organist of the town's principal Lutheran church. Aside from learning to play the organ, harpsichord, violin, and oboe, young Handel also studied composition, writing church cantatas and numerous small-scale instrumental works.

Out of respect for his father's wish, Handel enrolled at the University of Halle in 1702. At the end of his first year, however, he withdrew from the university and went to Hamburg to pursue his interest in music.

Musical activity in Hamburg, as in most cosmopolitan cities of the time, centered on the opera house, where Italian opera thrived. Soon after Handel arrived in Hamburg in 1703, he obtained a position as violinist in the theater orchestra and industriously set about learning the craft of opera composition. His first opera, *Almira* (1704), reflected the curious mixture of native German and imported Italian musical styles then prevalent in Hamburg; the recitatives were set in German, the arias in Italian. The work was a popular success, and three other operas soon followed. In 1706, feeling that he had learned all that Hamburg had to offer, Handel decided to go to Italy.

His three-year stay in Italy was amazingly successful. Traveling back and forth between Florence, Venice, Rome, and Naples, he met many of Italy's greatest composers and was the frequent guest of cardinals,

Figure 7.2 An engraving of Handel.

princes, and ambassadors. Much of his popularity stemmed from the success of his operas *Rodrigo* (Florence, 1708) and *Agrippina* (Venice, 1709).

Through one of the friends he made in Italy, Handel obtained the position of musical director to the Electoral Court of Hanover, Germany. He had just taken up his duties in 1710, however, when he asked permission from Elector Georg Ludwig to visit London. Italian opera was then in great vogue with the English aristocracy, and the success of his opera *Rinaldo* (1711) led Handel to ask permission for another leave of absence the following year. Though promising to return "within a reasonable time," Handel stretched out his second London visit indefinitely.

In 1714 Queen Anne died, and Elector Georg Ludwig of Hanover ascended to the throne as George I of England. How Handel settled the embarrassing problem of his long-neglected contract with the Electoral Court is unknown. But the annual pension Queen Anne had given him was continued and even increased by George I, and within several years he was in high favor at the royal court.

During his years in England (he became a subject in 1726), Handel was involved in no less than four operatic enterprises. The most significant of these, the Royal Academy of Music, was organized by British nobility under the sponsorship of the king. During its eight-year existence (1720–1728), Handel's career as an opera composer reached its highest point.

Despite Handel's many personal successes, each of his four opera companies collapsed. A major reason for their collapse was the declining taste of the English for Italian opera. The enormously successful 1728 pro-duction of John Gay's *The Beggar's Opera* undoubtedly hastened the extinction of Italian opera in England. A parody of Italian style, *The Beggar's Opera* was widely imitated, and a new form of light, popular musical entertainment was created in English.

Though Handel continued to compose Italian operas for more than a decade after the appearance of *The Beggar's Opera,* he turned increasingly to the oratorio. His first English oratorio, *Haman and Mordecai* (later revised and renamed *Esther*), was composed in 1720. Others followed during the 1730s, but it was not until 1739, with the completion of *Saul* and *Israel in Egypt,* that he seemed to sense the full musical and dramatic possibilities of this form. Neither of these works was an immediate success, but others that followed were. In 1742, *Messiah* received high critical praise after its first performance in Dublin. By 1746, with the performance of *Judas Maccabaeus,* Handel had found a new public in the growing English middle class.

In his last years Handel was universally recognized as England's greatest composer. His popularity with all segments of English society steadily grew, and the royal patronage of George I was followed by that of George II. Despite declining health and the eventual loss of his eyesight, Handel continued to maintain a heavy schedule of oratorio performances, which he conducted himself from the keyboard. While attending a performance of *Messiah* on March 30, 1759, he suddenly grew faint and had to be taken home. He died two weeks later and was buried with state honors in Westminster Abbey. His will revealed that he had accumulated a substantial private fortune, which was dispersed—along with his music manuscripts—among friends.

HANDEL'S WORK

Today the fame of George Frideric Handel rests largely on the half-dozen oratorios—still in concert repertory (particularly *Messiah*), several *concerti grossi* (see chapter 8), some organ concertos, and two orchestral suites, *Water Music* and *Royal Fireworks Music.* These amount to only a fraction of his total work.

With few exceptions, Handel's operas followed the pattern laid down by Italian composers of the seventeenth century. Their plots, drawn from classical mythology, were developed through a series of paired recitatives and arias. His gifts for melody and his imaginative, resourceful orchestration were acclaimed in his own time, and his ability to dramatize in music the psychological and emotional states of his characters was unexcelled.

The bulk of Handel's oratorios are dramatic, with specific characters and plots. Although most of them, including *Samson, Saul, Solomon, Belshazzar,* and *Jeptha,* are based on stories drawn from the Old Testament, they were not written as church music. Instead, they were intended to be performed for the public in music halls and auditoriums.

Handel's two nondramatic oratorios are *Israel in Egypt* and *Messiah.* In *Israel in Egypt* the chorus dominates, narrating and describing the events. The solo voices do not represent specific characters as they would in a dramatic oratorio. Instead, they complement and act as a foil for the chorus. The unusually large orchestra is used brilliantly to depict the plagues that were inflicted upon Egypt, particularly in the sections representing the buzzing of the flies and the fire and hailstones.

MESSIAH

Handel's other nondramatic oratorio, *Messiah,* is based on the life of Christ. In *Messiah* the solo voices do not represent specific characters (with the exception of the passage in which the angel appears to the shepherds), nor is the orchestra used for pictorial narration. Although we might expect that the text for this oratorio would come from the Gospels of the New Testament, where the life of Christ is recorded, the bulk of the libretto consists of prophetic passages from the Old Testament. As a result, the events in Christ's life and his role as Redeemer are suggested symbolically rather than portrayed realistically.

Messiah was composed in only twenty-four days. It was a success in Handel's lifetime and has become one of the most loved and popular pieces of music in the history of Western civilization. At its first London performance in 1743, King George II was so moved by the opening of the "Hallelujah" chorus that he stood during its performance, a precedent that most audiences follow still.

Altogether, *Messiah* represents about three hours of music for four solo voices (SATB), chorus (SATB), and orchestra. The oratorio is in three parts comprising fifty-three movements. (A **movement** is an independent section of a larger composition.) The movements include arias, recitatives, choruses, and orchestral sections. Part I deals with the prophecy of the coming of the Messiah and his birth; part II, the sacrifice of Jesus and the salvation of humanity through his suffering and death; part III, the certainty of eternal life through faith in the risen Christ.

Aria

The aria received ingenious treatment in the oratorios of Handel. He modified the standard da capo form (ABA), often avoiding the expected return to the A section. In *Messiah* the arias are rich in expression and marvelously varied in mood. Among the many vocal gems are the joyous contralto aria "O Thou that tellest good tidings to Zion," followed immediately by a choral version of the same musical material; the stirring aria for bass "The trumpet shall sound"; and the serenely beautiful "I know that my Redeemer liveth."

Recitative

In *Messiah,* Handel employs both secco and accompanied recitatives. The secco recitatives are quite short and function merely as brief introductions to ensuing arias. The accompanied recitatives are longer and achieve a higher level of musical interest, at times even rivaling the expressiveness of the arias they introduce. This is true of such recitatives as "Thus saith the Lord," "For, behold, darkness shall cover the earth," "Thy rebuke hath broken His Heart," and "Comfort ye," the recitative that initiates the action of *Messiah* immediately after the overture.

Chorus

A primary factor that stamps Handel's oratorios as historically unique is the use of the chorus as a major element in the dramatic and musical structure. Certainly this is true of *Messiah.* In *Messiah,* choral movements perform a variety of functions. They serve as the climactic element in a three-part complex consisting of a recitative, an aria, and a chorus. A second use of the chorus is as a structural "frame," beginning and ending a large section. Part II of *Messiah,* for example, begins with the restrained and sorrowful "Behold the Lamb of God" and concludes with the joyous and triumphant "Hallelujah." These two choruses constitute a frame for the entire middle section of the oratorio. Occasionally, Handel joins two or more choruses into a larger unit in which each chorus depends upon the one preceding or following it. This is the case in part II of *Messiah* with "Surely, He hath borne our griefs," "And with His stripes we are healed," and "All we like sheep have gone astray."

Many of *Messiah's* choral movements have extraordinary emotional impact and musical appeal. Such well-known choral movements as "And the glory of the Lord," "For unto us a child is born," and the magnificent "Hallelujah" help account for the tremendous popularity of *Messiah.*

Orchestra

Because of the limited orchestral resources available to him in Dublin, where *Messiah* had its premiere, Handel employed a modest instrumental ensemble consisting of oboes, bassoons, trumpets, timpani, strings, and continuo. Two movements in the oratorio were written for orchestra alone—the overture that begins the work and the short, eloquent *"Pastorale"* that sets the scene in part I in which the angel appears to the shepherds.

Organization

Part of the genius of *Messiah* derives from Handel's ability to unify a complex musical structure consisting of numerous individual movements. Frequently he employed the pattern recitative-aria-chorus to organize a long stretch of music. The recitative introduces the aria, which progresses to a culminating choral movement. Each movement possesses its own internal organization and interest but also contributes to the larger structure. This organizational procedure dominates the first part of *Messiah* and is well illustrated by the movements that immediately follow the overture:

Overture	Recitative	Aria	Chorus
	Comfort ye	*Ev'ry valley*	*And the glory of the Lord*

HANDEL:

Messiah, First Movement

Cassette 1/B, Track 3

CD 1, Tracks 10–12

The first movement (recitative) displays Handel's masterful handling of baroque techniques. The text is divided into two parts.

A: Comfort ye, comfort ye my people, saith your God; speak ye comfortably to Jerusalem, and cry unto her, that her warfare is accomplish'd, that her iniquity is pardon'd.

B: The voice of him that crieth in the wilderness, Prepare ye the way of the Lord, make straight in the desert a highway for our God. ISAIAH 40:1–3

Part A, in the key of E major, is very much like an arioso in that it is quite lyrical and its tempo is steady. Both the orchestra and the tenor voice convey the feelings inherent in the words. This is evident from the tenor's opening motive:

Example 7.1

Com-fort ye

which not only matches the rhythmic inflection of the text but also conveys the feeling of serenity of the first part of the movement.

Another example of musical treatment of words to reflect their expressive quality is shown in the phrase:

Example 7.2

and cry un-to her

The large upward leap on "and cry" and the long note on "cry" reinforce the drama of the joyful announcement.

This part of the movement is unified by the statement and reappearance of material played by the orchestra:

Example 7.3

The first portion of this material (sometimes only the first five notes) reappears several times, either giving way to the tenor voice:

Example 7.4

or coming in "on top" of it:

Example 7.5

The last appearance of the material is a full statement which, after the various fragment versions, imparts a feeling of completion and concludes the first part of the movement.

In the second part of the movement the decisive emotional change in the text is reflected in the musical structure. The lyricism and serenity of the "comfort" section give way to dramatic assertiveness in the B section. The voice executes short, clipped phrases while the orchestra punctuates with short chords in the strings (example 7.6).

Example 7.6

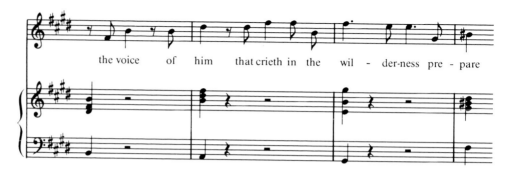

the voice of him that crieth in the wil - der-ness pre - pare

This procedure is typical of the recitative style, as is the ending, with its downward motion of the voice followed by two concluding chords (dominant to tonic) from the orchestra:

Example 7.7

for our God

Thus, Handel uses both arioso and recitative in one movement to exploit the contrasting character of the two sections of text. In addition, the recitative portion not only brings the movement to a close but leads naturally into the next movement, the aria "Ev'ry valley:"

Ev'ry valley shall be exalted and ev'ry mountain and hill made low, the crooked straight, and the rough places plain. ISAIAH 40:4

Probably the most immediately striking aspect of this aria is its use of word painting, a device we encountered earlier in our discussion of Renaissance secular music. The word *exalted* is set to a long ascending sixteenth-note melisma, which gives a feeling of rising:

Example 7.8

shall be_____ ex - alt - - - - -

- - - - - - - - ed.

The words *crooked* and *plain* (meaning "level") also receive musical treatment that reflects their meaning and spirit:

Example 7.9

the crook-ed straight, the crook-ed straight and rough pla-ces plain _____

The angular figure on *crooked* contrasts sharply with the static, simple melody on *plain.*

Word painting is used again in the setting of the phrase "and every mountain and hill made low," in which the melody rises to a peak on *mountain* and then descends to a tone an octave below on *low:*

Example 7.10

and ev-'ry moun-tain and hill _____ made low.

The use of individualized musical figures to reflect the emotional feeling or physical characteristics of a word or phrase was common in the Baroque period, and indeed is found in music of virtually every baroque composer. Extended melismas and highly ornamented figures provided the perfect vehicle for virtuoso soloists to display their remarkable vocal skills.

"Ev'ry valley" is followed immediately by the allegro choral movement in A major, "And the glory of the Lord:"

And the glory of the Lord shall be revealed, and all flesh shall see it together, for the mouth of the Lord hath spoken it. ISAIAH 40:5

This choral movement is based upon four melodic ideas, each with its own set of words:

Example 7.11

a) and the glo - ry, the glo - ry of the Lord

b) shall be re - veal - ed.

c) and all flesh ___ shall see ___ it to - geth - er

d) for the mouth of the Lord hath spo - ken it.

Handel contrasts these ideas in a variety of ways, perhaps the most striking of which is the use of both polyphonic and homophonic textures. The first polyphonic section of the movement is based upon "a" and a combination of "a" and "b."

Example 7.12

Here the texture is very thin, with no more than two voice parts singing at the same time and the orchestra reduced to continuo only. This thin polyphonic texture is maintained until the climactic point when all four parts of the chorus and the full orchestra join in a *homophonic* phrase, which brings the first section of the movement to a close (example 7.13). The change from thin texture to full chorus and orchestra and the sudden switch from polyphony to homophony provide a powerful climax.

Chapter 7

Example 7.13

The rest of the movement consists of several sections organized in roughly the same manner. Each is characterized by imaginative and flexible use of the four melodic ideas and their combinations. And each involves the same alternation between polyphonic imitation and strong homophonic endings, each more powerful than the one before. The movement culminates in a passage of almost breathtaking force:

Example 7.14

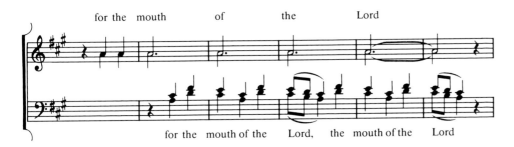

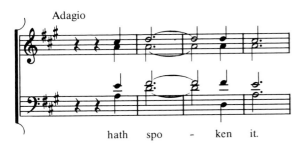

Just before the final statement of "hath spoken it," Handel brings the music to a sudden and surprising halt, followed by silence, creating a feeling of excitement and suspense. This suspense is resolved by a prolonged cadence on "hath spoken it," as all parts of the chorus and the full orchestra combine to provide a stirring conclusion to the entire three-movement complex.

Of course, we have discussed only a small portion of this work. The rest of *Messiah* is full of equally glorious music, masterfully crafted. Certainly it is no wonder that *Messiah* is one of the world's most beloved pieces of music.

LUTHERAN GERMANY

While the seed of baroque style sown in Italy at the beginning of the seventeenth century came to fruition in England in the operas and oratorios of Handel, it grew and flowered differently in Germany, culminating in the music of Johann Sebastian Bach.

The traditions of the Lutheran church into which Bach was born and for which he composed almost all of his vocal music rested heavily upon the principle of direct and active participation by the congregation in church ceremonies. To this end, religious services were conducted in the *German* language as opposed to *Latin* as in the case of Catholicism. And to this end there needed to be a kind of religious music simple and direct enough for the congregation to sing, regardless of the degree of musical talent or training.

THE CHORALE

Martin Luther (1483–1546) began the development of a body of such music as part of the reforms that initiated the Protestant movement. The **chorale,** a simple hymn tune with spiritual words, provided this kind of music not only as part of the church service but also for devotional activity in the home.

Chorale melodies came from a variety of sources. Some were adapted from Gregorian chants, others came from secular tunes, and many were newly composed. Luther himself is responsible for many chorales, and his still-famous "Ein' Feste Burg ist Unser Gott" ("A Mighty Fortress Is Our God") typifies the simplicity and strength of the chorale.

By Bach's time, these well-known chorale melodies and their texts functioned not only as the basis for congregational singing, but also provided a rich body of materials from which larger and more complex vocal and instrumental musical structures could be built. Thus, they were used in much the same way as the Gregorian chant had been during the Renaissance.

The most important forms of vocal music in baroque Germany were the cantata, the opera, and the Passion. The Italian influence that spread throughout Europe was felt in Germany. Italian music and Italian musicians held sway particularly in the field of opera. So strong was this influence that early attempts to establish opera in the German language failed, and it was not until the later part of the period that German opera enjoyed any sustained popularity and then only for a brief span of time.

The Italian style also influenced German Protestant religious music but to a lesser extent. The polyphonic tradition was never completely abandoned and remained a strong element in the music of the church, particularly among the more conservative composers such as J. S. Bach.

THE PASSION

The **Passion** is a musical setting of the story of the suffering and crucifixion of Jesus Christ as told in the Bible by the gospels. The Passion was particularly important during Holy Week, especially on Good Friday. The early settings of the Passion text, for instance those of the great German master of the early baroque, Heinrich Schütz (1585–1672), employed only the biblical text with an introductory and concluding chorus. By Bach's time, musical settings of the Passion had expanded to include *nonbiblical* texts in the form of commentary about the events described in the Gospel.

In Bach's monumental *Passion According to St. Matthew,* the Gospel account of the betrayal, arrest, trial, and crucifixion of Christ is told by soloists in recitative, secco for all characters except Christ, who is accompanied by a string quartet. The chorus assumes various roles such as the crowd and the disciples. The nonbiblical contemplations are interspersed between sections of the Gospel story in the form of da capo arias sung by soloists and numerous chorales in which the congregation joins the choir and orchestra.

Bach's *St. Matthew Passion* joins Handel's *Messiah* in representing the culmination of baroque vocal music.

THE CANTATA

Like the opera and the oratorio, the cantata went through considerable transformation from early to late baroque, reaching its height in Germany in the works of Dietrich Buxtehude (ca. 1637–1707) and J. S. Bach. By Bach's time, the sacred cantata often included the standard baroque elements of recitative, aria, chorus, and instrumental ensemble. Frequently, cantatas were built upon one of the many well-known chorale tunes.

Cantata texts related to specific feast days of the church year, and for church musicians such as Bach, the writing of cantatas was a routine professional obligation. Between 1704 and 1740, Bach composed cantatas on a regular basis for the churches he served. He is believed to have written more than 300, although only 195 have been preserved.

Bach's Cantata no. 4 was written early in his career and does not employ the recitative and da capo aria that typify his later compositions. Using as its theme the chorale tune and text *Christ lag in Todesbanden,* it is an example of Bach's contrapuntal technique, a skill that ultimately marked him as one of the great musical craftsmen in history. The cantata was intended to be performed as part of the Easter Sunday service.

The work is scored for four solo voices (SATB), chorus (SATB) doubled by four brass instruments, and a string ensemble with continuo. It consists of seven movements (one for each verse of the chorale text) and a **sinfonia,** a short instrumental introduction, according to the following plan:

BACH:
Cantata no. 4: *Christ lag in Todesbanden (Christ Lay in Death's Bondage)*
Cassette 1/B, Track 4
CD 1, Tracks 13–15

Sinfonia	Verse I	II	III	IV	V	VI	VII
	chorus	duet	solo	quartet	solo	duet	chorus
	SATB	SA	T	SATB	B	ST	with
							congregation

CHRIST LAG IN TODESBANDEN

VERSUS I

Christ lag in Todesbanden
Für unsre Sünd gegeben,
Er ist wieder erstanden
Und hat uns bracht das Leben;
Des wir sollen fröhlich sein,
Gott loben und ihm dankbar sein
Und singen Halleluja,
Halleluja!

VERSUS II

Den Tod niemand swingen kunnt
Bei allen Menschenkinden,
Das macht alles unsre Sünd,
Kein Unschuld war zu finden.
Davon kam der Tod so bald
Und nahm über uns Gewalt,
Hielt uns in seinem Reich gefangen,
Halleluja!

VERSUS III

Jesus Christus, Gottes Sohn,
An unser Statt ist kommen
Und hat die Sünde weggetan,
Damit dem Tod genommen
All sein Recht und sein Gewalt,
Da bleibet nichts denn Todsgestalt,
Den Stachl hat er verloren.
Halleluja!

VERSUS IV

Es war ein wunderlicher Krieg,
Da Tod und Leben rungen,
Das Leben behielt den Sieg,
Es hat den Tod verschlungen.
Die Schrift hat verkündigt das,
Wie ein Tod den andern frass,
Ein Spott aus dem Tod ist worden.
Halleluja!

CHRIST LAY IN DEATH'S BONDAGE

VERSE I

Christ lay in death's bondage,
For our sins given;
He is again arisen
And has brought us life;
For which we should rejoice,
Praise God and give him thanks,
And sing Hallelujah,
Hallelujah!

VERSE II

No one could overcome Death
Among all mortal children;
This was caused by all our sins,
No innocence was to be found.
Hence came Death so soon
And over us achieved dominion,
Held us in his realm imprisoned,
Hallelujah!

VERSE III

Jesus Christ, God's Son,
In our stead has come
And has done away with sin;
Thus from Death seizing
All its prerogatives and power;
There remains nothing but Death's
  image,
Its sting has been lost,
Hallelujah!

VERSE IV

It was a wondrous war,
With Death and Life embattled;
Life achieved the victory,
It swallowed up Death.
The scripture has proclaimed this,
How one Death consumed another;
A mockery has Death become.
Hallelujah!

VERSUS V

Hier ist das rechte Osterlamm,
Davon hat Gott geboten,
Das ist hoch an des Kreuzes Stamm
In heisser Lieb gebraten,
Das Blut zeichnet unser Tür,
Das hält der Glaub dem Tode für,
Der Würger kann uns nicht mehr
    schaden.
Halleluja!

VERSUS VI

So feiern wir das hohe Fest
Mit Herzensfreud und Wonne,
Das uns der Herre scheinen lässt,
Er ist selber die Sonne,
Der durch seiner Gnade Glanz
Erleuchtet unsre Herzen ganz,
Der Sünden Nacht ist verschwunden.
Halleluja!

VERSUS VII

Wir essen und leben wohl
In rechten Osterfladen,
Der alte Sauerteig nicht soll
Sein bei dem Wort der Gnaden,
Christus will die Koste sein
Und speisen die Seel allein,
Der Glaub will keins andern Leben.
Halleluja!

VERSE V

Here is the true Easter lamb
That God has offered us,
Which high on the stem of the cross
Is roasted in burning love;
His blood marks our door,
Faith holds this up to death,
The destroyer can no longer harm us.
Hallelujah!

VERSE VI

Therefore we celebrate the high feast
With joyous heart and rapture,
Which the Lord lets shine for us;
He is himself the sun,
Who through the splendor of his grace
Fully illumines our hearts,
The night of sin has disappeared.
Hallelujah!

VERSE VII

We eat and live well
By the true Passover bread,
The old leaven shall not endure
Beside the word of grace;
Christ will be the feast
And he alone will feed the soul,
Faith is sustained through no other.
Hallelujah!
    Martin Luther

The tune itself (example 7.15) is a short, simple, and sturdy melody. Its use as the fundamental musical material in each of the movements unifies the work. The changes in the melody from movement to movement not only ensure musical variety but also reflect the changing nature of the words and intensify the spiritual message they convey.

The *sinfonia* is very brief. Its key (E minor), tempo (slow), and dynamic level (piano) establish a somber mood for the beginning of verse I of the cantata. Bach's use of the chorale in the sinfonia is limited to only the first phrase of the melody which appears, slightly decorated, in the first violin about halfway through the movement.

Verse I uses the entire chorale melody in a variety of fascinating ways. Throughout most of the movement, each phrase of the chorale is stated in long note values by the soprano part against a background of lively contrapuntal material played and sung by the other parts of the ensemble. This contrapuntal material varies in its melodic relationship

Example 7.15

Christ lag in To-des - ban-den für un-sre Sünd ge - ge - ben, er

ist wie-der er - stan-den, und hat uns bracht das Le - ben;

des wir sol-len fröh-lich sein, Gott lo-ben und ihm dank-bar sein, und

sin-gen Hal-le - lu - ja! Hal - le - lu - ja!

to the chorale tune. Sometimes it is entirely different; at other points, it merely hints at the chorale tune for only a few notes; and in some sections of the movement, it is very closely related to the tune, using the entire phrase—but *always* employing shorter note values than those in the soprano.

Except for the very beginning, the lower voices of the chorus start the new line of text prior to its appearance in the soprano, thereby providing an introduction to and a background for the elongated statement of the chorale melody in the soprano part.

As the movement progresses, the relationship between the soprano and the rest of the ensemble becomes a consistent and predominant characteristic of the musical flow, and the listener anticipates its continuation. This anticipation is upset with startling effect in the midst of the phrase "und singen Hallelujah." Here, as the chorale tune is passed from tenor to alto to bass, the strong expectation on the part of the listener is that the soprano will enter with the chorale phrase in long sustained tones in conformity with the arrangement that has prevailed in the piece thus far. Instead, the soprano enters with the same *short* note values as the rest of the chorus and, for the first time, joins in the polyphonic interplay with the rest of the ensemble on the fragmented hal-le—lu-jah. This sudden change comes as a surprise and imparts a sense of excitement that is intensified when, at the beginning of the last phrase (Hallelujah), the tempo is abruptly increased and the beginning of each statement of the melody is syncopated, imbuing the ending of the movement with a sense of musical and psychological exhilaration.

In contrast to the exuberant ending of the first verse, verse II returns to the general mood of the sinfonia, reflecting the cantata text with its concentration on Death and Sin. The movement is scored for soprano and alto duet with continuo. The piece employs a rhythmic **basso ostinato**—a phrase repeated persistently in the bass. Over this ostinato, the soprano sings a variation of the chorale melody while the alto imitates the soprano melody or sings counterpoint against it.

Verse III is a good example of the way Bach gives a particular word or thought special significance by the manner in which he treats it musically. The movement begins in a joyous mood created by a rapidly moving violin melody over a steady ostinato figure in the continuo.

Example 7.16

Between the upper violin line and the continuo, the tenor sings the chorale tune in clear-cut phrases. The driving motion continues without any pause or interruption for over half the movement, when suddenly and surprisingly there is an abrupt halt at the word *nichts* ("nothing"). Everything stops! After a suspense-filled silence, the words *denn Tod'sgestalt* ("but death's image") are set to a slow and intense version of the chorale phrase.

Example 7.17

Immediately, the lively motion is resumed, imparting a heightened sense of joy that is intensified when the last phrase of the chorale, Hallelujah, is decorated so as to give it the same exuberant character of the violin figure.

Example 7.18

Such examples of masterful manipulation of musical materials to reflect and enhance the meaning of the words abound in the cantatas of Bach.

The "wondrous war" between Death and Life is portrayed in verse IV, in which the unadorned chorale melody is executed by the alto voice part imbedded within a busy contrapuntal texture supplied by the soprano, tenor, and bass parts. As was the case in verse II, the instrumental component in this movement is limited to the continuo.

Baroque Vocal Music

Verse V employs the rich sound of the full string ensemble in support of the solo bass voice. Its triple meter, moderate tempo, and the manipulation of the chorale melody give it a more relaxed and lyrical quality than is characteristic of the rest of *Christ lag in Todesbanden*. For most of the movement, the bass voice and the first violin alternate in stating each phrase of the tune:

Example 7.19

Bach's penchant for giving selected ideas special musical treatment is present in this movement. *Kreuzes* ("cross") is emphasized by a lengthening and decoration of the note on which the word occurs:

Example 7.20

Of particular interest is the setting of the words *dem Tode für,* with the extreme downward leap to and elongation of *Tode* ("death"):

Example 7.21

And the elongation of the first syllable of *Würger* (destroyer) is very dramatic:

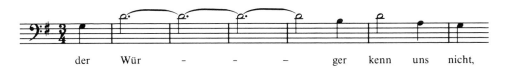

Example 7.22

Verse VI, scored for soprano, tenor, and continuo, expresses very beautifully the light-hearted joy embodied in the text of this movement. The chorale tune is passed back and forth between the two solo voices, and the end of each phrase is extended and decorated by a melismatic triplet figure.

In verse VII, the last movement, we finally encounter the chorale tune in its pure form. The melody is located in the soprano voice and the first violin part, with the rest of the chorus, doubled by instruments, providing simple harmonic support.

Example 7.23

In comparison to the elaborate settings in the previous movements, the final verse is considerably less complex, allowing the congregation to join the choir in singing the last verse of the cantata. This active participation provides the climactic religious and spiritual fulfillment of the experience as a whole.

SUMMARY

The Baroque era began in Italy around the year 1600. Fundamental style changes were brought about by a reaction against Renaissance vocal polyphony and a desire to make music serve and reflect the mood and meaning of the words. This attitude resulted in the monodic style, in which a single voice is accompanied by a group of instruments called basso continuo. The new prominence of the major and minor modes, the establishment of a tonic, and the devices of modulation and dissonance permitted the development of larger musical structures.

Many new vocal forms developed during the Baroque period, notably the speechlike recitative and the lyrical arioso. The da capo aria is an expansion of the arioso and is characterized by an ABA form. These became important features of the large vocal forms of the Baroque—the opera, the oratorio, and the cantata.

The opera is an elaborately staged dramatic form based on secular themes. The first great opera was *Orfeo,* written by the Italian Claudio Monteverdi. The oratorio is a sacred dramatic work presented without scenery or stage action. It reached its height in the works of George Frideric Handel, particularly with his *Messiah.* The cantata is smaller in scale than either the opera or oratorio and used both sacred and secular texts.

The Protestant movement in Germany promoted the use of simple hymn tunes for congregational singing. These tunes, known as chorales, formed the basis for larger, more elaborate vocal works. Such works as the *St. Matthew Passion* and the numerous cantatas by Johann Sebastian Bach represent the finest in German baroque vocal music.

NEW TERMS

monodic style	opera
basso continuo (continuo)	oratorio
figured bass	cantata
recitative	libretto (libretti)
secco recitative	movement
accompanied recitative	chorale
arioso	Passion
aria (da capo aria)	sinfonia
da capo	basso ostinato

SUGGESTED LISTENING

Bach, Johann Sebastian

Magnificat in D. This setting of the Latin canticle of the Virgin Mary is one of Bach's finest and most melodious works. It is scored for soloists, chorus, and orchestra.

Cantata 140, *Wachet auf, ruft uns die Stimme* (*Sleepers Awake*). Movements 1, 4, and 7 are based upon the chorale melody. Movements 3 and 6 are duets in ABA form. Each duet is introduced by a short recitative (movements 2 and 5).

Carissimi, Giaccomo

Jepthe. An oratorio that tells the Old Testament story of Jepthe's pledge to God. If allowed to return from battle victorious, he will sacrifice the first person who greets him upon his return. The first person turns out to be his daughter. The piece ends with a lament sung by the daughter, followed by a moving chorus.

Handel, George Frideric

Israel in Egypt. An oratorio based upon the Old Testament account of the flight of the Jews from captivity in Egypt. Of particular interest is the description of the plagues.

Purcell, Henry

Dido and Aeneas. Purcell wrote this opera to be performed by a school for young gentlewomen— all but one of the roles are for female voices. Surprisingly, it is the only opera in English written during the Baroque period. Dido's beautiful lament near the end of the opera has become famous in its own right and is often performed independently from the opera at song recitals.

Schütz, Heinrich

Historia von der Geburt Jesu Christi (*The Christmas Story*). One of the earliest masterpieces of baroque oratorio, this work is divided into eight sections with opening and closing choruses. The recitatives are written in a masterful, flowing style, and the vocal arias and ensembles have very colorful instrumental accompaniments.

Strozzi, Barbara

Cantatas found in *Harmonia Mundi 1114*. Interesting music by a prolific composer of baroque secular cantatas.

BAROQUE INSTRUMENTAL MUSIC

CHAPTER

8

The Baroque era was not only a period of magnificent achievement in vocal composition; it also saw the gradual development of a significant body of instrumental music. The Baroque was the age of the great violin makers, among them the members of the Stradivari family. Improvements were made in the construction of virtually every wind and brass instrument, and the organ and the harpsichord became the basic keyboard instruments. By the end of the Baroque era, instrumental music had gradually equalled or surpassed vocal music in importance, and the style of vocal music itself was very much influenced by the instrumental idiom.

KEYBOARD MUSIC

A large body of music for keyboard instruments—the organ and harpsichord (the piano had not yet been invented)—was written during the Baroque period. These pieces appeared with various titles—**fantasia, prelude, toccata**—that were carryovers from the names given to lute music in the sixteenth century. The terms described the style and character of a piece rather than its form, for pieces bearing these titles were cast in "free form," with no standard formal design.

The term *toccata* derives from the Italian verb *toccare* ("to touch") and implies a piece full of scale passages, rapid runs and trills, and massive chords. The fantasia was a piece characterized by displays of virtuosity. The prelude customarily introduced another piece or group of pieces.

The prelude, fantasia, and toccata were improvisatory in nature and were often used as an introduction to a **fugue,** one of the great intellectual musical structures of the Baroque era.

FUGUE

A fugue is a piece of music consisting of the polyphonic development of a melodic phrase called the **subject.** Fugues are composed for a certain number of voice parts: two-voice fugue, three-voice fugue, and so on. The precise manner in which the subject is developed among these voice parts varies from piece to piece. However, the initial section of virtually every fugue follows a plan that is more or less standard. This section is called the **exposition.**

Vast technical improvements in wind, brass, and keyboard instruments, as well as the development of the violin, encouraged the growth of instrumental music during the Baroque era. Pictured here is an imaginary instrument-maker's workshop.

The exposition begins with a single voice part stating the subject. As the subject ends, a second voice part enters in imitation, stating the subject while the first voice continues with contrasting melodic material called the **countersubject.** This process of imitative entrances of each voice part in turn continues until all voice parts have stated the fugue subject, at which point the exposition has been accomplished. Without pause, the piece continues with a number of sections that function either as new statements of the fugue subject or some variation of it, or as transitions between statements of the subject. The transition sections are called **episodes,** and most frequently modulate from the key of one statement of the subject to the key of the next statement. The melodic material in the episodes may be derived from the subject, the countersubject, or entirely different material.

A number of techniques were available for the development of the fugue subject. For example, the subject can be elongated—stretched out with longer note values—a technique called **augmentation.** Or just the opposite can occur—condensed through the use of shorter note values—called **diminution.** It can be turned upside down (**inversion**) or even played backward (**retrograde**). Sometimes statements of the subject overlap; before one voice finishes, another enters—a device known as **stretto.** It is important to note that, while the general pattern of the exposition is part of virtually every fugue, what follows the exposition is quite free and varies greatly from fugue to fugue.

In listening to a fugue, the primary interest lies in following the life of the fugue subject as it appears and reappears in different surroundings and in different forms throughout the course of the piece.

The fugue was a very popular form utilized in both choral and instrumental literature. Although it originated in the Baroque period, it has held a high place in all musical eras after the Baroque, up to and including the present time. The unchallenged master of the baroque fugue was Johann Sebastian Bach.

BACH (1685–1750)

Johann Sebastian Bach (fig 8.1) was the most distinguished member of a family of musicians that reached back four generations before him and was carried forward by three of his sons. His father, Johann Ambrosius, was a musician in service to the town council of Eisenach, a small community in Thuringia, now part of eastern Germany. Little is known about Bach's early life, but it seems that his father, an excellent violinist, taught him to play stringed instruments, and another relative, the organist of Eisenach's leading church, began instructing him at the organ.

Orphaned when he was only ten, Bach was sent to live with his eldest brother, Johann Christoph, an organist at the nearby town of Ohrdruf. He remained there five years, taking organ and harpsichord lessons from his brother, earning some money as a soprano, and studying at the town's famed grammar school. He did so well at the school that he was offered a scholarship to St. Michael's, a secondary school in Lüneburg, a city in northern Germany.

In 1703 Bach obtained his first musical position, as violinist in the small chamber orchestra of the ducal court of Weimar, but when a post as church organist became available in Arnstadt in August of 1703, he accepted the position. Dissatisfied with working conditions

Figure 8.1 Johann Sebastian Bach.

in Arnstadt and the poor state of the church choir, Bach left in 1707 to become organist at the church of St. Blasius in the Free Imperial City of Mühlhausen. In that same year he married a cousin, Maria Barbara Bach.

Soon entangled in a feud between factions within the Lutheran church, Bach left Mühlhausen in 1708 to become court organist, and later concertmaster, in the ducal chapel of Weimar. His nine years in Weimar constitute his first major creative period. Here he composed a number of cantatas and many of his greatest organ works, and he worked intensively with singers and instrumentalists as a conductor.

Because of his evident talent as a composer, performer, and conductor, Bach expected to be offered the top position of *Kapellmeister* (chapelmaster) at Weimar when it became available in 1716. However, he was passed over in favor of another. The following year he accepted the position of court conductor to the small principality of Anhalt-Cöthen.

Bach had enjoyed a growing reputation as an organist and composer of church cantatas, and had made annual performing tours to important centers such as Kassel, Leipzig, and Dresden. His duties at Cöthen, as conductor and composer for the eighteen-member court orchestra, led to a shift in emphasis toward instrumental music. Much of his finest orchestral music dates from this period, including the six Brandenburg Concertos.

The happy and productive years at Cöthen were marred by the death of his wife in 1720. Bach soon remarried, however, and his new wife, Anna Magdalena, proved to be a hardworking, cheerful companion who raised Bach's four children by Maria Barbara along with her own. She gave birth to thirteen children in all, six of whom survived.

In 1723 Bach was offered the position of cantor (director of music) at St. Thomas Church in Leipzig, one of the most important musical posts in Protestant Germany. However, it was not a completely auspicious beginning for Bach, as the city council turned to him only after it had received refusals from two other composers. His duties included composing cantatas for St. Nicholas Church as well as St. Thomas Church, supervising the musical programs in all the municipal churches, and teaching Latin in the St. Thomas choir school.

Despite the irksome nature of some of his duties and his uneasy relationship with his superiors, the Leipzig town council, Bach remained in Leipzig for the rest of his life. He personally supervised the musical education of his most gifted sons, Wilhelm Friedemann, Carl Philipp Emanuel, and Johann Christian, and saw them embark on promising musical careers. Though, like Handel, he went blind in old age, his creative powers remained undimmed. His last composition, dictated to a son-in-law a few days before his death, was a chorale prelude, "Before Thy Throne, My God, I Stand."

Bach at the organ in St. Thomas Kirche Leipzig. This superb instrument stimulated Bach's musical genius for more than a quarter of a century.

BACH'S WORK

BACH:
Fugue in G Minor
Cassette 1/B, Track 5
CD 1, Track 16

Bach's profound genius extended to nearly every form of musical composition prevalent in the Baroque period. His vocal music is best represented by his Mass in B Minor, his Passions, and his many cantatas. In his instrumental music he was equally prolific and far-ranging in style.

His consummate skill is clearly seen in the Fugue in G Minor (ca. 1709), subtitled "The Little" to distinguish it from his longer fugue in the same key.

The Fugue in G Minor is a four-voice piece for organ based upon the following subject:

Example 8.1

Voice I (in this case the highest, or soprano voice) states the subject in the tonic key of G minor and continues with the countersubject where voice II enters in imitation with the subject in D minor (example 8.2).

Example 8.2

After a brief modulation back to G minor, voices III and IV follow the same pattern of stating the subject and countersubject as indicated in example 8.3:

Exposition of the Fugue in G Minor

Example 8.3

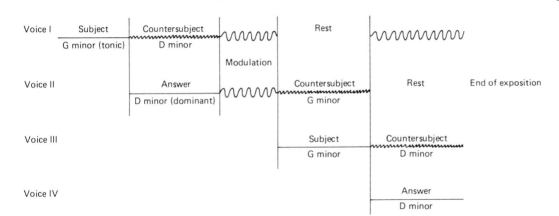

Note that this musical organization is heavily dependent upon the device known as imitation—voice II imitates voice I, and each voice in turn imitates the one before it in stating the subject.

There is no pause at the conclusion of the exposition. The flow of music is continuous. After a modulation back to the key of G minor, there appears to be an entry of the subject in voice III. However, after the first few notes, voice III continues, not with the subject but the countersubject, while voice I "steals" the subject and goes on with a full statement. Aside from this "false entry," the piece consists of a number of sections in which episodes prepare for and lead to statements of the subject in a variety of keys, ending with the final statement of the subject in the bass voice in the tonic of G minor (example 8.4).

Example 8.4

| Episode | False entry (Voice III), full statement (Voice I) | Episode | Subject (Voice II) | Episode | Subject (Voice IV) |

| Episode | Subject (Voice I) | Episode | Final statement of subject (Voice IV) |

Aside from the structural fugal procedures, this little piece illustrates a major stylistic feature of much baroque instrumental music—namely, an unbroken, uninterrupted, steady flow of music from the first note to the last chord. Quite unlike later styles, in which sections of music are separated by pauses, the polyphonic instrumental style of the baroque is characterized by continuous motion and progression from beginning to end.

Baroque organ literature included many works intended for performance in conjunction with religious ceremonies, and many of these pieces were based upon chorale melodies. For instance, as an introduction to the service, the organist would play a work based upon the particular chorale tune appropriate for the specific day in the church year—hence the *chorale prelude, chorale partita,* and *chorale fantasia.*

SUITE

A popular form among composers of music for the harpsichord was the **suite,** a series of movements with each based upon a particular dance rhythm and style. Usually it included the German **allemande,** the French **courante,** the **sarabande** (originally from Spain), and the English or Irish **gigue** (jig). Many suites also included the **gavotte,** and at times, non-dance movements such as the prelude were employed. This series of movements was designed to offer interesting contrasts in meter, tempo, and texture.

The dance movements of the suite were not intended to accompany actual dancing. Composers simply adapted the rhythm and character of the dances, turning them into well-wrought compositions for listening.

While harpsichord suites were very popular in the late Baroque period (J. S. Bach's so-called *English* and *French Suites*), the suite was by no means confined to the keyboard. Rather, suites were written for a wide range of solo instruments, chamber ensembles, and orchestra. Handel's orchestral suites—*Water Music* and *Music for the Royal Fireworks*—remain popular today.

BAROQUE SONATA

In the beginning of the Baroque period, the term **sonata** was applied to instrumental pieces that varied greatly in structure, character, and the number and type of instruments. Usually it was a multimovement work, but the number of movements varied from piece to piece.

Gradually there developed a distinction between the sonata written for the church, **sonata da chiesa,** and that intended for the chamber, **sonata da camera.** The sonata da camera became essentially a dance suite, and the sonata da chiesa a four-movement work in which the movements alternated in tempo: slow-fast-slow-fast.

Toward the later part of the Baroque period, three types of sonatas were predominant: the sonata for unaccompanied instrument; the **solo sonata** for one solo instrument (usually the violin) and continuo; and the **trio sonata,** usually employing two violins for the upper voices and a cello and keyboard instrument for the continuo. Corelli, Vivaldi, Handel, and Bach all made important contributions to the sonata literature.

At the very end of the Baroque period, the emphasis shifted to the solo sonata, setting the stage for its development as a primary musical form during subsequent periods of music history.

CONCERTO

Baroque innovations in the realm of instrumental music included the **concerto,** a type of musical form based upon the contrast between relatively large and small bodies of sound. This principle of contrast manifested itself in the **concerto grosso** and the **solo concerto.**

CONCERTO GROSSO

The concerto grosso is a multimovement work in which a small group of solo instruments, called the **concertino,** and the full ensemble, called the **ripieno** (Italian for "full"), are contrasted. The basic outlines of the concerto grosso were established by Arcangelo Corelli (1653–1713), whose *Christmas Concerto* remains a favorite today. Corelli's concertino consisted of two solo violins and violoncello with either organ or harpsichord (continuo), contrasting with a small string orchestra (with its own continuo) playing the role of ripieno. The actual contrast between the solo group and the string orchestra in Corelli's concerti was slight in comparison to the concerti of later composers, and the number of movements employed by Corelli varied from piece to piece.

Giuseppe Torelli (1658–1709) established a three-movement pattern—allegro-adagio-allegro (fast-slow-fast)—and the **ritornello form** as the structure of the first movement. In general, ritornello form follows the pattern outlined below:

A	B	A	C	A	
ritornello	concertino	ritornello	concertino	ritornello	etc.

The thematic material given to the ripieno (the "ritornello") returns between sections played by the solo group of instruments—an example of alternation (see page 27). The ritornello statements *within* the movement are often fragmentary, consisting of only part of the original material, and can be in different tonalities. Nevertheless, the returns of the ritornello theme, even though somewhat changed, give the movement a great sense of unity. The final ritornello is usually complete and is always in the same tonality in which the movement began.

Antonio Vivaldi (1669–1741) was a great master of the concerto grosso. He adopted the three-movement form and the ritornello pattern just described. He also made a greater distinction between the ripieno and the concertino in terms of the increased degree of complexity of the musical material played by the concertino. Vivaldi's music had a strong influence on J. S. Bach.

THE BRANDENBURG CONCERTOS

In 1721 Bach completed six works dedicated to Christian Ludwig, the Margrave of Brandenburg. Although Bach referred to these pieces as "concertos for several instruments," they have come to be known as the Brandenburg Concertos. Three of them (nos. 2, 4, and 5) follow the tradition of Vivaldi in that they contrast a group of solo instruments (concertino) against a full ensemble (ripieno).

The Brandenburg Concerto no. 5 is scored for a concertino consisting of flute, violin, and harpsichord contrasting with a string orchestra with continuo as the ripieno. By his choice of instruments for the concertino, Bach created a contrast in timbre *within* the solo group as well as *between* the solo group and the ripieno. He maintains the fast-slow-fast three-movement structure established by earlier composers.

First Movement

The first movement is in ritornello form and uses as the returning thematic material the following:

BACH:
Brandenburg Concerto
no. 5, First Movement
Cassette 2/A, Track 1
CD 2, Track 1
*See Listening Guide on
page 158.*

Example 8.5

At the beginning, in the middle, and at the end of the movement, the ripieno presents a complete statement of this material in the key of D major, the tonic key of the movement. These full statements act as thematic and harmonic pillars providing the movement with a solid and unified structure. In between these complete statements, the solo instruments of the concertino develop and expand upon melodic and rhythmic ideas derived from the ritornello theme, punctuated by the ripieno with periodic fragmentary statements of the ritornello theme itself in a variety of keys.

As the movement progresses, the equality among the three solo instruments gradually gives way to the almost total predominance of the harpsichord. In fact, toward the end of the movement the violin, the flute, and the ripieno cease altogether, and the harpsichord is heard as a solo instrument in passages that require great virtuosity, such as:

Example 8.6

The long solo section by the harpsichord climaxes in the final entry of the ritornello theme played by the entire ensemble ("tutti").

Like much baroque instrumental music, this entire movement is characterized by a constant spinning out of music with no stopping points or pauses of any kind—a relentless rhythmic drive from beginning to end.

Second Movement

In accordance with the concerto grosso plan, the second movement contrasts markedly. It is in a different key (B minor), it is slow in tempo (marked affettuoso—"tenderly"), and it employs only the three solo instruments of the concertino, the harpsichord performing the dual function of solo instrument and continuo. The essence of this short movement is drawn from two distinctive rhythmic motives:

Example 8.7

Example 8.8

They are contrasted and combined in a variety of ways by the three solo instruments.

Third Movement

The third movement returns to the tempo (allegro) and key (D major) of the first movement. It is very much in the spirit of a *gigue* based upon:

Example 8.9

It features the solo instruments, particularly the harpsichord, with the ripieno devoted to light accompanying support except in a few climactic places where it joins with or rivals the concertino. Structurally, the movement is a large three-part form, ABA. It has the same kind of continuous rhythmic drive as the first movement, with the exception of an obvious stop and pause immediately before the return of the A section—quite a surprise in this style!

This work, along with the second and fourth Brandenburg concertos, represents the culmination of this fascinating form.

SOLO CONCERTO

The solo concerto is organized along the same lines as the concerto grosso, with the notable exception that it is written for only *one* solo instrument—contrasting with a full instrumental ensemble. Antonio Vivaldi wrote hundreds of solo concertos that became the models for later baroque composers, including Handel and Bach.

Le Quattro Stagione

VIVALDI:
Le quattro stagione
(*The Four Seasons*):
Spring, First Movement
Cassette 2/A, Track 2
CD 2, Track 2
See Listening Guide on page 159.

Of all Vivaldi's concertos, the group called *Le quattro stagione (The Four Seasons)* is perhaps the most interesting because of the extramusical basis of its inspiration. Vivaldi was one of the first to try to depict by musical means the feelings and sounds of the changing seasons. These four violin concertos are an early example of baroque descriptive or *program music,* and the music for the solo violin, which calls for virtuoso playing, demonstrates Vivaldi's skill at writing for the instrument. In spite of their descriptive intent, all of the concertos follow the three-movement formal outline—fast, slow, fast, with the outer movements being in the same key.

Each of the four concertos bears the title of one of the seasons—spring, summer, winter, fall—and each is preceded by a sonnet describing that particular season. For instance, the concerto entitled *Spring* has the following introduction:

First Movement—Allegro

Spring has come, and the birds greet it with happy songs, and at the same time the streams run softly murmuring to the breathing of the gentle breezes.
Then the sky being cloaked in black, thunder and lightning come and have their say; after the storm has quieted, the little birds turn again to their harmonious song.

Second Movement—Largo

Here in a pleasant flowery meadow, the leaves sweetly rustle, the goatherd sleeps, his faithful dog at his side.

Third Movement—Allegro

Nymphs and shepherds dance to the festive sound of the pastoral musette under the bright sky that they love.

The three movements present sharp contrasts not only in tempo but also in meter (4/4, 3/4, 12/8), key (E major, C♯ minor, E major), and general dynamic level (forte, piano, forte). The second movement is quite unusual in that it does not employ the basso continuo. The third movement is titled *Danza Pastorale* (*Pastoral Dance*) and uses a dance rhythm as its ritornello material.

The birds' songs, murmuring streams, gentle breezes, the storm, and the return to serenity are all vividly represented by the solo violin and the full ensemble. But all of this descriptive writing takes place within the ritornello structure consisting of nine sections as follows:

I   Ritornello (*Spring has come*)   E major

The beginning of the movement includes a full statement of what appears to be the ritornello material, which consists of two contrasting phrases (a) and (b), each of which is stated *forte* and immediately repeated *piano* in echo fashion.

Example 8.10

As the movement unfolds, we will discover that only phrase (b) is used as ritornello material, returning from time to time during the movement as the primary unifying element. Phrase (a) never appears again in the course of the movement.

II   "Bird Songs"   E major

In this section, the solo violin (violino principale) is joined by violins from the ensemble to present the description of a variety of bird songs. During this section, the rest of the ensemble is silent and remains so until the ritornello (example 8.11).

Example 8.11

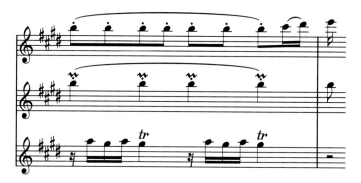

III   Ritornello   E major

IV   "Streams and Breezes"

Example 8.12

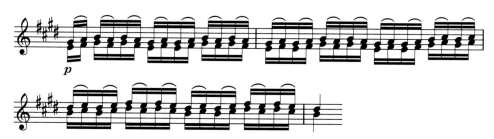

V   Ritornello   B major

VI   "Storm"

The thunder is depicted by all the strings on a tremulo figure played forte,

Example 8.13

while lightning follows in the upper strings:

Example 8.14

As this section continues, the solo violin provides the lightning,

Violino principale

Example 8.15

while the full ensemble continues to supply thunder with tremulo entrances.

This section is characterized by modulation in preparation for the next ritornello statement,

VII   Ritornello   C♯ minor

ending the storm.

VIII return of birds in harmonious song

Here again the principal violin solo is joined by solo violins from the ensemble in presenting musical representation of a variety of bird calls leading to a section played by the full ensemble—a section that acts as a kind of ritornello, although the material is not drawn from the ritornello material:

Example 8.16

This section ends with a short, cadenza-like passage featuring the solo violin completing the modulation back to the principal key in preparation for the final appearance of the ritornello:

IX   Ritornello

In this final statement, the phrase appears in its original form—stated twice, first forte, then piano—bringing the movement to a convincing conclusion.

In this movement, Vivaldi has cleverly balanced virtuoso writing for the solo violin, material designed as descriptive in function, and the standard ritornello form typical of the baroque solo concerto.

The fates of the solo concerto and the concerto grosso beyond the Baroque period were quite different. The concerto grosso ceased to occupy the attention of composers to any appreciable extent, while the solo concerto thrived during subsequent stylistic periods.

Listening Guide

BACH: Brandenburg Concerto no. 5

First Movement: Fast
Quadruple meter
Ritornello form

Concertino: Flute, violin, harpsichord

Ripieno: String orchestra with continuo

Review: Example 8.5 (the ritornello theme)
Example 8.6 (virtuoso passage on harpsichord)

CD 2 (Cassette 2/A, Track 1)

1	①	0:00	**Ritornello theme** **Ripieno**	1a	Complete statement in tonic; vigorous melody surges upward, setting rhythmic drive in motion
		0:21	**Contrasting section** **Concertino**	b	Fragments from ritornello theme; imitation between flute and violin, with harpsichord an independent third part in constant motion
	②	0:46	**Ritornello theme**	2a	Partial statement from beginning of theme
		0:51	**Contrasting section**	b	Continued imitation between flute and violin; more extended than *1b*
	③	1:12	**Ritornello theme**	3a	Partial statement, begins where *2a* left off
		1:19	**Contrasting section**	b	Harpsichord enters; flute and violin echo in single notes, then develop other fragments
	④	1:39	**Ritornello theme**	4a	Partial statement, taken from where *3a* left off
		1:46	**Contrasting section**	b	Interplay between violin and flute; fast notes, virtuosic display, draw attention to harpsichord
		2:29	**Ritornello theme**	5a	Partial statement from middle of theme
	⑤	2:35	**Contrasting section**	b	Figures tossed back and forth between flute and violin; new melodic fragment introduced and developed; extended length; final trills lead to:
		4:19	**Ritornello theme**	6a	Partial statement from beginning of theme
		4:24	**Contrasting section**	b	Continued imitation between violin and flute
		5:11	**Ritornello theme**	7a	Full statement in tonic key
		5:23	**Contrasting section**	b	Continued imitation between flute and violin moving smoothly into:
		5:52	**Ritornello theme**	8a	Partial statement from middle of theme
	⑥	5:59	**Contrasting section**	b	The longest contrasting section; virtuosic display draws attention to harpsichord; flute and violin drop out, leaving harpsichord, with trills and passage work, long preparation on dominant for return of:
		9:31	**Ritornello theme**	9	Complete statement in tonic

Listening Guide

VIVALDI: *Le quattro stagione (The Four Seasons): Spring*

First Movement: Allegro (fast)
Quadruple meter
Ritornello form

Concertino: Solo violin (joined occasionally by 2 more solo violins)

Ripieno: String orchestra with continuo

Review: Example 8.10 (ritornello theme, phrases a and b)
Example 8.11 (bird songs)
Example 8.12 (streams and breezes)
Example 8.13 (thunder)
Example 8.14 (lightning, upper strings of orchestra)
Example 8.15 (lightning, solo violin)
Example 8.16 (ritornello-like theme)

CD 2 (Cassette 2/A, Track 2)

2	1	0:00	**Ritornello**	1	Orchestra, first phrase of optimistic spring theme, stated forte; echoed piano
		0:16			Second phrase of spring theme, stated forte; echoed piano
	2	0:33	**Contrasting section**	2	3 solo violins, high pitch, trills, suggest bird calls
		1:10	**Ritornello**	3	Orchestra, second phrase of spring theme, forte
	3	1:18	**Contrasting section**	4	Orchestra, smoothly flowing, soft note pairs suggest streams and breezes
		1:43	**Ritornello**	5	Second phrase of spring theme, orchestra
	4	1:51	**Contrasting section**	6	Forte tremolo in orchestra for thunder, scales rushing upward for lightning; solo violin added with new lightning theme, tremolo continues in orchestra
	5	2:19	**Ritornello**	7	Orchestra, second phrase of spring theme, minor key
		2:28	**Contrasting section**	8	3 solo violins suggest bird calls, sustained note in bass
		2:45			Orchestra, forte, ritornello-related theme
		2:57			Solo violin with continuo, passage work
		3:11	**Ritornello**	9	Orchestra states second phrase of spring theme forte; echoed softly to conclude

SUMMARY

The Baroque era saw the rise of instrumental music of all kinds, due in part to the development and improvement of existing instruments.

The harpsichord and the organ were the chief keyboard instruments of the Baroque period. Single movement works written for them include the fantasia, the prelude, and the toccata. Chorale tunes formed the basis for a large body of literature written for the organ. The suite is an example of the multimovement keyboard form that became popular for other solo instruments and ensembles. A form that often appears in keyboard, instrumental, and vocal works is the fugue. The fugue, in which a melodic subject is presented and developed in a variety of ways, is one of the most significant forms of the Baroque.

The baroque sonata is a multimovement work for one or more instruments. Two of its early forms are the sonata da camera and the sonata da chiesa. Later developments include the sonata for unaccompanied instrument, the solo sonata, and the trio sonata.

The concerto grosso is a multimovement work that pits a small group, the concertino, against a full ensemble, the ripieno. A solo concerto differs from the concerto grosso in that the concertino is reduced to a single instrument. The three-movement pattern of the concerto (fast-slow-fast) and the use of the ritornello form in the first movement influenced the development of subsequent musical forms.

Arcangelo Corelli, Giuseppe Torelli, and Antonio Vivaldi all contributed to the development of instrumental music in the Baroque, especially in the areas of the solo concerto and the concerto grosso. An acknowledged master of baroque instrumental music is Johann Sebastian Bach.

NEW TERMS

fantasia

prelude

toccata

fugue
  subject
  exposition
  countersubject
  episode
  augmentation
  diminution
  inversion
  retrograde
  stretto

suite
  allemande
  courante
  sarabande
  gigue
  gavotte
sonata (da chiesa, da camera)
  solo sonata
  trio sonata
concerto (solo, grosso)
  concertino
  ripieno
  ritornello

SUGGESTED LISTENING

Bach, Johann Sebastian

Orchestra Suite no. 3 in D Major. One of Bach's best-known suites, especially because of its third movement, *Air on the G String.*

Organ Works: Toccata and Fugue in D Minor; Passacaglia and Fugue in C Minor; Prelude and Fugue in E-flat ("St. Anne"). These works span Bach's most active period of organ compositions.

Corelli, Arcangelo

Concerto Grosso in G Minor op. 6, no. 8, "*Christmas Concerto.*" Written to be performed at midnight Mass on Christmas Eve. The final movement ("Pastorale") is often interpreted as an evocation of the angels hovering over Bethlehem.

Handel, George Frideric

Orchestral Suites: *Water Music; Fireworks Music.* The *Water Music,* actually a compilation of three individual suites, was first performed at a royal boating party. The *Fireworks Music,* a shorter work, was originally scored for a large wind band and later revised to include strings.

Music of the

Classical Era

Mozart and His Sister Playing before Maria Theresa. Painting by Borkmann.
(North Wind Picture Archives.)

The Classical Era: Reason and Revolution

The Classical era in the arts lasted from about 1750 to the end of the first quarter of the nineteenth century. These turbulent generations witnessed the breakdown of the baroque style and the return to classically inspired forms in building, statuary, and painting. The upheaval of the late eighteenth century was highlighted by the American and French Revolutions; at the same time, the application of the steam engine to industrial production and transportation was transforming the nature of European life. In this seventy-five-year period, every quarter of the continent breathed change.

European intellectuals of the eighteenth century were the first to consider themselves fully emancipated from the Middle Ages. They spoke of themselves as living in Enlightenment and an Age of Reason. They were confident believers in human control over a reasonable world, in the marvelous machine of a universe they thought they understood, where God was not so much the awesome Father and Judge as the cosmic Watchmaker. But the discord and irrationality in France in the 1790s made reason a questionable proposition. In the early nineteenth century, many intellectuals dismissed those who had absolute faith in reason as naive at best and hypocritical at worst.

BEFORE THE FRENCH REVOLUTION (1750–1789)

In the eighteenth century, towns grew, interregional trade quickened, fortunes were made, and the bourgeoisie (the middle class) enjoyed more economic power than ever before. Towns like London and Amsterdam bustled with high finance, warehouses, trading marts, and ship movements. Taste, however, was determined in France, the country that had become the leading cultural center of the continent. Fashion, in dress, design, and ideas, radiated from Paris and Versailles. It was the aristocracy rather than the busy entrepreneurs of the middle class that had the money and time for the cultivation and refinement of life.

It is wrong, however, to imagine the members of the upper class as wicked pleasure-seekers. In townhouse and palace, they strove for worldly perfection in art and thought as well as in manners. In fact, the eighteenth century was a period of vigorous intellectual activity. Scientific advance continued with even greater velocity; more important, the century was energized by the active philosophical debate over the nature of reform and progress.

Some thinkers believed that the human race could attain perfection through the application of common sense to social problems, a viewpoint eloquently championed by the German mathematician Leibnitz and brutally satirized by Voltaire in *Candide*. Diderot and other brilliant French philosophers undertook the *Encyclopédia*, a massive enterprise of twenty-four volumes that tried to codify accumulated knowledge from the past and current ideas in the present. Rousseau, a harbinger of nineteenth-century romanticism, challenged the ultra-refined world around him. He believed that human beings enjoyed a godlike character that had been corrupted and deadened by civilization. He wanted to abandon the cerebral world of logic and analysis and return to the more natural, instinctual, primitive world of the aborigine. All these different points of view appear contradictory on the surface; however, they all assumed that the human condition could be improved or perfected. The eighteenth century glorified the power of the individual to control and order the world, a viewpoint that nurtured both economic growth and the notion that governments should reflect the will and interests of the people.

For much of this period, the visual arts, dominated by the late baroque style called rococo, did not mirror the rising tide of reason and simplicity. The rococo style emphasized elegance rather than clarity, delicacy rather than strength, softness rather than severity, and playfulness rather than solemnity. French interiors were decorated with beautiful gold-and-white curved woods, crystal chandeliers, and gilt ceilings (see page 167).

The French painters Boucher and Fragonard, who idealized the joy and sweetness of aristocratic life, were deluged with commissions (see pages 168 and 169).

Rococo art, though, became less popular in the last decades of the eighteenth century. Cream colors and rich velvet grew less fashionable. The new taste of the 1770s and later, called neoclassicism, borrowed from the seventeenth-century French artist Poussin (see Prelude II, page 113), as well as from Greek temples and Roman statuary. In short, the last quarter of the eighteenth century rejected baroque design and began to work from "more noble" classical models.

Music, with all its evocative powers, held a high position in the *ancien régime* ("the old order," a phrase later used to summarize the elegance and grandeur of France before 1789). The two greatest composers of the late eighteenth century were both Austrian: Wolfgang Amadeus Mozart (1756–1791) and Franz Joseph Haydn (1732–1809). Both depended on commissions in their early careers, Mozart as a concertmaster to the Archbishop of Salzburg and Haydn as a music director for a Hungarian prince.

Both Mozart and Haydn ended their careers in Vienna. This eastern city, the seat of the Hapsburgs and the capital city of the Holy Roman Empire, was a magnet for first-rate musicians, since the Hapsburg court and the Viennese townspeople placed a very high premium on musical achievement and excellence. The prestige of the composer, musician, and performer—from whatever background—was high. The demand for new compositions, frequent concerts, and the competition among the private orchestras of the nobility made it the first city of European music by the end of the eighteenth century.

THE FRENCH REVOLUTION AND ITS AFTERMATH (1798–1825)

In the first half of the eighteenth century, royal governments were able to exercise tremendous power over their subjects. In 1776, however, leaders in England's North American colonies, convinced that London no longer represented their economic interests and infuriated that it was trying to extinguish their local political rights, declared their independence from George III and his Parliament. Thirteen years later, the French bourgeoisie acted to wrest lawmaking power from Louis XVI. This was the beginning of a political struggle that reduced France to a state of anarchy in the 1790s and made for war throughout Europe.

The progress of the French Revolution is confusing and, like most revolutionary periods, often irrational. In the first stage the bourgeoisie established a limited monarchy; later, after Louis XVI tried to escape to the company of royalists and fight against the rebels, the monarchy was abolished and the king was executed for "treason." In the 1790s, revolutionaries argued among themselves while they tried to stamp out aristocratic and peasant opposition to their programs; the result was a busy guillotine and political chaos.

At the same time, a revolutionary French army battled the armies of a more conservative European continent. From these contests there emerged a new French hero and leader—Napoleon Bonaparte. Napoleon's mind was tenacious and perfectly ordered; his spirit was dazzling. By 1799, he had enough power to take over the French government. In the next fifteen years he came to control almost all of Europe.

In the last quarter of the eighteenth century, the visual arts underwent as radical a change as European politics. The rococo faded entirely, to be replaced by that neoclassicism that idealized ancient Athens and Rome and attempted to recreate a heroic world based on antiquity.

In the 1790s Napoleon's counterpart in the arts was Jacques-Louis David (1748–1825), a painter who became a kind of art dictator during the Revolution and whose style was undisputed before the 1820s. David avoided the "capricious ornament" of earlier art. Instead, he built solemn scenes of noble sacrifice and great historical moments in a clear, balanced, linear style (see page 170). To David and his fellow revolutionaries, the excellence of antiquity was a guide to the perfection of the human race. In politics and art the French Revolution was a culmination of the spirit of reform of the preceding generations.

In some respects the use of the term *classical* to describe the milieu of the late 1700s and early 1800s is misleading. The word classical suggests clarity, harmony, evenness, and tranquility—all qualities for which this period is not known. It was an age of ferment, of differing values, of change. Nevertheless, the *music* of the

This reconstruction of an eighteenth-century French interior is a magnificent example of the elegant decoration of the rococo. Tapestries, mirrors, chandeliers, curved woods, and gilt all contributed to the luxury of the Parisian townhouses.

Classical period attaches great importance to balance and clarity of structure. The symphonic form reached its zenith and became a kind of music that later composers could only elaborate on or reject.

No musician of the nineteenth century could ignore the impact of Beethoven (1770–1827). It was Beethoven who brought the classical musical style to completion; moreover, for many musicians and critics of the nineteenth century, he served as a model and a beacon of musical perfection.

Are They Thinking About the Grape? by François Boucher (1747), oil on canvas, 80.8 cm × 68.5 cm. Boucher was the most popular painter at the court of Versailles in the middle of the eighteenth century. His style is consummately rococo—light, delicate, playful, and colorful. Its innocence and sensuality were dismissed by later generations as frivolous and trivial. (© 1988 The Art Institute of Chicago, Martha E. Leverone Endowment, 1973.304. All rights reserved.)

Before his death in poverty and obscurity, Jean-Honoré Fragonard (1732–1806) developed a highly individual style well represented in his painting *The Bathers,* executed around 1765. (Oil on canvas, 25½″. × 31½″. The Louvre, Paris.)

Jacques-Louis David's *The Death of Socrates* (1787) was exhibited in
Paris just two years before the French Revolution broke out. It
exemplifies the neoclassical style in its classical subject matter. It was
also a political statement, memorializing the heroism of a great man who
died for ideas that an oppressive state could not accept. (Oil on canvas,
51″ × 77¼″. The Metropolitan Museum of Art; Wolfe Fund, Catherine
Lorillard Wolfe Collection, 1931 [31.45].)

MOZART AND HAYDN

T he term *classical* is applied to music in several different ways. In one sense, we speak of a "classic" as any work of lasting value. Classical sometimes designates so-called *serious* or concert music, as opposed to *popular* music. In this case, the term is applied without regard to historical or stylistic factors, so that composers of different style periods—Bach, Beethoven, and Tchaikovsky, for example—may all be considered classical composers. In a narrower and more accurate sense, the term is applied to music in either of two meanings. First, it describes those historical periods in which music emphasized formal clarity, balance and structure, lucid design, objectivity, and traditionalism, as opposed to the romantic qualities of sentimentalism, exaggerated emotionalism, subjectivism, and experimentation. The late Renaissance and late Baroque periods were periods of classicism. Second, the term designates the music of the Viennese classic school (that is, the music of Haydn, Mozart, and to an extent, Beethoven and Schubert) from about 1770 to 1830. It is the second meaning that is intended when we refer to the "Classical era."

As we discussed in chapters 7 and 8, the style of the Baroque period began as a reaction against the vocal polyphony of the late Renaissance. Gradually, the homophonic style of early baroque music was transformed into a new kind of polyphony based upon the major-minor harmonic system and shaped by the maturing instrumental idioms.

Similarly, the style of the Classical era was the result of a reaction to the instrumental polyphony that we encountered in the late Baroque period, particularly in the music of Johann Sebastian Bach.

The new style, the classical style, was essentially homophonic rather than polyphonic; it was based upon the idea of successive *contrasting* thematic ideas rather than the contrapuntal expansion of *one* germinal melodic idea. In general, classical musical forms are sectional, with clear divisions between the sections as opposed to the frequent baroque manner of one continuous flow of music without pauses and stopping points from beginning to end.

Although the basso continuo was gradually abandoned in the Classical era, the major-minor system with its reliance on the dominant-tonic relationship continued to be a fundamental structural element. These stylistic features are embodied in the sonata style of the Classical period.

THE CLASSICAL SONATA

The meaning of the word *sonata* varies from age to age in music history. Originally, *sonata* meant something to be *played,* as opposed to *cantata,* something to be *sung.* The term had various applications throughout the Baroque period, but in the Classical era it took on a very specific and important meaning.

The classical **sonata** is a multimovement work in one of two schemes:

Three-movement plan

First movement	*Second movement*	*Third movement*
Fast tempo	Slow tempo	Fast tempo
Key of tonic	Contrasting key	Key of tonic

Four-movement plan

First movement	*Second movement*	*Third movement*	*Fourth movement*
Fast tempo	Slow tempo	Minuet and trio	Fast tempo
Key of tonic	Contrasting key	Key of tonic	Key of tonic

SONATA-ALLEGRO FORM

In both plans, the first movement is invariably cast in what has become known as **sonata-allegro form.** Sonata-allegro form (often referred to as simply **sonata form**) is based upon the scheme of the statement of musical materials; the exploration and manipulation of the materials; and the restatement of the materials. This general scheme is realized in three specific sections of the movement: (1) the **exposition,** (2) the **development,** and (3) the **recapitulation** (fig. 9.1).

Exposition

The exposition introduces the thematic material that forms the basis of the entire movement. This thematic material usually consists of two contrasting themes or groups of themes connected by a **bridge.** The first theme establishes the overall tonality for the movement as a whole; the second theme is always in a different key. If the first theme is in a *major* key, the second theme will almost always be in its *dominant* key. If the first theme is in a *minor* key, the second theme will usually appear in the relative *major* key. In some cases, sonata-allegro movements contain only one melody, which functions as both first and second themes. In such cases, the key relationships explained above are maintained. The bridge serves the function of modulating from the key of the first theme to the new key of the "second theme." Usually there is a clear and definite cadence, pause, or both separating the bridge and the second theme. Frequently, a short section called a **codetta** is employed after the second theme to bring the exposition to a close.

In almost all cases the exposition is immediately repeated so that the basic thematic ideas are firmly established, enabling the listener to follow the use of these ideas in the development section.

Figure 9.1 Sonata-allegro form.

Exposition	Development	Recapitulation
Theme I (tonic)	Transformation of expositional material	Theme I (tonic)
Bridge (modulates to new key)		Bridge (extended)
	Rapid modulations	Theme II (tonic)
Theme II (new key)		*Coda*
Codetta to cadence		Final cadence (tonic)
Exposition repeated		

Development

The development concentrates on some of the materials of the exposition and manipulates them in a variety of ways. Themes may be fragmented, small melodic or rhythmic motives expanded, or counterpoint added. Changes in timbre, rhythm, and dynamics are among the many devices that may be employed. No two development sections are the same; however, what is common to all of them is the process of *modulation.* Frequent and often extreme modulation is the rule.

Recapitulation

The recapitulation is a restatement of the whole exposition, with one important change—the second theme appears in the *tonic* rather than in a contrasting key as in the exposition. This reaffirmation of the tonic key and the return of the melodic material in its original form lends great unity to this formal structure. In some pieces, a concluding section, the **coda** ("tail"), is added as an extended conclusion of the movement, as shown in figure 9.1.

Occasionally the sonata-allegro movement is preceded by a slow introduction. The introduction, however, is not part of sonata-allegro form and is not included in the repetition of the exposition or in the recapitulation.

OTHER SONATA MOVEMENTS

The second movement of a sonata is slower and often more lyrical than the first. It always contrasts in key with the first movement. Theme and variations, or an alternating form such as ABA or ABACA, is commonly used, although sonata-allegro form is occasionally employed.

In the four-movement sonata plan, the third movement is usually a **minuet-and-trio** in the key of the first movement. It is in the stately style of the minuet in triple meter and cast in ternary form:

A	B	A
Minuet	Trio	Minuet

Typically there are repeated small sections within the first minuet and the trio but not within the second minuet:

A	B	A
Minuet	Trio	Minuet
aabb	ccdd	ab

The term *trio* is a carryover from the seventeenth century, during which the second of two alternating dances was scored for three instruments. In the classical sonata, the trio is rarely a three-voice piece but does contrast with the minuet in a variety of ways.

The minuet-and-trio plan is typical of works by Haydn and Mozart and of early works by Beethoven. However, Beethoven experimented with this movement a great deal and eventually adopted, in place of the minuet, a much faster type of piece known as a **scherzo.** As we shall see, the scherzo and trio became a movement of great power and drama in the works of Beethoven.

The last movement of the sonata returns to the general quality of the first movement. It is fast and in the key of the first movement. It is often a **rondo,** an extended alternating form in fast tempo, usually ABACA or ABACABA. It is generally spirited and often playful. Occasionally, the last movement of a sonata employs the sonata-allegro form.

The sonata principle (fig. 9.2) was an all-pervasive concept that served as a procedure for the composition of thousands of works of music during the Classical and Romantic periods. The four-movement plan became the basis for the **symphony** (sonata for orchestra) and the **string quartet** (sonata for four stringed instruments). The three-movement scheme,

Figure 9.2 The complete classical sonata.

First movement	Second movement	Third movement	Fourth movement
Sonata-allegro form	Theme and variations, alternating form, or sonata-allegro form	Minuet and trio or scherzo and trio	Rondo or sonata-allegro
Fast tempo		Triple meter (minuet)	Fast tempo
Dramatic	Slow tempo	Fast tempo (scherzo)	Spirited, playful
	Lyrical	Light, cheerful	Key of first movement
	Key contrasts with first movement	Key of first movement	

omitting minuet-and-trio, was typical of works for solo piano (piano sonata), for solo instruments and the piano (e.g., sonata for violin and piano), and for the **concerto** (sonata for solo instrument and orchestra).

PIANOFORTE

In the Classical period, the harpsichord of the baroque gave way to the new **pianoforte** (or simply **piano**) as the preferred keyboard instrument. The greater dynamic range and ability to sustain sounds for a longer period of time made the piano popular as a solo instrument, a chamber music participant, and a solo concerto instrument. The change of sound quality represented by the piano was an important element in the nature of classical style and influenced the course of music history in later stylistic periods. Equally important was the development of the orchestra.

THE CLASSICAL ORCHESTRA

In the Baroque era, instrumental music had become an independent idiom, and a vast literature for instrumental ensembles was produced. But the baroque orchestra, aside from the usual complement of strings, had no fixed makeup.

In the Classical era, the composition of the orchestra became standardized to a great extent. Its development was largely the work of Johann Stamitz (1717–1757), a violinist, composer, and conductor of the orchestra at the German city of Mannheim. Under his direction, the Mannheim orchestra became the most celebrated musical ensemble in Europe. The excellence of its playing was praised by the leading composers of the day.

By baroque standards, the Mannheim orchestra was of large dimensions. In 1756 it consisted of twenty violins, four violas, four cellos, and four basses. The wind section included four horns in addition to pairs of flutes, oboes, clarinets, and bassoons. Trumpets and timpani were also used. The German poet and musician D. F. D. Schubert (1739–1791) recorded his impressions of the orchestra in his *Essay on Musical Esthetics:*

> No orchestra in the world ever equalled the Mannheimers' execution. Its forte
> is like thunder, its crescendo like a mighty waterfall, its diminuendo a gentle
> river dissappearing into the distance, its piano is a breath of spring. The wind
> instruments could not be used to better advantage; they lift and carry, they
> reinforce and give life to the storm for violins.

While the technical improvement of the instruments during the Baroque period contributed to the creation of a significant body of solo and chamber music, the development of this collective instrument, the orchestra, enabled the growth of a vast body of symphonic compositions. These compositions centered in the cities of Berlin, Mannheim, and Vienna. The Berlin or North German composers, of whom C. P. E. Bach, the son of J. S. Bach, was the leading figure, retained the more conservative three-movement structure and preserved elements of the contrapuntal style. The Mannheim group, under the leadership of Stamitz, employed the four-movement structure. The Viennese symphonists also favored the four-movement form. One of the greatest Viennese composers was Wolfgang Amadeus Mozart.

MOZART (1756–1791)

Born in Salzburg, Austria, Wolfgang Amadeus Mozart (fig. 9.3) began his musical career as one of the most celebrated child prodigies in eighteenth-century Europe. His father, Leopold, a highly respected composer and violinist, recognized his son's extraordinary talent and carefully supervised his musical education. Mozart began harpsichord lessons when he was four and wrote his first compositions when he was five. At the age of six, he and his older sister, Maria Anna ("Nannerl"), were taken by their father on a concert tour of Munich and Vienna.

From this first public performance until he was fifteen, Mozart was almost constantly on tour, playing prepared works and improvising. While the harpsichord and later the piano remained Mozart's principal instruments, he also mastered the violin and the organ. In addition to keyboard pieces, he wrote church works, symphonies, string quartets, and operas. In 1769, on a long trip to Italy, Mozart composed his first major opera, *Mitridate,* which was performed in Milan in 1770. His success in Italy, as triumphant as Handel's had been some sixty years earlier, brought him a number of commissions for operas.

His father, court composer and vice chapelmaster to the Archbishop of Salzburg, obtained a position for his son as concertmaster in the Archbishop's orchestra. But the new Archbishop of Salzburg, installed in 1772, failed to appreciate Mozart's genius. Relations between the haughty churchman and the high-spirited young composer steadily deteriorated until, in 1781, despite his father's objections, Mozart quit his position and settled in Vienna.

The first years in Vienna were fairly prosperous. Mozart was in great demand as a teacher; he gave numerous concerts, and his German **Singspiel**—a German comic opera with spoken dialogue, *Die Entführung aus dem Serail (The Abduction from the Harem,* 1782) — was a success. He married Constanze Weber, a woman he had met several years earlier on a concert tour, and looked forward to a happy family life. But Constanze was a careless housekeeper, and Mozart was a poor

Figure 9.3 This portrait of Mozart at the clavier shows the young prodigy in his early teens.

manager of finances. Intrigues at the Viennese court kept him from obtaining a permanent post. Public taste changed, and his teaching began to fall off. Except for occasional successes—his opera *Le Nozze di Figaro (The Marriage of Figaro,* 1786) and the Singspiel *Die Zauberflöte (The Magic Flute,* 1791)—the last ten years of his life were spent, for the most part, in poverty.

In 1788 Mozart gave up public performances, relying on a meager income from teaching and loans from various friends to sustain himself and his family. In spite of these troubles, he continued to compose, but his health began to decline. When he died in 1791 at the age of thirty-five, he was buried in an unmarked grave in a part of the cemetery reserved for the poor.

MOZART'S WORK

Unlike the meticulous Haydn, who kept a chronological list of all his compositions, Mozart never bothered to organize his musical papers in any consistent fashion. In the nineteenth century, Ludwig von Köchel compiled a roughly chronological listing of Mozart's music (numbering up to 626 pieces). This catalogue, along with substantial revisions and additions by later musicologists, remains in use today, the number of each work being preceded by "Koch" or the initial "K."

RELIGIOUS MUSIC

Mozart composed almost all of his church music at the beginning of his career, when he was working in Salzburg. Unfortunately, his two greatest choral works were left incomplete. The first of these was the gigantic *Mass in C Minor* (1782), intended as an offering of thanks for his marriage to Constanze Weber. The second is also his last work, the *Requiem in D Minor.* In 1791 Mozart accepted a commission to write this work on behalf of a nobleman who wished to remain anonymous. Mozart died before the work was finished. On his deathbed Mozart extracted a promise from his wife that Franz Süssmayr, his favorite pupil, would be selected to finish the piece. Süssmayr did so, making some additions of his own.

OPERA

Mozart's operas are the only eighteenth-century works in this genre that have remained consistently in the general repertory. For the most part, they fall into one of three categories: (1) Italian *opera seria,* based on serious plots, including *Mitridate* (1770), *Idomeneo* (1781), and *The Clemency of Titus* (1791); (2) comic Italian opera, including *The Marriage of Figaro* and *Cosi fan tutte* (1790); and (3) German *Singspiel,* including *The Abduction from the Harem.* Two of Mozart's most popular and significant operas resist such classification. *Don Giovanni* (1787), subtitled "humorous drama," vacillates between high comedy and genuine tragedy in following the career of the legendary Don Juan. *The Magic Flute,* though cast in the form of a *Singspiel* with intermittent spoken dialogue, might better be considered a morality play bound up in a fairy-tale setting. In many ways, *Don Giovanni* may be regarded as the greatest of the eighteenth-century Italian operas; *The Magic Flute* may be considered the first great German opera.

INSTRUMENTAL MUSIC

The amazing fluency with which Mozart composed his operas is also evident in his instrumental music. He was able to carry around finished compositions in his head, once remarking that "the committing to paper is done quickly enough. For everything is already finished, and it rarely differs on paper from what it was in my imagination." His instrumental music includes forty-one symphonies, twelve violin concertos, over twenty-five piano concertos, some fourteen concertos for other instruments, twenty-six string quartets, seventeen piano sonatas, over forty violin sonatas, and numerous other chamber music works.

Many of the piano concertos were composed for his own use in his public performances. These concertos demonstrated many of Mozart's most progressive ideas. His string quartets also reveal his mastery of musical forms.

His final three symphonies—nos. 39, 40, and 41 (the *Jupiter* Symphony)—were composed during the summer of 1788, three years before his death. They stand among Mozart's finest contributions to instrumental music.

SYMPHONY NO. 40 IN G MINOR

MOZART: Symphony no. 40 in G Minor, Movement I
Cassette 2/A, Track 3
CD 2, Track 3
See Listening Guide on pages 196–197.

Mozart's G Minor Symphony follows the four-movement plan outlined earlier: fast-slow-medium-fast. It is scored for an orchestra consisting of flute, two oboes, two clarinets, two bassoons, two horns, and strings.

First Movement (Allegro): Sonata-Allegro Form

Exposition
The opening theme centers on two phrases.

Example 9.1

They are the same *length;* they are identical in *rhythm;* but they differ in melodic shape. Melodically, the first phrase is static until the end when it leaps upward; the second is active until the end when it becomes static, repeating the same tone. These paired phrases and elements drawn from them—especially the rhythmic motive ♫ | ♩ —are crucial to the spirit and structure of the entire first movement.

The first theme begins with this pair of phrases played softly by the violins against an agitated background in the lower strings. The phrases are stated and repeated, and then interrupted by a new phrase that is stated and extended by the woodwinds with a crescendo to a half-cadence in the dominant key of D major.

Example 9.2

Chapter 9

There is an immediate return to the key of G minor and the paired phrases. Again they are stated and repeated, this time to be interrupted by a sudden forte and the beginning of the *bridge*, which modulates to the key of B♭ major:

Example 9.3

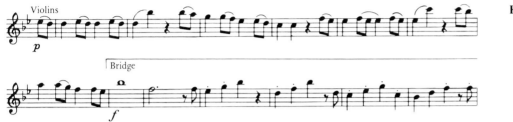

After an emphatic cadence and a pause, the second theme appears. The first part of the theme is a soft, lyrical, and expressive melody shared by the strings and woodwinds:

Example 9.4

The strings and winds exchange roles in a repetition of this melody, which is extended through a long crescendo leading to the second part of the second theme, in which the rhythmic motive from the first phrase is employed:

Example 9.5

Closing material brings the exposition to a definite ending, and the entire exposition is then repeated, followed by the development section.

Development

The development section can be thought of as a kind of drama during which the central character undergoes various changes. Through several stages of development, the two phrases from the first theme are manipulated and are eventually reduced to their smallest musical component— ♫ | ♩ .

In *stage one,* the phrases appear very much as they were at the beginning of the exposition. The subtle change is due to modulation.

Stage two comes as a complete surprise at an abrupt change in dynamics (from piano to forte), and the phrases are "tossed" back and forth between violins and cellos and basses—from high to low and back again in a contrapuntal texture:

Example 9.6

Almost unnoticed, the *third stage* of development takes place when the *active* melodic parts of both phrases are combined into one new phrase—a composite. The two phrases are reduced to one active phrase:

Example 9.7

This is immediately followed by another kind of reduction when the *static* parts of both phrases are combined in the fourth development stage to produce:

Example 9.8

The *melodic activity* of the composite phrase has been reduced to the most static form inherent in the two original phrases.

During the remaining development stages, the composite static phrase is gradually and systematically reduced in length to ♫ | ♩ .

To end the development, the flute and clarinets answer each other with the basic ♫ | ♩ in the process of smoothly and gently returning to the first theme and the beginning of the recapitulation. Thus, the "drama" of the development section ends.

Recapitulation

The recapitulation begins with a statement of the first theme as it was heard in the exposition. A bridge, similar to but longer than the bridge in the exposition, leads to the second theme, which remains in the tonic key of G minor.

Coda

A brief coda, also based on the first phrase of theme one, brings the movement to a close.

The organizational power and expressive possibilities inherent in the sonata-allegro form are beautifully illustrated in this movement.

Second Movement (Andante)

In accordance with the four-movement sonata plan (outlined in figure 9.2), the second movement contrasts with the first. It is slower in tempo (andante), different in meter (6/8), and in a contrasting key (E♭ major). Like the first movement, it is cast in sonata form, yet it differs strongly in content and mood.

The first theme begins with imitative entrances of a quiet, expressive melodic phrase beginning with violas, then second violins followed by first violins (see A in example 9.9). The next phase of the theme consists of short melodic fragments separated by rests (see B in example 9.9). As the theme continues, a small melodic figure appears (see C in example 9.9).

Example 9.9

This figure, almost unnoticeable when it first occurs, gradually assumes more and more importance as the exposition progresses. It becomes more noticeable as the first theme draws to a close; it permeates the bridge:

Example 9.10

It is integral to the tender second theme in B♭ major:

Example 9.11

And it is included in the codetta that brings the exposition to a close. In fact, this small chirplike motive is included in every part of the exposition—sometimes barely noticeable, sometimes dominating the melodic material—tying together the entire exposition and unifying the movement as a whole.

MOZART: Symphony no. 40 in G Minor, Movement III

Cassette 2/A, Track 3

CD 2, Track 4

See Listening Guide on page 197.

Third Movement: Menuetto (Allegretto)

The third movement returns to the original key of G minor and conforms to the general formal outline—minuet-trio-minuet—described earlier. It is unusual in its character and in the striking contrast between its two major sections.

The minuet is in G minor. Its loud dynamic level, constant use of the full orchestra, syncopated rhythms, and pronounced dissonances give it a driving and intense character that is unusual in this type of movement:

MENUETTO

Example 9.12

The trio provides a calming contrast. In addition to the change from G minor to G *major,* the trio is soft in dynamic level (piano) and has a graceful flowing mood that is enhanced by striking alternations between the strings and winds of the orchestra. The serenity of the trio makes even more pronounced the agitated character of the minuet when it returns to conclude the movement.

Fourth Movement (Allegro Assai)

The last movement of this symphony confirms the key of G minor, is fast in tempo, and is cast in sonata-allegro form.

Exposition

The first theme consists of two melodic ideas: the triad of G minor played in a rapidly rising "rocket" figure, which is played *piano,* and a contrasting figure, which is played *forte.*

Example 9.13

After the theme is repeated several times, a new element adds dynamic contrast, moving from loud to soft. A bridge leads to a cadence and pause, and the second theme begins, played by reduced orchestra, first only the strings and then only the woodwinds. A closing, based on the bridge material, leads to a repetition of the exposition.

Development and Recapitulation

The "rocket" motive of theme 1 and an extensive modulation are the basis of the short development section. Passed from one section of the orchestra to another, the motive is treated polyphonically with overlapping entrances. Gradually, it leads to a pronounced pause that separates the development from the recapitulation. Mozart intended that the entire development, recapitulation, and coda be repeated.

The G Minor Symphony not only provides a superb example of Mozart's craft, but also illustrates general characteristics of the classical style and the classical symphony:

1. The four-movement plan of the sonata (fast-slow-medium-fast) is followed, the first movement being cast in sonata-allegro form.

2. There is *no thematic relationship* among the movements; each movement is self-contained, and none of the materials of one movement appear in any other movement.

3. Structurally, the main unifying force is *key;* movements 1, 3, and 4 are in the common key of G minor, creating *tonal unity.*

4. Within individual movements, clarity and balance are probably the most pronounced stylistic features. Contrasting materials and sections are for the most part clearly and carefully set off from each other—often with the help of such musical devices as changes in dynamics, cadences, and pauses—without the blurring of relationships we will encounter in later periods of music.

HAYDN (1732–1809)

Franz Joseph Haydn (fig. 9.4) was born in Rohrau, a small Austrian village located near the Hungarian border southeast of Vienna. His parents, both of peasant stock, seem to have encouraged their son's musical ability and entrusted his earliest musical training to a relative, Johann Franck, a schoolteacher and choirmaster in the nearby town of Hainburg. At age six, Haydn was already singing in Franck's church choir and had begun playing the *clavier* (an early keyboard instrument) and violin.

In 1740, the composer and choirmaster at St. Stephen's Cathedral in Vienna stopped in Hainburg to recruit singers for his choir. Impressed with Haydn's voice, he arranged to take the young boy back with him to Vienna.

For the next nine years, Haydn immersed himself in the routine of a Catholic choirboy. He received a smattering of elementary education at St. Stephen's choir school and continued with violin and voice lessons, but his training in composition and theory was erratic and largely self-taught. In 1749, when his voice began to mature, Haydn was abruptly dismissed and turned out onto the street.

The following years were hard ones. At first Haydn made his living teaching clavier by day and playing in

Figure 9.4 Portrait of Haydn.

Mozart's symphony demonstrates the organizing power and wonderful flexibility of sonata-allegro form. Three of the work's four movements are organized by this formal procedure, all of them solid in design, yet completely different from each other in their expressive qualities.

CHAMBER MUSIC

Even after the orchestra had emerged, music for smaller ensembles continued to thrive as wealthy patrons commissioned works to be performed in their salons for private audiences.

The multimovement sonata structure that we encountered in the symphony was also used in chamber music for a wide variety of instrumental combinations. The string quartet, consisting of a first and second violin, a viola, and a cello, became in the Classical era the most important chamber music medium. Its popularity continued well into the twentieth century in the works of Bartók, Hindemith, and others.

Franz Joseph Haydn was the first great master of string quartet composition, which occupied him throughout most of his long and creative life.

street bands and serenading parties by night. His reputation as a teacher and vocal accompanist, however, gradually spread, and he started serious composition. In 1759, he was appointed *Kapellmeister* and chamber composer to a Bohemian nobleman, Count Morzin. He composed his first symphonies for the count's small orchestra.

In 1760, Haydn married Maria Anna Keller, but the marriage, which lasted forty years, was a tragic mistake. They were incompatible in temperament and finally separated.

The unhappy marriage was offset by his appointment in 1761 as assistant music director to Prince Paul Anton Esterhazy, head of one of the most powerful and wealthy Hungarian noble families. Haydn's contract stipulated that he was to compose whatever music was required of him (which would become the property of his patron), keep the musical instruments in good repair, train singers, and supervise the conduct of all of the musicians.

Despite the rigid and burdensome requirements of his contract, Haydn enjoyed his work and was to say later, "My prince was pleased with all my work, I was commended, and as conductor of an orchestra I could make experiments, observe what strengthened and what

weakened an effect and thereupon improve, substitute, omit, and try new things; I was cut off from the world, there was no one around to mislead and harass me, and so I was forced to become original."

Haydn remained in the employ of the Esterhazy family for almost thirty years, serving first Prince Paul Anton and then his brother, Prince Nikolaus. Despite his isolation at their country estate, his fame gradually spread throughout Europe. He was able to fulfill commissions from other individuals and from publishers all over the continent. When Prince Nikolaus died in 1790, Haydn was retained as nominal *Kapellmeister* for the Esterhazy family, but he was now independent. Moving to Vienna, he resumed his friendship with Mozart, whose talent he had admired since their first meeting in 1781. Haydn also gave lessons to a young, rising composer named Ludwig van Beethoven. He made two successful trips to London (1791–1792, 1794–1795), where he conducted a number of his own symphonies, written on commission for the well-known impresario Johann Salomon. After his second London visit, he ceased writing symphonies, turning instead to the composition of Masses and oratorios. After 1800, his health began to fail, and he lived in secluded retirement. He died in 1809 at the age of seventy-seven.

HAYDN'S WORK

The great majority of Haydn's work was composed during his service to the Esterhazy princes. The biweekly concerts and opera performances at Esterhaz, Prince Nikolaus's country estate, engendered a prodigious flow of instrumental and vocal music. Most of Haydn's 104 symphonies were written for the small but excellent Esterhazy orchestra.

SYMPHONIES

The symphonies form a remarkably complete record of Haydn's development as a composer, ranging in unbroken continuity from his earliest, somewhat crude efforts to the rich and masterful works of the 1780s and 1790s. Many of the more popular symphonies bear identifying nicknames; the *Horn Signal* (no. 31, 1765), the *Farewell* (no. 45, 1772), the *Surprise* (no. 94, 1791), and the *Drumroll* (no. 103, 1795) are but a few. His greatest works in this genre are the last twelve symphonies, called the *London* Symphonies, which were written for his two London visits.

CHAMBER MUSIC

While many of Haydn's experiments with musical form were carried out in the symphonies, his chamber music, particularly the string quartets, was equally significant in his development as a composer. In his eighty-three quartets, Haydn laid down many of the fundamental principles that were taken up by younger composers such as Mozart and Beethoven. The six works making up opus 20[1] (the *Sun* Quartets, 1772) are among his masterworks in this genre. The later sets of opus 33 (the *Scherzo* or *Russian* Quartets, 1781) and opus 50 (1787) represent still further advances in Haydn's musical development.

Among Haydn's other chamber works are more than twenty *divertimenti*. As their title suggests, these were light "diversionary" pieces written in a simple, popular style. Other chamber music included a multitude of trios and sonatas for various instruments. Of some sixty sonatas written for piano, fifty-two survive.

Though he was a good string player, Haydn did not consider himself a virtuoso performer. Consequently, his solo concertos are few. A good many concertos have been lost, and still others attributed to Haydn have not yet been authenticated as coming from his hand.

---

1. The term *opus* refers to a musical composition numbered to show its place in the composer's published work.

Haydn, shown here directing the rehearsal of a string quartet, spent many of his most productive years composing for and conducting the orchestra of the Esterhazy princes.

OPERAS

Opera was a highly important part of musical activity at the Esterhazy palace, and Haydn was for a long time quite proud of his more than twenty stage works. Austrian Empress Maria Theresa reputedly said, "If I want to hear a good opera, I go to Esterhaz." However, when Haydn became familiar with Mozart's incomparable genius for opera composing, he realized that his own works were of lesser quality. Today they are all but forgotten.

MASSES AND ORATORIOS

Haydn's Masses and oratorios present a different story. The last six of his twelve Masses, composed between 1796 and 1802, are his crowning achievement as a church composer—works of old age, demonstrating a mastery of form and technique accumulated over more than fifty years of composing. Several of them—*Missa in tempore belli* (*Mass in Time of War,* 1796), the *Missa in Augustiis* (*Nelson Mass,* 1798), and the *Harmoniemesse* ("Wind-Band" Mass, 1802)—rank among Haydn's masterworks. Stimulated by Handel's oratorios, some of which he had heard during his London visits, Haydn produced two of his own.

Titled *The Creation* (1796–1798) and *The Seasons* (1798–1801), they have remained in concert repertoire to this day. Contemporary with these major vocal works was Haydn's gift to the Austrian people, the national anthem *Gott erhalte Franze den Kaiser* (*God Save the Emperor Franz,* better known as the *Austrian Hymn*). He wrote it on his own initiative as a patriotic gesture when Napoleon's armies invaded Austrian territory in 1796. During the French bombardment of Vienna in 1809, he played it to comfort himself. It was the last music he heard before he died.

STRING QUARTET OP. 33

Haydn developed the string quartet from the eighteenth-century *divertimento,* giving more substance to the light, popular form and scoring it for two violins, a viola, and a cello. His eighty-three quartets, written over the course of his creative lifetime, evolved slowly into a sophisticated form. Together they constitute one of the most important bodies of chamber music literature.

The quartets of Haydn's opus 33 are collectively known as *Gli Scherzi* (*The Scherzos*) because Haydn uses the more rapid scherzo rather than the minuet-and-trio. Number 3 of this set became known as "The Bird," owing to the birdlike trills and ornaments in the first, second, and fourth movements:

Example 9.14

First Movement

Exposition

The clarity and balance that we encountered in the music of Mozart are again evident here in the clearly separated, repeated phrases, the sudden contrast and extension of one phrase, and the use of dynamics to reinforce structure.

The "bird" ornaments heard in the first theme provide a unifying element among the contrasting sections of the movement.

The first theme begins with soft, short, repeated notes in the second violin and viola. Against this background, the first violin enters with the main melodic material. Characteristically, the bridge between themes 1 and 2 uses elements from theme 1. The second theme makes abundant use of the ornamental ("bird") element of the first theme. The exposition closes with material derived from the very end of the bridge. The entire exposition is then repeated.

Development

Although relatively short, the development section draws from all three stages of the exposition. It begins with a statement of the A phrase of theme 1. Then elements of theme 2 and the bridge are combined, after which theme 2 is stated first in the high strings, then in the low strings. Elements from theme 1 and the closing material are briefly combined and lead into successive statements of the ornamental notes at rising pitch levels. The rising feeling is helped along by a crescendo leading to two long chords that create a sense of suspense. The suspense is quieted by an apparent return to theme 1, but the return turns out to be false. Instead, the passage leads to a development of the bridge, which then leads to genuine recapitulation.

Recapitulation

The recapitulation is rather standard except that the second part of theme 1 is omitted. After the entire development and recapitulation are repeated, there is a coda consisting of (1) an exploitation of the "bird" ornament, (2) a fragment of the closing material, (3) a crescendo and cadence, and (4) a complete statement of the A phrase of theme 1. The movement ends in the original key of C major.

Second Movement

The six quartets of opus 33 depart from sonata structure in two respects. First, the minuet-and-trio movement is replaced by the scherzo and trio. Second, the positions of the second and third movements are reversed: The scherzo and trio is second, and the slow, lyrical movement is third.

This scherzo movement is a wonderful example of Haydn's ability to use instrumental range, color, articulation and musical texture, dynamics, and form for expressive purposes. The movement has a three-part scherzo-trio-scherzo structure (example 9.15), with the sections set off from each other by obvious cadences and pauses. The contrast between them is marked. The scherzo employs all four instruments in a low register and homophonic texture. It is dark, smooth, sustained, and thick. The trio is reduced to two violins playing in the higher part of their ranges, within a polyphonic texture using staccato articulation. It is light, bright, thin, and brittle, employing ornamental trills reminiscent of the first movement.

Example 9.15

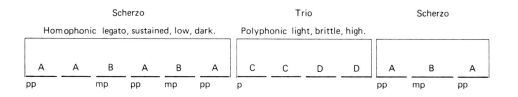

Third Movement

The slow third movement is a theme and variations. The first violin, which spins out the long theme, is clearly prominent. The theme is lyrical, almost aria-like in its melodic arches and contours. In the two variations the shape of the melody is altered. Those sections that are preserved are extensively varied, mostly through the addition of decorative notes, creating a much more florid melodic line. Throughout the entire movement, the first violin is a solo instrument and the other three strings provide accompaniment.

Fourth Movement

HAYDN: String Quartet op. 33, no. 3 in C Major ("The Bird"), Fourth Movement
Cassette 2/B, Track 2
CD 2, Track 9
See Listening Guide on page 198.

The last movement of the quartet is an intriguing example of Haydn's sense of humor in music. The melodies are jocular, the tempo very fast, and the texture light. A series of tricks and surprises fascinate the listener up to the concluding measures.

Technically, the movement combines the rondo principle of alternating themes with the development and recapitulation of sonata-allegro procedures. It starts with a gay, bouncy two-part theme in C major; the second part combines materials of the first part with the "bird" figure of the first movement. After both parts are repeated, theme A ends with a pause. Theme B begins without a bridge passage. This theme, also in two parts, is in A minor. The first part is repeated, and the second part develops material from the first part. Toward the end of the section, the rhythmic material that began theme A is passed back and forth among the instruments. The intent of this is to suggest the return of theme A, but the listener is kept in suspense as to *when* it will return. The suspense increases when the rhythmic figure is shortened to a two-note version, the dynamic level changes suddenly from forte to piano, and a dominant chord is outlined that cries for resolution to the tonic. At this point, when it appears that the music will plunge into the A theme, there is instead a sudden, unexpected pause, after which the A theme enters at last.

Example 9.16

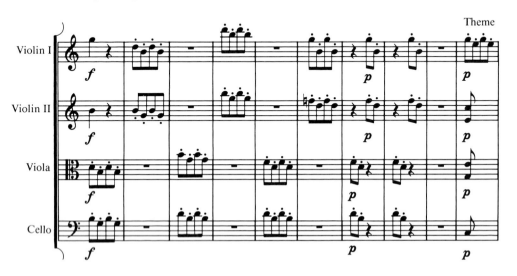

This "trickery," involving the reappearance of theme A, is again evident later in the movement. After the restatement of themes A and B, another developmental section occurs that leads back to A. This presentation of the theme ends in a cadence and a pause. But after this convincing ending, Haydn launches into a coda beginning with the two-note "bird" motive and moving to the more active rhythmic material from theme A. A feeling of conclusion is created by the increase of activity as all four instruments play the rhythmic material. The crescendo pushes forward, but instead of ending, Haydn stops not on the expected C major chord but on a chord in a different key. The chord is full of suspense and implies anything but a conclusion. After a pause, which intensifies the suspense, there is a drive to a forceful cadence in the tonic C major, and apparently, the long-delayed ending. But this is followed by yet another section, played very softly, to give an extra unexpected ending, a kind of final chuckle from the composer.

THE CLASSICAL CONCERTO

During the Baroque era, the term *concerto* referred to both the concerto grosso and the concerto for solo instrument. Bach's Brandenburg Concerto no. 5 and Vivaldi's *The Four Seasons* are examples of the two types.

In the Classical era, composers continued to develop the solo concerto while the concerto grosso fell into virtual disuse. The violin and piano were the favored solo instruments, but concertos were also written for other instruments such as the cello, trumpet, bassoon, horn, and clarinet.

Typically, the classical concerto follows the three-movement sonata plan outlined on page 172, and consisted of a fast-slow-fast movement sequence *without* minuet-and-trio.

The contrast between the solo instrument and the orchestra was an essential element in the concerto, and the formal structure of each movement was contrived to exploit this feature. First movements combined elements of the baroque ritornello principle with sonata-allegro characteristics often involving two expositions. In the first exposition, the thematic material is set forth by the orchestra alone in one key. In the second exposition, the themes are stated by both the solo instrument and the orchestra. The *solo* exposition includes a modulating bridge leading to the second theme in a new key. Thus, the exposition takes the following form:

I	II
A bridge B	A bridge (modulation) B (new key)
Orchestra	Solo instrument and orchestra

The double exposition is *not* repeated.

In addition to the manipulation of the thematic materials, the development section exploits the opposition between the orchestra and solo instrument. The first movement ends with a recapitulation usually based upon features of both expositions but always involving the solo instrument.

The first and last movements of the classical concerto (and occasionally the middle movement) include an additional section called the **cadenza.** Played by the solo instrument, without accompaniment, the cadenza offers the perfect vehicle for the virtuoso soloist. It has the quality of an improvised performance; even if written out or at least well planned in advance, it is supposed to sound as if it were being made up by the performer on the spot. The exact placement of the cadenza in the sonata-allegro movement varies, but it always occurs toward the end of the movement, usually after the recapitulation, and is followed by closing material:

Recapitulation

A   bridge   B   cadenza   closing material

The cadenza is "set up" by a sustained chord in the orchestra, followed by a pause. The main musical ingredients of the cadenza are fragments of the thematic material from the movement proper combined with the free use of the instrument in executing rapid scale passages, arpeggios, trills, and other technical feats. The tempo is erratic, the beat is often obscured, and modulation occurs. Typically, the cadenza increases in intensity, ending on a trill that leads to the return of the orchestra for the concluding portion of the movement.

It was Mozart who, in his more than forty concertos, established the general form and style of the classical concerto. His concertos for piano are among the most enduring works of the Classical era.

CONCERTO IN B-FLAT MAJOR

Mozart's piano concertos span virtually his whole productive life. The Concerto in B-flat Major, written in his last year, is his final contribution to the form.

The piece is in three movements and is scored for flute, oboes, bassoons, French horns, strings, and solo piano.

First Movement

The first movement is in sonata-allegro form with a double exposition. Its tempo is fast (allegro), and it is set in the tonic key of B-flat major. The first theme is stated by the violins and answered by the winds. When the solo piano enters, beginning the second exposition, it plays a slightly decorated version of the first theme.

Example 9.17

With the entrance of the piano, the orchestra drops out altogether until the strings take over the answering function first performed by the winds.

The alternation between piano and orchestra, in which one is silent while the other is active, is a device favored by Mozart and typifies this particular movement. In the previous example, we saw how the orchestra and piano alternate in rather large blocks of music; in other parts of the movement, they often "share" a phrase. In example 9.18, the piano begins a phrase that is completed by the flute; in example 9.19, the reverse is true: The orchestra initiates the phrase, which is finished by the solo piano.

Example 9.18

Example 9.19

In this movement, the solo instrument and the orchestra rarely work together for any appreciable length of time. When they do, the solo instrument is almost always dominant. The most obvious place where the solo piano "shines" is the cadenza, which occurs after the recapitulation and leads into the closing material. The cadenza that is usually played is one written by Mozart himself. It exhibits all the qualities outlined earlier and provides a convincing and exciting conclusion to the first movement.

Second Movement

The second movement is a glorious example of Mozart's lyrical use of the piano as a "singing" instrument. The movement is slow in tempo (larghetto) and in the contrasting key of E-flat major. Its structure is a large ABA form, with each section containing a rich variety of melodic materials.

The B section features the solo instrument, supported throughout by unobtrusive orchestral accompaniment. The A section that frames the movement is more elaborate, both in the variety of its materials and in the relationship between the orchestra and the piano. As in the first movement, the solo instrument and orchestra tend to alternate rather than work together.

MOZART: Piano
Concerto no. 27 in
B-flat Major (K. 595),
Second Movement
Cassette 2/A, Track 4
CD 2, Track 5
*See Listening Guide on
page 199.*

The most important thematic material is the simple melody played by the solo piano at the beginning of the movement (example 9.20). The flowing beauty of this short melody sets the mood for the entire movement.

Example 9.20

Third Movement

The third movement returns to the key of B-flat major and is fast (allegro), conforming to the three-movement plan of the classical concerto. Its brisk tempo is intensified by a jocular, dancelike rhythm, giving the piece a lively quality:

Example 9.21

The movement, which begins with solo piano, is essentially a rondo, but includes developmental sections that impart a flavor of sonata-allegro form. Of particular interest is the fact that the movement includes *two* cadenzas, both of which reintroduce the principal theme.

Mozart's last piano concerto is one of his most serene and sublime works, well deserving of its honored place in the repertoire.

Characteristics of Classical Music

Texture	Largely homophonic, but flexible, with shifts to polyphony
Tonality	Major-minor system with frequent modulations to related keys; heavy dependence on tonic-dominant relationship
Rhythm	Variety of rhythmic patterns within a work
Melody	Composed of short, balanced phrases; melodic phrases often contrasted with each other Melodies often lyrical and expressive; less ornamentation of notes
Mood	Expression of variety of moods within a work and sudden changes of mood
Dynamics	Gradual dynamic changes
Large Works	Sonata, symphony, concerto, string quartet, Mass, oratorio, opera
Instruments	Piano and violin favored for solo concerto; makeup of orchestra becomes standardized; development of orchestra favors growth of symphonic works
Formal Structures	Sonata principle (multimovement structure for long pieces); sonata-allegro form (first movement form); rondo; minuet-and-trio; scherzo and trio; theme and variations; cadenza and double exposition used in concertos
Symphonic Style	Follows four-movement plan, with first movement in sonata-allegro form Each movement self-contained Key is main unifying device Clarity and balance are major stylistic features

Listening Guide

MOZART: Symphony no. 40 in G Minor

First Movement: Allegro (fast)
                 Duple meter
                 Sonata form

Classical Orchestra

Review: Example 9.1 (theme 1, two phrases)
         Example 9.2 (half-cadence, middle of theme 1)
         Example 9.3 (theme 1 interrupted by bridge)
         Example 9.4 (theme 2)
         Example 9.5 (second part of theme 2)
         Example 9.6 (contrapuntal passage from development)
         Example 9.7 (composite of two previously separate phrases)
         Example 9.8 (static reduction of Example 9.7)

CD 2 (Cassette 2/A, Track 3)

				Exposition		
3	1,4	0:00	2:09	*Theme 1*	1a	Agitated accompaniment; violins state symmetrical melody, phrase leaping upward and phrase moving downward; similar phrases answer with extension; woodwinds answer, loud chords
	2	0:34	2:44	*Bridge*	b	Violins begin symmetrical melody
		0:24	2:35		2	Forte, upward-leaping motive in violins; rushing string scales, emphatic close
	3	0:54	3:05	*Theme 2*	3a	Flowing melody mostly in violins; woodwind answer begins, moves in new direction
		1:18	3:30		b	Strings take over, crescendo, build twice to high point; soft descending scale
		1:32	3:44		c	Rhythmic motive from symmetrical melody traded among woodwind instruments and strings, alternating soft and loud
		1:52	4:04	*Closing*	4	Rushing downward string scales, emphatic closing chords

(*Exposition is repeated*)

			Development		
	5	4:23		1	Piano, symmetrical melody in violins, new harmonies
		4:39		2	Sudden forte, symmetrical melody traded between low strings, violins, low strings; violins extend with composite of two phrases into one
		5:10		3a	Soft, static version of phrase traded between violins and woodwinds
		5:22		b	Woodwind answer reduced to three-note motive
		5:28		c	Sudden forte, three-note motive traded between violins and low strings
		5:38		4	No strings, flute and clarinets trade three-note motive descending into:

Continued on next page

⑥	5:45	*Theme 1*	1a	Violins state symmetrical melody piano, second phrase extended; woodwinds answer, loud chords
	6:09		b	Violins begin symmetrical melody, move in new harmonic direction
	6:18	*Bridge*	2a	Forte, upward-leaping motive in violins; upward-leaping motive in low strings; motive tossed between low strings and violins; violins take over
	6:28		b	Rushing string scales, emphatic close
⑦	7:04	*Theme 2*	3a	Flowing melody mostly in violins; woodwind answer begins, moves in new direction
	7:28		b	Strings take over, crescendo, build twice to high point; soft descending scale
	7:48		c	Rhythmic motive from symmetrical melody traded among woodwind instruments and strings, alternating soft and loud
⑧	8:08	*Coda*	4a	Rushing string scales, build to woodwind chord
	8:21		b	Violins begin symmetrical melody, answered by violins, violas, woodwinds; sudden forte, emphatic closing chords

Third Movement: Menuetto (allegretto) (minuet, moderately fast and light)
Triple meter
Ternary form (minuet and trio)

Review: Example 9.12 (first theme of minuet)

4	①	0:00	**Minuet (A)**	a	Intense phrase, minor key, orchestra, forte
				a	Intense phrase repeated
		0:40		b a′	Second phrase, more dissonant; moves directly to return of first phrase, varied with added dissonances; soft ending in woodwinds
		1:21		b a′	Second phrase and varied first phrase repeated
	②	2:01	**Trio (B)**	c	Relaxed, lyrical phrase, major key, strings, continued by woodwinds, then strings
				c	Lyrical phrase repeated
		2:55		d c′	Lower strings begin, answered by woodwinds; woodwinds complete the phrase; horns join strings in varied return of lyrical phrase; phrase completed by horns with woodwinds, then strings
		3:31		d c′	Strings and woodwinds repeat second phrase; horns with strings, then woodwinds, repeat varied return of first phrase
	③	4:08	**Minuet (A)**	a	Intense phrase, minor key, forte
		4:28		b a′	Second phrase; moves directly to return of first phrase, forte, with added dissonances; soft ending in woodwinds

Listening Guide

HAYDN: String Quartet op. 33, no. 3 ("The Bird")

Fourth Movement: Presto (very fast)
                          Duple meter
                          Sonata-rondo form (A-B-Development-A)

String Quartet

Review: Example 9.18 (return of A
              theme after unexpected pause)

CD 2 (Cassette 2/B Track 2)

9	①	0:00	**A**	a a	Bouncy theme, staccato, repeated
		0:13		b b	Repeated-note bird calls, motive from bouncy theme accompanies; repeated, clear stop at end
		0:35	**B**	c c	Minor theme, more flowing, repeated; goes directly into:
	②	0:57	**Development**		Opening motive of bouncy theme and repeated-note fragment developed in rapid-fire polyphony; four-note motive tossed back and forth, reduced to two-note motive; sudden pause
		1:24	**A**	a	Bouncy theme
		1:30		b	Repeated-note theme, goes directly into:
		1:41	**B**	c	Flowing minor theme, goes directly into:
	③	1:52	**Development**		Long notes in first violin, bouncy-theme motive accompaniment; minor-theme motive repeated, reduced to repeated monophonic note, transition back to:
		2:06	**A**	a	Bouncy theme
		2:12		b	Repeated-note theme, clear stop at end
		2:23	**Coda**		Two-note motive and bouncy motive tossed back and forth, move quickly to pause; moves further to apparent emphatic closing; piano, bouncy motive and repeated-note motive to actual quiet close

Listening Guide

MOZART: Piano Concerto in B-flat Major (K. 595)

Second Movement: Larghetto (slow)
Quadruple meter
Ternary form

Solo Piano; Classical Orchestra

Review: Example 9.20 (opening theme)

CD 2 (Cassette 2/A, Track 4)

5	①	0:00	**A**	aa	Simple, quiet theme stated by solo piano, then by orchestra
		1:00		b	Second part of melody by solo piano
		1:29		a	First half returns, solo piano
	②	1:55	**Transition**		Repeated-note figure begins orchestral transition; continues based on 3-note fragment:

Moving to clear pause

	③	2:59	**B**	c c	Piano sings melody accompanied by orchestra; repeated
		3:35		d	Second part of melody begins with repeated note, also by piano with orchestra
		4:04		e	Piano melody moves gently up and down with long notes by instruments; piano trills prepare for:
	④	5:02	**A**	a	Simple melody by piano solo; short orchestral transition
		5:33		b	Second half by piano with orchestra; piano and orchestra echo each other; orchestral chord then piano transition
		6:19		a	Simple melody in flute, violin, and piano
	⑤	6:46	**Coda**		Repeated-note figure begins coda; material based on three-note transition fragment as piano and orchestra together move gradually toward gentle, unadorned close

SUMMARY

Instrumental music arrived at a new level of maturity during the Classical period. The ranges and technical capabilities of many instruments were improved greatly, and composers began to score their works for standard groupings. The makeup of the orchestra became standardized and included an increased number and variety of instruments. Because of the social customs of the day, chamber music also flourished and encouraged sophisticated compositions in which each player performed an individual part.

Sonata-allegro form and the multimovement structure became the main basis for music composed in the early Classical period. The two great masters of the Classical era—Haydn and Mozart—developed and refined sonata-allegro form in their symphonies, string quartets, and concertos.

NEW TERMS

sonata
sonata-allegro form (sonata form)
    exposition
    development
    recapitulation
    bridge
    codetta
    coda
minuet-and-trio

scherzo
rondo
symphony
string quartet
concerto
pianoforte (piano)
Singspiel
cadenza

SUGGESTED LISTENING

Haydn, Franz Joseph

Symphony no. 45 in F-sharp Minor (*Farewell*). One of Haydn's most dramatic and unorthodox symphonies. The opening movement introduces an extended new theme in place of the usual development section; and in the final movement, the tempo suddenly changes from presto to adagio, and the instruments drop out (say farewell) one by one, leaving only two violins to conclude the work.

Mozart, Wolfgang Amadeus

Symphony no. 41, K.551. The *Jupiter* was the last of Mozart's symphonies and is often grouped with symphonies no. 39 and 40 as the finest examples of Mozart's symphonic compositions.

Eine Kleine Nachtmusik (*A Little Night Music*). This string serenade was written as outdoor entertainment. Its character is light.

CLASSICAL VOCAL MUSIC

T he Classical era was predominantly a period of instrumental music. The new instrumental style and forms became the area of greatest concentration for the major composers of the time. Vocal music occupied a position of lesser importance. The Lieder (songs) written by Haydn, Mozart, and Beethoven are considered a relatively secondary part of their compositional efforts. The operas composed by Haydn to entertain the guests at Esterhazy have vanished into history, and Beethoven wrote only one opera, *Fidelio.* However, the age was not without significant and lasting achievements in the area of vocal music. Specifically, some of the large choral works of Mozart, Haydn, and Beethoven and many of Mozart's operas made lasting contributions to the body of vocal literature.

CHORAL MUSIC OF HAYDN

Of the three giants of the Classical era, Haydn contributed the largest number of compositions to the choral music repertoire. Two of his oratorios, the *Creation* and the *Seasons,* are still widely performed; together with his Masses, they constitute his most important contribution to vocal music.

MISSA IN ANGUSTIIS (NELSON MASS)

Haydn's *Missa in Angustiis* (*Mass in Time of Peril*) is one of the choral masterpieces of the Classical period. Better known as the *Nelson Mass,* it was written in 1789 during the naval Battle of the Nile. When Lord Nelson visited Eisenstadt Castle in 1800, this Mass was among the works performed in his honor.

The orchestration of Haydn's Masses varied from work to work according to the instruments and players available to him at the time. The *Nelson Mass* is scored for a comparatively small orchestra consisting of three trumpets, timpani, organ, and strings, together with four solo voices (SATB) and four-part chorus (SATB). The organ is used alternately as a continuo instrument, filling in chords—a carryover from baroque practice—and as an ensemble or solo instrument.

The text is divided into six main sections and five subdivisions, constituting eleven movements in all:

Kyrie	Credo	Benedictus
Gloria	Et incarnatus	Agnus Dei
Qui tollis	Et resurrexit	Dona nobis
Quoniam tu solus	Sanctus	

Kyrie

The prevalence of sonata-allegro procedure in instrumental music was well established in the previous chapter, but its organizing force was by no means confined to instrumental music. The first movement of the *Nelson Mass* is an example of how the sonata-allegro principle was applied to vocal composition.

The first theme, in D minor, is characterized by short, emphatic pronouncements by the chorus on the text "*Kyrie eleison*" ("Lord have mercy"). The trumpets and timpani sound a prominent figure (♩♫ ♫♫ | ♩), which alternates with sharp chords in the strings. The organ, meanwhile, plays sustained chords. The second theme is dominated by the soprano solo voice, singing elaborate virtuoso passages, quite instrumental in character:

Example 10.1

Allegro Moderato
Soprano solo

Chri - ste e - lei - son, e - lei - son

The light texture, the *piano* dynamic level, the key change (to the relative F major), and the concentration on the solo voice are in marked contrast to the driving force of the first theme:

Ky - ri - e e - lei - son

The prominent elements of the development are sung by the chorus. The solo part from the second theme is now played by the violins. Imitative entrances in the chorus lead to a climax where all four parts come together. The drive that results from these insistent overlapping entrances of the voices is enhanced by constant modulation.

The key returns to D minor for the recapitulation. Here the second theme resembles the original theme in texture, dynamics, and the relationship of the solo soprano voice to the orchestra, but new melodic material is involved.

The coda ends with the entire orchestra hammering out the rhythmic figure ♩♫ ♫♫ | on which the movement began in the orchestral introduction.

HAYDN: *Missa in Angustiis (Nelson Mass)*
Cassette 2/B, Track 1
CD 2, Tracks 6–8

Gloria, Qui Tollis, and Quoniam Tu Solus

Although the second, third, and fourth movements each appear to be self-contained, they are actually parts of one three-movement complex.

202

The driving tension and restlessness that characterized the *Kyrie* are immediately dispelled at the striking beginning of the Gloria. The important thematic material of the A section, on the text "*Gloria in excelsis Deo*" ("Glory to God in the highest"), is introduced in dialogue fashion between the soprano soloist and the chorus.

Example 10.2

The dynamic level drops to *piano* for the contrasting B section, "*et in terra pax hominibus*" ("and on earth peace to men"). The emphasis is on the solo tenor and bass parts, whose imitative entrances grow into a moving, expressive duet.

The chorus enters in octaves in the C section, loudly proclaiming in short, clipped statements "*laudamus te*" ("we praise Thee") and "*adoramus te*" ("we adore Thee"), and the section builds to an ending on an extended setting of "*glorificamus te*" ("we glorify Thee").

A kind of development begins with successive statements of the A melody, utilizing new words and modulating into different keys. It opens with the solo alto, who is answered by the soprano, and then, more fully, by the chorus. After expanded statements of B by the solo voices, the chorus brings the movement to a rather abrupt close, without the expected return of the A theme.

The slow, quiet *Qui tollis* movement is, structurally, a straightforward example of alternating themes. The solo bass has the dominant part, often paired with the first violins. Frequently the bass voice and first violins answer each other back and forth. The organ is used as a solo instrument in conjunction with the choral entrances, and while the choral entrances are expressive in themselves, they also constitute a considerable surprise element in the movement. It is impossible to anticipate either when they will occur or whether they will occur softly in unison or loudly in full harmony on statements of "*miserere nobis*" ("have mercy on us") and "*deprecationem nostram*" ("our prayer").

The *Qui tollis* has no real conclusion, but ends instead on a chord of suspense, the dominant. Its resolution comes at the opening of the *Quoniam tu solus* movement, which, in addition, returns to the melody from the *Gloria*. Thus, the lack of conclusion in the preceding movement, coupled with the reappearance of the original theme of the *Gloria,* acts as a powerful unifying element in the three-movement complex.

Example 10.3

After the solo and choral statements of the A theme, a quiet transition section on the words "*cum sancto spiritu*" ("with the holy spirit") leads to a long, vigorous fugue. The coda, which uses material from the *Gloria* movement, creates further unity and builds to one of Haydn's brilliant and exhilarating endings on ♩ ♩ ♪ ♩ ♩ .
A - men A - men

Credo

The *Credo* is divided into three parts, which constitute the fifth, sixth, and seventh movements. The fifth movement, which begins with *Credo in unum Deum* ("I believe in one God"), is a two-part canon. The sopranos and tenors sing the first part against the altos and basses on the second. The tempo is fast, and there is a driving rhythm throughout, with much activity in the orchestra.

In contrast to the fifth movement, the sixth, *Et incarnatus* ("and was incarnate"), is slow and quiet. An atmosphere of lyricism and melodic grace pervades. The first theme is stated in turn by the orchestra, the solo soprano, and the chorus. A concluding coda adds weight to the movement's mood.

The seventh movement, *Et resurrexit tertia die* ("and on the third day He arose"), bursts forth *forte,* in a fast tempo, and with great musical activity to convey the atmosphere of triumph and resurrection. This movement is particularly interesting for the abundance of technical devices employed to organize it: Imitative entrances are used to build momentum; homophonic texture and choral declamation set off the meaning of the text; and striking differences in dynamics and pitch contrast the *vivos* ("living") with the *mortuos* ("dead"). The movement ends with a brilliant "Amen."

Sanctus and Benedictus

The eighth and ninth movements consist of five subsections:

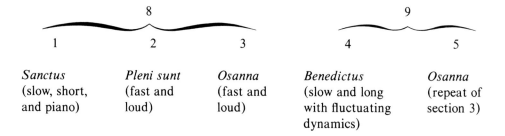

1	2	3	4	5
Sanctus (slow, short, and piano)	*Pleni sunt* (fast and loud)	*Osanna* (fast and loud)	*Benedictus* (slow and long with fluctuating dynamics)	*Osanna* (repeat of section 3)

The *Sanctus* is a slow introductory section. The *Pleni sunt* is an allegro choral section with an active orchestral background. This section merges without a break into the *Osanna.*

The *Benedictus,* which follows, is very much like the sonata-allegro movement of a concerto. It consists of a double exposition (the first in the orchestra, the second in the solo soprano and chorus), a short development section, a genuine recapitulation, and a dramatic coda. The *Benedictus* stops on a dominant chord, followed by a pause. The resulting suspense is dispelled when the *Osanna* returns, bringing the entire complex to a stirring ending.

Agnus Dei and Dona Nobis

The quietest section of the entire Mass, the *Agnus Dei,* is the only movement that does not include the chorus, trumpets, or timpani. Adagio in tempo and lyrical in expression, it is the perfect foil for the loud and buoyant finale.

The *Dona nobis* is a fast, loud, choral fugue set against intense orchestral activity. The imitative entrances of the soprano, alto, tenor, and bass are followed by a jocular, homophonic section in the chorus, while the violins play a kind of chirp in the background. This lightheartedness turns into gaiety near the end, when there is a sudden and unexpected halt, followed by a pause, then a resumption of the very quiet statements of "*Dona nobis pacem*" ("grant us Thy peace") by the chorus, with interjections of the chirping figure by violins:

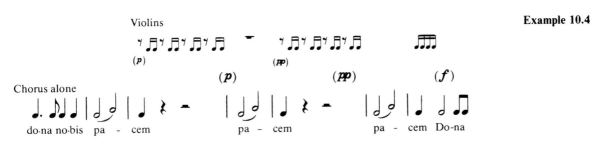

Example 10.4

Finally, there is an energetic push to a brilliant ending.

OPERA

The greatest composer of opera in the Classical era was Wolfgang Amadeus Mozart who, with his finest works, took each type of operatic form to its epitome:

Opera seria (serious opera)
   Idomeneo, 1781
Opera buffa (Italian comic opera)
   Le Nozze di Figaro (The Marriage of Figaro), 1786
   Don Giovanni, 1787
   Così fan tutte (Thus do they all), 1790
Singspiel (German opera)
   Die Entführung aus dem Serail (The Abduction from the Harem), 1782
   Die Zauberflöte (The Magic Flute), 1791

THE MARRIAGE OF FIGARO

The opera *Le Nozze di Figaro* is based upon a French play by Beaumarchais, translated into Italian and cast in the form of an opera libretto by Lorenzo da Ponte, a popular librettist at the time. The plot is typically intricate and amusing, including a pair of lovers, intrigues between servants and masters, a case of discovered identity, and a few unlikely coincidences.

The Characters

    The Count Almaviva, *a Spanish nobleman (*baritone*)*
    The Countess Almaviva, *his wife (*soprano*)*
    Susanna, *the Countess's maid (*soprano*), promised in marriage to*
    Figaro, *the Count's servant (*bass*)*
    Cherubino, *the Count's page (*soprano*)*
    Marcellina, *housekeeper (*soprano*)*
    Bartolo, *a Doctor from Seville (*bass*)*
    Basilio, *a music teacher (*tenor*)*
    Don Curzio, *a lawyer (*tenor*)*
    Barbarina, *a daughter of Antonio (*soprano*)*
    Antonio, *the Count's gardener and Susanna's uncle (*bass*)*
    Chorus of country people and peasants

The Plot

The opera is set in Count Almaviva's country house near Seville. Figaro, a valet to Count Almaviva, is preparing to marry Susanna, the countess's chambermaid. Figaro has borrowed a large sum from Marcellina, the old castle housekeeper, promising to repay the money by a certain date or marry her if he defaults. The count has designs on Susanna and tries to seduce her, but she tells Figaro and the countess, and together they scheme to frustrate the count's plans.

Since Susanna will not yield to him, the count decides to take Marcellina's side in the financial dispute and force Figaro to marry her. This plot is foiled by the discovery that Marcellina and her advocate, Dr. Bartolo, are actually Figaro's long-lost parents, from whom he was kidnapped as an infant.

Meanwhile, Susanna and the countess have been conniving; their trick involves a case of disguised identity. Susanna promises to meet the count in the garden that night, but it is the countess, dressed as Susanna, who actually keeps the appointment. Figaro learns of the meeting and thinks that Susanna is deceiving him. The count is caught red-handed by his wife, confesses his attempted infidelity, and begs forgiveness, which she laughingly grants. It all ends happily when Figaro marries Susanna.

The Music

The dramatic action is expressed musically through recitatives (both secco and accompanied), arias, duets, and larger ensembles. The orchestra not only provides instrumental accompaniment for the voices but also intensifies the character of the action on stage.

An examination of a portion of act III illustrates Mozart's use of these musical forces to portray the dramatic action and reveal and underscore its character. At the beginning of act III, Susanna and the countess arrange for Susanna to meet the count that night. Their dialogue, and the subsequent conversation between the count and Susanna, are in

Count Almaviva (Thomas Hampson) rages at his wife, the countess (Carol Vaness), in a scene from *The Marriage of Figaro*. (© 1992 Beth Bergman.)

secco recitative. In the duet that follows, the count rejoices at Susanna's agreement to meet him, while she (in an aside to the audience) asks forgiveness for her lie. Each character has distinctive music, so that it is quite clear that they are singing about two different things.

The next recitative ends with Susanna mentioning to Figaro, as they leave, that he has won his case. The count overhears her remark and sings a recitative expressing his fury and plotting to force Figaro to marry Marcellina. This recitative is accompanied by the full orchestra and includes many sudden changes of key, tempo, and dynamics. It leads to an aria by the count in which he explains how jealous he is of his happy servant Figaro, how he will get revenge, and how happy the thought of revenge makes him. The aria is in two large sections; the second section is faster than the first and is repeated with an extended and ornamented cadence. The style of the accompaniment changes frequently to reflect the count's different thoughts.

As the count finishes, he meets the judge, Don Curzio, who has just upheld Marcellina's right to repayment or marriage. Figaro mentions that he cannot get married without his parents' consent and he has not been able to locate them since he was kidnapped as a child. He describes the circumstances, and Marcellina and Dr. Bartolo realize that he is their child. This dramatic action is covered quickly in recitative, and then a large ensemble begins: The reunited family rejoices together ("beloved son," "beloved parents").

Susanna enters, sees Figaro embracing Marcellina, and misunderstands the situation. During the next section, a sextet, Susanna and the count both rage furiously, with a jagged, dotted musical line,

Example 10.5

Fre-mo, Sma-nio dal fu - ro - re

("I fret, I rave with fury"), while Figaro and his parents calmly note that Susanna's jealousy is a sure sign of her love. The judge joins the count, making the balance in the sextet even—three against three. Finally, Susanna listens to their explanation that Marcellina is Figaro's mother. Scarcely believing it, she questions each one of them in turn: "Sua madre?" Each one answers "Sua madre!" and the pitch level rises with each statement. The same device is used when Dr. Bartolo is introduced as Figaro's father.

The sextet ends with all characters singing, but the balance has changed from three and three to four and two, since Susanna has changed sides and is no longer angry. The musical setting makes their different feelings perfectly clear. The happy four sing smoothly and lyrically, with Susanna (the highest soprano) expressing her joy with an ornamented musical line. The count and the judge sing another jagged, dotted line to express their anger. At the end, where both groups have identical words, the different meanings are expressed by the speed of the notes: The angry men sing much faster than the others.

Example 10.6

MOZART: *Le Nozze di Figaro (The Marriage of Figaro)*
Cassette 3/A, Track 1
CD 3, Track 1

Excerpt from Act III[1]

SCENA PRIMA	**SCENE 1**
Salotto, ornato per una festa nuziale	*A large hall, decorated for a wedding*
RECITATIVO	**RECITATIVE** (*secco*)
Conte (*passeggiando*)	**Count** (*pacing up and down*)
Che imbarazzo è mai questo!	*What a mix-up this is!*
Un foglio anonimo . . .	*An anonymous letter . . .*
La cameriera in gabinetto chiusa . . .	*the maid locked in the closet . . .*
La padrona confusa . . . un uom che salta	*my lady flustered . . . a man jumping down*
Dal balcone in giardino . . . un altro appresso	*from the balcony into the garden . . . then*

1. English translation copyright by Lionel Salter. Reprinted by permission.

Che dice esser quel desso . . .
Non so cosa pensar: potrebbe forse
Qualcun de'miei vassalli . . . a simil
razza
È comune l'ardir . . . ma la
Contessa . . .
Ah, che un dubbio l'offende . . .
Ella rispetta troppo sè stessa;
E l'onor mio . . . l'onore . . .
Dove diamin l'ha posto umano
errore!

another who claims it was he . . .
I don't know what to think: it might
have been one of my vassals . . . such
rabble
are bold enough . . . but the
Countess . . .
No, to doubt her is an insult . . .
she has too much respect for herself
and for my honour . . . my honour
in which, dammit, human frailty
exists!

SCENA SECONDA

LA CONTESSA, SUSANNA, E IL CONTE

*La Contessa e Susanna s'arrestano in
fondo alia scena non vedute
dal Conte*

Contessa
Via, fatti core; digli
Che ti attenda in giardino.

Conte (*sempre tra sè*)
Saprò se Cherubino
Era giunto a Siviglia: a tale oggetto
Ho mandato Basilio

Susanna
Oh cielo! e Figaro . . .

Contessa
A lui non dèi dir nulla, invece tua
Voglio andarci io medesma.

Conte
Avanti sera
Dovrebbe ritomar . . .

Susanna
Oh Dio! non oso.

Contessa
Pensa ch' è in tua mano il mio riposo. (*si
nasconde*)

Conte (*sempre tra sè*)
E Susanna? chi sa ch'ella tradito
Abbia il segreto mio . . . Oh, se ha
parlato
Gli fo sposar la vecchia.

SCENE 2

THE COUNTESS, SUSANNA, AND THE
COUNT

*The Countess and Susanna stay in the
background, unseen by
the Count*

Countess
Go on, take courage: tell him
to meet you in the garden.

Count (*to himself*)
I'll find out if Cherubino
went to Seville: I've sent
Basilio to enquire . . .

Susanna
Oh heavens! if Figaro . . .

Countess
Say nothing of it to him: I myself
intend going in your place.

Count
Before this evening
he should be back . . .

Susanna
Oh dear! I dare not.

Countess
Reflect that my happiness is in your
hands. (*She hides.*)

Count (*still to himself*)
And Susanna? Who knows if she has
betrayed my secret? . . . If she's
spoken
I'll make him marry the old woman.

Susanna *(tra sè)*	**Susanna** *(aside)*
Marcellina!	*Marcellina!*
(forte)	*(aloud)*
Signor . . .	*My lord! . . .*
Conte *(serio)*	**Count** *(firmly)*
Cosa bramate!	*What do you want?*
Susanna	**Susanna**
Mi par che siate in collera!	*I believe you're angry!*
Conte	**Count**
Volete qualche cosa?	*What have you come for?*
Susanna	**Susanna**
Signor . . . la vostra sposa	*My Lord . . . my lady*
Ha i soliti vapori,	*has the vapours, as usual,*
E vi chiede il fiaschetto degli odori.	*and requests your smelling salts.*
Conte	**Count**
Prendete.	*Take them.*
Susanna	**Susanna**
Or vel riporto.	*I'll bring them back at once.*
Conte	**Count**
Eh no, potete	*No, you may keep them*
Ritenerlo per voi.	*for yourself.*
Susanna	**Susanna**
Per me?	*For me?*
Questi non son mali	*Such ailments are not*
Da donne triviali.	*for girls in my position.*
Conte	**Count**
Un' amante, che perde il caro sposo	*A girl who loses her bridegroom*
Sul punto d'ottenerlo . . .	*on the point of winning him . . .*
Susanna	**Susanna**
Pagando Marcellina	*Paying Marcellina off*
Colla dote che voi mi	*with the dowry you promised*
prometteste . . .	*me*
Conte	**Count**
Ch'io vi promisi? quando?	*That I promised you? When?*
Susanna	**Susanna**
Credea d'averlo inteso . . .	*That's what I understood.*
Conte	**Count**
Si, se voluto aveste	*Yes, if you had cared*
intendermi voi stessa.	*to come to an understanding.*
Susanna	**Susanna**
E mio dovere,	*It's my duty,*
E quel di sua eccellenza èil mio	*and my lord's wish is my*
volere.	*command.*

16. DUETTINO

Conte
Crudele! perchè finora
Farmi languir così?

Susanna
Signor, la donna ognora
Tempo ha di dir di si.

Conte
Dunque, in giardin verrai?

Susanna
Se piace a voi, verrò.

Conte
E non mi mancherai?

Susanna
No, non vi mancherò.

Conte
Verrai?

Susanna
Si.

Conte
Non mancherai?

Susanna
No.

Conte
Dunque verrai?

Susanna
No!

Conte
No?!

Susanna
Si!!
Se piace a voi, verrò.

Conte
Mi sento dal contento
Pieno di gioia il cor.

Susanna (piano)
Scusatemi se mento,
Voi che intendete amor.

RECITATIVO

Conte
E perchè fosti meco
Stamattina si austera?

16. DUET (with orchestra)

Count
*Cruel one, why have you
caused me thus to languish?*

Susanna
*My lord, a woman always
needs time before she says Yes.*

Count
Then you'll come into the garden?

Susanna
If it pleases you, I'll come.

Count
You won't fail me?

Susanna
No, I won't fail you.

Count
You'll come?

Susanna
Yes.

Count
You'll not fail?

Susanna
No.

Count
You'll really come?

Susanna
No!

Count
No?!

Susanna
*Yes!
If it pleases you, I'll come.*

Count
*In contentment I feel
my heart full of joy.*

Susanna (aside)
*Forgive my deception,
you who truly love.*

RECITATIVE (secco)

Count
*Then why were you
so distant to me this morning?*

Susanna
Col paggio ch'ivi c'era . . .

Conte
Ed a Basilio,
Che per me ti parlò . . .

Susanna
Ma qual bisogno
Abbiam noi che un Basilio . . .

Conte
È vero, è vero.
E mi prometti poi . . .
Se tu manchi, o cor mio . . .
Ma la contessa
Attenderà il fiaschetto.

Susanna
Eh, fu un pretesto:
Parlato io non avrei senza di questo.

Conte *(La prende per mano.)*
Carissima!

Susanna
Vien gente.

Conte *(tra se)*
È mia senz'altro.

Susanna *(tra se)*
Forbitevi la bocca, o signor scaltro.
*(vuol partire, e sotto ia porta
s'incontra in Figaro)*

SCENA TERZA

FIGARO, SUSANNA, ED IL CONTE

Figaro
Ehi Susanna, ove vai?

Susanna
Taci. Senza avvocato
Hai già vinta la causa. *(parte)*

Figaro
Cosa è nato? *(la segue)*

SCENA QUARTA
17. RECITATIVO ED ARIA

Conte
Hai già vinta la causa! cosa sento!
In qual laccio cadea! perfidi! io voglio
Di tal modo punirvi! a piacer mio

Susanna
With the page there . . .

Count
*And to Basilio,
who spoke on my behalf . . .*

Susanna
*But what need have we
of a Basilio . . .*

Count
*That's true, indeed.
Promise me again . . .
If you fail me, my dear . . .
But the Countess
will be waiting for the smelling salts.*

Susanna
*Oh, that was just a pretext; I couldn't
have spoken to you without one.*

Count *(taking her hand)*
Dearest!

Susanna
Someone's coming.

Count *(aside)*
She's mine, I'm sure now.

Susanna *(aside)*
*Wipe off that smile, my cunning master.
(about to exit, she meets Figaro
at the door)*

SCENE 3

FIGARO, SUSANNA, AND THE COUNT

Figaro
Susanna, where are you going?

Susanna
*Hush. We've won our case
without a lawyer (exit)*

Figaro
What's happened? (He follows her)

SCENE 4
17. RECITATIVE AND ARIA *(with orchestra)*

Count
*We've won our case! What do I hear!
I've fallen into a trap! The traitors!
I'll punish them so! The sentence will*

La sentenza sarà . . . Ma s'ei pagasse La vecchia pretendente?
Pagarla! in qual maniera? . . . è poi v'è Antonio
Che a un incognito Figaro ricusa
Di dare una nipote in matrimonio. Coltivando l'orgoglio Di questo mentecatto . . .
Tutto giova a un raggiro . . .
Il colpo è fatto.

Vedrò mentr'jo sospiro, Felice un servo mio?
E un ben, che invan desio,
Ei posseder dovrà?
Vedrò per man d'amore
Unita a un vil oggetto
Chi in me destò un affetto,
Che per me poi non ha?
Ah no, lasciarti in pace
Non vo' questo contento!
Tu non nascesti, audace!
Per dare a me tormento,
E forse ancor per ridere
Di mia infelicità.
Già la speranza sola
Delle vendette mie
Quest'anima consola
E giubilar mi fa.

(Vuol partire, e s'incontra in Don Curzio)

SCENA QUINTA

IL CONTE, MARCELLINA, DON CURZIO, FIGARO, E BARTOLO

RECITATIVO

Curzio *(entrando)*
È decisa la lite.
O pagarla, o sposarla. Ora ammutite.

Marcellina
Io respiro

Figaro
Ed io moro.

Marcellina *(tra se)*
Alfin sposa io sarò d'un uom che adoro.

---

be at my pleasure . . . But supposing he has paid off the claims of the old woman?
Paid her? How . . . and then there's Antonio
who'll refuse to give his niece in marriage to a Figaro, of whom nothing is known. If I play on the pride of that half-wit . . .
Everything favours my plan . . . The die is cast.
Must I see a serf of mine made happy while I am left to sigh,
and see him possess a treasure which I desire in vain?
Must I see her, who has roused in me a passion
she does not feel for me, united by the hand of love to a base slave?
Ah no, I will not give you the satisfaction of this contentment!
You were not born, bold fellow, to cause me torment
and indeed to laugh at my discomfiture.
Now only the hope of taking vengeance eases my mind and makes me rejoice.

(About to leave, he meets Don Curzio)

SCENE 5

THE COUNT, MARCELLINA, DON CURZIO, FIGARO, AND BARTOLO

RECITATIVE *(secco)*

Curzio *(entering)*
The case is decided.
Pay up, or marry her. That's all.

Marcellina
I breathe again.

Figaro
And I'm done for.

Marcellina *(aside)*
At last I'll be married to the man I love.

Figaro
Eccellenza, m'appello . . .

Conte
È giusta la sentenza.
O pagar, o sposar. Bravo,
Don Curzio.

Curzio
Bontà di Sua Eccellenza.

Bartolo
Che superba sentenza!

Figaro
In che superba?

Bartolo
Siam tutti vendicati.

Figaro
Io non la sposerò.

Bartolo
La sposerai.

Curzio
O pagarla, o sposarla. Lei t'ha prestati
Due mille pezzi duri.

Figaro
Son gentiluomo, e senza
L'assenso de' miei nobili parenti . . .

Conte
Dove sono? chi sono?

Figaro
Lasciate ancor cercarli:
Dopo dieci anni io spero di trovarli.

Bartolo
Qualche bambin trovato? . . .

Figaro
No, perduto, Dottor, anzi rubato.

Conte
Come?

Marcellina
Cosa?

Bartolo
La prova?

Curzio
Il testimonio?

Figaro
My lord, I appeal . . .

Count
The judgment is fair.
Pay up, or marry her. Quite right.
Don Curzio.

Curzio
Your lordship is too kind.

Bartolo
An excellent judgment!

Figaro
In what way excellent?

Bartolo
We are all avenged.

Figaro
I won't marry her.

Bartolo
Oh yes, you will.

Curzio
Pay up, or marry her. She lent you
two thousand pieces of silver.

Figaro
I am of gentle birth, and without
the consent of my noble parents . . .

Count
Where are they? Who are they?

Figaro
Let me go on looking for them;
for ten years I've been hoping to find them.

Bartolo
Were you a foundling? . . .

Figaro
No, lost, Doctor, or rather stolen.

Count
Stolen?

Marcellina
What's that?

Bartolo
Your proof?

Curzio
Your witness?

Figaro
L'oro, le gemme, e i ricamati
panni,
Che ne' più teneri anni
Mi ritrovaro addosso i masnadieri,
Sono gl'indizi veri
Di mia nascita illustre, e sopra tutto
Questo al mio braccio impresso
geroglifico.

Marcellina
Una spatola impressa al braccio destro?

Figaro
E a voi ch' il disse?

Marcellina
Oh Dio!
È desso . . .

Figaro
È ver, son io.

Curzio
Chi?

Conte
Chi?

Bartolo
Chi?

Marcellina
Rafaello.

Bartolo
E i ladri ti rapir?

Figaro
Presso un castello.

Bartolo
Ecco tua madre.

Figaro
Balia?

Bartolo
No, tua madre.

Conte e Curzio
Sua madre!?

Figaro
Cosa sento!

Marcellina
Ecco tuo padre.
(Marcellina corre ad abbracciare Figaro)

Figaro
*The gold, the jewels, and the
embroidered clothes which, in my
infancy, the bandits found upon me
are the true indications of my noble
birth, and moreover this mark upon
my arm.*

Marcellina
A spatula on your right arm?

Figaro
Who told you that?

Marcellina
*Great heaven!
It's he . . .*

Figaro
It's I, indeed.

Curzio
Who?

Count
Who?

Bartolo
Who?

Marcellina
Rafaello.

Bartolo
And robbers stole you?

Figaro
Near a castle.

Bartolo
There stands your mother.

Figaro
My nurse? . . .

Bartolo
No, your mother.

Count and Curzio
His mother!?

Figaro
Do I hear aright?

Marcellina
And there stands your father.
(She runs to embrace Figaro)

18. SESTETTO

Marcellina
Riconosci in questo amplesso
Una madre, amato figlio.

Figaro
Padre mio, fate lo stesso,
Non mi fate più arrossir.

Bartolo
Resistenza la coscienza
Far non lascia al tuo desir.

Curzio *(tra śe)*
Ei suo padre, ella sua madre: L'imeneneo
   non può seguir.

Conte *(tra śe)*
Son smarrito, son stordito: Meglio è
assai di qua patir. *(Il Conte fa per
partire, Susanna l'arresta)*

Marcellina e Bartolo
Figlio amato!

Figaro
Parenti amati!

Susanna
Alto, alto, signore Conte, Mille doppie
qui son pronte. A pagar vengo per
Figaro, Ed a porlo in libertà.

Conte e Curzio
Non sappiam come'è la cosa. Osservate
un poco là.

Susanna *(si volge e vede Figaro che abbraccia
Marcellina)*
Già d'accordo colla sposa? Giusti dei;
che infedeltà! Lascia, iniquo!
(vuol partire)

Figaro
(la trattiene; ella lo forza)
No, t'arresta Senti, o cara.

Susanna *(da uno schiaffo a Figaro)*
Senti questa!

18. SEXTET *(with orchestra)*

Marcellina
*Dearest son, in this embrace
recognize your mother.*

Figaro
*Father dear, do the same, do not leave
me longer here to blush.*

Bartolo
*Do not let conscience stand in the way
of your desire.*

Curzio *(aside)*
*He's his father, she's his mother: the
   wedding can't go forward.*

Count *(aside)*
*I'm astounded, I'm amazed: to leave
here would be for the best. (He makes
to leave, but Susanna detains him)*

Marcellina and Bartolo
My beloved son!

Figaro
My beloved parents!

Susanna
*Just a moment, pray, my lord. I have
the money ready here. I've come to
pay for Figaro and set him free.*

Count and Curzio
*We don't know where we are.
Just look over there.*

Susanna *(turns and sees Figaro embracing
Marcellina)*
*Already reconciled to her as wife? Great
   heaven, how faithless! Leave me,
   wretch!*
(She starts to go.)

Figaro
(detains her; she struggles)
Stay a moment. Listen, my dearest.

Susanna *(boxes Figaro's ears)*
Listen to that!

Marcellina, Bartolo, e Figaro
È un effetto di buon core, Tutto amore
è quel che fa.

Conte e Curzio
Fremo, smanio dal furore, Il destino me la
   (gliela) fa.

Susanna
Fremo, smanio dal furore,
Una vecchia a me la fa.

Marcellina
Lo sdegno calmate, Mia cara figliuola,
Sua madre abbracciate, Che vostra or
sarà.
(Marcellina corre ad abbracciare Susanna)

Susanna
Sua madre?

Tutti
Sua madre.

Figaro
E quello è mio padre,
Che a te lo dirà.

Susanna
Suo padre?

Tutti
Suo padre.

Figaro
E quella è mia madre,
Che a te lo dirà
(Corrono tutti e quattro ad abbracciarsi)

Susanna, Marcellina, Bartolo, e Figaro
Al dolce contento
Di questo momento, Quest' anima
appena
Resistere or sa.

Conte e Curzio
Al fiero tormento
Di questo momento Quest' anima
appena
Resistere or sa.

Marcellina, Bartolo, and Figaro
It's the result of her full heart;
what she did, she did for love.

Count and Curzio
I rage, I burn with fury; fate has
   overcome me (him).

Susanna
I rage, I burn with fury;
this old woman has overcome me.

Marcellina
Dearest daughter, calm your bitterness,
and embrace his mother,
who now will be yours too.
(She runs to embrace Susanna)

Susanna
His mother?

All
His mother.

Figaro
And this is my father,
who'll tell you it's true.

Susanna
His father?

All
His father.

Figaro
And this is my mother,
who'll tell you it's true.
(All four embrace)

Susanna, Marcellina, Bartolo, and Figaro
My heart
scarcely can support
the bliss
of this moment.

Count and Curzio
My heart scarcely can support
the raging torment
of this moment.

SUMMARY

Although the main area of concentration for most classical composers was instrumental music, the age did produce lasting achievements in vocal music as well.

Haydn's *Nelson Mass* well represents the classical treatment of the Mass. In the six main sections, comprising eleven movements, the listener is carried from themes of driving force to adagio passages of light texture, from exhilarating and dynamic movements to slow and expressive sections. Considered a masterpiece, this work is a favorite in contemporary choral repertoires.

The greatest composer of opera in the Classical era was Mozart. His first comic opera, *The Marriage of Figaro,* stands out among opera buffa for its realistic characters, amusing libretto, delightful solo and ensemble music, and skillful use of orchestral devices to enhance the characterization.

NEW TERMS

opera seria
opera buffa

SUGGESTED LISTENING

Haydn, Franz Joseph

Die Schöpfung (The Creation). This oratorio (one of three by Haydn) depicts and tells the story of the creation of the world. From the overture (Representation of Chaos) to the final triumphant chorus, Haydn uses soloists, chorus, and orchestra to impart the story vividly and dramatically.

Mozart, Wolfgang Amadeus

Requiem in D Minor, K.626. In spite of the fact that Mozart died before he could finish this piece (it was completed by a student), it became and still is one of the great settings of the Requiem for the Dead. It is scored for soloists, chorus, and orchestra.

Exsultate, Jubilate. This motet is written for soprano soloist and an orchestra consisting of strings, oboes, and horns. Its last movement, *Alleluja,* calls for brilliant vocal technique on the part of the soprano.

Don Giovanni. The story of Don Juan, the Spanish lover, and his downfall, in what many consider Mozart's best opera.

THE MUSIC OF BEETHOVEN

P robably no single composer has influenced the course of musical events more than Ludwig van Beethoven. His evolving style had a profound effect on the musicians of his time, and the music he left to the world has continued to influence musicians and to have great public appeal. In 1970, concert halls around the world presented programs of his music to commemorate the two-hundredth anniversary of his birth in 1770. Athough he is considered a representative of the Classical era, Beethoven in many ways was a precursor of romanticism. His life bridged two centuries almost equally, and his spirit seemed more in tune with the upheaval that followed the French Revolution than with the relative stability of the Age of Reason. While he injected a new freedom into the classical forms, Beethoven continued to adhere to them. His great contribution was to carry forward the tradition of Mozart and Haydn, building on the structures they had developed and elevating them to new heights of power and expressiveness.

BEETHOVEN'S WORK

In comparison to the productivity of Mozart and Haydn, Beethoven's works seem surprisingly few. This is partly due to his method of composing. Mozart never lacked musical inspiration, and ideas flowed from his pen with miraculous ease; Haydn confessed to the necessity of resorting to prayer at difficult moments, but he kept to a regular schedule of composition. Beethoven, however, had to struggle. Ideas did not come easily, and he filled innumerable pages with slowly evolving sketches. Even his finished compositions were continually rewritten and revised (see fig. 11.2). The second reason for limited production was his attitude toward composition. He regarded music, above all, as art, and he generally took on only those commissions that he personally wished to fulfill.

If Beethoven's works took longer to write than was usual at the time, they were also more substantial, both in content and length. His works include nine symphonies; nine concert overtures; five piano concertos; one violin concerto; sixteen string quartets; ten sonatas for violin and piano; five sonatas for cello and piano; thirty-two sonatas for solo piano; twenty-one sets of variations for piano; one opera, *Fidelio;* an oratorio, *Christus am Ölberg* (*Christ on the Mount of Olives*); *Choral Fantasia* for piano, chorus, and orchestra; and two Masses, one in C major, the other, entitled *Missa solemnis,* in D major.

Most musical scholars divide Beethoven's career into three periods: the first extending to about 1802, the second extending to 1814, and the last ending with his death in 1827. The first period was a time of assimilation of the classical tradition of Mozart and Haydn and includes the string quartets of opus 18 (1798–1800), the First Symphony (1799), and his first three piano sonatas.

BEETHOVEN (1770–1827)

L udwig van Beethoven (fig. 11.1) was born in the Rhineland city of Bonn, the son of a singer in the Electoral Court chapel. His musical education was taken over by his father, who hoped to make his boy into a child prodigy like Mozart. Though never fulfilling his father's hope, young Beethoven did learn piano and violin quickly. He received instruction from several musicians at the court, and by the age of twelve, he was substituting at the chapel organ. In 1784 he was appointed to a permanent position as assistant organist and had already begun to make his mark because of his virtuoso improvisations at the piano. After his mother died, in 1787, his father's alcoholism grew worse, and Beethoven's home life became increasingly unbearable.

The year 1790 marked a turning point in the young composer's career. Haydn, passing through Bonn on his way to London, urged the Elector to send Beethoven to Vienna for further study. Two years later, at the age of twenty-two, Beethoven moved to Vienna, where he remained the rest of his life. At first he studied composition with Haydn; but, unsatisfied with the older man's methods, he turned to other composers for instruction. Though he was a frequent performer at musical evenings held by prominent Viennese nobility, Beethoven did not play in public until 1795, when he performed one of his early piano concertos.

Figure 11.1 Beethoven's music encompasses both the classical love of form and the fiery passion of romanticism. The force and intensity of his stormy personality are evident in this engraving.

Unlike Mozart, Beethoven always retained his popularity with both the general public and the aristocracy of Vienna; and unlike Haydn, he never had to endure the rigors of the eighteenth-century system of musical patronage. Though he may have yearned at times for the prestige and security of a court position, he remained proudly and fiercely independent throughout his life.

During most of his career he was able to count on annual stipends from a small circle of aristocratic friends and admirers. He seemed to enjoy moving about in the upper echelons of Viennese society, remarking that "it is good to mingle with aristocrats, but one must know how to impress them."

Beethoven was one of the first composers to demand and obtain an equal footing with this aristocracy solely on the basis of his genius. It was his fortune to come upon the world in a time of rapidly changing values and increasing social mobility. The emerging middle-class audience and the growth of public concerts provided ample opportunities for performance of his music. The rising demand for his works enabled him to live off the sale of his music to publishers.

During the first years of the nineteenth century, when Beethoven seemed to be approaching the height of his career, he became aware that he was growing deaf. He became deeply depressed when he realized that his career as a performer would end. In a moving letter to his two brothers, written from the small town of Heiligenstadt outside Vienna and intended to be read after his death, Beethoven confessed:

My misfortune pains me doubly, in as much as it leads to my being misjudged. For me there can be no relaxation in human society, no refined conversations, no mutual confidences: I must live quite alone and may creep into society only as often as sheer necessity demands; I must live like an outcast. If I appear in company I am overcome by a burning anxiety, a fear that I am running the risk of letting people notice my condition. . . . Such experiences almost made me despair, and I was on the point of putting an end to my life— The only thing that held me back was my art. For indeed it seemed to me impossible to leave this world before I had produced all the works that I felt the urge to compose, and thus I have dragged on this miserable existence.[1]

After his affliction became painfully obvious, Beethoven gave up conducting and playing in public. His principal means of communication became a notebook in which his few visitors were invited to write their remarks. As he withdrew into his art, his works became more complex, more abstract, and more incomprehensible to his fellow musicians. He never married, and when total deafness set in after 1820, he became almost a recluse. Beethoven died in 1827 at the age of fifty-seven.

1. Emily Anderson (ed. and trans.), *The Letters of Beethoven,* 3 vols., Vol. 3, p. 1352. Copyright © 1961 St. Martin's Press, New York, NY. Reprinted by permission of MacMillan London Publishers, London, England.

The second period was perhaps the happiest of Beethoven's life; it was certainly the most productive. During it, he wrote masterpiece after masterpiece: seven more symphonies, including the gigantic *Eroica* (no. 3, 1803) and the Fifth (1805); the *Rasoumovsky Quartets* of opus 59 (1806); his opera *Fidelio* (with no fewer than three versions appearing from 1805 through 1814); and the "Waldstein" and "Appassionata" piano sonatas of 1804.

Beethoven's last creative period, a time of great personal troubles including his deafness, was less productive, but in many ways it was the most important of the three. It culminated in his monumental Ninth Symphony (1823), the equally immense *Missa solemnis* (completed in 1824), and increasingly abstract late quartets and piano sonatas. In these works he developed many of the musical ideas that influenced the coming romantic movement. The innovations they contained in form and harmonic structure were not fully understood or appreciated until almost half a century after his death.

ELEMENTS OF BEETHOVEN'S STYLE

Beethoven's music reveals several original stylistic characteristics. One that is immediately apparent is size. His works tend to be much longer than those of Haydn or Mozart.

Another striking characteristic is the prevalence of the developmental process. Beethoven lengthened the development section of sonata-allegro form, giving it a weight equal to that of the exposition and recapitulation, and used development in other parts of the movement, especially the coda. In many of his works, the coda is not a short, tacked-on ending but is extended into a second development section, sometimes followed by a second coda that acts as a genuine coda—a short, concluding section.

In general, Beethoven adhered to the schemes of separate, self-contained movements, unrelated thematically. But there are exceptions: the Sixth Symphony (the *Pastoral*) has five movements, and there is no break between the last two. And the Fifth Symphony, which we shall discuss later in this chapter, was a striking departure from the principle of thematic independence among the movements.

Within the four-movement scheme, Beethoven radically transformed the *third* movement. The short, stately minuet and trio was replaced by a scherzo and trio movement of an entirely different character. Swift of tempo, and fully proportioned in their length, Beethoven's scherzos are the equal of the other movements, performing a more important structural and expressive role in the overall scheme of the work.

Beethoven's music is characterized by an intense, dramatic use of fluctuating dynamics. Frequently he used special dynamic effects, such as a crescendo that is not allowed to climax, but is aborted by a sudden change to pianissimo. He also used long crescendos for structural and expressive purposes. A crescendo slowly builds momentum and energy, culminating in the appearance of an important event, such as the beginning of the recapitulation. Under these circumstances, the beginning of the recapitulation would also serve as a climactic ending of the development section.

Beethoven was ingenious in the use of *silence*. In his music, silence functions both as a structural element, separating sections, and as an expressive element, building suspense.

The qualities that we have outlined here are characteristic of Beethoven's work in general. Other, more specific qualities can be seen in his orchestral works.

ORCHESTRAL STYLE

Beethoven's orchestral sound is more powerful and dramatic than that of Mozart or Haydn. This increased intensity was the result of larger orchestras and a change in the ways in which the instruments were used. More players were added to the string section, and two horns (sometimes four), two trumpets, and timpani were included as standard parts of the orchestral ensemble. The normal woodwind section was comprised of two flutes, two oboes, two clarinets, and two bassoons. For extra color and power, Beethoven occasionally added piccolo, contrabassoon, and three trombones. The trumpets, horns, and trombones assumed a greater role than they had previously, and the timpani, which formerly merely reinforced the trumpets, were used independently, even as solo instruments.

Working with this expanded orchestra, Beethoven made important contributions to the craft of **orchestration**—writing and arranging music for orchestra to achieve the most effective overall combinations. In this area he greatly influenced later composers in the Romantic era for whom orchestration became a major component of musical composition.

The increased dimensions, extended use of development, advanced exploitation of dynamics, employment of suspense-building devices, and powerful use of an expanded orchestra are among the most important stylistic features of Beethoven's symphonies. Beginning with the Third and culminating in the Ninth, they revolutionized orchestral writing and playing.

SYMPHONY NO. 5 IN C MINOR

BEETHOVEN:
Symphony no. 5 in
C Minor, Movement I
Cassette 2/B, Track 3
CD 2, Track 10
*See Listening Guide on
pages 235–237.*

Beethoven's Fifth Symphony, which he began in 1804, was first performed in Vienna in December, 1808. It is probably the most popular of Beethoven's symphonies, not only for its terse and memorable themes, but also for its unity.

First Movement

The first movement of the symphony is an excellent example of Beethoven's skill at building a large structure out of a small motive, in this case the famous ♪♪♪ 𝅗𝅥 .

    Its stark and forceful announcement, played fortissimo by all strings and clarinets, stands at the beginning of the movement.

Example 11.1

After these two statements, there is a change to *piano* as the motive is used to create the initial phrase of the first theme in the principal key of C minor.

Example 11.2

The theme is soon abruptly driven to a dramatic halt by a crescendo, leading to three loud, separated chords. The last chord lingers on a long-held note in the first violin, creating a feeling of suspense that is dispelled when the full orchestra, fortissimo, hammers out the motive:

This dramatic and isolated statement of the motive draws attention to it, interrupting the flow of the theme. With another extreme change, from full orchestra playing fortissimo to strings playing piano, the theme is resumed, building on the motive (example 11.3).

Example 11.3

1st Violin

Shortly after the resumption of the theme, several important features of Beethoven's style appear. The intensity increases, underlined by the gradual addition of instruments, stepped-up rhythmic activity, and climbing pitch level, all combining in a mighty crescendo that envelops the bridge and culminates in two sharp chords separated by silence and followed by silence, dramatically setting off the appearance of the second theme.

The second theme, in E-flat major, is launched by the four-note motive announced by the horns.

Example 11.4

The second theme continues with a lyrical legato melody in the first violins and the woodwinds. The basic motive is still present as a kind of punctuation in the lower strings.

Example 11.5

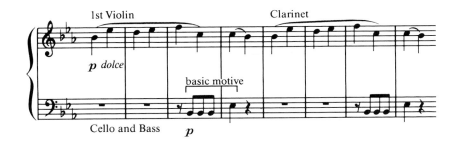

As the rhythmic activity of the theme increases, the basic motive reasserts itself, commanding full attention in the closing material ending the exposition, which is then repeated.

Example 11.6

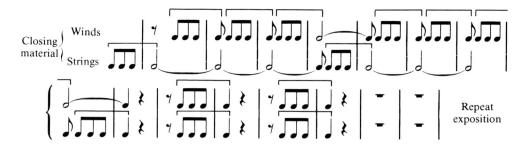

The first phase of the development concentrates on the basic motive, in a manner similar to theme 1, gradually leading to the winds and strings answering each other.

The second phase of development begins with the opening phrase of theme 2 and turns it into one of the most intense examples of suspense building in the history of musical composition. After the violins state the phrase twice, each time followed by rhythmic punctuations in the winds and lower strings, the phrase

is transferred to the winds, where it is played fortissimo in a shortened form. The strings answer with the two long notes of the phrase, and the winds and strings continue to alternate this two-note pattern.

Example 11.7

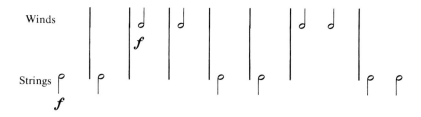

This stretch of music creates the atmosphere of suspense and expectation that is intensified when the dynamic level is progressively lowered through a diminuendo ($>$) and the musical material is reduced to one chord.

Example 11.8

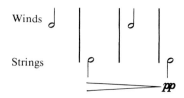

There is no "theme," no "motive," only the seemingly endless answering back and forth on this barest of fragments. Finally there is a jolting, forte entrance of

ff

and it would appear that all the suspense is ended, but the music immediately reverts to softly alternating winds and strings. Again the suspense returns, finally to be ended with another entrance of the basic motive that now crescendos to a climactic

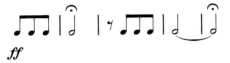

ff

Here Beethoven shows complete mastery of form and structure—the simple four-note motive acquires an awesome impact as he develops it. Its reappearance constitutes the climactic ending of this development and at the same time the beginning of the recapitulation.

The recapitulation is quite straightforward, with the addition of a short oboe solo and minor changes in orchestration. But the closing material does not end the movement. Instead, there is a long coda, which is actually a new development section treating the basic motive, followed by the lyrical first phrase of the second theme. This becomes the new driving element, which builds to yet another climactic statement of the opening figure. There is then a short second coda based on the first theme and a crescendo to a final appearance of the basic motive.

Second Movement

Superficially, the second movement follows the classical style: It is in a contrasting key (A-flat major) and meter (3/8); it is slower in tempo (andante con moto) and, at least in the beginning, establishes a lyrical, relaxed atmosphere in relation to the first movement. However, as the movement unfolds, it displays characteristics that are unique.

The movement begins as a theme and variations, with a two-part theme containing several distinctive contrasting elements. The first part begins with a lyrical, flowing melody played by violas and cellos, followed by a contrasting phrase initiated by the woodwinds. The second half of the theme is dominated by a loud phrase, played by horns and trumpets in C major and employs the ♪♪♪|♩ motive from the first movement. This is followed by a soft, suspenseful ending that leads into the first variation.

In the first variation, only the viola-cello melody is varied. With minor changes in the accompaniment, the rest of the theme is merely repeated in its original form. The second variation begins with a rhythmic intensification of the first variation of the viola-cello melody.

Example 11.9

Up to this point, the movement appears to consist of a clear theme and variations. But after the beginning of the second "variation," the theme never again appears intact, in either varied or original form. Only parts of it are used.

The music that follows is more characteristic of development than of variation. Fragments as well as whole phrases of the theme are manipulated in a variety of ways. Modulation, change of tempo, fluctuating dynamics, crescendos climaxing in the dramatic appearance of part of the theme are all used in building the movement. The movement closes with a return to the "woodwind" phrase, followed by a coda based on the viola-cello theme.

Third Movement

BEETHOVEN:
Symphony no. 5 in
C Minor, Movement III
Cassette 2/B, Track 3
CD 2, Track 11
*See Listening Guide on
pages 236–237.*

As we pointed out earlier, the third movements of Beethoven's symphonies utilize scherzo and trio rather than the minuet and trio found in the symphonies of Haydn and Mozart. In this symphony Beethoven employs a most unusual technique for his time—he relates the third movement to the first by reintroducing the familiar motive from the first movement (♪♪♪ |♩). Another distinguishing feature of this movement is that it is not self-contained, but leads directly into the last movement without a break. Furthermore, it is a fascinating example of how dynamics and orchestration influence musical structure.

The literal meaning of the word *scherzo* is "joke," and the early pieces (for instance, those by Haydn) had a frolicsome character. Many of Beethoven's scherzos also reflect a playful, often whimsical atmosphere. However, the scherzo of the Fifth Symphony has a brooding, almost ominous quality.

Like the minuet and trio, the scherzo and trio has a three-part structure: scherzo-trio-scherzo. It, too, is in the key of the first movement, but the similarities end there.

The first scherzo alternates two contrasting ideas: A quiet, brooding, mysterious section (A) with a faltering, "stop-and-go" quality is followed by the loud, vigorous, driving thrust of the second theme (B), which is based on the familiar motive: ♪♪♪ |♩ (example 11.10).

Example 11.10

The trio shifts to the key of C major and begins with a short section consisting of fugal entrances of thematic material beginning with cellos and basses followed in turn by violas, second violins, and first violins, and ending with a melodic fragment utilizing the familiar rhythmic motive from the first movement. This section is repeated.

After two false beginnings:

Example 11.11

the second section proceeds with an expansion of the material in the first section and ending with ♪♪♪ ♩ at a forte dynamic level.

What follows begins as a repetition of this section but turns into a transition passage in which the dynamic level becomes very soft and the orchestral sound is gradually reduced so that only cellos and basses are left for a quiet return to the scherzo (A).

In the repeat of the scherzo, the themes no longer contrast dynamically; both are now pianissimo. The ♪♪♪ ♩ motive, originally so loud and bold as played by the horns, is now subdued as it is shared by the clarinet and pizzicato first violins. By reducing the dynamic level and subduing the orchestration throughout the entire repeat of the scherzo, Beethoven has profoundly changed the character of the music and created an atmosphere of almost excruciating restraint and expectation.

The scherzo does not "end" but turns into one of those suspense-ridden stretches of music of which Beethoven was a master. Here he uses the technique called *pedal point,* in which a long tone is maintained in the bass against changing harmonies in other parts. In this case, the timpani continually plays the note C. Over this pedal point, a long melodic arch gradually unfolds, played by the first violins, first in fragments, and then as a continuous rising line pulling against the timpani roll. Higher and higher this line pulls, eventually joined by the rest of the orchestra on a long dominant chord and a crescendo that climaxes with breathtaking force in the triumphant and stirring C major melody that begins the last movement. The third and fourth movements are thus united with dramatic effect.

Example 11.12

Fourth Movement

The last movement is fast and is in the key of C major rather than making the expected return to C minor. Beethoven tended to end large works brilliantly in major keys. To provide greater color and strength to the movement, he added a piccolo, contrabassoon, and three trombones to the orchestration.

The movement is a sonata-allegro movement with three themes. Two of them draw upon the basic motive of the first movement for part of their material. In theme 1, the motive is "hidden" within the theme,

Example 11.13

but in theme 2 the motive constitutes the primary melodic and rhythmic substance.

Example 11.14

The motive is not used in theme 3, although later in the movement, the material from this theme is used in association with the motive.

Example 11.15

The bridge between themes 1 and 2 is exceptionally long, and its melodic importance rivals that of the themes themselves.

Example 11.16

The bridge modulates from C to G major, ending with repetitions of the motive as it leads to the second theme.

After the repeat of the exposition (many conductors do not make this repetition), the closing section flows directly into the development section—indeed, there is almost no indication of where one ends and the other begins.

The development section makes forceful use of the orchestra, with emphasis on winds and brasses, extended use of dynamics and modulation. Toward the end of the development section, a loud, fanfare-like section leads to a remarkable phase of development. There is a direct quote of the end of the *third* movement. Using this quote, the development builds through a long crescendo to the recapitulation. Again, as in the beginning of the fourth movement, because of the way it is approached, the first theme produces a "victorious" effect.

The piece does not end with the conclusion of the recapitulation. Instead, there is a long coda that is actually a new development section. It is characterized by an exhilarating increase in tempo leading to what is without question one of the longest and most emphatic endings in music history—and bringing to a close one of the most remarkable compositions of all time.

COMPOSITIONS FOR PIANO

A significant portion of Beethoven's output was devoted to works for the piano. For this instrument he wrote thirty-two solo sonatas, five piano concertos, and a host of other works for solo piano including the *Thirty-Three Variations on a Waltz by Diabelli.* Added to this list are many works in which the piano was employed as a collaborating instrument, such as sonatas for violin and piano, cello and piano, and horn and piano.

All of the stylistic elements noted previously are evident in his writing for the keyboard. In his hands, the piano became a more dramatic and dynamic instrument than it was in the keyboard works of Mozart and Haydn.

PIANO SONATA OP. 57 ("APPASSIONATA")

Both as a virtuoso pianist and as a composer, Beethoven preferred the heavier piano developed in England to the lighter Viennese instrument played by Mozart. The English design and construction resulted in an instrument of great brilliance and dynamic power which Beethoven exploited to the fullest extent, as illustrated in his Piano Sonata op. 57 to become known as the "Appassionata."

The sonata maintained the three-movement plan—fast, slow, fast—without, however, the usual break between the second and third movements.

BEETHOVEN:
Piano Sonata op. 57
("Appassionata")
Cassette 2/B, Track 4
CD 2, Track 12
*See Listening Guide
on page 238.*

First Movement (Allegro assai)

The first movement, in the key of F minor, is in sonata-allegro form, including two contrasting themes, the first ominous:

Example 11.17

the second, flowing:

Example 11.18

The abrupt changes of mood, sudden and frequent change in dynamic level, dramatic pauses, and suspense building we encountered in much of the Fifth Symphony are in abundance in this movement. In addition, Beethoven makes full use of the extremes of pitch level—very high to very low—of which the piano is capable (examples 11.19, 11.20, and 11.21).

Example 11.19

Example 11.20

Example 11.21

Two stretches of music in this movement are very much like cadenzas. One ends the development and introduces the recapitulation, and the second ends the recapitulation and introduces the allegro finale. The closing coda is a tour de force for the virtuoso pianist, as it races at breakneck speed and with fortissimo dynamics. The theme is doubled in octaves and sounded in the most brilliant register of the piano. In a gesture typical of Beethoven, it then progresses from its point of climax to one of repose. In the last measures, the dynamic level drops from fortissimo to pianissimo to triple piano. The theme is sent soaring to the heights of the keyboard, then plummeting to a final whispered cadence five octaves below.

Second Movement

The second movement is a lyrical theme and variations in D-flat major. In this movement Beethoven exploits the lower range of the piano and creates striking effects by juxtaposing high and low sections. The initial somber theme is stated in the rich and sonorous lower register of the keyboard. The theme is in two parts, each of which is repeated.

The first variation preserves the theme's contour but alters the rhythm. The right hand transforms the legato articulation into short, detached notes. The left hand, meanwhile, syncopates the rhythm of the theme, so that notes now appear slightly after the beat.

The second variation returns to the smooth legato of the opening, with the right hand playing chordal figures while the left hand retains the original bass line with slight rhythmic alterations. The material in both hands has been transposed one octave higher than in the original, thus creating a lighter, less massive texture.

In the first two variations, the repetition structure of the theme is retained, but in the final variation this is no longer the case. Beethoven uses a motive based on the opening of the theme as a superstructure around which he weaves rapid chordal and scale figurations; here again we witness his exploration of development possibilities.

The magic that sometimes results from the juxtaposition of high and low registers emanates from the last simple statement of the theme at the close of the movement. The first three chords of each phrase are high, the next low, and this continued alternation between high and low registers gives the theme itself a quiet, fragmented quality of suspense. This feeling is heightened by the fact that the movement doesn't "end"; rather it pauses in anticipation on two long, arpeggios—one very soft, the second very loud—that call for resolution:

Example 11.22

a resolution that comes only at the beginning of the concluding movement with a return to a fast tempo.

Third Movement (Allegro ma non troppo)

The beginning of the last movement constitutes a continuation of the introductory character of the end of the second movement. Not until twenty measures into the movement does the theme of the last movement appear.

Example 11.23

This passage, or some variant of it, seems omnipresent throughout the entire movement, blurring the distinctions between exposition and development and between development and recapitulation. The movement sounds like one continuous development of this material, with other thematic elements imbedded within or grafted onto it. The movement ends with a presto finale in a climax of brilliance and excitement.

Listening Guide

BEETHOVEN: Symphony no. 5 in C Minor

First Movement: Allegro con brio (fast, fiery)
Duple meter
Sonata form

Classical Orchestra

Review: Example 11.1 (opening, with basic motive)
Example 11.2 (initial phrase of first theme)
Example 11.3 (continuation of first theme)
Example 11.4 (horns announcing second theme)
Example 11.5 (legato second theme with basic motive in basses)
Example 11.6 (closing material of Exposition)
Example 11.7 (2–note Development pattern)
Example 11.8 (reduction to 1–note pattern)

CD 2 (Cassette 2/B, Track 3)

Exposition

10 ① 0:00	③ 1:32		*Theme 1*	1a	Basic motive stated twice, forte
0:07	1:39			b	Piano, motive sounds throughout strings; crescendo, three forte, separated chords, long-held note by violins on last chord
0:20	1:53			c	Motive, fortissimo; piano, motive builds theme in strings; instruments gradually enter, crescendo, pitch rises; two separate chords, fortissimo
			Bridge		
② 0:47	2:20		*Theme 2*	2a	Horn call, basic motive with extension, fortissimo
0:50	2:23			b	Legato theme in violins, then clarinet, then flute; basic motive in low strings; fragment of theme in strings, other instruments gradually enter, crescendo
1:11	2:44		*Closing*	3a	Loud chord, strings in strong descending passage, repeated
1:22	2:54			b	Basic motive descends in winds answered by strings; repeated; 2 separate statements of motive
					(Exposition is repeated)
④ 3:05			**Development**	1	Basic motive in horns, strings, fortissimo; motive developed among instruments, piano, slight crescendo, return to piano for further development
3:26					Strings and winds toss motive back and forth, crescendo to strings hammering on repeated note
3:44				2a	Horn call from theme 2 developed, with answer from low strings; reduced to 2–note fragment echoed between winds and strings; reduced to 1–note echo, suspense builds through diminuendo to pianissimo

Continued on next page

	4:18		b	Horn call erupts in full orchestra; 1–note echo resumes; basic motive repeated fortissimo, directly into:
		Recapitulation		
⑤	4:32	*Theme 1*	1a	Trumpets and timpani added for 2 statements of basic motive
	4:42		b	Motive through strings with countermelody in oboe, piano; three separated chords, oboe cadenza concludes countermelody on last chord
	5:05		c	Motive, piano, builds theme in strings; instruments gradually enter, crescendo, pitch rises; two separate chords, fortissimo
⑥	5:28	*Theme 2*	2a	Horn call (bassoon in some recordings), basic motive with extension, fortissimo
	5:31		b	Legato theme traded between violins and flute, basic motive in low strings; fragment of theme divided between strings and flute, crescendo in strings as other instruments gradually enter
	5:28	*Coda*	3a	Loud chord, strings in strong descending passage, repeated
	6:09		b	Basic motive descends in woodwinds answered by strings; repeated
⑦	6:13	*Second development*	4	Separate statements of motive extended fortissimo to hammer on repeated note, basic motive piano, repeated note forte, motive piano
	6:33			Horn call from theme 2 in cellos and violas, new countertheme in violins; repeated; countertheme vigorously developed, full orchestra
	7:00			Fragment of countertheme tossed between winds and strings; repeated note leads directly into:
⑧	7:26	*Second coda*	5a	Basic motive stated twice, fortissimo
	7:37		b	Piano, basic motive in strings; fortissimo, full orchestra states basic motive three times with final chords

Third Movement:		Allegro (fast)		
		Triple meter		
		Ternary form (scherzo and trio)		
Review:		Example 11.10 (two themes of scherzo)		
		Example 11.11 (two false starts, then opening of scherzo theme)		
		Example 11.12 (opening theme of fourth movement)		
11 ①	0:00	**Scherzo (A)**	a	Quiet, mysterious theme (minor key) rises from low strings, answered by high strings, pause; dialogue repeated
	0:22		b	Insistent, martial theme, forte, horns; orchestra extends theme, moves directly to:
	0:40		a	Mysterious theme with answer, pause; mysterious theme repeated and extended, with added oboe line, connects with:
			b	Bold theme, forte, orchestra, extended and moving directly to:

Continued on next page

1:21		a	Mysterious theme, low strings, answered by woodwinds, taken and developed mainly by strings; crescendo into:
		b	Bold theme, forte, orchestra; woodwinds provide quiet close
② 1:52	**Trio (B)**	c c	Rough, boisterous theme (major key) in basses and cellos, fugal imitations up through strings; repeated
2:24		c'	Two false starts, then boisterous theme with fugal imitations, extended to full orchestra, forte
2:52		c"	Two false starts, boisterous theme with fugal imitations, piano, extended and continues into woodwinds; transition cascades down through woodwinds to pizzicato bass strings
③ 3:24	**Scherzo (A')**	a'	Mysterious theme, low strings, answered by woodwinds, pause; mysterious theme, bassoon, answered by pizzicato strings
		b'	Insistent theme now pianissimo, more threatening, pizzicato strings and woodwinds
4:02		a'	Mysterious theme, pizzicato strings, shortened, overlaps into:
		b"	Insistent theme, pizzicato strings and woodwinds, with development; final statement with strings and bassoon echoes, cadences into:
④ 4:34	**Bridge**		Sustained pedal point in strings, timpani with short-short-short-long motive, pianissimo; turns to threatening repeated note; violins gradually unfold long melodic arch, based on mysterious theme; tension builds as melody pulls higher and higher; orchestra, crescendo
5:12			Triumphant, majestic opening theme of fourth movement

Listening Guide

BEETHOVEN: Piano Sonata op. 57 ("Appassionata")

First Movement: Allegro assai (rather fast)
Quadruple meter
Sonata form

Piano

Review: Example 11.17 (first theme)
Example 11.18 (second theme)
Examples 11.19–20–21 (use of extreme pitch ranges of piano)

CD 2 (Cassette 2/B, Track 4)

Exposition

12 (1)	0:00	*Theme 1*	1a	Ominous theme, pianissimo; repeated; four-note motive in bass; sudden loud "cadenza," long chord
	0:37		b	Ominous theme developed; alternating soft and loud fragments
	0:53	*Bridge*	2	Repeated-note accompaniment, fragments leap high and low; diminuendo
(2)	1:14	*Theme 2*	3	Sweet, flowing theme, piano; suddenly breaks off, trills, long descending scale
(3)	1:47	*Closing*	4a	Robust, powerful theme, forte
	2:06		b	Brilliant passage work descends, diminuendo, to held note

Development

(4)	2:19		1	Ominous theme fragmented, developed, sudden changes of register, dramatic interruptions
	3:18		2a	Repeated-note accompaniment and leaping fragments from bridge, extended development, crescendo
	3:50		b	Sudden piano, flowing second theme developed at length, shifting harmonies, gradual crescendo
	4:18		3a	Sudden loud arpeggios rise higher in pitch, then fall lower
	4:31		b	Insistent repetition of four-note motive

Recapitulation

(5)	4:42	*Theme 1*	1a	Ominous theme pianissimo, repeated-note accompaniment; four-note motive, sudden loud cadenza, long chord
	5:16		b	Ominous theme developed; alternating soft and loud fragments
	5:39	*Bridge*	2	Repeated-note accompaniment, fragments leap high and low; diminuendo
(6)	6:01	*Theme 2*	3	Sweet, flowing theme, piano; suddenly breaks off, trills, long descending scale
	6:35	*Coda*	4a	Robust, powerful theme, forte
	6:50		b	Brilliant passage work descends, diminuendo, smoothly into:
(7)	7:03	*Second development*	5a	Ominous first theme increasingly fragmented, pianissimo
	7:19		b	Flowing second theme developed, gradual crescendo
	7:33		6	Loud arpeggios erupt moving gradually higher; brilliant arpeggios sweep up and down the keyboard; four-note motive quietly
(8)	8:31	*Second coda*	7	Four-note motive fortissimo, faster tempo; ominous theme developed; fragments echo violently high and low; opening of ominous theme, piano, descends to quiet conclusion

SUMMARY

Ludwig van Beethoven expanded nearly every aspect of classical composition. His works are longer and larger in scale than those of his contemporaries and predecessors. Beethoven's compositions place great emphasis on developmental procedures and use such effects as dynamics to reach new heights of expressiveness. Beethoven often used a lively scherzo rather than a minuet in the third movement. This movement also becomes more important structurally in the overall work. Devices such as movements flowing together without a break and movements sharing the same thematic material were used by Beethoven to unify a work.

Improvements in instruments and instrumental techniques directly influence Beethoven's compositions. The orchestra had a larger number and greater variety of instruments, which reflects in Beethoven's masterful orchestrations. The piano developed into an instrument with a greater dynamic range and improved expressive qualities; Beethoven, a virtuoso pianist, fully exploited this new brilliance and power in his many piano works.

NEW TERMS

orchestration

SUGGESTED LISTENING

Beethoven, Ludwig van

Symphony no. 9 in D Minor op. 125. Perhaps the greatest symphony ever composed, this work remained a source of inspiration to subsequent composers throughout the nineteenth century. Its most striking innovation is the choral finale on Schiller's "Ode to Joy"; the three preceding movements are on an equally grand scale; the second is an immense scherzo built around a single rhythmic motive, and the third is a set of variations on a double theme.

Egmont Overture. This is part of the incidental music Beethoven wrote for Goethe's play *Egmont,* the story of a hero's struggle against tyranny. Enforcing Goethe's theme, Beethoven has written a strong musical statement for freedom and brotherhood. Although the play ends in tragedy, part of the overture is then repeated as a "Victory Symphony."

Violin Concerto in D. Often called Beethoven's most serene work, this was the longest and most symphonically organized concerto that had yet been written. The entire first movement grows from the first, simple motive: five taps of the timpani.

String Quartet in F Major op. 59, no. 1. The three string quartets of Beethoven's opus 59 were dedicated to the Russian ambassador to Vienna, Count Rasoumovsky. The quartets are, therefore, known as the *Rasoumovsky Quartets.* The count was an ardent chamber music player and often played second violin during chamber music evenings in his home.

Music of the Romantic Era

On the Seine at Bennecourt (Au bord de l'eau, Bennecourt), by Claude Monet, French (1840–1926). Oil on canvas, 1868, 81.5 × 100.7 cm. (Mr. & Mrs. Potter Palmer Collection, 1922.427. The Art Institute of Chicago. Photograph © 1992. All rights reserved.)

PRELUDE IV The Arts of the Romantic Era

Voltaire, the preeminent essayist of eighteenth-century France, held that feelings and passions were not significant in the discussion of existence and experience. He maintained that the world was intelligible only through reasoned, clear analysis. The romantics, led first by Rousseau, disagreed. Like the Spanish artist Francisco Goya, whose early nineteenth-century etching shows a sleeping man haunted by bats, owls, and other nocturnal apparitions (see page 245), they were often preoccupied with the irrational side of human nature. For them, "the sleep of reason produces monsters."

The term *romanticism* describes a school of thought that infused much of the philosophy, literature, and visual arts of the early nineteenth century.[1] The romantics were particularly drawn to "the exception to the rule." They were excited by the turbulence that followed the French Revolution in European politics. They were fascinated by the power of the individual, especially the man or woman of feelings, who dwelt in a private world of emotions and solitary dreams, and the hero, who represented the grandest possibilities of the individual. They searched for the exotic, the mysterious, and the unfamiliar. They were adventurers drawn to experience that affected their senses and stimulated their passions.

The romantics mused over landscape and nature. Great doubts about progress, civilization, and industrialization moved them from the salon to the field and hillside, where the delights of refined society were replaced by private reverie, melancholy introspection, and contemplation of the overwhelming heart. Landscape painting, which had been merely decorative backdrop to eighteenth-century portraits and aristocratic idylls, became independent and respectable subject matter. Writers sought inspiration in nature and found in its changes metaphors for their own moods and motions. For some romantics, like the poet Wordsworth, nature was elevated into a religion. Rejecting absolutely the Age of Reason, Wordsworth wrote:

> *One impulse from a vernal wood*
> *May teach you more of man,*
> *Of moral evil and of good,*
> *Than all the sages can.*
> *Sweet is the lore which Nature brings;*
> *Our middling intellect*
> *Misshapes the beauteous forms of things:*
> *We murder to dissect.*

---

1. Musical romanticism had a longer lifespan, extending across the entire century.

This romantic point of view has gained new currency in our own generation. For many, particularly those born after World War II, the romantic drive toward a harmonic reconnection of humankind and nature has fresh appeal in a world in which the individual seems progressively devalued.

The two greatest landscape painters of the early nineteenth century were John Constable (1776–1837) and J.M.W. Turner (1775–1851), both Englishmen unconstrained by the powerful influence of the neoclassical painter David. Constable was a realist who believed that accurate representation of nature was scientific as well as poetic. Unlike painters who drew their inspiration, color schemes, and compositions from old masters, Constable went to the countryside, where he made sketches of meadows, trees, and clouds that he later reworked in his studio (see page 246).

Turner was a very different kind of landscapist. His paintings celebrated the sublime, the elemental force of nature that overpowers man in the cosmos. His work, full of storms, wind, fire, and water, dramatically veiling concrete reality, is sometimes breathtaking in its dazzling color and advanced abstraction (see page 247).

The most radical painter in early nineteenth-century France was Eugène Delacroix (1799–1862), who rejected the neoclassical principles by which the artist was enjoined to imitate classical models and to subordinate color and brushstroke to composition and line. Delacroix painted in a free and colorful manner that sometimes makes his work indistinguishable from that of Rubens, whom Delacroix revered (see page 248).

Accordingly, some art historians have called the romantic style in French painting and sculpture a neobaroque movement.

Romantic writers, fascinated by the macabre and fantastical, depicted a world of the supernatural in works like Poe's "The Masque of the Red Death" and Walpole's *The Castle of Otranto.* These authors were especially drawn to outstanding individuals. It was an age that made Napoleon and Beethoven divine! In literature, a significant character type was the Byronic hero, who towered above ordinary human beings in his unique abilities and his capacity for feeling, especially suffering. The Byronic hero was driven by violent passions that were ultimately fatal to himself and others; nonetheless, mortals could not resist his powerful personality. Lord Byron himself introduced this figure in poems such as Childe Harold's *Pilgrimage* and *Don Juan.* In Emily Brönte's *Wuthering Heights,* he is personified in the brooding, tormented Heathcliff.

Romantic music displayed the features of the movement in special ways. As the couplets of Alexander Pope gave way to the musings of Keats and Shelley, the formal structures of classical music gave way to new emotionalism. Berlioz experimented with the different possibilities of musical instruments and greatly expanded the size of the orchestra. In his *Symphonie fantastique,* a young musician dreams that he is at a witches' sabbath attended by fearful monsters and grotesques, all awaiting his burial. In the Romantic era, musical virtuosos like Franz Liszt and Niccolò Paganini became international celebrities who attracted huge audiences by their extraordinary technical showmanship.

During the nineteenth century, there was a close relationship among all the arts. The romantic poetry of Byron and Goethe inspired the art of Delacroix, who likewise painted his friend Chopin. Franz Schubert was enchanted by the poetry of Schiller and created many beautiful songs from the texts of his lyric poems. Romanticism gave new life to opera, and the great German composer Richard Wagner envisioned opera as a fusion of all the arts.

Romanticism as a general movement was countered in the middle of the nineteenth century by the fashion of realism. Realism discarded the earlier movements of neoclassicism and romanticism on the grounds that both invented a world rather than reflecting the world in which people live. To the realists, the vulgar and commonplace were legitimate subjects for high art and literature; they despised what they called the sentimentality and mock heroism of earlier nineteenth-century art.

The high priest of realism in French art was Gustave Courbet (1818–1877), who, to the disgust or discomfort of the critical establishment in Paris, chose provocative subjects of peasants and common laborers (see page 249).

Charles Dickens and Émile Zola wrote about the brutal lives of the working class; Georges Bizet's opera *Carmen* tells the story of a girl who works in a cigarette factory.

Where romanticism had imagined a grander, more mysterious world beyond, realism sought factual truth. Realism presaged the material objectivity of the modern world, a world that has been liberated by the technological wonders of the applied sciences and engineering, but a world curiously uneasy in its wealth. Because the realist viewpoint is practical, it has had tremendous influence on the thinking of industrial society. Because romanticism has more feeling, it still has appeal to those who remained convinced that "the heart is the proper guide."

The Sleep of Reason Produces Monsters, by Francisco Goya,
1746–1828. (Vanni/Art Resource, N.Y.)

Stoke-by-Nayland, by John Constable, British, 1776–1837. Oil on canvas, 49½″ × 66½″. (Mr. and Mrs. W. W. Kimball Collection, 1922.4453. © 1991 The Art Institute of Chicago. All rights reserved.)

J. M. W. Turner's painting of a Swiss avalanche (*The Fall of an Avalanche in the Grisons,* 1810) is typical of his explosive, highly abstracted scenes that reflected the power of nature. His practice of painting light and atmosphere in patches of pure color anticipated the impressionists by about forty years. (The Clore Collection of The Tate Gallery, London/Art Resource, N.Y.)

Eugène Delacroix (French, 1798–1863), the leader of the French
Romantics, rejected the neoclassical style of David and instead used the
bright colors and forms of Rubens as his models. He was especially
attracted by action-packed scenes in exotic, foreign locales, as shown in
this late example, *The Lion Hunt* (1861), oil on canvas, 76.5 × 98.5 cm.
(© 1988 The Art Institute of Chicago; Potter Palmer Collection.
All rights reserved.)

The Stone Breakers, by Gustave Courbet, 1899. Oil on canvas, 5'3″ × 8'6″. (Gustave Courbet/Archiv/Photo Researchers, Inc.)

SONG AND PIANO MUSIC

12

The Romantic period in music roughly coincided with the nineteenth century. In some respects, it was a logical extension of the principles established during the Classical era. In other respects, however, it represented a fundamental departure from those principles. Even within the outlines of the basic musical structures of the Classical period—sonata-allegro form and theme and variations—formal balance and clarity of structure gave way to spontaneity, emotional depth, and richness, qualities foreshadowed in the later works of Beethoven. In addition, the Romantic era saw the classical forms abandoned altogether by some composers. Instead, there was a heavy reliance on literature, nature, visual images, and the supernatural as sources for musical inspiration and as frameworks for musical forms.

ROMANTIC INNOVATIONS

Romantic composers made some of their most remarkable achievements in harmony and tone color, and the harmonic vocabulary became increasingly rich during the nineteenth century. Chromatic harmonies, modulations to distant keys, and complicated chords all tended to blur the outlines of the harmonic system of major and minor keys. Harmony became as much a means of expression as an element of musical structure.

The romantic interest in tone color is shown by the phenomenal growth of the orchestra during this period. Instrumental color was regarded as an important element of music, on a par with melody, harmony, and rhythm. Instruments were improved, new ones were invented, new combinations were discovered, and the art of orchestration became a prime preoccupation for many composers of the age.

The Romantic period is often described as the age of the art song and the short piano piece (fig. 12.1), since these two genres constitute some of the most interesting musical literature of the nineteenth century. This fascination with the smaller forms is one of the two major aspects of the romantic spirit; the other aspect centered upon the larger forms, which offered greater scope in which to expand and develop. (We will discuss the larger forms in succeeding chapters of this unit.) These small pieces had an intimate quality, as though the composer were speaking directly to a small group of friends. The media that seemed most suitable to them were the piano and the solo voice.

Figure 12.1 The short piano piece was tremendously popular during the Romantic period. The social intimacy created by this smaller musical form is well illustrated by this romanticized painting entitled *A Schubert Evening in a Viennese Home.*

ART SONG

The **art song** is a musical setting of a poem for solo voice and piano. The German words **Lied** and **Lieder** (plural), which we previously encountered in chapter 6, became the standard terms for this type of song. The Lied became an important musical genre in the work of major composers early in the nineteenth century.

In the mid-eighteenth century, the Lied had been a simple song with keyboard accompaniment. The musical setting used **strophic form,** with the same melody repeated for every stanza (or strophe) of the poem. The text was treated syllabically (one note for each syllable), and the accompaniment served merely to support the singing voice.

Toward the end of the eighteenth century, the **ballad,** a narrative poem set to music, became popular in Germany. The ballad was long, emphasized dramatic situations, and alternated in structure between narration and dialogue. These characteristics required greater musical resources than the strophic procedure offered. Hence, the ballads were **through-composed;** that is, each section of the text had new music that was different from the music preceding and following.

Both the strophic and through-composed procedures were used in the nineteenth century Lied. The earliest and, in many respects, the most important Lieder composer was Franz Schubert.

SCHUBERT (1797–1828)

In many ways, the circumstances of Franz Peter Schubert's life were the very essence of the romantic's view of an artist's condition. During his brief and troubled lifetime, Schubert (fig. 12.2) lived in poverty and was unrecognized, except by a small circle of friends; only after his death was his genius more widely acknowledged. He was born in a suburb northwest of Vienna, the fourth surviving son of an industrious and pious schoolmaster. His formal musical training, never very systematic, began with violin lessons from his father and piano instruction from an older brother.

In 1808, at the age of eleven, Schubert obtained a place in the choir of the Imperial Court Chapel and was thereby privileged to attend the *Stadt-Konvict* (City Seminary), one of Vienna's most prestigious boarding schools. In addition to his regular studies and music lessons, he became a violinist in the school orchestra, later assuming the duties of conductor on various occasions. The numerous works he composed during these years at the *Konvict* include songs, overtures, religious works, an operetta (light opera), and six string quartets. His first symphony was written in 1813, the year he left the *Konvict,* and his first Mass was successfully performed in 1814.

After leaving the *Konvict,* Schubert returned home to live, first attending a training college for primary school teachers and then teaching at his father's school. The regimen of the classroom was not suited to his temperament, and in 1816 he applied for the musical directorship of the new State Normal School at Laibach (now Ljubljana in Yugoslavia), but was turned down.

Unable to find any other permanent employment at that time, Schubert resolved to earn his living by taking music students, selling his compositions, and writing for the theater. In 1817, he moved to Vienna.

During the early 1820s, performances of Schubert's solo songs and vocal quartets for male voices aroused considerable public interest, and his name became widely known throughout Vienna. Two of his operettas were produced with moderate success, and a number of songs and piano works were published. These successes were offset by his continuing inability to obtain a salaried position. In 1822, a serious illness, probably syphilis,

Figure 12.2 Franz Schubert. His Lieder exemplify the spontaneity and lyricism of the romantic movement.

necessitated a stay in the hospital and a prolonged period of recuperation. The following year, *Rosamunde,* a play with incidental music by Schubert, failed dismally, closing after only two performances. It was his last work for the theater.

The last four years of Schubert's life were a continual battle against ill health and poverty. Though his music, particularly the songs, continued to draw high praise from fellow musicians, including Beethoven, it was not until 1828 that a public concert of his works was given. He was unable to live on the pitifully small income from his music publications, but he continued to compose at a feverish pace. Despite his weakening health, he seemed at the height of his creative power. In the fall of 1828, Schubert became ill, and he died on November 19, at the age of thirty-one. His last wish, to be buried near Beethoven, was granted, and on his tombstone was written: "The art of music here entombed a rich possession but even far fairer hopes."

SCHUBERT'S WORK

During the seventeen years between 1811, when he was fourteen, and 1828, the year of his death, Schubert composed about one thousand works. They include nine symphonies, fifty chamber works and piano sonatas, a large number of short piano pieces, several operas and operettas, six Masses and about twenty-five other religious works, nearly one hundred choral compositions, and more than six hundred songs.

Schubert's symphonic style displays a romantic gift for lyric melody and a love of interesting patches of color and harmony. Nevertheless, his symphonies were written in the classical forms. His famous Symphony no. 8 in B Minor was written in 1822, when the composer was twenty-five years old, but he never chose to extend it beyond the original two movements. Nicknamed "The Unfinished," the work was not performed until 1865, forty-three years after his death.

Schubert is best known, however, for his abundant body of Lieder. He set to music the poetry of the great literary figures of his time, Goethe and Schiller among them. In addition to settings of individual poems, Schubert wrote two **song cycles** (a series of art songs that tell a story), *Die Schöne Müllerin* (*The Maid of the Mill,* 1823) and *Die Winterreise* (*Winter Journey,* 1827).

Schubert employed both the strophic form (with considerable flexibility) and through-composed forms with great imagination. His songs also reflected the supremacy of the poem as the generating force. The shape and quality of the melodic line, the choice of harmonic progressions, the rhythmic character of the work, and the entire structure were fashioned to serve the poem. And the piano accompaniment, now no longer a mere harmonic background for the voice, joined with the voice, virtually as a full partner, bringing to musical life the essence of the poem.

''GRETCHEN AM SPINNRADE''

One of the finest examples of the use of the piano is found in "Gretchen am Spinnrade" ("Gretchen at the Spinning Wheel"). Gretchen, who in Goethe's play has fallen in love with Faust, sings as she sits at her spinning wheel.

Gretchen am Spinnrade	Gretchen at the Spinning Wheel[1]
Meine Ruh ist hin,	*My peace is gone,*
Mein Herz ist schwer;	*my heart is heavy;*
Ich finde sie nimmer	*never, never again*
Und nimmermehr.	*Will I find rest.*
Wo ich ihn nicht hab;	*Where I am not with him*
Ist mir das Grab,	*I am in my grave,*
Die ganze Welt	*the whole world*
Ist mir vergällt.	*turns to bitter gall.*
Mein armer Kopf	*My poor head*
Ist mir verrückt,	*is in a whirl,*
Mein armer Sinn	*my poor thoughts*
Ist mir zerstückt.	*are all distracted.*

1. Gretchen am Spinnrade (Schubert) from *The Penguin Book of Lieder* by S. S. Prawer, editor and translator, 1964, London, p. 33. Copyright © 1964 S. S. Prawer. Reproduced by permission of Penguin Books Ltd.

Meine Ruh ist hin,
Mein Herz ist schwer,
Ich finde sie nimmer
Und nimmermehr.

Nach ihm nur schau' ich
Zum Fenster hinaus,
Nach ihm nur geh'ich
Aus dem Haus.
Sein hoher Gang,
Sein' edle Gestalt,
Seines Mundes Lächeln,
Seiner Augen Gewalt,
Und seiner Rede
Zauberfluss.
Sein Händedruck,
Und ach, sein Küss!

Meine Ruh ist hin,
Mein Herz ist schwer,
Ich finde sie nimmer
Und nimmermehr.

Mein Busen drängt
Sich nach ihm hin!
Ach drüft' ich fassen
Und halten ihn,
Und küssen ihn,
So wie ich wollt',

An seinen Küssen
Vergehen sollt'!

An seinen Küssen
Vergehen sollt'!

Meine Ruh ist hin,
Mein Herz ist schwer . . .

My peace is gone,
my heart is heavy;
never, never again
Will I find rest.

I seek only him when I look
out of the window,
I seek only him when I leave
the house.
His noble gait,
his fine stature,
the smile of his lips,
the power of his eyes,
and the magic flow
of his speech,
the pressure of his hand,
and oh, his kiss!

My peace is gone,
my heart is heavy;
never, never again
Will I find rest.

My bosom yearns
towards him.
If only I could seize him
and hold him
and kiss him
to my heart's content—

Under his kisses
I should die!

Under his kisses
I should die!

My peace is gone.
My heart is heavy. . . .

The piano accompaniment, which represents the spinning wheel, mirrors her growing agitation. As Gretchen conjures up her lover, a running sixteenth-note figure (the sound of the wheel) gradually intensifies. As the voice rises higher and higher, the sound of the whirling wheel crescendos, stops, and Gretchen cries out, *"und ach, sein Küss!"* ("and oh, his kiss"). Gretchen sits transfixed by her passion, as does the listener.

It is not the voice but the piano that tells us that Gretchen returns to her senses. The spinning motive in the piano (pianissimo) makes two false starts; then with the third, the song is in motion again, with the spinning reintroducing the voice on *"Meine Ruh ist hin"* ("My peace is gone").

The words *Meine Ruh ist hin* and their melody begin each verse and act as a unifying element throughout the song. Gretchen repeats these words once more at the end of the song in a sigh of resignation. As the sound of her voice fades away, the whirring of the piano's spinning motive closes the piece as it began.

''DIE FORELLE'' (1817)

The romantic love of nature is evident in "Die Forelle" ("The Trout"), one of Schubert's shorter Lieder. The poem concerns the struggle between a fish and a fisherman; typically, the romantic poet's sympathy lies with the fish.

Die Forelle	**The Trout[2]**
In einem Bächlein helle,	*In a bright little stream,*
Da schoss in froher Eil'	*in joyous haste,*
Die launische Forelle	*a playful trout*
Vorüber wie ein Pfeil.	*flashed past me like an arrow.*
Ich stand an dem Gestade	*I stood by the shore*
Und sah in süsser Ruh	*and in sweet contentment I watched*
Des muntern Fischleins Bade	*the little fish bathing*
Im klaren Bächlein zu.	*in the clear stream.*
Ein Fischer mit der Rute	*A fisherman with his rod*
Wohl an dem Ufer stand,	*stood on the bank*
Und sah's mit kaltem Blute,	*and coldly watched*
Wie sich das Fischlein wand.	*the trout's windings.*
So lang' dem Wasser Helle,	*So long as the water*
So dacht ich, nicht gebricht,	*—I thought—remains clear,*
So fängt er die Forelle	*he will not catch the trout*
Mit seiner Angel nicht.	*with his line.*

2. Die Forelle (Schubert) from *The Penguin Book of Lieder* by S. S. Prawer, editor and translator, 1964, London, p. 37.
    Copyright © 1964 S. S. Prawer. Reproduced by permission of Penguin Books Ltd.

Doch endlich ward dem Diebe	*But at last the thief*
Die Zeit zu lang. Er macht'	*grew impatient. He*
Das Bächlein tückisch trübe,	*treacherously dulled the clear stream,*
Und eh' ich es gedacht,	*and before I could think it*
So zuckte seine Rute,	*his rod quivered*
Das Fischlein zappelt' d'ran,	*and the fish was struggling on his hook.*
Und ich mit regem Blute	*I felt the blood stir within me*
Sah die Betrogne an.	*as I looked at the cheated trout.*

In form, "Die Forelle" is almost strophic. The first two verses have identical music: a simple melody with a very simple harmonic background. The accompaniment makes use of a short, rising figure that seems to sparkle and babble like a brook, conveying a mood of cheerful calm.

The third verse of the poem is much more excited, as the fish is caught. Schubert echoes this change of mood by putting aside the strophic form. The new melody is backed by a more agitated, more chromatic accompaniment. For the last two lines of the song, however, Schubert returns to the original melody and accompaniment. Although the text of the poem does not repeat the opening lines, the reappearance of the first melody rounds out the form of the song. In 1819, Schubert used this song as a basis for a set of variations in the Quintet in A Major (op. 114), the famous "Trout" Quintet for Piano and Four Strings.

"ERLKÖNIG"

SCHUBERT:
"Erlkönig"
Cassette 3/A, Track 2
CD 3, Track 2

While two of the Romantic period's favorite themes, nature and painful love, occupy "Die Forelle" and "Gretchen am Spinnrade," the supernatural is involved in Schubert's setting of "Erlkönig" ("King of the Elves"). The poem, a ballad by Goethe, tells the story of a father riding through a storm on horseback carrying his sick child in his arms (fig. 12.3). As they hurry through the stormy night, the delirious boy imagines that the Erlkönig (who symbolizes death) appears and tries to entice him away with promises of fine games and pleasures. When the father and son finally arrive home, the boy is dead in his arms.

The poem has four separate characters, all sung by one voice: the narrator, who introduces and closes the song, the frightened child, the frantic father, and the sinister Erlkönig.

Narrator

Wer reitet so spät durch Nacht und
    Wind?
Es ist der Vater mit seinem Kind;
Er hat den Knaben wohl in dem Arm
Er fasst ihn sicher, er hält ihn warm.

Narrator[3]

*Who rides so late through the night and
    the wind?*
It is the father with his child.
He holds the boy in his arm, grasps
him securely, keeps him warm.

Father

"Mein Sohn, was birgst du so bang dein
    Gesicht?"

Father

*"My son, why do you hide your face so
    anxiously?"*

---

3. Erlkönig (Schubert) from *The Penguin Book of Lieder* by S. S. Prawer, editor and translator, 1964, London, p. 34.
Copyright © 1964 S. S. Prawer. Reproduced by permission of Penguin Books Ltd.

Figure 12.3 Illustration of Goethe's poem "Erlkönig."

Son

"Siehst, Vater, du den Erlkönig nicht?
Den Erlenkönig mit Kron' und Schweif?"

Father

"Mein Sohn, es ist ein Nebelstreif."

Elf King

"Du liebes Kind, komm, geh' mit mir!
Gar schöne Spiele spiel' ich mit dir;
Manch' bunte Blumen sind an dem
    Strand,
Meine Mutter hat manch' gülden
    Gewand."

Son

"Mein Vater, mein Vater, und hörest du
    nicht,
Was Erlenkönig mir leise verspricht?"

Father

"Sei ruhig, bleibe ruhig, mein Kind:
In dürren Blättern säuselt der Wind."

Son

"Father, do you not see the Elf-King?
The Elf-King with his crown and train?"

Father

"My son, it is only a streak of mist."

Elf King

"Darling child, come away with me!
I will play fine games with you.
Many gay flowers grow by the shore:

my mother has many golden robes."

Son

"Father, father, do you not hear

what the Elf-King softly promises me?"

Father

"Be calm, dear child, be calm—
the wind is rustling in the dry leaves."

Elf King

"Willst, feiner Knabe, du mit mir gehn?

Meine Töchter sollen dich warten schön;
Meine Töchter führen den nächtlichen
    Reihn'
Und wiegen und tanzen und singen dich
    ein."

Son

"Mein Vater, mein Vater, und siehst
    du nicht dort
Erlkönigs Töchter am düstern Ort?"

Father

"Mein Sohn, mein Sohn, ich seh' es
    genau:
Es scheinen die alten Weiden so grau."

Elf King

"Ich liebe dich, mich reizt deine schöne
    Gestalt;
*Und bist du nicht willig, so brauch'
    ich Gewalt.*"

Son

"Mein Vater, mein Vater, jetzt fasst
    er mich an!
Erlkönig hat mir ein Leids gethan!"—

Narrator

Dem Vater grauset's, er reitet geschwind
Er hält in den Armen das ächzende Kind,
Erreicht den Hof mit Müh' und Not;

In seinen Armen das Kind—

                     war tot.

Elf King

*"You beautiful boy, will you come with
    me?
My daughters will wait upon you.
My daughters will lead the nightly
    round,
they will rock you, dance to you, sing you
    to sleep."*

Son

*"Father, father, do you not see
the Elf-King's daughters there, in
that dark place?"*

Father

*"My son, my son, I see it clearly:
it is the grey gleam of the old
willow-trees."*

Elf King

"I love you, your beauty allures me,

*and if you do not come willingly, I shall
    use force."*

Son

"Father, father, now he is seizing me!

The Elf-King has hurt me!"—

Narrator

*Fear grips the father, he rides swiftly,
holding the moaning child in his arms;
with effort and toil he reaches the
    house—
the child in his arms—*

                    was dead.

In form, "Erlkönig" is through-composed. As in "Gretchen am Spinnrade," the piano is a crucial element. It sets the atmosphere at the beginning: the wild wind, the galloping horse, and the anxiety of the father.

Example 12.1

The triplet figure in the right hand occurs in various forms throughout, sustaining the highly charged atmosphere until the final moments of the song. The figure in the left hand appears periodically to indicate the running horse and to unify the piece musically.

Schubert portrays the characters and sets them off from each other by a number of devices, particularly by manipulating the piano accompaniment. Whenever the Erlkönig enters, for example, the dynamic level drops to pianissimo, the accompaniment changes, and the vocal line becomes smooth and alluring.

Schubert reflects the son's mounting terror by repeating the same melodic material at successively higher pitch levels each time he cries out to his father. An upward leap on *"Mein Sohn"* and *"Sei ruhig"* marks the father's utterances that act as modulatory bridges linking the passages of child and Erlkönig.

The father's final statement ends with the strong drop of the interval of a fifth doubled by the left hand of the piano. The same figure recurs as the Erlkönig utters his last words as he seizes the boy,

Example 12.2

and is repeated once more in the boy's cry as he is taken in death.

Example 12.3

The last verse shows Schubert's sense of drama and the manipulation of the song's elements to heighten the emotional impact. The piano is silent as the narrator sings "the child in his arms," a single chord sounds, increasing the feeling of suspense, and the narrator concludes "was dead."

PIANO MUSIC

The piano, which had replaced the harpsichord as the basic keyboard instrument in the Classical era and was written for extensively by such composers as Mozart and Beethoven, increased in importance during the Romantic period. The huge body of romantic piano music falls into two broad categories; one consists of short, intimate, lyrical pieces similar in scope to Lieder, while the other includes larger, more brilliant exhibition pieces written for virtuoso performers. Virtually every major composer of the nineteenth century contributed to the piano repertory.

Three composers stand out as major contributors to the piano literature and the development of piano technique: Franz Liszt, Robert Schumann, and Frédéric Chopin.

FRANZ LISZT (1811–1886)

Pianist, conductor, and composer, the colorful personality of Franz Liszt made a great impact upon the musical society of his time. As a pianist, he overwhelmed the public with his brilliant virtuosity; as a conductor, he led the first performance of important new works such as Richard Wagner's opera *Lohengrin* in 1850; and as a composer, he made significant contributions to the symphonic and piano literature. His symphonic poem, *Les Préludes* (*The Preludes*), is still a part of the standard orchestral repertory (see chapter 14).

Liszt's piano music includes an enormous variety of forms and styles: variations on well-known symphonic works and brilliant showpieces, technical studies, and tone poems. The *Transcendental Études,* the *Hungarian Rhapsodies,* and *Liebestraum* (*Love Dream*), along with the Sonata in B Minor, were important contributions to the literature for solo piano. His works for piano and orchestra include two concertos, *Hungarian Fantasia* and *Totentanz* (*Dance of Death*), a large-scale paraphrase of the medieval funeral chant, the *Dies Irae.*

In his contributions to piano style and sonority, Liszt created a grander, more dramatic style that exploited the orchestral possibilities of the instrument and demanded enormous technical skill on the part of the performer.

ROBERT SCHUMANN (1810–1856)

Along with Chopin and Liszt, Robert Schumann (fig. 12.4) was one of the creators of modern piano technique. Almost all of his most popular and greatest works for piano date from his early years as a composer, up to 1840. They range from miniature **character pieces** (pieces portraying a single mood, emotion, or idea) whose titles establish them as wholly romantic—*Papillons* (*Butterflies*), *Carnaval, Kinderscenen* (*Scenes from Childhood*)—to large, classically oriented works such as the three piano sonatas, the Fantasy in C Minor, the Symphonic Études, and the Piano Concerto in A Minor. Schumann considered the *Fantasiestücke* (*Fantasy pieces*) to be among his best works for piano.

Much of Schumann's music was inspired by poetry, and the titles of his piano pieces are often derived from extramusical sources. His style is very free and flexible, almost kaleidoscopic, with rapid alternations between the characteristic romantic extremes of intimacy and brilliance.

Figure 12.4 Robert and Clara Wieck Schumann.

In addition to his works for piano, Schumann composed four symphonies, several song cycles of which *Dichterliebe* (*Poet's Love*) ranks with those of Schubert, a goodly amount of chamber music, and the oratorio *Das Paradies und die Peri* (*Paradise and the Peri*).

CLARA WIECK (1819–1896)

Clara Wieck married Robert Schumann in 1840 over the violent objections of her father. Clara had received extensive musical training in her youth and became widely recognized as a virtuoso pianist, including among her admirers Felix Mendelssohn, Frédéric Chopin, and Schumann, her future husband. She was an accomplished composer.

Clara's marriage to Schumann and the subsequent birth of eight children placed considerable limitations on her musical activities. Nevertheless, she continued to perform, teach, and compose, leaving behind a sizeable collection of songs, piano pieces, and chamber and orchestral works. After the death of Robert, she toured extensively as a pianist, championing the music of her husband and her close friend and companion, Johannes Brahms.

CHOPIN (1810–1849)

Frédéric Chopin (fig. 12.5) was one of the most creative and original composers in the history of music. Almost none of his mature works rely on traditional devices or forms; he created an entirely new musical idiom. His style is unique and easy to identify; every phrase is characteristically his. Chopin's art is inescapably linked to the sonority of the piano, the only possible means of expression for him. Although his life was marked by fame and the friendship of some of the greatest artists of the time, it ended in a mortal illness and an early death. When he died at the age of thirty-nine, he left behind him a literature for the piano unequaled before or since, and his critics, borrowing a character from Shakespeare's *The Tempest,* dubbed him the "Ariel of the piano."

Chopin was born near Warsaw on February 22, 1810, of a French father and a Polish mother. His father, Nicolas, had come to Poland to teach French to the sons of the Polish nobility, and it was in these surroundings that young Frédéric received his formal education. He studied piano at the Warsaw School of Music, showing an early

Figure 12.5 An engraving of Chopin.

talent for the instrument. He gave his first public concert at the age of seven. By the age of fifteen, he had already

CHOPIN'S WORK

Chopin wrote almost exclusively for the piano. His only major works that include orchestra are the Piano Concertos in F Minor and E Minor (Warsaw, 1830), written when he was twenty. These works still appear in the concert repertory.

The bulk of Chopin's music falls into one of four categories. The first consists of technical studies or **études.** Each of the études is built upon a single technical problem and usually develops a single musical motive. In many ways they summarize Chopin's conception of the technical possibilities of the piano. But they are more than mere exercises; they are also a series of miniature, abstract tone poems.

The second category consists of works composed in small, intimate forms, including preludes, waltzes, polonaises, and mazurkas. The influence of Polish melodies and rhythms on Chopin's style is most clearly demonstrated in the **polonaises** and **mazurkas.** These are Polish national dances in triple meter, with Slavic rhythmic patterns and folklike melodies.

published some compositions, and by nineteen, he had achieved eminence in both composition and performance. He traveled widely throughout Europe and was received enthusiastically wherever he played. So cordial was the reception at Chopin's first concert in Paris in 1831, that he decided to make that city his home and never again returned to Poland.

The public and his peers immediately recognized Chopin's genius, and he was in constant demand as a teacher and performer. He played frequently in Parisian salons, which had become the meeting places of the artists, musicians, and writers devoted to romanticism. His circle of friends included the writers Victor Hugo, Honoré de Balzac, and Alexandre Dumas; the composers Liszt, Berlioz, and Schumann; and the painter Delacroix. Reviewing some of Chopin's works, Schumann wrote that he was the "boldest and proudest poetic spirit of the time." His admirers were legion, and he was the recipient of almost fanatical acclaim.

Among the influential members of Parisian society was a woman novelist, Mme. Aurore Dudevant, who wrote under the name of George Sand. Through Liszt, Chopin met George Sand in 1837, when he was twenty-eight and she was thirty-four. It was a relationship that was to have a profound effect on his life, and though happy at first, their relationship became increasingly bitter. By the time Chopin developed tuberculosis in 1847, their once deep affection had deteriorated completely.

In 1848, with the full knowledge that he was in failing health, Chopin traveled to England and Scotland, where he stayed for seven months. There his concerts and strenuous activities sapped his fast-ebbing strength. Heartbroken over the bitterness that accompanied the conclusion of his relationship with George Sand, his energies exhausted, he returned to Paris, where he spent his remaining months. The funeral following his death on October 17, 1849, was attended by the elite of Paris society, artists as well as aristocrats; only Mme. Sand was absent from among the mourners. As a final gesture to his homeland, Chopin wished his heart to be returned to Poland, while his body was buried in Père Lachaise Cemetery in Paris.

The simple dance forms are frequently expanded into fantasies and tone poems. Chopin's most intimate pieces are the **nocturnes** (night pieces). These were character pieces of melancholy mood with expressive melodies sounding over an arpeggiated accompaniment.

The third category consists of works written in relatively large, free form. It includes scherzos, **ballades,** and fantasies. The ballades and scherzos demonstrate Chopin's ability to work within large-scale forms. He was apparently the first to employ the term *ballade* for an instrumental piece. All of his ballades are in 6/4 or 6/8 meter, and Chopin borrowed freely from the existing sonata-allegro, rondo, and song forms to create this new and epic genre. Good examples of these large-form works are the Ballade no. 1 in G Minor (opus 23, 1831) and the Ballade no. 2 in F Major (opus 38, 1836–1839). Chopin adopted the scherzo, a piece in 3/4 meter moving at a rapid tempo, from Beethoven.

Two other pieces stand in a category by themselves: the Fantaisie in F Minor (opus 49, 1840–1841) and the *Polonaise fantaisie* (opus 61, 1845–1846). These two pieces are among Chopin's most monumental works.

It is significant that, contrary to the prevailing fashion of the time, none of Chopin's pieces bears a fanciful, romantic title. Chopin, a master at creating expressive atmosphere and mood, resisted using programmatic elements in his pieces.

There are no real precedents for Chopin's works. His compositions depend on no large standard forms. His music is whimsical, elegant, and enchanting. In the large compositions, beautiful melodies and sparkling harmonies weave arbitrary, free-flowing forms. In both the smaller and larger works there is considerable repetition, often with just a touch of ornamentation to add interest to the repeat. Chopin's pieces give the illusion of being improvised (something every romantic composer longed to be able to do), but actually they are carefully and consciously constructed.

Chopin's music expresses sentiments ranging from melancholy to exultation, but he avoids empty virtuosity. The subtle qualities of his music are enhanced by the use of the performance technique called **rubato,** in which the melody is permitted to forge ahead or lag behind very slightly, while the accompaniment maintains a steady beat.

BALLADE NO. 1 IN G MINOR

CHOPIN: Ballade no. 1 in G Minor, op. 23
Cassette 3/A, Track 3
CD 3, Track 3
See Listening Guide on page 266.

This ballade is one of Chopin's larger works. The repetition of three themes forms the structure of the ballade. Chopin deliberately obscures the form by interspersing beautiful and lengthy episodes, transitions, and a coda between the statements of themes. The emphasis on nonstructural material, as well as the absence of pauses between the sections, reinforces the sense of continuity and the apparently free-flowing and evolving character of the work.

The piece opens with a short, improvisatory introduction; the subsequent first theme is a waltzlike melody in a minor key.

Example 12.4

A long transition section builds to a climax and then subsides to a quiet imitation of horn calls. Theme 2, in a major key, is soft and lyrical, with an accompaniment of slowly arpeggiated chords in the left hand.

Example 12.5

Theme 3 follows immediately, still very soft but in somewhat faster note values and with a triplet figure in the melody.

Example 12.6

Theme 1 returns, this time over a pedal point, and is stated much more dramatically; there are several sudden changes of dynamics. Eventually it builds up to a *forte* restatement of theme 2, with full chords in both hands. A very long episode follows, with brilliant passage work[4] and modulations; a long descending scale leads into another restatement of theme 2, still *forte,* and with a faster-moving accompaniment than before. Theme 3 follows again, this time *forte,* but grows quieter and introduces the final and abbreviated return of theme 1, again over a pedal point. The coda is long, fast, and full of scales and arpeggios, utilizing the full range of the piano.

4. Passage work refers to rapidly moving melodies using many notes.

Listening Guide

CHOPIN: Ballade no. 1 in G Minor

Single Movement: Largo; moderato; presto con fuoco (very slow; moderate; very fast, with fire)
Triple meter
Irregular alternating form: ABCABBCA

Piano

Review: Example 12.4 (first theme)
Example 12.5 (second theme)
Example 12.6 (third theme)

CD 3 (Cassette 3/A, Track 3)

③	①	0:00	**Introduction**	Thoughtful monophonic melody; soft chords
	②	0:32	A	Quiet, waltzlike theme; ends with cadenza-like rapid notes
		2:01	**Transition**	More rapid notes, quickly becomes agitated, loud; extended development; "horn calls" in left hand; intensity decreases; "horn calls" alone
	③	3:03	B	Tender, lyrical melody, pianissimo
	④	3:38	C	Faster rhythms in melody, with triplets, alternates with left-hand arpeggios
		4:12	A	Waltzlike theme, pianissimo, repeated note (pedal point) in bass; gradual crescendo into:
		4:43	B	Tender melody now passionate, fortissimo; ends with upward-surging scales, then downward-falling arpeggio
	⑤	5:16	**Episode**	Faster; begins pianissimo, gradual crescendo, fast passage work; extensively developed; pounding left-hand chords, fast notes build to high pitch, rapid downward scale
		6:01	B	Tender melody again passionate, fortissimo
		6:28	C	Triplet melody, accompanied by left-hand arpeggios; slowing, diminuendo
		7:01	A	Waltzlike theme, pianissimo, repeated note (pedal point) in bass; intensity builds to short descending scale
	⑥	7:42	**Coda**	Suddenly faster, passage work leaping from high to low, extended development, mounting tension; cadenza-like scales up, down, up again
		8:22		Quiet chords; loud fragment, rapid scale up; quiet chords; loud fragment; extreme high and low pitches approach each other, join in descending chromatic scale; closing cadence

SUMMARY

While classical musical forms were retained by some, many romantic composers drew their inspiration for the form and content of their works from literature and nature. A richer, expanded harmonic system and a preoccupation with instrumental color are hallmarks of the Romantic era.

The art song, in particular the Lied, attracted many romantic composers. In the Lied of Franz Schubert, the music is generated from and reflects the meaning of the text, and the piano accompaniment becomes the equal of the voice.

The piano, which was ideally suited to both the intimate and brilliant aspects of romanticism, was the favorite instrument of the period. The literature produced for the piano consisted of two main types: short, lyric pieces, similar in scope and feeling to the Lieder, and larger exhibition pieces written for virtuoso performers. Three composers in particular realized the capabilities of the piano and developed a new type of literature for it.

The piano music of Franz Liszt includes a variety of forms and styles. In these works he creates a grander, more dramatic style that exploits the orchestral possibilities of the piano and demands enormous technical skill of the pianist.

Robert Schumann wrote works ranging from miniature character pieces to large, classically oriented sonatas and concertos. His style was free and flexible, alternating between the romantic extremes of intimacy and brilliance.

Frédéric Chopin wrote almost exclusively for the piano. His work falls into three main categories, consisting of études, intimate forms, and large, free forms. With their rhapsodic melodies, his pieces often give the illusion of being improvised, but were actually very carefully constructed.

NEW TERMS

art song
Lied (Lieder)
strophic form
ballad (vocal)
through-composed
song cycle
character piece

étude
polonaise
mazurka
nocturne
ballade (instrumental)
rubato

SUGGESTED LISTENING

Chopin, Frédéric

Piano Études, op. 25. The second set of twelve studies, each concentrating on a specific feature of piano technique.

Liszt, Franz

Hungarian Rhapsody, no. 2. Liszt began to love "gypsy music" as a boy and later studied it exhaustively. His *Hungarian Rhapsodies* combine traits of gypsy music with virtuoso piano style.

Schubert, Franz

Die Winterreise (*Winter Journey*). A cycle of twenty-four songs on the general theme of loneliness. One of the great song cycles. "Gretchen am Spinnrade" ("Gretchen at the Spinning Wheel"), see pages 253–255; "Die Forelle" ("The Trout"), see pages 255–256.

Schumann, Robert

Carnaval, op. 9. This work consists of twenty short piano pieces. Some describe a carnival (clowns, sphinxes); others relate to Schumann's friends, such as Chopin and Clara Wieck.

THE ROMANTIC TRADITIONALISTS

A mong romantic composers, attitudes toward the classical forms developed by Haydn and Mozart and expanded by Beethoven vary considerably. As we shall see in later chapters, some of the more radical composers abandoned these traditions altogether, turning instead to other sources of inspiration and organization.

At the same time, a stream of classical tradition continued to flow through the Romantic period, as a number of composers cultivated and expanded the traditional forms. In doing so, they utilized elements from both the Classical and the Romantic eras. Though essentially classical in broad design, their works were richly endowed with romantic harmonies, color, dynamics, and orchestration. The leading composers in this group were Franz Schubert, Felix Mendelssohn, Johannes Brahms, and the Russian Peter Ilyich Tchaikovsky.

THE ROMANTIC SYMPHONY

The romantic symphony grew in the shadow of Beethoven's symphonic writing. Virtually all the early romantic composers were affected by Beethoven's music, some by his use of the orchestra, others by his expansion of form.

Early in the Romantic period, the symphonic writing of Franz Schubert was influenced first by Haydn and Mozart and finally by Beethoven. Schubert's last two symphonies, "The Unfinished" Symphony (1822) and the big C Major (1828), take a place along with those of Beethoven in the repertoire.

If Schubert was the outstanding symphonist of the beginning of the Romantic period, Johannes Brahms deserves that honor for the latter part of the century. Brahms occupies a unique place in the history of the romantic movement. Although he was much admired by his contemporaries, he had no wish to seek new forms of musical expression and new sources of musical inspiration. He disagreed with the popular romantic notion—championed by more radical composers such as Berlioz and Wagner—that literature, the visual arts, and philosophy should be united with music. In a period of experimentation and change, he looked back to Beethoven and the Classical era, finding in traditional forms new and worthwhile ideas to express.

BRAHMS (1833–1897)

Born and raised in Hamburg, Johannes Brahms (fig. 13.1) received his earliest musical training from his father, a double-bass player. The family was not wealthy, and at an early age, Brahms had to contribute to the family income by playing the piano in local taverns. At the age of twenty, he met the famed Hungarian violinist Eduard Reményi and toured Germany as Reményi's accompanist. On one of his tours, his first attempts at composition were heard by Joseph Joachim, the foremost violin virtuoso of the time. Through Joachim, Brahms was introduced to Franz Liszt and Robert Schumann, who were both greatly impressed by the young composer. Schumann, always eager to do what he could to advance the career of young, promising composers, wrote a laudatory article heralding Brahms as the coming genius of German music.

Schumann and his wife Clara welcomed Brahms into their home. After Schumann suffered a mental collapse, the devoted friendship of Brahms enabled Clara to survive the tragedy of her husband's illness. Their friendship grew to love even though she was fourteen years Brahms's senior. When Schumann died in a Bonn asylum, Brahms was at Clara's side. After Schumann's death, however, the passion subsided into a lifelong friendship.

In his thirties, Brahms took several posts in various German towns, conducting and organizing choral groups and music societies. He spent much of his time in Vienna, finally settling there in 1878. His reputation as a composer grew to international proportions, and in 1878 Cambridge University offered him the degree of Doctor of Music. He declined, being reluctant to make the long journey, but he accepted a similar honor from the University of Breslau, acknowledging it by writing the celebrated *Academic Festival Overture,* which is based in large part on popular German student songs.

Brahms was not a controversial figure, as so many of his contemporaries were, and he had no enemies. Yet, in his dealings with others, his characteristic charm could give way to the most acerbic sarcasm. To one musician who was trying to maneuver Brahms into paying him a compliment, he said, "Yes, you have talent, but very

Figure 13.1 Johannes Brahms.

little." But when the daughter of Johann Strauss (the "Waltz King" of Vienna) presented him with her fan so that he might autograph it, he wrote on it the first few measures of Strauss's *Blue Danube Waltz* and signed it, "Not, alas, by Johannes Brahms."

Brahms remained a bachelor all his life, living simply and composing methodically. He enjoyed the respect and admiration of his peers, inspiring the noted conductor Hans von Bülow to coin his famous phrase, "the Three B's of Music," which placed Brahms on the same level of genius as Bach and Beethoven. After his death, his fame grew, as many societies were founded to publish and perform his works. In the concert repertoire, Brahms's symphonies occupy a place second only to that of his acknowledged master, Beethoven.

BRAHMS'S WORK

With few exceptions, Brahms composed in all the familiar instrumental and choral idioms of the nineteenth century. He was a careful and disciplined composer who frequently revised his earlier works.

Brahms did not attempt to compose symphonies until quite late in his life. His first symphony (in C minor) took him twenty-one years to write and was not finished until 1876. Three others followed during the next nine years: no. 2 (in D major, 1877), no. 3 (in F major, 1883), and no. 4 (in E minor, 1884–1885). These works remain some of the most frequently performed symphonies in modern times.

Brahms's masterful symphonic style was developed through the composition of serenades, concertos, and overtures. His first orchestral composition was a Serenade in D Major (1857–1858), followed by his first piano concerto (in D minor, 1858). His other concertos include the renowned Violin Concerto in D Major (1878), the second piano concerto (in B-flat major, 1878–1881), and the Double Concerto in A Minor for violin and cello (1887). His overtures include the *Academic Festival Overture* (1880) and the *Tragic Overture* (1880–1881). Falling into none of these categories is the very popular *Variations on a Theme by Haydn* (1873).

Choral music, both sacred and secular, attracted Brahms throughout his career. His *Ein Deutsches Requiem* (*A German Requiem,* 1857–1868), discussed in chapter 16, ranks as one of the choral masterpieces of the nineteenth century.

Brahms's contributions to chamber music repertory were the most substantial of those made by any nineteenth-century composer after Beethoven. Among them are duos, trios, quartets, and quintets for a variety of instrumental combinations. His piano works reveal a mastery of contrapuntal texture and require virtuoso performance technique. They include variations on themes by Schumann, Paganini, and Handel; three sonatas; and a number of short lyric pieces, including ballades, rhapsodies, fantasies, and intermezzi.

SYMPHONIC STYLE

Brahms retained the traditional four-movement structure of the late classical symphony: fast-slow-scherzolike-fast. In many ways, his style is a direct outgrowth of the symphonic style of Beethoven. He continued to expand sonata-allegro form, enlarge the orchestra, and use dynamics and sonorities as structural elements.

Brahms's use of sonata-allegro form involves some changes, primarily in the treatment of the bridge section and the coda. The bridge becomes much more important; its material often sounds like a genuine theme, and it is often difficult to distinguish between the bridge and the second theme on first hearing. The first and second themes are still contrasted in the classical manner, but there is often no obvious separation (such as a rest) between them.

The beginning of the recapitulation is sometimes obscure because Brahms tends to lead into it unobtrusively; frequently, the exposition material reappears with different instrumentation, a device Beethoven used. The coda is extended, as in Beethoven's works, and often used as a second development section. In contrast to Beethoven, however, Brahms often ends movements very quietly.

One of Brahms's favorite structural devices is to build new themes out of short motives taken from earlier material. This brings an additional element of unity to a movement, beyond that provided by sonata-allegro form. Brahms often incorporates the motive into themes in a subtle way, and it appears in many rhythmic variations.

Brahms uses a larger orchestra than Beethoven but one that is much smaller than that used by Berlioz in the colossal works described in chapter 14. His orchestra consisted of two flutes, two oboes, two clarinets, two bassoons, four horns, two trumpets, three trombones, tuba, timpani, and strings. In his use of the orchestra, the lower strings, woodwinds, and brasses are given important roles. Timpani are often treated independently from the brass instruments and even have solo passages.

SYMPHONY NO. 2 IN D MAJOR

His second symphony beautifully illustrates Brahms's symphonic skill and expressiveness.

The symphony conforms to the basic sonata outline of the classical tradition. It has four movements in the traditional fast-slow-scherzolike-fast pattern. The first and last movements are in D major; the middle movements are in contrasting keys.

First Movement (Allegro non troppo)

The standard outlines of sonata form we encountered in the works of Mozart, Haydn, and Beethoven are clearly evident in this movement, with its exposition (repeated), development, and recapitulation. Brahms also uses a short motive to unify the thematic material.

BRAHMS: Symphony no. 2 in D Major, Movement I
Cassette 3/B, Track 1
CD 3, Track 4
See Listening Guide on pages 288–289.

Example 13.1

Theme 1 is divided between groups of instruments. It begins with the basic three-note motive in the cellos and basses, and continues first in the horns and bassoons and then in the upper winds.

Example 13.2

It is typical of Brahms to dispense a theme among several instruments or instrumental groups. Their instrumental colors become part of the character of the theme itself, and thus the theme can be effectively varied by changing its instrumentation.

The second theme, which is longer than the first theme and the bridge combined, consists of sharply contrasting thematic materials in an ABA form. The A section is flowing and serene, only at the end increasing in volume with a crescendo that introduces the second section (B), which is loud, vigorous, and rhythmically complex. At its conclusion there is an abrupt and unexpected return to the calmer A section, followed by a short codetta, ending the exposition that Brahms indicates should be repeated.

Development

The development section concentrates on materials drawn from the first theme and the bridge. In it Brahms applies all the technical and dramatic tricks of the development trade: frequent modulation to a great variety of keys; fragmented themes; expanded motives; inverted (turned upside-down) melodic elements; polyphonic treatment of themes; and dramatic changes in volume, articulation, and orchestral color. All of these elements produce the dramatic tension characterized by the developmental process.

Toward the end of the section, Brahms plays a "trick" on his listeners by introducing what at first appears to be the recapitulation, but it is a **false recapitulation** and goes on to more development that prepares the way for the genuine recapitulation.

Recapitulation

In typical romantic fashion, Brahms produces a recapitulation section that is *not* an exact replica of the exposition. The character of the music is altered in a variety of ways. The first theme is reorchestrated, and the bridge is quite different from that found in the exposition. Only the second theme, with its ABA structure, is more or less intact.

While Beethoven habitually used the coda for further *development* of the movements' thematic materials, Brahms often introduced *new* themes in the coda. Such is the case with the first movement of this symphony, the coda of which includes two very beautiful new themes—one for horn (example 13.3).

Example 13.3

The other theme is played by the first violins accompanied by the original basic motive in the bass:

Example 13.4

The quiet intensity of these themes enriches the movement.

Second Movement (Adagio non troppo)

The second movement is a wonderful example of romantic symphonic lyricism, of which Brahms was a master. In character, it provides the kind of contrasts traditionally expected of a second movement; it is slower in tempo and in a contrasting key. However, in terms of structure, it follows no standard formal procedure, such as sonata form, or theme and variations. Instead, it is rather freely based upon the principle of contrasting themes and the development process.

A long, flowing melody played by cellos (A) begins the movement.

Example 13.5

The horn begins theme B, which is treated polyphonically, with imitative entrances of the melody in the oboe, flute, and cello following the horn.

The winds and strings alternate in presenting theme C with its prevailing syncopated triplet pattern.

Example 13.6

And finally, the intensely expressive theme D,

Example 13.7

with its push into a stretch of music given over to the development of themes A, C, and D. A short coda based on material from theme A provides a quiet conclusion.

Third Movement (Allegretto grazioso— Presto ma non troppo)

With this movement, Brahms has cleverly produced a kind of cross between the minuet of the earlier classical symphony and the scherzo of Beethoven. It is organized into a five-part alternating form:

A B A C A

and the sections are clearly distinguished by marked changes in meter and tempo. This movement is further offset from the rest of the symphony by the fact that Brahms employs a reduced orchestra, leaving out trumpets, trombones, tuba, and timpani.

Fourth Movement (Allegro con spirito)

The final movement of the Second Symphony is one of the most confident and jubilant movements Brahms ever wrote. It returns to the key of D major, its tempo is fast, and the full orchestra is brought back into play. Sonata-allegro form is followed, and the contrast between the two major themes is striking—the first is brisk and sparkling—the second is lyrical and expressive.

Both themes and the bridge make subtle use of the three-note basic motive from the first movement, thereby providing an added degree of unity to the entire work. This desire to make a single entity out of a multimovement work is typical of much romantic music. After a rather straightforward development and recapitulation, a long coda ends with a great, crashing finale in which the horns and trumpets play a stirring version of the second theme.

OTHER ROMANTIC SYMPHONISTS

ANTON BRUCKNER

Anton Bruckner (1824–1896), an Austrian composer and organist, joined Brahms in the effort to retain classical forms within an expanded harmonic and structural framework. Bruckner was a simple and very religious man, deeply involved with Catholic mysticism. Symphonic in technique, his three Masses are of sufficient caliber to rank Bruckner as the most important church composer of the late nineteenth century.

Bruckner's nine symphonies show his kinship to classical tradition in their formal design, but their exceptional length and weighty orchestration mark them as romantic works. Wagner was one of Bruckner's idols, and Bruckner's emphasis on chromatic tones and shifting tonalities shows Wagner's influence. Bruckner, in turn, influenced later composers in his native Vienna, particularly Mahler and Schoenberg.

GUSTAV MAHLER

The Austrian Gustav Mahler (1860–1911) was a conductor as well as a symphonic composer. His nine completed symphonies are immense and complex, and encompass a vast emotional range. Although the symphonies follow the classical outline and have separate movements, their style incorporates many elements from vocal music, including opera. His symphonies contain long, lyrical melodies, often treated contrapuntally; four of them have parts for voices as well as instruments. Mahler's works span the spectrum of emotions, from ecstasy to despair. He tried to make each symphony a complete world in itself, with all types of themes and techniques. These large-scale works are unified, to some extent, by the use of recurring themes and motives.

Mahler is also famous for his songs and song cycles; the *Kindertotenlieder* (*Songs on the Death of Children,* 1902) and *Das Lied von der Erde* (*The Song of the Earth,* 1908) are particularly outstanding. Themes from the songs are often quoted in the symphonic works. Mahler's last works—the Ninth Symphony, the unfinished Tenth, and *Das Lied von der Erde*—are in a more contrapuntal style than his earlier compositions. They also show a weaker sense of tonality and thus point toward the important developments in atonal music in the early twentieth century.

Figure 13.2 Niccolò Paganini's unusual appearance—he was tall, pencil-thin, and habitually dressed in black—combined with his unearthly virtuosity, gave rise to rumors that his violin was the devil's consort and that the phenomenal Italian violinist was the devil himself. The German poet Heine called him "a vampire with a violin."

THE ROMANTIC CONCERTO

As we pointed out in chapter 12, romantic audiences were dazzled by exhibitions of virtuosity. All through the Romantic era there was a steady growth of virtuoso technique, particularly on the piano and the violin. The trend was begun by Beethoven, whose works were considerably more difficult to play than Mozart's. It was spurred on in 1820 by the arrival on the European concert stage of Niccolò Paganini (1782–1840); this phenomenal Italian violinist astounded and enchanted all who heard him by the incredible speed and brilliance of his playing (fig. 13.2).

The concerto for solo instrument and orchestra, with the improvised quality of its cadenza section, lent itself especially well to displays of technical skill. Composers wrote very difficult solo parts in their concertos. Unfortunately, many second-rate romantic composers mistook virtuosity for substance; thus, the majority of romantic concertos were either pleasant pieces or bombastic tirades, full of technical acrobatics but essentially meaningless.

The master composers of the period, however, joined virtuoso technique to lyric and expressive writing. Robert Schumann, Johannes Brahms, Felix Mendelssohn, and Peter Ilyich Tchaikovsky all wrote outstanding concertos.

MENDELSSOHN (1809–1847)

Unlike most of the great composers of his generation, Felix Mendelssohn (fig. 13.3) not only achieved artistic success but also lived a life of relative ease and financial security. Born into a wealthy and cultured Jewish family—his father was a banker, his grandfather, Moses Mendelssohn, a distinguished philosopher—he and his brother and two sisters were brought up as Christians. The remarkable musical abilities of Felix and his elder sister Fanny were quickly recognized by the children's mother, Leah, who began teaching the children piano when they were quite young. After the family moved to Berlin in 1812, Felix and Fanny's formal musical training was entrusted to Carl Zelter, an eminent composer, teacher, and head of the famous *Singakademie*.

The Mendelssohn home was the meeting place for musicians and poets at which concerts of chamber music were organized and directed by Leah Mendelssohn. Felix and Fanny's earliest compositions were performed at these musicales.

By 1821, Felix had composed trios, quartets, sonatas, and operettas. His debut as a concert pianist had been made even earlier—at the age of nine—and he mastered both violin and viola while still in his teens. The first striking demonstration of Felix's genius as a composer was the overture to Shakespeare's *A Midsummer Night's Dream,* written in 1826 when he was seventeen. Three years later, he made his mark as a conductor when he revived J. S. Bach's *St. Matthew Passion.* This performance of the Passion, a great triumph for Mendelssohn, was the first given since Bach's death almost eighty years earlier and began a wide-scale revival of Bach's music.

Early in the 1830s, Mendelssohn traveled extensively throughout Europe. He conducted his concert overture *Fingal's Cave (The Hebrides)* in London and met Hector Berlioz in Italy. Returning to Berlin in 1833, Mendelssohn decided to seek a permanent post and applied for the directorship of the *Singakademie.* He was turned down—one of his few failures—but in the same year he was asked to become town musical director and conductor at Düsseldorf. Two years later, he accepted

Figure 13.3   A child prodigy, Mendelssohn made his debut as a concert pianist at the age of nine. His magical concert overture *A Midsummer Night's Dream* was written when he was seventeen.

an offer to become conductor of the famous *Gewandhaus* Orchestra in Leipzig.

In 1837, Mendelssohn married Cécile Jeanrenaud, the daughter of a French Protestant clergyman. In 1841, they moved to Berlin where, at the request of Kaiser Friedrich Wilhelm IV, Mendelssohn took charge of the music division of the newly established Academy of Arts. The position did not require close supervision, and he was able to develop his plans for a conservatory at Leipzig. In 1843, the conservatory opened with a distinguished faculty in residence, and several years later, Mendelssohn moved his family back to Leipzig.

Though his health began to deteriorate after 1846, Mendelssohn continued to immerse himself in his work. The death of Fanny, to whom he was deeply attached, was a major shock. Falling into a severe depression, he soon became bedridden and died in Leipzig at the age of thirty-eight.

MENDELSSOHN'S WORK

Despite his relatively short life, Mendelssohn produced many works, ranging from large-scale symphonies and oratorios to intimate chamber works and Lieder. His first published symphony (in C minor, 1824) was actually the thirteenth he had written. Of the four symphonies that still remain, one—apparently influenced by Beethoven's Ninth—is for chorus and orchestra, entitled *Lobgesang* (*Hymn of Praise*, 1840). The others are descriptive: no. 3 (*Scottish*, 1830–1842), no. 4 (*Italian*, 1833), and no. 5 (*Reformation*, 1830–1842). His imaginative and original *concert overtures* (see page 283) include *A Midsummer Night's Dream* (1826), *Calm Sea and Prosperous Voyage* (1830–1832), *Fingal's Cave* (*The Hebrides*, 1830–1832), and the overture to Victor Hugo's play *Ruy Blas* (1839).

Along with these major orchestral works, Mendelssohn composed many chamber pieces, the octet for strings (opus 20, 1825) being one of his most original and delightful works.

Mendelssohn's long-standing appreciation of Bach's music shows up in his several collections of preludes and fugues for piano. The bulk of his piano music, however, consists of short character pieces in a highly romantic vein. The most popular of these are the eight collections of *Songs Without Words*, published between 1829 and 1845. His finest large-scale work for piano is the *Variations sérieuses* (opus 54, 1841).

Although he composed many religious works and an equally substantial number of art songs, Mendelssohn's reputation as a vocal composer rests on his two oratorios, *St. Paul* (1836) and *Elijah* (1846). In them, Mendelssohn incorporated elements of Bach's Passion style and Handel's oratorio form. They are generally considered the most successful nineteenth-century works of their kind.

Many of Mendelssohn's later works, composed in the 1840s, appear to be somewhat uninspired. In one work, however, he fully recaptured the magical verve of the *Midsummer Night's Dream* overture: The incidental music he wrote for the same play in 1842, including the famous "Wedding March," stands as a fitting companion to his youthful masterpiece. And one of his greatest concertos is the Violin Concerto in E Minor (opus 64, 1844).

VIOLIN CONCERTO IN E MINOR

Mendelssohn's violin concerto retains the fast-slow-fast movement structure of the classical concerto except for the fact that there is no definite break between the first and second movements. The work is scored for solo violin and orchestra of modest proportions, consisting of two flutes, two oboes, two clarinets, two bassoons, two horns, two trumpets, timpani, and strings.

First Movement (Allegro molto appassionato)

Exposition
The first movement is in sonata form but does not include the orchestral introduction involved in the classical double exposition. Rather, after only a few measures of orchestral introduction, the violin enters with a statement of the first theme, in which the violin is prominent against an unobtrusive orchestral accompaniment (example 13.8).

Example 13.8

Allegro molto appassionata

The bridge is quite long and provides for considerable display of violinistic virtuosity in the midst of modulating to G major for the statement of the second theme.

The theme is introduced by the winds and then taken up and extended by the solo violin.

Example 13.9

Violin solo

pp tranquillo

Here again, Mendelssohn is careful to maintain a careful balance between the solo instrument and the orchestra so that the expressive violin melody is foremost in the listener's mind.

Development

Much of the development section is characterized by orchestral statements of parts of the first theme against brilliant and rapidly moving violin figurations. Of particular interest is the placement of the cadenza and its relationship to the development and recapitulation. In essence, the cadenza grows out of the development and blends into the beginning of the recapitulation where the orchestra begins the first theme while the violin continues to play the material of the cadenza.

Example 13.10

Solo Violin   End of Cadenza   Recapitulation

1st Violin, Oboe, Flute

The dramatic division between development and cadenza, and cadenza and recapitulation found in the classical tradition are thereby blurred, and the music takes on a more continuous character.

Recapitulation

The bridge in the recapitulation is divided between orchestra and solo instrument (in that order) and modulates to E major, in which the second theme appears in an expanded version. What follows is a rather long coda very reminiscent of Beethoven in that it contains an additional development of the first theme.

The end of the coda is characterized by an increase in tempo leading to the dramatic end of a well-crafted piece of music.

Second Movement (Andante)

The first movement appears to end but doesn't—not really. A single note from the final chord played by the bassoon "hangs over" and forms a suspenseful link to the next movement.

The slow movement is in the key of C major and is a three-part alternating form—ABA—with coda.

Section A consists of a beautifully spun melody for the solo violin with quiet support provided by the strings.

Example 13.11

In section B, the orchestra and solo instrument alternate in stating phrases of the new thematic material. This section includes a good deal of modulation through a variety of keys, eventually returning to C major for the return of section A. As is often the case in romantic music, this is not a literal repetition of the initial material. Rather, the theme is rearranged and shortened and leads to a short coda, drawing a compact and expressive movement to a close.

Third Movement (Allegro non troppo— allegro molto vivace)

Introduction

The use of a short, slow introduction preceding a sonata form movement was a frequent occurrence in the Classical period, and Mendelssohn uses it in the final movement of this concerto. This introductory section for solo violin and strings also serves the purpose of modulating from C major, the key of the second movement, to E major for the last movement.

Exposition

The beginning of the last movement proper retains an introductory flavor in which the orchestra and solo violin alternate in leading to the first theme (example 13.12).

MENDELSSOHN:
Violin Concerto
in E Minor, op. 64,
Third Movement
Cassette 3/A, Track 4
CD 3, Track 5
*See Listening Guide
on page 290.*

Example 13.12

After a bridge based upon elements of the first theme, the orchestra introduces the second theme, which is then taken up by the solo violin.

Example 13.13

Development

The design of the first part of this development section is similar to that found in the first movement—against a light orchestral background consisting of fragments of theme 2, the solo violin executes brilliant solo passages.

New thematic material not found in the exposition is introduced by the violin,

Example 13.14

and is taken up by the orchestra while the violin develops the thematic material leading to the recapitulation.

Recapitulation

The first and second themes are linked by a shortened bridge. The second theme leads to a new development section followed by a coda to bring the movement to a close, resulting in the overall form:

Slow Intro   Exposition   Development   Recapitulation   Development   Coda

Throughout this concerto, Mendelssohn maintains a good balance between virtuosity and musical substance, integrating those elements into a musical work of enduring value and popularity among performers and audience alike.

CONCERT OVERTURE

Prior to the nineteenth century, the overture had been an instrumental piece that functioned as an introduction to a longer musical work (such as an opera or oratorio) or, in some instances, as "incidental music" to spoken drama. Although this type of overture continued to be written during the nineteenth century, the Romantic period gave rise to a new type of overture, one that was not an introduction to something else. The **concert overture** was a one-movement, self-contained musical work intended for performance in the concert hall. As such, it took its place alongside the symphony and the concerto as one of the major symphonic forms of the period.

Some concert overtures were written for specific festive occasions. Beethoven's *Consecration of the House* is one such work. Others, such as Mendelssohn's *Hebrides Overture,* attempted to evoke some aspect of nature. And still others, including Brahms's *Tragic Overture,* expressed a generalized mood or human condition.

Many concert overtures have programmatic and descriptive elements and in some respects resemble the symphonic poem (see chapter 14). But unlike the symphonic poem, the concert overture retains the strong musical organization embodied in sonata-allegro form. In this respect, the concert overture is much like the first movement of a symphony, except that it is complete in itself.

One of the most popular concert overtures written during the Romantic era, *Romeo and Juliet,* was composed by the Russian Peter Ilyich Tchaikovsky. During the Romantic period there were two schools of musical thought in Russia. The nationalists (who will be discussed in chapter 15) attempted to create a music that was totally Russian in character and style. The cosmopolitans, on the other hand, looked to the Western European tradition for their inspiration, and composed in the general romantic style. Tchaikovsky was the outstanding composer of the cosmopolitan school and the first Russian composer to gain an international reputation.

TCHAIKOVSKY (1840–1893)

Born in Votkinsk, in a remote province of Russia, Peter Ilyich Tchaikovsky (fig. 13.4) received his earliest musical training from a French governess. When he was ten, his family moved to St. Petersburg, where he was enrolled in a school of jurisprudence. Upon graduation at the age of nineteen, he became a government clerk but soon decided to pursue a musical career. He was accepted at the age of twenty-one to the newly established St. Petersburg Conservatory, where he began serious composition under Anton Rubinstein (1829–1894), the institution's founder and an eminent pianist and composer.

He graduated in 1865, winning a gold medal for a cantata based not on a Russian subject but, significantly, on a German one—Schiller's *Hymn to Joy*. The following year he became a professor of harmony at the Moscow Conservatory, a position he was to hold for twelve years. His early works, which include overtures, string quartets, and a programmatic symphony, demonstrate little of the individual style that marked his later achievements. He widened his experience, however, through frequent trips abroad.

In 1876, Tchaikovsky acquired the support of an unusual benefactress, Nedezhda von Meck, a widow who had inherited an immense fortune. Impressed by his music and told by a third party that the composer was in financial need, she commissioned several works at large fees. She arranged to pay him a fixed annuity so that he could devote himself completely to composition. Their relationship, lasting thirteen years, was carried on entirely by letter. They agreed never to meet, and except for several accidental encounters in public places, the bargain was kept.

In 1877, Tchaikovsky married Antonia Milyukova, a conservatory student who threatened suicide if he would not marry her. The marriage was a disastrous failure, for Tchaikovsky's sympathy for the girl quickly turned to revulsion, in part because of his homosexuality. After he himself made an attempt at suicide by plunging into the Moscow River, a legal separation was arranged. With the financial help of Mme. von Meck, he then embarked on a trip to Italy, Paris, and Vienna.

Figure 13.4 Peter Tchaikovsky wrote in the Western romantic style, yet he often incorporated folk songs of his homeland, which gave his works a Russian flavor.

Despite an increasing tendency toward depression, Tchaikovsky remained a highly productive composer. His Fourth and Fifth Symphonies (1877 and 1888) and the ballets *Swan Lake* (1876) and *The Sleeping Beauty* (1889) were soon performed all over Europe. By the 1880s, he had reached the height of his career. Suddenly, for reasons that have never been fully explained, Mme. von Meck withdrew her support and friendship. Though her action was a severe blow to his pride, Tchaikovsky was by now able to afford the financial loss, and his capacity for work remained undiminished. During 1891 and 1892, he undertook several concert tours in America, Poland, and Germany. When he went to St. Petersburg in 1893 to conduct the premiere of his Sixth Symphony, the *Pathétique,* he fell ill and died, a victim of the cholera epidemic that had been raging in the city.

Figure 13.5 Since its premiere in old St. Petersburg, Russia, in 1892, Tchaikovsky's ballet *The Nutcracker* has become a perennial favorite with audiences throughout the world.

TCHAIKOVSKY'S WORK

Tchaikovsky's best-known works are his last three symphonies, his three ballets, his two symphonic fantasies, his violin concerto, his concert overtures, and his first piano concerto. He composed his first three symphonies between 1866 and 1875. The fourth was completed in 1877, the fifth in 1888, and the sixth (the *Pathétique*) in 1893.

Although Tchaikovsky followed traditional procedures in his symphonies, his main efforts were directed at creating beautiful melodies and brilliantly orchestrated textures. The Fourth Symphony has an elaborate program wedged into the traditional symphonic format. Tchaikovsky's Fifth Symphony uses a single theme to link the four movements, much as Beethoven and Brahms had done in the symphonies previously studied.

His ballets—*Swan Lake, The Sleeping Beauty,* and especially *The Nutcracker* (1891–1892) (fig. 13.5)—remain among the most celebrated works of their kind, and the orchestral suites drawn from them are basic items in present-day repertoire as well.

Of Tchaikovsky's ten works for a solo instrument with orchestra, the most popular with performers and audiences alike are the Piano Concerto no. 1 in B-flat Minor (1875) and the Violin Concerto in D (1878). Of his several operas, only *Eugene Onegin* (1877–1878) and *The Queen of Spades* (1890) continue to be performed regularly. Few of his chamber works are performed today, but *None But the Lonely Heart,* one of the more than one hundred songs written during his career, is still a favorite.

Although Tchaikovsky is best remembered for his last three symphonies, the ballet scores, and the piano and violin concertos, two of his concert overtures have also become an almost indispensable part of symphonic repertoire: the *1812 Overture* and the overture-fantasy *Romeo and Juliet*.

Romeo and Juliet is a relatively early work (1870), composed at the suggestion (almost the insistence) of the Russian composer Mili Balakirev (1837–1910), to whom Tchaikovsky dedicated the piece. The composer revised the work in 1881, and it is this later version that is performed today.

Despite its title, *Romeo and Juliet* is programmatic only in that it selects some of the basic elements of Shakespeare's drama for musical treatment. But the drama is not used to organize the piece. Rather, these elements are worked out in strictly musical ways within the highly organized yet flexible structure of sonata-allegro form.

The piece begins with a long introduction whose generally "religious"-sounding texture is usually held to represent Friar Laurence. The expressive use of the full romantic orchestra, including harp, is immediately obvious even in this early part of the piece. After several changes of tempo, the introductory section builds into the agitated first theme of the exposition, played by the full orchestra—the feud between the Montagues and Capulets.

TCHAIKOVSKY:
Romeo and Juliet
Overture
Cassette 4/A, Track 1
CD 4, Track 1
See Listening Guide on pages 291–292.

Example 13.15

This feud theme is contrasted with the exquisite, flowing love theme of Romeo and Juliet, first stated briefly by solo English horn and muted violas.

Example 13.16

Very shortly, the love theme appears again, greatly extended and lushly orchestrated. This time the horns provide a countertheme, thus creating a love duet.

Example 13.17

The love music is closely associated with the short, atmospheric section played by muted strings.

Example 13.18

This short stretch of music separates the first two statements of the love music and is used again later in the movement.

The development focuses on the feud theme and the Friar Laurence material from the introduction. As the piece unfolds, the feelings of anger and chaos gradually dominate until, at the end of the recapitulation, a coda clearly signifies that the lovers are dead. The final few measures, with their isolated chords, are often held to represent a final union of the lovers, transfigured through death.

Tchaikovsky makes full use of the richness of the romantic orchestra as well as other romantic techniques: changes of tempo, sharply contrasting dynamic levels, dynamic crescendos, and long, lyrical melodies. In *Romeo and Juliet* he has created a fascinating example of the romantic concert overture as well as a clear illustration of the romantic sensibility. This piece is an example of program music, the subject of the next chapter.

Listening Guide

BRAHMS: Symphony no. 2 in D Major

First Movement: Allegro non troppo (rather fast)
                         Triple meter (often obscure)
                         Sonata form

Romantic Orchestra

Review: Example 13.1 (three-note unifying motive)
          Example 13.2 (theme 1)
          Example 13.3 (first new theme in coda)
          Example 13.3 (second new theme in coda)

CD 3 (Cassette 3/B, Track 1)

4	①	0:00	*Theme 1*		1	Unifying motive in cellos and basses; melody in horns and bassoons, then woodwinds, as motive continues underneath; restated by same instruments with minor-sounding harmony
		0:32				Dissolves, falling down through strings; single-note timpani solos, unifying motive in woodwinds
	②	1:20	*Bridge*		2	Lyrical melody in violins answered by flute, dissolves; suddenly loud, unifying motive in slow and fast rhythms; staccato chords in oboes based on motive
	③	2:23	*Theme 2 (ABA)*	A	3	Serene, almost waltzlike melody in lower strings; continues in woodwinds and strings; short crescendo to:
		3:20		B		Loud, vigorous; development of unifying motive builds to climax
		4:28		A		Sudden soft return of serene, waltzlike melody in strings with flowing countermelody in flute; melody in woodwinds, dissolves into:
	④	4:58	*Closing*		4	Very quiet downward-moving scales with unifying motive
						(Exposition may be repeated)
	⑤	5:18	**Development**		1	Sections of theme 1 (including unifying motive) developed in horn and other instruments; builds to:
		6:27			2	Loud, intense development of unifying motive in slow and fast rhythms; lyrical melody from bridge loud, gradually becoming softer
		7:18			3	Suddenly loud; extended development of fragment from beginning of theme 1; soft statement of fragment by horns and trumpets, a false recapitulation interrupted by further development of lyrical melody from bridge
					4	Soft downward scales in winds lead seamlessly into:

Continued on next page

		Recapitulation			
⑥	8:33	*Theme 1 and Bridge*		1	Melody in oboes then strings; first part restated by oboes with minor-sounding harmony, dissolves into unstable, fragmented passage ending in timpani solo and soft brass chords
⑦	10:02	*Theme 2*	A	2	Serene, waltzlike melody in lower strings; continues in woodwinds; builds to:
	11:08		B		Loud, vigorous full orchestra; extended development of unifying motive leads to climax
	12:09		A		Suddenly soft, return of waltzlike melody in winds, then in cellos and violas with flowing countermelody in flute; downward scales flow into:
⑧	12:52	*Coda*		3a	Soft return of theme 1 fragment builds, dies away to:
	13:10			b	A first new theme stated softly by horn
	13:59			c	A second new theme sung by violins
	14:42			d	Fragment from bridge and unifying motive developed in staccato woodwind and horn chords, pizzicato strings; final chord sounds softly in full orchestra

Listening Guide

MENDELSSOHN: Violin Concerto in E Minor

Third Movement: Allegretto non troppo; allegro molto vivace (lightly, not too fast; fast and very lively)
Quadruple meter
Sonata form with introduction

Solo Violin; Romantic Orchestra

Review: Example 13.12 (first theme)
Example 13.13 (second theme)
Example 13.14 (new theme from Development)

CD 3 (Cassette 3/A, Track 4)

5	1	0:00	**Introduction**		Slow, simple theme, violin and strings; pause
			Exposition		
	2	0:45	*Introductory section*	1	Fanfare-like introduction, orchestra and violin alternate, crescendo into:
	3	0:56	*Theme 1*	2	Joyful, scherzolike violin melody with orchestra; solo violin scales; joyful melody continues at length, crescendo to loud chord and cadence
		1:40	*Bridge*	3	Fast notes in violin; orchestra adds fragments of joyful theme; ascending scale by violin alone
	4	2:00	*Theme 2*	4	Marchlike beginning, full orchestra fortissimo; bouncy continuation in violin
	5	2:40	**Development**		Brilliant passage work in violin, opening fragment of march theme in orchestra; orchestra subsides, scales in violin; violin develops joyous theme
	6	3:16			Broad, new melody in violin as orchestra develops fragments of joyful theme; violin takes over joyous theme, strings sing broad melody
		3:45			Violin scales descending, then ascending
			Recapitulation		
	7	3:53	*Theme 1*	1	Joyful, scherzo-like theme in violin, combined with broad melody in strings; brilliant violin scales
		4:17	*Theme 2*	2	Marchlike theme, full orchestra; bouncy continuation, violin; less active transition
		4:44	**Development**		Marchlike fragments in orchestra, excited scales and arpeggios in violin; introductory fanfare; ascending trills in violin
		5:15			Trill continues over joyful theme; descending scales, orchestra subsides; long timpani roll
		5:33			March fragments alternate with scales; repetitive motive and crescendo; full orchestra, timpani, emphatic cadence
		6:03	*Coda*		March fragments tossed between winds and strings, virtuoso passage work in violin; emphatic closing chords

Listening Guide

TCHAIKOVSKY: *Romeo and Juliet* Overture

Single Movement: Tempo varies (slow introduction; fast)
Quadruple meter
Sonata form with introduction

Full Romantic Orchestra

Review: Example 13.15 (feud theme)
Example 13.16 (love theme)
Example 13.17 (love theme with countertheme)
Example 13.18 (theme associated with love music)
Outline of program, pages 286–287.

CD 4 (Cassette 4/A, Track 1)

Introduction

1	1	0:00	*Friar Laurence*	1a	Hymnlike, homophonic theme softly in clarinets and bassoons
		0:37		b	Foreboding fragments begin in low strings, build gradually to winds with harp arpeggios
		2:03		c	Strings pizzicato, Friar Laurence theme more agitated in woodwinds
		2:34		d	Foreboding music returns, then with harp arpeggios
		3:55		2a	Timpani roll introduces intense, threatening motives climaxing in loud, fast passage
		4:25		b	Timpani, threatening motives: woodwind-string echoes build directly to:

Exposition

	2	5:14	*Theme 1: Feud between Montague and Capulet families*	1a	Agitated feud theme in orchestra; strings rush up and down; agitated feud theme; rising three-note motive tossed between strings and winds
		5:37		b	Fragments of feud theme and rushing strings combined, developed with three-note motive; full orchestra with cymbal crashes in loud chords and rushing strings build to climax
		6:15		c	Feud theme explodes in full orchestra; transition with rushing strings; feud theme builds to close
		6:36	*Bridge*	2	Energy released in woodwind development of three-note motive; low strings take over
	3	7:25	*Theme 2: Love of Romeo and Juliet*	3a	Flowing love theme in English horn and muted violas, pulsating horns accompany

Continued on next page

	7:46		b	Harp arpeggio introduces muted strings with tender love music
	8:28		1c	Flutes and oboes surge upward to love theme with countertheme in French horn creating a love duet; greatly extended with lush orchestration
	9:31	*Closing*	4	Harp chords and soft tones in strings and winds subside to restful close
④	10:33	**Development**	1	Fragments of feud theme; fast scales in strings accompany Friar Laurence theme intoned softly in horn; theme extended and developed
	11:44		2	Three-note motive interrupts in cellos and basses, with fragments of feud theme; downward rushing strings added and builds to climax
⑤	12:00		3	Cymbal crash, full orchestra develops feud theme fragment; Friar Laurence theme combined forte in trumpet; rushing strings with loud chords in orchestra lead directly into:
		Recapitulation		
⑥	12:33	*Theme 1*	1	Agitated feud theme in full orchestra with cymbal crashes; strings rush downward
	12:55	*Theme 2*	2a	Tender love music in oboes and clarinets; intensity grows as other winds enrich the sound; strings rise intensely upward into:
	13:31		b	Love theme soars in strings and flute with countertheme in horn and throbbing woodwind accompaniment; grows to full, rich orchestration
	14:27		c	Love theme fragment in cellos answered by flute; extended with fragments and horns answered by flute; strings begin love theme but it dissolves
⑦	15:02	*Coda*	3	Fragments of feud and love themes vie with each other in full orchestra; feud theme emphatically takes over, then combined with Friar Laurence theme in brass; extended development as feud music takes over; furious activity decreases to ominous timpani roll
⑧	16:20		4a	Drumbeat continues as in a funeral march; fragments of love theme sound brokenly in strings, drumbeat ceases as woodwinds answer with a variation of tender love music; rising harp arpeggios signal union of the lovers; strings yearningly sing fragment of love theme
	18:51		b	Drum roll crescendo to strong final chords, recalling the feud theme

SUMMARY

A stream of classical thought continued to flow through the Romantic period. Although some composers discarded the classical forms, one group cultivated and expanded them in both orchestral and chamber music settings. The leading composers in this group were Schubert, Mendelssohn, Brahms, and Tchaikovsky.

Nearly all of the early romantic composers were influenced by Beethoven, either his use of the orchestra or his expansion of form. Brahms, the greatest of the late romantic symphonists, retained the four-movement symphonic structure. He continued to expand sonata-allegro form, enlarge the orchestra, and define structures by means of dynamics and instrumental colors.

The interest of romantic audiences in virtuosity encouraged composers to write concertos containing very difficult solo parts. While many romantic concertos were second rate, those written by Schumann, Brahms, Mendelssohn, and Tchaikovsky were outstanding.

The Romantic era gave rise to a new type of overture, one that did not introduce a longer work but was instead a self-contained work in one movement, intended for performance in the concert hall. The concert overture, exemplified by Tchaikovsky's *Romeo and Juliet,* often had programmatic elements but retained the sonata-allegro form of organization.

NEW TERMS

false recapitulation
concert overture

SUGGESTED LISTENING

Brahms, Johannes

Piano Quintet in F Minor, op. 34. A wonderful example of romantic chamber music.

Variations on a Theme of Haydn, op. 56a. A fascinating set of eight variations and a finale on a simple theme (*Chorale St. Antonio*) probably not by Haydn. Each variation is not merely a reworking of the theme but an emotional transformation of the original melody. The orchestration is brilliant.

Mahler, Gustav

Das Lied von der Erde (*The Song of the Earth*). A wonderful example of a romantic orchestral song cycle.

Mendelssohn, Felix

Hebrides Overture (*Fingal's Cave*). In this concert overture, Mendelssohn describes his impressions of a sea journey to Fingal's cave. The interplay of the two main themes—one restless, the second severe—evoke the play of wind and sun on water.

Tchaikovsky, Peter Ilyich

The Nutcracker Suite. Excerpts from one of the most famous ballets in history.

Piano Concerto no. I in B-flat Minor. Along with his violin concerto, two of the most frequently performed works by this composer.

PROGRAM MUSIC

The Romantic era gave rise to the establishment of a fascinating genre of music that has become known as **program music.** In program music, musical materials and techniques are employed with the intent of depicting or portraying an extramusical phenomenon such as a dramatic incident, a poetic image, a visual object, or some element in nature. Poems, dramatic plots, visual objects, and natural phenomena provided for the composer not only the general suggestive impulse for pieces of music but also became the dominating idea, determining the specific flow and form of the composition. Program music was thus contrasted to **absolute music**—music conceived by the composer and understood by the listener *without* reference to extramusical features. As we shall see, however, much absolute music is subject to programmatic interpretation by the imaginative listener, and the best program music can be understood and appreciated in purely musical terms without an awareness of the extramusical element.

Neither the principle nor the techniques of descriptive or program music originated in the Romantic period. In fact, they extended back into the medieval and Renaissance eras. For example, we have already encountered Clement Jannequin's *Chant des oiseaux* (page 101), in which human voices imitate bird calls. In the Baroque period, Antonio Vivaldi's *The Seasons* depicted the scenes and activities of each season of the year in the context of a violin concerto. Beethoven's Sixth Symphony (Pastoral), with its descriptive title for each movement, is regarded as a type of program music. But these pieces were rare and isolated examples.

In the Romantic period, program music became a major branch of instrumental musical composition, engaging the imagination and energy of many of the finest composers of the era, among them Hector Berlioz, Franz Liszt, and Richard Strauss.

BERLIOZ (1803–1869)

Hector Berlioz (fig. 14.1) grew up in a small town near Grenoble, France. Hector was expected to follow his father's profession and was sent to medical school in Paris. However, by his own inclinations he was drawn to the opera and the music library. When he appeared in class, he would annoy his fellow students by humming at the dissecting table. Finally, to the fury of his father, he quit the study of medicine to become a composer.

At twenty-three, Berlioz began what he called "the great drama of my life." At a performance of *Hamlet,* he was overwhelmed, both by "the lightning-flash" of Shakespeare's genius and "the dramatic genius" of Harriet Smithson, who played Ophelia. Berlioz tried to meet the actress, but his wild letters convinced her that he was a lunatic.

In 1830, on his fifth attempt, Berlioz won the Prix de Rome, a composition prize offered at the Paris Conservatory. In that year he also wrote the *Symphonie fantastique,* the outpouring of his passion for Harriet Smithson. When the composition was performed in Paris two years later, Harriet Smithson was in the audience. Realizing that the music was about her, she felt (according to Berlioz) "as if the room reeled." They were married a year later, but the romantic dream faded, and several years later, they separated.

Although he had become successful, Berlioz had difficulty getting his work performed. His music soon ceased to appeal to most of "the frivolous and fickle public." Both to support his family and to promote an understanding of the kind of music he advocated, Berlioz wrote musical criticism. He also wrote a fascinating prose autobiography. In it he emerges as a romantic hero, falling in love, scheming murder, talking politics, passionately

Figure 14.1 In his passionate emotionalism, daring experimentation, and rich imagination, Berlioz epitomized the nineteenth-century romantic spirit.

composing. He conducted performances of his own works throughout most of Europe, but in Paris he was overlooked for various honors and conducting posts. Increasingly bitter, his energies spent, Berlioz did not compose during the last seven years of his life.

BERLIOZ'S WORK

Perhaps Berlioz's greatest contribution to music was in the art of orchestration. In his music, tone color was as prominent an element as melody or harmony. He experimented extensively with individual instruments and devised many unusual blends, combining bells with brasses and directing violinists to strike the strings with their bow sticks. In 1844, he wrote his treatise on orchestration, the first comprehensive text on the subject and a work that is still in use today.

Berlioz's ideas were grandiose, and he wanted to carry them out on a grandiose scale. The first performance of *Symphonie fantastique* was thwarted because there were not enough chairs and music stands for the performers. At a time when orchestras usually numbered sixty players, Berlioz's ideal (never realized) was an orchestra of 240 strings, thirty harps, thirty grand pianos, and wind and percussion to scale!

Berlioz's major works are immense and dramatic. He usually composed from a literary text, favoring plays, epic poems, and novels. Works inspired by Shakespeare include the "dramatic symphony" *Romeo and Juliet* (1839), the *King Lear* Overture (1831), and the opera *Beatrice et Benedict* (1860–1862). The *Waverly* and *Rob Roy* overtures (c. 1827 and 1832) are based on the novels of Sir Walter Scott, and the symphony, *Harold in Italy* (1834), is based on the poem by Byron.

SYMPHONIE FANTASTIQUE

BERLIOZ: *Symphonie fantastique*, Fourth Movement
Cassette 3/B, Track 2
CD 3, Track 6
See Listening Guide on page 304.

The *Symphonie fantastique* is a program symphony in five movements. It is based upon a program, supplied by Berlioz out of his personal experience:

Program of the Symphony

A young musician of morbidly sensitive temperament and fiery imagination poisons himself with opium in a fit of lovesick despair. The dose of the narcotic, too weak to kill him, plunges him into a deep slumber accompanied by the strangest visions, during which his sensations, his emotions, his memories are transformed in his sick mind into musical thoughts and images. The loved one herself has become a melody to him, an *idée fixe* ("fixed idea") as it were, that he encounters and hears everywhere.

Part I. Reveries, Passions

He recalls first that soul-sickness, that *vague des passions,* those depressions, those groundless joys, that he experienced before he first saw his loved one; then the volcanic love that she suddenly inspired in him, his frenzied suffering, his jealous rages, his returns to tenderness, his religious consolations.

Part II. A Ball

He encounters the loved one at a dance in the midst of the tumult of a brilliant party.

Part III. Scene in the Country

One summer evening in the country, he hears two shepherds piping a *ranz des vaches* in dialogue; this pastoral duet, the scenery, the quiet rustling of the trees gently brushed by the wind, the hopes he has recently found some reason to entertain—all concur in affording his heart an unaccustomed calm, and in giving a more cheerful color to his ideas. But she appears again, he feels a tightening in his heart, painful presentiments disturb him—what if she were deceiving him?—One of the shepherds takes up his simple tune again, the other no longer answers. The sun sets—distant sound of thunder—loneliness—silence.

Part IV. March to the Scaffold

He dreams that he has killed his beloved, that he is condemned to death and led to the scaffold. The procession moves forward to the sounds of a march that is now somber and fierce, now brilliant and solemn, in which the muffled sound of heavy steps gives way without transition to the noisiest clamor. At the end, the *idée fixe* returns for a moment, like a last thought of love interrupted by the fatal blow.

Part V. Dream of a Witches' Sabbath

He sees himself at the sabbath, in the midst of a frightful troop of ghosts, sorcerers, monsters of every kind, come together for his funeral. Strange noises, groans, bursts of laughter, distant cries which other cries seem to answer. The beloved melody appears again, but it has lost its character of nobility and shyness; it is no more than a dance tune, mean, trivial, and grotesque: it is she, coming to join the sabbath.—A roar of joy at her arrival.—She takes part in the devilish orgy.—Funeral knell, burlesque parody of the *Dies irae*,[1] sabbath round-dance. The sabbath round and the *Dies irae* combined.

The five movements are linked together by the use of one melody that represents the hero's image of his beloved. This melody, the *idée fixe,* appears in each movement of the symphony in various transformations—in the second movement, it is a waltz tune; in the fourth, it appears fleetingly just before the fall of the executioner's blade; and in the fifth movement, it becomes a grotesque witches' dance combined with the medieval chant *Dies irae* ("Day of Wrath"). The technique of theme transformation intensifies the effectiveness of the musical representation of the program and lends a purely musical unity to the symphony. Example 14.1 shows the *idée fixe* as it appears in each movement.

Throughout the work, Berlioz's masterful use of the orchestra portrays a wide range of images and emotional states—from the fluctuating, dreamlike introduction to the grotesque and macabre Witches' Sabbath.

---

1. Hymn sung in the funeral rites of the Catholic church.

Example 14.1

FRANZ LISZT

The major achievement of Franz Liszt (1811–1886) (fig. 14.2) as an orchestral composer was his development of the **symphonic poem** or **tone poem,** an extended, single-movement, programmatic work. In the symphonic poem, Liszt abandoned altogether old forms such as sonata-allegro and relied instead on the principle of **theme transformation** as an organizing technique. His symphonic poem, *Les Préludes,* uses a three-note motive as the germ for themes depicting a variety of situations. In one section it suggests love; in another, a pastoral theme; in still another, a marchlike character.

In his rejection of the traditional multimovement organization and sonata-allegro form in favor of the single movement with flexible form based upon theme transformation, Liszt charted a new course that had a substantial impact upon the Romantic period and beyond.

LES PRÉLUDES

LISZT: *Les Préludes*
Cassette 3/B, Track 3
CD 3, Track 7
*See Listening Guide on
pages 305–306.*

Les Préludes was originally written as the orchestral overture to a choral work, but Liszt later decided to publish it separately. Looking for a suitable program, he was struck by the parallel construction of one of Alphonse de Lamartine's *Méditations poétiques*. He translated it freely and adopted it as the program for his composition:

> *What is our life but a series of Preludes to that unknown song, the first solemn note of which is sounded by Death? The enchanted dawn of every existence is heralded by Love, yet in whose destiny are not the first throbs of happiness interrupted by storms whose violent blasts dissipate his fond illusions, consuming his altar with fatal fire? And where is to be found the cruelly bruised soul, that having become the sport of one of these tempests does not seek oblivion in the sweet quiet of rural life? Nevertheless, man seldom resigns himself to the beneficent calm which at first chained him to Nature's bosom. No sooner does the trumpet sound the alarm, than he runs to the post of danger, be the war what it may that summons him to its ranks. For there he will find again in the struggle complete self-realization and the full possession of his forces.*

Liszt composed *Les Préludes* for a full romantic orchestra: flutes, oboes, clarinets, bassoons, four horns, trumpets, trombones, tuba, timpani (three drums), harp, and strings. For the finale (the section analogous to the call to battle), a side drum, cymbals, and a bass drum are added. The manner in which the orchestra is used is also typically romantic. The winds are often used as solo instruments; the horn, a favorite romantic instrument, is particularly prominent; fluctuations in tempo and dynamics occur frequently.

The stages of life mentioned in the poem correspond to the sections of Liszt's piece. It opens with a brief introduction, built on a three-note motive:

Example 14.2

that will later be used in the construction of most of the themes in the composition. The opening is slow and tentative. The motive gradually expands by enlarging its second interval,

Example 14.3

and eventually leads to the first theme. It is an expansive and majestic melody, vaguely related to the opening motive. The accompanying figure includes a direct statement of the motive.

Example 14.4

The next section, which reflects the mention of love in the poem, contains two themes. The first,

Example 14.5

is introduced by the low strings and then is treated as a horn solo in another key. The opening motive is quite prominent in this theme. The second theme (played by the four horns, and the violas divided into four sections) has the notes of the motive spaced out, with other material in between.

Example 14.6

X indicates the notes of the basic motive.

Eventually, these two themes are used simultaneously.

In the section of the piece corresponding to the storm, rushing chromatic patterns are interlaced with brief statements of the basic motive. Frequent changes of tempo increase the sense of agitation. As the storm subsides, the first love theme returns and leads to a section corresponding to the "sweet calm of rural life." The beginning of this lovely section, with its pastoral theme,

Example 14.7

features the woodwinds. Soon the strings join in, and the second love theme is added to the pastoral tune.

A gradual increase in tempo, dynamics, and intensity leads to the climactic finale, the call to battle. The final section opens with a transformation of the first love theme into a march sounded by the horns and trumpets.

Example 14.8

A bridge leads to a marchlike variation of the second love theme, with drums and cymbals added to the rest of the orchestra. Eventually, the section returns to the majestic first theme, accompanied by the basic motive, and the piece comes to a vigorous conclusion.

RICHARD STRAUSS

Although the life of the late romantic composer Richard Strauss (1864–1949) extended nearly halfway through the twentieth century, the bulk of his tone poems were written in the nineteenth century. These works exhibit the influences of both the detailed descriptions of Berlioz and the less specific descriptions of Liszt. Thus, *Tod und Verklarung* (*Death and Transfiguration,* 1889) and *Also sprach Zarathustra* (*Thus Spake Zarathustra,* 1896) have general, philosophical programs, while the comic *Till Eulenspiegel's lustige Streiche* (*Till Eulenspiegel's Merry Pranks,* 1895) and *Don Quixote* (1897) have more specific programs.

Strauss was a skilled composer, a virtuoso at writing effectively for large orchestra. Although his thematic inventions were rarely profound, they were always fresh and un-inhibited. A practical musician, Strauss realized that he was not innovative enough to follow in Liszt's steps, with essentially programless tone poems. He therefore chose to continue the detailed programs of Berlioz, but incorporated some of the supreme musicianship that marks Liszt's works.

A knowledge of the program is essential to the understanding of a Strauss tone poem. The explanations and comments are an integral part of the work and help give it coherence.

Figure 14.3 Strauss was not the only one to be attracted to Cervantes's foolish but invincible character Don Quixote. The addlepated knight was also a favorite subject of the painter and lithographer Honoré Daumier, who depicts him riding forth toward another imagined adventure.

DON QUIXOTE, OP. 35

The program of Richard Strauss's tone poem *Don Quixote* is taken from the great Spanish satirical novel of the same title, written in the early seventeenth century by Miguel de Cervantes. Don Quixote is a gentle, dignified, and rather simpleminded old man who becomes slightly addled by reading about the Age of Chivalry. He decides that he must become a knight, seeking adventure and revenging wrongs (fig. 14.3).

Strauss selected a series of episodes from Cervantes's tale and depicted them in a set of ten freely constructed variations on two themes, which represent Don Quixote and his squire, Sancho Panza. These musical characterizations are enhanced by assigning particular instruments to each man. A solo cello portrays Quixote, described as "The Knight of the Sorrowful Countenance"; Sancho Panza is depicted by a solo viola, with occasional help from the bass clarinet and tenor tuba.

The variations on these two themes are freer than those encountered in earlier music; no attempt is made to preserve the structure or the harmonic pattern of the themes. In fact, it might be more accurate to consider these "fantastic variations" (as Strauss himself subtitled them) as short episodes or rhapsodies on the themes, transformed to suit the particular adventures the composer selected.

Listening Guide

BERLIOZ: *Symphonie fantastique*

Fourth Movement: March to the Scaffold
Allegretto non troppo (not too fast)
Duple meter
Ternary form

Romantic Orchestra, Expanded Percussion

Review: Example 14.1 (*idée fixe* in all movements)
Outline of program, pages 296–297

CD 3 (Cassette 3/B, Track 2)

6	①	0:00	**Introduction**	Soft funeral drum rolls echo with horn calls in fragment from later march theme; interaction quickens; drum rolls crescendo into:
	②	0:28	**A**	Powerful descending scale theme in low strings; repeated in low strings, countermelody in bassoon
		0:54		Theme now in major key in upper strings, new countermelody in low strings, closed by fortissimo chords; stated again in upper and lower strings, closed by fortissimo chords
		1:19		Scale now ascends in pizzicato strings, countermelody in bassoon; strings rush upward into:
	③	1:39	**B**	March theme played twice by wind instruments, no strings; loud brass chords lead to:
		2:11		Downward scale (from A section), soft, scattered through the orchestra
		2:21		March theme played twice by full orchestra; loud brass chords lead to:
		2:53		Downward scale, soft, scattered through the orchestra; forte transition develops scale theme, crescendo in timpani explodes into:
		3:14	**A**	Fortissimo return of powerful downward scale, suddenly grows softer, erupts into upward version of scale, moves smoothly to:
		3:39	**Coda**	Galloping theme, loud punctuating chords; echoes between wind instruments and strings, growing softer; sudden loud climax
	④	4:16		*Idée fixe* softly in clarinet recalls beloved, suddenly cut off by death blow
		4:28		Drums thunder out the execution of the prisoner, with fortissimo concluding chords

Listening Guide

LISZT: *Les Préludes*

Single Movement: Tempo varies
Meter varies
Tone poem (symphonic poem)

Romantic Orchestra

Review: Example 14.2 (three-note motive, introduction)
Example 14.3 (three-note motive expanded)
Example 14.4 (first theme and accompaniment)
Example 14.5 (the first love theme)
Example 14.6 (the second love theme)
Example 14.7 (pastoral theme)
Example 14.8 (march theme)
Outline of program, pages 300–301

CD 3 (Cassette 3/B, Track 3)

7 ①	0:00	**Introduction**		Two pizzicato notes; ominous theme in strings opens with three-note motive, answered by woodwinds; same a step higher in pitch; ominous theme in strings joined by harp and brass, each entrance higher; emphatic ritard
②	2:36	**Life/Death**		Majestic, expansive melody in high winds, paired with powerful transformation of ominous theme in low brass and strings; timpani beats, trumpet fanfares; diminuendo
③	3:27	**Love**	a	Lyrical first love theme sung by violins, basses interject ominous three-note motive; lyrical theme sung by horn
	4:52		b	Fragile second love theme in horn and viola harmonies; fragile theme in woodwinds, yearning responses in violins and flutes
	6:01		c	Tender woodwind motives interrupted by ominous threatenings; lyrical and fragile love themes combined in strings and horn
④	7:30	**Storm**	a	Distant rumblings in cellos, tremolo strings; woodwinds and strings rush up and down, loud explosions in horns
	8:00		b	Full orchestra, forte, three-note motive in horns, loud chords, drum rolls, extended development
	8:28		c	Full orchestra explosion; trumpet fanfares, drumbeats, storm at its height; fanfares in strings, drumbeats answer; diminuendo

Continued on next page

⑤	9:24	**Calm of Rural Life**	a	Oboe sings tentative version of lyrical love theme accompanied by woodwinds, then strings accompanied by harp
	10:30		b	Playful melody in horn, then oboe, then clarinet, peaceful accompaniment in strings and harp; flutes answer with second half of playful melody, then oboes; playful motives tossed among woodwinds and strings; becomes extremely fragmented
	12:03		c	Fragile love theme in duet with playful melody in strings; woodwinds and harp join strings in warmer sound; horns added further enrich sound; full orchestra exults in combined melodies, with trumpet fanfares and drum rolls
⑥	14:02	**Call to Battle**	a	Rushing strings, trumpet fanfares answered by trombones and tuba; suddenly piano, more fragmented texture, constantly rising tension erupts into:
	14:38		b	Battle march with cymbals and drums; more majestic statement of march theme
	15:06		c	Suddenly piano, fragmented texture returns, constantly rising tension; final buildup of intensity
⑦	15:36	**Full Self-Realization**		Majestic, expansive theme combined with transformed ominous theme from first main section, sounded triumphantly by full orchestra; final chords

SUMMARY

Because they chose to abandon the classical forms, some romantic composers were forced to find new ways of unifying their larger instrumental works. A favorite method was to correlate the music with a nonmusical idea, frequently a story. Such music is known as program music.

The more radical romantic composers used the programmatic technique more directly. Hector Berlioz's major works are immense and dramatic and were often inspired by a literary text. His *Symphonie fantastique* derives its unity from the *idée fixe*, a melodic idea appearing in various transformations throughout the work.

Franz Liszt wrote single-movement works in a new and relatively free form that he devised, called the symphonic or tone poem. Each piece was unified by a single theme or melody that Liszt continuously transformed through changes in tempo, dynamics, and orchestration. This technique, called theme transformation, was also employed by other romantic composers.

Richard Strauss combined influences from both Berlioz and Liszt in the tone poems he wrote near the turn of the century. Unlike Liszt, however, Strauss depended heavily on the text to unify his works. The explanations and comments are integral parts of his tone poems, helping to give them coherence.

NEW TERMS

program music
absolute music
idée fixe

symphonic poem (tone poem)
theme transformation

SUGGESTED LISTENING

Mussorgsky, Modest

Pictures at an Exhibition. This work for piano, now more familiar in an orchestral version, portrays both particular paintings and the composer's reactions upon viewing them. A short musical theme called a *Promenade* introduces the work and is used as a transition from one painting to the next.

A Night on Bald Mountain. This symphonic poem tells the legend of St. John's Night when witches assembled to hold their sabbath and glorify Satan.

Rimsky-Korsakov, Nikolai

Schéhérazade, op. 35. *Schéhérazade* is a symphonic suite based on the tale, *A Thousand and One Nights,* in which a sultan's plan to kill each of his wives is foiled by Schéhérezade, who keeps him so interested in her stories that he rescinds the death sentence.

Sibelius, Jean

Finlandia. Finland's greatest composer is best known for his many symphonies and tone poems, many of which were inspired by Finnish mythology. *Finlandia* was written during the Russian domination of Finland and became a symbol for Finnish nationalism and independence.

Strauss, Richard

Don Quixote. See page 303.

NATIONALISM

During the later part of the Romantic era, nationalism became an important force in music. *Nationalism* in this context refers to any musical expression that is intended to emphasize the unique character and interests of a particular nation. There had been some stylistic differences in the music of different nations ever since the early fifteenth century. In the seventeenth century, France and Italy had dominated the European musical scene. Germany became an important force by about 1750 and assumed the dominant position in music at the beginning of the nineteenth century. But the classical style, as established by Mozart, Haydn, and Beethoven, had no distinctive national characteristics—it was international and cosmopolitan.

During the Romantic era, self-conscious and even aggressive nationalistic feeling flared up in both literary and musical circles. The reaction took different forms in different countries, although there were some common features. They ranged from the use of national subjects for operas and symphonic poems, and the occasional quoting of folk music material, to more general traits, such as the adoption of characteristic national idioms (in melody, harmony, rhythm, form, and tonal color) into the mainstream of Germany's romantic musical language.

The most important and obvious effect of the nationalistic movement took place in countries that did not have strong musical traditions of their own. Before the nineteenth century, areas such as Russia, Bohemia, and the Scandinavian countries had been musically dependent on the leaders of European culture, particularly Germany and Italy. They had imported their music and their musicians to perform it.

Many important nationalistic composers were not founders of schools of composition but were isolated figures. The whole nationalistic movement was rather short-lived, soon joining the prevailing currents of the more strongly established European cultures. Nevertheless, nationalism enriched the central musical language with new idioms and procedures and added works of lasting value to the repertory.

RUSSIA

Russia is the classic example of a nation that was suddenly exposed to Western civilization and became culturally dependent before first having a chance to find its own national voice. Prior to the reign of Peter the Great (1672–1725), Russia had been isolated from the West; Peter forced Western customs and ideas on his people and eliminated national traditions. This pressure created the beginnings of a cultural division between the liberal, Western-oriented aristocracy and the more traditional, conservative masses. The split was reflected almost immediately in Russian literature, and it gradually appeared in music as well.

European music was introduced to Russia late in the seventeenth century, and Italian opera was particularly popular at the Imperial Court. Music was definitely a luxury in Russia, imported for the upper classes and monopolized by foreigners. But in the nineteenth century, a new sense of national pride began to grow, demanding that there be something "Russian" about the music produced for Russian consumption. At about this time, the first significant Russian composer, Glinka, appeared.

MIKHAIL GLINKA

Although Mikhail Glinka (1804–1857) studied with German and Italian musicians, he became closely associated with the members of a nationalistic literary movement in St. Petersburg. At their urging, he wrote a "national opera," which he filled with the spirit and melody of the Russian people. His opera *A Life for the Tsar* was first performed in 1836. Russia had a vast supply of folk music and liturgical chant (for the Orthodox church), and Glinka was one of the first to draw on these resources.

THE SPLIT BETWEEN NATIONALISTS AND COSMOPOLITANS

About the time of Glinka's death, the Russian musical world divided into two camps. Some Russian composers wanted to be completely independent of the West, writing Russian music addressed to Russians only. Others were convinced that Slavic culture should be abandoned for the cosmopolitan culture of Western Europe. This split was paralleled in literary circles, in which the novelist Dostoyevsky was a leading nationalist, while Turgenev represented the more conservative faction. The outstanding composer of the cosmopolitan school was Peter Ilyich Tchaikovsky, who was discussed in chapter 13.

THE RUSSIAN "FIVE"

The leaders of the nationalistic school of composition in Russia, who professed to have no interest in the music of the West, were a strange group. Known as "the Five," they were not professional musicians, except for their leader and teacher, Mili Balakirev (1837–1910). The rest were professionally employed in other fields: Alexander Borodin (1834–1887) was a chemistry professor at a medical school; César Cui (1835–1918) was a military engineer; Modest Mussorgsky (1839–1881), an army officer; and Nikolai Rimsky-Korsakov (1844–1908), a naval officer. The most significant of these composers were Borodin, Rimsky-Korsakov, and Mussorgsky. Borodin's best works are an opera, *Prince Igor* (1890), and a symphonic sketch, *In the Steppes of Central Asia*. The music for the Broadway musical *Kismet* is taken from his work. Rimsky-Korsakov, who employed opulent and overwhelming orchestrations, is best known for his orchestral tone poem *Schéhérazade* (1888).

MUSSORGSKY (1839–1881)

Modest Mussorgsky (fig. 15.1), the outstanding composer of the Russian nationalistic school, is often called the founder of modern musical realism. Mussorgsky was born in Pskof to an aristocratic family. His mother gave him his first piano lessons, and at thirteen, Mussorgsky studied with one of the better piano teachers in St. Petersburg. He acquired facility on the piano and became familiar with German music, but received no training in musical theory. At seventeen, Mussorgsky became an army officer, indulging in such regimental pastimes as boasting, drinking, and wenching. He soon resigned his post to devote full time to composing, but when the emancipation of the Russian serfs in 1861 left his family in financial trouble, Mussorgsky became a government clerk, a position he held almost until his death.

At twenty-one, Mussorgsky became a pupil and friend of Balakirev. However, Balakirev never completely trusted Mussorgsky's judgment—either musically or personally—and eventually the two grew apart.

Some of Mussorgsky's earliest nationalistic feelings were expressed in a letter to Balakirev on his first trip to Moscow. He was equally moved by the tombs of the tsars and by the common people, who had, he said, "a strange demeanor, a nimbleness of motion. I was a cosmopolitan; now I feel reborn, and quite close to all that is Russian." Increasingly, Mussorgsky began to base his music on Russian themes—its literature, legends, folk songs, and the memories of his own childhood.

At twenty-nine, Mussorgsky began his greatest wor the opera *Boris Godunov*. He wrote the libretto himse basing it loosely on Pushkin's drama of Boris, wl became tsar in 1598 by arranging the murder of the chi heir to the throne. The opera was finally performed 1874. It was acclaimed by the public, but panned by mc critics, especially César Cui, Mussorgsky's old friend. was dropped from the repertory shortly after his deat but revived some years later.

Figure 15.1 Modest Mussorgsky. His new kind of music—based on Russian themes and full of dissonance and rhythmic variety—initially met considerable resistance from musical conservatives. But his harmonic and rhythmic innovations pointed the way for later composers.

ore disor-
alternated
ng. He felt
1881, he

Metropolitan Opera setting of the Coronation Scene from *Boris Godunov*.

MUSSORGSKY'S WORK

"My music," Mussorgsky wrote, "must be an artistic reproduction of human speech in all its finest shades, that is, the sounds of human speech, as the external manifestations of thought and feeling, must, without exaggeration or violence, become true, accurate music. . . ."

This credo helps to explain Mussorgsky's disdain for the conventions of the conservatory. His music is full of strange dissonances and rhythmic innovations that seemed to his contemporaries inexplicable and crude. But with these sounds, Mussorgsky attempted to evoke Russian speech, folk music, and real and imagined happenings—bells clanging for Boris's coronation, a witches' sabbath, the laughter of peasant girls.

Mussorgsky strove for complete realism in his music. His programmatic orchestral suite *Night on Bald Mountain* retells the legend of St. John's Night, when witches assembled to glorify Satan and hold their sabbath. His song cycle *The Nursery* describes different aspects of the life of an aristocratic child. His program work for piano (now more familiar in its orchestral version), *Pictures at an Exhibition,* describes both particular paintings and the composer's thoughts as he looks at them. In *Boris Godunov,* the realism is evident on all levels. His vocal lines follow the accents of natural speech, and his portrayal of crowd scenes is intensely real. On a deeper level, he expresses musically the deep and often unutterable sufferings and passions that rage in the human soul.

p. 546
Instrumental music associated with a nonmusical idea, this idea often being stated in the title or in an explanatory program note.

MUSSORGSKY:
Boris Godunov
Cassette 4/A, Track 2
CD 4, Track 2

BORIS GODUNOV

The drama *Boris Godunov,* which contains a prologue and four acts, centers on the character of Boris, his psychological disintegration and eventual death. We see Boris become tsar after arranging for the murder of the rightful heir to the throne. We watch him from the moment of his coronation to his death, tormented by hallucination, fear, and guilt from within and political intrigue from without.

But aside from the powerful figure of Boris and the realistic dramatization of his spiritual and physical deterioration, at the heart of the opera is the other central protagonist—the Russian people. Indeed, they are the drama's real hero. In choral sections and solo arias, Mussorgsky realistically depicts a variety of Russian types and sympathetically evokes the struggle and suffering of an oppressed people.

One of the opera's most powerful scenes in this regard is the brilliant Coronation Scene, which occurs in the prologue to act 1. As the prologue begins, it is clear that Boris, the son-in-law of the tsar, has devised the murder of the child Dmitri, the rightful successor to the throne. Upon the death of Tsar Feodor, Boris pretends to withdraw into seclusion but secretly contrives for the police to arouse the people to implore him to assume the throne. Thus, the stage is set for the Coronation Scene.

The scene opens with a clamorous orchestral introduction based on the alternation of two dissonant chords. As bells peal, the curtain rises on a courtyard of the Kremlin with the Cathedral of the Assumption and the Cathedral of the Archangels at either side. The people kneel between the great churches, and a procession of brilliantly dressed boyars (noblemen) and churchmen moves across the courtyard toward the Cathedral of the Archangels. From the cathedral porch, Prince Shuiski turns to proclaim, "Long life to Tsar Boris Feodorovich." The crowds (prodded by police) and the boyars respond by singing a hymn of praise based on a Russian folk tune:

Example 15.1

As the chorus and orchestra reach the height of a crescendo, Boris, accompanied by his two children and robed in magnificent cloth of gold, appears before the kneeling throng.

The atmosphere changes to one of quiet intensity. In an introspective monologue, Boris sings of the anguish, guilt, and fear that grip his heart. He invokes the aid of his departed father to help him rule justly and with glory. Then, singing a stronger, more resolute melody, Boris bids the people, boyar and beggar alike, to be his guests at a royal feast.

To the renewed peals of the great bells, the royal procession moves on to the Cathedral of the Archangels. The people arise and again sing in praise of Boris. The chorus and orchestra surge to a climax, and the scene ends with the continued reverberation of the cathedral bells.

Prince Shuiski
Da zdrávstvuyet Tsar Borís Feódorovich!

Chorus
Zhiví i zdrávstvui, Tsar násh bátyushka!

Prince Shuiski
Long life Tsar Boris Feodorovich!

Chorus
Long live the Tsar, our little father!

Prince Shuiski
Slávte!

Prince Shuiski
Glory to you!

Chorus
Uzh kák na nébe sólntsu
krásnomu,
Sláva!
Uzh i sláva no Rusí Tsaryú
Borísu!
Sláva!

Chorus
*Even as glory to the radiant sun in the
sky,
Glory!
So glory to Tsar Boris in Russia!*

Glory!

*(An imperial procession from the Cathedral. Police officers keep the people in line on both sides
of the procession.)*

Zhivi i zdrávstvui!
Ráduisya, veselísya pravoslávnyi lyud!
Velichái Tsaryá Borísa i sláv!

*Long live the Tsar! Rejoice and make
merry, all ye faithful of the Russian
church, and glory to the great Tsar
Boris.*

Nobles *(from the porch)*

Da zdrávstvuyet Tsar Borís Feódorovich!

Nobles

All hail to Tsar Boris Feodorovich!

Chorus
Da zdrávstvuyet!

Chorus
All hail!

(Boris now appears and crosses the stage.)

Uzh, kák na Rusí tsaryú Borísu!
Sláva, sláva, Tsaryú!
Sláva, sláva, sláva!

*Glory to Tsar Boris in all Russia!
Glory, glory, to the Tsar!
Glory, glory, glory!*

Boris
Skorbít dushá!
Kakói-to strákh nevólnyi
Zlovéschim predchúvstviyem
Skovál mne sérdtse.
O právednik, o mói otts derzhávnyi!
Vozzrí s nebés na slyózy vérnykh slug
I nisposhlí ty mné
svyaschénoye na vlást
Blagoslovénye.
Da búdu blag i práveden kak tý,
Dá v sláve právlyu svói naród.
Tepér poklónimsya pochíyuschim
Vlastítelyam Rusíyi.
A tám szyvát naród na pir,
Veskh, ot boyár do nischevo
sleptsá,
Vsem vólnyi vkhod, vse gósti dorogíye.

Boris
*My soul is torn with anguish!
Involuntary fears and sinister
forebodings clutch my heart.
Oh, righteous and sovereign Father,
look down from heaven and behold
the tears of these your faithful servants!
Bestow Thy sacred
blessings upon me and my
dominion! Help me to be kind and
just like Thyself, and rule over my
people in glory! And now let us bow
in homage to the great departed
rulers of Russia. Then let us
summon the people, from the noble
to the blind beggar, to a feast. All
are free to come and be my dear
and welcome guests.*

(Bells are rung on stage as the procession continues to the Archangels Cathedral.)

313

Chorus
Zhiví zdrávstvui Tsár nash bátyushka.

Chorus
Long live the Tsar, our little father!

(Police officers try to restore order, but the people break away and dash towards the Archangels Cathedral.)

Uzh kák na nébe sólntsu
krásnomu,
Sláva, sláva!
Uzh, kák na Rusí Tsaryú Borísu,
Sláva, sláva, i mnógaya léta!

*Even as glory to the radiant sun in the
    sky,*
Glory, Glory!
So glory to Tsar Boris in Russia!
Glory, glory and a long life!

(Great commotion. The police officers struggle with the people. Boris emerges from the Archangels Cathedral and proceeds to his chambers.)[1]

The *Coronation Scene* has achieved great popularity in its own right and is frequently performed in concert form (without costumes or scenery) as an independent concert piece.

NATIONALISM IN OTHER COUNTRIES

The distinctive nature of Russian folk music and Slavic culture made the nationalist movement there very obvious. But Russia was not the only country in which nationalistic forces influenced the musical scene. Ralph Vaughan Williams in England, Jean Sibelius in Finland, Edvard Grieg in Norway, Manuel de Falla of Spain, and Ottorino Respighi in Italy each reflected in some way the particular nationalistic flavor of their native countries.

Ralph Vaughan Williams (1872–1958) was the most important English composer of the late nineteenth and early twentieth centuries. In many of his works, his interests focused on English folk music. But the nationalistic aspect of his music was not merely a matter of quoting folk literature; it was a philosophical position indirectly expressed in music. His symphonic style involves a nontraditional approach to tonality within a general romantic idiom. His nine symphonies and his other large orchestral works are balanced by an extensive collection of vocal music ranging from simple, folklike settings to operas, songs, and many large choral works, including some with orchestra.

In particular, the early works of the Spanish composer Manuel de Falla (1876–1948) were strongly nationalistic and employed the idioms of Andalusian folk music and dance very effectively. His best-known works are the ballet *El amor brujo* (usually translated as *Love the Magician,* 1915), which features the ritual Fire Dance, and *Noches en los jardines de Espana* (*Nights in the Gardens of Spain,* 1916) for piano and orchestra, which effectively blends impressionism with native musical elements.

In Italy, Ottorino Respighi (1879–1936) was an outstanding composer of both instrumental and vocal music. His most successful opera is *La Fiamma* (1934), but he is best known for his trilogy of nationalistically oriented symphonic poems: *Fontane di Roma* (*The Fountains of Rome,* 1917), *Pini di Roma* (*The Pines of Rome,* 1924), and *Feste Romane* (Roman Festival 1929), all three of which are characterized by brilliant writing for large symphony orchestra.

---

1. From Mussorgsky, Modest Petrovich, *BORIS GODUNOV*, Coronation Scene, from Louis Biancolli, trans., *BORIS GODUNOV* (RCA Victor, LM 6403, 1952). Copyright © Louis Biancolli. Reprinted by permission.

The forces of nationalism also influenced musical developments in Bohemia. Bohemia (an area that is now part of Czechoslovakia) had been an Austrian colony for centuries, and thus had always been in touch with the mainstream of European music. Many fine musicians were produced in this region, but until the Romantic era, no distinctively Czech national style had developed. Even when a nationalist movement did arise, no extreme effort was made to avoid Western influence.

The two composers who led in the formation of a national style were Bedřich Smetana and Antonín Dvořák. Both were fully trained in traditional methods. Smetana's style was closely related to Liszt's, while Dvořák's was much closer to that of Brahms.

SMETANA (1824–1884)

Regarded as the founder of the Czech national school, Bedřich Smetana (fig. 15.2) was a composer dedicated to merging the spirit of Bohemian folk music with the innovations of the European musical pioneers of his day. A gifted pianist from childhood, Smetana performed the works of the classical masters. His traditional orientation was supplanted, however, when on a visit to Prague, he had the opportunity to hear Liszt and Berlioz. Smetana came to share with these men not only a fascination with progressive musical ideas but a spirit of nationalism, to which his dream of a Bohemia free from Austrian rule responded.

The spirit of Czech nationalism was widespread in Austrian-ruled Bohemia, and rising unrest culminated in the revolution of 1848. The uprising was a failure and left in its wake a long period of repression that Smetana eventually found unbearable. In 1856, he traveled to Sweden, where he worked as a teacher and conductor. He returned to his homeland after six years, this time finding a new and dynamic liberalism in the air. Shortly after his return, a Czech national theater for opera, drama, and ballet was established, and Smetana began work on an opera in the Czech language.

Over the next twenty years, the composer produced ten operas, eight of them on patriotic themes. *The Bar-*

Figure 15.2 Bedřich Smetana.

tered Bride (1866), which told of a village romance and recounted the comic antics of local Bohemian peasants, was instrumental in establishing his reputation.

In 1874, Smetana suddenly became deaf. But, like Beethoven before him, he continued to compose until nearly the end of his life.

SMETANA'S WORK

Aside from his operas, Smetana is best known for his famous cycle of symphonic poems, *Má vlast* (*My Country,* 1879). The six works in this cycle celebrated his country's legendary past, its splendid rivers and hillsides, and great moments in Bohemian history. One of the finest of the six is called *Vltava* (*The Moldau*). It traces musically the course of the river Moldau from its sources through central Bohemia to Prague and on to join the Elbe.

VLTAVA (THE MOLDAU)

SMETANA: *Vltava (The Moldau)*
Cassette 5/A, Track 1
CD 5, Track 1
See Listening Guide on pages 324–325.

Although *The Moldau* is just one part of a large work and has some thematic relationship to other parts of the cycle, it stands complete in its own right and has become one of the most popular works in symphonic repertoire. The piece is a reflection of the composer's love for his country and an expression of the Czech national character. In addition, it is a good example of program music.

As Smetana himself indicates in the score, the work consists of eight sections. It begins with (1) a depiction of the two sources of the river, played by the flutes,

Example 15.2

which are joined by clarinets and lower strings, gradually flowing into (2) the river itself, represented by the following melody in E minor:

Example 15.3

Beneath this flowing melody (the Moldau theme), the sixteenth-note motive (example 15.2) that began the piece continues. In fact, with two notable exceptions, this "swirling" water motive acts as a unifying element throughout the work, continuing as a background against which events of greater importance take place.

The river flows through a hunting forest (3), where the horns and trumpets sound hunting calls above the swirling water figure.

In the course of the river's flow, the forest is replaced by (4) a rustic village in which a wedding celebration is taking place. The celebration is represented by joyous, dancelike music (example 15.4).

Example 15.4

In this section, the sixteenth-note motive, which has characterized the piece thus far, is absent, and as a result, there is a feeling of repose.

The simple wedding scene gives way to an even more serene, almost unearthly section (5), "moonlight and the dance of the water sprites." The sixteenth-note figure now appears in an entirely different guise—as a gently rippling accompaniment to the "moonlight" theme played by the high strings, which are muted and have a shimmering effect.

Example 15.5

In the midst of this quiet and relaxed section, the horns and trombones slip in, almost without notice, repeating the water-sprite dance motive pianissimo. The serenity and quiet intensity of this section offer the perfect foil for the excitement and drama that follow.

As the water-sprite dance section draws to a close, the swirling motive begins to assert itself; the strings and brass contribute to a general increase in momentum, and the "river" theme (again in E minor) appears afresh (6). Then, abruptly, the entire orchestra interrupts the serene melodic flow with a theme suggesting great turbulence. We have reached St. John Rapids (7). Here Smetana uses the full resources of the romantic orchestra to evoke swirling rapids of chaotic and frightening proportions.

Soon, however, the rapids give way to the most beautiful and expansive part of the river (8). The river melody appears in its most stirring form, this time in E major, played forte by the full orchestra. At its broadest point, the river flows past the Vysihrad, the glorious castle that symbolizes Bohemian grandeur, proclaimed in a hymnlike passage for brass.

Example 15.6

The combination of the river theme and the Vysihrad motive produces a stirring conclusion that elegantly expresses Smetana's love of his country and his skill as a composer of program music.

DVOŘÁK (1841–1904)

The desire to establish a distinctive Czech national school was the ambition of yet another Bohemian composer, Antonín Dvořák. Born in a small village near Prague, Dvořák journeyed to Prague at the age of sixteen to study music and to become a master of the German Classical tradition. Yet, this man, who was one day to establish Czech prominence in the areas of symphonic and chamber music, found musical recognition elusive for many years.

The Prague public first became aware of Dvořák with the performance of his patriotic choral work *Hymnus* in 1873. This success prompted a grant from the Austrian ministry of fine arts, which supplied the composer with a small income. However, it was the patronage of Brahms, whom he met a year later, that thrust Dvořák into musical prominence. In 1878, Brahms persuaded a German music publisher to print the composer's *Moravian Duets* and *Slavonic Dances*. This allowed Dvořák to spend the 1880s touring Europe conducting his own work, and eventually he obtained the position of professor of composition at the Prague Conservatory.

Dvořák's career ultimately brought him to America, where he served from 1892 to 1895 as artistic director of the National Conservatory of Music in New York. One of his students at the conservatory was Henry T. Burleigh, a black composer and baritone who introduced him to American Negro spirituals. Dvořák was much impressed, too, by the melodies of the American Indians. In these traditions, he believed, lay the basis of a new musical school capable of expressing the unique spirit of the American people. His own nationalistic fervor impelled him to urge his American students toward the creation of a national style that would draw on these musical resources.

Homesick for his native country, Dvořák left the United States after three years. In 1901, he was appointed to the directorship of the Prague Conservatory. His death in 1904 at the age of sixty-three was mourned throughout his beloved Bohemia.

DVOŘÁK'S WORK

Dvořák's versatility is reflected in his legacy of concertos for violin, cello, and piano; his fourteen string quartets; his four great oratorios; his five symphonic poems; his cantata, *The Spectre's Bride* (1884); his four piano trios and two quintets; and his eleven operas and nine symphonies, among a multitude of other works.

"NEW WORLD SYMPHONY"

Dvořák's greatest contribution was in the art of the symphony. The best known of his works in this form, indeed one of the most famous in all of symphonic literature, is his Symphony no. 9 in E Minor, opus 95. The symphony, written in 1893 after Dvořák had come to the United States as director of the National Conservatory, is subtitled "From the New World."

As we said earlier, Dvořák was very much interested in the music of American Indians and American blacks. Indeed, these elements helped shape his "American style" and gave the "New World Symphony" much of its particular flavor. In a letter written while he was composing the symphony, he declared: "I should never have written the symphony like I have, if I hadn't seen America." However, the influence of American music was general rather than specific. Some of the melodies were suggested by but not quoted from American folk music. The influences of Czech and American music are also evident in the folklike character and syncopated rhythms of portions of the work.

First Movement

The first movement, in E minor, begins with a slow (adagio) and dramatic introduction that foreshadows the first phrase of the initial theme of the movement proper. The main body of the movement is fast (allegro molto) and is cast in sonata-allegro form. It is based on three main themes:

Example 15.7

The three themes are rather simple and tuneful, each employing syncopated rhythm. They are worked out in straightforward sonata-allegro fashion, complete with repeated exposition, development, recapitulation, and a coda that concentrates on the first part of theme 1. This phrase is not only important in the first movement, it also reappears and gains in importance as the symphony progresses.

From the beginning of the work, Dvořák uses the romantic orchestra with great skill and imagination. Abrupt dynamic changes, energetic crescendos, full employment of brass and percussion, and a strong sense of orchestral color are evident throughout.

Second Movement

The character of the second movement differs sharply from that of the first. Although it employs internal changes of tempo and dynamic contrasts, it is slow (largo) and subdued in character. The movement consists of three sections (ABA).

A somber succession of chords in the low winds and brasses leads to the beautifully melodious theme of the first A section, featuring the English horn accompanied by muted strings.

Example 15.8

This flowing melody of which the Negro spiritual "Goin' Home" is reminiscent, is expanded by the strings, then returns to the English horn. Section A ends in an increasingly subdued mood with two horns, muted, echoing the opening motive of the melody.

The B section has more rhythmic and melodic activity, and, like the first movement, employs a diversity of materials. The opening melody in the flutes and oboes with a slight increase in tempo,

Example 15.9

contrasts with the more relaxed melody that follows in the clarinets.

Example 15.10

Both themes are in strong contrast to the last portion of the B section, beginning with the sprightly, staccato oboe theme,

Example 15.11

which is then combined with trills in the flute.

Example 15.12

These materials are repeated several times, culminating in the sudden appearance of motives from the initial theme of the first movement combined with the beginning of the main theme of the second movement, which now assumes a livelier character.

Example 15.13

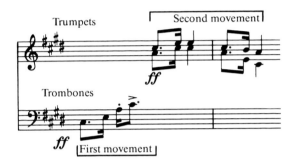

This dramatic combination of motives from two movements is an example of **cyclical treatment,** a procedure in which the same material recurs in succeeding movements. Cyclical technique is used here to effectively unify the two movements.

A decrescendo leads to a shortened repeat of the A section. The movement ends mournfully with a return to the somber chords that appeared at its beginning.

Third Movement

The third movement is a scherzo and trio in E minor. It is very fast (molto vivace), high-spirited, and dramatic. Its most important thematic material is the beginning of the scherzo.

Example 15.14

This driving phrase is the germ out of which the A section is built, and it reappears throughout the movement. The B section is more lyrical and flowing.

Example 15.15

Nationalism

The trio also consists of two contrasting sections.

Example 15.16

Winds

Example 15.17

But instead of following the usual pattern of

Scherzo   Trio   Scherzo
ABA   ABA   ABA

Dvořák varies this structure again, using cyclical technique. Between the first scherzo and trio there appears a short transition, like a bridge, that employs not only the materials of the scherzo movement but also the motive obviously derived from theme 1 of the first movement.

Example 15.18

Cello

In the coda he again features this material from the first movement in an obvious and dramatic way, combining it with the ♪♩♩|♩.♩ scherzo motive. Thus, he achieves unusual unity; motives from the first movement not only permeate that movement but also lend coherence to the second and third movements.

Fourth Movement

DVOŘÁK: Symphony no. 9 in E Minor (op. 95), Fourth Movement
Cassette 4/A, Track 3
CD 4, Track 3
See Listening Guide on pages 326–327.

The fourth movement is an enormous sonata-allegro in E minor, returning to a fast tempo (allegro con fuoco—fast, with fire). A short, fiery introductory section leads to the first theme, which is strong and marchlike.

Example 15.19

Trumpet and Horns

The contrasting second theme is tender in nature. It is stated first by the clarinet and immediately taken up by the strings, leading to a third and final theme straight out of a Czech village dance.

Example 15.20

At first the development concentrates on the marchlike first theme, but as the section progresses, themes from *all three* previous movements are introduced in various combinations and rhythmic alterations.

Example 15.21

Perhaps the most climactic moments in the symphony occur in the coda, when these two ideas are combined in dramatic fashion.

Example 15.22

There follows the final drive to the end that, surprisingly, fades away to the softest possible sound on the last chord.

As we have seen, the use of themes from the earlier movements in the later ones lends great unity to the work. This procedure is used most strikingly in the last movement, which includes themes from all four movements. Even more importantly, one idea—the opening phrase of theme 1 of the first movement—is central throughout the symphony. Partly due to its original appearance, but also because of its treatment in the later movements, this motive, particularly its rhythmic structure ♩. ♪♪♩ ⃒ ♩. ♪♪♩. , is the strongest unifying factor in the work.

The "New World Symphony" was immediately popular at the time of its creation and has remained so to this day. The world of music is richer for the fact that a Czech by the name of Dvořák came to the New World.

Listening Guide

SMETANA: *Vltava (The Moldau)*

Single Movement: Tempo varies with program
                      Duple meter
                      Tone poem (symphonic poem)

Orchestra

Review: Example 15.2 (springs where river begins)
           Example 15.3 (the Moldau theme)
           Example 15.4 (melody in Czech folk dance style)
           Example 15.5 (moonlight theme with sixteenth-note accompaniment)
           Example 15.6 (hymnlike theme of Vysihrad Castle)
           Outline of program, pp. 316–317

CD 5 (Cassette 5/A, Track 1)

1	①	0:00	**Two Springs, Sources of the River**	1a	Flutes portray cold spring bubbling up; harp and pizzicato strings accompany
		0:26		b	Clarinets enter to portray warm spring; two springs remain separate, then blend together to form single stream
	②	1:00	**The Moldau**	2	Triangle note, flowing accompaniment suggests movement of water; the Moldau theme in minor key

Continued on next page

---

③	3:00	**Forest Hunt**	3	Hunting horns suddenly heard from the forests along the river, as flowing accompaniment continues; louder trumpet calls increase excitement; calls and accompaniment die away
④	4:04	**Peasant Wedding**	4	Music in style of Czech folk dance portrays peasant wedding celebration on the banks of the river; dies away to single notes in bass; transition in woodwinds
⑤	6:00	**Moonlight, Dance of Water Sprites**	5a	Serene melody high in violins, quietly undulating woodwind accompaniment, occasional harp arpeggios portray calm of river in moonlight
	7:34		b	Distant brass fanfares, pianissimo, recall the ruins of ancient castles reflected in the water and bygone days of chivalry; timpani roll and crescendo in woodwinds lead to:
	8:39	**The Moldau**	6	Return of the Moldau theme, original minor form, flowing accompaniment
⑥	9:30	**St. John Rapids**	7	Sudden brass calls, fortissimo, cymbal roll, signal the white water turbulence of the St. John Rapids; sudden drop to pianissimo, then upward rushing crescendo
⑦	10:45	**The Moldau; Vysihrad Castle**	8a	The Moldau theme now in major key, the river flows majestically through the great city of Prague
⑧	11:15		b	Brasses peal forth the theme of Vysihrad Castle, home of great heroes of Bohemia's history
	12:05	**Coda**	c	Fragment of Moldau theme sweeps up and down through the strings, gradually softening and slowing as the river flows into the distance; two closing chords, forte

Listening Guide

DVOŘÁK: Symphony no. 9 in E Minor ("From the New World")

Fourth Movement: Allegro con fuoco (fast, with fire)
                              Quadruple meter
                              Sonata form
Romantic Orchestra

Review: Example 15.7 (Theme 1 of first movement)
             Example 15.8 (second-movement theme, "Goin' Home" spiritual)
             Example 15.19 (Theme 1 of fourth movement)
             Example 15.20 (Theme 3, Czech village dance-style theme)
             Example 15.21 (development of themes from all four movements)
             Example 15.22 (first- and fourth-movement themes combined in coda)

CD 4 (Cassette 4/A, Track 3)

			Exposition		
3	①	0:00	*Introduction*		Two-note motive stated, expanded with faster rhythms, timpani roll
	②	0:14	*Theme 1*	a a	Emphatic, marchlike theme in brass, powerful chords from orchestra, minor key; repeated
		0:40		b	Strings state contrasting second phrase of theme
		0:53		a	First phrase returns in orchestra, brass chords
		1:09	*Bridge*		Jaunty triplet theme in violins, woodwinds, violins; energy dissipates, soft cymbal crash
	③	1:43	*Theme 2*		Clarinet sings tender melody, comments from cellos with triplet motive from Bridge; violins take over melody; drum roll leads to:
	④	2:38	*Theme 3*	a	Czech village dance theme, first phrase closes with three-note motive moving down scale; repeated
		2:51		b	Second phrase closes with same three-note motive descending
	⑤	3:01	**Development**	1	Three-note motive continues in low strings, vigorous new counter melody in violins; three-note motive shifts to winds, returns to low strings with countermelody; countermelody winds down to pianissimo
		3:28		2a	Three-note motive in pizzicato strings, then woodwinds with high trills; horns suddenly intone opening theme, forte
		3:53		b	Three-note motive softly in woodwinds; opening motive forte in horns
		4:06		3	Opening motive in faster notes alternates with triplet motive from Bridge

Continued on next page

(6)	4:25		4a	Flutes softly sing "Goin' Home" theme from second movement, strings alternate in fragment from third movement
	4:48		b	Crescendo with faster rhythm; brass blares out "Goin' Home" fragment; these two ideas then repeated
	5:11		c	Opening motive developed in simultaneous fast and slow rhythms, crescendo into forte statement of fragment from first movement; development of opening motive takes over with powerful chords, crescendo
		Recapitulation		
(7)	5:49	*Theme 1*		Trombones proclaim marchlike theme; rhythmic motive developed as energy subsides
	6:42	*Theme 2*		Tender melody in strings, answered by woodwinds with triplet melody; intensity grows, then fades
	7:40	*Theme 3*	a	Village dance theme now in slower, reflective version
	7:59		b	Second phrase, closes into horn call softly recalling theme from first movement; three-note motive excitedly developed as transition
		Coda		
(8)	8:39	*Second development*	1a	Brass proclaims opening marchlike theme, strings respond with triplet theme from Bridge
	8:54		b	Trombones triumphantly blast out theme from first movement; orchestra continues to develop opening motive with powerful chords; timpani figure and rushing strings lead to climactic chord; energy dissipates
	9:32		2	Clarinet in "Goin' Home" theme of second movement set against fragment from third movement
(9)	9:48	*Second recapitulation and coda*	1a	Horn softly intones opening marchlike theme; orchestra restates theme forte
	10:18		b	Themes of first and fourth movements, now in major, boldly stated simultaneously
	10:30		2	Triumphant cadence closes movement; long-held chord dies away

SUMMARY

Nationalism was most evident in countries that did not have strong musical traditions of their own.

Russia began early in the nineteenth century to produce music in a unique national idiom. Mikhail Glinka drew from his country's vast supply of folk music and liturgical chant to write the opera *A Life for the Tsar,* first performed in 1836. A group of Glinka's successors formed a nationalistic school known as "the Five." The outstanding members of this group were Alexander Borodin, Nikolai Rimsky-Korsakov, and Modest Mussorgsky. Mussorgsky, composer of the opera *Boris Godunov,* is often considered the founder of modern musical realism.

The forces of nationalism were also felt in other European countries. In particular, a national style developed in Bohemia through the efforts of Bedřich Smetana and Antonín Dvořák, and nationalistic influences were also felt in Spain, Italy, Finland, the Scandinavian countries, and England.

NEW TERMS

cyclical treatment

SUGGESTED LISTENING

de Falla, Manuel

Noches en los jardines de Espana (*Nights in the Gardens of Spain*)

Respighi, Ottorino

Fontane di Roma (*The Fountains of Rome*)

Pini di Roma (*The Pines of Rome*). Two poems depicting important aspects of the city of Rome.

Sibelius, Jean

Finlandia. Finland's greatest composer is best known for his many symphonies and tone poems, many of which were inspired by Finnish mythology. *Finlandia* was written during the Russian domination of Finland and became a symbol for Finnish nationalism and independence.

Vaughan Williams, Ralph

Dona Nobis Pacem. This large work for chorus, soloists, and orchestra is a moving antiwar piece, the text of which draws on poetry of Walt Whitman.

ROMANTIC OPERA AND CHORAL MUSIC

O pera was one of the most important musical genres of the Romantic period. In the eighteenth century, each of the three leading countries of musical Europe—France, Italy, and Germany—had its own operatic style. These national styles became even more distinct during the Romantic period.

FRENCH OPERA

During the first half of the Romantic era, Paris was the operatic capital of Europe. Beginning about 1820, with the rise of a large and influential middle class, a new type of opera developed. Called **grand opera,** it concentrated on the spectacular elements of the production: crowd scenes, ballets, choruses, and elaborate scenery. The integrity of the drama and the music was often sacrificed for these special effects. Giacomo Meyerbeer (1791–1864), a German composer who had studied and worked extensively in Italy before coming to France, introduced grand opera to Paris with such operas as *Les Huguenots* (1836) and *Le Prophète* (1849). One of the longest grand operas of the early Romantic period was *Guillaume Tell* (*William Tell,* 1829) by an Italian, Gioacchino Rossini. The overture to *William Tell* remains popular today.

Although grand opera received the lion's share of Parisian attention, the less pretentious **opéra comique** (comic opera) continued to be popular. The distinguishing feature of opéra comique was its use of *spoken* dialogue rather than sung recitative. Both the music and the plot tended to be simpler than in grand opera. Despite the word *comique,* many operas in this form had serious plots.

Later in the nineteenth century, a new form developed as a compromise between the overwhelming spectacle of grand opera and the lightness of opéra comique. Called **lyric opera,** it evolved from the more serious type of opéra comique. Using plots taken from romantic drama or fantasy, these works relied primarily on the beauty of their melodies. One of the finest lyric operas of the period, Charles Gounod's *Faust* (1859), was based on the first part of Goethe's famous play.

NATURALISM

Toward the latter part of the century, a new literary movement, **naturalism,** developed in France. Naturalist writers rebelled against the romantic tendency toward escapism and emphasis on individual feeling. They sought to depict life as it is, objectively and truthfully. Often they portrayed characters from the lower classes whose lives were controlled by impersonal social forces as well as by their own passions.

Georges Bizet (1838–1875) introduced naturalism to opera in his masterpiece *Carmen* (1875). Whereas grand operas often portrayed historical and mythological figures, with the performers using stylized gestures to express their feelings, Bizet's main character was a gypsy girl whose fiery temper and passionate nature were dramatized realistically. Bizet's brilliant orchestration and his vital melodies and rhythms effectively complement the characterization and dramatic action.

BIZET (1838–1875)

Born and brought up in Paris, Georges Bizet entered the Paris Conservatory at the age of ten, and by seventeen, had written his first symphony. His work revealed such talent and ingenuity that he was awarded the Prix de Rome, enabling him to study at the Italian capital. Unfortunately, this brilliant beginning was soon clouded by the cold reception of his audiences, who were startled and offended by the boldness of his realism and the starkness of the emotions displayed in his early operatic works.

Following his youthful compositions, Bizet created three operas: *The Pearl Fishers* (1863), *The Fair Maid of Perth* (1867), and *Djamileh* (1872). Of the three, only *The Fair Maid of Perth* was well received, but Bizet's skill in orchestration and musical structure began to build his reputation. Success came in 1872 when he composed the incidental music for *L'Arlesienne,* a piece filled with exotic harmonies and bold orchestration. This won him an offer to do an opera based on a libretto adapted from Prosper Mérimée's novel about a fiery gypsy girl.

The realism of the libretto, dealing as it did with earthy figures and driving passion, was a perfect vehicle for Bizet's imagination and love of folk melodies. He undertook the assignment, and the opera, entitled *Carmen,* was produced in 1875. The subject scandalized the audience, and the themes of desire, love, and hate proved too bold for its time. The touch of scandal that surrounded it, however, kept the opera running for several months, and Bizet was subsequently offered a contract for his next work.

But the opera's reception was a great blow to the composer, and emotionally exhausted by so many months and years of work, he was stricken by a heart attack and died. At the age of thirty-eight, he had created the greatest French opera of his century and what is now one of the best-loved operas in the world. His inspired vocal ensembles, his use of the orchestra to comment on the action on stage, his pounding rhythms, his masterly scoring, and his eminently singable melodies assured him musical immortality. Five years after its unfavorable reception in Paris, *Carmen* returned to that city and was received with great enthusiasm.

ITALIAN OPERA

By the nineteenth century, opera was virtually the only important musical form being cultivated in Italy. The distinctions between *opera seria* and *opera buffa* were still maintained, although both were influenced by French grand opera. The orchestra began to play a more important and colorful role, and the chorus was also used more effectively.

ROSSINI, DONIZETTI, AND BELLINI

The most outstanding Italian opera composer of the early part of the nineteenth century was Gioacchino Rossini (1792–1868). His sense of melody and effective staging made him an instant success. Opera buffa seemed to be a natural outlet for his talents, and *Il Barbiere di Siviglia* (*The Barber of Seville,* 1816) ranks with Mozart's *The Marriage of Figaro* as a supreme example of Italian comic opera. As with Mozart's work, the skillful treatment of ensembles and the exposition of comic situations and characters make *The Barber of Seville* an exceptional opera.

In his thirty-two operas and oratorios, Rossini sought to cultivate the aria to its highest possible level. Its function was to delight audiences with melodious and spontaneous music. This **bel canto** style, which emphasized beauty and purity of tone and an agile vocal technique, was also exemplified in the work of two of Rossini's contemporaries: Gaetano Donizetti (1797–1848), composer of some seventy operas, including *Lucia di Lammermoor* (1835); and Vincenzo Bellini (1801–1835), whose lyric and expressive style is particularly evident in his *La Sonnambula* (*The Sleepwalker,* 1831) and *Norma* (1831).

However, the greatest Italian opera composer of the second half of the nineteenth century was Giuseppe Verdi.

VERDI (1813–1901)

Born of a poor family in a little hamlet in Bussetto, Italy, Giuseppe Verdi (fig. 16.1) began his musical training as the apprentice of the local church organist. His hard work and talent were rewarded with a stipend contributed by his town to enable the continuation of his studies at the Milan Conservatory. He was subsequently turned down by the examiners, but through the financial aid of a friend, he continued his studies by means of private lessons.

Verdi's first opera, *Oberto* (1839), written when he was twenty-six, was an instant success. To this musical triumph he added another, with the presentation of his third opera, *Nabucco,* in 1842. It was this work that brought him not only musical recognition, but national fame. The story dealt with the plight of the Jews in Babylon, but the parallel with the Milanese crusade for freedom from Austrian rule was so striking that Verdi was exalted as a patriot and champion of the Italian cause. His name soon became linked with the cry for independence, and his evident sympathies, as they were reflected in his works, brought him under police suspicion.

After producing a number of successful works, Verdi settled on a country estate in 1849. There he continued to pursue his political activities and produced, in succession, three of his best-known works: *Rigoletto* (1851), *Il Trovatore* (1853), and *La Traviata* (1853). These productions are regarded as the culmination of his first creative period.

Years of intensive musical productivity followed, during which such memorable works as *Un Ballo in Maschera* (*A Masked Ball,* 1859), *La Forza del Destino* (*The Force of Destiny,* 1861), and *Don Carlos* (1867) were created. In 1872, Verdi's masterpiece of spectacular grand opera, *Aida,* was written. With its cohesive dramatic structure, wealth of melodic, harmonic, and orchestral color, and subtle characterizations, this work is regarded as the height of his second creative phase.

Figure 16.1 Verdi was beloved not only as an operatic composer but also as a champion of the cause of Italian freedom.

Following this triumph, Verdi produced no operatic work for sixteen years. Then, in 1893, *Otello,* an opera unlike any he had previously written, was performed in Milan. Regarded by many critics as the pinnacle of Italian tragic opera, its sense of continuity surpasses that of his earlier works, while its orchestration still never obscures the singing voices. Verdi's last opera, *Falstaff,* written in 1893 when the composer was nearly eighty, is one of the finest in the comic opera genre.

VERDI'S WORK

Verdi's style is frequently contrasted with that of his German contemporary Richard Wagner. While each of these composers brought romantic opera to its height in his native country, they used quite different approaches. Wagner's plots usually involved larger-than-life, mythological characters whose activities were meant to symbolize underlying philosophical issues. Verdi's plots favored real people cast in dramatic, action-filled situations. Although Wagner's plots are more strictly ordered, Verdi's are notable for their spontaneity and sure sense of effective drama.

Verdi and Wagner disagreed on the relative importance of the singers and the orchestra. Wagner used orchestration to convey his philosophical ideas, sometimes overshadowing the singers, whose role was to move the surface action along. By contrast, Verdi's operas are dominated by the singing voice. Melody is the vehicle for expressing a vast range of emotions, and singers are rarely forced to compete with the orchestral background.

LA TRAVIATA (THE FALLEN WOMAN)

On a visit to Paris in 1852, Verdi saw the play *La Dame aux Camélias* (*Lady of the Camellias*), by Alexandre Dumas, the son of the famous author. Verdi was so taken with the drama and its subject matter that he decided to use it as the basis for a new opera, and within a year he produced *La Traviata* on a libretto by Francesco Maria Piave, Verdi's most frequent librettist.

The opera had its first performance in Venice on March 6, 1853. Mainly because of incompetent singers, it was a disastrous failure. A year later, it was performed in the same city—this time, a triumph! *La Traviata* achieved great international popularity and remains one of the most frequently performed and greatly admired works in today's operatic repertoire.

The plot of *La Traviata* focuses on two central characters: Violetta Valery (soprano), a beautiful, free-living Parisian courtesan, and Alfredo Germont (tenor), her ardent admirer who, in the course of the opera, becomes her lover. Secondary persons are Giorgio Germont (Alfredo's father), Gastone, Viscount de Letorières (Alfredo's friend), Baron Douphol (a rival of Alfredo), Flora Bervoix (Violetta's friend), and Annina (confidante of Violetta). Added to these are the many guests and servants of Violetta who form the chorus which, along with the orchestra in the pit, has important dramatic and musical functions in the opera.

The opera is cast in three acts: act 1 in August, act 2 in January, and act 3 in February. The action takes place around 1850 in and around Paris.

Act 1 is set in Violetta's splendid house, opening in the midst of a lively party with many guests. During the party, Baron Douphol arrives with Flora, followed shortly by Gastone, who introduces Alfredo to Violetta as "one who admires you greatly." As the guests seat themselves at the table, Violetta is placed between Gastone and Alfredo, opposite Flora and the Baron. As the feast proceeds, Violetta and Gastone engage in quiet conversation during which Gastone tells Violetta of Alfredo's great admiration for her and how, when she was ill, Alfredo rushed to her house daily to ask about the state of her health. Surprised, Violetta asks Alfredo, "Is this true?"

Later the guests rise from the table to dance in the adjacent ballroom. As Violetta moves toward the door, she turns pale and falters. Sitting down to rest, she urges the others to go ahead; she will join them shortly. They all leave, except for Alfredo, who stays behind, expressing concern for Violetta's health and declaring his love for her. Violetta dismisses the idea of love but flirtatiously invites him to return the next day. Alfredo, ecstatic at the thought of seeing her again, leaves. After the party, Violetta, alone, ponders Alfredo's expression of love but insists to herself that her life is one of only passing pleasures, not real love. As she does so, however, she hears Alfredo singing his love theme below the balcony.

Act 2 finds Violetta and Alfredo living in unmarried bliss on a country estate outside Paris. By chance, Alfredo learns from Annina that Violetta has secretly sold all her belongings to support their life together. In a fit of shame, Alfredo dashes off to Paris to raise the money to make things right. In his absence, his father, Germont, appears and convinces Violetta that her affair with Alfredo is not only ruining his reputation but is endangering Alfredo's innocent sister and her chance for marriage as long as he is involved in such a disreputable relationship.

In grief and despair, but out of love for Alfredo, Violetta decides to abandon him, leaving behind a note telling him she is returning to the Baron and her former life. Ignorant of his father's intervention and believing that he has been betrayed by his mistress, Alfredo follows Violetta to Flora's apartment where, in the midst of yet another party, he insults Violetta, wounds the Baron in a duel, and is forced to leave the country because of the ensuing scandal.

VERDI: *La Traviata*
Cassette 4/B, Track 1
CD 4, Track 4

The tragic love affair comes to its conclusion in act 3. Alfredo's father has revealed to his son the truth about Violetta's noble sacrifice for him and his family. Hope for Alfredo's return to her sustains Violetta, who is seriously ill. Alfredo, after learning the truth, returns to Violetta—too late—she dies!

The last part of act 1, beginning with Alfredo's declaration of love, is a good illustration of Verdi's operatic style. Alfredo has lingered with Violetta while the other guests have gone off to dance. He expresses concern for her health and declares his love for her:

Example 16.1

Later in the same aria, a melodic line constitutes the opera's love theme and reappears several times, sung by both Alfredo and Violetta:

Example 16.2

Violetta replies to this declaration of love in an aria that includes **coloratura** (brilliantly florid) singing, which characterizes much of the music assigned to this heroine and the kind of vocal writing Verdi used frequently:

Example 16.3

The chorus and orchestra restore the festive atmosphere after the parting of Alfredo and Violetta, preparing for the next scene, which finds Violetta alone, pondering the situation. Both dramatically and musically, the structure of this scene is interesting and makes for a very effective ending of act 1.

a. Accompanied recitative (allegro).

b. Aria (andantino), which includes music from Alfredo's love aria.

c. Accompanied recitative (allegro) ending with a cadenza-like passage:

Example 16.4

preparing for the next section.

d. Aria (allegro brillante) in which Violetta is interrupted by Alfredo singing his love theme (andantino) from outside, below the balcony.

Example 16.5

e. Short, accompanied recitative (allegro), ending with the same cadenza, leading to a repetition and extension of Violetta's previous aria (allegro brillante), this time *joined* by Alfredo, bringing act 1 to an exciting end (example 16.6).

Example 16.6

Violetta

dee ___ vo - lar,   dee ___ vo - lar,

Alfredo

A - mor è pal - pi-to   del - i'u - ni - ver - so,

Alfredo
Un dì felice, eterea
Mi balenaste innante,
E da quel di tremante
Vissi d'ignoto amor.
Di quell'amor, quell'amor ch'è palpito
Dell'universo, dell'universo interno
Misterioso, altero,
Croce e delizia al cor.

Violetta
Ah se ciò è ver, fuggitemi . . .
Solo amistade io v'offro;
Amar non so, nè soffro
Un cosi eroico amore.
Io sono franca, ingenua;
Altra cercar dovete;
Non arduo troverete
Dimenticarmi allor.

Alfredo
Oh amore misterioso,
Misterioso, altero,
Croce e delizia al cor.

Violetta
Non arduo troverete
Dimenticarmi allor.

Gastone appears.

Gastone
Ebben? che diavol fate?

Violetta
Si folleggiava . . .

Gastone
Ah! ah! . . . sta ben . . . restate . . .

Alfredo[1]
One day, happy and ethereal,
You appeared before me,
And since that day I've lived,
Trembling, in an unknown love.
In that love which is the pulse
Of the universe, the whole universe,
Mysterious, aloof.
The heart's cross and delight.

Violetta
Ah, if that is true, flee from me. . .
I offer you only friendship;
I cannot love, nor can I bear
Such a heroic love.
I am frank, simple;
You must look for another woman;
You won't find it difficult
To forget me then.

Alfredo
Oh, mysterious love,
Mysterious, aloof,
The heart's cross and delight.

Violetta
You won't find it difficult
To forget me then.

Gastone
Well? What the devil are you doing?

Violetta
We were talking nonsense . . .

Gastone
Ha! Ha! . . . very well . . . stay . . .

He goes back in.

1. *La Traviata* (Verdi). From *Seven Verdi Librettos* by Giuseppe Verdi. Copyright © 1963 by William Weaver. Used by permission of Doubleday, a division of Bantam Doubleday Dell Publishing Group, Inc.

Violetta
Amor dunque non più . . .
Vi garba il patto?

Alfredo
Io v'obbedisco . . . Parto

Violetta

A tal giungeste?
Prendete questo fiore.

Alfredo
Perche?

Violetta
Per riportarlo.

Alfredo
Quando?

Violetta
Quando sarà appassito.

Alfredo
Oh ciel! . . . Domani . . .

Violetta
Ebben . . . domani.

Alfredo

Io son, io son felice!

Violetta
D'amarmi dite ancora?

Alfredo

Oh, quanto, quanto v'amo!

Violetta
Partite?

Alfredo

Parto.

Violetta
Addio.

Alfredo
Di più non bramo.

Violetta and Alfredo
Addio. Addio.

Violetta
No more love then. . .
Does this agreement suit you?

Alfredo
I obey you . . . I'm leaving . . .

Violetta
(takes a flower from her bosom)

You go that far?
Take this flower.

Alfredo
Why?

Violetta
To bring it back.

Alfredo
When?

Violetta
When it has withered.

Alfredo
Heaven! . . . tomorrow . . .

Violetta
Very well . . . tomorrow . . .

Alfredo
(ecstatically taking the flower)
I . . . I am happy!

Violetta
You still say you love me?

Alfredo
(about to leave)
Ah, how much, how much, I love you!

Violetta
Are you going?

Alfredo
(comes back to her and kisses her hand)
I go.

Violetta
Good-bye.

Alfredo
I long for nothing more.

Violetta and Alfredo
Good-bye. Good-bye.

Alfredo goes out. The others, flushed from their dancing, come back from the other room.

All

Si ridesta in ciel l'aurora,
E n'è forza di partire;
Mercè a voi, gentil signora,
Di sì splendido gioir.
La città di feste è piena,
Volge il tempo dei piacer;
Nel reposo ancor la lena
Si reitempri per goder.

All

Dawn is reawakening in the sky,
And we must leave;
Our thanks to you, kind lady,
For such splendid entertainment.
The city is filled with parties,
The season of pleasures is coming;
We must restore our vigor by resting
So that we can enjoy ourselves more.

They go out. Violetta is alone.

Violetta

È strano! . . . è strano! . . . in core

Scolpiti ho quegli accenti!
Saria per me sventura un serio amore?

Che risolvi, o turbata anima mia?

Null'uomo ancor t'accendeva . . .
Oh gioia ch'io non conobbi,
Esser amata amando!
E sdegnarla poss'io
Per l'aride follie del viver mio?
Ah fors'è lui che l'anima

Solinga ne'tumulti
Godea sovente pingere
De' suoi colori occulti
Lui, che modesto e vigile
All'egre soglie ascese,
E nuova febbre accese
Destandomi all'amor.
A quell'amor, quell'amor ch'è palpito
Dell'universo, dell'universo intero,
Misterioso, altero,
Croce e delizia al cor.

Violetta

It's strange! . . . strange . . . those words

are carved in my heart!
Would a serious love be a misfortune for me?

What are you resolving, O my anguished spirit?

No man ever aroused you before . . .
Oh joy I did not know,
To be loved and to love! . . .
And can I spurn it
For the barren follies of my life?
Ah, perhaps he is the one whom my spirit,

Alone amid tumults,
Often enjoyed painting
With its mysterious colors. . .
He who, modest and constant,
Came to my sickroom door,
And kindled a new fever
Waking me to love.
To that love which is the pulse
Of the universe, the whole universe,
Mysterious, aloof,
The heart's cross and delight.

She is lost in thought for a moment, then she recovers herself.

Follie! . . . follie!
Delirio vano è questo! . . .
Povera donna, sola,

Folly! . . . folly! . . .
This is vain raving! . . .
A poor woman, alone,

Abbandonata in questo
Popoloso deserto
Che appellano Parigi,
Che spero or più?
Che far degg'io? . . . Gioire!
Di voluttà ne' vortici perir!
Gioir! . . . gioir!
Sempre libra degg'io
Folleggiare di gioia in gioia,
Vo' che scorra it viver mio
Pe' sentieri del piacer.
Nasca il giorno, o il giorno muoia,
Sempre lieta ne' ritrovi,
A diletti sempre nuovi
Dee volar il mio pensier.

Alfredo

Amore è palpito dell'universo,
Dell'universo intero,
Misterioso, altero,
Croce e delizia al cor.

Violetta
Follie! . . . follie! . . . follie!
Giorir! . . . gioir!
Sempre libra degg'io
Folleggiare di gioia in gioia.
Vo' che scorra il viver mio
Pe' sentieri del piacer,
Nasca il giorno, o il giorno muoia,
Sempre lieta ne' ritrovi,
A diletti sempre nuovi
Dee volar pensier

Alfredo
Amor e palpito dell'universo.

Violetta
Ah! ah! il pensier,
Il mio pensier.

Abandoned in this
Crowded desert
That they call Paris,
What more can I hope for now?
What must I do?. . .Enjoy myself!
Perish in the giddy whirl of pleasure!
Enjoy myself . . . Enjoy!
Always free I must
Dart lightheadedly from joy to joy,
I want my life to glide
Along the paths of pleasure
Whether the day is born or dying,
Always gay at parties,
My thought must fly
Always to new delights.

Alfredo
(below the balcony)

Love is the pulse of the universe,
The whole universe,
Mysterious, aloof,
The heart's cross and delight,

Violetta
Folly! . . .folly!. . .folly!
Enjoy! . . .enjoy!
Always free I must
Dart lightheadedly from joy to joy,
I want my life to glide
Along with the paths of pleasure,
Whether the day is born or dying,
Always gay at parties,
My thoughts must fly
Always to new delights,

(together)

Alfredo
Love is the pulse of the universe.

Violetta
Ah! ah! new delights,
Always seeking.

THE VERISMO MOVEMENT

Toward the end of the nineteenth century, a movement toward naturalism and realism took place in Italian literature, similar to the movement in France. Called **verismo** (realism), it quickly penetrated Italian opera. Bizet's *Carmen* served as a model for the three Italian composers who led the movement: Giacomo Puccini (1858–1924), Ruggiero Leoncavallo (1858–1919), and Pietro Mascagni (1863–1945). Leoncavallo is remembered for *I Pagliacci* (*The Clowns* 1892) and Mascagni for *Cavalleria Rusticana* (*Rustic Chivalry,* 1890). Puccini, the most successful of the verismo composers, effectively united grand opera and realism.

PUCCINI (1858–1924)

One of the most celebrated and successful of Italian opera composers, Giacomo Puccini was descended from a line of musicians that stretched back over five generations. During most of his childhood, Puccini showed only a modest talent for music; nevertheless, his mother insisted that he continue his studies, and by the age of sixteen he was composing in earnest—chiefly organ music for church services.

In 1880, Puccini obtained a scholarship to enter the Milan Conservatory. Once graduated from the Conservatory, he entered an opera competition with *Le Villi* (*The Vampire,* 1884), a work based on a Slavonic legend. He failed to win the contest, but the opera was produced in Milan on May 31, 1884. The success of the premiere persuaded the well-known publisher Giulio Ricordi to commission a second opera by Puccini. Largely because of a poor libretto, *Edgar* (1884–1888) was not a success; however, Ricordi continued to support the composer, and both men worked over the book for the next work, *Manon Lescaut.* Its premiere on February 1, 1893, was an immense triumph.

Although *Manon Lescaut* made Puccini famous in Italy, his next opera, *La Bohème* (*Bohemian Life,* 1893–1896), brought him worldwide fame. He completed the work in his magnificent new villa next to Lake Massaciuccoli in northern Italy.

Ironically, Puccini's only serious failure was his favorite opera, *Madame Butterfly* (1904). Despite the hisses and catcalls of the premiere, however, the work became quite popular outside Italy. His next opera, *La Fanciulla del West* (*The Girl of the Golden West,* 1910), was based on a play by David Belasco, as was *Madame Butterfly.* Its premiere at the Metropolitan Opera in New York was one of the most glittering events of 1910, with Arturo Toscanini conducting and Enrico Caruso singing the lead male role.

During World War I Puccini remained in Italy, working quietly on more operas. His last work, *Turandot,* was left incomplete at his death. In 1923 he began suffering from what turned out to be cancer of the throat, and the following year he died of a heart attack. The task of finishing the final scenes of the work was entrusted to Franco Alfano, a distinguished younger composer. The opera was produced under Arturo Toscanini at La Scala, Milan, on April 25, 1926.

Figure 16.2 A scene from
La Bohème.

PUCCINI'S WORK

Puccini's operas reflect his realistic bent and his fascination with exotic settings. *Madame Butterfly,* for example, is set in Japan, and *Turandot* in China. The opera that brought him international acclaim, *La Bohème* (fig. 16.2), combines rich and sensuous romantic melodies with realistic details of plot and characterization.

LA BOHÈME

The Plot

The opera is set in the Latin Quarter of Paris (the artists' district on the Left Bank) in the 1830s. Rodolfo (a struggling young poet) and his friend Marcello (a painter) are freezing in their garret studio on Christmas Eve. Suddenly a friend enters with money, groceries, and firewood, and insists they all go out to celebrate. Rodolfo stays to finish an article he is writing but is interrupted by a knock at the door. The caller is Mimi, a neighbor, whose candle has blown out. She asks for a light, and he invites her in. She is ill and faints. When she feels strong enough to leave, they discover that her key has fallen. As they search for it on the floor, their hands meet, and they give up the search to wait for more light from the moon. Rodolfo tells Mimi about his life and hopes. She describes her life as a maker of artificial flowers and her longing for spring and sunshine. Rodolfo declares his love and Mimi responds passionately. As the act ends, they leave to join his friends at the cafe.

The next act opens with a holiday crowd in the streets near the cafe. Marcello sees his old flame, Musetta, with a wealthy old codger in tow. She tries to attract Marcello's attention, embarrassing her escort and amusing the spectators. Finally she sings a provocative waltz and, having sent her escort off on a fool's errand, leaps into Marcello's eager arms.

Some months later, Rodolfo's jealousy has caused Mimi to leave him. She seeks out Marcello to ask his help and tells him of Rodolfo's unbearable behavior; Rodolfo arrives and Mimi hides. He starts to complain to Marcello of Mimi's flirting but admits that he is actually in despair over her failing health. When Mimi's coughing reveals her presence, Rodolfo begs her to stay with him until spring, and she agrees.

Act 4 is set in the garret the following fall. Rodolfo and Marcello are in the studio. Their fellow artists arrive for dinner, and a hilarious evening begins. Musetta interrupts their gaiety, announcing that Mimi has collapsed on the stairs. They carry her in; all except Rodolfo leave to pawn their treasures to buy medical supplies. Rodolfo and Mimi recall their first meeting; their friends return and Mimi drifts off to sleep. She dies, and Rodolfo embraces her while the others weep.

The Music

Much of the music of *La Bohème* follows the natural inflections of the words of the libretto. Often Puccini attempts to give the impression of normal spoken conversation in a kind of recitative style. Much of the action is delivered in short phrases, often sung on one or two notes. Characters constantly interrupt one another. Little musical ornamentation is used. Frequently, in these passages, the orchestra has the most important musical material and creates subtle transitions between recitative and arias in which the voice assumes primary melodic importance. All of this is well illustrated in the last half of act 1.

While Mimi and Rodolfo grope in the dark for her keys, they speak to each other in short, clipped phrases: *"Your neighbor is troublesome—don't mention it"; "Are you looking—I am looking."* In the midst of this searching, Rodolfo finds the key and secretly puts it in his pocket! *"Have you found it?—No."*

While Rodolfo is seeking Mimi's hand, the orchestra prepares a change of mood, leading to Rodolfo's aria. By the time he captures her hand, his aria flows naturally out of the preceding orchestral texture (example 16.7).

Example 16.7

RODOLFO Che ge - li - da ma - ni - na, se la la - sci ris - cal - dar
(What a frozen little hand, let me warm it)

Rodolfo goes on to tell Mimi about his life and hopes, and his aria builds to a climax as he is swept up in a wave of emotion.

Example 16.8

Ta - lor dal mio for - zie - re ____ ru-ban tut-ti i gio -

iel - li due la - dri: gli oc - chi bel - li.
("Now and then two thieves will rob me of all the jewels from my strongbox: two beautiful eyes.")

Mimi responds with her own lovely aria, "Mi chiamnao Mimi" ("They call me Mimi"). As Mimi ends her aria, Rodolfo's friends shout to him from the street, momentarily breaking the spell. After this interruption, Rodolfo turns from the window and is transfixed by the sight of Mimi bathed in the glow of moonlight. He begins to sing and soon is joined by Mimi in a beautiful love duet based on the climactic phrase of Rodolfo's aria (compare example 16.9 with example 16.8).

Example 16.9

Con anima
(Ah! love alone commands me!)
MIMI: Ah! tu sol co - man-di,a - mor

RODOLFO: Fre - mon già nel - l'a - ni - ma ____
(Trembling in my soul)

This sensuous melody becomes the love theme of the opera. The duet ends in a kiss, and act 1 closes as the lovers leave to join their friends, singing the word *amor* ("love").

The following excerpt is from the last half of act 1 of *La Bohème*.[2]

*Rodolfo pretends to continue searching and gropes his way nearer to Mimi;
finally he manages to touch her hand in the darkness.*

PUCCINI: *La Bohème*
Cassette 4/B, Track 2
CD 4, Track 5

Mimi
Ah!

Mimi
Ah!

Surprised, she stands up.

Rodolfo

Che gelida manina, se la lasci riscaldar.
   Cercar che giova? Al buio non si trova.
Ma per fortuna, è una notta di luna
. . . e qui la luna, l'abbiamo vicina.
Aspetti, signorina, le dirò con due
parole chi son, chi son, e che faccio,
come vivo. Vuole? Chi son? Chi son?
Sono un poeta. Che cosa faccio?

Scrivo. E come vivo? Vivo. In povertà mia
lieta scialo da gran signore rime ed
inni d'amore. Per sogni e per chimere e
per castelli in aria l'anima ho
millionaria. Talor dal mio forziere
ruban tutti i gioielli due ladri: gli occhi
belli. V'entrar con voi pur ora, ed i
miei sogni usati, e i bei sogni miei tosto
si dileguar! Ma il furto non m'accora
poichè—poichè v'ha preso stanza la
dolce speranza! Or che mi conoscete,
parlate voi, deh! Parlate! Che siete? Vi
piaccia dir!

Rodolfo

*What a frozen little hand, would you let
   me warm it? What's the good of
searching? We won't find it in the
dark. But by luck it is a moonlit night,
and we'll have the moon near us here.
Wait, Miss, and I'll tell you in a
couple of words who I am—who I am,
and what I do, how I live. Would you
like that? Who am I? Who am I? I'm
a poet. What do I do?*

*I write. And how do I live? I live. In my
poverty I feast as gaily as a grand
lord on rhymes and hymns of love. For
dreams and fancies and castles in the
air, I have a millionaire's soul. Now
and then two thieves rob all the jewels
from my strongbox: two beautiful
eyes. They came in with you, just now,
and my old dreams, my beautiful
dreams, quickly dissolved. But the
theft doesn't hurt me, since—since
such sweet expectation has taken its
stead. Now that you know me, come,
you speak. Who are you? Please tell!*

Rodolfo releases Mimi's hand, and she drops into a chair.

Mimi
Si. Mi chiamano Mimì, ma il mio nome è
Lucia. La storia mia è breve. A tela o
a seta ricamo in casa e fuori. Son
tranquilla e lieta ed è mio svago far
giglie e rose—Mi piaccion quelle cose
che han sì dolce malìa, che parlano

Mimi
*Yes. They call me Mimi, but my name is
Lucia. My story is brief. I embroider
silk or linen at home and outside. I'm
contented and happy, and it's my
pleasure to make lilies and roses. I
like those things that have sweet*

2. La Bohème (Puccini). Translation from Ellen Bleiler, *Dover Opera Guide Libretto Series,* 1962. Dover Publications, New
   York, NY. Reprinted by permission.

d'amor, di primavere, che parlano di sogni e di chimere—quelle cose che han nome poesia—Lei m'intende?

Rodolfo

Sì.

Mimi

Mi chiamano Mimì, il perchè non so. Sola, mi fo il pranzo da me stessa. Non vado sempre a messa ma prego assai il Signor. Vivo sola, soletta, là in una bianca cameretta: guardo sui tetti e in cielo, ma quando vien lo sgelo il primo sole è mio—il primo bacio dell'aprile è mio! Il primo sole è mio! Germoglia in un vaso una rosa. Foglia a foglia la spiro! Così gentil il profumo d'un fior! Ma i fior ch'io faccio, ahimè, i fior ch'io faccio, ahimè, non hanno odore! Altro di me non le saprei narrare: sono la sua vicina che la vien fuori d'ora a importunare.

charm, that speak of love, of springtimes, that speak of dreams and fancies—those things that are called poetry. Do you understand me?

Rodolfo

Yes.

Mimi

They call me Mimi, but I don't know why. All alone, I make dinner for myself. I don't always go to Mass, but I often pray to the Lord. I live alone, all by myself, in a little white room over there. I look on the roofs and into the sky, but when the thaw comes, the first sunshine is mine—the first kiss of April is mine. The first sunshine is mine! A rose opens in a vase. Leaf by leaf I sniff its fragrance. So lovely is the perfume of a flower. But the flowers that I make—alas! the flowers that I make—alas! have no odor. I wouldn't know anything else to tell you about myself—I'm your neighbor who comes at this odd hour to trouble you.

Voices are heard from outside.

Schaunard

Ehi! Rodolfo!

Colline

Rodolfo!

Marcello

Olà! Non senti? Lumaca!

Colline

Poetucolo!

Schaunard

Accidenti al pigro!

Schaunard

Hey! Rodolfo!

Colline

Rodolfo!

Marcello

Hey there! Don't you hear? Snail!

Colline

Paltry little rhymester!

Schaunard

Confound the slowpoke!

Rodolfo goes to the window and calls down.

Romantic Opera and Choral Music

Rodolfo	**Rodolfo**
Scrivo ancor tre righe a volo.	*I still have three lines to write in a flash.*

Mimi comes to the window beside Rodolfo.

Mimi	**Mimi**
Chi son?	*Who are they?*
Rodolfo	**Rodolfo**

To Mimi

Amici.	*Friends.*
Schaunard	**Schaunard**
Sentirai le tue!	*You'll get yours!*
Marcello	**Marcello**
Che te ne fai li solo?	*What are you doing up there all alone?*
Rodolfo	**Rodolfo**
Non son solo. Siamo in due. Andate a Momus, tenete il posto, ci saremo tosto.	*I'm not alone. There are two of us. Go to Momus, hold a place, we'll be there soon.*
Marcello, Schaunard and Colline	**Marcello, Schaunard and Colline**
Momus, Momus, Momus, zitti e discreti, andiamocene, via!	*Momus, Momus, Momus, quiet and discreet, let's get away from here, away!*
Schaunard and Colline	**Schaunard and Colline**
Momus, Momus!	*Momus, Momus!*
Marcello	**Marcello**
Trovò la poesia!	*He found poetry!*

Their voices fade into the distance.

Schaunard and Colline	**Schaunard and Colline**
Momus, Momus, Momus!	*Momus, Momus, Momus!*

A moonbeam shines through the window on Mimi. Rodolfo, turning, sees her.

Rodolfo	**Rodolfo**
O soave fanciulla . . .	*O gentle girl . . .*
Marcello	**Marcello**

From far away.

Trovò la poesia!	*He found poetry!*
Rodolfo	**Rodolfo**
O dolce viso di mite circonfuso alba lunar, in te ravviso il sogno ch'io vorrei sempre sognar.	*O sweet face surrounded by mild white moonlight, the dream I would always dream comes to life in you.*

Mimi	**Mimi**
Ah! tu sol commandi, amor!	*Ah! love, you alone may rule!*
Rodolfo	**Rodolfo**
Fremon già nell'anima—le dolcezze estreme . . .	*Already extreme joys are thrilling in my soul . . .*
Mimi	**Mimi**
Tu sol commandi, amore!	*Love, you alone may rule!*
Rodolfo	**Rodolfo**
Fremon nell' anima . . .	*Are thrilling in my soul . . .*
Mimi	**Mimi**
Oh! Come dolci scendono le sue lusinghe al core, tu sol commandi, amor!	*Oh! How sweetly your soft words sink into my heart, love, you alone may rule!*
Rodolfo	**Rodolfo**
—dolcezze estreme—fremon dolcezze estreme, nel bacio freme amor.	*—extreme joys—extreme joys are thrilling, love thrills in the kiss.*

He kisses Mimi.

Both thematically and musically, *La Bohème* is unified by recurring motives. The last act is in many ways the mirror image of the first. In the same garret Rodolfo and the dying Mimi relive their first meeting. As in their first encounter, Mimi's hands are cold, but a muff is quickly brought, and as she drifts into her last sleep, she murmurs, "My hands are all warm. . . ."

GERMAN OPERA

While the Italian verismo composers were influenced by the realist movement in literature, nineteenth-century German opera drew much of its inspiration from the ideals of the romantic movement.

The first significant composer of German Romantic opera was Carl Maria von Weber (1786–1826). A nationalist and romanticist, he built his style on the legends and songs of the German people and on romantic elements. His opera *Der Freischütz* (*The Freeshooter,* 1821) incorporates aspects of the supernatural, a typically romantic fascination.

German Romantic operas, such as *Der Freischütz,* tended to stress mood and setting. Nature was represented as a wild and mysterious force, and supernatural beings mixed freely with ordinary mortals. Human characters often symbolized supernatural forces of good and evil, and the hero's victory meant salvation or redemption. Harmony and orchestral color were the primary means of dramatic expression, with the voice often relegated to a secondary role.

In the latter part of the nineteenth century, one of the most powerful personalities in the history of music emerged—Richard Wagner. In his works, German Romantic opera reached its highest point.

WAGNER (1813–1883)

Born in Leipzig, Richard Wagner (fig. 16.3) was the son of a clerk in the city police court who died when his son was only six months old. Richard's mother later married Ludwig Geyer, a gifted actor, playwright, and painter. It was rumored that Geyer was the composer's real father, and Wagner himself considered this likely. Wagner was a precocious child who showed an early interest in literature, writing a tragedy in the style of Shakespeare at the age of fourteen. In his formal musical training he was among the least systematic of the great nineteenth-century composers. He began piano lessons at age twelve but never became a first-rate performer on any instrument. Like that of Berlioz, his great French contemporary, his music brought into play the full resources of the orchestra.

Lack of adequate technical preparation did not prevent Wagner from making early attempts at composition. By 1832, several of his works—including two overtures and a symphony—had been performed publicly. The following year, at age twenty, he began his professional career, becoming chorus master for the Würzburg theater. Positions at Magdeburg, Königsberg, and Riga followed in succession, and he began composing operas.

While in Königsberg, he married the actress Minna Planer and began work on an opera based on Bulwer-Lytton's historical novel, *Rienzi, Last of the Tribunes.* The years 1839 to 1842 were spent in Paris, where he tried vainly to have the work performed. His financial situation became desperate—partly because of his increasingly spendthrift ways—and the first serious breakdown in his marriage occurred.

Rienzi was finally accepted, not in Paris but in Dresden, Germany, and Wagner returned to Germany to supervise the production. The success of both *Rienzi* (1842) and his next opera, *Der fliegende Holländer* (*The Flying Dutchman,* 1843), led to his appointment as conductor to the King of Saxony. For the next six years, Wagner busied himself producing operas and writing two more himself: *Tannhäuser* (1842–1844) and *Lohengrin* (finished in 1848). Wagner's active participation in the

Figure 16.3 An informal photograph of Wagner taken when he lived in Switzerland. He often posed for at-home pictures in the velvet jacket and beret.

revolutionary uprising of 1848–1849 forced him to flee to Switzerland.

While in exile, he turned to literary activity and wrote a number of essays, the most influential of which were *Das Kunstwerk der Zukunft* (*The Art-Work of the Future,* 1850) and *Oper und Drama* (*Opera and Drama,* 1851). In these he laid the foundations for "music drama," the term he used for his unique type of opera.

During his ten years in Switzerland, Wagner began putting his artistic theories into practice. By 1852 he had completed the poems of an epic cycle of four music dramas, entitled *Der Ring des Nibelungen* (*The Ring of the Nibelung*). The music for the first two dramas, *Das Rheingold* (*The Rhine Gold*) and *Die Walküre* (*The*

Figure 16.4 Built in 1876, the Bayreuth Festspielhaus was designed under Wagner's direction specifically for the performance of his operas.

Valkyrie), and for part of the third, *Siegfried*, was completed by 1857. The entire cycle was completed seventeen years later, in 1874, with the composition of *Die Götterdämmerung* (*The Twilight of the Gods*). These works place heavy demands on the performers, and since the individual dramas last three to five hours each, the whole tetralogy requires four separate days for its performance.

In the intervening years, Wagner wrote two other works that remain perhaps his most popular and most frequently performed: *Tristan und Isolde* (1856–1859) and *Die Meistersinger von Nürnberg* (*The Mastersingers of Nuremberg,* 1862–1867).

Although highly prolific, Wagner experienced great difficulty in arranging performances of his works. Most were formidable in scale, requiring theatrical and musical resources beyond the means of even the largest opera houses. As he approached the age of fifty, he became discouraged. His debts continued to pile up, and he separated from his wife and even contemplated suicide.

Then in 1864, his fortunes changed. The new king of Bavaria, Ludwig II, a devoted admirer of Wagner's music, invited the composer to Munich with the promise of financial and artistic support. At this time, Wagner fell in love with Cosima von Bülow, the daughter of Franz Liszt and wife of one of Wagner's close associates. Cosima left her husband to join Wagner, completely devoting herself to his career. They were finally married in 1870, and together they raised enough money to build an opera house devoted exclusively to producing his works. Located in the small Bavarian town of Bayreuth, the *Festspielhaus,* as it was called, was the scene of the first complete performance of the Ring cycle, in 1876 (fig. 16.4). One of the great artistic events of the century, this performance was the fulfillment of Wagner's lifelong dream. He completed one more work, *Parsifal* (1882), before illness forced him to travel to Italy in hope of regaining his health. He died quite suddenly, in Venice, on February 13, 1883.

WAGNER'S WORK

Although his most significant works were operas and music dramas, Wagner also wrote some orchestral and choral music. His most important instrumental piece is *Siegfried Idyll,* a short work composed for Cosima's birthday celebration of December 25, 1870. His most outstanding nonoperatic vocal work is a collection of five settings of poems by Mathilde Wesendonk, with whom Wagner had a passionate love affair in the late 1850s. Composed during 1857–1858, the collection is known today as the *Wesendonk Lieder.*

Wagner's early operas—*Die Feen* (*The Fairies,* 1833), *Das Liebesverbot* (*Love Prohibited,* 1836), and *Rienzi* (1842)—were written under the influence of Meyerbeer, Bellini, and Donizetti, the masters of grand opera whose works dominated the European opera houses of the early nineteenth century. His next three operas—*The Flying Dutchman, Tannhäuser,* and *Lohengrin*—represent a culmination of the German Romantic opera tradition that Wagner inherited from Carl Maria von Weber.

In the Ring cycle, Wagner began to apply his innovative theories of operatic style and structure. The plots of the Ring cycle (all of which were his own creations, not those of a librettist) dealt with German mythology or historical legend. Underlying the surface plot were philosophical issues that he considered to be of fundamental importance: the struggles between the forces of good and evil and between the physical and spiritual, and the idea of redemption through unselfish love. In the Ring cycle, Wagner attempted to symbolize the corruption of modern society through characters drawn from Teutonic mythology: giants, dwarfs, gods, and warriors.

WAGNER'S STYLE

Wagner believed that a music drama should be a *Gesamtkunstwerk* (universal artwork) combining elements from all the arts. The most important element should be drama, with the music serving to reinforce the dramatic expression. This view was directly opposed to that held by many earlier opera composers, including Mozart, who believed that the drama should serve as a framework for the music.

In Wagner's works the music is essentially continuous throughout each act, with one section moving smoothly into the next. In place of the traditional arias and recitatives, Wagner developed a musical line he called *Sprechsingen* (singing speech). This style combined the lyric quality of the aria and the speaking quality of the recitative and permitted a continuous musical flow that Wagner termed "endless melody."

The voices and orchestra each play a specific role in conveying several levels of meaning. The singers often have the lesser role; through their actions and words, they explain only the surface events of the drama. The orchestra is used to express the inner meaning of the events, which the characters themselves often do not understand. In addition, the orchestra serves as the major unifying force of the opera. The fabric of the orchestral music is held together by the use of the **leitmotif** (leading motive), a melodic fragment that represents a specific character, object, or idea; it is a kind of musical label that sounds every time its object appears in the drama. This technique was not original with Wagner; Verdi, Puccini, Weber, and Berlioz had used recurring themes to unify their works. But Wagner used the leitmotif much more consistently.

Apart from identifying characters or objects, leitmotifs are also used in more subtle ways. As musical phrases, they can be varied or developed in the usual symphonic fashion; with every variation and every change of context, they take on added shades of meaning. Wagner also uses them to suggest ideas to the audience. For example, the connection between two objects may be suggested by a similarity between their leitmotifs.

Although leitmotifs are woven into the orchestral fabric, they do not provide enough unification for works of such vast dimensions as Wagner's operas. Wagner therefore imposes formal structures on larger portions of the music dramas (such as whole acts), usually constructing them in either AAB or ABA form. On such a large scale, forms are not obvious to the listener; nevertheless, they lend a feeling of balance and proportion to the work.

Another aspect of Wagner's style that deserves special mention is his use of chromatic and dissonant harmonies. Wagner continued to expand the chromatic idiom used by other romantic composers, particularly Liszt in his symphonic poems. In *Tristan and Isolde,* discussed in the following section, Wagner produced a new ambiguity of tonality by constantly shifting keys and by introducing dissonant chords in places where the listener would normally expect resolution to consonance. Indeed, Wagner's use of chromatic harmony represents an important step toward the development of the new, atonal systems that evolved in the twentieth century (see chapters 20 and 21).

TRISTAN AND ISOLDE

Tristan and Isolde (fig. 16.5) is an outstanding example of Wagner's mature style. In this work the complex web of leitmotifs is ever-present, but they are subordinated to a constant flow of emotions and inspired orchestral writing. The mood of tragic gloom is sustained by the highly chromatic quality of the writing.

The Plot

The libretto is based on a medieval legend. The opera opens on shipboard, where the knight Tristan is escorting the Irish princess Isolde to Cornwall. There she is to marry his lord and uncle, King Marke. Isolde explains to her maid Brängane that she has met Tristan before; he had come to her, unknown and wounded, and she had healed him. When she later discovered that he was the one who killed her fiancé in combat, she became furious and tried to kill him. But when he looked into her eyes, she was unable to; she felt love instead. Isolde orders Brängane to prepare a death potion so that she may kill Tristan and herself. They drink the potion and are condemned to a fate worse than the death she had planned, for Brängane has substituted a love potion, and their attraction becomes an irresistible passion.

The second act opens in Isolde's garden, where she and Tristan plan to meet in secret that night; King Marke and the courtiers are off on a hunt. Brängane advises caution, but Isolde signals to her lover and he comes. Their long love scene is interrupted by the return of the hunting party, which includes Melot, a jealous knight who has warned King Marke about the affair. The king, revealing that he married Isolde only to satisfy the people of his

Figure 16.5 A nineteenth-century engraving depicting a scene from *Tristan and Isolde*.

kingdom, questions Tristan. Tristan does not defend his disloyalty but asks Isolde if she will follow him to the "wondrous realm of night." She agrees; Tristan pretends to attack Melot, drops his guard, and permits himself to be seriously wounded.

The final act takes place at Tristan's ancestral castle in Brittany. His squire Kurvenal has sent for Isolde; the dying and delirious Tristan recalls their love and his longing. As Isolde arrives, the dazed hero rips off his bandages and dies in her arms. King Marke, Melot, and the others arrive in a second ship, and Kurvenal and Melot kill each other. Marke forgives the unhappy lovers, and Isolde joins Tristan in death.

Such a simplified account of the plot gives no indication of the wealth of detail and symbolism with which Wagner imbued it. The story actually represents a philosophy of life: an all-encompassing love inevitably leads to unsatisfied longing, then to death, and a final transfiguration of two into one. This deeper level of meaning is symbolized by constant references to day and night. Day is the world of conventional life and values, while night is the inner world in which such a love exists. When Tristan asks Isolde to follow him to the "wondrous realm of night," he means the death in which their union can be complete.

In *Tristan and Isolde,* Wagner makes extensive use of leitmotifs. With slight variations, they seem to represent several different things. The opening passage of the opera is a case in point. The two motives here are often called Tristan and Isolde, or grief and desire. Together, they represent yearning, or the love potion (example 16.10).

WAGNER:
Tristan and Isolde
Cassette 4/B, Track 3
CD 4, Track 6

Example 16.10

Many basic emotions such as suffering, ecstasy, and desire are closely linked, and their motives are also related. Even the day and night motives are similar.

Example 16.11

In the last scene of the second act, several other leitmotifs are employed. Three come from the great love duet of the preceding scene; they represent love's peace, love-death, and ecstasy.

Example 16.12

The other two are associated with King Marke and his grief over Tristan's betrayal.

Example 16.13

The last scene begins at the very climax of the love duet. As the singers reach their final notes, the orchestra plays a loud and unexpectedly dissonant chord, Brängane screams, and Kurvenal shouts to Tristan to protect himself. Marke, Melot, and the courtiers enter. The music grows quiet as the two groups study each other. The love-death and ecstasy themes are heard softly in the orchestra. They are followed by the day theme, as Tristan sings *"Der ode Tag zum letzten Mal"* ("The bleak day for the last time").

Marke, shattered, tells how deeply Tristan's betrayal affects him, while the bass clarinet sounds his grief motive. Tristan answers violently that this is all a bad dream; significantly, he calls it a day phantom, a morning vision, rather than a nightmare.

Marke, the innocent victim of fate, is a "day" person, with no control over his unhappy situation. Repeatedly he asks what he has done to deserve this. Marke can never know the answer to his question. At the same time, the orchestra answers the question for the audience by playing the grief and desire motive from the opening of the opera.

Tristan then asks Isolde if she will follow him; as he begins, the violins play the leitmotif associated with love's peace. In a lyric arioso passage he describes the dark land to which they will go. Isolde gives her assent in a similar section; he kisses her as the ecstasy motive is heard. The infuriated Melot urges the King to defend his honor. Tristan challenges Melot and finally lets himself be mortally wounded.

Wagner's music has been unusually influential. His harmonic style, continuous but irregular melodic writing, symphonic use of leitmotifs, and superb sense of orchestral color all influenced several later generations of composers. He attained his ideal of the *Gesamtkunstwerk,* although his music had a force that his librettos did not. Since he intended that his music should serve the drama, it is ironic that today we sometimes hear the music alone performed in concerts, while the librettos could never stand alone as plays. But despite some errors in judgment, Wagner's accomplishments were truly outstanding, expressing the universal state of ecstasy toward which all romantic artists had been striving.

CHORAL MUSIC

The choral literature of the nineteenth century presents a fascinating array of compositions ranging in scope and size from short, modest pieces for unaccompanied chorus to compositions of colossal proportions in which the chorus is part of a huge musical apparatus involving gigantic orchestral forces (fig. 16.6). Although choral music continued to occupy a position of secondary importance to instrumental music, virtually every major composer made significant contributions to choral literature and the choral tradition.

The oratorio tradition established in the Baroque period by Handel and continued through the Classical era by Haydn received the attention of such composers as Franz Liszt (*Legend of St. Elizabeth*), Hector Berlioz (*Childhood of Christ*), and Felix Mendelssohn, whose oratorio *Elijah* became very popular and is often performed today.

In many instances the chorus was incorporated into the symphonic portrayal of secular themes in dramatic works such as Robert Schumann's *Scenes from Faust,* Franz Liszt's *A Faust Symphony,* and Hector Berlioz's *Romeo and Juliet.*

The great religious texts of the Catholic church, including the *Mass, Requiem, Te Deum,* and *Stabat Mater,* were set for soloists, chorus, and orchestra by a wide variety of composers such as Anton Bruckner, Franz Schubert, Antonín Dvořák, and Gioacchino Rossini. Verdi's *Requiem,* in memory of the author Alessandro Manzoni, is a large and dramatic setting of the moving requiem text.

In three great works, *The Damnation of Faust* (1846), the *Requiem* (*Grande messe des morts,* 1837) and the *Te Deum* (1855), Hector Berlioz reached the epitome of the colossal romantic choral style. The musical forces involved in these works are gigantic. The *Requiem* was written for 210 singers, a large orchestra, and four brass bands positioned in various locations and representing the calls to the Last Judgment. The *Te Deum* requires two choruses of one hundred singers each, six children's voices, and an orchestra of 150 players. The effects Berlioz achieved with his masterful skill at orchestration were truly dazzling.

BRAHMS

Johannes Brahms composed some of the most enduring choral music of the Romantic period. He wrote for a wide variety of choral combinations and in diverse styles. Smaller works include a cappella choruses for various voice combinations, motets, canons, part songs, and psalm settings, many employing various types of instrumental accompaniment. One of the most popular of these works is the *Liebeslieder Walzer* (*Lovesong Waltz,* 1868–1869) for piano, four hands, and either mixed solo quartet or chorus. Brahms composed several large works for chorus and orchestra, some with several soloists. Among these are the cantata

Rinaldo (opus 50), the incomparable *Schicksalslied* (*Song of Destiny,* opus 54) for chorus and orchestra, and *Triumphlied* (*Song of Triumph,* opus 55). The most important of his large-scale choral compositions was one of his early works, *Ein Deutsches Requiem* (*A German Requiem,* opus 45). It was composed over a period of eleven years and was finished in 1868, when Brahms was thirty-five. It not only preceded much of his other choral writing, but was written a full eight years before his first symphony.

EIN DEUTSCHES REQUIEM (A GERMAN REQUIEM, OPUS 45)

Unlike the Requiems of Mozart, Berlioz, Verdi, and later Fauré, Brahms's setting does not employ the traditional Latin text, which is actually a mass for the dead (*Missa pro defunctis*). Rather, it is a setting of nonliturgical German texts Brahms selected from the Lutheran Bible. A comparison of the Brahms text with the Roman Catholic liturgy shows a marked difference in intention and feeling: The Latin text prays for the soul of the dead, while Brahms's text is designed to console the living.

The opening words of the two texts confirm this:

ROMAN CATHOLIC TEXT	**BRAHMS TEXT**
(Missa pro defunctis)	*(Ein Deutsches Requiem)*
Requiem aeternam dona eis Domine	Selig sind, die da Leid tragen, denn sie
(Give them eternal rest, O Lord)	sollen getröstet werden
	(Blessed are they that mourn, for they shall be comforted)

BRAHMS: *Ein Deutsches Requiem*, Sixth Movement
Cassette 5/A, Track 2
CD 5, Track 2

Brahms's entire composition conveys this pervasive feeling of consolation in both the text and the music.

The work consists of seven movements and is scored for soprano and baritone soloists, chorus, and a large orchestra. The chorus and orchestra participate in all seven movements, although the orchestration varies somewhat from movement to movement. By comparison, the role of the soloists is minimal, with the baritone appearing in the third and sixth movements and the soprano appearing only in the fifth. Brahms builds a sense of overall unity into the piece by linking the first and last movements in spirit and in key (F major), and by including in the last movement thematic material from the first.

Sixth Movement

In many respects, the sixth movement is the most dramatic of the entire work. It is characterized by extreme contrasts and driving climaxes, and its power is intensified by its position between the gentle fifth movement and the quiet, consoling seventh, with its remembrance of the first movement.

Denn wir haben hier keine bleibende
Statt, sondern die zukünftige suchen wir.

For here we have no lasting city, but we seek that which is to come.

HEBREWS 13:14

Siehe, ich sage euch ein Geheimnis:
Wir werden nicht alle entschlafen, wir
 werden aber alle verwandelt werden;
 und dasselbige plötzlich, in einem
 Augenblick, zu der
 Zeit der letzten Posaune.[3]

Denn es wird die Posaune schallen, und
 die Toten werden auferstehen
 unverweslich, und wir werden
 verwandelt werden.

Dann wird erfüllet werden das Wort, das
 geschrieben steht: Der Tod ist
 verschlungen in dem Sieg.

Tod, wo ist dein Stachel?
Hölle, wo ist dein Sieg?

I CORINTHIANS 15:51–55

Herr, du bist würdig zu nehmen
 Preis und Ehre und Kraft,
 den du hast alle Dinge geschaffen, und
 durch deinen Willen haben sie das
 Wesen und sind geschaffen.

REVELATION 4:11

Behold, I tell you a mystery:
We shall not all sleep, but we shall all be
 changed in a moment, in the twinkling
 of an eye, at the time of the last
 trumpet.

For the trumpet shall sound, and the
 dead shall be raised incorruptible, and
 we shall be changed.

Then shall come to pass the saying that
 is written: Death is swallowed up in
 victory.

Death, where is thy sting?
Hell, where is thy victory?

Lord, Thou art worthy to receive glory
 and honor and power, for Thou hast
 made all things, and by Thy will they
 were given substance and were created.

The movement consists of three large sections; the first two involve the solo baritone, while the third is an extended fugue for chorus and orchestra. The first section is moderate in tempo (andante) and subdued in dynamics (pp); the texture is thin, with the upper strings muted and the cellos and basses playing pizzicato doubling the chorus.

Example 16.14

The second section begins with the solo baritone announcing *"Siehe, ich sage euch ein Geheimnis"*: *"Wir werden nicht alle entschlafen."* The melodic activity of the last word is reduced while the winds introduce a contrasting phrase (example 16.15).

---

3. "Posaune" is German for *trombone*. In this context it is by tradition translated to read *trumpet*.

Example 16.15

Wir wer·den nicht al - le ent - schla — — — fen.

The chorus repeats the same text on static chords against which the strings play the baritone's original melody, again answered by the winds. The alternations (between baritone and chorus, strings and winds) continue during the phrase *"wir werden aber alle verwandelt werden."*

The baritone's next phrase, *"und dasselbige plötzlich,"* still quiet and slow, marks the beginning of a drive to an engulfing climax. The momentum begins to pick up, with the appearance of the original baritone melody at double speed in the violins and then flutes.

Example 16.16

A gradual crescendo in the lower strings carries the momentum as far as the word *"Augenblick."* After an abrupt pause, the soloist begins alone with the text *"zu der Zeit der letzten Posaune";* he is joined, appropriately enough, by the trombones and tuba. The tempo begins to accelerate, along with a gradual crescendo (*poco a poco*—"little by little"), and the chorus takes over from the soloist. The full orchestra joins in for a fortissimo climax on *"Po-sau---ne."* As the momentum continues to increase, the strings begin a rapid rising and falling tremolo figure, while the rest of the orchestra punctuates with short chords. This leads directly into the second large section of the movement.

The rushing string figure continues into the next section, which is marked *vivace* and is in triple meter. The chorus, singing *"Denn es wird die Posaune,"* is supported by the winds, brasses, and timpani. The choral parts are a mixture of straightforward declamation, tightly woven legato lines, and sharp, stinging exclamations, all very loud.

Example 16.17

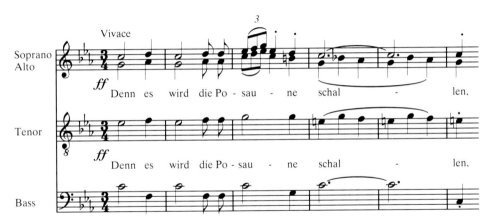

This driving passage is interrupted by the baritone's final appearance; over a soft orchestral background, he sings *"Dann wird erfüllet,"* with melodic material reminiscent of his earlier passage, *"Siehe, ich sage euch."* His last word is engulfed by a resumption of the furious string passage work, which leads to a repetition of the material that opened the section, this time with the words *"Der Tod ist verschlungen."*

This section is extended beyond the repeat, concentrating on the contrast between the two phrases, *"Tod, wo ist dein Stachel?"* with its very short, hard notes, and *"Hölle, wo ist dein Sieg?,"* which is very lush and legato. The accompaniment in the string section also differs for these two phrases. Gradually the emphasis shifts to the single word *"wo."*

wo . . . . wo . . . . . . wo . . . .
Wo ist dein Sieg?

All the forces come together to emphasize these words, and out of this climax emerges the final section of the movement, a long and triumphant fugue in C major. In general, the fugal voices are doubled by wind instruments, while the strings play accompaniments and countersubjects. The fugue subject is a broad, majestic statement, while the countersubjects are lighter and faster moving.

Example 16.18

As a contrast to the emphatic quality of the fugal opening, the section *"Denn du hast"* is very soft and legato; this material occurs several times during the course of the fugue. Further contrast is provided by the homophonic setting that is sometimes given to the text *"zu nehmen Preis und Ehre und Kraft,"* particularly at the powerful ending of the movement.

Example 16.19

Perhaps more than any other, this movement demonstrates Brahms's unique ability to combine classical design—its carefully balanced and contrasting elements—with the expressive qualities of the romantic spirit.

Ein Deutsches Requiem, like the great sacred choral works by Schütz and Bach in the Baroque period, was inspired by a deep concern for the state of the human soul; the more humanistic orientation of the Romantic age led Brahms to direct his words to the mourners rather than to the deceased. The texts of consolation and hope that he chose have an eloquent beauty of their own, and his music enhances this beauty still more.

Characteristics of Romantic Music

Tonality	Major-minor system with less firm sense of tonal center
Texture	Largely homophonic
Rhythm	Frequent fluctuations in tempo; use of rubato
Pitch	Greatly expanded pitch range
Harmony	Use of chromatic harmonies Modulations to distant keys Complicated chords Harmony used as expressive element
Tone Color	Fascination and experimentation with instrumental color; color rivals other elements in importance
Melody	Lyrical, expressive, flowing; sometimes ornamented
Dynamics	Wide range of dynamics Frequent fluctuations in dynamic level Dynamics used as structural element
Small Works	Art song (Lied) Character pieces and miniatures for piano
Large Works	Concerto, symphony, program symphony, symphonic poem (tone poem), opera, choral works, chamber works, concert overture
Instruments	Piano was favorite instrument; large orchestra; unusual instrument groupings; emphasis on orchestration and color
Performance Style	Steady growth of virtuoso technique
Formal Innovations	Carefully constructed classical forms were freely manipulated and expanded; cyclical procedure; theme transformation; development of programmatic and descriptive music as manifested in the program symphony and tone poem; *verismo* movement in opera; development of nationalism in music.

SUMMARY

During the early part of the Romantic era, Paris was the operatic capital of Europe. French opera concentrated on spectacular productions featuring crowd scenes, ballets, choruses, and fantastic scenery. These grand operas, however, gradually gave way to lyric operas that emphasized romantic plots and beautiful melodies. Toward the end of the century, a naturalistic style developed, of which Georges Bizet's *Carmen* is a prime example.

In Italy, Gioacchino Rossini was the outstanding composer of the early part of the nineteenth century. His *Barber of Seville* is an excellent example of the Italian *opera buffa*. The dominant figure in Italian opera during the second half of the century was Giuseppe Verdi. His realistic, action-filled plots were dominated by the singing voice, which became the primary vehicle for emotional expression. Toward the end of the century, a movement toward naturalism penetrated Italian opera. Called *verismo,* it is best exemplified in the works of Giacomo Puccini.

Romantic opera in Germany was strongly influenced by the romantic movement itself. The composer who first established a genuinely Germanic style was Carl Maria von Weber. German opera reached its highest point in the works of Richard Wagner, who sought to write "music dramas" that would encompass all the arts in a unified whole. To Wagner, the most important element was the drama, with the music serving the dramatic expression. Dramatic unity was enhanced by the use of leitmotifs, or melodic fragments associated with persons, objects, or ideas. Wagner's use of chromatic harmonies represented a significant step toward the development of new tonal systems in the twentieth century.

The lush sound of a large chorus was well suited to the romantic style, and nearly every composer of the period wrote choral music in some form. Hector Berlioz frequently utilized a large chorus combined with an enormous orchestra in his works. Oratorios and settings of Catholic liturgical texts were written by such composers as Mendelssohn, Liszt, Berlioz, Schubert, Bruckner, and Verdi. Choruses also were used in programmatic symphonic works.

Some of the most enduring choral music of the Romantic era was written by Johannes Brahms. The greatness of his most significant work, *Ein Deutsches Requiem,* rests on its masterful and eloquent marriage of the music and texts. In contrast to the traditional Catholic funeral Mass, Brahms's *Requiem* uses texts from the Old and New Testaments that give a message of comfort and consolation to the bereaved mourners.

NEW TERMS

grand opera
opéra comique
lyric opera
naturalism

bel canto
coloratura
verismo
leitmotif

SUGGESTED LISTENING

Berlioz, Hector

Requiem (Grande messe des morts): Mass for the Dead. This monumental Mass for the dead requires over two hundred voices in the chorus and an immense orchestra with eight pairs of timpani and four brass ensembles scattered around the stage. Berlioz, a superb orchestrator, uses this huge force to the best effect, supporting the drama of the texts in this powerful work.

Bizet, Georges

Carmen. This *opéra comique* is based on Prosper Merimée's tragic novel about a fiery, beautiful, amoral gypsy woman and the tormented soldier who gives up everything for her. Bizet's last work is his greatest and, despite its initial failure (which contributed directly to his death), has become one of the most popular operas in the repertoire.

Leoncavallo, Ruggiero

I Pagliacci (The Clowns)

Mascagni, Pietro
Cavalleria Rusticana (Rustic Chivalry)

I Pagliacci and *Cavalleria Rusticana*, two short, powerful operas, are almost always presented together. Both are in verismo style, and both deal with love betrayed and its tragic revenge. *I Pagliacci* contains one of the most famous arias of Italian opera, "Vesti la giubba," in which the betrayed husband pours out his grief.

Mendelssohn, Felix

Elias (Elijah). This oratorio is Mendelssohn's most important choral work, incorporating elements of Bach's Passion style and Handel's oratorio form. Written for an English music festival, *Elias* had a brilliant premiere and remained extremely popular for a number of years. It remains one of the best-known oratorios due to its inspired blending of musical and dramatic elements.

Rossini, Gioacchino

Il Barbiere di Siviglia (The Barber of Seville). This opera, based on the famous Beaumarchais play, is an example of *opera buffa* at its finest. It tells of the wooing of the beautiful and rich Rosina by Count Almaviva in spite of the opposition of Rosina's old guardian, who wants to marry her himself. Love finds a way with the help of the crafty barber Figaro, whose comic opening aria is the famous "Largo al factotum."

Verdi, Giuseppe

Aida, Verdi's masterpiece of spectacular grand opera. Regarded as the height of his second creative period.

Wagner, Richard

Die Meistersinger von Nürnberg. This work remained one of Wagner's most popular and accessible operas. The libretto, by Wagner himself, is based on historical figures from the sixteenth-century Nuremberg guild of mastersingers. The famous overture is frequently performed as a concert piece.

Music of the Early Twentieth Century

Three Musicians, by Fernand Léger, 1944, oil on canvas,
68½ × 57¼ in. (Collection, The Museum of Modern Art, New York.
Mrs. Simon Guggenheim Fund.)

The Genesis of the Modern Era

A lthough romanticism infused the music of the entire nineteenth century, by mid-century other art forms began to take a new direction. Rejecting emotionalism, realist writers and artists chose to portray everyday life—and low life—as objectively and unsentimentally as possible.

Realism included an interest in portraying scenes of nature accurately and unpretentiously. What this interest led to was the awesome impressionist departure of the 1870s. Strongly influenced by Edouard Manet (1832–1883), who played down careful perspective and abandoned the usual gradations of light and shadow in his efforts to give the illusion of three-dimensionality, the impressionists went a step further. In their landscape painting, they concentrated on producing an overall sense of what the eye sees rather than what the mind knows is there. In a way, the real subject of the impressionists was not nature itself, but light. Leaving their studios for the out-of-doors, they carefully noted how sunlight illuminates an object and tried to duplicate that effect by applying their bright, pastel-colored pigment in tiny flecks. To give their paintings spontaneity and immediacy, they consciously blurred or distorted their images. The most accomplished of the impressionists was Claude Monet (1840–1928). (See page 367.)

In his later career, Monet was so eager to capture the way objects change their appearance in response to changes in light and atmosphere that he undertook to paint whole series of canvases devoted to a given subject—a cathedral, a haystack, a poplar tree—as it appeared at different times of the day.

Artists trained at the official academies and most critics in Paris were both contemptuous of and hostile toward the impressionists, dismissing their exhibitions as the work of madmen, frauds, and incompetents. Nevertheless, though it was scorned in the 1870s, impressionism began to achieve a measure of success and recognition in the 1880s. Meanwhile, a counterpart to impressionism could be discerned in literature, in the movement called symbolism. Symbolist poets, among whom were Charles Baudelaire (1821–1867) and Arthur Rimbaud (1854–1891), attempted to achieve "musical" effects by manipulating the rhythm and sounds of words. The basic idea or emotion of each poem was suggested by clusters of images and metaphors.

By the end of the nineteenth century, many art collectors actively sought out impressionist works. The academic viewpoint, which held that art should be concerned only with religious, historical, literary, and patriotic themes, had started to fade, and the impressionist experiments of the 1870s had stimulated painters to explore a wide range of different styles. Vincent van Gogh (1835–1890) worked with agitated, distorted shapes and brilliant color to arouse the feelings of the observer (see page 368).

Paul Gauguin (1848–1903) introduced large areas of bright, flat color, and his scenes of primitive life in Brittany and Tahiti conveyed an overpowering sensuality (see page 369).

Georges Seurat (1859–1891) and Paul Cézanne (1839–1901), on the other hand, were more interested in new formal combinations than in the expression of feelings. Seurat, deeply influenced by the color theory of contemporary physicists, applied tiny dots of pure color to the canvas to build scenes that shimmered with light. Cézanne, whose goal was to capture on canvas the solidity of the forms found in nature, retained the color of the impressionists but concentrated on conveying a sense of the mass of objects (see page 370).

The work of the impressionist and postimpressionist artists helped prepare the way for the tremendous amount of experimentation that marked all the arts of the early twentieth century. Indeed, it is fair to say that few centuries have witnessed more basic changes in the arts than the twentieth. In painting and sculpture, the depiction of actual objects was abandoned for nonrepresentational abstraction. In literature, traditional narrative forms were sometimes discarded for radical new approaches, such as James Joyce's stream-of-consciousness technique. In music, traditional harmony and tonality were redefined or rejected in favor of atonality and serialism. Indeed, it seems that the quest for innovation and new systems of expression has sometimes made newness the most important standard of quality. Since World War II, the range of expression in all the arts has become so vast that consensus among critics and patrons has nearly disappeared.

In the first years of the twentieth century, young artists, influenced by the impressionists and the avant-garde postimpressionists, exhibited styles of painting that were more daring and varied than any seen in the preceding generation. Beginning around 1905, the painters known as the Fauves ("wild beasts"), most notably Henri Matisse (1870–1954), worked in an expressionist style, which distorted contours and colors with the intent of creating visual excitement and expressing inner feeling rather than reproducing reality.

One Russian-born expressionist, who worked both in Paris and in Munich, was Wassily Kandinsky (1866–1944). In 1910, he took the drastic step of completely abandoning representational painting. Thereafter, it was recognized that the subject of the painter could be simply shapes and colors—with all the freedom and variety that this kind of abstraction implies. (See page 371.)

A different current of twentieth-century painting developed from the experiments of Paul Cézanne, who, after a giant retrospective in Paris at the turn of the century, was now recognized as a "master." In the decade preceding World War I, Pablo Picasso (1881–1973) and others developed a style called cubism. In this style, illustrated by the striking *Les Demoiselles d'Avignon* (see page 372), a composition was broken into angular, geometric shapes presented from several simultaneous viewpoints.

Cubism differed from expressionism in giving primary attention to form. Instead of trying to excite the passions of the observer or reveal the inner soul of the artist, cubism tried to reformulate the world in terms of fundamental shapes: spheres, cones, cubes, and cylinders. This concern with abstract structure held broad possibilities, and cubism thus remained a strong influence on advanced painting throughout the first half of the century.

The most provocative sculptor in late-nineteenth-century France was Auguste Rodin (1848–1917), because he explored human form more intuitively than his contemporaries, whose sculpture was often pedantically exact and mock-heroic. By 1900, Rodin was the most renowned artist in Paris (see page 373).

But how different sculpture became in the next few years! Matisse designed bronzes of highly abstract human figures, and in 1909 Picasso applied the cubist approach to a bronze head. Umberto Boccioni (1882–1916) attempted to display figures in the process of movement (see page 374), and the Romanian sculptor Constantin Brancusi (1876–1957) developed forms that were nearly nonrepresentational.

In architecture, designers began moving away from the historicism of the previous century, with its emphasis on the revival of earlier styles. One architectural eccentric, Antonio Gaudi of Spain (1852–1926), rejected historical building vocabularies entirely, in favor of free-flowing, almost organic forms. More influential in the development of a contemporary architecture, however, was the Bauhaus, a German school that designed buildings and objects in a functional style that was consistent with the era of mass production and made use of industrial materials. More than any other single institution, the Bauhaus helped create the so-called international style, an architecture of steel framing, glass, and concrete. Twentieth-century apartments, office buildings, factories, civic centers, department stores, and schools designed in this functional, antihistorical style have changed the appearance of cities all over the world (see page 374).

Changes in the music of the late nineteenth and early twentieth centuries were just as substantial as those in the visual arts. Whereas the romantic mode prevailed before 1900, the turn of the century brought new directions. Musical impressionism was introduced in the compositions of Claude Debussy, who began to experiment with a new harmonic vocabulary and to move away from traditional forms and procedures. Later, such composers as Hindemith, Bartók, and Stravinsky redefined tonality and changed the way that a tonal center was established. Arnold Schoenberg took an even more radical direction, rejecting tonality altogether and eventually developing a revolutionary new system of musical organization called serialism.

When Claude Monet's *Impression: Sunrise* was exhibited in 1874,
one critic who was appalled by its "unfinished" qualities
denounced the new style and coined the term "impressionism"
in disgust.

Between 1850 and 1950, the Industrial Revolution transformed the nature of
work and the standard of living for the overwhelming majority of people in Europe
and America. The great cities, railroad systems, and factories created an environment entirely different from that of the primarily agricultural world that existed
before the mid-nineteenth century. It is hard for those of us who have known no
other life to appreciate how complex our industrial world is. Its diversity and complexity, however, help to explain the breakdown of the classical and romantic styles
and their replacement with a bewildering variety of movements and directions in all
the arts.

In the 1880s, French artists, using impressionism as a starting point, developed far more radical designs. Vincent van Gogh's late paintings of the dazzling light and color of the Provençal countryside— as in *The Starry Night* (1889)—demonstrate the agitation and emotional power of his highly individual style. (Oil on canvas, 29 × 36¼ in. Collection, The Museum of Modern Art, New York; acquired through the Lillie P. Bliss Bequest.)

*D*ay of the Gods (*Mahana no Atua*), by Paul Gauguin, French,
1848–1903. Oil on canvas, 1894, 68.3 × 91.5 cm.
(Helen Birch Bartlett Memorial Collection, 1926.198.
Photograph © 1992, The Art Institute of Chicago.

Bathers, by Paul Cézanne, 1898–1905.
Oil on canvas, 82 × 98 in.

Composition 238: Bright Circle, by Wassily Kandinsky, 1921. Oil on canvas, 54½ × 70⅞ in. (Yale University Art Gallery. Gift of Collection Societe Anonyme).

Les Demoiselles d'Avignon, Paris, painted by Pablo Picasso in 1907,
fractures and dislocates form into planes and geometrical blocks.
Early critics dubbed the new style cubism. The figures on the right
reflect the influence of African sculpture. (Oil on canvas, 8′ × 7′ 8″.
Collection, The Museum of Modern Art, New York; acquired
through the Lillie P. Bliss Bequest.)

The Burghers of Calais, by Rodin, 1884–1886.
Bronze, 82½ × 95 × 78″.

Unique Forms of Continuity in Space, by Umberto Boccioni (1913).
Bronze (cast 1931), 43⅞ × 34⅞ × 15¾″. Boccioni tried to show the
human figure in motion by suggesting several different moments of time
in one sculpture. This bronze seems to have been shaped by rushing air
whose currents extend beyond the fluttering shapes of the metal.
(Collection, The Museum of Modern Art, New York;
acquired through the Lillie P. Bliss Bequest.)

The Bauhaus Workshop, built by Walter Gropius in the 1920s,
dramatized the principle of building a structural skeleton of steel and
then giving it a floor-to-ceiling glass wall. This kind of functional
architecture was later called the international style.
(The Museum of Modern Art, New York.)

BRIDGING THE GAP BETWEEN CENTURIES

Toward the end of the nineteenth century, the center of cultural activity in Europe was Paris. Two different musical styles were current. One was the basically German-Italian late romantic style, strongly influenced by the monumental achievements of Richard Wagner. The leaders of this pan-European style of music in Paris were César Franck (1822–1890) and his pupils. The other was the specifically French tradition, as cultivated by Camille Saint-Saëns (1835–1921), Jules Massenet (1842–1912), and Gabriel Fauré (1845–1924). The underlying spirit of the French tradition was more classical and orderly than romantic and expressive. The music was subtle and understated, full of lyric melodies and carefully wrought details.

IMPRESSIONISM AND SYMBOLISM

The musical culture of France was closely connected to the other arts, particularly painting and literature. One of the outstanding artistic movements of the turn of the century was **impressionism,** in which painters sought to capture the visual impression, rather than the literal reality, of a subject. Although their work and methods were at first ridiculed by the critics, the impressionists persisted in their exploration of the play of light and their use of patches and dabs of color to build up an image. They also continued their habit of working out-of-doors and utilizing bright afternoon light; mood and atmosphere and the richness of nature were among their major inspirations. Meanwhile, **symbolist** poets were experimenting with rhythm, sound, and the clustering of images to suggest moods or emotions.

Coming slightly later than the movements in art and literature, the impressionist movement in music was similarly characterized by experimentation and by the rejection of past viewpoints. It, too, emphasized mood and atmosphere more than structure, and it, too, adopted nature as a frequent subject. Impressionist music was recognizable by its fragile and decorative beauty, its sensuous tone colors, its subdued atmosphere, its elegance and refinement. It cast off the more pompous, heavy, and serious quality of the German tradition. The influence of impressionism extended to England, Spain, Italy, and America, but France produced the most important composers: Claude Debussy and Maurice Ravel.

DEBUSSY (1862–1918)

Claude Debussy (fig. 17.1) was born in St. Germain-en-Laye, near Paris, and was educated at the Paris Conservatory, where he received traditional training in the cosmopolitan late romantic style. He absorbed it well enough to win the Prix de Rome at the age of twenty-two, but soon after, he began to reject the Germanic tradition in general and Wagner's philosophy in particular.

Debussy was put off by the grand themes and ponderous quality of German Romantic music. For him the primary goal of music was to give pleasure, to appeal to the senses. An incisive critic, Debussy wrote articles on music that were published in the leading French journals. His reaction to Wagner's use of the leitmotif is characteristically witty and caustic: "Remember, [Wagnerian characters] never appear unless accompanied by their damnable leitmotiv, and there are even those who sing it! It's rather like those silly people who hand you their visiting cards and then lyrically recite key information they contain."

Opera was one of Debussy's lifelong interests, and his operatic style was very much a reaction against Wagner's influence. *Pelléas et Mélisande* (1902), which Debussy worked on during the 1890s, is taken from a symbolist play by Maurice Maeterlinck, and the vague references and images of the text are matched by the strange harmonies and restrained colors of the music. Throughout the work, the voices dominate over a continuous orchestral background. The first performance of the opera met a mixed reaction; some critics attacked it for its lack of form and melody and its unconventional harmonies, and others were enchanted by its subtle, elusive quality. The opera caught on and established Debussy as the leader of the impressionist movement in music.

Figure 17.1 Claude Debussy. He broke with the German Romantic style to create evocative impressionistic music characterized by its sensuous tone colors, elusive chromatic harmonies, and freedom of form.

Debussy was deeply devoted to his country, and the onset of World War I disturbed him so profoundly that for a time he felt incapable of writing music. But his sense of nationalism impelled him to return to his art, and he began composing again with furious energy—an effort spurred on by the fact that he was slowly dying of cancer. His death came in March 1918, as Paris was being bombarded by German artillery.

DEBUSSY'S WORK

Debussy's compositions for piano are among the most significant works for that instrument written during the present century. His early (nonimpressionistic) works include the *Suite Bergamasque* (1893) and a suite *Pour le piano* (1901). *Clair de lune* (*Moonlight,* 1890) is perhaps his best-known work for piano. The impressionistic style is fully evident in works published between 1903 and 1913: *Estampes* (*Engravings*), two collections of *Préludes,* and two of *Images.*

Debussy's important orchestral works are all impressionistic, beginning with the *Prélude à l'après-midi d'un faune* (*Prelude to the Afternoon of a Faun,* 1894), and continuing with the three *Nocturnes*—*Nuages* (*Clouds*), *Fêtes* (*Festivals*), and *Sirenes* (*Sirens*)—and *La Mer* (*The Sea,* 1905), a set of symphonic sketches. In chamber music his greatest achievement was the Quartet in G Minor for Strings (1893). The first performance of this work left its audience puzzled and critics complaining of an "orgy of modulations." A forerunner of his musical impressionism, it came to be recognized in the twentieth century as one of the most important string quartets since those of Brahms.

Although Debussy loved opera, he completed only one of the many operatic projects he started, *Pelléas et Mélisande.* He also wrote incidental music for a play as well as art songs set to poems by Mallarmé, Villon, Verlaine, Baudelaire, and others.

DEBUSSY'S STYLE

The music of Claude Debussy is programmatic, but in a very general way; there is little attempt to tell a story or express specific feelings. Rather, his music creates a "mood" or atmosphere to correspond with its subject or program.

Although Debussy's style is unique, many influences helped form it. Most important were the romantic pianists Chopin and Liszt and the composers in the French tradition. Paris was a center for Russian music, and Mussorgsky's idiom pointed Debussy in new directions. His interest in exotic music was stimulated by the Javanese orchestra (called a *gamelan*), which he heard at the Paris Exposition of 1889.

One of the strongest influences on Debussy's style was not musical at all, but literary; he was closely associated with a group of artists centered around Stéphane Mallarmé, the symbolist poet. Through this connection, Debussy became interested in expressing the unique sounds and rhythmic patterns of the French language in music. French generally avoids strong accents, making use of vowels of different lengths for rhythm and stress. Debussy's choice of subject matter for many of his pieces also reflects his close association with this important literary movement.

Debussy was the first European composer to break with the old system of tonality, and the new language he developed had a profound influence on almost every other composer of the twentieth century. His music is organized around sound patterns; he works with blocks of color and shifts from one to another very subtly. The harmonic basis of his music is entirely new, building on the symmetrical patterns of the whole-tone scale (example 17.1).

Example 17.1

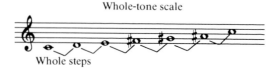

Whole-tone scale

Whole steps

Notice in example 17.1 that the *dominant* (G♮) and the *leading tone* (B) are not included in the whole-tone scale. Thus, instead of relying on the traditional tonic-dominant-tonic sequence of harmonies, Debussy often uses a series of chords built on adjacent degrees of the scale. These parallel chains of chords leave the piece without any clearly defined tonal center for extended periods. Other elements of the music must therefore function as form-building devices—particularly rhythm, dynamics, texture, and instrumental timbre.

In one sense, of course, Debussy's style is clearly an offshoot of the romantic movement; the emphasis on color and the lack of interest in traditional forms and procedures are evidence of this, as are the literary associations of most of his works. But in another sense, Debussy represents the beginning of the new and radically different music of the twentieth century. His use of nonfunctional harmonies took music into new and uncharted areas, and his freer forms and concentration on timbre influenced almost all later composers.

PRÉLUDE À L'APRÈS-MIDI D'UN FAUNE

DEBUSSY: *Prélude à l'après-midi d'un faune*
Cassette 5/A, Track 3
CD 5, Track 3
See Listening Guide on pages 381–382.

This brief work was inspired by Mallarmé's poem *L'après-midi d'un faune,* published in 1876. Debussy first intended to write an opera based on the poem but soon abandoned this project for a smaller one; he described the *Prélude* as a "very free illustration of Mallarmé's beautiful poem." The faun of the title is the sensual forest deity of pagan mythology, half man, half goat. Awakening from sleep, his mind befuddled by wine, the faun recalls two nymphs he had seen earlier in the day. Did he carry them off to his lair or was it only a fantasy? "Is it a dream that I love?" he asks. But the afternoon is warm, the effort to remember too great, so once again he drifts off to sleep. Without following the events of the poem literally, Debussy evokes a musical impression of each scene.

In the *Prélude,* which was his first orchestral work, Debussy had not completely broken with traditional ideas of form; the piece is very roughly in an AA′BA″ pattern, although there is no literal repetition. However, the character and significance of the work lie, not in its formal structure, but in those elements that give it its impressionistic quality.

The choice of instruments is in itself unusual and indicative of the nature of the piece. The winds consist of three flutes, two oboes, English horn, two clarinets, and two bassoons; there are four horns, but the rest of the brasses (trumpets, trombones, and tuba) are omitted and the percussion is limited to a pair of tiny "antique cymbals," which produce a delicate rather than a smashing sound. Two harps and strings complete the instrumentation.

Debussy also departs from the standard orchestral practice in his *use* of these instruments. Virtually all the main melodic material is assigned to solo winds, primarily flute and oboe, with the horn also playing an important role. The strings are often muted and divided. The use of the harps helps evoke the langorous atmosphere, which is the essence of the piece.

The opening theme is a sensuous melody first played by the solo flute and heard later in various transformations throughout the work (example 17.2).

Example 17.2

The lyric theme of the middle section is first located in the wind instruments in unison and repeated later by the strings.

Example 17.3

In general, the piece has a delicate, restrained, dreamlike quality. The dynamic level is subdued, only occasionally rising to a forte or fortissimo. There are frequent subtle changes of tempo and dynamics, a relaxed, almost vague rhythmic movement without a strong beat, and many dissonant harmonies, which provide color more than a strong sense of progression. All of these contribute to the floating, evocative nature of the work.

Along with Debussy's later orchestral works, the *Prélude* had a profound and lasting effect on the subsequent development of orchestral music.

MAURICE RAVEL

Maurice Ravel (1875–1937) is often linked with Debussy as the other major figure who most fully realized the possibilities of musical impressionism. But Ravel's music, especially the compositions written in his later years, combines the sonorous impressionism of Debussy with a classical orientation toward form and balance.

Philosophically, Ravel had much in common with Debussy. Both composers agreed that music should serve an aesthetic purpose, that the creation of beautiful sound was the ultimate aim. They considered themselves rebels against German Romanticism and the Wagnerian school. They shared an attraction to the medieval modes and the novel scales employed by nationalistic composers of other countries. The rhythms of Spanish dance music also intrigued them, as did Oriental modes and colors.

But the similarities between the two composers were limited. While Ravel made use of all the impressionist devices, his compositional procedures were quite different in a number of ways from those of Debussy. Ravel's work features less use of the whole-tone scale and sparing use of dissonance. His use of orchestral color is more brilliant and dynamic than

Debussy's. For musical texture, he relied on melodic lines rather than on the parallel blocks of sound that Debussy favored. Ravel also displayed a firmer sense of key and employed broader melodies, more distinct harmonic movement, and more emphatic rhythms than his predecessor.

Ravel created many compositions for the piano. *Pavane pour une Infante défunte* (*Pavane for a Dead Princess,* 1899), *Jeux d'eaux* (*Fountains,* 1901), and *Miroirs* (1905) are among the works that earned him his reputation as one of the outstanding composers of piano music of the twentieth century.

Songs were also a source of fascination to Ravel, and he continued their composition until the end of his life. *Schéhérazade* (1903) is a song cycle for voice and orchestra. Ravel also succeeded in combining chamber music with voice, as in the *Trois poèmes de Stéphane Mallarmé* (1913) and the sensuous *Chansons madécasses* (*Songs of Madagascar,* 1926).

Despite his popular repertoire of piano works, songs, and chamber music, Ravel is unquestionably best known for his orchestral works. His *Rapsodie espagnole* (*Spanish Rhapsody,* 1907) remains a favorite today. So, too, does his *Mother Goose Suite* (1912) for orchestra, adapted from his own piano composition. One of his most ambitious undertakings was *Daphnis et Chloë* (1912), a ballet from which were taken two frequently performed orchestral suites. Two of his most enduring compositions are *La Valse* (1920) and *Boléro* (1928). In both, the artist made use of unusual elements. *La Valse* is notable for its unusual combination of traditional waltz rhythms and arresting and disturbing harmonic and textural elements. *Boléro,* drawing its inspiration from the Spanish dance of the same name, employs a gradual uninterrupted crescendo and a repetitive single melody. To this great body of work must also be added the famous Piano Concerto in G (1931) and the *Concerto for the Left Hand* (1931), two virtuosic masterpieces.

OTHER TRENDS IN THE EARLY TWENTIETH CENTURY

The effects of Debussy's musical innovations were lasting. Conceptions of tonality broadened in the wake of his break with the harmonic tradition that culminated in the romanticism of the music dramas of Richard Wagner. However, by 1918, the year of Debussy's death, impressionism was giving way to other styles.

A group of young French composers known as "The Six"—Georges Auric, Louis Durey, Arthur Honegger, Darius Milhaud, Francis Poulenc, and Germaine Tailleferre—shared the common goal of creating lighthearted, "simple" music, free of the emotional intensity of romanticism and the vague qualities of impressionism.

Each member of The Six composed in a variety of forms and styles. Honegger's and Poulenc's music became conservative as their careers progressed. Milhaud remained an experimenter. He explored polytonality, incorporated jazz elements, and, late in his career, wrote electronic music. Tailleferre was not an innovator. Her works remained within the original boundaries of the group. She cultivated a style characterized by simple melodies and uncomplicated harmony and rhythm. Auric achieved distinction as a composer of film scores, and Durey turned to musicological research instead of composing.

The mentor who brought The Six together was Eric Satie (1866–1925). Like his younger colleagues of The Six, Satie created "unserious" music that was antisentimental and displayed an ironic sense of humor. The objectivity and simplicity of his style are exemplified in his piano music.

In contrast to the objectivity and wit of Satie are the compositions of Lili Boulanger (1893–1918). Her vocal works are passionate settings of themes of humility, sadness, and despair. Her religious works include psalm settings for various combinations of vocal soloists and orchestra. Her last work, *Pie Jesu* (1918), is scored for solo voice, string quartet, harp, and organ.

Much of Boulanger's music employs typical romantic techniques such as use of leitmotifs in combination with impressionistic harmonies and flexible rhythmic progressions. Boulanger's song cycle *Clairières dans le Ciel* (*Rifts in the Sky*) is a 1914 setting of thirteen poems from symbolist poet Francis James's poetic cycle *Tristesses* (*Sadnesses*). Boulanger won the Prix de Rome in 1913 for her cantata *Faust et Heline*. Her music was championed by her older sister, Nadia Boulanger, the great recitalist, conductor, and teacher.

Listening Guide

DEBUSSY: *Prélude à l'après-midi d'un faune (Prelude to the Afternoon of a Faun)*

Single Movement: Changing tempo
Meter irregular and unclear
Modified ternary form

Orchestra with modified instrumentation (diminished brass and percussion)

Review: Example 17.2 (A theme)
Example 17.3 (B theme)
Outline of program, p. 378

CD 5 (Cassette 5/A, Track 3)

3	①	0:00	**A**	Languid, sensuous flute melody floats down and up; horn calls and harp glissandos; sensuous melody again in flute with quiet tremolo in strings; crescendo in orchestra as intensity builds, then fades away
	②	1:35	**A′**	Sensuous melody, flute, with added decoration, accompanied by occasional harp arpeggios
		2:48	**Bridge**	Splashes of instrumental color through the orchestra grow in volume and animation, suggest faun's awakening senses, then subside; slow, dreamlike clarinet solo with delicate strings moves directly into:
	③	4:33	**B**	Lyric, long-breathed melody in woodwinds with gently pulsing string accompaniment, crescendo; suddenly soft as lyric melody repeats in strings with harp arpeggios and pulsing woodwinds

Continued on next page

	5:54	**Bridge**	Fragments from previous bridge in strings, then in various woodwind colors; solo violin longingly sings beginning of lyric melody
	6:22		Harp arpeggios accompany flute in anticipation of sensuous melody; woodwind fragments of melody and staccato chords interrupt; harp arpeggios accompany opening of sensuous melody in oboe; again soft interruptions
(4)	7:39	**A″**	Sensuous melody in flutes, with the delicate ring of antique cymbals and subdued tremolo in strings, yearning solo violin counterpoint; melody repeated in flute and cello, flute wanders drowsily off, melody completed by oboe
	9:05	**Coda**	Harp and strings in floating, static notes, fragment of sensuous melody in horns, ringing antique cymbals, pizzicato in low strings

SUMMARY

Around the turn of the century, the musical culture of France was closely related to the other arts. Two of the dominant movements at the time were impressionism in painting and symbolism in literature, both of which influenced the development of impressionism in music. Impressionist music is characterized by its fragile beauty, sensuous tone colors, subdued atmosphere, and elegance. It cast off the more pompous, heavy, and serious quality of the German tradition. Claude Debussy is the composer primarily associated with impressionistic style. His use of nonfunctional harmonies and free forms led to the development of organizational procedures built around sound patterns and blocks of color. Other organizational devices used by Debussy are rhythm, dynamics, texture, and instrumental color. Maurice Ravel, who is often linked with Debussy, incorporated many impressionistic devices in his music, but also displayed a classical orientation toward form and balance.

Debussy's innovations had a profound impact on a number of composers. By the time of his death, some composers were rejecting both the vague qualities of impressionism and the emotional intensity of romanticism. Eric Satie and the group of French composers known as "The Six" created lighthearted, antisentimental, and sometimes ironic compositions. Lili Boulanger in France produced significant works, particularly in the area of vocal music.

NEW TERMS

impressionism
symbolism

SUGGESTED LISTENING

Boulanger, Lili

Clairières dans le ciel (*Rifts in the Sky*). This work is a setting of the thirteen poems from symbolist poet Francis James's poetic cycle *Tristesses* (*Sadnesses*). The songs are about a poet's despair as he mourns the disappearance of his lover. (Leonarda Productions.)

Debussy, Claude

Pelléas et Mélisande. An opera in five acts based on a medieval legend. It epitomizes the subtlety of impressionism—each act is a continuum of musical narrative employing leitmotifs.

Ravel, Maurice

Daphnis et Chloë. Ravel's most ambitious work, this "ballet symphony" was commissioned for the Russian ballet.

TOWARD THE
MODERN PERIOD

CHAPTER

18

Although specific points of view have dominated the musical scene at various times since 1900, trends in twentieth-century music do not seem, like those of previous periods, to lead in a single direction. In fact, music since 1900 has been characterized by an unprecedented diversity of styles and points of view. Different styles are displayed by individual composers working at the same time; styles have changed from one five-year period to the next; and differences in style are sometimes found in the musical output of a single composer. Radical or conservative trends have come rapidly to the fore and then have receded into relative obscurity, only to reemerge or even become blended with one another. Popular music and concert music have gone their separate ways as the musical audience itself has expanded and diversified.

DISTINGUISHING FEATURES OF TWENTIETH-CENTURY MUSIC

Despite the diversity of styles to which we have just referred, it is possible to identify three characteristics that distinguish the concert music of our century from that of earlier style periods: tonality, dissonance, and rhythmic complexity.

TONALITY

The tonal system, which had been fundamental to the music of previous centuries, related all notes and chords to a single note, the central or tonic note of the key. Harmonic progressions away from and then back toward the tonic implied motion and rest, departure and arrival. Virtually all the formal structures developed during the Baroque, Classical, and Romantic periods depended on tonality as a major structural element. Fugal procedure, sonata-allegro form, and even the tone poem were all based on certain assumptions about tonality that were shared by composer and listener alike. Although much romantic music strained the boundaries of functional tonality by the introduction of increasing numbers of chromatic notes and by more frequent modulations to distant key areas, it nevertheless retained a strongly tonal character. Many composers of the twentieth century have, by contrast, completely abandoned the assumptions on which this tonal system is based.

Two primary paths were open to a composer who rejected the basic concepts of functional tonality. One was to avoid traditional tonality altogether, denying the importance of any one tone over the others. The music of Arnold Schoenberg evolved along these lines,

384

eventually leading to his formulation of a system called twelve-tone technique or serialism to replace tonality as a structuring force (see chapter 19). But other important composers chose a different course; they maintained the idea of a tonal center or point of rest but significantly altered the methods by which the center was established. Composers in this category include Igor Stravinsky, Béla Bartók, Benjamin Britten, Paul Hindemith, and others.

DISSONANCE

Before the later part of the Romantic period, consonance was considered the norm and dissonance a departure from the norm. Dissonant harmonies were expected to return to, or resolve into, consonance. To varying degrees and in differing stylistic manifestations, this convention regarding the use of dissonance was adhered to by Palestrina, Bach, Mozart, Beethoven, and Brahms, as well as all other composers from each of these eras.

The late romantic styles of Richard Wagner and Richard Strauss placed more emphasis on dissonance. Dissonances became more prolonged, and frequently a series of dissonances would occur before the ultimate resolution to a consonant harmony. As composers included more dissonant tones and chords in their vocabulary of sound, the traditional relationship between consonance and dissonance broke down. Eventually, in the twentieth century, the use of dissonance became independent of the use of consonance. The old tendency to resolve dissonances into consonances was abandoned.

The result was a greater variety of "harmonic sonorities" than had existed before and more complex combinations than had been previously possible. In fact, in much music, harmonic progressions take place from dissonance to dissonance. Thus, the music is heard as a series of dissonances, varying in their complexity from mild to exceedingly tense.

RHYTHMIC COMPLEXITY

The greater degree of dissonance and the use of dissonance apart from consonance in modern music are closely allied to the change in attitudes toward tonality. Quite separate from these developments is the third important distinguishing feature of twentieth-century music—its increased rhythmic complexity. In their search for fresh expression, composers have become interested in breaking up the steadiness of the metrical flow by grouping the beats together in measures of different lengths, or else they have avoided any kind of recurring pulse at all, thus producing an impression of extreme vagueness in the rhythmical flow. Sometimes successive single beats are divided into different numbers of equal parts, giving melodies a free, improvisatory quality. And very often, a number of unusual rhythms are superimposed, making for a more complex texture than had been heard before. Thus, in much modern music it is sometimes difficult to detect regular metrical patterns, or even the actual beat. These rhythmic features contribute significantly to the extraordinary excitement and power characteristic of much of the music of our century.

To summarize, rhythmic complexity, harmonic dissonance, and a less clearly defined or nonexistent tonal center are three distinguishing characteristics of much twentieth-century music.

Figure 18.1 Pablo Picasso, *La Toilette,* 1906. Oil on canvas, 59½″ × 39″. Neoclassicism, which reinterpreted older styles to develop a new, modern idiom, was reflected in art, literature, and music. This 1906 painting by Picasso has a strong classical flavor, its figures suggestive of ancient Greek vase painting. (Albright-Knox Art Gallery, Buffalo, NY; Scala/Art Resource, N.Y.)

NEOCLASSICISM

During the period between the two world wars, a new movement in music grew up as a reaction against romanticism and impressionism. Many leaders in the visual arts had already taken a new direction, into the abstraction and formalism of cubism (painting and sculpture) and the international style (architecture). Now music, too, turned away from the emotionalism of the nineteenth century. Like the artists of the late eighteenth century, who had embarked on a Neoclassical era in painting after the excesses of the Baroque period (fig. 18.1), composers now sought to revive the objectivity and restraint of the Classical era in music.

Neoclassical composers often avoided the huge romantic orchestra in favor of smaller instrumental combinations. They preferred absolute music, which received its impetus from purely musical ideas, to the descriptive elements so prevalent in much romantic and impressionistic music. They looked on musical composition as an intellectual challenge to be approached systematically and rationally, with irrelevant emotions held in check. The neoclassical composers were especially attracted to the forms of the Baroque and Classical periods. But they did not simply resurrect these old forms; they varied them to develop a new and distinctly modern idiom.

STRAVINSKY (1882–1971)

I gor Stravinsky is, along with Arnold Schoenberg, one of the two towering figures in twentieth-century music (fig. 18.2). His career, like that of his great Spanish contemporary Pablo Picasso, spanned three generations; in their respective fields each played a dominant role in almost all significant trends of the first half of this century.

Stravinsky, the third son of one of the most celebrated bass baritones in the Imperial Opera, was born in a small Russian town on the Gulf of Finland near St. Petersburg. He began piano lessons at the age of nine, but his parents, though encouraging his piano studies, regarded his musical activity as a sideline and decided that he should study law at the University of St. Petersburg. At the university, Stravinsky had the good fortune to make friends with the youngest son of Rimsky-Korsakov; he soon met the composer himself, then the leading figure in Russian music and one of the members of the "Five" (see chapter 15). By 1903, Stravinsky was studying orchestration with Rimsky-Korsakov. They became close friends, and the elder composer acted as best man at Stravinsky's wedding to a cousin, Catherine Gabrielle, in 1906.

After completing his university studies in 1905, Stravinsky decided on a career as a composer. His earliest serious works were written under Rimsky-Korsakov's supervision. In 1909, he met Sergei Diaghilev, the impresario of the newly formed Ballets Russes, who commissioned the young composer to write music for a ballet based on an old Slavic legend. The work, entitled *L'oiseau de Feu (The Firebird),* had its premiere at the Paris Opera the following year. It was so successful that Stravinsky became a celebrity almost overnight.

Two more ballets quickly followed: *Petrouchka* (1910–1911) and *Le Sacre du printemps* (*The Rite of Spring,* 1912–1913). The premiere of *The Rite of Spring* created an unprecedented riot by its use of novel orchestration and aggressive, "primitive" rhythms. Undeterred by what proved to be only temporary criticism, Stravinsky kept up a continuous flow of composition. Until the outbreak of World War I, he divided his time

Figure 18.2 Throughout his life, Igor Stravinsky was one of the most productive and influential composers of the twentieth century.

among Switzerland, Russia, and France. A member of the most distinguished musical and artistic circles of Europe, he came in close contact with Debussy, Ravel, de Falla, the writer Jean Cocteau, and Picasso.

From the outbreak of World War I until 1919, Stravinsky lived in Switzerland. The difficulty in gathering together large groups of performers during this period of world conflict contributed to his evolving compositional style. He turned from his earlier penchant for huge orchestral works to compositions scored for instrumental ensembles of more modest size.

At the end of the war, Stravinsky returned to Paris, where he became a French citizen (he had given up his Russian citizenship at the time of the Russian Revolution of 1917). Much of his time during the 1920s and 1930s was spent on tour through the principal cities of Europe and America. When World War II began, he moved again, this time to Hollywood, California. Deciding to remain in the United States permanently, he gave up his French citizenship to become a naturalized American in 1945.

Stravinsky continued to compose well into his later years, and he conducted concerts of his music all over the world into his eighties. He died in 1971 at the age of eighty-eight, leaving a musical legacy of monumental proportions.

STRAVINSKY'S WORK

Stravinsky's work constitutes a unique variety of styles, genres, musical forms, and instrumental and vocal combinations. By and large, his most popular works continue to be the music he composed for the three early ballets, written before World War I. These works, which include Russian and Oriental elements, are characterized by exotic and colorful melodies and harmonies, glittering orchestration, and striking, often primitive-sounding rhythmic patterns.

Most of the works that he wrote between 1913 and 1923—including three ballets as well as some short piano pieces, songs, and chamber music—were scored for small instrumental ensembles of various types. One of his most popular works for stage composed during this period is *L'histoire du soldat* (*The Soldier's Tale,* 1918) "to be read, played, and danced"; it is scored for a chamber ensemble of seven instruments.

His ballet *Pulcinella* (1919), based on music by the eighteenth-century composer Giovanni Battista Pergolesi, and the *Octet for Wind Instruments* (1923) began his neoclassical period, which lasted until 1951. His compositions during this long creative period incorporate references to many older materials and styles, all transformed in a uniquely Stravinskian way. Many of these works demonstrate an austere style, clear—even dry—texture, and meticulous craftsmanship. Some show the influence of jazz; others make a deliberate return to baroque or classical models; still others represent an attempt to strip music of any subjective or emotional appeal whatever. The opera *Oedipus Rex* (1927) is based on the ancient Greek tragedy. *The Rake's Progress* (1950), titled after a series of engravings by the English artist William Hogarth and structured after the conventions of Italian opera, represents the essence of neoclassicism.

The most important orchestral works to come out of Stravinsky's neoclassical period include *Symphonies of Wind Instruments* (1920), *Concerto for Piano and Wind Orchestra* (1924), *Dumbarton Oaks Concerto in E-flat* (1938), *Symphony in C* (1940), and *Symphony in Three Movements* (1945).

Stravinsky's first major choral work, an undisputed masterpiece, was the *Symphony of Psalms* (1930), written for chorus and orchestra. This three-movement setting of three psalms exhibits several innovations in tonality and rhythm. Instead of being based on traditional functions (such as the tonic-dominant relationship), the tonality is established by the frequent repetition of a particular pitch as a center of reference. An important structural technique is the simultaneous use of several different *ostinato* patterns (persistently repeated figures) as building blocks; these patterns overlap and produce shifting accents and conflicting rhythms.

LE SACRE DU PRINTEMPS

During the early years of the twentieth century, many artists and intellectual leaders became fascinated with nonliterate, "primitive" cultures. Henri Matisse and Pablo Picasso incorporated into their early paintings the stylized forms of African sculpture (see page 372). Similarly, Stravinsky's imagination was stirred by the frenzied, irregular rhythms found in non-Western music. *The Rite of Spring,* the third in the series of ballet scores written by Stravinsky for Diaghilev's Ballets Russes, is perhaps the premier example of musical

primitivism. Subtitled *Pictures of Pagan Russia,* it depicts the cruelty of the primitive Russian peasants' rites to celebrate the coming of spring, culminating in the sacrifice of a young virgin, who dances herself to death while the tribal elders watch.

The Rite of Spring was a revolutionary landmark in the history of musical style. Its unconventional use of the large orchestra, its dramatic rhythmic complexities, and its consistent use of dissonant harmonies made the ballet a wild and exciting piece of music—one that confounded the Parisian audience at its first performance in 1913 and greatly influenced successive generations of composers.

The instrumentation for which Stravinsky composed *The Rite of Spring* is unusually large,[1] consisting of:

2 piccolos	8 horns
3 flutes	5 trumpets
1 alto flute	1 bass trumpet
4 oboes	3 trombones
2 English horns	4 tubas
4 bassoons	large percussion section
2 contrabassoons	very large string section

Stravinsky drew upon the richness and variety of sounds available to him in such a large ensemble to portray the quality of primitive ceremonies his imagination conjured up—"I saw in imagination a solemn pagan rite: wise elders, seated in a circle, watching a young girl dance herself to death. They were sacrificing her to propitiate the god of spring." As was the case with Hector Berlioz in the Romantic period, Stravinsky's orchestration was an integral part of the process of composition, and Stravinsky exploited the lowest and highest registers of the instruments (particularly woodwinds) to produce unorthodox sounds in portraying primitive actions and scenes.

The rhythmic complexity in *The Rite of Spring* was an aspect of the work that confused and alienated early audiences but fired the imagination of musicians and composers. Very often the number of beats in the measure changes, resulting in a series of measures of *different* sizes:

$$\frac{7}{8} \quad \frac{3}{8} \quad \frac{5}{8} \quad \frac{3}{8} \quad \frac{4}{8} \quad \frac{5}{8} \quad \frac{6}{8} \quad \frac{5}{8} \quad \text{etc.}$$

An even greater degree of rhythmic complexity results when the value of the beat itself varies—

$$\frac{7}{8} \quad \frac{3}{4} \quad \frac{6}{8} \quad \frac{2}{4} \quad \frac{6}{8} \quad \frac{3}{4} \quad \text{etc.}$$

—a complexity that is often compounded by the use of syncopation.

Its rhythmic complexity, combined with a high degree of harmonic dissonance and vagueness of tonality, mark *The Rite of Spring* as a forerunner in the development of twentieth-century music.

---

1. To facilitate performance of *The Rite of Spring* by orchestras of moderate size, a revised edition with reduced instrumentation was published in 1974.

The Rite of Spring is laid out in two large parts, each of which has several contrasting movements (scenes) that follow each other without pause. The first half is called "Worship of the Earth"; after a slow introduction, the scenes are "Auguries of Spring—Dances of the Young Girls," "The Ritual of Abduction," "Roundelays of Spring," "Contest of Rival Clans," "Cortege of the Sage," and "The Sage—Dance of the Earth." The second part, "The Great Sacrifice," opens with a long, slow introduction ("The Pagan Night"), followed by five movements entitled "Mystic Circle Dance of the Young Girls," "Glorification of the Chosen One," "Evocation of the Ancestors," "Ritual Dance of the Ancestors," and "Sacrificial Dance."

STRAVINSKY:
Le Sacre du printemps
Cassette 5/B, Track 1
CD 5, Track 4
See Listening Guide on pages 412–413.

Part I: Worship of the Earth

A. Introduction
The introduction is dominated by woodwinds, horns, and trumpet; the strings have a minor role; the rest of the brass and percussion are not involved at all. It begins with a solo bassoon in its highest register

Example 18.1

and is immediately followed by English horn.

Example 18.2

Additional prominent melodic materials are added as the movement progresses (examples 18.3–18.5).

Example 18.3

Example 18.4

Examples 18.1–18.4 from Igor Stravinsky, *Le Sacre du printemps*. (Copyright 1921 by Edition Russe de Musique. Copyright assigned 1947 to Boosey & Hawkes, Inc.)

Example 18.5

The melodic "fragment" in example 18.5 is used as an ostinato figure, repeated over and over throughout most of the rest of the movement. From this point onward, the listening impression is one of expansion and growth as more instruments are added, increasing the volume and density of the texture. This process ends suddenly, and the solo bassoon plays a shortened version of its original melody (example 18.1), followed by the violins stating a figure that links the introduction to the next movement.

Example 18.6

This violin figure becomes an ostinato figure throughout most of the second movement, at times quite prominent, at other instances barely audible as part of the general background.

B. Auguries of Spring—Dances of the Young Girls
A strong rhythmic pattern is established by the strings repeating the same dissonant chord with strong, irregular accents (>) intensified by the horns.

Example 18.7

During the first portion of this movement, the material in example 18.7 is used as the constant part of an alternating scheme. Each time it appears, it becomes background against which new melodic material is introduced.

Example 18.8

Examples 18.5–18.8 from Igor Stravinsky, *Le Sacre du printemps.* (Copyright 1921 by Edition Russe de Musique. Copyright assigned 1947 to Boosey & Hawkes, Inc.)

The second phrase of the melody introduced by bassoons (example 18.8) is used contrapuntally by bassoons, trombones, and oboes, bringing the music to a surprising halt.

For the rest of the movement, the violin motive (♪ ♪) in one form or another is used as an ostinato figure, repeated over and over, against which other melodic material is added (example 18.9).

Example 18.9

And finally:

Example 18.10

Examples 18.9 and 18.10 from Igor Stravinsky, *Le Sacre du printemps.* (Copyright 1921 by Edition Russe de Musique. Copyright assigned 1947 to Boosey & Hawkes, Inc.)

The rest of the movement is one huge crescendo to the "end," which is the "beginning" of the next movement. Here again, the movement does not end in the normal sense. It simply "gives up" in suspense, and we go on to something else.

C. The Ritual of Abduction

The beginning of this section comes as the climactic end of the previous movement. In fact, the listening impression interprets movement C as a kind of fast coda of movement B, leaving it to the actions of the dancers on stage to define the character of this stretch of music (C) as a separate structural unit.

The music of "The Ritual of Abduction" uses the full orchestra, is very fast (presto) and loud, and changes both the beat and measure frequently:

$$\frac{9}{8} \quad \frac{4}{8} \quad \frac{5}{8} \quad \frac{7}{8} \quad \frac{3}{4}$$

Again there is increasing momentum to the end of the movement, which, of course, does not really end but is tied into the beginning of the next movement.

The culminating movement of this exciting work is the finale of part II, the "Sacrificial Dance," in which the chosen one dances herself to death. Stravinsky's use of the musical materials to create and sustain the frenzied atmosphere demanded by the ballet plot is masterful. What on first hearing may seem chaotic, is in fact a carefully crafted piece of music. Cast in five-part alternating form, ABAC²A, the movement employs and epitomizes the techniques already encountered in the work: sectionalization, repetition, rhythmic complexity, harmonic dissonance, obscure tonal center, and unconventional use of the orchestra.

Although *The Rite of Spring* was conceived of as a ballet, today it is most often performed as a tone poem, a concert piece for orchestra without dancers. As an artistic conception, it stands as an early twentieth-century masterpiece, one that had a profound impact on generations of composers.

2. Section C includes a brief quotation from section A.

BARTÓK (1881–1945)

The most significant composer to emerge from eastern Europe in the twentieth century was Béla Bartók (fig. 18.3). He was born in Hungary, the son of the director of a government agricultural school. His first piano lessons, begun at the age of five, were given by his mother. Following the death of his father in 1888, the family moved to Bratislava (now in Czechoslovakia), where Bartók began formal studies in music. While a student at Bratislava, he made his first public appearance as a composer and pianist in 1892, playing one of his own works, and formed a close friendship with Ernö Dohnányi, in later years one of Hungary's most noted pianists and composers.

In 1899, though admitted to the prestigious Vienna Conservatory, Bartók decided to follow Dohnányi to the Royal Academy of Music in Budapest. In Budapest he became strongly attracted to the music of Wagner and Richard Strauss. He also was caught up in the nationalistic movement in politics, literature, and the arts then sweeping through Hungary. His first major composition, an immense orchestral tone poem entitled *Kossuth* (1903), commemorated the nationalist leader of the unsuccessful revolution of 1848. He became friends with Zoltán Kodály (1882–1967), the third member (with Dohnányi and Bartók himself) of the great trio of modern Hungarian composers.

Both Bartók and Kodály developed a strong interest in the problem of creating a national music and began collecting and analyzing Hungarian folk music. The earliest product of their research was a joint publication of arrangements, *Twenty Hungarian Folksongs* (1906). Bartók's interest in folk music began to have an immediate effect on his own work; side by side with the most current devices in composition appeared folk-derived rhythms and melodic patterns.

Following his graduation in 1902 from the Royal Academy, Bartók began a series of concert tours throughout major European cities that lasted for the next several years. During this period, he became increasingly influenced by the French impressionistic music of Debussy and his contemporaries. Bartók's own effort at composition, however, did not seem to get off the ground during this period, and for a while he

Figure 18.3 Béla Bartók's lifelong interest in eastern European folk music had a profound effect on his composing, especially his approach to tonality.

leaned toward a career as a concert pianist rather than a composer.

In 1907, Bartók accepted an appointment as a piano teacher at the Budapest Academy, a post that he held for nearly thirty years. In 1909, he married Márta Ziegler, one of his pupils, and settled into a routine of teaching, composing, researching folk music, and making extensive concert tours. In 1923, he was divorced and married another of his piano students, Ditta Pásztory. They often toured together, playing works for two pianos, and in 1927, they traveled to America for a series of solo recitals and appearances with various orchestras.

The political turmoil of the late 1930s, brought on by the expansionist policies of Nazi Germany, convinced Bartók that he had to leave Hungary. In 1940, he emigrated to the United States, where he was soon given an appointment at Columbia University. While in New York, however, he developed leukemia and his health began declining seriously. He died in September 1945.

BARTÓK'S WORK

Béla Bartók was primarily an instrumental composer; with a few exceptions, almost all of his music falls into one of the following categories: music for solo piano, chamber music for strings (often with piano), concertos, orchestral works of various types, and stage works.

His works for piano range from technical studies and beginners' pieces to difficult recital pieces and concertos. His major contribution to piano literature is the six-volume *Mikrokosmos* (1926–1937), a collection of 153 pieces graded in order of difficulty.

Among his chamber works, the most outstanding pieces are the six string quartets. Since they span a large portion of his creative life, they offer a comprehensive picture of his development as a composer. In particular, the *Fifth String Quartet,* written in 1934, is considered a pivotal point in his stylistic development, after which his music assumes qualities that make it much more accessible to the listener. The *Sixth String Quartet* (1939) is in many ways the culmination of Bartók's life and work; it displays the ingenuity and self-discipline that are among his finest contributions to the literature in the modern era.

His ten concertos are major works, and many of them are frequent items in twentieth-century repertory. *The Second Concerto for Violin* (1937–1938) is one of the finest in the modern idiom.

Bartók's stage works include a one-act opera and two ballets. His one major choral work, *Cantata profana* (1930), based on a Hungarian legend, requires a double mixed chorus, tenor and baritone soloists, and a large orchestra.

Kossuth, an orchestral tone poem and Bartók's first major work for orchestra, was highly acclaimed at performances in England and Budapest. The much later *Concerto for Orchestra* (1943) was his orchestral masterpiece and is considered one of the great works of this century. Two other popular works, both written for smaller forces, round out his orchestral music: *Music for Strings, Percussion, and Celesta* (1936), and the *Divertimento for String Orchestra* (1939).

BARTÓK'S STYLE

Throughout his life, Bartók studied the folk music of eastern Europe. The effects of his studies on his own compositions were profound, especially in his approach to tonality. Most eastern European folk music is based on modes and scales that lie outside the familiar major-minor system, and Bartók realized the impossibility of using this material within the tonal system. He formed his own type of harmonic organization, one that could accommodate melodies not based on a major-minor tonality.

Bartók's studies also influenced his style of melodic writing, which sometimes has a folklike character. He rarely used actual folk songs in his compositions, but he understood how they were constructed and effectively imitated them.

The diverse, irregular rhythms of Hungarian folk music also had a significant impact on his work. In a single passage, the meter may change almost from measure to measure, lending his music a strongly primitive, rhythmic impulse. Syncopations and ostinato patterns are imaginatively employed as well.

Bartók's mature style is compact and economical. Often he derives his melodic material from just one or two very short motives and uses them extensively throughout a composition. He structures large-scale pieces cyclically, bringing back the same material in several movements. Bartók's writing is essentially contrapuntal, with greater emphasis on melodic line than on harmony. He frequently employs dissonances that range from relatively mild to exceedingly tense.

Traditional devices and forms are an important part of Bartók's style, and in this sense he can be called a neoclassicist. He employed fugue, canon, and other contrapuntal procedures and also made use of the sonata-allegro principle. These formal schemes were modified to adapt to and accommodate other elements of Bartók's style.

Another aspect of earlier music that appears in Bartók's writing is the baroque device of separating an ensemble into two antiphonal groups in order to make the contrapuntal lines more distinct. Bartók used this device in his outstanding *Music for Strings, Percussion, and Celesta.*

Music for Strings, Percussion, and Celesta was written in 1936 on commission for the celebration of the tenth anniversary of Switzerland's Basle Chamber Orchestra. It was Bartók's first major work after the *Fifth String Quartet* and displays the same kind of tightly organized structure.

The piece is written for two separate string groups and two sets of percussion instruments, specified by the composer to be arranged in the following manner:

BARTÓK:
Music for Strings, Percussion, and Celesta
Cassette 5/B, Track 2
CD 5, Track 5
See Listening Guide on page 414.

	Double Bass I	Double Bass II	
Cello I	Timpani	Bass Drum	Cello II
Viola I	Side Drums	Cymbals	Viola II
Violin II	Celesta	Xylophone	Violin IV
Violin I	Piano	Harp	Violin III
	Conductor		

This plan allows for many possible instrumental combinations; in addition, the choice of instruments such as the piano, harp, xylophone, and celesta creates the opportunity for exploiting fascinating instrumental effects and sonorities, an opportunity the composer used with great imagination.

MUSIC FOR STRINGS, PERCUSSION, AND CELESTA

First Movement

The first movement (Andante tranquillo) is fuguelike, with the strings playing the major role. It is based upon the following subject with its four short phrases:

Example 18.11

Béla Bartók, *Music for Strings, Percussion, and Celesta.* Copyright 1937 by Universal Edition; renewed 1964. Copyright and renewal assigned to Boosey & Hawkes, Inc., for the U.S.A.

This melody is the basis for the entire first movement. After its first statement by muted violas, the piece proceeds with successive entrances of the melody, each time at the interval of the fifth higher or lower. The first entrance is on A, the second on E (a fifth above A), the third on D (a fifth below A), the fourth on B (a fifth above E), the fifth on G (a fifth below D), and so on, until the most remote and climactic entrance on E-flat. As each new voice part enters, the texture grows thicker and the dynamic level increases until the climactic point when the E-flat section is reached. After this climax, there is a short transition, based on the *inversion* of the first phrase, which leads to successive entrances on the inverted fugue subject.

Example 18.12

Béla Bartók, *Music for Strings, Percussion, and Celesta*. Copyright 1937 by Universal Edition; renewed 1964. Copyright and renewal assigned to Boosey & Hawkes, Inc., for the U.S.A.

This part of the movement reverses the pattern of dynamics of the first part. There is a long diminuendo to the end of the movement. The concluding portion uses both the original and the inverted forms of the second phrase of the theme, dying away to the pitch A, which was the starting point.

Example 18.13

Béla Bartók, *Music for Strings, Percussion, and Celesta*. Copyright 1937 by Universal Edition; renewed 1964. Copyright and renewal assigned to Boosey & Hawkes, Inc., for the U.S.A.

As previously noted, this movement is dominated by the strings, which work together as a homogeneous group. Only toward the end, after the climax, does the celesta enter, playing an elaborate accompaniment to the strings.

Second Movement

The second movement is high-spirited (Allegro) and follows the basic outlines of sonata-allegro form. The first theme is characterized by the alternation of the two string groups answering back and forth. The second theme, which is clearly set off from the first, is rather delicate and playful (example 18.14).

Violin I Example 18.14

Béla Bartók, *Music for Strings, Percussion, and Celesta*. Copyright 1937 by Universal Edition; renewed 1964. Copyright and renewal assigned to Boosey & Hawkes, Inc., for the U.S.A.

There is a full-fledged development section and a clear-cut recapitulation. In addition to the strings, there is extensive use of the harp, the piano, and some of the percussion instruments in this highly rhythmic movement.

Third Movement

The slow third movement (Adagio) is an ABCDCBA form, with snatches of the theme from the first movement appearing between the various sections. The movement begins and ends with solo xylophone; glissandos on the piano and harp combine with interesting runs on the celesta to create evocative and unusual sonorous effects.

Fourth Movement

The last movement is fast (Allegro molto) and hard driving, with many contrasting sections. The most important materials are the dancelike:

Allegro molto Example 18.15

Béla Bartók, *Music for Strings, Percussion, and Celesta*. Copyright 1937 by Universal Edition; renewed 1964. Copyright and renewal assigned to Boosey & Hawkes, Inc., for the U.S.A.

and the return to a simplified and expanded version of the theme of the first movement in a slower tempo:

Molto moderato Example 18.16

Béla Bartók, *Music for Strings, Percussion, and Celesta*. Copyright 1937 by Universal Edition; renewed 1964. Copyright and renewal assigned to Boosey & Hawkes, Inc., for the U.S.A.

The piece concludes with a dramatic coda based on the main thematic material in example 18.15, ending fortissimo.

Figure 18.4 Although Benjamin Britten composed a good deal of instrumental music, his finest compositions are those for voices, either solo or in chorus.

During the last ten years of his life, Bartók did not compose a great deal of music, but the works he produced were of a very high order. *Music for Strings, Percussion, and Celesta* is perhaps the masterwork of that period of his life.

BENJAMIN BRITTEN

The most outstanding English composer of the twentieth century was Benjamin Britten (1913–1976; fig. 18.4). In spite of a considerable output in instrumental music, Britten's best works were composed for voices or voices and instruments. Indeed, Britten is widely regarded as a master at setting English texts to music in the tradition, and at times the manner, of his great English predecessor Henry Purcell. His operas, particularly *Peter Grimes* (1945), are among the best twentieth-century works in the traditional operatic format.

Britten's style bears an original stamp. Superficially, his music is rather simple and appealing, with a wide variety of forms and procedures and an essentially tonal harmonic language. But beneath the surface lie complex and carefully worked-out structures.

Britten's *War Requiem* (1963) is an outstanding example of the elaborate forces that may be involved. This work juxtaposes the Latin text of the Mass for the Dead with antiwar poems in English by Wilfred Owen, a young soldier-poet who wrote and died during World War I. This contrast is reflected in the orchestration: The traditional Latin text is performed by full orchestra, chorus, boys' choir, and solo soprano; the English poetry is assigned to tenor and baritone soloists (representing soldiers) and a separate chamber orchestra. The styles employed range from Gregorian chant to fugue to aria. The result is a highly dramatic work depicting the horror of war in a unique and very moving way.

Almost all of Britten's major works involve voices, either solo or chorus. Some are on a large scale, particularly the *Spring Symphony* (1949) and *Ballad for Heroes* (1939), an unusually effective antiwar piece for large orchestra, chorus, and soloist. On a much smaller scale is *A Ceremony of Carols,* for boys' chorus and harp, and the cantata *Rejoice in the Lamb,* for soloists, chorus, and organ.

SERENADE FOR TENOR, HORN, AND STRINGS

Britten made several important contributions to the literature of orchestrally accompanied song, the best known of which is *Serenade for Tenor, Horn, and Strings,* op. 31, composed in 1943. The piece was written for the virtuoso hornist Dennis Brain and tenor Peter Pears, an intimate associate of Britten.

For this work, Britten combined six poems by different authors: Charles Cotton (1630–1687), Alfred Tennyson (1809–1892), William Blake (1775–1827), Ben Jonson (1572–1637), John Keats (1795–1821), and an anonymous poet of the fifteenth century. Although different in style and historical period, these poems have in common aspects of night, the prevailing theme of the song cycle, and hence the title "Nocturne."

Throughout his life, Britten was sensitive to words and challenged by the task of setting them to music. The musical setting he provided for these separate poems galvanized them into one unified, expressive whole.

The settings of the poems are framed by a prologue and epilogue played by the solo horn, on stage at the beginning, off stage from a distance at the end. Although these sections are exactly the same, they differ greatly in impact. The epilogue is colored by all the music that separates it from its twin, and it comes from a distance, as an echo of the prologue, enhancing the emotional flavor of the conclusion.

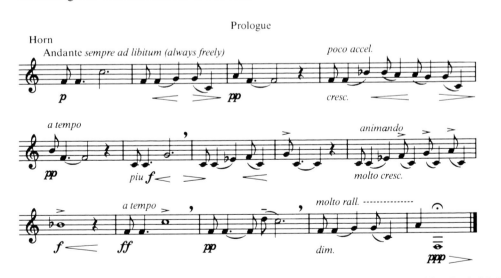

Prologue

Example 18.17

BRITTEN: *Serenade for Tenor, Horn, and Strings,* op. 31, Prologue
Cassette 6/A, Track 1
CD 6, Track 1

Toward the Modern Period

Pastoral (Cotton)

The Day's grown old; the fainting Sun
Has but a little way to run,
And yet his Steeds, with all his skill,
Scarce lug the Chariot down the hill.

The shadows now so long do grow,
That brambles like tall cedars show;
Molehills seem mountains and the ant
Appears a monstrous elephant.

A very little, little flock
Shades thrice the ground that it would stock;
Whilst the small stripling following them
Appears a mighty Polypheme.[3]

And now on benches all are sat,
In the cool air to sit and chat,
Till Phoebus,[4] dipping in the West,
Shall lead the way to rest.

Pastoral centers on night as the ending of the day—the fading sun with distorting shadows, closing with the god of light dipping in the west, leading the world to rest. Britten represents the day-ending flavor effectively. Out of the four stanzas of the poem, he fashions a three-part musical form:

A	**B**	**A**
stanzas one & two	stanza three	stanza four

The pastoral mood is established by muted strings, which provide a gently syncopated introduction that continues as background against which the tenor sings a melody that beautifully reflects both the inflection and the spirit of the words. The downward movement of the voice on "The day's grown old" is echoed by the horn (example 18.18).

3. Cyclops, a one-eyed giant.

4. Phoebus Apollo, Olympian god of light; originally a god of shepherds and flocks.

Serenade, Opus 31, for Tenor, Horn, and Strings by Benjamin Britten. © Copyright 1944 by Hawkes and Son (London) Ltd.; copyright renewed. Boosey & Hawkes, Inc.

The horn continues to interject this sunset motive throughout the A section and into the B section.

At the beginning of the B section, the tempo becomes faster, the strings have contrasting material played pizzicato (plucked), and the voice takes on a playful character while the horn continues to dwell on the sunset motive:

Serenade, Opus 31, for Tenor, Horn, and Strings by Benjamin Britten. © Copyright 1944 by Hawkes and Son (London) Ltd.; copyright renewed. Boosey & Hawkes, Inc.

until it is used to characterize the words "appears a mighty Polypheme" by sounding a low tone that is held and rearticulated through the rest of the B section and through the repeated A section to the very end of the piece. Meanwhile, the tenor and strings, at the words, "And now on benches, . . ." resume the music of section A, the violins taking over the sunset motive in place of the horn. At the very end of the movement, after the voice is finished, the strings return to the initial motive, and the horn "sets the sun" one final, syncopated time to close the movement.

It is typical of Britten that tempo, texture, rhythmic patterns, melodic contour, consonance/dissonance, and tonality serve the essence of the poetry in a well-balanced musical form.

Cassette 6/A, Track 1
CD 6, Track 3

Nocturne (Tennyson)

The splendor falls on castle walls
And snowy summits old in story:
The long light shakes[5] across the lakes,
And the wild cataract[6] leaps in glory;
Blow, bugle, blow, set the wild echoes flying,
Bugle, blow, answer, echoes, answer, dying.

O hark, O hear! how thin and clear,
And thinner, clearer, farther going!
O sweet and far from cliff and scar[7]
The horns of Elfland faintly blowing!
Blow, let us hear the purple glens replying:
Bugle, blow; answer, echoes, answer, dying.

O love, they die in yon rich sky,
They faint on hill or field or river:
Our echoes roll from soul to soul
And grow for ever and for ever.
Blow, bugle, blow, set the wild echoes flying,
And answer, echoes, answer, dying.

Britten takes ingenious advantage of the structure of this poem: The first three lines of each stanza receive similar but not identical melodic treatment; each fourth line ends with the tenor singing a fanfare-like figure that leads to a cadenza in which the voice and horn answer each other, the horn adopting the fanfare in response to the voice (example 18.20).

5. Trembles.

6. Waterfall.

7. Bare rocks on the side of a mountain.

Chapter 18

Example 18.20

and the wild cat-ar-act leaps in glo - ry: Blow bu-gle,

p accel.------- rit.

blow, set the wild ech-oes fly-ing, Bu-gle, blow,

più f

Serenade, Opus 31, for Tenor, Horn, and Strings by Benjamin Britten. © Copyright 1944 by Hawkes and Son (London) Ltd.; copyright renewed. Boosey & Hawkes, Inc.

In each stanza, the cadenza increases in intensity (tempo and volume), climaxing at "answer, echoes, answer," after which the music subsides through successive "dying, dying, dying." With the exception of this dynamic pattern in the cadenza, the second stanza is pianissimo and, in the cadenza, the horn is muted, intensifying the contrast of the second section to the first and last.

Elegy (Blake)

Cassette 6/A, Track 1
CD 6, Track 4

O Rose, thou art sick;
The invisible worm
That flies in the night,
In the howling storm,
Has found out thy bed
Of crimson joy;
And his dark secret love
Does thy life destroy.

Britten exploits the interval of the half-step and the fluctuation between major and minor harmony to symbolize the intense images in Blake's grim poem. In particular, he manipulates the half-step between G and G♯ as it distinguishes an E *major* chord with a G♯ or an E *minor* chord with a G♮.

The movement is laid out as a three-part plan:

A	B	A
horn and strings	*voice and strings*	*horn and strings*
	recitative	*exact repetition of A*
		with a short extension

The A section features the solo horn playing a long melody that employs the extremes of the horn range and makes repeated use of the half-step in establishing and maintaining the sentiment of the poem.

Example 18.21

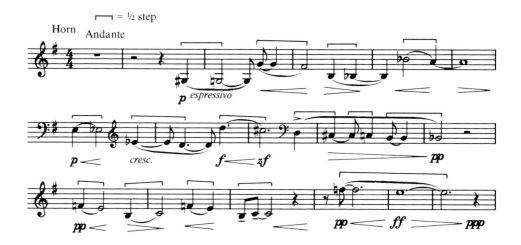

Serenade, Opus 31, for Tenor, Horn, and Strings by Benjamin Britten. © Copyright 1944 by Hawkes and Son (London) Ltd.; copyright renewed. Boosey & Hawkes, Inc.

The voice takes up the half-step progression (G♯–G♮) at the beginning of the recitative on "O Rose," changing the underlying E chord from major to minor. And at the end, on "life destroys" the reverse, G♮–G♯, prepares the way for the reentrance of the horn with its G♯–G♮ to begin the repetition of A (example 18.22).

Example 18.22

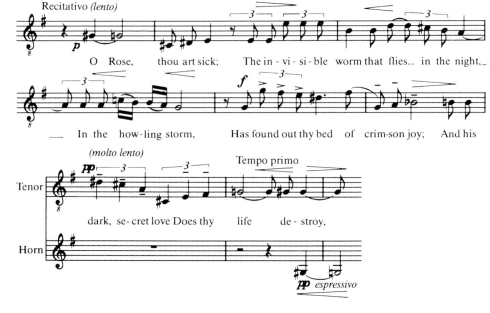

Serenade, Opus 31, for Tenor, Horn, and Strings by Benjamin Britten. © Copyright 1944 by Hawkes and Son (London) Ltd.; copyright renewed. Boosey & Hawkes, Inc.

The emotional quality of this movement is intensified at the very end, when the horn dwells on the half-step motion:

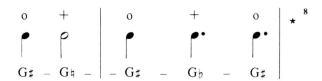

finally ending the movement in E major.

Dirge (Anonymous, 15th Century)

Cassette 6/A, Track 1
CD 6, Track 5

This ae[9] nighte, this ae nighte,
Every nighte and alle,
Fire and fleet[10] and candle-lighte,
And Christe receive thy saule.[11]

8. o = open bell.
  + = stopped bell by right hand of player, producing a muffled, eerie sound.

9. ae, Middle English word for "one."

10. Fleet should be *sleete* for salt, a plate of which was placed on the breast of the corpse as a symbol of enduring life and a means of keeping away the devil.

11. Saule, soul.

When thou from hence away art past,
Every nighte and alle,
To Whinny-muir[12] thou com'st at last;
And Christe receive thy saule.

If ever thou gav'st hos'n and shoon,[13]
Ever nighte and alle,
Sit thee down and put them on;
And Christe receive thy saule.

If hos'n and shoon thou ne'er gav'st nane,[14]
Every nighte and alle,
The whinnes[15] sall prick thee to the bare bane;[16]
And Christe receive thy saule.

From Whinny-muir when thou may'st pass,
Every nighte and alle,
To Brig o'Dread[17] thou com'st at last;
And Christe receive thy saule.

From Brig o'Dread when thou may'st pass,
Every nighte and alle,
To Purgatory fire thou com'st at last;
And Christe receive thy saule.

If ever thou gav'st meat or drink,
Every nighte and alle,
The fire sall never make thee shrink;
And Christe receive thy saule.

If meat or drink thou ne'er gav'st nane,
Every nighte and alle,
The fire will burn thee to the bare bane;
And Christe receive thy saule.

This ae nighte, this ae nighte,
Every nighte and alle,
Fire and fleet and candle-lighte,
And Christe receive thy saule.

The half-step G♮–G♯ ending *Elegy* is recast as G♮–A♭ (the same half-step notated differently) and used to generate the melodic material that begins *Dirge* (example 18.23).

12. Whinny-muir, a moor of prickly plants.

13. Hos'n and shoon, stockings and shoes.

14. Nane, none.

15. Whinnes, prickly plants.

16. Bane, bone.

17. Brig o'Dread, Bridge of Dread.

Example 18.23

Alla morcia grave
(as in a lament)

This ae nighte, this ae nighte, Ev - er - y nighte and alle

fire and fleet and can - dle-lighte, And Christe re - ceive thy soule When

thou from hence a - way art past,

Serenade, Opus 31, for Tenor, Horn, and Strings by Benjamin Britten. © Copyright 1944 by Hawkes and Son (London) Ltd.; copyright renewed. Boosey & Hawkes, Inc.

All nine stanzas are sung to this melody. Against it, Britten writes an instrumental fugue, using as a subject:

Example 18.24

ppp marc.

cresc. *fpp*

Serenade, Opus 31, for Tenor, Horn, and Strings by Benjamin Britten. © Copyright 1944 by Hawkes and Son (London) Ltd.; copyright renewed. Boosey & Hawkes, Inc.

The fugal process of successive entrances and development of the subject increases the momentum, which climaxes with the entrance of the fugue subject by the horn at "From Brig o'Dread" in the tenor. This is followed by a gradual relaxation until only the tenor and string basses with a fragment of the fugue subject remain to end the movement, pianissimo.

Hymn (Ben Jonson)

Queen and huntress,[18] chaste and fair,
Now the sun is laid to sleep,
Seated in thy silver chair,
State in wonted manner keep:

18. Diana, goddess of the sun.

Hesperus[19] entreats thy light,
Hesperus entreats thy light,
Goddess, goddess, goddess, excellently bright.

Earth, let not thy envious shade
Dare itself to interpose;
Cynthia's[20] shining orb was made,
Heav'n to clear when day did close:

Bless us then with wishèd sight,
Bless us then with wishèd sight,
Goddess, goddess, goddess, excellently bright.

Lay thy bow of pearl apart,
And thy crystal shining quiver;
Give unto the flying hart
Space to breathe, how short so ever:

Thou that mak'st a day of night,
Thou that mak'st a day of night,
Thou that mak'st, Thou,
Goddess, goddess, goddess, excellently bright.

This scherzo-like movement is very fast and humorous. Throughout, the strings provide a light pizzicato background for the voice-horn interchange. Each segment of this ABA plan ends with a spectacular bit of melismatic tone painting on "excellently bright." The brisk pace and lighthearted brilliance of this movement are calculated to give the last movement extreme contrast.

Cassette 6/A, Track 1
CD 6, Track 6

Sonnet (Keats)

O soft embalmer of the still midnight,
Shutting with careful fingers and benign
Our gloom-pleas'd eyes, embower'd from the light,
Enshaded in forgetfulness divine:

19. Greek for Venus, the evening star.

20. Cynthia, the moon personified.

O soothest Sleep! if so it please thee, close
In midst of this thine hymn my willing eyes,
Or wait the "Amen" ere thy poppy throws
Around my bed its lulling charities.

Then save me, save me, or the passèd day will shine
Upon my pillow, breeding many woes,
Save me, save me from curious Conscience, that still lords
Its strength for darkness, burrowing like a mole;

Turn the key deftly in the oilèd wards,
And seal the hushèd Casket of my Soul.

Britten's sensitivity to poetry and his mastery of setting it to music are nowhere better illustrated than in his rendering of Keats's sonnet as the last movement of this fine work.

The horn is absent,[21] leaving the strings (often divided into many parts) and the voice to interpret the dreamlike poem. The music is through-composed, its unity ensured by the frequent appearance of a distinctive harmonic progression with which the movement begins and ends

Strings

Example 18.25

Serenade, Opus 31, for Tenor, Horn, and Strings by Benjamin Britten. © Copyright 1944 by Hawkes and Son (London) Ltd.; copyright renewed. Boosey & Hawkes, Inc.

firmly establishing and confirming the prevailing tonality of D major.

The inspired joining of music to words so that they enrich each other is a profound testament to Britten's craftmanship and artistry (example 18.26).

The ethereal closing of the sonnet is followed by a distant echo of the beginning of the *Serenade*—from the horn—off stage.

21. In part, to allow the player to get off stage for the epilogue.

PAUL HINDEMITH

The leading German composer of the first half of the twentieth century was Paul Hindemith (1895–1963). In many respects, Hindemith's music is conservative. Tonality, harmonic tension (consonance/dissonance), rhythmic patterns, and texture (homophony/polyphony) were calculated to serve the formal plan of the work. For the most part, Hindemith conceived his music in terms of traditional formal procedures: contrasting themes in different tonalities often connected by transitions (bridges), development, and confirmation of thematic materials. Much of his music employs traditional contrapuntal devices as part of the theme or as a method of developing thematic material. His music is a rational combination of traditional formal concepts with new harmonic, tonal, and rhythmic elements characteristic of twentieth-century music.

Hindemith wrote in virtually all traditional genres of music and contributed important works to the twentieth-century repertoire of almost all musical instruments. He wrote extensively for the piano, including several sonatas and *Ludis Tonalis,* subtitled "Studies in Counterpoint, Tonal Organization, and Piano Playing."

His ten operas include *Mathis der Maler* (*Matthias the Painter*). The orchestral suite of excerpts from this opera, the *Symphonic Metamorphosis on Themes by Weber,* and the dance compositions, *The Four Temperaments* and *Nobilissima Visione* on St. Francis of Assisi, are his best-known works for orchestra. His vocal works include *Das Marienleben* (*The life of Mary*), a song cycle for soprano and piano, and the large-scale choral-orchestral work *When Lilacs Last in the Dooryard Bloom'd,* an American requiem with text from Walt Whitman.

Hindemith's chamber music is extensive and includes sonatas for solo instruments, duos and trios, seven string quartets, and a series of works for miscellaneous instrumental ensembles.

SERGEI PROKOFIEV

The Russian composer Sergei Prokofiev (1891–1953) is best known for two works, *Classical Symphony* (1918) and *Peter and the Wolf* (1936), a symphonic fairy tale for narrator and symphony orchestra. The popularity of these pieces has overshadowed Prokofiev's most important compositions, such as the opera *The Love of Three Oranges* (1919), the *Scythian Suite* (1914), music for two ballets, *Romeo and Juliet* and *Cinderella,* and film music for *Lieutenant Kije* (1934) and *Alexander Nevsky* (1938).

DMITRI SHOSTAKOVITCH

Another Russian composer who was even more deeply affected by the criticism of Soviet authorities was Dmitri Shostakovitch (1906–1975). His earliest works were neoclassical and tonal, but his ironic sense of humor led him to use more dissonance and a more vigorous idiom.

Shostakovitch's opera *Lady Macbeth of the Mtsensk District* (1930–1932) was not favorably received, and he was attacked steadily by the Soviet regime until he evolved a new, more politically acceptable "heroic" style, first evident in his Fifth Symphony (1937). In all, Shostakovitch wrote fifteen symphonies as well as a variety of chamber works and a ballet. His Seventh Symphony and his Fifth Symphony rank as his most important works.

Listening Guide

STRAVINSKY: *Le Sacre du printemps* (*The Rite of Spring*)

First Part: Introduction and three movements; tempo varies
Irregular and changing meter
Sectional form, follows program

Extremely Large Orchestra

Review: Example 18.1 (Introduction, opening theme)
Example 18.2 (Introduction, second theme)
Examples 18.3 and 18.4 (Introduction, additional fragments)
Example 18.5 (Introduction, melodic fragment used as ostinato)
Example 18.6 (back-and-forth motive, ostinato in second movement)
Example 18.7 (irregular accents, barbaric rhythm)
Example 18.8 (mocking melody, second movement)
Example 18.9 (smooth melody, second movement)
Example 18.10 (flirtatious melody, second movement)

Outline of program, pp. 390–392

CD 5 (Cassette 5/B, Track 1)

4	①	0:00	**Introduction**	1a	Gentle, springlike melody in high bassoon; clarinet, high bassoon; new melody begins in English horn; bassoon; English horn completes its melody
		1:45		b	Additional melodies polyphonically in woodwinds; trill in violin; woodwind polyphony continues at length
		1:57		c	Oboe introduces fragment, high woodwinds only; clarinet squeals answer
		2:34		d	Low chord in double basses supports woodwind polyphony of previous fragments
		2:54		e	High bassoon alone in gentle opening theme; clarinet trill; back-and-forth motive in pizzicato violins, directly into:
	②	3:30	**Auguries of Spring—Dances of the Young Girls**	1a	Pounding barbaric rhythm in strings, loud horn punctuations; back-and-forth motive, English horn; barbaric rhythm, flirtatious melody in muted trumpet, oboes

Continued on next page

	3:55		b	Back-and-forth motive, violent trumpet fanfares and woodwind shrieks
	4:08		c	Barbaric rhythm; mocking melody in bassoons, echoed in trombone, bassoons, bassoons again, oboes, trombone, oboes
	4:47		2a	Violent interruption, drumbeats, long note in trombone
	4:52		b	Shrieks down through winds, violin solo trill, back-and-forth motive in English horn, with interruptions
	5:08		c	Back-and-forth motive in strings, smooth melody in horn, answered by flute; flirtatious melody in oboes and trumpet; smooth melody in alto flute
	5:39			Activity mounts; heavy melody in trumpets, added triangle and cymbals
	6:00		d	Suddenly piano, strings, loud punctuations; smooth melody in piccolo, extended and developed, mounting whirling activity, full orchestra, crescendo
③	6:40	**The Ritual of Abduction**	1a	Very fast, sustained brass chord, violent drum beats, shrieking woodwinds, raucous trombones
	6:54		b	Horn calls answered by woodwinds and strings; violent drum beats, raucous trombones return
	7:10		c	Violent, polyphonic activity continues
	7:16		2a	Full orchestra suddenly coheres in frantic rhythms
	7:24		b	Suddenly reduced, softer, horn calls; loud, descending interruption
	7:37		3	Fanfare-like in brass, drum interruptions; whirling strings, violent interruptions; solitary trill in flute continues into the next section, *Roundelays of Spring.*

Listening Guide

BARTÓK: *Music for Strings, Percussion, and Celesta*

Third Movement: Overall slow tempo, with variation
                       Quadruple meter prevails; sections in triple and quintuple meters
                       Arch form (ABCDCBA)

Two string orchestras separated by piano, harp, celesta, percussion

Review: Example 18.11 (theme quoted from first movement)

CD 5 (Cassette 5/B, Track 2)

[5] (1)	0:00	**A**		Repeated notes on xylophone increase and decrease rhythmically; timpani glissandos
	0:27			Halting, fragmented theme in violas; theme is extended through imitation among strings, accompanied by timpani rolls and glissandos, and repeated xylophone notes; repeated notes in xylophone, increasing rhythm
	1:51	**Transition**		Opening phrase of first-movement theme
(2)	2:01	**B**		Ghostly trills and glissandos in violins; eerie, sinuous theme in celesta and high solo violins
	2:50	**Transition**		Repeated xylophone notes, timpani glissandos, fragments in piano; second phrase of first-movement theme
(3)	3:13	**C**		Glissandos in celesta, harp and piano; wandering, chromatic theme softly in tremolo strings; gradual crescendo; glissandos stop as chromatic theme takes over, builds quickly to:
(4)	3:58	**D**		Cymbal crash, climactic dissonant chord, sudden drop to piano; five-note bell-like motive echoes through the instruments, slow and fast rhythms, played forward and backward, builds to great intensity, softens as celesta and pizzicato strings predominate
	4:49	**Transition**		Third phrase of first-movement theme, bowed strings
(5)	4:57	**C/B**		Sinuous B theme very softly and expressively imitated between high strings on left and low strings on right, glissandos in celesta, harp, and piano, wandering C theme in high solo violins tremolo on right
	5:52	**Transition**		Fourth phrase of first-movement theme, celesta and piano, pianissimo; loud, startling pizzicato chord
(6)	6:09	**A**		Fragments from halting A theme imitated among string, timpani glissandos; repeated notes, xylophone, increasing rhythm, sustained close

SUMMARY

Music since 1900 is characterized by an unprecedented diversity of styles and points of view. Three distinguishing features of modern music are its rhythmic complexity, its free use of dissonance, and its vaguely defined or nonexistent tonal center.

An important movement in music between the two world wars was neoclassicism. Neoclassical composers believed musical composition should be approached systematically and rationally, with irrelevant emotions held in check. They varied the forms of the Baroque and Classical eras to develop a distinctly modern idiom.

The Russian-born composer Igor Stravinsky was one of the towering figures in twentieth-century music. His early works, Russian in flavor, combined glittering orchestration and unusually complex rhythms. His later works, written in the neoclassical style, are austere and clear-textured.

Béla Bartók, the leading composer to come out of eastern Europe in the twentieth century, was profoundly influenced by Hungarian folk music. His mature style was compact, often dissonant, and rhythmically inventive and complex.

Benjamin Britten, an outstanding English composer, is best known for his works for voices or voices with instruments. He was sensitive to words and is regarded as a master at setting English texts to music. Britten's unique style incorporated a variety of forms and procedures and an essentially tonal harmonic structure.

Three other modern European composers who have contributed lasting works to the repertoire are the German Paul Hindemith and the Russians Sergei Prokofiev and Dmitri Shostakovitch.

NEW TERMS

neoclassicism
primitivism

SUGGESTED LISTENING

Bartók, Béla

Concerto for Orchestra, a work for large orchestra in five movements. This piece from 1943 is Bartók's symphonic masterpiece.

Britten, Benjamin

A Ceremony of Carols. See page 399.

Hindemith, Paul

Das Marienleben (*The Life of Mary*). A cycle of fifteen songs written to poems by Rainer Maria Rilke, arranged into four groups. Each group is organized as a unit within the overall scheme of the cycle. Hindemith subjected the piece to many revisions, finally publishing a completed revision in 1948.

Mathis der Maler. Hindemith's best-known symphony, based on his opera of the same name.

Prokofiev, Sergei

Symphony no. 1 in D, op. 25 (*Classical Symphony*). Prokofiev decided to write his first symphony in the style and spirit of Haydn. The work is both an appreciation and a parody of classical style.

Shostakovitch, Dmitri

Symphony no. 5. A powerful work that has become part of the standard orchestral repertoire.

Stravinsky, Igor

Symphonie de Psaumes (Symphony of Psalms). This work for chorus and orchestra was written in 1930 for the fiftieth anniversary of the Boston Symphony Orchestra. The orchestration is unusual—two pianos and a harp are used instead of violins and violas. The text is taken from the Book of Psalms and is sung in Latin. The psalms form a sequence of prayer, testimony, and praise.

SERIALISM

I n their efforts to create a new kind of "tonality," it occurred to many twentieth-century composers that they might be able to avoid the traditional concept of tonality completely. But the idea of the tonal center was so fundamental to musical organization that it could not simply be dropped. Rather, it had to be replaced by an organizing principle of equal strength and validity. The search for such an alternative was the life work of several Viennese composers in the early 1900s. Their work took place at the same time that Stravinsky, Bartók, Hindemith, and others were expanding the idea of tonality. These two simultaneous developments determined the course of musical composition for the first half of the twentieth century.

SCHOENBERG'S WORK

The work of Arnold Schoenberg—amounting to fifty opus numbers, several early unpublished pieces, and three unfinished compositions—includes stage works, art songs, choral pieces, works for piano, a number of orchestral compositions, and an extensive variety of chamber music. His early works, up through the first years of the century, stand in the late German Romantic tradition of Wagner, Brahms, and Mahler. They are tonally based and use many of the romantic forms. The tone poem *Verklärte Nacht* (*Transfigured Night,* 1899), written for string sextet and later revised for string orchestra, is based on a literary program and uses a recurring theme to link the sections of the work. The harmonic style is related to that of Wagner's *Tristan and Isolde.* Schoenberg's symphonic poem *Pelléas und Mélisande* was inspired by the same Maeterlinck drama that interested Debussy. The symphonic cantata *Gurrelieder* (*Songs of Gurre,* 1900–1901) is a gigantic and complex work for vocal soloists, chorus, and huge orchestra.

ATONALITY AND EXPRESSIONISM

Beginning in about 1905, Schoenberg evolved radically different procedures that were regarded by his contemporaries as quite revolutionary. Two different terms are often used to describe his new approach. The first, **atonality,** refers to the systematic avoidance of any kind of tonal center. This is accomplished by excluding simple, familiar chords, major or minor scales, and octave leaps. When these principles are combined with dissonance and a rapid succession of chords, the ear cannot find any stable point (tonic) to use as a center of reference. In this way the twelve tones of the chromatic scale are made equal, rather than consisting of seven tones "belonging" to the key of a piece and five others "not belonging."

SCHOENBERG (1874–1951)

A t the start of his career, Arnold Schoenberg (fig. 19.1) was closely allied with late German Romanticism, although he moved farther from it than almost any of his contemporaries. Together with two of his students, Alban Berg and Anton von Webern, Schoenberg took the fateful step of rejecting the concept of tonality completely and wrote in what is called an atonal style. He later developed a new system of musical organization to replace tonality that involves arranging the twelve chromatic tones in a chosen order, and then using them in various ways. This system is called **serialism, twelve-tone technique,** or **dodecaphony.**

Almost single-handedly Arnold Schoenberg effected a radical and significant change in basic concepts of music. His development of the twelve-tone technique opened the door to new methods of composing and new ways of constructing harmonic relationships. He himself viewed his new method of composing not as a dramatic, revolutionary gesture against the past, but as a logical consequence of nineteenth-century chromatic developments in harmony. He developed his method over many years through a number of compositions, each of which explores new techniques. Some of these techniques were to form part of his serial procedures.

Schoenberg was born into a Viennese middle-class family; although both of his parents loved music, neither

Figure 19.1 One of the most important and innovative figures in twentieth-century music, Schoenberg also enjoyed painting.

provided much guidance in his early training. While in grammar school, he studied the violin and cello and was soon composing and playing in chamber ensembles. When Schoenberg was in his late teens, a friend, Alexander von Zemlinsky, who directed an amateur orchestral society, first interested him in serious musical study; and after working several years as a bank employee, Schoenberg decided in 1895 to embark on a musical career.

The two great influences on his early composition were the giants of late-nineteenth-century German music: Brahms and Wagner. During the 1890s, he wrote several string quartets and piano works and a small number of songs. In 1901 he married his friend's sister, Mathilde von Zemlinsky. Shortly afterward, he was engaged as a theater conductor in Berlin. There he became acquainted with Richard Strauss, who helped him obtain a teaching position and expressed great interest in his work. In 1903, Schoenberg returned to Vienna to teach musical composition. Gustav Mahler became a supporter of his music, and, more importantly, Schoenberg took on as students two younger men, Alban Berg and Anton von Webern. Both pupils would later adopt Schoenberg's twelve-tone methods and would develop them in their own individual ways; Webern would decisively influence the future course of music.

During the first decade of the twentieth century, Schoenberg began turning away from the late romantic style of his earlier works and gradually developed his new twelve-tone method. Although his name spread among composers and performers, public acclaim eluded him. His famous song cycle *Pierrot Lunaire* (*Moonstruck Pierrot*), which drew invectives from critics but praise from avant-garde sympathizers, employed a half-sung, half-spoken technique called **Sprechstimme** (literally, "speech voice").

Schoenberg's reputation was beginning to grow when his career was interrupted by World War I, in which he served with the Austrian army; but soon after he was again active as a composer, lecturer on theory, and teacher. The 1920s marked a new direction. He went to Berlin in 1925 to teach composition at the State Academy of the Arts, taking with him his second wife, Gertrude Kolisch. (His first wife had died in 1923.)

In 1933, Schoenberg's career again took another direction. When the Nazi party assumed power, Schoenberg, being a Jew, was dismissed from his post and emigrated first to France, then to the United States. Although his reputation as a teacher and a "modernist" preceded him, he nevertheless had financial difficulty. After working in Boston and New York, he joined the faculty of UCLA. He died in Los Angeles at the age of seventy-seven.

As previously noted, Schoenberg considered his new harmonic style to be a logical extension of tendencies already apparent in late German Romanticism. In the music of Wagner and Strauss, brief atonal passages can be found, although they are embedded in a tonal context. Schoenberg simply increased the amount of dissonance and chromaticism in his music until the listener could no longer perceive the difference between stable tones ("belonging") and unstable tones ("not belonging"). Since dissonances were no longer resolved in the traditional manner, they became "emancipated." The ordering of successive intervals, not the traditional relationship of dissonance to consonance, became the chief organizing principle.

The second term used to describe Schoenberg's works in the period from 1905 to about 1912 is **expressionism.** Borrowed from the field of art criticism, the term refers to a school of German artists and dramatists who tried to represent the artist's innermost experience. Often expressionist artists used unusual, even revolutionary, methods—such as harsh colors and distortion of the human image—to achieve an intense emotional effect. The subject matter of expressionism was modern humanity in its varied psychological states: isolated, irrational, rebellious, tense. The artist did not attempt to produce beautiful or realistic art, but only to penetrate and reveal inner feelings. Schoenberg shared the goals of the expressionistic artists; his atonal music was the stylistic means of reaching those goals.

The problem that Schoenberg eventually had to face, having abandoned tonality, was the loss of the form-building properties that the old system had provided. Without tonal centers and modulations, the traditional forms could not really exist. Without such simple but useful devices as the dominant-tonic chord progression, there was no harmonic guide to help distinguish a cadence from any other point in a phrase.

At first Schoenberg found only temporary solutions. He wrote short pieces and depended heavily on outside material (either literary or dramatic) to impose form on the music. In addition, he used intricate motivic development and contrapuntal procedures to unify his "free" atonal compositions. These devices had been part of his romantic style, but they became even more important as this expressionistic style emerged. Some of his works from this middle period are characterized by the dominance of a particular interval. Others contain canons and ostinato figures.

Schoenberg creates incredible variety within each piece. Rarely is the same texture maintained for more than a single phrase. Instead, contrapuntal patches are interspersed with accompanied melody. Rhythm and dynamics are also subject to the same rapid variation. Two consecutive phrases are rarely equal in length. Schoenberg almost never uses literal repetition or any other formal symmetry, even when a repeated text in vocal music invites such treatment.

An excellent example of Schoenberg's expressionistic style is *Pierrot Lunaire* (1912), a setting of twenty-one surrealistic poems for vocalist, piano, flute, clarinet, violin, and cello. Schoenberg provides for further variety by having some players switch to other instruments: piccolo, bass clarinet, and viola. The singer (a woman) uses the *Sprechstimme* technique. Both the rhythms and the pitches are precisely notated. The pitches, however, are points that the singer may center on, then fall away from. The effect of *Sprechstimme* in *Pierrot Lunaire* is haunting and eerie.

DEVELOPMENT OF THE TWELVE-TONE METHOD

Schoenberg continued to be very much aware of the limitations his free atonal style placed on him; he wanted to write longer pieces, but he lacked a formal framework on which to build them. Form was very important to Schoenberg. He believed that some underlying organization was essential, no matter what radical changes took place in the harmonic idiom.

Gradually he evolved a system he described as a "method of composing with twelve tones that are related only with one another, not to a central tone: a tonic." The rudiments of this method are simple: The composer arranges the twelve pitches of the chromatic scale in a particular order (example 19.1).

Example 19.1

This arrangement is known as a **tone row** or **series** or **set** for a specific piece. The row can be transposed to any pitch level, and it may be used upside down (*inversion*), backward (*retrograde*), or upside down and backward (*retrograde inversion*). For instance, the tone row and its various forms for *Variations for Orchestra,* opus 31, is:

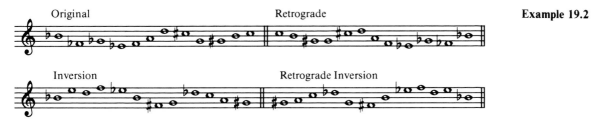

Example 19.2

Used by permission of Belmont Music Publishers. Copyright 1928 by Belmont Music Publishers.

The notes of the series (or any of its variations) are sometimes used sequentially, both in full or in segments, to form a melody or theme, and they are also used simultaneously in clusters to form chords. The system does not impose similar limits on rhythm, dynamics, or textures that the composer will choose, so it is not a mechanical music-producing method, as it might seem at first. A composer who writes with the serial technique is no more limited than one who chooses to write tonally. The basic tone row provides some coherence, in the same way that tonality does, but there is still room for tremendous variety.

Schoenberg had formulated his twelve-tone method by 1923, and he used it in most of his compositions thereafter. It was applied in part to the *Five Piano Pieces* (opus 23, 1923) and the *Serenade for Seven Instruments and Bass Voice* (opus 24, 1923). The *Suite for Piano* (opus 25, 1924), which uses baroque forms, and the *Wind Quintet* (opus 26, 1924) use the system throughout.

No longer expressionistic, the works written in the 1920s have a marked air of confidence and playfulness. A traditional spirit is also evident. Schoenberg used forms resembling classical ones—theme and variations and sonata form, for instance—and contrasted his themes in a classical manner, while continuing to write in a very dissonant idiom with serial techniques. In 1928, he completed the powerful *Variations for Orchestra,* opus 31, a serial work for full orchestra consisting of a theme and ten variations.

He also used the twelve-tone system in a number of important works written in the United States during the 1930s and 1940s, including the *Concerto for Violin and Orchestra* (1936), the *String Quartet no. 4* (1937), the *Concerto for Piano and Orchestra* (1942), and *A Survivor from Warsaw* (1947), a cantata for speaker, chorus, and orchestra. His death left uncompleted his major opera, *Moses und Aron* (begun in 1931).

SCHOENBERG:
A Survivor from Warsaw
op. 46
Cassette 5/B, Track 3
CD 5, Track 6

A Survivor from Warsaw was composed by Schoenberg in 1946–1947 and was first performed in 1947. It is a short but dramatic cantata written for a male narrator, men's chorus, and an orchestra consisting of two flutes (piccolos), two oboes, two clarinets, two bassoons, three trumpets, four horns, three trombones, tuba, a large percussion section, and a body of strings the exact number and distribution of which the composer was careful to specify: ten first violins, ten second violins, six violas, six violoncelli, and six string basses.

The composer fashioned the text himself using as a basis reports of the atrocities of the Warsaw ghetto uprising. The piece is a twelve-tone work built upon the tone row:

Example 19.3

1 2 3 4 5 6 7 8 9 10 11 12

© Copyright 1949 by Bomart Music Publications; copyright assigned 1955 to Boelke-Bomart, Inc. Revised edition © copyright 1974 by Boelke-Bomart, Inc.; newly revised edition © copyright 1979 by Boelke-Bomart, Inc.

The row is divided into sections that function as melodic and harmonic material, creating the orchestral texture.

After a brief orchestral introduction, the narrator recites the account of horror against a dramatic instrumental background. For the most part, the speech rhythm and the vocal inflection of the narration are precisely indicated by the composer. As a result, the text and its rendition are integral to the overall structure and musical flow. At several dramatic points, the narrator assumes the identity of a German soldier, barking orders and hurling threats at the Jews:

"Achtung! Stilljestanden! Na wirds mal?
  Oder soll ich mit dem Jewehrkolben
  nachhelfen? Na jutt; wenn ihrs
  durchaus haben wollt!"

*"Watch out! Stand at attention! How
  about it? Or do you want me to help
  you with the rifle butt? Okay, if that's
  the way you want it!"*

(The sergeant and his subordinates hit everybody, young or old, quiet or nervous, guilty or innocent.)

"Abzählen!"	*"Count off!*
"Achtung!"	*Watch out!*
"Rascher! Nochmol von anfangen! In	*Faster! Once again from the beginning!*
einer Minute will ich wissen, wieviele	*In one minute I want to know how*
ich zur Gaskammer abliefere!	*many I am going to deliver to the gas*
Abzählen!"	*chamber. Count off!"*

The men's chorus is held in reserve until late in the work—the climactic moment when, as the culmination of the narration, it breaks forth with the ancient Hebrew prayer "Shema Yisroel" ("Hear, O Israel"), set to a clear statement of the tone row:

Hear, O Israel: The Lord is our God, the Lord is One!
Blessed is His glorious kingdom forever and ever!
You shall love the Lord your God with all your mind, with all your strength,
with all your being.
Set these words, which I command you this day, upon your heart. Teach them
faithfully to your children; speak of them in your home and on your way,
when you lie down and when you rise up.
Bind them as a sign upon your hand; let them be a symbol before your eyes;
inscribe them on the doorposts of your house, and on your gate.

A Survivor from Warsaw is among Schoenberg's most personal, dramatic, and gripping works, inspired by bitter experience as a Jew living through the hellish nightmare of World War II.

ALBAN BERG

Alban Berg (1885–1935; fig. 19.2) was a pupil of Schoenberg's who adopted most of his methods of construction but used them with a great deal of flexibility. His works allow for a sense of tonality and combine Schoenbergian techniques with established formal procedures from earlier musical periods, including the suite, the march, the rondo, and the passacaglia. Much of his music has a warmth and lyricism that stem from the romantic tendencies of Schoenberg. In addition, such elements as his ability to sustain large forms and his use of large orchestras reinforce the romantic aspect of his style. As a result, much of Berg's music is more accessible to the listener than some of Schoenberg's and most of Webern's.

Berg's principal works are his *Lyric Suite for String Quartet* (1926), his *Violin Concerto* (1935), and his two operas, *Lulu* (1929–1935, uncompleted) and *Wozzeck. Lulu* was not allowed to be completed until after the death of Berg's widow in 1976, and it was not until 1979 that the completed version by Friedrich Cherha was premiered.

Figure 19.2 Alban Berg's use of the twelve-tone technique incorporated a great degree of warmth and lyricism.

BERG: *WOZZECK*

The opera *Wozzeck* is considered by many to be Berg's greatest work. It was written between 1917 and 1921 and was unquestionably influenced by the environment created in Europe by World War I. In its psychological probing of the unconscious and its presentation of a nightmarish world, it is the finest manifestation of expressionism in opera form.

The central character is Wozzeck, the soldier who represents "We poor people." He is belittled and abused by his superior, the captain; used as a hired guinea pig in medical "experiments" by his doctor; betrayed by his mistress, Marie; and eventually driven to murder and suicide by a completely hostile society.

Berg himself constructed the libretto, fashioning it from bits and pieces of a drama by Georg Büchner (1813–1837). Only a musician with substantial mastery of his craft could have formulated such a libretto. As designed by Berg, the opera has three acts that follow the scheme:

Act 1—Exposition
Act 2—Development
Act 3—Catastrophe

Each act consists of five scenes and is organized along the lines of a specific musical form. For example, act 2 (the longest) takes the form of a symphony in five movements, the individual scenes of which are:

Sonata Movement (scene 1)
Fantasia and Fugue (scene 2)
Largo (scene 3)
Scherzo (scene 4)
Rondo with introduction (scene 5)

Acts 1 and 3 are organized along similar lines.

Actually there is continuous music throughout each act. The intervals between scenes are filled with orchestral transitional passages that function either as a coda to the scene just finished or as an introduction to the ensuing scene.

Each of the musical structures (scenes) is used as the vehicle through which the plot of the opera is advanced and the spirit of the action is portrayed. The "delivery" of the lines of the libretto by the actor-singers and their stage actions take place within this musical framework.

The vocal style of *Wozzeck* depends heavily on the *Sprechstimme* technique, which in *Wozzeck* alternates with ordinary speech and conventional singing in an extremely expressive manner. The prevailing mood of *Wozzeck* is one of cynicism, irony, helplessness, and depression.

Catastrophe (the title of act 3) aptly describes the conclusion of this tale of bitterness. Like acts 1 and 2, it consists of five scenes with orchestral interludes indicating the changes of scenes.

Scene 1 centers on Marie, who sits in her room with her child, the son of Wozzeck, reading the Bible. Essentially, she alternates between reading the story of Mary Magdalene, the sinner, and begging Christ's forgiveness for her own sin—adultery. The scene ends with Marie's torturous cry, "Savior! as Thou hadst mercy on her, have mercy on me, Lord!"

A short orchestral interlude leads to scene 2, probably the most highly charged dramatic point in the entire work. Wozzeck and Marie are on a forest path by a pool at dusk. Marie is anxious and wants to move on, but Wozzeck insists that they stay. Driven to madness by a tormenting world and Marie's infidelity, he plunges a knife into her throat, crying out, "Not me, Marie! Then no other either!" The scene is extended by the orchestra as Marie sinks into death, and finally Wozzeck bends over her and in a cold whisper says, "Tot!" ("Dead!") and rushes silently away, ending the scene.

Scene 3 finds Wozzeck in a tavern, with patrons drinking and dancing to a fast polka. Wozzeck joins in the revelry until Margaret notices that there is blood on his hands and clothes, which Wozzeck attributes to a cut. The crowd at the tavern comments that it "smells of human blood," whereupon Wozzeck in fright flees from the tavern to find and hide the murder weapon, lest he be discovered as a murderer—thereby ending the scene.

Scenes 4 and 5 bring the opera to its tragic conclusion. In scene 4, Wozzeck frantically returns to the murder scene to find the weapon and hide it, lest it be discovered and he be condemned. In searching for the knife, he encounters the body of Marie, whereupon he speaks to her as if she were still alive. At this point he cries out in agonizing self-condemnation, "Mörder! Mörder!" ("Murderer! Murderer!") and again begins to look for the knife. He finds it and throws it into the pond. After deciding the knife is too near the shore and could be easily found, he wades into the pool to hide it better and drowns, moaning, "Woe! Woe! I wash myself with blood."

Afterward, the Captain and the Doctor, Wozzeck's tormentors, appear and engage in a frightened exchange as they hear groans from the pool (Wozzeck drowning): "It is a long time since anyone was drowned." They depart, ending the scene, whereupon the orchestra provides a lengthy interlude (designated by Berg as "Invention on a Key"), leading to scene 5.

This concluding scene can be described as the ultimate in cynical despair. In it we find a group of children, including the son of Wozzeck and Marie, in front of Marie's house, with the boy riding his hobby horse while the rest of the children sing and shout, "Ring-a-ring-a-roses, All fall down!" Other children appear and announce the news that Marie is dead. Her son continues to ride his hobby horse, singing, "Hopp, Hopp." After the rest of the children run off to find and look at Marie's body, her son continues to ride, still singing, "Hopp, Hopp," until he notices that he is alone. He then follows the children, leaving the stage empty while the orchestra ends the opera with a brief passage that simply dies away.

BERG: *Wozzeck*,
Act III, Scenes 4–5
Cassette 6/A, Track 2
CD 6, Track 8

SCENE FOUR[1]

Forest path by the pool. Moonlit night as before. Wozzeck staggers on hastily, and then stops as he searches for something.

Wozzeck

Das Messer? Wo ist das Messer? Ich hab's dagelassen. . . Näher, noch näher. Mir graut's! Da regt sich was. Still! Alles still und tot. . . Mörder! Mörder!! Ha! Da ruft's. Nein, ich selbst. (*wankt suchend ein paar Schritte weiter und stösst auf die Leiche*) Marie! Marie! Was hast Du für eine rote Schnur um den Hals? Hast Dir das rote Halsband verdient, wie die Ohrringlein, mit Deiner Sünde! Was hängen Dir die schwarzen Haare so wild? Mörder! Mörder! Sie werden nach mir suchen. . . Das Messer verrät mich! (*sucht fieberhaft*) Da, da ist's (*am Teich*) So! Da Hinunter! (*wirft das Messer hinein*) Es taucht ins dunkle Wasser wie ein Stein. (*Der Mond bricht blutrot hinter den Wolken hervor. Wozzeck blickt auf*) Aber der Mond verrät mich. . . der Mond ist blutig. Will denn die ganze Welt es ausplaudern?!—Das Messer, es liegt zu weit vorn, sie finden's beim Baden oder wenn sie nach Muscheln tauchen. (*geht in den Teich hinein*) Ich find's nicht. . . Aber ich muss mich

Wozzeck

Where is it? Where has the knife gone? Somewhere here I left it . . . . Somewhere here, somewhere. Oh, horror! There something moved! Still! All is still and dead! . . . . Murder! Murder! Ah, who cried? No, 'twas me. (Still searching, he staggers forward a few more steps, and comes upon the corpse.) Marie! Marie! What is that so like a crimson cord round your neck? And was that crimson necklace well earned, like the gold earrings: the price of sinning! Why hangs your fine black hair so wild on your head? Murder! Murder! For me they'll soon be searching . . . . That knife will betray me! (Seeks it feverishly.) Ah! It's here! (At the pool.) Down to the bottom! (Throws the knife in.) It sinks through deep, dark water like a stone. (The moon comes up blood-red through the clouds.) See how the moon betrays me . . . . The moon is bloody! Must then the whole wide world be blabbing it?—The knife there, too near to the shore! They'll find it when bathing, maybe when they

1. Berg, *Wozzeck*, English by Blackall and Harford. Copyright 1923, 1931 by Universal Edition A. G., Wien. English translation copyright 1952 by Alfred A. Kalmus, London. Copyrights Renewed. All Rights Reserved. Used by permission of European American Music Distributors Corporation, sole U.S. and Canadian agent for Universal Edition Vienna, and for Alfred A. Kalmus.

waschen. Ich bin blutig. Da ein Fleck. . . und noch einer. Weh! Weh! Ich wasche mich mit Blut! Das Wasser ist Blut. . . Blut. . . (*er ertrinkt.*)

are musselgath'ring. (He wades into the pool.) It's gone now. I ought to wash my body. I am bloody. Here's a spot. . . and here. . . something. Woe! Woe! I wash myself with blood! The water is blood. . . blood . . . . (He drowns.)

After a short time, the Doctor enters, followed by the Captain.

Captain

Halt!

Captain

Stop!

Doctor

(*bleibt stehen*) Hören Sie? Dort!

Doctor

(Stands still.) Do you hear? There!

Captain

Jesus! Das war ein Ton. (*bleibt ebenfalls stehen*)

Captain

Heavens! There was a sound. (Stands still.)

Doctor

(*auf den Teich zeigend*) Ja, dort!

Doctor

(Pointing to the pool.) Yes, there!

Captain

Es ist das Wasser im Teich. Das Wasser ruft. Es ist schon lange Niemand ertrunken. Kommen Die, Doktor! Es ist nicht gut zu hören. (*will den Doktor mit sich ziehen*)

Captain

It is the water in the pool. The water calls. It is a long time since anyone was drowned. Come, Doctor, This is not good to hear. (He tries to drag off the Doctor.)

Doctor

(*Bleibt aber stehen und lauscht*) Das stöhnt. . . als stürbe ein Mensch. Da ertrinkt Jemand!

Doctor

(Stands still and listens.) It groans. . . like a dying man. There's someone drowning!

Captain

Unheimlich! Der Mond rot und die Nebel grau. Hören Sie?. . . Jetzt wieder das Ächzen.

Captain

It's uncanny! The moon is red, and the mist is grey. Do you hear?. . . That groaning again.

Doctor

Stiller . . . jetzt ganz still.

Doctor

It's getting softer. . . and now quite gone.

Captain

Kommen Sie! Kommen Sie schnell. (*zieht den Doktor mit sich*)

Captain

Come away! Quick! (Drags the Doctor off with him.)

Scene Change—Orchestral Epilogue: Invention on a key

SCENE FIVE

In front of Marie's door. Bright morning. Sunshine. Children are playing and shouting. Marie's child is riding a hobby horse.

Children	Children
Ringel, Ringel, Rosenkranz, Ringelreih'n!	*Ring-a-ring-a-roses, all fall down!*
Ringel, Ringel, Rosenkranz Rin. . .	*Ring-a-ring-a-roses, all. . .*

They stop, and other children come rushing on.

One of These
Du Käthe! . . . Die Marie. . .

One of These
Katie! . . . Marie. . .

Second Child
Was ist?

Second Child
What is it?

First Child
Weisst' es nit? Sie sind schon Alle 'naus.

First Child
Don't you know? They've all gone out there.

Third Child
(*zu Mariens Knaben*) Du! Dein Mutter ist tot!

Third Child
(To Marie's child.) Hey! Your mother is dead.

Marie's Child
(*immer reitend*) Hopp, hopp! Hopp, hopp! Hopp, hopp!

Marie's Child
(Still riding his horse.) Hop, hop! Hop, hop! Hop, hop!

Second Child
Wo is sie denn?

Second Child
Where is she now?

First Child
Draus' liegt sie, am Weg, neben dem Teich.

First Child
Out there, on the path by the pool.

Third Child
Kommt, anschaun! (*Alle Kinder laufen davon.*)

Third Child
Let's go and look! (All the children run off.)

Marie's Child
(*reitet*) Hopp, hopp! Hopp, hopp! Hopp, hopp! (*zögert einen Augenblick und reitet dann den anderen Kindern nach.*)

Marie's Child
(Continues to ride.) Hop, hop! Hop, hop! Hop, hop! (Hesitates a moment, and rides off after the other children.)

Surely, few portrayals of life as meaningless, hopeless, and cynical can match that of Wozzeck. Partly in spite of this feeling and partly because of it, *Wozzeck* is an extremely exciting theater piece that speaks forcefully to our own troubled times.

ANTON VON WEBERN

Anton von Webern (1883–1945; fig. 19.3) was also a pupil of Arnold Schoenberg in Vienna. While Berg came to represent a link to the past among the followers of Schoenberg, Webern represents a more radical denial of and departure from established compositional procedures and concepts. His mature works crystallize the serialist constructionist approach to musical composition inherent in the twelve-tone technique as originally postulated by Schoenberg.

Figure 19.3 Like his teacher Schoenberg, Webern achieved little recognition during his lifetime. Yet, a decade after his death, he came to be regarded as one of the principal influences on contemporary composers.

While Berg was writing in long forms for large musical forces, Webern was striving for economy of material and extreme compactness of form. He felt strongly that each individual note in a composition was important in itself; he added nothing for "general effect." As a result of this preoccupation, most of his works take on the quality of "miniatures." Indeed, Webern's music is the epitome of clarity, economy of material, spareness of texture, and brevity.

It is not surprising, then, that Webern wrote very little music and that all of his works tend to be quite short, some individual pieces lasting less than a minute and some of the "longest" works not exceeding ten minutes. His complete output has been recorded on only four long-playing records, which means that his entire creative effort produced perhaps four hours of music.

Webern's compositions are about equally divided between vocal and instrumental pieces. His vocal music includes collections of solo songs with various types of instrumental accompaniment, the choral work *Das Augenlicht* (*Light of the Eyes*, 1935), and two cantatas for soloists, chorus, and orchestra. The most important instrumental works are the *Symphonie,* op. 21 (1928) for nine solo instruments; *String Quartet,* op. 28 (1938); the *Concerto for Nine Instruments,* op. 24 (1934); and the *Piano Variations,* op. 27 (1936).

Almost without exception, Webern's works are on the scale of chamber music, another manifestation of economy of means and compactness. His instrumentation often includes highly unorthodox combinations of instruments, such as in his *Quartet,* op. 22 (1930), which is scored for clarinet, saxophone, violin, and piano.

As we noted before, Webern's music depends heavily on serialism. His style is essentially contrapuntal and is marked by an exceptional sensitivity to instrumental color. Often a single melodic line, derived from a twelve-tone row, is divided among several instruments, each assigned only one or two notes at a time; the changes of timbre from instrument to instrument give the melody added interest.

Serialism   **429**

The first movement of the *Symphonie,* opus 21, demonstrates the spareness of Webern's style and the distribution of the melodic line over a number of instruments.

Example 19.4

WEBERN: *Symphonie,*
op. 21, Movement I
Cassette 5/B, Track 4
CD 5, Track 7
*See Listening Guide on
page 432.*

During his lifetime, Webern suffered the same lack of public recognition as Schoenberg, but his music, like that of his teacher, became increasingly influential after World War II. In particular, in the seventies and eighties, many young composers, captivated by the lean character of his style and his isolation of the single note as an important musical event, adapted features of his music and expanded the techniques of serialism to suit their own purposes. The twelve-tone technique initiated by Schoenberg and advanced by Berg and Webern became a powerful force in the world of music and still influences some composers today.

ELIZABETH LUTYENS

Elizabeth Lutyens (1906–1983) appears to be the first British composer to adopt atonality as a compositional principle. Independently from Schoenberg, Berg, and Webern, she experimented with using all twelve tones, discarding such devices as the dominant-to-tonic relationship. Her *Three Symphonic Preludes* (1945) and *Concerto for Viola* (1950) are among the most important of her atonal works.

Characteristics of Twentieth-Century Music (to World War II)

Tonality	Major-minor system retained by some composers, but methods of establishing tonal centers altered; other composers employed atonal systems, including serialism
Texture	Both homophonic and contrapuntal textures employed; variety of textures within a single work
Rhythm	Complex rhythms; rhythmic patterns used to build form; frequent absence of well-defined beat; frequent change of meter
Harmony	High dissonance levels; new methods of chord construction in addition to triadic harmony
Tone Color	Instruments sometimes played in extreme registers; unusual instruments, instrument groupings, and colors. Tone color a primary structural element, particularly in the music of Debussy
Melody	Melodic material sometimes derived from very short motives; melodies often not songlike
Dynamics	Dynamic extremes employed; rapid dynamic fluctuations
Ensembles	Wide variation in size of ensembles from very small to gigantic
New Organizational Procedures	Serialism (twelve-tone technique)
General Stylistic Trends	Impressionism Neoclassicism Expressionism
Vocal Style	Combination of ordinary speaking, conventional singing, and *Sprechstimme*

Listening Guide

WEBERN: *Symphonie*, op. 21

First Movement: Ruhig schreitend (moving quietly)
Duple meter
Modified sonata form

Clarinet, bass clarinet, two horns, harp, strings (no double basses)
In some performances, only a string quartet is used; in any case, the string group is always quite small

Review: Example 19.4 (opening bars)

Note: This work requires concentrated and repeated listening in order not to seem like simply a lovely web of disconnected tone colors. It makes better sense to listen to it in a linear manner, as three- or four-note melodic fragments in one instrument imitated or answered by another instrument. These fragments may be difficult to follow, since they jump between widely separated pitches. In this Listening Guide, the word *answer* indicates the use of *contrary motion:* that is, where the movement of the first fragment is up, the answering fragment moves down, and vice versa. The guide does not try to indicate all of these relationships, but simply keeps you on track as the music progresses. It is a good idea to listen several times without the guide as well.

CD 5 (Cassette 5/B, Track 4)

7	①	0:00	**Part I** **(Exposition)**	1	Overlapping statement and answer in horns, followed by same in clarinets; mostly pizzicato strings and harp form background; above overlaps with cello statement answered by violas, similar pair in clarinets
	②	0:47		2	Short passage of single notes; viola statement answered by cellos; movement slows and thins out
	③	1:09			Part 1 repeated
	④	2:20	**Part II** **(Development)**	1	Generally faster notes; three-note motive (very long-short-short) twice in clarinets answered by lower strings; two-note (long-short) jump between violins and clarinets; pause
	⑤	2:46		2	Wide jump, short-long, stated and answered among various instruments, continues at length
		3:06			While above continues, three-note short-short-long idea between clarinet and cellos; pause
	⑥	3:23		3	Development of two-note leap continues; climax at forte dynamics (first in the piece), busier texture
	⑦	4:02		4	Muted solo violin passage, pianissimo, thinner texture to close
	⑧	4:18			Part II repeated; texture thins, movement slows for conclusion

SUMMARY

The development of the atonal style was led by Arnold Schoenberg, a Viennese composer who, along with Igor Stravinsky, was a dominant figure in twentieth-century music. Schoenberg rejected the concept of tonality completely and devised a new system, ultimately called serialism, to organize his works.

Schoenberg's early works are in the late romantic tradition and are tonally based. During the first decade of the twentieth century, he began to develop a "free" atonal style that systematically avoided any tonal center, thereby equalizing all twelve tones. He depended heavily on literary or dramatic material, motivic development, and contrapuntal procedures to impose form and organization. His works from 1905 to about 1912 are also described as expressionistic, reflecting his association with the school of German artists and dramatists who were attempting through their art to represent the psychological experience of modern humanity.

Schoenberg was aware that the free atonal style placed certain limitations on his work. Tonality had provided a means of making structural distinctions. In its absence he needed to develop a formal framework on which to build. His solution was to arrange the twelve pitches of the chromatic scale in a particular order, known as the tone row, series, or set for a specific piece. The twelve tones of the series could be used in sequence, forming a melody or theme, or simultaneously in groups to form chords. Furthermore, the system did not impose limitations on rhythm, dynamics, or texture. As a result, the tone row provided coherence in the same way that tonality does but still left room for great variety. Schoenberg had formulated his twelve-tone method by 1923 and used it in most of his compositions thereafter. *A Survivor from Warsaw,* op. 46, is a good example of the use of the twelve-tone method in a dramatic work for narrator, men's chorus, and orchestra.

Although he received little recognition during his lifetime, Schoenberg has had a major influence on contemporary composition. Much of that influence has been transmitted through the music of his pupils and colleagues. Anton von Webern and Alban Berg represent the further development of two divergent aspects of Schoenberg's style: Webern the abstract constructionist as evidenced in his *Symphonie,* op. 21, and Berg the romanticist who produced the great opera *Wozzeck.* The British composer Elizabeth Lutyens also experimented with twelve-tone techniques and atonality.

NEW TERMS

atonality
serialism (twelve-tone technique,
  dodecaphony)

Sprechstimme
expressionism
tone row (series, set)

SUGGESTED LISTENING

Berg, Alban

Lyric Suite for String Quartet (1926) in six movements.

Violin Concerto (1935) in two movements. The first concerto to be based on the twelve-tone technique, it quotes the German chorale "Es ist genug" ("It is enough") also used by J. S. Bach in one of his cantatas.

Schoenberg, Arnold

Variations for Orchestra, op. 31. A complex and powerful orchestral work using the twelve-tone technique.

Suite for Piano, op. 25, which combines the twelve-tone technique with baroque forms.

Webern, Anton von

String Quartet, op. 28.

Concerto for Nine Instruments, op. 24.

Music in America

© 1992, Art Montes de Oca, "Fourth of July," FPG International Corp.

PRELUDE VI # American Culture before World War II

I n the seventeenth century, Europeans colonized and settled the eastern seaboard of North America. By 1700, more than a million colonists were scattered up and down the Atlantic coast, living mainly on farms, sometimes in villages, and occasionally in trading towns like Boston, New York, and Charleston. In the eighteenth century, the imperial health of England depended more and more on American shipbuilding and exports of agricultural commodities. To many Europeans, the economic promise of the New World seemed limitless.

The cultural record of the American colonies is more spare. There exists some rather naive local portraiture and some expressive tomb sculpture; the architecture, modeled on that of European masters like Palladio and Wren, is sometimes outstanding. On balance, however, little American art of the seventeenth and eighteenth centuries stands beside the masterwork across the Atlantic.

On the other hand, the American colonies had a rich local tradition in the crafts. Even today, the names Paul Revere and Duncan Phyfe suggest excellence in silversmithing and furniture-making. Likewise, native composers, mainly self-taught, traveled the countryside, organizing singing assemblies and getting tune books published. These singing masters, of course, were most inclined toward choral music and hymn singing.

American painting came into its own in the late eighteenth century. The best American painters, though, had to leave the colonies and travel to London to make their reputations. John Singleton Copley (1738–1815) moved to England in 1774 (see page 440). Benjamin West (1738–1820) became president of the Royal Academy and court painter to George III (see page 441).

Purely American scenes did not become fashionable until the early nineteenth century. Then, painters of the untraveled West found a large and enthusiastic audience. George Caleb Bingham (1811–1879) painted scenes of Missouri flatboatmen, river ports, trappers, and local elections.

Hudson River landscapists like Thomas Cole (1801–1848) and Asher Durand (1796–1886) began a school of American nature painting that celebrated the wonder of the wilderness—in a more and more melodramatic way as the nineteenth century progressed. The paintings of later landscapists like Frederic Church (1826–1900) and Albert Bierstadt (1830–1902; see page 442) were sometimes first displayed in the manner of the contemporary film premiere and were immensely popular, even if these works gave many Easterners a distorted and grandiloquent vision of Western topography.

In its pantheism and nature worship, early-nineteenth-century American painting reflected elements of the romantic movement. So also did literature, as Washington Irving, James Fenimore Cooper, and Edgar Allan Poe wrote tales of the wild, exotic, and supernatural. Not until 1830, however, did New England enter its greatest literary period. The brilliant speculations of transcendentalist Ralph Waldo Emerson, the radical primitivism of Henry David Thoreau, and the thoughtful fiction of Nathaniel Hawthorne and Herman Melville created a rich literary environment of far-reaching significance.

Achievements in American music came later and were more modest. The most notable composer in the United States before the Civil War came out of the slightly vulgar realm of the minstrel show. Stephen Foster (1826–1864), a dreamer and alcoholic outcast, wrote more than two hundred songs, including tunes like "Camptown Races" and "Oh! Susanna" that have formed the bedrock of American popular music. The first American composers to achieve a reputation abroad were Edward MacDowell (1861–1908) and Amy Beach (1867–1944), who composed in the style of the German Romantics at a time when the romantic mode was no longer in the European avant-garde. Even in the late nineteenth century, most American composition continued to respond to European fashion. It was Charles Ives (1874–1954) who broke away from European tradition and helped initiate an independent American avant-garde. Ives's extraordinarily original compositions were far ahead of their time, and not until World War II did his work gain wide critical acceptance. Since then, his influence has been extensive, and composers today continue to draw inspiration from his bold experimentation.

When the colonies achieved independence in the late eighteenth century, the country had begun to outgrow its character as a collection of separate, often competing provinces and to move toward greater centralization. But it was not until the end of the Civil War (1865) that federal supremacy was ensured. Then, with the rise of great railroad networks, new corporations emerged that delivered manufactured goods to rapidly growing cities all over the continent. With the settlement of the American interior from coast to coast, the United States became an urban, industrial power very different from the land of yeoman farmers that Thomas Jefferson had dreamed of at the beginning of the nineteenth century.

Significantly, American industrial captains of the nineteenth century collected art to decorate their great townhouses and country estates. Just as significantly, they were much more interested in buying renaissance and baroque work by established masters than in commissioning work that reflected American realities! Most American designers, especially architects, emulated (sometimes with slavish reverence) the models of the French academicians and l'École des Beaux-Arts (the prestigious French school of fine arts). A few farsighted collectors bought the controversial work of the impressionists; however, most connoisseurs were attracted to the culturally "safe" style dictated by the well-entrenched art establishment in Paris. The distinction between "local color" and the "made-in-Europe" label was visible in music as well, as the upper class that built majestic concert halls and subscribed to operas and symphonies clearly demonstrated its preference for the imported styles.

At the turn of the century, the favored painter in the United States was John Singer Sargent (1856–1925), whose handsome portraits of the landed, powerful, and financially secure were eagerly sought and displayed in the best New York and Boston townhouses (see page 443).

At the same time, a very different style of art was being produced by the Ashcan School, so called after its raw, graphic scenes of proletarian New York. These paintings disturbed the average art patron, who felt that vulgarity and low life were not proper subjects for the painter. The European avant-garde was threatening, too. In 1913, a large exhibition of European art, including the cubist work of Pablo Picasso and the fauvist work of Henri Matisse, stupefied and revolted most of New York's influential critics—in the same way the impressionists had scandalized Paris thirty years earlier. Nevertheless, the Armory Show, as it was called, began to redirect American painting, and Europe's new modernism became a force that no serious painter could ignore.

Most American architecture of the early twentieth century was historical in concept, using a diverse vocabulary of styles that were revived from antiquity, the Middle Ages, the Renaissance, and the Baroque period. Two architects broke this mold, and in so doing, they created the prototypes for many of the buildings seen in America today. Louis Sullivan (1856–1924) rejected highly ornamented details when he built impressive skyscrapers whose lines clearly echoed their steel skeletons, and Frank Lloyd Wright (1867–1959) invented the low, relatively rustic residence that has since become a standard style of housing in suburban America (see page 444).

The building of cities slowed or halted during the Great Depression, although some projects, such as Rockefeller Center in New York, went forward. In the 1930s, the federal government, as part of its public works program, also commissioned murals and decorations for public buildings. These were primarily in the regional style, of which Thomas Hart Benton and Grant Wood were leaders.

Although the work of Benton and Wood was more abstract than earlier American art, it reflected nostalgic realism that was uneasy with European experiments. Edward Hopper (1882–1967) understood the structural logic of cubism, but his great talent lay in evoking the mystery inherent in commonplace aspects of American life (see page 445).

In the 1930s painters were also drawn to political subjects. Some idealized the worker as the backbone and real hero of the American people. Others, such as Paul Starrett Sample, concentrated on nostalgic regionalism, often in sentimental fashion (see page 446).

Between the two world wars, some American painters, especially in New York, were aware of concurrent French work, and in the 1930s, the Museum of Modern Art was founded in New York. New York, however, did not outshine Paris until after 1945. Then the United States, which despite its commercial power remained on the periphery of Western art, would become the cultural center of the Atlantic Community.

Portrait of Paul Revere, the political activist and silversmith, by John S. Copley, American. Oil on canvas, 35″ × 28½″. (Gift of Joseph W., and William B. and Edward H. R. Revere. Courtesy Museum of Fine Arts, Boston.)

The Death of General Wolfe, the British commander who died on the
battlefield of Quebec in 1759, by Benjamin West, 1770. Oil on
canvas, 59½″ × 84″. (National Gallery of Canada, Ottawa. Gift of the
2nd Duke of Westminster, Eaton Hall, Cheshire, 1918.)

The Last of the Buffalo (ca. 1885), by Albert Bierstadt, oil on
canvas. In the nineteenth century, Americans living in eastern
cities provided artists with an enthusiastic audience for exotic and
dramatic scenes of western life and landscapes. In 1800, the American
frontier was just beyond the Appalachians; by 1900, it was gone.
(Corcoran Gallery of Art; gift of Mrs. Albert Bierstadt, 1909.)

Portrait of Lady Agnew, by John Singer Sargent,
c. 1892–1893. Oil on canvas, 49½″ × 39½″. (National Gallery
of Scotland.)

Frank Lloyd Wright designed the Kaufman House at Bear Run, Pennsylvania, 1936–37, as an organic extension of nature. Massive cantilevers support the floors that hover above the waterfall; a skeleton of concrete, glass, and native rock further integrates the house with the landscape. (Western Pennsylvania Conservancy/Art Resource, N.Y.)

As shown in his *Early Sunday Morning,* 1930, Edward Hopper painted
harsh, simplified forms in flat, bright light. Although his paintings
have an abstract quality, Hopper remained distant from the
experiments of such European innovators as Picasso and Matisse.
(Collection, Whitney Museum of American Art; purchase with
funds from Gertrude Vanderbilt Whitney.)

Janitor's Holiday, by Paul Starrett Sample, 1936. Oil on canvas,
H. 26, W. 40 in. A gentle scene of a New England countryside.
(The Metropolitan Museum of Art; Arthur Hearn Fund,
1937 [37.60.1].)

AMERICAN MUSIC BEFORE WORLD WAR II

Striking contrasts run through the history of music in the United States. Imitation of European models has contrasted with attempts to produce a more uniquely American idiom; conservative and radical strains have alternated or vied for dominance; concert music, jazz, and popular music have tended to go their separate ways, though occasionally cross-fertilizing. As America has grown in expanse and population, so has the breadth and significance of her musical expression. In the twentieth century, American music, written in the many different musical languages that characterize our multicultural nation, stands in the forefront of important and influential artistic movements throughout the world.

THE SEVENTEENTH CENTURY

The religious dissenters who settled New England in the early seventeenth century had come from a world rich in music and the other arts. The Pilgrims, for example, loved and practiced music, but had little spare time for entertainment in their new land. Their music was functional and used mostly for worship in church and at home. It consisted primarily of psalms and hymns, with tunes taken from older hymns or folk songs brought over from England and Holland.

The first book printed in the Colonies was a new rhymed translation of the psalms called the *Bay Psalm Book* (1640; fig. 20.1), to which music was added in a 1698 edition. Its publication underscores the strong ties between music and religion in early America.

THE EIGHTEENTH CENTURY

Secular music began to flourish in the Colonies during the eighteenth century, particularly in such major cities as New York, Boston, Philadelphia, and Charleston. Through shipping and trading, the people in these cities remained in close contact with the artistic life of Europe. As the cities prospered, the growing middle class acquired both the leisure and the money to support the arts.

Figure 20.1 A page from the *Bay Psalm Book*, the first book printed in the American colonies.

Beginning in the 1730s, many concerts, operas, and other musical events featured immigrant musicians. These professionals worked both as performers and as "professors" of music. They taught music to gentlemen amateurs who, in turn, supported the rapid growth of music in America. Their supporters included Thomas Jefferson, one of the outstanding music patrons of his day and an amateur violinist himself, and Benjamin Franklin, who served capably as a performer, inventor of an instrument (the glass harmonica), and music critic. Another of the gentleman amateurs, Francis Hopkinson (1737–1791), wrote genteel songs and claimed to be the "first native of the United States who has produced a musical composition."

By 1770, there was a group of native American composers with enough in common to be considered a school. The leader of this group was a fascinating man—William Billings of Boston (1746–1800).

FANEUIL HALL, BOSTON.

With regard to traditional styles and rules of composition, Billings and his compatriots were mavericks. Proclaiming his musical independence, Billings asserted that he was "not confined to any Rules for Composition by any that went before him" and "Nature is the Best Dictator, for all the hard dry rules will not enable any Person to form an Air without Genius. Nature must inspire the thought." The result of this attitude was a distinctive style of music that was often considered crude and inept by traditional European taste and standards. But it was music that had its own profound power and grace and had a lasting effect on the development of American music.

Billings, a tanner by trade, published a number of collections of his own compositions, among them *The New England Psalm Singer* (1776), engraved by Paul Revere; *Singing Masters Assistant* (1778); and *The Psalm Singers Amusement* (1781). These publications contained hymns, anthems, rounds, and "fuging tunes"—hymns or psalm tunes with brief polyphonic sections that have imitative entrances.

BILLINGS:
"When Jesus Wept"
Cassette 6/A, Track 3
CD 6, Track 9

One of Billings's most beautiful and popular compositions is the round (canon) "When Jesus Wept" from *The New England Psalm Tune:*

When Jesus wept, the falling tear, in mercy flowed beyond all bound;
When Jesus groaned, a trembling fear seized all the guilty world around.

"When Jesus Wept," the anthem "Be Glad Then America," and the hymn tune "Chester," all by Billings, were used by the twentieth-century American composer William Schuman in his orchestral work *New England Triptych.*

THE NINETEENTH CENTURY

The musical culture of nineteenth-century America was marked by two significant phenomena. The first was the division between what we now call "classical" and "popular" music. Classical music was meant either for serious study and listening or for religious purposes, while popular music aimed only to entertain. Earlier music had served both functions. For example, the eighteenth-century fuging tunes were written for worship and enlightenment, but learning and singing them was also an enjoyable social function.

The second phenomenon of nineteenth-century music was the imitation of German music by American composers, a trend that became most evident after the Civil War. By that time, the pattern of immigration to the United States had changed, as more people came from the European mainland and fewer from Great Britain. The Europeans brought to America the ideas of the romantic movement, which was strongest in Germany. Soon romanticism influenced every area of American musical life.

AMERICAN COMPOSERS BEFORE THE CIVIL WAR

In the years preceding the Civil War, many extremely sentimental songs were written and published primarily for use by amateurs in their own homes. The one great songwriter of the period did not follow in the European tradition, but wrote for the parlors and minstrel shows of America.

Stephen Foster (1826–1864; fig. 20.2) wrote music that appealed to a large segment of the American population—those who were from neither the sophisticated Eastern cities nor the frontier. He articulated the uneasy feelings of dislocation and transition in a rapidly changing country.

FOSTER: "I Dream of Jeanie"
Cassette 6/A, Track 4
CD 6, Track 10

Although his formal musical training was not extensive, he had an unmistakable gift for melody. Many of his songs are filled with nostalgic yearning, often for an unattainable love. Both the text and music of his best-known songs, like "I Dream of Jeanie," are gentle and tender. Foster also wrote many songs for the minstrel shows that were a popular form of entertainment in the North, both before and after the Civil War. The music of minstrel shows had a robust quality that was missing from the household songs of the period. Dance tunes and songs using the dialects of black Americans were the basis of the shows, and Foster contributed many of the latter, including his well-known "Oh! Susanna" and "Camptown Races."

While Foster wrote in a vernacular style and drew from uniquely American experience, composers of sacred music centered their attention on European styles. The Civil War and Reconstruction years were marked by a growing taste for hymns adapted from the music of the great European composers, from Palestrina to Mendelssohn. Lowell Mason (1792–1872) composed and adapted many such hymns. His efforts also brought music education into the public school curriculum for the first time.

Figure 20.2 Stephen Foster composed many popular songs, a number of which are still familiar and sung today. (Attributed to MMK Major and Knapp Lithography Co., active 1864–1871, after photo lithograph with tintatone $7^3/_5 \times 6^5/_8$ in. National Portrait Gallery, Smithsonian Institution, Washington, D.C./Art Resource, N.Y.)

Much American music—original compositions, arrangements of songs and dances, and sets of variations on well-known tunes—was written for the piano, the favorite instrument of the Romantic era. American piano builders became some of the best in the world. One of the most colorful and talented figures in American music before the Civil War was a virtuoso pianist from New Orleans, Louis Moreau Gottschalk (1829–1869), who adopted many of the mannerisms of Liszt. He composed numerous works for both piano and orchestra, many of which contained exaggerated sentimentality, and he also used such exotic musical materials as African-Caribbean rhythms and Creole melodies.

Most of the music performed by American orchestras was by European composers, although the works of the American George Bristow (1825–1898) were sometimes performed. Bristow wrote six symphonies in a style almost identical to Mendelssohn's. The New York Philharmonic, of which he was a member, was founded in 1842. A typical orchestral program in this period carefully mixed "heavy" music (single movements of symphonies, never complete ones) with "lighter" music (marches and overtures).

AFTER THE CIVIL WAR

From the end of the Civil War to World War I, German Romantic music had its greatest influence. Symphony orchestras were formed in many of the major cities, and large concert halls were built, including Carnegie Hall in New York (1891). Conservatories were established, and music departments appeared in colleges and universities.

A group of romantic composers formed in Boston under John K. Paine (1839–1906), a conservative and serious craftsman who became the first professor of music at Harvard. Other talented members of the Boston group were Horatio Parker (1863–1919) of Yale and George Chadwick (1854–1931). These men composed instrumental and choral music: symphonies, sonatas, chamber music, and oratorios. Stylistically, they were closely allied with the early German Romantics, such as Schubert, Mendelssohn, and Schumann.

Amy Beach (1867–1944) also lived in Boston and composed in the conservative romantic tradition. Her output included more than one hundred songs, short piano pieces, sacred and secular choral works, a piano quintet, and a symphony (1894). Her works for chorus and orchestra, *Three Browning Songs* (1900) and *The Canticle of the Sun* (1928), were among her most widely known works. Beach was recognized as a gifted pianist and composer both in the United States and Europe, which she toured from 1910 to 1914. Beginning in 1885, much of her music was published by Arthur P. Schmidt, an early champion of American composers, including such women as Beach, Margaret Ruthren Lang, Helen Hood, Clara Kathleen Rogers, and others.

Beach very much admired the work of the English poet Robert Browning (1812–1889). In 1900, she set three of his poems to music and dedicated the music to the Browning Society of Boston. The group of three songs begins with "The Year's at Spring," with its famous line "God's in His Heaven, all's right with the world!," and ends with an effective musical rendering of "I send my heart up to Thee." As a center piece, Beach chose the poem "Ah, Love, but a Day."

BEACH: "Ah, Love, but a Day"
Cassette 6/B, Track 1
CD 6, Track 11

As example 20.1 shows, the composer manipulated the text by repeating certain words and lines to facilitate the musical structure she designed to convey the overall quality of the poem. The piece consists of two larger sections. Each begins quietly, builds to a climax, then subsides. Between them is a brief refrain, on the words:

"Ah, Love, but a day
And the world has changed!"

Example 20.1

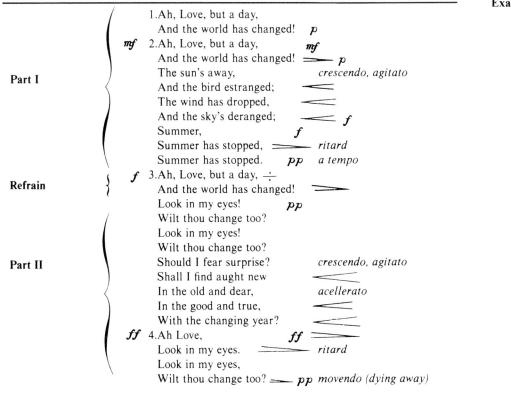

Part I

mf

1. Ah, Love, but a day,
And the world has changed!   *p*
2. Ah, Love, but a day,   *mf*
And the world has changed!   *p*
The sun's away,   *crescendo, agitato*
And the bird estranged;
The wind has dropped,
And the sky's deranged;   *f*
Summer,   *f*
Summer has stopped,   *ritard*
Summer has stopped.   *pp*   *a tempo*

Refrain

f

3. Ah, Love, but a day,
And the world has changed!
Look in my eyes!   *pp*

Part II

Wilt thou change too?
Look in my eyes!
Wilt thou change too?
Should I fear surprise?   *crescendo, agitato*
Shall I find aught new
In the old and dear,   *acellerato*
In the good and true,
With the changing year?

ff

4. Ah Love,   *ff*
Look in my eyes.   *ritard*
Look in my eyes,
Wilt thou change too?   *pp*   *movendo (dying away)*

In addition to the dynamic pattern of each individual section, there is a musical progression that transcends the separate segments and ties them into a larger dynamic structure. This progression consists of the differing musical treatments of the words "Ah, Love."

Example 20.2

Each successive setting of "Ah, Love" is heard as an increase of musical energy, growing toward a climax. The second "Ah, Love" is louder and higher than the first; the third is louder and longer; the fourth, the loudest, longest, and highest, is the climax of this progress and of the entire song.

The craftsmanship exemplified in "Ah, Love, but a Day" made Beach a respected and popular composer during her lifetime.

Edward MacDowell (1861–1908) also came under the influence of German Romanticism but avoided the established instrumental forms in favor of program music. Having studied in Germany, he went on to achieve success there as a pianist, composer, and teacher. In contrast to the Boston group, MacDowell allied himself with the tradition of Wagner and Liszt. He wrote several tone poems for orchestra, a well-known piano concerto (in D minor), and many songs and choral pieces. But this American "tone poet" became primarily the composer of small character pieces for piano, most with programmatic titles. His *Woodland Sketches,* containing "To a Wild Rose" and "To a Water Lily," and *New England Idyls* are among his best-known works in this vein.

Late in the century, a few American musicians began to react against the domination of German ideals and attitudes. Some American composers decided to make use of American Indian and Negro themes—a challenge put forth by Czech composer Antonín Dvořák on his visit to America from 1892 to 1895. Arthur Farwell (1872–1951) was an American composer who accepted Dvořák's challenge and concentrated on using Indian themes in his works. Those who reacted against the German influence also took interest in the new musical ideas from France and Russia. Charles T. Griffes (1884–1920), whose creative talents were cut short by his premature death, showed in his early works the influence of Debussy, Ravel, and Stravinsky. He also developed an interest in Oriental music, and his last works, especially the *Sonata for Piano* (1918, revised 1919) and the *Poem for Flute and Orchestra* (1919), contain the seeds of a synthesis of his various interests.

THE EARLY TWENTIETH CENTURY

During the first two decades of the twentieth century, as we have just noted, the German Romantic tradition continued to hold sway within the American musical establishment both among the concertgoing public and in academic circles. Eventually, the influence of French impressionism made some inroads via the music of Charles T. Griffes. Later, French traditions and the neoclassicism of Stravinsky would be transmitted to American composers through influential French teachers and would supplant German attitudes.

But American musical pioneers were at the same time beginning to discover and invent new and radical kinds of music of their own, independent of and in some cases even before their European counterparts. From about 1900 to 1920, in such widely separated places as Danbury, Connecticut, and San Francisco, California, a few Americans were tinkering with an assortment of "ultramodern" sounds and methods of composition.

One of these bold figures was Charles E. Ives, one of the most extraordinary and original composers America has produced. Not only did Ives use such advanced techniques as atonality, free dissonance, and extreme rhythmic complexity, he dipped into home-grown music as well. Indeed, his music contains elements drawn from the entire gamut of his musical and personal experience—from popular American songs and marches to hymn tunes to quotations from famous European classics. In a statement reflecting his open-minded approach, Ives said, "There can be nothing 'exclusive' about a substantial art. It comes directly out of the heart of experience of life and thinking about life and living life." Thus, even within the same composition, Ives might shift from atonality to simple, hymnbook harmonies for evocative purposes. Ives, with his acceptance of all musical sources as valid and his rejection of dogmatic and exclusive methods, continues to influence composers here and beyond our borders.

IVES (1874–1954)

Charles Ives (fig. 20.3) was raised in the small town of Danbury, Connecticut, where his father was town bandleader, church organist, music teacher, and composer. His father had an unusual interest in musical experimentation and a fascination with unconventional sounds, which he transmitted to his son. This was undoubtedly one of the most important musical influences in Ives's life.

The young Ives studied music at Yale and then launched a successful career in life insurance. He deliberately chose to earn his living in an enterprise separate from his composing, on the theory that both efforts would be better for it, and he never regretted the decision. He composed furiously during evenings and weekends, storing his manuscripts in his barn. Ives's music was totally unknown until he published his *Concord Sonata,* a volume of songs, and a collection of essays in the early 1920s. Even then, his works were not readily accepted; only since World War II has his music become widely performed, published, and recorded. As his works became better known, Ives's influence increased, and successive generations of composers still draw inspiration from various aspects of his wide-ranging musical language. His work is considered so important among musicians and so popular with the concertgoing public that the one-hundredth anniversary of his birth was widely celebrated in 1974.

The musical isolation in which Ives worked led to the development of an unusual philosophy of music. Ives idealized the strength and simple virtue of ordinary people. He had little regard for technical skill, either in

Figure 20.3 Charles Ives, perhaps the boldest and most original of American composers, drew his musical elements and inspiration from the entire stage of his musical and personal experiences.

composition or in performance, but placed high value on the spirit and earnestness with which amateurs sang and played their popular hymns and songs. The freedom that Ives permitted himself in the choice of musical materials, he extended to performers of his works. Undismayed by an enthusiastic but inaccurate performance of *Three Places in New England* (1903–1914), Ives remarked approvingly, "Just like a town meeting—every man for himself. Wonderful how it came out!"

IVES'S WORK

Ives wrote several engaging orchestral works, including his four numbered symphonies, another symphony titled *New England Holidays,* and *Three Places in New England.* The latter contains the famous musical representation of two marching bands coming down Main Street on the Fourth of July, each playing in a different rhythm and key! Ives produced a considerable amount of chamber music as well, some for such traditional combinations as string quartet. But he also enjoyed creating new and unusual groupings of instruments. In *The Unanswered Question* (1906), a solo trumpet "asks the question" with an atonal melody, and four flutes attempt an answer in successive flurries of confusion, all against a tonal background played by offstage strings. In *Hallowe'en* (1907?), for string quartet, piano, and optional bass drum, each of the strings plays in a different key. Ives wrote over one hundred songs, several violin sonatas, and works for piano, including the great Second Sonata (1909–1915), subtitled *Concord Mass., 1840–60.*

IVES: *Variations on "America"*
Cassette 6/B, Track 2
CD 6, Track 12

Like much of his music, *Variations on "America"* displays an intriguing sense of humor. The piece was composed for organ in 1891 but is best known today in the transcription for symphony orchestra made in 1963 by the American composer William Schuman.

A typical theme and variation begins with the statement of a theme allowing the listener to become sufficiently familiar with the basic musical material in order to follow and appreciate it as it is varied in subsequent sections of the composition. On the assumption that just about everyone in the United States knew the tune to "America" ("My country 'tis of thee"), Ives dispensed with this traditional process and began the piece not with a simple statement of the theme but with an introduction that is in itself a kind of variation of segments of the melody.

Example 20.3

Each section of the **ABA** plan of the introduction begins with this variant of the beginning of "America." The second A ends on a dominant chord, ♩ which resolves into a statement of the entire melody with its traditional harmonization in the clear-cut key of F major. The instrumental tone quality of the theme, however, is anything but traditional. To match the strange sound Ives wanted from the organ, the transcriber uses muted trumpets and trombones combined with strings played not with the *hair* of the bow but with the *wood* of the bow drawn over the strings (*col legno,* meaning "with wood"), producing an eerie sound from the string section. To heighten this effect, bells make unexpected entrances at the end of each phrase of the tune. The effect of this familiar and simple tune combined with such strange and unorthodox orchestration provides an overall impression that can best be described as weirdly incongruous.

In variation 1, the theme is presented by the strings against rapid decorative material played by oboes, clarinets, bassoons, and xylophone, with trumpets and snare drum coming in with a finishing touch. In this variation, the theme itself is not altered. Variation results from the new and varied material played *against* the theme. The key of F major is clearly maintained.

Variation 2 is quite different in several interesting aspects. While the overall tonic key of F major is maintained, the harmonic vocabulary is much richer and more complex than that normally associated with this simple tune. This is particularly true at the end of each section, where the style is reminiscent of "barbershop harmony."

The sectional nature of the tune is emphasized by the orchestration. In the first section, the tune (somewhat simplified) is played by solo clarinet, doubled by solo horn, and accompanied by strings. The instruments employed in the second section create an entirely different tone quality. In the second section, the tune (somewhat fragmented) is played by muted solo trumpet accompanied by horns, trombones, and tuba (all muted), with the solo clarinet making a surprise entrance at the very end. Difference in dynamic level, *pp* in section one, *mf* in section two, intensifies the contrast between sections.

Thus far, the introduction, the theme, and variations 1 and 2 have maintained the key of F major as the prevailing tonic. Variation 3 is quite clearly in a different key—D-flat major. In between variation 2 (F major) and variation 3 (D♭ major), Ives inserts an interlude in which both F major and D♭ major are used simultaneously, a device known as **polytonality.** In this polytonal texture, Ives employs *canon,* an imitative contrapuntal device in which flutes, oboes, clarinet, trumpets, and violins play the tune in F major, followed one measure later, by the tune in D♭ major played by horns, trumpet, and trombones.

Example 20.4

The dissonance that normally results from polytonality is well illustrated in the interlude's final chord, which consists of a combination of the chords of F major and D♭ major.

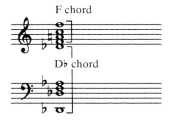

Example 20.5

While the tone F is common to both chords, the D♭ and A♭ of the D♭ chord and the A♮ and C of the F chord clash harshly so that the overall sound is quite dissonant. The interlude is further set off from its two neighbors (variations 2 and 3) by its *fff* dynamic level.

The fun begins in earnest when variation 3 provides relief of comic proportions after the harsh and loud interlude. The change of key from F major to D♭ major keeps company with a switch in meter, from 3/4 to 6/8. The melody is transformed into a lively "dance tune" played by the oboe against a repeated jocular figure in the cello (example 20.6).

The rest of the strings provide pizzicato accompaniment. The first statement by the tune ends 𝄐 followed by a deliciously flippant phrase by solo flute.

Example 20.7

The second time around, the clarinet and second violin have the tune, and the first violins add increased rhythmic activity.

Example 20.8

In the second half of the tune, the glockenspiel adds to the *ff* level; the flippant ending is played by the trumpet and extended by the piccolo—to close a jolly musical episode.

Without pause we are launched into variation 4 in the style of a polonaise. The tune is played in F minor by solo trombone and tuba against the traditional polonaise rhythm provided by strings, horns, and percussion.

Example 20.9

The second half of the tune is repeated by oboes, clarinets, and bassoons while the flutes, piccolo, and trumpet enliven the background by adding ♪♪⁷♪♪|♩. The combination of the tune in a minor key against such a "foreign" background makes the movement grotesquely funny.

A very brief interlude, in which the brass section confirms the key of F minor, prepares for variation 5, the last, longest, and most brilliant, to finish the piece majestically. Variation 5 consists of two statements of the theme, the second of which is extended and climaxes in a surprise return of the original introduction. The introduction in turn leads to a coda, with full orchestra, fortissimo, ending the composition.

Example 20.10

Variations on "America" gives us an intriguing glimpse of a unique and fascinating musical personality, one that continues to grow in stature as a figure in the history of American music.

THE MUSIC OF BLACK AMERICANS

The important contributions to popular music in this country by black Americans is well known and recognized, as we shall see in chapter 22. But black Americans produced and continue to produce important works in the field of concert music—art songs, chamber music, symphonies, operas, and choral music—although, because of the nature of American society, publication and performance have often been difficult to obtain.

Curiously, it was the work and the personage of a black Englishman that supplied much of the impetus for black Americans in the composition of serious music. Samuel Coleridge-Taylor (1875–1912) was the son of a Negro doctor of medicine from Sierra Leone who settled in London and married an Englishwoman. He studied violin at an early age, and in 1890, he became a student at the Royal College of Music in London. In 1898, he wrote the first part of a long choral work on poetry by Longfellow. "Hiawatha's Wedding Feast" gained great popularity and established the reputation of Coleridge-Taylor all over the English-speaking world. In 1904, he was appointed conductor of the prestigious Handel Society in London.

Coleridge-Taylor made three visits to the United States as a guest conductor in 1904, 1906, and 1910, performing much of his own music. He had a tremendous influence on black American musicians, particularly Henry T. Burleigh (1866–1946) and R. Nathaniel Dett (1882–1943), whose activities became excellent models for other black composers.

The early decades of the twentieth century saw the rise of many gifted black composers such as Burleigh, Dett, Scott Joplin, William Dawson, Howard Swanson, Margaret Bonds, Florence B. Price (the first black woman to write a symphonic work to be performed by a major symphony orchestra), and William Grant Still (1895–1978), who came to be known as the "Dean of Afro-American Composers."

WILLIAM GRANT STILL

Throughout a long career, William Grant Still (fig. 20.4) proved himself to be a versatile and resilient human being and musician. He played in theaters, orchestras, and dance bands; wrote arrangements for radio shows; composed for films (*Lost Horizon,* 1935; *Pennies from Heaven,* 1936; *Stormy Weather,* 1943) and television ("Gunsmoke" and the "Perry Mason Show"); and authored a large number and wide variety of concert works, among them operas, music for ballets, chamber music, and vocal and choral music, including many art songs, and symphonic works.

Afro-American Symphony

Still is perhaps best known for his first symphony, *Afro-American Symphony* (1930). In addition to being an interesting piece of music, this work is historic in that it was the first symphonic work by a black American to be performed by a major symphony orchestra, the Rochester Philharmonic in 1931. In this work, Still fully employed black musical ingredients, including spirituals, blues, work songs, ragtime, and jazz within a general style that is often described as neoromantic. He was also the first composer to introduce the tenor banjo into the ranks of a symphony orchestra.

The *Afro-American Symphony* (which Still revised in 1969) is laid out in four movements and is scored for large symphony orchestras consisting of three flutes (with one piccolo), two oboes, English horn, two clarinets, bass clarinet, two bassoons, four horns, three trumpets, three trombones, tuba, a large percussion section including vibraphone, celesta, harp, tenor banjo, and strings.

After the piece was finished, Still chose selected parts of poems by Paul Laurence Dunbar to reflect the spirit of each movement, giving the piece a kind of programmatic flavor:

Movement I—Moderato assai

All my life long twell de night has pas'
Let de wo'k come ez it will,
So dat I fin' you, my honey, at las',
Some whaih des ovah de hill.

Movement II—Adagio

It's moughty tiahsome layin' 'roun'
Dis sorrer-laden earfly groun',
An' oftentimes I thinks, thinks I
'Twould be a sweet t'ing des to die
An' go 'long home.

Movement III—Animato

An we'll shout ouah halleluyahs,
On dat mighty reck'nin' day.

(Incidentally, this rousing movement became so popular that it is often performed as an independent piece.)

Movement IV—Lento, con risoluzione

Be proud, my Race, in mind and soul.
Thy name is writ on Glory's scroll
In characters of fire.
High mid the clouds of Fame's bright sky
Thy banner's blazoned folds now fly,
And truth shall lift them higher.

Still adds as a kind of postscript: "He who develops his God-given gifts with view to aiding humanity, manifests truth."

The pronounced blues character of the piece is clearly evident at the onset of the movement in a brief introductory section by the English horn.

STILL: *Afro-American Symphony,* First Movement
Cassette 6/B, Track 3
CD 6, Track 13
See Listening Guide on pages 469–470.

Example 20.11

Reproduced by permission of Novello & Co. Ltd.

This flavor is maintained in the first theme played by muted trumpet, with syncopated [r]hmic figures punctuating at the end of melodic phrases and between them by the horns.

Reproduced by permission of Novello & Co. Ltd.

The theme is repeated by the clarinet, with flutes and oboes providing different flourishes at phrase endings and between phrases. After a brief transition, the violins have a slightly altered version of the theme against accompaniment supplied primarily by the brass section ending in a short "bridge" modulating to a different key and ending with a brief pause in preparation for the second theme.

The second theme is set forth by the oboe against flute counterpoint and with melodic/rhythmic insertions by clarinet and horn all accompanied by the harp and quiet lower strings.

Example 20.13

Reproduced by permission of Novello & Co. Ltd.

The strings then begin what can be described as a development section, with versions of the themes (particularly the second theme) played by upper strings, lower strings, and harp, leading to an allegro section in which the upper strings and French horns alternate in stating fragments of the themes, and finally the entire orchestra joins in the developmental process.

The end of the development section is marked strikingly by the celesta that completes the modulation back to the central key of the movement and the recapitulation.

In the recapitulation, the second theme appears first in a very expressive and somewhat altered form stated by the strings. But one of the most striking features of the movement is the transformation of the second theme into a really jazzy version featuring the trumpet section (example 20.14).

Original

Example 20.14

Recapitulation

Reproduced by permission of Novello & Co. Ltd.

After this transformed second theme, the movement ends with a quiet coda.

This movement and the rest of the *Afro-American Symphony* comprise a fascinating work. In form it is quite conventional—two contrasting themes, development and recapitulation—sonata-allegro form! But its *character* is unique, permeated by elements indigenous to black culture.

GEORGE GERSHWIN

As we shall see in chapter 22, the blues, jazz, and other forms of popular music became important ingredients in American culture. Just as the blues was a pronounced element in the concert music of William Grant Still and others, jazz became influential in the works of many composers, prominent among them George Gershwin (1898–1937). Gershwin was a composer of popular songs and made many contributions to American musical theater, including the musical comedies *Of Thee I Sing, Strike Up the Band* and, in particular, his "folk opera" *Porgy and Bess* (1935).

In addition, Gershwin incorporated the musical idioms of jazz into the concert hall in works such as *Jazz Piano Preludes* (1936), the symphonic poem *An American in Paris* (1928), *Concerto in F* for piano and orchestra (1925), and his best-known work, the jazz piano concerto *Rhapsody in Blue* (1924).

GERSHWIN:
Rhapsody in Blue
Cassette 6/B, Track 4
CD 6, Track 14
See Listening Guide on pages 470–471.

AARON COPLAND

Aaron Copland (1900–1990; fig. 20.5) was the first of a stream of Americans who traveled to France to study with the famous teacher Nadia Boulanger. He developed an abstract, neoclassical style. Among his works in this style are the brilliant *Piano Variations* (1930) and the rhythmically complex *Short Symphony* (1933).

By the mid-1930s, however, Copland began to be dissatisfied with the growing distance between the concertgoing public and the contemporary composer. "I felt that it was worth the effort to see if I couldn't say what I had to say in the simplest terms possible," Copland wrote. Increasingly thereafter, he drew on themes of regional America. His best-known scores are three ballets: *Billy the Kid* (1938) and *Rodeo* (1942) use actual cowboy songs, while *Appalachian Spring* (1944) depicts life in rural Pennsylvania and is among the most beautiful and enduring representatives of Americana in our musical heritage.

Figure 20.5 One of Aaron Copland's abiding concerns has been to bridge the gap between the concertgoing public and the modern composer.

Copland also wrote film scores during this period, such as *Of Mice and Men* (1939), *Our Town* (1940), and *The Red Pony* (1948). Several patriotic works, including the *Lincoln Portrait* (1942) and *Fanfare for the Common Man* (1942), were occasioned by the entry of the United States into World War II. Almost all these works used American subjects and were aimed at the wider audience provided by such media as film. Like Stravinsky, Copland turned to serial composition after 1950. The *Connotations for Orchestra* (1962) adapts the twelve-tone technique to his special musical style. During the last several decades of his life, Copland spent much of his time conducting concerts of his own music all over the world.

APPALACHIAN SPRING

COPLAND:
Appalachian Spring, Part I
Cassette 7/A, Track 1
CD 7, Track 1
See Listening Guide on pages 472–473.

Appalachian Spring, the last of Copland's three ballets on American frontier themes, was written on commission for Martha Graham's modern dance company. The work, choreographed by Miss Graham, premiered in October 1944.

Scored originally for a chamber orchestra of thirteen instruments, the ballet was later revised by Copland as a suite for symphony orchestra and is best known today in this form. The ballet itself is virtually plotless, having for its characters a young bride (originally danced by Miss Graham), her farmer husband-to-be, an older pioneering woman, and a preacher with his followers.

The music, evoking a simple, tender, and pastoral atmosphere, is distinctly American in its use of folklike themes, suggesting barn dances, fiddle tunes, and revival hymns. Only one piece is actually a genuine folk tune: the Shaker song "Simple Gifts," which forms the basis for a set of five variations. Not only Copland's melodic material, but also his compositional techniques suggest a distinctly American musical style. The orchestral texture is, by and large, open and transparent, with the different instrumental choirs—string, woodwind, brass, and percussion (chiefly piano and harp)—scored as individual units and juxtaposed with one another. The vigorous, four-square rhythmic patterns, particularly in the music for the revivalist preacher and his followers, could not have originated anywhere but in the folk music of the American frontier.

The orchestral suite falls into eight distinct sections set off from one another by changes in tempo and meter. The opening section, marked "very slowly," introduces the characters, one by one. Over a luminous string background, solo woodwind and brass instruments enter one by one—paralleling the balletic action—with slowly rising and falling figures that outline different major triads. It is not until the solo flute and violin enter that these triadic figures coalesce into any kind of definite theme.

Example 20.15

(Solo Violin doubles an octave higher.)

From Aaron Copland *Appalachian Spring,* Boosey & Hawkes, Inc., sole publishers and licensees.

The serene mood of the introduction is suddenly broken by a vigorous, strongly accented theme sounded in unison in the strings and piano.

Example 20.16

From Aaron Copland *Appalachian Spring,* Boosey & Hawkes, Inc., sole publishers and licensees.

The action of the ballet now gets under way. The theme—initially built on the notes of an A-major triad—is soon broken down into smaller motives with the rhythmic figure predominating.

Musical development intensifies as these motives are passed back and forth between different orchestral choirs and solo instruments. Constant changes in meter and shifts in rhythmic accents add to the increasing momentum of this section.

Then follows a *pas de deux* (a dance for two performers) for the bride and her husband-to-be, and their mixed feelings of tenderness and passion are expressed in a lyrical melody originating in the clarinet.

Example 20.17

From Aaron Copland *Appalachian Spring,* Boosey & Hawkes, Inc., sole publishers and licensees.

The melody gradually expands and takes a definitive shape through numerous changes in tempo, culminating in a statement divided among the oboe, clarinet, and flute.

The revivalist preacher and his followers take over, announced by a cheerful tune that seems to have come right out of a country fiddlers' convention. Though heard first in the oboe and then the flute, the tune is not given fully until the entry of the violins.

Example 20.18

From Aaron Copland *Appalachian Spring,* Boosey & Hawkes, Inc., sole publishers and licensees.

As in the second section, the rhythmic aspects of the tune soon prove to be more important than the melodic ones. The pace becomes more frenetic; cross-accents and syncopations soon predominate; and the section ends in a very Stravinskian manner, with alternating meters of 2/4 and 5/8.

An extended solo for the bride follows, in which she expresses extremes of joy and fear, and exaltation at her coming motherhood. A presto theme forms the basis for most of this section,

Example 20.19

From Aaron Copland *Appalachian Spring,* Boosey & Hawkes, Inc., sole publishers and licensees.

but toward the end, a lyrical theme—very much like that of the earlier *pas de deux*—enters in the solo violin and oboe, gradually leading into a short recapitulation of the introduction.

A solo clarinet presents the melody of the Shaker song "Simple Gifts."

Example 20.20

From Aaron Copland *Appalachian Spring,* Boosey & Hawkes, Inc., sole publishers and licensees.

The action of the ballet at this point—scenes of daily activity for the bride and her intended—seem perfectly reflected in the tune. The text of the song runs as follows:

'Tis the gift to be simple,
'Tis the gift to be free,
'Tis the gift to come down where we ought to be,
And when we find ourselves in the place just right,
'Twill be in the valley of love and delight.
When true simplicity is gain'd,
To bow and to bend we shan't be asham'd,
To turn, turn will be our delight
'Till by turning, turning, we come round right.

The five variations following the statement of the tune present the melody in a variety of contrasting textures and accompanying figures, often with new lines of counterpoint. At the end, the full orchestra blazes forth in a broad, chorale-like setting of the tune.

In the final section, the bride takes her place among her neighbors, and they depart quietly, leaving the young couple alone. Once again the luminous sonorities of the introduction return, and the work concludes in the atmosphere of serenity with which it began.

To the list of conservative American composers of the early twentieth century should be added William Schuman (1910–1992) and the neoromanticists Samuel Barber (1910–1981) and Gian Carlo Menotti (b. 1911), known primarily for his operas for both stage and television.

THE EXPERIMENTERS

Other composers at the beginning of the century were taking more radical approaches to compositional techniques and musical style.

Henry Cowell (1897–1965), a West Coast composer, experimented with many radical compositional procedures that would later have considerable influence. His most well known device, found mainly in his piano works, is the **tone cluster.** This dense, indistinct sound can be produced by playing a large group of adjacent notes on the piano with the flat of the hand. It is said that Béla Bartók wrote Cowell asking permission to use this "invention" of his American colleague. Cowell wrote energetically about modern music and published it as well, especially promoting the work of Charles Ives and Edgard Varèse.

Edgard Varèse (1883–1965) was born in Paris but came to New York to live in 1915 and became one of the most innovative and influential composers of the twentieth century. Varèse challenged conservative musical traditions by defining music as "organized sound." This meant *all* sound, including some sounds previously classified as nonmusical noises, such as Cowell's tone clusters.

Many of Varèse's compositions employ unusual combinations of instruments, which often play at the extremes of their registers. The musical idiom is characterized by violent, screechingly dissonant, and blocklike chords spanning many octaves. Varèse's titles often reflect an interest in science: *Hyperprism* (1923), *Integrales* (1925), *Ionisation* (1930–1933), and *Density 21.5* for solo flute (1936). The sound of the music tends to recall the

Figure 20.6 Ruth Crawford Seeger, one of the first experimenters in the area of serialism in the first half of twentieth century.

noises of mechanized society. *Ionisation,* written for percussion ensemble, employs a huge battery of standard orchestral percussion and exotic instruments as well, such as the "lion's-roar" (a primitive kind of friction drum) and three sirens. The sirens illustrate Varèse's passion for expanding sound resources beyond those of the normal orchestra. Later, the development of more sophisticated electronic means inspired Varèse to write such masterpieces as *Déserts* (1949–1954) and *Poème électronique* (1957–1958).

Wallingford Riegger (1885–1961) adapted serial procedures freely in such works as *Dichotomy* for chamber orchestra (1932) and his Third Symphony (1948).

Ruth Crawford Seeger (1901–1953; fig. 20.6) was one of the most remarkable American composers of the first half of the twentieth century. Her works include compositional techniques not heard again until thirty years later. Her *String Quartet* of 1931 is recognized as one of the most outstanding works in American chamber music literature. Her close friendship with the poet Carl Sandburg resulted in several songs based on Sandburg poems.

Roger Sessions (1896–1985) easily ranked alongside the most important European composers of his generation and was one of America's most respected composers and teachers. His early works show the influence of Stravinsky. His eight symphonies, two operas, and his setting of Walt Whitman's poem "When Lilacs Last in the Dooryard Bloom'd," for vocal soloists, chorus, and orchestra, form an impressive legacy.

As a teacher, Sessions influenced several generations of American composers, including Miriam Gideon, Hugo Weisgal, Vivian Fine, Donald Martino, and Ellen Taaffe Zwilich, all of whom have outstanding careers as composers.

Listening Guide

STILL: *Afro-American Symphony*

First Movement: Tempo varies
Quadruple meter
Sonata form

Orchestra

Review: Example 20.11 (introductory theme, based loosely on first theme)
Example 20.12 (first theme)
Example 20.13 (second theme)
Example 20.14 (first theme in original and "swinging" rhythms)

CD 6 (Cassette 6/B, Track 3)

			Exposition		
13	①	0:00	**Introductory theme**	1	Slow, bluesy melody in English horn, begins monophonically; closes with accompaniment interjections
	②	0:22	**Theme 1**	2a	Muted trumpet states Theme 1 in three short phrases, syncopated responses between phrases
		1:03		b	Clarinet repeats Theme 1, over rhythmic string accompaniment with "clicking" sound, syncopated woodwind responses between phrases
		1:23	**Bridge**	3a	Transitional fragments circle through woodwinds, ending with bassoon
		1:47		b	Strings develop three-note pattern over long timpani roll, tempo accelerates; changes to two-note motive, tempo ritards to cadence
	③	2:25	**Theme 2**	4a	Tender, singing theme in oboe, accompanied by harp arpeggio, responses from woodwinds, muted brass, solo violin; second half of theme sung in violins; variant of first part of theme in flute to close
		3:31		b	Cellos sing first half of theme; harp plays variant of second half of theme
	④	4:04	**Development**	1	Two-note motive accelerates to allegro, rhythmic accompaniment pattern; violins alternate fragments of Theme 2 with other sections of orchestra
		4:36		2	Violin fragments crescendo to full orchestra playing fragments of Theme 2, forte
		4:58		3	Fragments move to English horn, softer dynamic; bass clarinet alternates with celesta as tempo slows

Continued on next page

		Recapitulation		
⑤	5:10	**Theme 2**	1	Tender, singing theme in shortened form, violins
	5:39	**Bridge**	2	Slow transition in woodwinds, trill in low strings
⑥	5:50	**Theme 1**	3a	Two-note motive against strong rhythm accompaniment in pizzicato strings; muted trumpets play first theme (three phrases) in "swing" rhythm, interjected responses from other sections of orchestra
	6:37		b	Harp solo, slowing tempo provide transition
	6:44	**Introductory theme**	4	Yearning strings introduce slow, bluesy theme, bass clarinet; quiet concluding chords

Listening Guide

GERSHWIN: *Rhapsody in Blue* (Original Version)

Single Movement: Tempo varies
                Quadruple meter
                Irregular sectional form

Solo Piano, Jazz Orchestra

CD 6 (Cassette 6/B, Track 4)

14 ①	0:00	**Introduction**		Clarinet trill, glissando to bluesy theme; reaches climax on high note, held; repeated-note theme, muted horns; clarinet trill, glissando
②	0:47	**A**	1	Bluesy theme, muted trumpet; piano, five-note motive (de-de-de-daa-daa), extended; bluesy theme, orchestra; five-note motive developed; pianistic display ends in upward scale
	1:56		2	Bluesy theme and five-note motive alternate, ending in pianistic display
	3:07		3	Bluesy theme and five-note motive, faster tempo, orchestra
	3:37	**Bridge**		Short, exuberant aaba melody ends in brief arpeggios in piano, directly into:
③	4:03	**B**	1	Repeated-note theme (from Introduction), clarinet, against sustained chords

Continued on next page

	4:17		2	Assertive version of repeated-note theme, with motive from bluesy theme (A); sudden slowing at new idea ("wa-wa") in clarinet, muted trumpet, muted trombone; loud chords
④	5:02	C		Exciting, jazzy theme, low instruments; developed at length, builds in tension
	6:08	B		Piano enters on low note, rising passage to extended development of repeated-note theme; motion slows, meditative development of end of theme, pause
⑤	8:38	A/C	1	Bluesy theme, piano, woodwinds with piano running notes; piano solo, trills and runs, arpeggio plunging downward
	9:31		2	Piano develops jazzy theme (C) at length, mounting excitement and brilliance; short cadenza with soft, rising conclusion; pause
⑥	11:23	D	1	Warm, sensuous melody, orchestra, includes three-note "circular" motive; solo violin; orchestra, fuller instrumentation; transition, soft fragment of theme in bells
	13:17		2	Piano, develops circular motive; sensuous melody with added flourishes from piano; fragment developed
⑦	15:12	**Piano cadenza**		Rapid-fire repeated notes; short pause, five-note motive (A); rapid-fire notes, upward glissando
⑧	16:12	D		Orchestra returns with sensuous theme now in faster, exciting rhythm, piano figurations; builds to dissonant chord
	16:41	A		Agitated development of five-note motive; emphatic rising chords
	17:06	B		Exuberant statement of repeated-note theme
	17:33	A		Full orchestra, bluesy theme, Hollywood style; piano, five-note motive; climactic ending

Listening Guide

COPLAND: *Appalachian Spring*

First Part: Four sections; tempo varies
                  Meter varies
                  Sectional form, follows program

Large Orchestra

Review: Example 20.15 (flute and solo violin theme, first section)
              Example 20.16 (vigorous theme, second section)
              Example 20.17 (love theme, third section)
              Example 20.18 (country fiddle tune, fourth section)
              Outline of program, pp. 464–467

CD 7 (Cassette 7/A, Track 1)

1	①	0:00	**Introduction**		Slow, string background; quiet overlapping entrances in winds; serene melody high in solo violin and flute; overlapping entrances throughout orchestra; final cadence, clarinet solo
	②	2:45	**The Ballet Begins; Characters and Activities of the Town**	1a	Vigorous, leaping theme, forte, strings and piano; fragments tossed through strings and winds, vigorous theme by orchestra
		3:10		b	Soft, strings accompany vigorous theme in flutes and two solo violins; virile brass figure, forte, imitated; brass chords combined with vigorous theme
		4:01		c	Short motive, de-de-daa, developed; fragmented texture; vigorous theme in flute
		4:36		d	De-de-daa rhythm on repeated note; tension builds to syncopated whirlwind climax; long single high-pitched note
		5:03	*Transition*	2a	Quiet version of vigorous theme in flute; strings accompany in sustained, peaceful version of de-de-daa motive
		5:38		b	De-de-daa motive echoes through woodwinds, pianissimo
	③	5:49	**Pas de Deux; The Bride and Husband-to-Be**		Folk dance accompaniment alternates with love motive in clarinet, oboe; descending melody in flutes
		6:42			Threatening brass chord alternates with intensely passionate string theme; trumpet added

Continued on next page

	7:27			Descending melody, woodwinds; passionate theme, quiet strings; descending melody, woodwinds
	8:20			Love theme fully stated in oboe, clarinet, flute; tender close, strings, flute
(4)	9:26	**The Revivalist Preacher and His Followers**	1a	Staccato country fiddle tune fragments in oboe, flute, other solo winds and pizzicato violins; full statement in violins with woodblock; fragments continuously developed in brass and winds with triangle, fast scales up and down
	10:08		b	Dancelike accompaniment added, snare drum, trumpet calls
	10:16		c	Country dance, accompaniment in bassoons, then pizzicato strings
	10:36		2a	Suddenly slower, emphatic string chords, square dance; horn calls, full orchestra pairs of chords, trumpets join in, strings join in
	11:23		b	Lighter section, bass drops out, strings and brass continue dance
	11:35		c	Oom-pah oom-pah accompaniment in piano and brass; full orchestra square dance, more frenetic rhythmic activity to climax

SUMMARY

Music in seventeenth-century America was primarily functional, used mostly for worship in church and at home. Secular music began to flourish in the eighteenth century, especially in the larger cities. While a group of composers led by William Billings created their own American style, most American music continued to be subservient to European music.

Nineteenth-century American music was marked by two significant phenomena: a division between "classical" and "popular" music, and the imitation of German music by American composers. While the songs of Stephen Foster and the instrumental works of Louis Moreau Gottschalk incorporate many uniquely American elements, most composers imitated current European practice. In the post–Civil War years, the Boston area produced such notable composers as John Paine, Horatio Parker, George Chadwick, and Amy Beach, all of whom wrote in the style of German Romantics. In contrast, Edward McDowell wrote program music in the tradition of Liszt and Wagner. Late in the century, some composers reacted against the domination of German ideals and attitudes. Arthur Farwell used American Indian themes in his music, while the works of Charles Griffes were influenced by French impressionists.

Early-twentieth-century composers began to invent their own kinds of new music. Charles Ives was one of the most extraordinary and original composers that America has produced. His music contains elements drawn from a variety of American and European traditions. He used such advanced techniques as atonality, free dissonance, polytonality, and extreme rhythmic complexity, along with traditional procedures, in a free and undogmatic manner. Ives's works have had a profound impact on later composers.

In the early part of the twentieth century, black American composers began to make significant contributions to concert music. Chief among them was William Grant Still, who is best known for his *Afro-American Symphony,* the first symphonic work by a black composer to be performed by a leading symphony orchestra.

George Gershwin, a versatile composer of popular songs and musical comedies, incorporated many aspects of jazz into concert music, such as his piano concerto *Rhapsody in Blue.*

Other composers took more radical approaches to compositional techniques and musical styles. Henry Cowell, who experimented with many new procedures, is best known for his use of tone clusters. Edgard Varèse, an innovative and influential composer, defined music as "organized sound," which included all sounds. His works are characterized by unusual combinations of instruments and violent, dissonant, blocklike chords spanning many octaves. Several of Varèse's works feature electronic sounds. Other "radical" composers include Wallingford Riegger, Ruth Crawford Seeger, and Roger Sessions.

NEW TERMS

polytonality
tone cluster

SUGGESTED LISTENING

Billings, William

"Be Glad Then, America"; "When Jesus Wept"; "Chester." These three works by this early American composer are respectively an anthem, a canon, and a hymn tune. All three were used by the twentieth-century composer William Schuman as the basis for his symphonic work *New England Triptych*.

Copland, Aaron

Fanfare for the Common Man for brass and percussion. Copland wrote this stirring piece in 1942 as part of the war effort, and later incorporated it into the finale of his Third Symphony in 1946.

Cowell, Henry

Piano Music. This unique assortment of exciting pieces demonstrates the composer's "tone clusters" and the techniques of plucking, scraping, and strumming the piano strings.

Foster, Stephen

"Oh! Susanna"; "Camptown Races." See page 450.

Griffes, Charles

Poem for Flute and Orchestra. The early music of this composer showed the influence of Debussy, Ravel, and Stravinsky. *Poem for Flute and Orchestra* is Griffes's best-known piece.

Ives, Charles

Three Places in New England. Each of the three movements of this work illustrates a different facet of the composer's highly individualistic technique: The first (The "St. Gaudens" in Boston Common) presents a subtle and complex use of traditional American melodies; the second ("Putnam's Camp," Redding, Connecticut) depicts a lively Fourth of July celebration, complete with colliding brass bands; the last ("The Housatonic at Stockbridge") is a wonderfully evocative tone poem portraying a quiet New England river.

Schuman, William

New England Triptych. In this piece for symphony orchestra, Schuman used three works by the early American composer William Billings: "Be Glad Then, America," "When Jesus Wept," and the hymn tune "Chester." Each piece forms the basis for one of the movements.

Seeger, Ruth Crawford

String Quartet (1931). This work is recognized as one of the most outstanding works in American chamber music. In it the composer employs a number of compositional techniques that came into vogue much later in the century. The third movement features "dynamic counterpoint," in which the listener's attention moves from one voice to another because of dynamic level rather than melodic interest. The fourth movement is an example of "total serialization" in which all aspects of the piece (pitches, rests, rhythm, and dynamics) are serialized.

Swanson, Howard

Short Symphony. Howard Swanson is one of the first black composers to be recognized in the first half of the twentieth century. His *Short Symphony* (1948) is probably his best-known work.

Varèse, Edgard

Ionisation. This is one of the first pieces of Western music scored entirely for solo percussion instruments (including sirens, piano, gong, bongos, bass drums, maracas, and chimes).

American Music before World War II

Scott Joplin - Tex Arkana

Music of the Late Twentieth Century

Bach In Space. (© Joe Sohm/The Image Works, Inc.)

Art and Architecture

since 1945

Since 1945, more movements in the arts have been launched, more scientific discoveries have been made, and more changes in everyday life have taken place than in any other era of human history. During the half century that has passed since World War II, the United States has consolidated its position as the most powerful and culturally influential nation in the world. The Soviet Union, until recently the second most powerful nation militarily, has lost much of its empire. At the same time, Third-World countries, especially in the Middle East, have become enormously influential, while China and Japan have emerged from revolutions and defeats to play important social and economic roles around the globe. Art and architecture have reflected many of these developments; they have also inspired developments of their own.

During the late 1940s and 1950s, most serious painters in Europe and the United States became abstract expressionists or were influenced by that movement. American abstract expressionists—also known as "New York" artists (because so many of them lived in New York City) or members of the "New York School"—began where their predecessors left off. Like the original expressionists, including Vincent van Gogh (1853–1890; see Prelude V, page 368), abstract expressionists used heavy layers of bright or deeply colored paint. Like the cubists and abstractionists of the 1920s and 1930s, including Wassily Kandinsky (1866–1944; see page 371) and Pablo Picasso (1881–1973; see page 372), they rarely portrayed anything except nonrepresentative shapes and forms. But abstract expressionists of the post-1945 era were less inhibited than their predecessors. Jackson Pollock (1912–1956), the most notorious member of the New York School (a term he disliked), became famous for "action paintings"—canvases onto which he dripped, poured, and threw masses of paint in a frenzy of inspiration. *Full Fathom Five* (1947; see page 482), one of Pollock's most powerful works, suggests the depth and violence of the ocean in its vivid colors; like the ocean, it also seems to "move" on the canvas in random patterns of light and shadow.

Pollock's contemporary Willem de Kooning (b. 1904), an action painter who moved from Holland to America in 1926, was more interested in representational art. *Woman I* (1950–1952; see page 483) is part of a series of de Kooning paintings in which huge, threatening female figures emerge with ferocious energy from the "picture plane"—the surface of the paint-encrusted canvas.

However, not all abstract expressionists were action painters, and not all European and American artists of the 1950s were abstract expressionists. Mark Rothko (1903–1970), for example, often painted large areas of uniform color that suggest hovering forces or shapes. *Red, Brown, and Black* (1958; see page 484) is strikingly symmetrical, but Rothko's color areas are blurred, his forms organic rather than geometrical.

The sharp lines and primary colors favored by European abstractionists like Piet Mondrian (1872–1944), who worked for a while in New York City, seem cooler and more intellectual than Rothko's brooding color clouds. Another imaginative artist, perhaps the most important figure in modern American art, is Robert Rauschenberg (b. 1925). A friend and colleague of the composer John Cage (b. 1912), Rauschenberg borrowed heavily from Dada and surrealist practices of the early twentieth century. Among other works he produced during the 1950s were "paintings" consisting of *blank* canvases; the "pictures" were composed of shadows cast by spectators when those canvases were exhibited in New York in 1951. Rauschenberg's most famous work is probably *Monogram* (1955–1958), a "sculpture" constructed from a stuffed goat surrounded by an automobile tire. Like Cage, Rauschenberg has influenced many artists who grew up during the 1960s, opposed American involvement in Vietnam, and thus went on to become critics of American fads and fashions.

As early as the late 1950s, a few American artists challenged the influence of abstract expressionism and returned to more realistic subjects, especially subjects drawn from everyday experience. In the 1950s, Jasper Johns (b. 1930) launched the movement later known as "pop art" when he produced paintings of flags, maps, and other familiar culture signs. Unlike the rich, painterly style of Pollock and Rothko, pop art often makes use of smooth surfaces and a glossy finish. By the 1960s, pop art had become a household term, especially because of two younger American painters, Andy Warhol (1928–1987) and Roy Lichtenstein (b. 1923). Warhol and Lichtenstein refused to pour or drip paint; they applied it sparingly, when they applied it at all. Instead, Warhol frequently used the silk-screen process to turn photographs of Marilyn Monroe or Coca-Cola bottles into art.

Many of Warhol's works consist of images repeated over and over, as if to emphasize the repetitiveness and sterility of American life. Lichtenstein approached art as if it were newspaper or magazine illustration. His giant canvases, covered with tiny dots of color, recreate scenes from romance and adventure comic books. Pop artists also allied themselves with artists of other kinds: musicians, movie-makers, and animators (to name but three). Thus, pop illustrations appeared during the 1960s on record jackets for rock groups like Big Brother and the Holding Company, and they added color to "camp" films like *Batman* (1966) and *Yellow Submarine* (1969).

A few artists of the 1960s and early 1970s experimented with designs and images known as "optical illusions"—the simulation of motion, for example, by means of carefully arranged lines and shadows. These illusions gave rise to the phrase "op art." Op artists did not become as famous as their pop contemporaries, but designs taken from op drawings and paintings influenced such fields as clothing and interior decoration. For instance, *Untitled* (1965; see page 485), by Arnold Schmidt (b. 1930), calls to mind the appearance in the mid-1960s of "optical" designs for women's dresses.

Other unusual designs, some full of psychedelic colors, influenced hippie fashions of the Vietnam War years. Certain musical scores took on an op art appearance; for example, pages from the score of *Threnody for the Victims of Hiroshima* (1959–1960; see page 486), by Polish composer Krzysztof Penderecki (b. 1933), look almost as innovative as the piece sounds.

The uncompromising, experimental character of abstract expressionism and other avant-garde movements attracted a great deal of public attention after World War II, but few people purchased experimental art objects for their homes or offices. (Reactions to avant-garde movements of the 1950s and 1960s were parodied wittily by Tom Wolfe in his 1975 book *The Painted Word*.) On the other hand, pop art and op art were easier to understand and much more commercially successful. The fortunes (and critical acclaim) won by artists like Lichtenstein paved the way during the 1970s for a return to realism, and several new movements sprang up—among them "super-realism" and "photo-realism" (two terms that often mean much the same thing). To create their canvases, photo-realists use slides of everyday scenes like cars parked on deserted streets; they project these slide images onto large canvases, then "copy" them in so photographic a style that they defy detection as paintings even at short distances. Richard Estes's *Bus Reflection* (1972) is a good example of photo-realism. Examples of super-realism include the life-size sculptures in polyester resins or polyvinyl acetate cast by Duane Hanson (b. 1925). Hanson's *Tourists II* are so lifelike that they have been mistaken for real people by visitors to museums and galleries throughout Europe and the United States (see page 487).

Because so many abstract and avant-garde artworks were called "modern" during the 1940s and 1950s, realist paintings of more recent years have sometimes been called post-modern. One of the most influential postmodernist artists is the British painter, sculptor, and stage designer David Hockney (b. 1937). Hockney has produced works in several styles, but he has become best known for pleasant, pastel-colored paintings like *A Bigger Splash* (1967; see page 488).

During the 1970s and 1980s, Americans also became familiar with the carefully contrived works of Georgia O'Keeffe (1887–1986; see page 489), who began painting almost eighty years before she was honored in 1977 with a special celebration at the National Gallery in Washington, D.C.

But pop, op, and realist artists of the 1960s and 1970s did not displace avant-gardists and their movements altogether. The 1960s, for example, witnessed the birth of two new experimental art schools: minimalism and conceptual art. Minimalist artists specialize in creating large works out of small amounts of material; in music, minimalist composers like Philip Glass (b. 1937) and Laurie Anderson (b. 1947) have become pop heroes, and their works have been turned into MTV music videos. Conceptual composers, on the other hand, have never achieved the widespread success of visual artists like Christo (born Vladmirov Javacheff Christo in 1935). Like other conceptualists, Christo works primarily out-of-doors and creates short-lived constructions of a controversial character. Since the 1960s, he has specialized in "settings" and "wrapping"; in 1974, for instance, he constructed a giant curtain between the cliffs in a Colorado valley—hence the project's name, *Valley Curtain.* Another project, entitled *Running Fence* (1976), consisted of a steel and nylon-fabric fence that stretched for several weeks across more than twenty miles of northern California farmland, and in 1991, he mounted thousands of huge yellow umbrellas on the countryside of southern California and Japan as a spectacular artistic display.

Like the visual arts, architecture has changed dramatically since 1945. During the 1950s, the Bauhaus movement achieved enormous influence over European and American designers, and architects of the so-called International School were responsible for thousands of steel, glass, and concrete office towers, high-rise apartment buildings, and other commercial structures erected around the world. The Seagram Building, designed by Dutch-born Ludwig Mies van der Rohe (1886–1969), is an outstanding example of Bauhaus-influenced architecture in Manhattan's business district.

Like several other Bauhaus architects, Mies van der Rohe emigrated to the United States during the turbulent 1930s. But American architects never entirely abandoned other approaches to design. For example, Frank Lloyd Wright (1867–1959; see Prelude VI, page 444) refused to become involved with international-style structures. By the end of the 1960s, unusual, even fanciful buildings were being built in New York City. The AT&T Building (1979; see page 490), designed by Philip Johnson, is a high-rise office tower topped with a Chippendale-like ornament that has drawn protests from many conservative critics. (Tom Wolfe also satirized the rise and fall of international-style architecture in his 1981 book *From Bauhaus to Our House.*)

Full Fathom Five, by Jackson Pollock, 1947. Oil on canvas with nails, tacks, buttons, key, coins, cigarettes, matches, etc., 50⅞″ × 30⅛″. (Collection, The Museum of Modern Art, New York. Gift of Peggy Guggenheim.)

Woman I, by Willem de Kooning, 1950–1952. Oil on canvas,
75⅞″ × 58″. (Collection, The Museum of Modern Art,
New York, Purchase.)

Red, Brown, and Black, by Mark Rothko. Oil on canvas,
8'10⅝" × 9'9¼". (Collection, The Museum of Modern Art,
New York, Mrs. Simon Guggenheim Fund.)

Untitled, by Arnold Schmidt, 1965. Synthetic polymer paint on canvas, 48⅛″ × 8⅛″. (Collection, The Museum of Modern Art, New York. Gift of Mr. and Mrs. Herbert C. Bernard.)

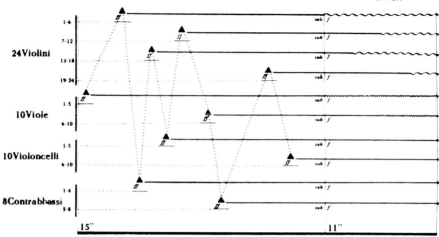

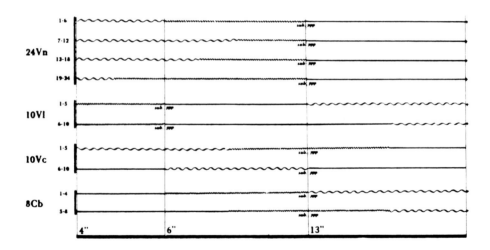

Threnody for the Victims of Hiroshima, by Krzystof Penderecki.
(Copyright © 1961. Copyright renewed by Deshon Music, Inc.
& PWM Editions. All Rights Reserved.)

Tourists II, by Duane Hanson, 1988. Plastic filler, polychromed in oil with accessories, life-size. (Courtesy, Gallery Neuendorf, Frankfurt, Germany.)

A Bigger Splash, by David Hockney, 1967. Acrylic on canvas, 96″ × 96″. (© David Hockney.)

Ladder to the Moon, by Georgia O'Keeffe.
(Photo by Malcom Varon, New York. © 1987.)

AT&T Building, New York.

Prelude VII

MUSIC IN THE SECOND HALF OF THE TWENTIETH CENTURY

CHAPTER
21

Music after World War II continued and extended trends that had originated during the first half of the twentieth century. These trends included atonality, serialism, rhythmic complexity, and the use of unconventional sounds as valid musical materials. Along with this continuation, new and more radical notions about the way music might be composed became increasingly important, and the rapidity with which new ideas were developed and put into practice was accelerated by the intrusion of electronic technology. The development of magnetic tape, the long-playing record, and high-quality playback equipment turned the mode of musical communication from live performance more in the direction of recording. The later availability of computer-controlled synthesizers made possible entirely new ways of composing and performing music.

The years immediately following World War II produced two opposing approaches to musical composition. One approach was **total serialism** (also called **total serialization**)—the complete, predetermined, and ultrarational organization of every aspect of a composition. The other approach was **indeterminacy**—the free, unpremeditated, and irrational occurrence of musical events that were deliberately meant to lie beyond the composer's immediate control. Other terms for *indeterminacy* are **chance music** and **aleatoric music** (*alea* is Latin for "game of chance").

Later, in the 1960s, a new approach to musical composition called **minimalism** was developed by a young generation of composers. This style and its various manifestations became important later in the century.

TOTAL SERIALISM

The French composer and conductor Pierre Boulez (b. 1925; fig. 21.1) described the feelings of younger postwar composers: "After the war we all felt that music, like the world around us, was in a state of chaos. Our problem was to create a new musical language. . . . We went through a period of seeking out total control over music."

Arnold Schoenberg's twelve-tone technique applied only to pitch and did not impose a similar mode of organization on rhythm, dynamics, tone color, or texture. It was the lean, lucid, and compact serial technique of Anton Webern that became the model for young composers in the pursuit of total serialism.

The first composer to apply serial procedures to all aspects of music was the American Milton Babbitt (b. 1916; fig. 21.2). Babbitt extended the system of organizing pitch (melody and harmony) to the systematization of rhythm, tempo, dynamics, and timbre. His *Second String Quartet* (1954) is considered a model of serial organization.

At about the same time, a French composer and teacher at the Paris Conservatory, Olivier Messiaen (1908–1992), was experimenting with total serialism. His students, Pierre Boulez and Karlheinz Stockhausen (b. 1928), became two of the most important figures

Figure 21.1 The music of Pierre Boulez was deeply influenced by the ideas of his teacher, Olivier Messiaen. Boulez's serial compositions and his conducting of twentieth-century orchestral works exhibit precision, clarity, and control.

Figure 21.2 Milton Babbitt at the huge RCA Mark II synthesizer. In several important works, including the rigorously serial *Philomel*, Babbitt has pitted a singer against recorded sound.

Figure 21.3 John Cage's experiments in indeterminacy have had enormous impact. Many current composers, including leading serialists, have adopted aspects of this "music of chance."

on the international music scene. Other prominent serial composers of the 1950s were the Hungarian György Ligéti (b. 1923), the Italians Luigi Nono (b. 1924) and Luciano Berio (b. 1925), and the American Gunther Schuller (b. 1925).

CHANCE MUSIC (INDETERMINACY)

The years immediately following the war saw the rise of chance music. In chance music, elements such as pitches, rhythmic values, and dynamic levels are determined by various extramusical methods such as throwing dice or tossing coins. Another type of chance music takes place during the performance as the performer determines aspects of the flow of the music.

JOHN CAGE

The chief figure in chance music is the American composer John Cage (1912–1992; fig. 21.3). His 1951 piano piece *Music of Changes* was the first work based in large part on random procedures. For it, Cage tossed coins and used the results to determine musical materials from the *I Ching* (Chinese *Book of Changes*). The map of the heavens supplied the note heads for *Atlas Eclipticalis* (1961–1962). This work consists of eighty-six instrumental parts "to be played in whole or part, any duration, in any ensemble, chamber or orchestral."

Cage has been one of the great innovators in the twentieth century. The roles of silence and of the unpredictable background noises that are always present are embodied in *4'33''*, Cage's famous 1952 example of pure "nonmusic." The piece consists entirely of whatever environmental sounds happen to be present during its performance, in which a pianist sits quietly before an open piano for four minutes and thirty-three seconds, then leaves the stage. The point of this gesture is to focus attention on the sounds around us, furthering the premise that any sound or no sound at all is as valid or "good" as any other.

Cage's pieces are all radically different from one another, but they have elements in common. They are programmed activities with certain boundaries set by the composer, who has only limited control over the outcome of the piece. Like the wind blowing a mobile and thereby changing its shape, the performers make decisions on the spur of the moment, thus avoiding rational control.

Cage's impact has been and continues to be great. Many serialist composers, such as Boulez and Stockhausen, as well as younger composers, such as Pauline Oliveros (b. 1932), have adapted aspects of chance music in varying degrees.

ELECTRONIC MUSIC

The development of advanced electronic technology in the 1950s and 1960s made possible radical changes in the way music could be composed and performed. Magnetic tape, synthesizers, and computers allowed the composer to control every aspect of music and made possible accurate rendition of the music without relying on live performers. The tape is both the piece of music *and* its performance.

MUSIQUE CONCRÈTE

An example of electronic music is **musique concrète.** Any kind of sound may be used in musique concrète, such as street noise, sounds from nature, human singing and speech, and usual or unusual sounds from traditional musical instruments, all of which can be manipulated and recombined on tape. After prerecording, sound alteration, cutting, and splicing are finished, the piece has been both composed and performed by the composer in a permanently accurate version. Early masterpieces of musique concrète are Stockhausen's *Gesang der Jünglinge* (*Song of the Youths,* 1956), Edgard Varèse's *Poème électronique* (1958), and Luciano Berio's *Omaggio a Joyce* (*Homage to Joyce,* 1958).

MUSIC FOR SYNTHESIZER

Because the medium of tape offered complete and accurate control over both the piece of music and its "performance," it attracted serialists such as Babbitt and Stockhausen (fig. 21.4), whose music had become incredibly difficult for performers to execute. These composers went beyond the sounds of musique concrète. Using the synthesizer, they invented entirely *new* sounds. Important synthesized electronic works of the 1950s and 1960s are *Electronic Studies I and II* by Stockhausen, *Composition for Synthesizer* by Babbitt, *Silver Apples of the Moon* by Morton Subotnick (b. 1933), and *Time's Encomium* by Charles Wuorinen (b. 1938).

Figure 21.4 Karlheinz Stockhausen, one of the foremost exponents of total serialism, has also made use of chance elements and minimalist techniques.

TAPE AND LIVE PERFORMERS

Taped sounds in combination with live performers have yielded many interesting and beautiful works. Edgard Varèse used such a combination in his *Déserts* (1954), in which music for winds, brass, and percussion alternates with taped musique concrète. Mario Davidovsky (b. 1934), with his series of *Synchronisms* (1963–1977), and Jacob Druckman (b. 1928), with his *Animus* series, have created brilliant works for live performance with prerecorded tape. Barbara Kolb (b. 1939) has produced a string of interesting works, including *Looking for Claudio* (1975), scored for seven guitars, mandolins, vibraphone, chimes, and three humming voices. All of the instruments except one solo guitar are provided by prerecorded tape. During the performance, the solo guitar part is supplied live, along with the tape.

MINIMALISM

Partly as a reaction against the extreme complexities of serialism on the one hand and chance elements on the other that characterized much music of the twentieth century, a new style was pioneered by four young American composers in the 1960s: La Monte Young (b. 1935), Terry Riley (b. 1935), Steve Reich (b. 1936), and Philip Glass (b. 1937; fig. 21.5). Because of its relative simplicity and use of limited musical material, this style was dubbed *minimalism* by critics and commentators, a term never accepted by the composers themselves but one that continued to be used nevertheless.

Figure 21.5 Philip Glass, an early minimalist, became widely known for his opera *Einstein on the Beach*.

In the early music of the minimalists, we hear seemingly endless repetitions of short musical fragments over an essentially static harmonic background. The basic material changes only gradually and over long time spans, and the listener tends to lose any sense of movement because of the almost hypnotic repetition and virtually imperceptible change.

Terry Riley's composition *In C* (1964) was one of the first pieces of music to be called minimalist, and it aptly fits the description just outlined. In it, each member of a musical ensemble is given short musical fragments numbered from one through fifty-three. Each player plays all fifty-three fragments in order. However, each performer is free to repeat each fragment any number of times at his or her discretion. These fragments are played against the constant pulsating of the tone C played on the piano throughout the entire piece. The effect of this procedure is endless repetition with very subtle change over a long stretch of time.

RILEY: *A Rainbow in Curved Air*
Cassette 7/A, Track 2
CD 7, Track 2

Along with *In C,* Riley's *A Rainbow in Curved Air* (1969) well represents the early minimalist style.

During the 1970s and 1980s, all of the minimalists developed individual and more complex styles of composition that bear varying degrees of similarity to the original minimalist concepts.

Philip Glass organized his own ensemble consisting of electronic keyboards, amplified voices, and wind instruments that produced a sound very similar to that of some rock groups. His ensemble recorded its first album, *Music with Changing Parts,* in the early seventies, and the ensemble remains popular as a touring group. Glass established himself as a major composer with his opera *Einstein on the Beach* (the first minimalist opera) in 1975. This was followed by several more operas as well as music for dance and films.

The stylistic turning point for Steve Reich came with *Music for 18 Musicians* in 1978, a major work exhibiting much greater harmonic movement than the early minimalist style. This composition led to the longer choral and orchestral works in the 1980s, culminating

Figure 21.6 Minimalist composer John Adams at a rehearsal of his opera *Nixon in China*, 1987.

in *Desert Music* (1984), a symphonic setting for large orchestra and chorus based on texts by William Carlos Williams. Since then, Reich has produced major works such as *The Four Sections* for orchestra (1987) and *Different Trains,* a fascinating and moving work for four "overdubbed" string quartets, train whistles, air-raid sirens, and taped speech fragments.

The new generation of minimalist composers is headed by John Adams (b. 1947; fig. 21.6). Adams's early works, such as *Phrygian Gates* (1977) for piano and the string septet *Shaker Loops,* give evidence of the early minimalist style except for the presence of a richer harmonic background and faster rate of change. The orchestral piece *Harmonielehre* (1985) and the opera *Nixon in China* (1987) established Adams as one of the important young composers of the late twentieth century. More recent works by Adams include *The Wound Dresser,* based on a poem by Walt Whitman about his experiences while nursing injured soldiers during the Civil War. The work is scored for solo violin, solo trumpet, baritone, and orchestra. The work *Fearful Symmetries* is characterized by a mixture of jazz elements and minimalism.

DIVERSITY OF STYLE

Atonality, serialism, chance music, electronic music, musique concrète, minimalism and its offshoots, and music that fits into none of these categories reflect the rich diversity of musical thought, techniques, and styles that characterize music of the second half of the twentieth century. This stylistic pluralism is well illustrated in the music of three American composers: Milton Babbitt, Leonard Bernstein, and Ellen Taaffe Zwilich.

MILTON BABBITT

Milton Babbitt (b. 1916) is one of the most influential composers of the second half of the twentieth century. He was attracted to serial music early in his career and was the first composer to apply serial techniques to all aspects of a composition in such works as *Three Compositions for Piano* (1947), *Composition for Four Instruments* (1946), and *Composition for Twelve Instruments* (1948). Babbitt was a pioneer in electronic music and has composed a number of works using tape and synthesizer. Many of his tape works include live performers. Among these works are *Vision and Prayer* (1961), *Philomel* (1964), and *Phonemena* (1974), all for tape and soprano.

BABBITT: *Phonemena*
Cassette 7/A, Track 3
CD 7, Track 3

    Phonemena is a short serial work, the title of which refers to *phonemes*—the smallest sound units of speech. For this piece, the composer arranged twenty-four consonants and twelve vowels into a "text" that forms part of the comprehensive serial organization. (The phonemes are not organized into words; they are used merely as sounds.) The work is a virtuoso piece for singer and is an elegant example of Babbitt's style.

LEONARD BERNSTEIN

From the age of forty when he became the youngest musician to be appointed artistic director of the New York Philharmonic, until his death in 1990 at the age of seventy-two, Leonard Bernstein (fig. 21.7) became probably the most famous musician in American history. Although a brilliant pianist and educator, Bernstein became known worldwide as a conductor and composer. As a conductor, he was eagerly sought by virtually every major orchestra in the world. As a composer, he left a large amount of music that demonstrated an amazing degree of versatility. His works include music for ballet, *Fancy Free* (1944) and *Facsimile* (1946); opera, *Trouble in Tahiti* (1952); comic operetta, *Candide* (1956); music for the theater, *On the Town* (1944), *Wonderful Town* (1953), and *West Side Story* (1957); three major symphonies, *Jeremiah* (1944), *Age of Anxiety* (1949), and *Kaddish* (1963); film music, *On the Waterfront* (1954); and a host of other works for a wide variety of media—all the while maintaining an extremely active schedule as a conductor. His was truly an extraordinary career.

    Among Bernstein's works is the interesting *Chichester Psalms,* one of his most outstanding choral works. It was commissioned in 1965 by the Cathedral of Chichester in Sussex, England, for the annual music festival in which it joins with the choral forces of its neighboring towns, Winchester and Salisbury.

Chichester Psalms

Chichester Psalms was originally conceived as a work for male chorus, organ, harp, and percussion. However, the work has gained its greatest popularity in Bernstein's second version, scored for boy soprano solo, mixed chorus, and an orchestra consisting of three trumpets, three trombones, percussion, two harps, and strings. This version was given its world premiere by the New York Philharmonic, with the composer conducting, in 1965.

    The work is laid out in three contrasting movements, each using the Hebrew versions of various psalms. The second movement is a particularly lovely example of Bernstein's writing for voices and instruments.

Figure 21.7 Leonard Bernstein, one of America's most versatile composers.

MOVEMENT II

BERNSTEIN:
Chichester Psalms,
Second Movement
Cassette 7/A, Track 4
CD 7, Track 4

SECTION A (Psalm 23, v. 1–4)

Boy Soprano

Adonai ro-i, lo ehsar.

Bin'ot deshe yarbitseini,

Al mei m'nuhot y'nahaleimi,
Naf'shi y'shovev,
Yan 'heini b'ma'aglei tsedek,

L'ma'an sh'mo.

Women's Chorus

Gam ki eilech
B'gei tsalmavet,

Lo ira ra,
Ki Atah imadi.
Shiv't'cha umishan'techa
Hemah y'nahamuni.

Boy Soprano with Women

(Adonai ro-i, lo ehsar.)

Boy Soprano

The Lord is my shepherd, I shall not want.
He maketh me to lie down in green pastures,
He leadeth me beside the still waters,
He restoreth my soul,
He leadeth me in the paths of righteousness,
For His name's sake.

Women's Chorus

Yea, though I walk
Through the valley of the shadow of death,
I will fear no evil,
For Thou art with me.
Thy rod and Thy staff
They comfort me.

Boy Soprano with Women

(The Lord is my shepherd, I shall not want.)

SECTION B (Psalm 2, v. 1–4)

Men's Chorus

Lamah rag'shu goyim
Ul'umim yeh'gu rik?
Yit'yats'vu malchei erits,
V'roznim nos'du yahad
Al Adonai v'al m'shilho.

N'natkah et mos'roteimo,
V'nashlichah mimenu avoteimo.
Yoshev bashamayim
Yis'hak, Adonai
Yil'ag lamo!

SECTION C (Psalm 23, v. 5–6)

Women's Chorus

Ta'aroch l'fanai shulchan

(Men's Chorus continuing)

Neged tsor'rai
Dishanta vashemen roshi

Boy Soprano

Cosi r'vayah.
Ach tov vahesed
Yird'funi kol y'mei hayai
V'shav'ti b'veit Adonai
L'orech yamim.

Women's Chorus

(Adonai ro-i, lo ehsar.)

Men's Chorus

Why do the nations rage,
And the people imagine a vain thing?
The kings of the earth set themselves,
And the rulers take counsel together
Against the Lord and against His
*   anointed.*
Saying, let us break their bands asunder,
And cast away their cords from us.
He that sitteth in the heavens
Shall laugh, and the Lord
Shall have them in derision!

Women's Chorus

Thou preparest a table before me

(Men's Chorus continuing)

In the presence of mine enemies,
Thou anointed my head with oil,

Boy Soprano

My cup runneth over.
Surely goodness and mercy
Shall follow me all the days of my life,
And I will dwell in the house of the Lord
Forever.

Women's Chorus

(The Lord is my shepherd, I shall not
*   want.)*

Coda

As shown, the movement consists of three main sections followed by a short orchestral coda. Sections A and B contrast sharply with each other. A is calm, quiet, and lyrical, moving at a moderate pace—andante con moto. In contrast, the B section is fast and characterized by extreme and dramatic changes in dynamic level, with rapid staccato exclamation of the text by the men's chorus.

The first part of section A features the boy soprano with quiet accompaniment. His melodic line has three components:

Andante con moto, ma tranquillo

Example 21.1

mp

A - do - nai ——— ro - i, lo eh - sar ———

Bi - n' ot de - she yar - bit - tsel - ni; ——— Al mei m' - nu - hot y' - na - ha - lei - ni,

Leonard Bernstein, *Chichester Psalms,* Boosey & Hawkes, Inc., New York, NY.

followed by:

Example 21.2

Naf' shi y' - sho - vev, ——— Ya - n' ——— hei - ni ———

etc.

— b' ma' - ag - lei — tse - dek, ——— l' ma' - an - sh' - mo. ———

Leonard Bernstein, *Chichester Psalms,* Boosey & Hawkes, Inc., New York, NY.

and ending with a lovely phrase, both the text and melody of which constitute a kind of refrain, acting as a unifying element for the entire movement.

Example 21.3

A - do - nai — ro - i, —— A - do - nai — ro - i, lo eh - sar. ———

Leonard Bernstein, *Chichester Psalms,* Boosey & Hawkes, Inc., New York, NY.

This material is immediately repeated by the sopranos of the chorus singing the first phrase in canon accompanied by quiet strings and harp. The second phrase is sung by the women of the chorus, the altos answering the sopranos until the refrain, which is again taken up by the soprano solo supported by the women of the chorus.

Without any pause, the B section bursts forth just as A concludes. Its appearance is in great contrast to the first in terms of tempo (allegro), dynamic level (forte), and musical forces—the first time the men of the chorus are utilized along with brass and percussion (example 21.4).

Example 21.4

Leonard Bernstein, *Chichester Psalms*, Boosey & Hawkes, Inc., New York, NY.

After this first outburst, the section continues, alternating between rapid enunciation of the text (pp) with strings, and loud shouts from the men supported by brass and percussion.

After a powerful climax on the words "Al Adonai v'al m'shilho. N'natkah et mos'roteimo, V'nashlichah mimenu avoteimo" ("Against the Lord and against His anointed. Saying, let us break their bands asunder, And cast away their cords from us"), the dynamic level decreases, the brass and percussion fall silent, and the rhythmic momentum diminishes to prepare the way for the last section of the movement (C).

Here the women of the chorus return (again in canon), singing a somewhat varied version of the first part of the A section, while the men and instruments continue with the same kind of general rhythmic activity that characterized the B section, again with a sudden forte outburst.

The soprano soloist returns to initiate the beginning of the second phrase—"Ach tov vahesed Yird'funi kil y'mei hayai" ("Surely goodness and mercy, Shall follow me all the days of my life"), leading to an extended version of the refrain, concluding with "Adonai ro-i, lo ehsar." This is sung as a kind of echo (pianissimo) by the women—sustaining the last syllable through the closing instrumental coda—pianissimo until the very last moment—a forte blast to end the movement.

In its entirety, Bernstein's *Chichester Psalms* is one of the most effective examples of music for voices and instruments composed in the second half of the twentieth century and again demonstrates the diversity of styles that has characterized that period of music history.

ELLEN TAAFFE ZWILICH

Ellen Taaffe Zwilich (b. 1939; fig. 21.8) has become one of the most accomplished and recognized American composers in the second half of the twentieth century. An accomplished violinist, she studied composition at the Juilliard School. In 1975, she was the first woman to receive the Doctor of Musical Arts degree from that prestigious institution. Her principal composition teachers were the distinguished composers Roger Sessions and Elliot Carter. She has received grants from the New York State Council on the Arts, the Martha Baird Rockefeller Fund for Music, and the National Endowment for the Arts, and in 1980–1981 she was the recipient of a Guggenheim Fellowship.

Among Zwilich's compositions are chamber music works such as the *Sonata for Violin and Piano* (1974), *String Quartet* (1974), *Divertimento* (1983), *Double Quartet for Strings* (1984), and *Passages* for soprano and instrumental ensemble. Her works for orchestra include *Celebrations,* commissioned by the Indianapolis Symphony (1984) for the dedication of its new hall, the Circle Theatre. In addition, Zwilich has composed two symphonies, the first of which, *Symphony No. I, Three Movements for Orchestra,* won the Pulitzer Prize in music (1983). She was the first woman to be so honored.

Symphony No. I

In the preface to the score of the first movement of her *Symphony No. I*, Zwilich states: "The first movement begins in a contemplative mood, with a 'motto': three statements of a rising minor third, marked accelerando. Each time the 'motto' appears in the first movement, an accelerando occurs, prompting slight evolutions of character until an *Allegro* section is established. After the *Allegro,* the movement subsides in tempo and ends as quietly as it began."[1]

The movement is laid out in three broad sections. The first section is introductory, concentrating on the various manifestations of the germinal idea, the interval of the minor third, and is characterized by an unstable tempo in which each major presentation of the germinal idea occurs within the framework of an acceleration of tempo, eventually leading to the establishment of a stable tempo—allegro—beginning the dramatic central section of the movement. This section consists of the presentation of many different thematic ideas. The final portion of the movement, a codalike section, is a calm return to the beginning of the movement in which the germinal idea of the basic interval of the minor third reasserts itself to bring about a convincing conclusion.

ZWILICH: *Symphony No. I,* First Movement
Cassette 7/A, Track 5
CD 7, Track 5
See Listening Guide on pages 506–508.

1. From full score of *Symphony No. I,* Ellen Taaffe Zwilich. © 1983, Margun Music, Inc. Used by permission.

Actually, the element of the germinating idea is rarely absent from the flow of the music, although it assumes a vast variety of guises—some very obvious, others hardly noticeable, if at all, to the listener.

On occasion, the interval of the minor third is extended by raising the upper tone an octave.

Example 21.5

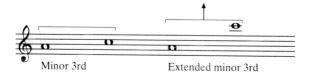

Minor 3rd   Extended minor 3rd

With the context of the flow of the music, they have the same general effect, the extended version being felt as an intensification of the original. Often the two versions are combined as in the very beginning of the movement.

Example 21.6

© 1983 Margun Music, Inc. Used by permission.

Frequently the minor third is an integral part of a larger melodic fragment.

Example 21.7

© 1983 Margun Music, Inc. Used by permission.

It can be dramatic in its appearance,

Example 21.8

with sharp dissonance clashes.
At times, several different minor thirds are spread out through a melodic fragment.

Example 21.9

A combination of minor thirds often appear as rhythmic punctuation

Example 21.10

or a very expressive melodic phrase.

Example 21.11

At the close of the Allegro, the minor third configuration is used very cleverly to lead smoothly into the rhythmic figure that eventually acts as background material throughout much of the coda.

Example 21.12

Music in the Second Half of the Twentieth Century

Finally the germinal minor third interval, which has permeated the fabric of the whole movement (obvious or obscure), is used very effectively to bring the movement to a tranquil close.

Example 21.13

Violas and 'celli

While it uses as a basic ingredient a small melodic element, this piece is certainly not minimalist. In spite of the frequently repeated material, the work has no real relationship to "serialism," and certainly no element of chance is involved. Rather, the piece represents an individual style—thorough in its craftsmanship and exciting in terms of its musical message—worthy of the honors bestowed upon it and deserving of its growing popularity.

Listening Guide

ZWILICH: *Symphony No. 1*

First Movement: Slow opening tempo gradually accelerates
Central section allegro (fast)
Duple meter prevails, triple measure often interpolated
Continuous motivic development through three sections

Orchestra

Review: Example 21.5 (minor-third germ motive, original and extended)
Example 21.6 (opening bars, motto in viola and harp)
Example 21.7 (part of repeated-note melody)
Example 21.8 (dramatic, dissonant development of germ motive)
Example 21.9 (interlocked minor third motive closes introduction)
Example 21.10 (motive of double minor thirds)
Example 21.11 (expressive cello melody)
Example 21.12 (germ motive linked to rocking motive of coda)
Example 21.13 (germ motive in tranquil conclusion)

CD 7 (Cassette 7/A, Track 5)

5	1	0:00	**Introductory Section**	1	Motto (germ motive of ascending minor third stated three times) played piano, continued with varied echo
		0:28		2	Motto begins in winds, covered by energetic violin theme climbing to high pitch, continues into intensely yearning melody that falls abruptly

Continued on next page

	0:50		3	Motto in violins echoed in basses; horns state a melody beginning with repeated notes; violins take over and climb to high pitch; trumpets proclaim repeated-note melody (varied)
	1:11		4	Motto in violins, high pitch, jumpy motive in flutes and piano, trumpet plays repeated notes; fast six-note idea tossed through orchestra in ascending, then descending pattern; repeated-note idea in bass instruments
	1:31		5	Strings state motto against gradually ascending line, jumpy motive in flutes and piano
	1:44		6	Trumpets open motto with dissonant chord, development of germ motive
	2:00		7	Motto in flutes, dissonant chord held in horns, sustained descending line in strings overlap into:
②	2:04		8	Expansion of motto in brass recalls opening bars, now faster; interjections from woodwinds and strings
	2:17		9	Brass continues, motto in trumpets, intensity builds; sudden pause
	2:22		10	Brass begins motto, others join as tension builds further; emphatic descent to short break
③	2:34	**Central Section (Allegro)**	1	Pizzicato strings accompany broad melody in horns, fast repeated notes also accompany; trumpet states broad melody; texture becomes fragmented
④	2:57		2	Four-note scale fragment rises and falls, echoed through the orchestra, while suspended cymbal tapping continues repeated-note accompaniment; three-note upward thrust in trumpet, plus repeated notes, abrupt descent
	3:07		3	Powerful chords hammered, downward-tumbling scale appears; vigorous development of minor third in various instruments; repeated-note tapping on suspended cymbal
⑤	3:22		4a	Extended development of minor-third motives combined with downward-tumbling scale and repeated-note motive in snare drum; cymbal crash and snare drum statement alone twice, with pauses
	3:38		b	Minor thirds and downward scales continue; rising and falling four-note scale fragment and suspended cymbal take over; repeated-note accompaniment moves to bass drum, downward scales return with hammered chords

Continued on next page

	4:02		c	Three-note upward thrust from basses, repeated bass drum notes; vigorous development of minor thirds in low strings; suspended cymbal returns; upward thrust in trombones continues into broad melody, repeated notes in brass and strings; hammered chords, downward scales, vigorous minor thirds in trombones, fragments into:
	4:34		d	Faster rhythms in strings, winds, and suspended cymbal; hammered chords crescendo to climax, upward thrust from trombones
⑥	4:44		5	Single chime and sustained chord dissipate energy; double third motive repeated, linked with new two-note motive rocking back and forth; chord dies away, chime strikes three times
⑦	5:25	**Coda**	1a	Chord dies away as two-note motive continues rocking movement; quiet chord in trombones
	5:45		b	Germ motive gently in oboe; motto (both ascending and descending minor third) in bass instruments; warm, sustained melody in cellos
	6:19		c	Rocking motive alternates with quiet final statement of motto, peaceful close

[Read Ron Cage]

SUMMARY

Music after World War II continued trends originated earlier in the century as well as developing new, radically different ideas and techniques. One new approach was total serialism, in which every aspect of a composition is predetermined by the composer. This technique was used by such prominent composers as Pierre Boulez, Milton Babbitt, and Karlheinz Stockhausen. Another approach was indeterminacy (chance or aleatoric music) in which most of the musical events of a piece lie beyond the immediate control of the composer. John Cage, one of the great innovators of modern music, is well known for his chance compositions.

Electronic technology in the form of magnetic tape, synthesizers, and computers has had a powerful impact on music composition. Musique concrète utilizes naturally occurring sounds that are manipulated on magnetic tape. Synthesizers are used to create entirely new sounds and to accurately control aspects of a composition. Tapes and synthesizers are frequently used with each other as well as with live performers.

Minimalism developed in the 1960s as a reaction against the complexities of much modern music. In minimalist music, short musical patterns are repeated over long time spans, with only gradual change. La Monte Young, Terry Riley, Steve Reich, and Philip Glass are considered the founders of minimalism. Each of these composers gradually expanded his music beyond the bounds of the early minimalist style. John Adams has emerged as the leader of the new generation of minimalist composers.

Many composers, such as Leonard Bernstein and Ellen Taaffe Zwilich, have developed their own individual styles without adhering to any specific technical approach.

NEW TERMS

total serialism

indeterminacy (chance music, aleatoric
   music)

minimalism

electronic music

musique concrète

SUGGESTED LISTENING

Babbitt, Milton

Philomel (1963–1964). The text of this work is by poet John Hollander and is drawn from Greek myth. Babbitt's ingenious setting is scored for live soprano, prerecorded soprano, and synthesized sounds. *Philomel* defies the notion that total serialism produces music that is any less communicative than that produced by other techniques.

Boulez, Pierre

Improvisation sur Mallarmé II, "Une dentelle s'abolit" ("A piece of lace disappears," 1958). Boulez incorporated this ten-minute piece, written for soprano and nine keyboard and percussion players, into his large-scale *Pli selon pii* (1957–1962). Both versions illustrate the composer's tempering of pointillism with lacy, bell-like sounds and almost Debussian colors.

Cage, John

Concerto for Prepared Piano and Chamber Orchestra (1951). The delicate percussive sounds of Javanese gamelan music inspired Cage's use of the piano. Chance operations determined many of the musical events.

Messiaen, Olivier

Turangalila-Symphonie for piano, ondes Martenot, and orchestra (1946–1948). This immense and extravagant work employs many of the composer's stylistic traits, including sumptuous harmony, personalized uses of serial and ostinato procedures, and bird calls (especially in the sixth movement, "The garden of the sleep of love"). The piano and the electronic instrument known as the ondes Martenot are given featured roles.

Riley, Terry

In C for any combination of instruments (1964). This attractive example of minimalism is open to performance by almost everyone because the "score," consisting of small fragments of melody played over and over, is printed right on the record album.

Stockhausen, Karlheinz

Gesang der Jünglinge (*Song of the Youths*) (1955–1956). A landmark "electro-acoustical" work, combining sung sounds with electronically produced sounds. The sung sounds—though often distorted in various ways—become comprehensible words from time to time. The text is based on the biblical account of Shadrach, Meshach, and Abednego being cast into the fiery furnace (Daniel 3).

Subotnick, Morton

Silver Apples of the Moon, electronic sounds on tape (1967). One of several albums commissioned specifically for recordings, this work illustrates the composer's rich and colorful palette of electronically produced sounds.

Pop Culture in American Music

Trumpeter John "Dizzy" Gillespie.

JAZZ AND ROCK

Jazz is considered by many to be America's greatest contribution to music. Its impact on American society has been enormous, and its influence on world culture has been far reaching. Its message has been direct, vital, and immediate, enabling it to hurdle cultural, linguistic, and political barriers.

THE ORIGINS OF JAZZ

The precise origins and early history of **jazz** cannot be chronicled because early jazz was neither notated nor recorded; it was *improvised* and existed only in performance.

It is clear, however, that what we now call jazz was rooted in southern America, was inspired by the experiences of black slaves, and resulted from the interaction of several cultures: African, white and black American, and European.

West African slaves arrived in the United States with only remnants of their culture intact. An important aspect of this culture was music appropriate for various daily activities and particular celebrations. Over time, this music adopted various aspects of European harmony and structure while maintaining many African elements, such as rhythm, vocal inflection, and a great emphasis on improvisation, which can be seen in the pattern of "call-and-response." In this pattern, a leader "calls" (sings) a first line, to which the chorus responds with an improvised "answer." This combination of elements is especially evident in various African-American folk music such as spirituals, which are greatly indebted to European harmony and structure, and in blues, which maintained the emphasis on improvisation and emotional expression that are vital to African music.

THE BLUES

The unique style of music known as the **blues** is the common strain running through virtually all American popular music. The style and phrasings of the blues can be found in the early music of the black churches, in country and western music, in songs by George Gershwin and other Broadway composers, and in current rock styles. But more than all else, the blues have influenced jazz styles, from the earliest to the most recent.

The blues can be seen as a direct outgrowth of the field hollers and work songs of the antebellum South. The first form that can be identified as blues has come to be known as "country blues." In this type of blues, the singer (who usually accompanies him/herself) relates the text in a very rhythmically and structurally loose manner, allowing the performer to improvise new lines of text or more elaborate accompaniment as seems appropriate. By around 1900, the blues featured a highly structured style, with distinct forms for both the lyrics and the melodies. The standard lyrical pattern consisted of two rhyming lines of poetry, with the first line (AAB), as in the following example:

Now listen baby, you so good and sweet,
Now listen baby, you so good and sweet,
I want to stay 'round you, if I have to beg in the street.

The form of the blues is typically based on a twelve-bar harmonic progression in three phrases of four measures each. Only three chords are involved: tonic (I), dominant (V), and subdominant (IV).

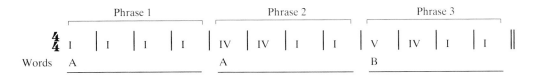

The blues are usually played in 4/4 time.

So-called **blue notes,** produced by flatting the third, fifth, or seventh notes of a major scale, are used extensively. These notes can be manipulated by allowing the performer to slide into them, rather than hitting them solidly. The result is "bent" or "glided" pitches that produce a highly distinctive sound.

The solidification of the blues structure introduced the opportunity for a more wide-reaching, "marketable" type of blues that evolved in the minstrel and vaudeville shows of the late nineteenth century. Entire bands began to accompany singers who were singing words with a more universal appeal than the highly personal, country blues lyrics. The "classic blues," as this form has come to be called, maintained the vocal emphasis of the country blues but made instrumental accompaniment more prominent.

One of the influential early classic blues singers was Bessie Smith (1894–1937), whose "St. Louis Blues" (*Smithsonian Collection of Classic Jazz*) features a classic illustration of "call-and-response" interplay between Smith's vocal and Louis Armstrong's trumpet. Vocalists such as Billie Holiday, Ella Fitzgerald, and Sarah Vaughn continued to expand this practice into the jazz era.

ARMSTRONG AND SMITH: "St. Louis Blues"
Cassette 7/B, Track 1
CD 7, Track 6

BILLIE HOLIDAY (1915–1959)

Women have usually played a part in jazz only as singers. Although there have been a few exceptions over the years (such as virtuoso pianist Mary Lou Williams and composer-bandleader Toshiko Akiyoshi), by far the widest avenue for women to enter the field has been as vocalists, and that remains the case even in our own "liberated" age.

Most of the leading jazz singers of the past few decades were greatly influenced by classic female blues singers such as Ma Rainey, Bessie Smith, and Ethel Waters. But the vocalist who brought the special art of the blues singer to its greatest heights and had the greatest influence on future jazz vocal styles was Billie Holiday (1915–1959; fig. 22.1).

Holiday was raised in the poorest section of Harlem, the daughter of a jazz guitarist with Fletcher Henderson's band who displayed little interest in Billie or her mother. She had a small, fragile voice and no musical training. Holiday got her start as a singer in 1933 at a club in Harlem, where her emotional rendition of "Body and Soul" had the customers in tears.

Figure 22.1 Billie Holiday's vocal styling was strongly influenced by the instrumental styles of Lester Young and Louis Armstrong.

RAGTIME

In the 1890s, a dance called the cakewalk, which had been translated from the antebellum South to the stages of the minstrel shows, became a dance craze. The music that accompanied this dance likewise became popular. It was called **ragtime.**

Ragtime is an excellent example of cross-pollination between African and European musical elements. The basic style comes from an attempt to translate the accompaniment of the antebellum cakewalk onto a single instrument, the piano. The steady "boom-chuck" rhythm of the pianist's left hand is an approximation of the hand clapping and foot stomping of the original (which was called "pattin' juba"), while the performer's right hand plays the "ragged" (syncopated) melodies that were originally played by banjos or fiddles. The

Shortly after she landed this job, the eighteen-year-old Holiday was discovered by talent scout John Hammond (who later discovered such talented contemporary performers as Aretha Franklin and Bob Dylan). Hammond arranged for her to record with Benny Goodman. Although these early records were disappointing, in 1936 Holiday recorded with an all-star band that included Roy Eldridge, Ben Webster, Benny Goodman, and Lester Young. It was Young who gave her the nickname that stuck, "Lady Day." The 1936 recordings and subsequent ones, such as *Lady Day* (Columbia CL 637), *Golden Years,* Vol. 1 (Columbia C 3L 21), and *The Billie Holiday Story* (MCA 4006E), demonstrate eloquently the unique vocal style that became her trademark.

After paying her dues as a band singer, first with Count Basie and then—as the first black female singer in a white band—with Artie Shaw, Holiday made a breakthrough as a single attraction. Throughout the 1940s, her personal life began to deteriorate, but her fame continued to spread. She performed such standards as "He's Funny That Way," "Crazy He Calls Me," and "Stormy Weather," and she also wrote her own material, including the deeply felt "God Bless the Child." The last

became a pop hit in the late 1960s for the rock group Blood, Sweat and Tears. But by then, Lady Day had passed from the scene, a victim of drug addiction, alcoholism, police harassment, and her own tragic self-destructiveness. Although she recorded extensively for producer Norman Granz during the 1950s, her career as well as her personal life had been deteriorating steadily, and on July 17, 1959, she died at the age of 44.

The events that surround her premature death have added a sordid luster to the legend of Billie Holiday and to some extent have obscured the very real contributions she made to jazz. Whereas most vocalists sang the music without embellishment ("straight"), Holiday made each song her own, improvising on the basic melody, changing the shape of a phrase, investing the song with her unique inflections and emotional quality. As she herself once put it, "I don't think I'm really singing. I feel like I'm playing a horn. I try to improvise like Les Young, like Louis Armstrong, or someone else I admire. What comes out is what I feel."[1]

---

1. Dan Morganstern, *Jazz People* (New York: Abrams, 1976), p. 240.

---

music takes its form from European marches that were popular at the time and borrows extensively from the standard harmonic vocabulary of the European tradition. Most important, though, is the fact that this was composed music, whose melodies and structure were written down, rather than improvised. This allowed ragtime music to be published, sold, and performed by anybody with a piano.

One of the most distinguished exponents of ragtime was Scott Joplin (1868–1917; fig. 22.2), a classically trained pianist whose compositions, including the classic "Maple Leaf Rag" (1899), earned him the title "King of Ragtime." Recently there has been a considerable revival of Joplin's music in concert halls, on records, on Broadway, and in films such as *The Sting.* Joplin also wrote an opera, *Treemonisha.* Other notable ragtime pianist-composers of the 1890s included James Scott, Tom Turpin, and Joseph Lamb.

JOPLIN:
"Maple Leaf Rag"
Cassette 7/B, Track 2
CD 7, Track 7

Figure 22.2 Scott Joplin's rags earned him the title "King of Ragtime."

JAZZ

NEW ORLEANS STYLE (DIXIELAND)

The major center of early jazz was the great cosmopolitan city of New Orleans. Around the beginning of the twentieth century, New Orleans possessed an international atmosphere. As a busy trading center located at the outlet of the Mississippi River into the Gulf of Mexico, it attracted elements of cultures as diverse as French, Spanish, Caribbean, Anglo-Saxon, and German that merged with the African traditions of the Creoles and recently emancipated slaves.

During this very early period, bands were used for such events as parades and funerals. On the way to the graveyard, the bands played mournful music. On the way back from the cemetery, however, they broke into a swinging rhythm that became an element of jazz. Bands began to play for social dancing, which became the rage. It was in the dance halls, gambling places, and brothels of the red-light district known as Storyville that New Orleans jazz was born and nurtured. The style of New Orleans jazz was established by cornetist Charles ("Buddy") Bolden (1877–1931) and his Rag Time Band. Bolden also fixed the instrumentation of the Dixieland jazz combo. One or two cornets (or trumpets), clarinet, and trombone formed the **front line,** while string bass, guitar or banjo (sometimes piano), and drums made up the **rhythm section.**

The most outstanding feature of New Orleans jazz was **group improvisation.** Against a background supplied by the rhythm section, the front-line players improvised on well-known tunes. Usually the cornet played variations of the tune, while the clarinet improvised an upper melodic line and the trombone supplied yet another improvised melody below the

Figure 22.3 Jelly Roll Morton and His Red Hot Peppers. From left: Andrew Hilaire, Kid Ory, George Mitchell, Johnny Lindsay, Morton, Johnny St. Cyr, and Omer Simeon.

cornet. All three instruments in the front line employed a lively, syncopated style against a steady beat maintained by the rhythm section. Collective improvisation, a kind of jazz polyphony, is a central element in New Orleans jazz.

Although Nick LaRoca and The Original Dixieland Jazz Band, a white group, made the first jazz recording in 1917, New Orleans jazz was created by black Americans, and black Americans have been at the forefront of all major jazz innovations. Products of New Orleans jazz have included Ferdinand ("Jelly Roll") Morton (1890–1941; fig. 22.3), the first jazz pianist and composer; Joseph "King" Oliver (1885–1938); and the great Louis Armstrong.

CHICAGO STYLE

A variety of factors, including the closing of the Storyville district in 1917, led to the migration of jazz musicians and their music to other parts of the country. In the Roaring Twenties, jazz spread over a wide geographic area, including Chicago, which became the scene of important jazz developments. Whereas the heart of the New Orleans sound was collective improvisation, the focus of attention shifted to the *individual* soloist. By far the most important jazz soloist was Louis Armstrong (1900–1971), a young cornetist from New Orleans who became one of the most influential stylists in the history of jazz.

LOUIS ARMSTRONG (1900–1971)

One individual whose name is universally associated with jazz is that of Louis Armstrong (1900–1971; fig. 22.4). To those familiar with Armstrong only as the smiling, genial entertainer of his later "Hello, Dolly" years, it is hard to imagine the enormity of his impact on the development of jazz. Armstrong's genius lay in his pioneering role in transforming jazz into a medium of personal expression.

Louis Armstrong was born in New Orleans on the first Fourth of July of the twentieth century. He was raised in a poor and unstable family, and soon became involved in the active street life of the city. At twelve he was sentenced as a juvenile offender and sent to the Colored Waifs' home. It was the director of the Waifs' Home Band who taught him to play the cornet.

After two years, Armstrong returned to the street, performing odd jobs and playing music whenever he got the chance. Eventually, the great Joe "King" Oliver took him under his wing. When Armstrong improved enough, Oliver sent him on jobs that he couldn't fill himself. At seventeen, Armstrong was firmly established as a competent New Orleans-style jazzman.

In 1919, Oliver moved to Chicago, and Armstrong took his place as cornetist in the best band in New Orleans. Two years later, Armstrong received a telegram from Oliver asking him to join Oliver's band there. He accepted and soon became famous among that city's jazz players and fans as a genius with a natural harmonic gift. In 1924, he accepted another offer, this time from Fletcher Henderson's orchestra in New York.

When he left Henderson's orchestra, Armstrong went on to lead his own groups and to record extensively. Some of his best work was done with a group known as the Hot Five—which also featured Johnny St. Cyr, Kid Ory, Johnny Dodds, and Armstrong's second wife, Lil Hardin—and with a later band known as the Hot Seven.

In the 1940s, Armstrong was featured on numerous radio shows and in films, and by the late 1950s, "Ambassador Satch" and the Armstrong All-Stars were traveling the world as goodwill emissaries of the United States government. Toward the end of his life, Armstrong became almost as prominent in that role as he had been earlier as a musician.

Figure 22.4 Louis Armstrong popularized individual soloist improvisation in the middle sections of each piece, leaving the beginning and end for ensemble playing.

But it is Armstrong's influence on jazz musicians and singers that remains his most important contribution. Rhythmically, his music was the embodiment of that elusive quality known as swing. His horn style, highly embellished, full of swoops, sudden dips, and darts, has affected the performing style of all later cornet and trumpet players and of other instrumentalists as well, as is evidenced by Earl Hines's adaptation of Armstrong's style to the piano. His playing also deeply influenced the vocal stylings of jazz singers like Billie Holiday and Ella Fitzgerald. Fine examples of Armstrong's recorded work are included on such albums as *The Louis Armstrong Story,* Vols. 1 and 2 (Col 851, 852) and *Louis Armstrong and Earl Hines* 1928 (Smithsonian R002).

In exploring the possibilities of solo freedom, Armstrong utilized an integrated ensemble at the beginning and end of each piece but reserved the middle sections for improvisations by soloists. Each member of the front line was given one chorus in which to improvise on either the theme or the harmonic structure of the piece, while the rest of the band either rested or played background rhythms. With the ascendance of the individual soloist, the beat became much less pronounced than ever before. The result was a flowing sound that later came to be called **swing.** These developments are evident in the extremely influential recordings of Armstrong's Hot Five and Hot Seven, which were recorded between 1925 and 1928.

As jazz gained in popularity during the 1920s, many white musicians began to take part in its development. One of the first of these was Leon "Bix" Beiderbecke (1903–1931), a virtuoso cornetist born in Davenport, Iowa. Another was bandleader Paul Whiteman (1890–1967), who in 1924 presented the first formal jazz concert. That concert featured the premiere of *Rhapsody in Blue,* a concert work by George Gershwin that incorporated jazz elements.

THE DEPRESSION YEARS

During the early years of the Great Depression, which began with the stock market crash of 1929, most club owners didn't have enough money to hire full-scale orchestras. As a result, the solo pianist came into vogue for a short time. The first important jazz piano styles were **stride** and **boogie-woogie.** In the stride style, the left hand alternated between a bass note and a chord played an octave or more above the bass, giving the effect of "striding" back and forth, while the right hand played the melody. The stride style, which was applied to blues, popular songs, and show tunes, allowed ample opportunity for improvisation.

Boogie-woogie was a blues piano style that used a rhythmic ostinato bass of eight notes to the measure in the left hand, while the right hand played a simple, often improvised melody. Typical left-hand patterns were:

 Left-hand patterns

The percussive bass part gave the sound and feel of the left hand "walking" over the piano keys. For this reason, boogie-woogie is sometimes called the "walkin' bass."

Certain players developed an assortment of regional styles by combining elements of the various styles of jazz piano playing, such as ragtime, stride, and boogie-woogie. These styles, which emphasized flashy technique and improvisation, were the result of stiff competition for jobs. "Cutting contests" became a proving ground where pianists would be expected to improvise on popular tunes and outdo, or "cut," the other players with their virtuosity. James P. Johnson, the "Father of Stride Piano" (1894–1955), Willie "the Lion" Smith (1897–1973), and Thomas "Fats" Waller (1904–1943) were the primary exponents of the "New York style," which emphasized stride, while Meade "Lux" Lewis (1905–1964) perpetuated the boogie-woogie style in Chicago, and later, in New York.

Another innovative jazz pianist was Earl "Fatha" Hines (1905–1983), who early in his career worked with Louis Armstrong. Hines was influenced by Armstrong's inventive cornet style, which he translated into the "trumpet style" for keyboard. In this style, the right hand played a melody line (much as a trumpet player or any single-line player might do) while the left hand played chords in flurries, punctuating and complementing the solo line. Pianists of the later bebop era drew from and expanded on this trumpet style of playing.

SWING

By the mid-1930s, with the economy slowly recovering, larger ensembles began to make a comeback. Gradually, jazz moved out of the saloons and into white as well as black ballrooms and dance halls. The "big band" sound, as it became known, soon reached an ever-larger audience via radio. During this period, New York became the cultural and communications center of America, replacing Chicago as the major jazz city. Thus began the swing era, which lasted roughly from 1935 to 1950.

Swing featured big bands of fifteen to seventeen players, with the old New Orleans front line of cornet, clarinet, and trombone increased dramatically to include whole brass sections of trumpets and trombones, as well as woodwind sections of clarinets and saxophones. The rhythm section included piano, string bass, guitar, and drums.

Stylistically, the big bands evolved in two directions. One style, which was shaped primarily by black bandleaders, was built around the solo performer. In a departure from traditional jazz, which was mostly improvised, loose arrangements of pieces were written down. Yet these arrangements were often modified by the bandleader to showcase the special talents of individual performers. A characteristic technique of these bands was the use of a **riff,** a short melodic line, usually rhythmic, that can be repeated over and over to form either the main melody or the background for improvised solos. The musical repertoire included many blues tunes and many original compositions.

Jazz as an art form has, since its inception, walked a fine line between popular and concert music. It has never received the widespread public recognition of most pop music, nor has it been fully admitted into the realm of academia as "serious" music in terms of acknowledgment and support. The music of Duke Ellington walked this line more closely than most.

DUKE ELLINGTON

Edward ("Duke") Ellington (fig. 22.5) was born in 1899, in Washington, D.C., to a relatively middle class family. As a child, he studied both art and music; his piano studies included the popular "ragged" and stride styles that eventually became jazz. Although an accomplished painter, he opted for a career in music and began to coordinate and lead bands for dances and social events, playing simple arrangements of popular tunes.

After relocating to New York in 1923, Ellington's band, the Washingtonians, began to incorporate some of the new jazz style that had started to become popular. This new approach came to the band via trumpeter James "Bubber" Miley and Sidney Bechet, both of whom worked with Ellington during this period after relocating from New Orleans, where they had learned about the new style firsthand. The other musicians in the band picked up many of the stylistic traits of these men, and Ellington incorporated them into his arrangements.

In 1927, the Ellington band started a five-year stint as the house band of Harlem's Cotton Club. During this time, Ellington's compositions and arrangements moved him and his orchestra into the forefront of the emerging big band style. Although the New Orleans men gradually departed, Ellington was able to find players to duplicate the "growling" effects that had become an integral part of his band's sound, and he recorded some of his most well known works, such as "Creole Love Call," "Mood Indigo," and "It Don't Mean a Thing if It Ain't Got That Swing," among others.

Upon leaving the Cotton Club, the band toured Europe and the United States and continued recording, producing such classics as "Ko-Ko," "In a Mellotone," and "Concerto for Cootie," the latter title indicating Ellington's growing interest in forms that extended beyond the confines of twelve-bar blues or thirty-two-bar popular song structures. This interest gradually became the focal point of his composing, with suites such as *Black, Brown, and Beige* and *The River* (a ballet) coming from this later period. Ellington also began to compose many religious works, presenting three concerts during the late 1960s and early 1970s.

By the time of his death in 1974, Ellington had heard himself called one of the great American composers. His orchestration of the jazz ensemble is certainly classic, manipulating timbres and "playing" the band like no one else in history. His large body of work, from popular songs to jazz suites to simple arrangements of the twelve-bar blues, will continue to be enjoyed for years to come.

ELLINGTON: "Take the 'A' Train"
Cassette 7/B, Track 3
CD 7, Track 8

THE BIG BAND ERA

The first of a long line of talented black bandleaders was Fletcher Henderson (1897–1952), an important innovator in band arranging in the 1920s and Benny Goodman's chief arranger in the late 1930s. Two other outstanding black musicians who gained fame in the swing era were William "Count" Basie (1904–1984), pianist and leader of a popular band, and saxophonist Lester Young, one of Basie's great soloists.

The other big band style is represented in the work of white bandleaders such as Benny Goodman (fig. 22.6), Harry James, Glenn Miller, Artie Shaw, Tommy Dorsey, and Woody Herman, all of whom drew on the black style but modified it for their predominantly white audiences. Their intricate, special arrangements were calculated to achieve a consistent and characteristic sound. Often the leader was showcased as the star personality and sometimes as the star soloist. A few other star soloists might also be featured, but the main emphasis was on the overall sound of the band as a unit. The music presented by this type of ensemble consisted of smooth, polished arrangements of popular tunes. The aim was to please the listening and dancing audience, a goal that tended to produce music that was commercially successful but not artistically innovative.

BOP

At the height of the swing era, many jazz musicians rebelled against the big band style and its commercialization. These young rebels began to organize small "combos" that offered more opportunity for individual expression. The result was **bebop,** or just **bop.**

It was in special after-hours clubs that young, adventuresome, experimental musicians like guitarist Charlie Christian (1916–1942), pianist Thelonious Monk (1917–1982), and drummer Kenny Clarke (1914–1985) found the freedom to explore their personal potentials. These and other musicians, notably trumpeter John "Dizzy" Gillespie (b. 1917) and saxophonist Charlie "Bird" Parker (1920–1955), would work all night with the swing bands in Manhattan nightclubs and ballrooms, then ride north to Minton's Play House in the early morning to participate in "jam sessions" in which they experimented with free-form solo work and harmonic improvisation. The new style they developed was given the name bebop (later shortened to bop). The bop combo consisted of one to three soloists supported by a rhythm section of drums and bass and sometimes piano or guitar.

Bop players sought to extend the role of the soloist in jazz, using the driving, harmonically oriented style of saxophonist Coleman Hawkins (1904–1969) as a starting point. They combined the Hawkins influence with jagged, uneven phrases, wide leaps in melodic intervals, and a great deal of rhythmic variety to develop a totally new sound. Kenny Clarke introduced an extraordinary rhythmic innovation with his technique of "dropping bombs"— that is, placing unanticipated bass drum accents before or after the beat. Almost single-handedly, Clarke moved the focus of jazz drumming away from the objective of simply keeping time. Drummers began to work around an implicit rather than a stated beat, and whatever basic timekeeping was necessary usually fell to the bass player.

Bop songs typically borrowed the chord changes from one of the popular songs of the day and added to them an entirely new melody. Whereas swing melodies were usually vocally conceived, the melodic conception of bebop was taken from an instrumental perspective and was, therefore, not very "hummable." Another bop innovation was the use of more complicated chords that added a higher degree of chromaticism to the music than had previously been present in jazz.

From among the group traditionally credited with starting the bop style, Charlie Parker had the greatest influence on subsequent players. His playing brought together all of the important bop innovations—harmonic complexity, rhythmic inventiveness, technical virtuosity—and combined them with a brilliant melodic sensibility. Several fine examples of his style are included on the *Smithsonian Collection of Classic Jazz,* including "Ko-Ko," "Parker's Mood," and "Shaw 'Nuff" (with Dizzy Gillespie).

GILLESPIE:
"Shaw 'Nuff"
Cassette 7/B, Track 4
CD 7, Track 9

A NEW ATTITUDE

Besides being musically advanced, bop was one manifestation of a larger social protest movement whose members later became known as the "beat generation." Part of the "beat" attitude was an insistence on a cool, detached manner. No longer did bandleaders extend the customary amenities to the audience, such as announcing song titles or hamming it up between tunes. The early bop players, though not outwardly rude to their audiences, intended to make no concessions or commercial compromises with their music.

At least part of the detached attitude and the militant image of the bop musicians was due to changes in the way they saw themselves. At the same time that traditional swing music structure was being abandoned, many black musicians were undergoing a shift in consciousness. Whereas older black players had been forced to play the sometimes unwanted role of entertainer for the amusement of their predominantly white audiences, the newer generation of players assumed a more self-assertive stance. As John Lewis of the Modern Jazz Quartet once put it:

"This revolution, or whatever you want to call it, in the 1940s took place for many reasons, not only musical ones. . . . For the younger musicians, this was the way to react against the attitude that Negroes were supposed to entertain people. The new attitude was: "Either you listen to me on the basis of what I actually do or forget it."[2]

2. Nat Hentoff, *Jazz Is* (New York: Random House, 1976), pp. 259–260.

Figure 22.7 Miles Davis, an outstanding trumpet player, retained a lyric style in his cool jazz and rock-jazz music while incorporating some of the avant-garde's modal and improvisatory techniques.

POST BEBOP

The flexibility of jazz and its ability to adapt to trends is evident in the period following World War II. At that time there was a revival of interest in Dixieland and Chicago style, and a number of swing bands were able to survive and are still active today. Bebop continued as the mainstream of jazz development, evolving in the 1950s into a style known as hard bop. **Hard bop** took the basic feel of bebop and added a more prominent blues influence, simplifying the harmonic activity and putting a greater emphasis on a straightforward, driving beat. Hard bop has continued into the 1990s as the embodiment of "straight-ahead jazz," perpetuated by Art Blakey (1919–1990) and his band. Alongside these styles, new styles evolved; the most popular of these were cool jazz, free jazz, and rock-jazz (fusion).

COOL JAZZ

Cool jazz came about as a reaction to bop. Whereas the boppers looked to the harmonic ideas of Coleman Hawkins for inspiration, the "cool" musicians followed the lead of one of Hawkins's contemporaries, Lester ("Prez") Young (1909–1959), whose airy tone and laid-back, melodic approach provided a more emotionally detached alternative to the aggression of the boppers. The leaders of this new style were pianist Lennie Tristano (1919–1978) and Miles Davis (1926–1991; fig. 22.7). It was Davis's nine-piece band that set the general style of cool jazz in the recordings known as *Birth of the Cool* in 1949–1950. Davis's group consisted of horn, trumpet, trombone, tuba, alto and baritone saxophones, piano, string bass, and drums, an ensemble that approximated the mellow sound of the Claude Thornhill orchestra.

Another group that contributed to the style was the Modern Jazz Quartet headed by pianist John Lewis (b. 1920). This group incorporated classical forms such as the rondo and fugue into jazz, even playing actual classical compositions with a jazz flavor. In addition, the Dave Brubeck Quartet made excursions into odd-metered music in such

Figure 22.8 John Coltrane is considered one of the major figures in the history of jazz. His incorporation of Indian and modal ideas and his innovative instrumental techniques have had a significant influence on both jazz and rock.

compositions as "Take Five" in 5/4 meter and "Blue Rondo à la Turk" in an irregular 9/8. And the American composer Gunther Schuller (b. 1925) made what is sometimes called "third stream" music, a combination of jazz and classical music.

FREE JAZZ

By the end of the 1950s, the standard structure and harmonies that had been the basis of jazz were beginning to limit the creativity of musicians. Players began to search for new forms of expression. One option that musicians explored was the substitution of harmonic and melodic material based on modes (scales) for the traditional major and minor harmonic material they had been using. Miles Davis, again at the forefront of new sounds, brought this approach to the jazz community with his *Kind of Blue* recording (1959), primarily the song "So What," which placed the soloists in a context with minimal harmonic information to play off of and required them to improvise in the Dorian mode.

Dorian Mode

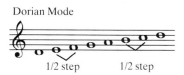

1/2 step   1/2 step

Example 22.1

A featured soloist on this recording, John Coltrane (1926–1967; fig. 22.8), quickly adopted the **modal jazz** approach and explored it extensively for the rest of his career, becoming one of the most important jazz musicians in history, with records such as *My*

Figure 22.9 Ornette
Coleman's free jazz style
emphasizes a free and
spontaneous melodic
improvisation that is usually
completely independent of
the underlying rhythm and
harmony.

Favorite Things (1961) and *A Love Supreme* (1964), the latter of which shows elements
of the other avenue that musicians began to explore in their quest for creative freedom—
free jazz.

Free Jazz (1960) was the name of a record by the Ornette Coleman Double Quartet.
The album's title has come to be the name of the musical style it introduced. The album
features a half hour of collective improvisation with no set harmonic center of rhythm,
bringing about many complex rhythms and abrasive dissonances and featuring a return to
the emotional cries of the field hollers and work songs of the antebellum South. Coleman
(b. 1930; fig. 22.9), along with Coltrane, became the most famous proponent of the new
music, although many important musicians experimented within this style in the 1960s,
including pianist Cecil Taylor (b. 1933) and trumpeter Don Cherry (b. 1936). The impetus
for this style stemmed primarily from the Civil Rights movement, with several African-
American jazz musicians seeking to reaffirm their African roots and abandon any "Euro-
peanisms" in their music. But as the Civil Rights movement lost momentum, so did the
music, and many musicians reverted to the modal style of Davis and Coltrane.

ROCK-JAZZ/ELECTRIC JAZZ/FUSION

The terms rock-jazz, electric jazz, and fusion have been used to describe a style of music
that resulted from combining the electronic sound and beat of rock with the improvisatory
nature of jazz. **Rock-jazz** came into being in 1969 and gained enormous popularity rivaling
that of swing in the big band era.

Miles Davis was again in the forefront of jazz innovations. His 1969 album *Bitches
Brew* used a full complement of electronic instruments. Many of the musicians associated
with Davis excelled in rock-jazz. Herbie Hancock (b. 1940) became one of the leaders in
the merger of rock rhythms with jazz. His 1973 recording *Head Hunters* sold nearly a
million copies and encouraged the later stampede of performers to the style. Saxophonist

Figure 22.10 Weather Report, founded in 1971 by Wayne Shorter and Joe Zawinul, was one of the foremost influential electric jazz groups.

Wayne Shorter (b. 1933) and Joseph Zawinul (b. 1932) went on to form Weather Report (fig. 22.10), a group that brought collective improvisation to a new level of interest in selections such as "Heavy Weather" and "Birdland."

Through the 1980s and into the 1990s, several types of music have been included under the general term jazz. Fusion continues to spawn new performers and groups, such as the Elektric Band of Chick Corea, with some artists carrying the fusion label over into the pop music charts, as Kenny G. did with his instrumental "Songbird." Younger performers, such as Anthony Davis, are creating a style called "new creative music," which combines elements of avant-garde European composition with the improvisational performance techniques of jazz. New Age music, a style perpetuated by pianist George Winston's *Windham Hill* record label, has been tossed into the jazz bin, although the music owes more to European minimalist music than to jazz. Many other young players, headed by trumpeter Wynton Marsalis (b. 1961) and his brother, saxophonist Branford Marsalis (b. 1960), are seeking new ways of expressing themselves within the limits of the mainstream ("hard bop") style.

Since its inception at the turn of the century, jazz in its various styles has been integral to American culture and has represented America in many parts of the world. Its flexibility and adjustability will undoubtedly ensure its continued growth in the future.

ROCK

In 1955, the movie *The Blackboard Jungle* opened with Bill Haley and the Comets' version of "Rock Around the Clock." Almost overnight, rock culture was born and the rock generation was on its way. As the main current of popular music, rock has continued to affect and reflect the attitudes, feelings, and values of a large portion of the younger generation.

Figure 22.11 One of the most important figures in the history of rock, Chuck Berry's aggressive and driving songs, innovative guitar techniques, and striking stage presence made him one of rock's earliest stars.

BERRY: "Johnny B. Goode"
Cassette 7/B, Track 5
CD 7, Track 10

While rock music became popular virtually overnight in 1955, it had developed over a considerable period of time. As was the case with jazz, much of rock's early history was the work of black musicians such as Chuck Berry (fig. 22.11) and Little Richard. Black **rhythm and blues** supplied an essential ingredient for rock—an insistently heavy beat, hard-driving sound, and earthy vocals with electric guitar. The other main component came from **country and western** music representing the white American folk tradition popularized in the "Grand Ole Opry" broadcasts and by such popular figures as Gene Autry and Roy Rogers.

ELVIS PRESLEY

The earliest rock records were remakes of African-American rhythm and blues tunes by white performers, who substituted driving guitar-and-drums accompaniments for the original jazz-tinged music and altered the lyrics, eliminating sexual innuendo and slang to make the text more acceptable to the mainstream white audience. The most famous of these performers was Elvis Presley (1935–1977; fig. 22.12), whose magnetic stage presence helped him achieve phenomenal popularity among teenagers and many adults.

The Presley craze opened the floodgates for rock music and musicians. A number of other white rockers became popular, among them Jerry Lee Lewis ("Great Balls of Fire"), Carl Perkins ("Blue Suede Shoes"), and Buddy Holly ("That'll Be the Day"). Black performers such as Chuck Berry ("Johnny B. Goode"), Little Richard ("Tutti Frutti"), and Fats Domino ("Blueberry Hill") began to see their records cross over from the rhythm and blues charts to gain acceptance with white audiences.

Figure 22.12 Elvis Presley's popularity as a rock performer created a cult that still continues, even though he died in 1977.

MOTOWN

By the end of the 1950s, the rock'n'roll craze had begun to be replaced with the smoother vocal sounds of such pop-ballad crooners as Fabian, Frankie Avalon, Frankie Valli and the Four Seasons, and Paul Anka. In response to the trend, Berry Gordy, Jr., created Motown Records—so called because it was based in Detroit, the "motor city." The subsequent "Motown sound" had a significant effect on rock music in the 1960s. It combined elements of gospel and rhythm and blues with the smooth vocal sound and slick production of the ballad singers, and it added the visual appeal of stylish appearance and engaging choreography in live performance. This appeal was characteristic of such groups as the Supremes ("Stop in the Name of Love") and the Temptations ("My Girl"), as well as solo performers like Marvin Gaye ("I Heard It Through the Grapevine").

THE BEATLES

The "British Invasion" of the mid-sixties saw the revival of the more straightforward country and rhythm and blues roots that had shaped the music of the early 1950s. Groups such as the Rolling Stones and the Animals became popular with remakes of songs by African-American blues artists like Howlin' Wolf and Bo Diddley. The most important new British group, however, was the Beatles (fig. 22.13). Almost overnight, these four young Englishmen from Liverpool changed the face of American popular music. Their first American recording, "I Wanna Hold Your Hand," sold a million copies after only ten days on the market.

Figure 22.13 The Beatles
in a recording session.

During 1964–1965, they recorded albums and singles that represented virtually every style of rock music of the sixties: rhythm and blues, "Roll Over Beethoven" (original version written by Chuck Berry), "Money," and "She's a Woman"; country and western (rockabilly), "I've Just Seen a Face" and "Words of Love"; folk, "I'll Follow the Sun"; and ballad, "And I Love Her," "If I Fell," and "Till There Was You."

The genius of the Beatles, particularly that of the songwriters John Lennon and Paul McCartney, emerged as they experimented with rock style. One of the best examples of such experimentation is their 1967 recording *Sgt. Pepper's Lonely Hearts Club Band.* In this, the first "conceptual" or "song cycle" rock album, each song relates to the next and to an overriding theme. The cycle included a range of diverse elements—an English music hall song ("When I'm Sixty-Four"), new "psychedelic" sounds using advanced electronic devices ("Lucy in the Sky with Diamonds"), large orchestration, Indian instruments ("Within You Without You"), and good old-fashioned rock 'n' roll (the album's title song, "Sgt. Pepper's Lonely Hearts Club Band"). After five years of unprecedented success and popularity, the Beatles disbanded in 1970.

The popularity of the British groups prompted a blues revival in the United States, with groups such as the Allman Brothers Band and Santana emerging. Still others were influenced more by the sound than by the style, and used the raw sound as a backdrop for their growing concerns with the politics of the time, such as the ever-present civil rights movement and the growing conflict in Vietnam.

The pronounced emotional style of gospel singing was combined with rhythm and blues to form **soul** music, which became an increasingly important source of support for the civil rights movement. Performers like James Brown ("Say It Loud, I'm Black and I'm Proud"), Otis Redding ("I Can't Turn You Loose"), Aretha Franklin ("Respect") (fig. 22.14), and Wilson Pickett ("Til' The Midnight Hour") were all important proponents of this style.

Figure 22.14 Aretha Franklin, whose roots are in gospel music, has successfully performed rock, jazz, rhythm and blues, and soul. Her powerful vocal style has earned her the title "Queen of Soul."

The hippie movement of the late 1960s was reflected in the musical style of the **psychedelic rock** bands, such as Jefferson Airplane, the Grateful Dead, and Big Brother and the Holding Company (featuring Janis Joplin). Lyrically, these bands voiced the concerns of their audience while musically creating extended, repetitious pieces with an emphasis on improvisation. The most important musician from this scene was Jimi Hendrix, whose emotional, electrifying, blues-influenced guitar playing was far ahead of his peers and gave him a place in history as one of the most influential rock guitar players of all time before his untimely death in 1970. Large, multiband outdoor music festivals were frequent in this era, with the 1969 Woodstock festival being one of the most famous.

BOB DYLAN

The "folk-rock" style also became an important component of the music scene in the sixties, as singer-songwriter Bob Dylan (fig. 22.15) gained a great deal of popularity and critical acclaim with his songs of racial equality ("Blowin' in the Wind") and opposition to the war ("A Hard Rain's A-Gonna Fall") expressing the social climate of the times. Dylan began his career as a folk singer, later adding rock-oriented music and instrumentation (electric guitars, drums) to his lyrics of social awareness and political concern and gaining a much wider audience.

What some people believe to be the golden age of rock music came to a close in the early 1970s. The Beatles disbanded, and untimely death removed from the scene the stars Jimi Hendrix (fig. 22.16), Janis Joplin, and Jim Morrison. In addition, two meccas of rock music, the nightclubs Fillmore East and Fillmore West, were closed. Indeed, an era of rock history came to an end.

Figure 22.15 Bob Dylan's combination of folk-rock music with politically and socially conscious lyrics made him one of the pivotal figures in sixties rock and has inspired a whole generation of singer/songwriters.

Figure 22.16 Jimi Hendrix, the guitarist whose music helped define the "psychedelic" sound of the 1960s.

THE SEVENTIES

The early 1970s saw a continued interest in blues-based rock, with a number of British bands, such as Cream, The Who, and Led Zeppelin, grasping the raw-edged style that Jimi Hendrix had initiated. The result was a new style that became known as **hard rock.** The soul style of James Brown and others gradually evolved into a more rock-oriented style that came to be known as **funk.** Funk's predominant bass line and complex polyrhythms kept

Figure 22.17 The energetic music and often lewd stage performances of the Sex Pistols helped the group and "punk rock" receive great attention.

the music driving forward even though the harmonic motion gradually came to a virtual standstill. Sly and the Family Stone was one of the first funk bands, with bassist Larry Graham inventing the "slap-pop" bass technique that has become the calling card of funk-influenced music. Kool & the Gang was a later band that helped bridge the gap between funk and **disco.**

D I S C O

Disco became popular as a style of dance music in the city clubs in the early 1970s, but it was the 1977 movie *Saturday Night Fever* and its soundtrack, featuring the hit "Stayin' Alive" by the Bee Gees, that created the immense popularity of the style. Disco was essentially a highly polished, commercialized version of funk, with a subdued bass line and a danceable rhythm. Although the disco craze was relatively short-lived, it created careers for artists such as the Bee Gees, Donna Summer, and the Village People.

Several other forms were spawned during the 1970s. **Progressive rock** was created by performers with some formal European training, such as Yes and Emerson, Lake and Palmer (ELP). These bands combined classical and rock styles (usually drawing heavily on the baroque style) to create grandiose, extended rock "suites." At the other end of the spectrum was **punk rock,** which avoided everything associated with formal training in favor of raw, aggressive music designed as a vehicle for releasing frustration or anger with the government or society in general. Although the most famous 1970s punk band, the Sex Pistols (fig. 22.17), was noted more for its often obscene stage performances, many of the bands within the genre used the music as a means for pointed sociopolitical statements.

Figure 22.18 Hailed in the 1970s as "the next Bob Dylan," singer/songwriter Bruce Springsteen captured a large following with his driving music, perceptive lyrics, and kinetic live performances.

THE EIGHTIES

The 1980s did not see a great influx of new musical styles. Instead, the decade confirmed past styles. The blues-rock tradition of the late 1960s was kept alive by the continued success of the Rolling Stones, as well as by new artists like the Fabulous Thunderbirds; the folk-rock tradition was updated and revived by Bruce Springsteen (fig. 22.18), whose *Born in the U.S.A.* album sold millions of copies and helped him earn the title "voice of the decade" from *Rolling Stone* magazine; older soul and rhythm and blues sounds were revived and updated by the Commodores and Tina Turner; the early "rockabilly" was brought back by the Stray Cats; Prince kept a solid funk feel to his music; and disco split into two factions—the synthesizer-oriented dance music of Michael Jackson (fig. 22.19) and Madonna (fig. 22.20), and the more rock-based new wave of the Talking Heads and the Cars. However, one new style did break out of the underground and into the mainstream market: rap.

RAP

Rap music is very much a conglomeration of everything that preceded it. In fact, it is literally created using everything that has come before. A rap song consists of a rhyme-oriented text that is not sung, but is spoken, or "rapped," over the background of a constant drumbeat combined with "samples" or "dubs" from recordings of popular songs. This background is not created by a band, but by a disc jockey (DJ) who usually operates two turntables, manually turning the records of other artists to appropriate places to create the backdrop for the rap and occasionally slowing or accelerating the record by hand, a technique known as "scratching."

Figure 22.19 Michael Jackson, a multitalented singer, dancer, composer, actor, and producer, has been a rock star since the age of 11. His albums and music videos have gained enormous popularity.

Figure 22.20 Madonna, the "Material Girl," has gained fame for her funky, dance-oriented songs and her steamy, campy video and live performances.

A song called "Rapper's Delight" by the Sugar Hill Gang is generally acknowledged as the first commercial rap success, but the style's breakthrough record did not come until the late 1980s, with the exceptional popularity of Run-DMC's version of "Walk This Way" (originally by Aerosmith, a late-seventies hard-rock band). This song (aided considerably by the video that accompanied it) initiated the commercial success that rap has enjoyed through the late 1980s and into the 1990s.

L. L. COOL J:
"I'm Bad"
Cassette 7/B, Track 6
CD 7, Track 11

TELEVISION

In August 1981, **Music Television** (MTV) began broadcasting. This single channel and the multitude of video music channels around the world changed the way rock music is marketed, produced, performed, and experienced. Not only does MTV have the power to promote established artists and their latest music (as radio has for years), but MTV can give a new artist instant credibility through massive exposure. The MTV industry exemplifies the importance and power of the producer. Just as Berry Gordy created the Motown sound, people are now creating sounds for a number of new artists. Producers and production teams, such as L.A. and Babyface, Jimmy Jam and Terry Lewis, Beau Hill, and Quincy Jones, have become more important to the music the public hears than the musicians themselves. Without a doubt, MTV is having a significant effect on the lives of many young people in the 1990s.

SUMMARY

Perhaps the most significant American contribution to music is jazz, a musical language that grew out of the African-American experience. Among its early ancestors were the composed piano music known as ragtime and the improvisational vocal art known as the blues.

Dixieland, or New Orleans-style jazz, developed in the early 1900s and utilized a small jazz combo made up of front-line instruments and a rhythm section. The most important feature of New Orleans jazz is collective improvisation. The Chicago-style jazz of the 1920s saw the rise of the improvising soloist as a dominant force in jazz. The Depression years spawned the extension of jazz piano styles, notably stride and boogie-woogie. As the economy recovered, big bands emerged with an orchestrated style that came to be known as swing, the first jazz style to become popular with white audiences and performers. At the height of the swing era, a small group of musicians rebelled against the commercialism of the big bands and sought to reaffirm the African-American roots of the music. Their highly innovative rhythmic and harmonic experiments resulted in a small ensemble style called bebop (or bop), which brought the focus of jazz back to the soloist.

The 1950s and 1960s saw many experiments stemming from the bebop lead. Cool jazz, a reaction to the frenzied quality of bop, brought a more detached emotional quality and several European classical elements to the music, while hard bop reemphasized the music's African-American roots. The social climate of the sixties and the growing confinement of standard harmonies provoked jazz musicians to stretch into modal systems and a style called free jazz, which sought to release the musician from any musical boundaries.

Rock music has had a powerful impact on recent and current popular culture. Two major components in the development of rock were rhythm and blues and country and western music. In the mid-1950s, rock, then known as rock 'n' roll, became a popular style with white artists such as Elvis Presley producing remakes of rhythm and blues songs. Gradually, African-American artists began to be accepted by the public and added many new styles to the genre through the mid-1960s, notably the Motown sound and soul.

The "British Invasion" and the arrival of the Beatles in 1964 changed the face of American popular music. The Beatles' late recordings were a fusion of current rock styles and a variety of other musical styles and elements. The "British Invasion" rekindled an interest in rhythm and blues among American bands, which is evident in the psychedelic styles of the late 1960s, with the guitar playing of Jimi Hendrix paving the way for the guitar-oriented hard rock of the 1970s. The 1970s also saw disco, a refinement of the Motown sound, and punk rock, a rebellion against any sort of refinement.

The emergence of Music Television (MTV) as an important marketing tool did not establish any new styles, but did help reconfirm past styles. The one style that did emerge as a new development was rap, a rhythmic, spoken-word style that relies on a predominant beat and borrows extensively from past music by "dubbing." MTV has continued as an important medium into the 1990s, while stylistic boundaries have kept on diminishing.

NEW TERMS

jazz
blues
blue notes
ragtime
New Orleans style
front line
rhythm section
group improvisation
Chicago style
stride
boogie-woogie
swing
riff
bebop (bop)
hard bop
cool jazz

modal jazz
free jazz
rock-jazz (fusion)
rhythm and blues
country and western
rock 'n' roll
Motown
soul
psychedelic rock
hard rock
funk
disco
progressive rock
punk rock
rap music
Music Television (MTV)

SUGGESTED LISTENING

Smithsonian Collection of Classical Jazz

Armstrong, Louis

The Louis Armstrong Story

"S.O.L. Blues"

Count Basie

Moten Swing

Berry, Chuck

Maybelline; Johnny B. Goode; Roll Over Beethoven

Christian, Charlie

Solo Flight

Coleman, Ornette

Free Jazz

Coltrane, John

A Love Supreme; Ascension; My Favorite Things

Davis, Miles

The Complete Birth of the Cool; Kind of Blue; So What; Bitches Brew

Ellington, Duke

This Is Duke Ellington; Ellington at Newport

Hendrix, Jimi

Are You Experienced?

Holiday, Billie

Lady Day; The Golden Years, Volume I

"God Bless the Child"

Monk, Thelonious

Genius of Modern Music

"Monk's Dream"

Parker, Charlie

The Savoy Recordings

Run DMC

Walk This Way

Springsteen, Bruce

Born in the U.S.A., Nebraska

The Beatles

"I Wanna Hold Your Hand"; Sgt. Pepper's Lonely Hearts Club Band

Weather Report

Birdland

SUGGESTED READINGS

General Reading List

Apel, Willi, and R. T. Daniel. *The Harvard Brief Dictionary of Music.* Cambridge, Mass.: Harvard University Press, 1970. A succinct version of the *Harvard Dictionary of Music.*

Baker's Biographical Dictionary of Musicians, rev. by Nicholas Slonimsky. 7th ed. New York: Schirmer Books, 1984. Brief biographical information on thousands of musicians, from Bach to Jimi Hendrix. Good quick-reference source.

Bowers, Jane, and Judith Tick, eds. *Women Making Music: The Western Art Tradition, 1150–1950.* Urbana: University of Illinois Press, 1986. A series of essays by noted scholars on the role of women composers and performers in Western art music.

Einstein, Alfred. *A Short History of Music.* New York: Knopf, 1954; New York: Random House, 1954 (paper). One of the best concise histories of music, this work is a nontechnical chronological survey of important composers and musical genres from the Middle Ages through the nineteenth century.

Neuls-Bates, Carol, ed. *Women in Music: An Anthology of Source Readings from the Middle Ages to the Present.* New York: Harper & Row, 1982. A collection of writings by and about a variety of women musicians; arranged in chronological order.

The New Grove Dictionary of American Music. H. Wiley Hitchcock and Stanley Sadie, eds. London: Macmillan Press Ltd. and New York: Grove's Dictionaries of Music, Inc., 1986. Encyclopedia-style entries on important individuals in American music, as well as various styles (eg., rock, blues, rap). Concise, well-written entries and extensive bibliographies.

Randel, Don Michael, ed. *New Harvard Dictionary of Music.* Cambridge, Mass.: Belknap Press, 1986. A concise historical and bibliographical handbook of terms and concepts; biographical information is not included. Each major entry has a working definition, history, and bibliography.

Sadie, Stanley, ed. *New Grove Dictionary of Music and Musicians.* 20 vols. London: Macmillan, 1980. The most authoritative and comprehensive music reference tool in the English language. It is the first place to look for information on any music subject.

GENRES

Cuyler, Louise Elvira. *The Symphony.* New York: Harcourt Brace Jovanovich, 1973. Traces the two hundred-year development of the symphony, citing and analyzing the most important, representative compositions from each period by country and composer.

Grout, Donald Jay. *A Short History of Opera.* 2nd ed. New York: Columbia University Press, 1965. The standard English-language history of opera, this book surveys the most significant works and the major developments in operatic style from its beginnings through the early twentieth century.

Stevens, Denis, ed. *A History of Song.* rev. ed. New York: Norton, 1970. A technical, historical, and geographic survey of secular song in Western countries, with criticism and analysis.

Ulrich, Homer. *Chamber Music.* 2nd ed. New York: Columbia University Press, 1966. Ulrich defines and analyzes the growth of chamber music to 1930, using the works of Haydn, Mozart, Beethoven, and the Romantics as the core. Contemporary chamber music is also discussed.

Part 1: Fundamentals of Music

A. GENERAL WORKS

Copland, Aaron. *What to Listen for in Music.* New York: New American Library, 1964. A highly useful introductory guide to the elements of music, including chapters on basic structural forms (fugue, variation, sonata-allegro).

Erikson, Robert. *The Structure of Music: A Listener's Guide.* Westport, Conn.: Greenwood Press, 1977. Explores the nature of harmony, melody, and counterpoint from a nontechnical point of view.

B. MUSICAL INSTRUMENTS AND ORCHESTRATION

Carse, Adam. *The History of Orchestration.* New York: Dover, 1964. A largely nontechnical survey of the orchestra and the art of orchestration from the sixteenth century through the late nineteenth century.

The New Grove Dictionary of Musical Instruments. Stanley Sadie, ed. London: Macmillan Press Ltd. and New York: Grove's Dictionaries of Music, Inc., 1984. Enhanced versions of the articles that originally appeared in New Grove. Includes additional entries on non-Western instruments and electronic instruments.

Part 2: The Music of World Cultures

Hofmann, Charles. *American Indians Sing.* New York: The John Day Company, 1967. A study of the thought, religion, and culture of American Indians as revealed through their music, dances, and ceremonies. Well illustrated and very readable.

Malm, William P. *Music Cultures of the Pacific, the Near East, and Asia.* 2nd ed. Englewood Cliffs, N.J.: Prentice-Hall, 1977. Well illustrated, with both drawings and musical selections, this volume explores the anthropological, historical, and musical aspects of the subject cultures.

Nettl, Bruno, and Helen Myers. *Folk Music in the United States: An Introduction.* 3rd ed. Detroit: Wayne State University Press, 1976. An introducton to characteristics of folk music, its history, instruments, and singers.

Wade, Bonnie C. *Music in India: The Classical Traditions.* Englewood Cliffs, N.J.: Prentice-Hall, 1979. An introductory text, written for the uninitiated Western listener, which surveys the Hindustani and Karnatak traditions of classical Indian music. Includes a discography and filmography.

Warren, Dr. Fred, and Les Warren. *Music of Africa: An Introduction.* Englewood Cliffs, N.J.: Prentice-Hall, 1970. A lively account of African vocal and instrumental music.

Part 3: Medieval and Renaissance Music

Brown, Howard Mayer. *Music in the Renaissance.* Englewood Cliffs, N.J.: Prentice-Hall, 1976. Covers music from the early fifteenth century through 1600 and discusses the significant features and great composers of renaissance music.

Caldwell, John. *Medieval Music.* Bloomington: Indiana University Press, 1978. A well-written survey of medieval music.

Hoppin, Richard H. *Medieval Music.* New York: Norton, 1978. A well-written survey of medieval music.

Part 4: Music of the Baroque Era
A. GENERAL WORKS

Bukofzer, Manfred F. *Music in the Baroque Era.* New York: Norton, 1967. A comprehensive history of the important musical developments in the Baroque period.

Palisca, Claude. *Baroque Music.* 2nd ed. Englewood Cliffs, N.J.: Prentice-Hall, 1981. An overview of the principal styles of baroque music.

B. INDIVIDUAL COMPOSERS

Bach
Arnold, Denis. *Bach.* New York: Oxford University Press, 1984. Aimed at the general reader, Arnold does a fine job of pulling recent Bach research together in a concise, readable biography.

Handel
Hogwood, Christopher. *Handel.* New York: Thames and Hudson, 1985. Primarily a biography, Hogwood does a fine job of incorporating recent research into an excellent, accurate book.

Monteverdi
Tomlinson, Gary. *Monteverdi and the End of the Renaissance.* Berkeley: University of California Press, 1987. Discussion of Monteverdi's music, placing an emphasis on its relationship to the texts used. Contrasts his style and evolution to the cultural world of which he was a part.

Vivaldi
Talbot, Michael. *Vivaldi.* London: J. M. Dent, 1978. Good discussion of Vivaldi's life and works. A fair amount of musical examples enhance the discussions of his music.

Part 5: Music of the Classical Era
A. GENERAL WORKS

Pauly, Reinhard G. *Music in the Classic Period.* 2nd ed. Englewood Cliffs, N.J.: Prentice-Hall, 1973. A concise survey of the period in two parts, the first tracing the evolution of the classical style from the rococo through Haydn and Mozart, the second discussing the principal forms and genres of the period.

Rosen, Charles. *The Classical Style: Haydn, Mozart, Beethoven.* rev. ed. London: Faber & Faber, 1976. A comprehensive work on classical style by one of the foremost scholars in the area.

B. INDIVIDUAL COMPOSERS

Beethoven
Soloman, Maynard. *Beethoven.* New York: Schirmer Books, 1977. Wonderful biography on the composer's life, with separate sections at the end of each "period" that deal with the music. Extensive annotated bibliography.

Haydn
Landon, H. C. Robbins, and David Wyn Jones. *Haydn: His Life and Music.* Bloomington: Indiana University Press, 1988. The most recent contribution from a well-known Haydn scholar, this book brings together the facts of Haydn research in a more concise manner than Landon's four-volume work.

Mozart
Einstein, Alfred. *Mozart: His Character, His Work.* New York: Oxford University Press, 1965. A thoughtful, leisurely study of the composer, his character, musical development, and works.

Part 6: Music of the Romantic Era
A. GENERAL WORKS

Einstein, Alfred. *Music in the Romantic Era.* New York: Norton, 1974. Basic for the student wanting to comprehend the generating and sustaining forces of the Romantic period.

Longyear, Rey M. *Nineteenth-Century Romanticism in Music.* 3rd ed. Englewood Cliffs, N.J.: Prentice-Hall, 1988. A general work surveying romanticism and nationalism in music.

B. INDIVIDUAL COMPOSERS

Berlioz
Berlioz, Hector. *Evenings with the Orchestra.* Jacques Barzun, trans. Chicago: University of Chicago Press, 1973. Thoughts on contemporaneous musical ephemera. Delightful to read.

Brahms
James, Burnett. *Brahms: A Critical Study.* New York: Praeger, 1972. A standard biography assessing Brahms' artistic achievement and emphasizing his progressive tendencies and influence on Schoenberg, Webern, and Sibelius.

Chopin

Melville, Derek. *Chopin: A Biography, with a Survey of Books, Editions, and Recordings.* Hamden, Conn.: Shoe String, 1977. A concise biography tracing Chopin's musical development and works.

Dvořák

Clapham, John. *Antonin Dvořák, Musician and Craftsman.* New York: St. Martin's Press, 1966. A scholarly, comprehensive survey using Czech material, previously unpublished, for a close analysis of Dvořák's craft of composition. Includes biographical text, illustrations, and musical examples.

Liszt

Pereyni, Eleanor. *Liszt: The Artist as Romantic Hero.* New York: Little, Brown, 1974. A psychological exploration of Liszt in the framework of the romantic movement, probing the literary, musical, and social influences on Liszt's symphonic poems. Illustrated with comprehensive chronology.

Mendelssohn

Werner, Eric. *Mendelssohn: A New Image of the Composer and His Age.* Glencoe, Ill.: The Free Press, 1963. The comprehensive biography of Mendelssohn, containing many excerpts from the composer's correspondence not commonly available.

Mussorgsky

Calvocoressi, Michel Dmitri. *Mussorgsky.* rev. ed. London: J. M. Dent, 1974; Totowa, N.J.: Littlefield, 1974 (paper). A definitive study tracing all major works and many lesser compositions, describing and analyzing them in nontechnical language against the cultural background and musical climate of the age. A chapter on technique and style is included.

Schubert

Einstein, Alfred. *Schubert: A Musical Portrait.* New York: Vienna House, 1976. Einstein follows Schubert's creative development year by year, with a semitechnical analysis of the music.

Tchaikovsky

Abraham, Gerald, ed. *The Music of Tchaikovsky.* New York: Norton, 1974. Eminent music critics analyze the music by genre: chamber music, symphonies, songs, ballets, etc. With chronology and musical examples.

Verdi

Osborne, Charles. *The Complete Operas of Verdi.* New York: Knopf, 1970; New York: DaCapo, 1977 (paper). Lively prose and fine scholarship illuminate this discussion of Verdi's twenty-six operas, the Requiem, and other musical pieces, each given a literary and historical background to complement a play-by-play synopsis and nontechnical discussion of the music.

Wagner

Gurman, Robert. *Richard Wagner: The Man, His Mind, and His Music.* New York: Harcourt Brace Jovanovich, 1974. This provocative, nontechnical biography examines the nationalism and racism from which Wagner drew his most powerful symbols.

Part 7: Music of the Early Twentieth Century

A. GENERAL WORKS

Austin, William. *Music in the 20th Century: From Debussy Through Stravinsky.* New York: Norton, 1966. A detailed survey of modern music that is an essential reference source for comprehending the forces affecting it.

Salzman, Eric. *Twentieth-Century Music: An Introduction.* 3rd ed. Englewood Cliffs, N.J.: Prentice-Hall, 1988. A comprehensive survey of contemporary music.

B. INDIVIDUAL COMPOSERS

Bartók

Stevens, Halsey. *The Life and Music of Belá Bartók.* rev. ed. New York: Oxford University Press, 1967. This most important work on Bartók in English is divided into two sections: a biographical study and a categorized, subjective analysis of his music.

Berg

Reich, Willi. *Alban Berg.* Cornelius Cardew, trans. New York: Vienna House, 1974. An informative study of the life and works of Berg.

Debussy

Debussy, Claude. *Debussy on Music.* Collected and introduced by François Lesure; Richard Langham Smith, ed. and trans. New York: Knopf, 1977. A comprehensive collection of Debussy's lively musical criticism and interviews (written under the pseudonym M. Croche) liberally laced with annotations and anecdotes by Smith.

Schoenberg

Rosen, Charles. *Arnold Schoenberg.* Princeton: Princeton University Press, 1981. This study of stylistic phases (essentially nonbiographical) elucidates Schoenberg's composing technique and artistic philosophy through an exposition of musical ideas.

Stravinsky

White, Eric Walter. *Stravinsky: The Composer and His Works.* 2nd ed. Berkeley and Los Angeles: University of California Press, 1979.

Webern

Moldenhauer, Hans, and Rosaleen Moldenhauer. *Anton von Webern, a Chronicle of His Life and Work.* First American ed. New York: Knopf, distributed by Random House, 1979. A very thorough biography of this important composer, presenting documents from his lifetime to put the music into perspective.

Part 8: Music in America

A. GENERAL WORKS

Ammer, Christine. *Unsung: A History of Women in American Music.* Westport, Conn.: Greenwood Press, 1980. A history of the role played by women in American music as performers, composers, and teachers during the past two hundred years.

Brooks, Tilford. *America's Black Musical Heritage.* Englewood Cliffs, N.J.: Prentice-Hall, 1984. A detailed history tracing black music from its African roots through contemporary jazz. Also includes sections on black composers who wrote in the Western tradition and black musicians in American society.

Hitchcock, F. Wiley, ed. *Music in the United States: A Historical Introduction.* 3rd ed. Englewood Cliffs, N.J.: Prentice-Hall, 1988. An excellent and concise survey of American music. Particularly fine are the chapters on nineteenth-century popular music and Charles Ives.

Lowens, Irving. *Music and Musicians in Early America.* New York: Norton, 1964. A delightfully written collection of short studies concentrating on the colonial and Federalist periods.

The New Grove Dictionary of American Music, H. Wiley Hitchcock and Stanley Sadie, eds. London: Macmillan Press Ltd. and New York: Grove's Dictionaries of Music, Inc., 1986. Encyclopedia-style entries on important individuals in American music, as well as various styles (e.g., rock, blues, rap). Concise, well-written entries and extensive bibliographies.

B. INDIVIDUAL COMPOSERS

Gershwin

Jablonski, Edward. *Gershwin.* New York: Doubleday, 1987.

Ives

Hitchcock, H. Wiley. *Ives.* London, New York: Oxford University Press, 1977. A thorough study of the composer's work, divided into sections on each genre (chamber works, choral works, etc.). Brief biographical sketch at the beginning of the book provides information on the major points of his life.

Still

Arvey, Verna. *In One Lifetime.* Fayetteville: University of Arkansas Press, 1984. Written by Still's wife, this thorough biography provides unique insight into the circumstances in which the composer worked during his lifetime.

Brown, R. Donald. *William Grant Still.* Oral history program, California State University, Fullerton, 1984. Transcripts of two interviews conducted with the composer in late 1967. Provide valuable insight into the composer's perspective of his own music.

Part 9: Music of the Late Twentieth Century

A. GENERAL WORKS

Cope, David H. *New Directions in Music.* 4th ed. Dubuque, Ia.: Wm. C. Brown, 1984. An introduction and general survey of avant-garde and post–avant-garde music in the twentieth century. Contains many useful illustrations and photographs and lengthy bibliographies and discographies.

Salzman, Eric. *Twentieth-Century Music: An Introduction.* 3rd ed. Englewood Cliffs, N.J.: Prentice-Hall, 1988. This excellent and concise survey includes valuable chapters on avant-garde music through the early 1960s.

B. INDIVIDUAL COMPOSERS

Bernstein

Freedland, Michael. *Leonard Bernstein.* London: Harrap, 1987.

Boulez

Peyser, Joan. *Pierre Boulez.* New York: Schirmer Books, 1976. A chatty, controversial profile of the avant-garde composer, populated with famous friends and artistic figures, and enlivened by accounts of clashes of will and infighting.

Cage

Cage, John. *Silence.* Middletown, Conn.: Wesleyan Press, 1961. A collection of writings on experimental music, techniques of composition, and other miscellaneous topics. An invaluable source for the author's ideas on chance music.

Part 10: Jazz and Rock

Baraka, Imamu Amiri (LeRoi Jones). *Blues People.* New York: Morrow, 1971. Baraka places the entire continuum of African-American music in the context of cultural history, following changes in musical style by social and economic events. An excellent and intriguing thesis.

Charlton, Katherine. *Rock Music Styles: A History.* Dubuque, Iowa: Wm. C. Brown, 1990. Solid discussion of rock music by style, as opposed to a chronological survey. Good analyses of several songs.

Collier, Graham. *Inside Jazz.* London: Quartet Books, 1973. A readable, entertaining, general introduction to the world of jazz.

Dahl, Linda. *Stormy Weather: The Music and Lives of a Century of Jazzwomen.* New York: Pantheon, 1984. A fascinating look at jazzwomen vocalists and instrumentalists from the 1890s through the present. Includes a lengthy discography.

Garland, Phyl. *The Sound of Soul: The History of Black Music.* New York: Contemporary Books, 1969. A detailed, sensitive study of the roots and forms of black music in America. A masterfully stated discussion of the music of the early years serves as a prelude to a more extended treatment of the major "soul" singers of recent years.

Gridley, Mark C. *Jazz Styles.* Englewood Cliffs, N.J.: Prentice-Hall, 1978. A guide to appreciating jazz as well as an introduction to most styles that have appeared on recordings. Includes a discography and a guide to record buying.

Morgenstern, Dan. *Jazz People.* New York: Abrams, 1976. Combines an excellent tracing of the origins and subsequent history of jazz with a number of finely etched personality profiles. Includes graceful photographs by le Brask.

The New Grove Dictionary of Jazz. Barry Kernfeld and Stanley Sadie, eds. London: Macmillan Press Ltd. and New York: Grove's Dictionaries of Music, Inc., 1988. Updates and expands several jazz articles from *The New Grove Dictionary of American Music* and extends the number of important musicians covered. Excellent bibliographies and discographies, as well as detailed analyses of several players' styles, with musical examples.

Ostransky, Leroy. *Jazz City: The Impact of Our Cities on the Development of Jazz.* Englewood Cliffs, N.J.: Prentice-Hall, 1978. An interesting discussion of the possible reasons for the development and flourishing of jazz in New Orleans, Chicago, Kansas City, and New York.

Rolling Stone Illustrated History of Rock and Roll. rev. Jim Miller, ed. New York: Random House, 1981. A critical history bringing together the work of the finest rock writers in a pictorial record of the history of rock 'n' roll, soul, and rock and blues. Unique photos and discographies.

Shapiro, Nat, and Nat Hentoff, eds. *Hear Me Talkin' to Ya.* New York: Dover, 1966. A collection of first-person reminiscences by many major figures from the richest years of jazz history.

Williams, Martin. *The Jazz Tradition.* rev. ed. Oxford University Press, 1983. A clear and vivid narrative of developments in jazz from the early 1920s through the 1960s, with discussions of leading jazz figures from "Jelly Roll" Morton through Ornette Coleman.

GLOSSARY

A

a cappella Designating choral music without instrumental accompaniment.

absolute music Music that is entirely free of extramusical references or ideas.

accompanied recitative A type of recitative in which the voice is accompanied by instruments in addition to continuo.

accompaniment Musical material, usually instrumental, which harmonically supports a melodic line. See also *homophony*.

alternation A principle for building musical form in which a main section (A) alternates with contrasting sections (B, C, D, etc.). Ternary form (ABA) is a simple example.

aria A composition for solo voice and instrumental accompaniment.

arioso A vocal style that is midway between recitative and aria. Its meter is less flexible than that of recitative, but its form is much simpler and more flexible than that of the aria.

arpeggio A chord whose tones are played one after another in rapid succession rather than simultaneously.

art song A musical setting of a poem for solo voice and piano. The German words for song *Lied* and *Lieder* (plural) became the standard terms for this type of song.

atonal Lacking a recognizable tonal center or tonic.

augmentation A rhythmic variation in which the original note values of a theme are increased.

B

ballad (vocal) A narrative poem set to music.

ballade (instrumental) A relatively large, free-form instrumental work. The term was apparently used first by Chopin.

bar line The vertical line that separates the notes in one measure from those in the next.

basso continuo, continuo Continuous bass. A bass part performed by (1) a keyboard player who improvises harmony above the given bass notes, and (2) a string player—usually cello or viola da gamba—who reinforces the bass line.

basso ostinato A short melodic phrase that is repeated continually as a bass line, above which one or more voices have contrasting material.

battery The percussion section of an orchestra.

bebop (bop) A jazz style that emphasizes small ensembles, harmonic innovation, unusual chord structures, an implicit beat, and a "hard" sound.

bel canto "Beautiful song." A vocal technique emphasizing beauty and purity of tone and agility in executing various ornamental details.

binary form A basic musical form consisting of two contrasting sections (AB), both sections often being repeated (AABB); the two sections are in related keys.

blue note In blues and jazz music, any of the notes produced by flatting the third, fifth, or seventh notes of a major scale.

blues A lamenting, melancholy song characterized by a three-line lyrical pattern in AAB form, a twelve-bar harmonic progression, and the frequent use of "blue notes."

boogie-woogie A blues piano style that uses a rhythmic ostinato bass in the left hand while the right hand plays a simple, often improvised melody.

bridge In a musical composition, a section that connects two themes.

C

cadence A point of rest at the end of a passage, section, or complete work that gives the music a sense of convincing conclusion. Also, a melodic or harmonic progression that gives the feeling of conclusion.

cadenza A section of music, usually in a concerto, played in an improvisatory style by a solo performer without orchestral accompaniment.

call and response A song style found in many West African cultures (and black American folk music) in which phrases sung by a leader alternate with responding phrases sung by a chorus.

canon A contrapuntal technique in which a melody in one part is strictly imitated by another voice or voices.

cantata A choral work, usually on a sacred subject and frequently built upon a chorale tune, combining aria, recitative, chorus, and instrumental accompaniment.

chamber music Music written for a small group of instruments, with one player to a part.

chanson French for "song." A type of renaissance secular vocal music.

character piece A work portraying a single mood, emotion, or idea.

chorale A German hymn, often used as a unifying theme for a cantata.

chord A combination of three or more tones sounded simultaneously. See also *arpeggio*.

chorus, choir A vocal ensemble consisting of several voice parts with four or five or more singers in each section. Also, a section of the orchestra comprising certain types of instruments, such as a *brass choir*.

chromatic Designating melodic movement by half steps.

chromatic scale The scale containing all twelve tones within the interval of an octave.

church modes A system of eight scales forming the tonal foundation for Gregorian chant and for polyphony up to the Baroque era.

clef sign A sign placed at the beginning of a staff to indicate the exact pitch of the notes.

coda The concluding section of a musical work or individual movement, often leading to a final climax and coupled with an increase in tempo.

codetta The closing theme of the exposition in a sonata-allegro form movement.

concert overture A one-movement self-contained orchestral concert piece, often in sonata-allegro form.

concertino The solo instrument group in a concerto grosso.

concerto A work for one or more solo instruments and orchestra.

concerto grosso A multimovement work for instruments in which a solo group called the *concertino* and a full ensemble called the *ripieno* are pitted against each other.

consonance A quality of an interval, chord, or harmony that imparts a sense of stability, repose, or finality.

continuo See *basso continuo*.

cool jazz A restrained, controlled jazz style that developed during the 1950s.

counterpoint A musical texture consisting of two or more equal and independent melodic lines sounding simultaneously. See also *polyphony*.

countersubject In a fugue, new melodic material stated in counterpoint with the subject.

country and western A form of white popular music derived from the English/Scottish folk tradition of the Appalachian region and from cowboy ballads.

cyclical treatment A unifying technique of long musical works in which the same thematic material recurs in succeeding movements.

D

da capo "From the beginning." Indicates that a piece is to be repeated in its entirety or to a point marked *fine* ("end").

de capo aria An aria in ABA form; the original melody of A may be treated in a virtuosic fashion in the second A section.

development In a general sense, the elaboration of musical material through various procedures. Also, the second section of a movement in sonata-allegro form.

diminution A rhythmic variation in which the original note values of a theme are shortened.

dissonance A quality of an interval, chord, or harmony that gives a sense of tension and movement.

dodecaphony See *twelve-tone technique*.

dominant The fifth note of a given scale or the chord built upon it (dominant chord). It is the note that most actively "seeks" or creates the expectation of the tonic note.

drone A stationary tone or tones of constant pitch played throughout a piece or section of a piece.

dynamics See *volume*.

E

edge blown Describing a woodwind technique in which the player funnels a narrow stream of air to the opposite edge of the mouth hole.

electronic music Music produced by such means as magnetic tape, synthesizer, or computer.

end blown Describing a woodwind technique in which the air is blown into a mouthpiece.

episode In a fugue, a transitional passage based on material derived from the subject or based on new material, leading to a new statement of the subject.

étude A study piece for piano concentrating on a single technical problem.

exposition The first section in sonata-allegro form, containing the statement of the principal themes. Also, the first section in a fugue, in which the principal theme or subject is presented imitatively.

expressionism An artistic school of the early twentieth century that attempted to represent the psychological and emotional experience of modern humanity.

F

fantasia An improvised keyboard piece characterized by virtuosity in composition and performance; popular during the Baroque era. Also, a virtuoso piece for lute; popular during the renaissance.

fermata (⌢) A notational symbol indicating that a note is to be sounded longer than its normal time value, the exact length being left to the discretion of the performer.

figured bass, thorough bass A shorthand method of notating an accompanimental part. Numbers are placed under the bass notes to indicate the intervals to be sounded above the bass notes. See also *basso continuo*.

flat (♭) A notational sign indicating that a pitch is to be lowered by a half step.

form The aspect of music involving the overall structuring and organization of music.

frequency The rate at which a sounding body vibrates, determining the pitch of a musical sound.

front line In jazz bands, the instruments that carry the melodic material.

fugue A type of imitative polyphony based on the development of a single theme or subject.

G

glissando A rapid sliding up or down the scale.

grand opera A type of romantic opera that concentrated on the spectacular elements of the production.

Gregorian chant The music that accompanies the Roman Catholic liturgy, consisting of monophonic, single-line melodies sung without instrumental accompaniment.

H

half step, semi-tone One half of a whole step; the smallest interval in traditional Western music.

harmonic progression A series of harmonies.

harmony A composite sound made up of two or more tones of different pitch that sound simultaneously.

heptatonic scale A seven-tone scale, used in both Western and non-Western music.

heterophony Performance of a single melody by two or more individuals who add their own rhythmic or melodic modifications.

homophony A musical texture in which one voice predominates melodically, the other parts blending into an accompaniment providing harmonic support.

I

idée fixe A single, recurring motive; e.g., in Berlioz's *Symphony Fantastique*, a musical idea representing the hero's beloved that recurs throughout the piece.

imitation The repetition, in close succession and usually at a different pitch level, of a melody by another voice or voices within a contrapuntal texture.

Impressionism A late nineteenth-century artistic movement that sought to capture the visual impression rather than the literal reality of a subject. Also, in music, a style belonging primarily to Claude Debussy, characterized by an emphasis on mood and atmosphere, sensuous tone colors, elegance, and beauty of sound.

improvisation The practice of "making up" music and performing it on the spot without first having written it down.

incidental music Music written to accompany a play.

indeterminacy, aleatory, or chance music Music in which the composer sets out to remove the decision-making process from his or her own control. Chance operations such as throwing dice are employed to obtain a random series of musical events.

interval The distance in pitch between any two tones.

inversion Modification of a theme by reversing the direction of the intervals, with ascending intervals replaced by descending intervals, and vice versa.

K

key Tonality; the relationship of tones to a central tone, the tonic.

key signature The group of sharps or flats placed at the beginning of each staff to indicate which notes are to be raised or lowered a half step. The particular combination of sharps or flats indicates the key of a composition.

L

ledger lines Short horizontal lines added above or below the staff to indicate notes that are too high or too low to be placed within the staff.

legato "Linked, tied." Indicating a smooth, even style of performance, with each note connected to the next.

leitmotif "Leading motive." A musical motive representing a particular character, object, idea, or emotional state. Used especially in Wagner's operas.

libretto The text of an opera or similar extended dramatic musical work.

Lied, Lieder "Song." See *art song*.

lyric opera A type of French romantic opera that relied on beautiful melodies for its effect.

M

madrigal A polyphonic vocal piece set to a short poem; it originated during the renaissance.

major scale A scale having a pattern of whole and half steps, with the half steps falling between the third and fourth and between the seventh and eighth tones of the scale.

Mass The most solemn service of the Roman Catholic Church. The parts of the Mass most frequently set to music are the Kyrie, Gloria, Credo, Sanctus and Benedictus, and Agnus Dei.

mazurka In romantic music, a small piano piece based on the Polish dance form. Prominent in the works of Chopin.

measure A unit of time organization consisting of a fixed number of beats. Measures are separated from one another by vertical bar lines on the staff.

measured rhythm Regulated rhythm in which precise time values are related to each other.

melismatic Designating a melodic phrase in which one syllable of text is spread over several notes.

melody A basic musical element consisting of a series of pitches of particular duration that sound one after another.

meter The organization of rhythmic pulses or beats into equal, recurring groups.

microtone An interval smaller than a half step.

minimalism A late-twentieth-century movement that seeks to return music to its simplest, most basic elements.

minor scale A scale having a pattern of whole and half steps, with the half steps falling between the second and third and between the sixth and seventh tones of the scale.

minuet and trio A form employed in the third movement of classical symphonies, cast in a stately triple meter and ternary form (ABA).

modulation Gradual or rapid change from one key to another within a composition.

monodic style Designates a type of accompanied solo song that evolved in Italy around 1600 in reaction to the complex polyphonic style of the late renaissance. Its principal characteristics are (1) a recitativelike vocal line, and (2) an arioso with basso continuo accompaniment.

monophony A musical texture consisting of a single melodic line without accompanying material, as in Gregorian chant.

motet A polyphonic choral work set to a sacred text.

motive A short melodic or rhythmic figure that reappears frequently throughout a work or section of a work as a unifying device.

movement An independent section of a longer composition.

musique concrète "Concrete music." A musical style originating in France about 1948; its technique consists of recording natural or "concrete" sounds, altering the sounds by various electronic means, and then combining them into organized pieces.

N

natural (♮) A notational symbol indicating that a pitch that has been sharped or flatted is to be restored to its basic pitch.

neoclassicism In music of the early twentieth century, the philosophy that musical composition should be approached with objectivity and restraint. Neoclassical composers were attracted to the textures and forms of the Baroque and Classical periods.

nocturne "Night piece." A character piece for piano, of melancholy moods, with expressive melodies sounding over an arpeggiated accompaniment.

O

octave An interval between two pitches in which the higher pitch vibrates at twice the frequency of the lower. When sounded simultaneously, the two pitches sound very much alike.

opera A drama set to music and made up of vocal pieces such as recitatives, arias, duets, trios, and ensembles with orchestral accompaniment, and orchestral overtures and interludes. Scenery, stage action, and costuming are employed.

opera buffa Italian comic opera.

opéra comique (comic opera) A type of French romantic opera distinguished by its use of spoken dialogue rather than sung recitative. Many operas in this form had serious plots.

opera seria Italian opera with a serious (i.e., noncomic) subject.

oratorio An extended choral work made up of recitatives, arias, and choruses, *without* costuming, stage action, or scenery.

orchestration The arrangement of a musical composition for performance by an orchestra. Also, utilization of orchestral instruments for expressive and structural purposes.

organum The earliest type of medieval polyphonic music.

ostinato A musical phrase repeated persistently, usually at the same pitch.

overture The orchestral introduction to a musical dramatic work.

P

passion A musical setting of the story of the suffering and crucifixion of Jesus Christ.

pedal point A long-held tone, usually in the bass, sounding through changing harmonies in other parts.

pentatonic scale A five-tone scale. Various pentatonic scales are commonly employed in non-Western music.

phrase A musical unit consisting of several measures.

pitch The highness or lowness of a musical tone, determined by the frequency of vibration of the sounding body.

pizzicato A performance technique in which stringed instruments such as the violin are plucked with the fingers instead of bowed.

plainsong, plainchant See *Gregorian chant.*

pointillism A term borrowed from the visual arts and used to describe a melodic line made from isolated tones or chords.

polonaise In romantic music, a small piano piece based on the Polish dance form.

polyphony Many voices. A texture combining two or more independent melodies heard simultaneously; generally synonymous with counterpoint.

polyrhythm Two or more contrasting and independent rhythms used at the same time.

polytonality The simultaneous use of two or more different keys.

prelude A free-form piece that may introduce another piece or stand alone.

primitivism In music, the use of frenzied, irregular rhythms and percussive effects to evoke a feeling of primitive power, as in Stravinsky's *The Rite of Spring.*

program music Instrumental music associated with a nonmusical idea, this idea often being stated in the title or in an explanatory program note.

R

raga One of the ancient melodic patterns employed in Indian music.

ragtime A composed music of the 1890s, usually for piano, characterized by steady, marchlike accompaniment in the left hand and a decorated syncopated melody in the right hand.

rap A style of contemporary popular music that employs a spoken text delivered over a static drumbeat. Originated in the mid-1970s in New York, this style came to national attention in the mid-1980s.

recapitulation The third section of sonata-allegro form, which restates the entire exposition in the tonic key.

recitative A form of "singing speech" in which the rhythm is dictated by the natural inflection of the words.

rest A notational sign denoting the duration of silence.

retrograde A melody read backwards, beginning with the last note and ending with the first.

rhythm The element of music that encompasses all aspects of musical time.

rhythm and blues A form of black popular music that blends elements of jazz and the blues.

rhythm section In jazz bands, the instruments that supply the harmonic and rhythmic accompaniment.

ricercar A type of renaissance lute music, often polyphonic, that demonstrated the virtuosity of the performer.

riff A short melodic line, usually rhythmic, that can be repeated over and over to form either the main melody or the background for improvised solos.

ripieno The full ensemble in a concerto grosso.

ritornello "Return." A characteristic form for the first and sometimes the last movement of the baroque concerto grosso. The thematic material given to the ripieno returns between the passages played by the soloists.

rock 'n' roll (rock) Popular music characterized by a heavy beat, electronically amplified instruments, simple melodies, and often using elements from country music and the blues.

rondo An extended alternating form often employed in the fourth movement of classical symphonies; generally spirited and playful in character.

rubato "Robbed." A term indicating that a performer may treat the tempo with a certain amount of freedom, shortening the duration of some beats and correspondingly lengthening others.

S

scale The arrangement of adjacent tones in an order of ascending or descending pitches.

scherzo "Joke." A sprightly, humorous instrumental piece, swift in tempo; developed by Beethoven to replace the minuet.

secco recitative A recitative with only continuo accompaniment.

serialism See *twelve-tone technique*.

sharp (♯) A notational sign indicating that a pitch is to be raised by a half step.

sinfonia A short instrumental introduction to a baroque choral work.

singspiel German comic opera that employed spoken dialogue.

solo concerto A multimovement baroque work differing from concerto grosso in that the concertino consists of only one instrument (most often the violin or piano).

solo sonata A sonata for one instrument with continuo accompaniment.

sonata An instrumental work consisting of three or four contrasting movements.

sonata-allegro form A musical form encompassing one movement of a composition and consisting of three sections—exposition, development, and recapitulation—the last often followed by a coda.

sonata da camera "Chamber sonata." A baroque instrumental work, essentially a dance suite.

sonata da chiesa "Church sonata." A baroque instrumental work in four movements (slow-fast-slow-fast).

song cycle A series of art songs that tell a story.

soul A spirited, raw-edged form of rock music that features wailing vocals and hard-driving rhythm and brass sections.

sprechstimme "Speech voice." A vocal technique in which a pitch is half sung, half spoken. Developed by Arnold Schoenberg.

staccato "Detached." Indicating a style of performance in which each note is played in a short, crisp manner.

staff A graph, consisting of five lines and four intermediate spaces, on which music is notated.

stopping Changing the pitch of, for example, a violin string by pressing the string against the fingerboard.

stretto A type of imitation in which each successive voice enters before the phrase is completed in the previous voice; usually employed in fugues or fugal textures.

stride A jazz piano style in which the left hand alternates between a bass note and a chord played an octave or more above the bass, giving the effect of "striding" back and forth, while the right hand plays the melody.

string quartet A chamber ensemble consisting of a first and a second violin, a viola, and a cello. Also, the form which is a sonata for these instruments.

strophic Designating a song in which all verses of text are sung to the same music.

style Broadly, the manner of expression that distinguishes a particular work, composer, historical period, or artistic school.

subject In a fugue, the principal theme, introduced first in a single voice and then imitated in other voices, returning frequently during the course of the composition.

suite A series of instrumental movements, each based on a particular dance rhythm.

syllabic Designating a musical phrase in which each syllable of text is given one note.

symphonic poem See *tone poem*.

symphony A sonata for orchestra.

syncopation A deliberate disturbance of the normal metrical pulse, produced by shifting the accent from a normally strong beat to a weak beat.

T

tala One of the ancient rhythmic patterns employed in Indian music.

tempo The speed at which a piece of music moves.

ternary form A basic musical form consisting of three sections—ABA—the final A section being a repetition or slight variation of the first.

texture The relationship between the horizontal (melodic) and vertical (harmonic) aspects of a piece of music. The principal classifications are monophony, homophony, and polyphony.

theme A musical idea that serves as a starting point for development of a composition or section of a composition.

theme and variations A form based on a single theme and its subsequent repetition, with each new statement varied in some way from the original.

theme transformation The practice of varying a single theme or melody through the different sections of a piece; this procedure was used especially in romantic tone poems.

thorough bass See *figured bass.*

through-composed A term applied to songs in which new music is used for each successive verse.

time signature A numerical sign placed at the beginning of a composition to indicate the meter.

toccata A baroque keyboard piece full of scale passages, rapid runs and trills, and massive chords.

tonality The relationship of tones to a central tone called the tonic. See also *key.*

tone A pitch having a steady, constant frequency.

tone cluster A chord produced by playing a large group of adjacent notes on the piano with the flat of the hand. The resulting sound is dense and indistinct.

tone color, timbre The characteristic quality, or "color," of a musical sound as produced by a specific instrument or voice, or by a combination of instruments.

tone poem, symphonic poem A single-movement programmatic work, relatively long and very free in form, usually involving a dramatic plot or literary idea.

tone row (series, set) See *twelve-tone technique.*

tonic The tonal center. The tone that acts as a musical home base, or point of rest and finality, in a piece of music.

total serialism The complete, predetermined, and ultrarational systemization of every aspect of a composition: pitch, tempo, dynamics, articulations, and timbre.

transcription An arrangement of a composition for a medium other than that for which it was originally written.

tremolo A "trembling" effect produced on string instruments when the bow is moved rapidly back and forth across the strings.

trio sonata A sonata for two instruments with continuo accompaniment.

tritonic scale A three-tone scale, generally used in non-Western music.

twelve-tone technique, serialism, dodecaphony A system of composition developed by Arnold Schoenberg that consists of arranging the twelve pitches of the chromatic scale in a particular order (known as a tone row, series, or set).

V

verismo "Realism." An Italian operatic point of view favoring realistic subjects taken from everyday, often lower class, life.

vibrato A slight fluctuation in pitch that increases the "warmth" of a tone.

voice (voice part) A melodic line, either vocal or instrumental, in a contrapuntal piece such as a fugue.

volume (dynamics) Relative degrees of loudness or softness.

W

whole tone scale The scale in which the octave is divided into six consecutive whole steps.

word painting Representation of the literal meaning of a text through musical means.

ILLUSTRATORS

A-R Editions

Examples 2.5, 8.10, 8.11, 8.12, 8.13, 8.14, 8.15, 8.16, 13.1, 15.7, 15.16, 15.18, 16.1, 16.2, 16.3, 16.4, 16.5, 16.6, 16.14, 16.17, 16.19, 18.2, 18.11, 18.12, 18.13, 18.14, 18.15, 18.16, 19.4, 20.11, 20.12, 20.13, 20.14, 21.1, 21.2, 21.3, 21.4, 21.5, 21.6, 21.7, 21.8, 21.9, 21.10, 21.11, 21.12, 21.13, 22.1, Text Art 1.8, p. 11; 15.2, p. 322; 22.1, p. 513.

Rolin Graphics

Figures 4.1, 4.2, 5.4.

PHOTOS

Part Openers

1: © 1992, Michael Krasowitz, FPG International Corp.; **2:** © 1992, Keith Gunnar, FPG International Corp.; **4:** *The Lute Player,* Orazio Gentileschi, National Gallery of Art, Washington; Ailsa Mellon Bruce Fund.; **5:** North Wind Picture Archives; **8:** © 1992, Art Montes De Oca, FPG International Corp.; **9:** © Joe Sohm, *Bach in Space,* The Image Works; **10:** © Brock May, Photo Researchers, Inc.

Chapter 4

P. 30: © Beth Bergman 1992; **p. 32:** Courtesy IMG Artists, photograph by Christian Steiner; **p. 33:** Courtesy Sony Classical; **p. 33:** Courtesy Jane Davis, Inc. Artists Management, Newtown, Connecticut; **p. 34:** The Bettmann Archive; **p. 35:** © Wm. C. Brown. Photograph by James L. Shaffer; **p. 34:** © Topham/The Image Works; **p. 36:** Courtesy IMG Artists, photograph by Nick Sangiamo; **p. 36:** © James Shaffer; **p. 36:** © James Shaffer; **p. 37:** Courtesy Frank Salomon Associates, New York; **p. 37:** © James Shaffer; **p. 37:** Courtesy Fox Products; **p. 38:** © Steve Lanava, courtesy Worcester *Telegram and Gazette;* **p. 39:** Courtesy Stanton Consulting and Management, Astoria, New York; **p. 39:** © Martin Reichenthal/Gurtman and Murtha Assoc.; **fig. 4.3:** Courtesy Ludwig Industries; **p. 42:** Jan Lukas/Photo Researchers, Inc.; **p. 43:** Courtesy IMG Artists, photograph by Christian Steiner; **p. 43:** © Blair Seitz, Photo Researchers; **p. 44:** © Photographer Jack Mitchell, Juilliard String Quartet, New York; **p. 49:** Reuters/Bettmann.

Chapter 5

P. 56: H. Armstrong Roberts; **p. 57:** Courtesy of the Laura Boulton Collection, Archives of Traditional Music, Indiana University; **fig. 5.5:** Tom Cheek/Stock Boston; **fig. 5.6:** Copyright Marc & Evelyn Bernheim/Woodfin Camp; **fig. 5.7:** Copyright Marc & Evelyn Bernheim/Woodfin Camp.

Prelude I

P. 80: Scala/Art Resource, New York; **p. 81:** Scala/ Art Resource, New York; **p. 82:** © Ciccione/Photo Researchers; **p. 83:** Hirmer Verlag; **p. 84:** Scala/Art Resource, New York; **p. 85:** © Hieronymus Bosch/Archive/Photo Researchers.

Chapter 6

P. 90: Bob Coyle; **p. 95:** The Bettmann Archive; **p. 101:** Scala/Art Resource, New York; **p. 103:** Historical Pictures Service, Inc.

Prelude II

P. 111: Scala/Art Resource, New York; **p. 112:** Scala/Art Resource, New York; **p. 113:** The Metropolitan Museum of Art; Harris Brisbane Dick Fund, 1946. (46.160); **p. 114 (Bernini):** Scala/Art Resource, New York; **p. 114 (Borromini):** Scala/Art Resource, New York; **p. 115 (Rembrandt):** © Stadelsches Kunstinstitut, Frankfurt, West Germany; **p. 215 (Versailles opera house):** Scala/Art Resource, New York.

Chapter 7

Fig. 7.1: The Bettmann Archive.

Chapter 8

P. 145: The Bettmann Archive, 017.06, Three Lions, Inc.; **p. 148:** Historical Pictures Service, Inc.

Prelude III

P. 167: Art Resource, New York; **p. 169:** Scala/Art Resource.

Chapter 9

Fig. 9.3: North Wind Picture Archives; **fig. 9.4:** North Wind Picture Archives; **p. 187:** © The Bettmann Archive.

Chapter 10

P. 207: © Beth Bergman, 1992.

Chapter 11

Fig. 11.1: Historical Pictures Service, Inc.; **fig. 11.2:** Historical Pictures Services, Chicago.

Prelude IV

P. 245: Vanni/Art Resource, New York; **p. 247:** The Tate Gallery, London/Art Resource, New York; **p. 249:** © Gustave Courbet/Archiv/Photo Researchers.

Chapter 12

Fig. 12.1: © 1991, Historical Pictures Service; **fig. 12.2:** The Bettmann Archive; **fig. 12.3:** The Bettmann Archive; **fig. 12.4:** The Bettmann Archive; **fig. 12.5:** The Bettmann Archive.

Chapter 13

Fig. 13.2: Historical Pictures Service, Inc.; **fig. 13.4:** North Wind Picture Archives; **fig. 13.5:** © San Francisco Ballet Archives, SF Performing Arts Library Museum.

Chapter 14

Fig. 14.1: North Wind Picture Archives; **fig. 14.2:** Copyright Topham/The Image Works, Inc.; **fig. 14.3:** The Bettmann Archive.

Chapter 15

Fig. 15.1: Historical Pictures Service, Inc. © Winnie Klotz/Metropolitan Opera, New York; **fig. 15.2:** Historical Pictures Service.

Chapter 16

Fig. 16.1: Historical Pictures Service, Inc.; **fig. 16.2:** The Bettmann Archive, photo by Ron Scherl; **fig. 16.3:** Historical Pictures Service, Inc.; **fig. 16.4:** Historical Pictures Service, Inc.; **fig. 16.5:** Northwind Picture Archives; **fig. 16.6:** Northwind Picture Archives.

Prelude V

P. 367: Scala/Art Resource, New York.

Chapter 17

Fig. 17.1: Historical Pictures Service.

Chapter 18

Fig. 18.1: Scala/Art Resource, New York; **fig. 18.2:** Historical Pictures; **fig. 18.3:** Historical Pictures Service; **fig. 18.4:** The Bettmann Archive.

Chapter 19

Fig. 19.1: Historical Pictures Service, Inc.; **fig. 19.2:** Historical Pictures Service; **fig. 19.3:** The Bettmann Archive.

Prelude VI

P. 444: Art Resource, New York.

Chapter 20

Fig. 20.1: Historical Pictures Service, Inc.; **p. 449:** © James L. Shaffer; **fig. 20.3:** The Bettmann Archive; **fig. 20.4:** Courtesy William Grant Still Music; **fig. 20.5:** © Barcellona/Shooting Star; **fig. 20.6:** Courtesy Michael Seeger.

Prelude VII

P. 490: Courtesy of AT&T Archives.

Chapter 21

Fig. 21.1: © Gontier/The Image Works; **fig. 21.2:** Milton Babbitt, Princeton University; **fig. 21.3:** © Michael Weisbrot/Stock Boston; **fig. 21.4:** Michael Ochs Archive; **fig. 21.5:** The Bettmann Archive; **fig. 21.6:** Andrew Hopper/Picture Group; **fig. 21.7:** Howard Frank, Personality Photos, Inc.; **fig. 21.8:** © Cori Wells Braun.

Chapter 22

Fig. 22.1: Fred Tyon/Photo Researchers, Inc.; **fig. 22.2:** Institute of Jazz Studios, Rutger's University; **fig. 22.3:** Michael Ochs Archives; **fig. 22.4:** UPI/Bettmann Newsphotos; **fig. 22.5:** Michael Ochs Archives; **fig. 22.6:** Tadder/Archive Photos; **fig. 22.7:** © Barboza/Shooting Star; **fig. 22.8:** Institute of Jazz Studies, Rutgers University; **fig. 22.9:** Jon Chase/Stock Boston; **fig. 22.10:** Ray Avery, Jazz Archives; **fig. 22.11:** © Yoram Kahana/Shooting Star; **fig. 22.12:** © Dagmar/Shooting Star; **fig. 22.13:** © Topham/The Image Works, Inc.; **fig. 22.14:** © Thom Elder/Shooting Star; **fig. 22.15:** © Lester Cohen/Shooting Star; **fig. 22.16:** © Yoram Kahana/Shooting Star; **fig. 22.17:** © Topham/The Image Works; **fig. 22.18:** © Raul De Molina/Shooting Star; **fig. 22.19:** © Conrad Collette/Shooting Star; **fig. 22.20:** Shooting Star.

Disco, 533
Dissonance, 15, 117, 385
Diversity, 18, 497
Divertimento, 186, 188
Divertimento (Zwilich), 503
Divertimento for String Orchestra (Bartók), 394
Dixieland, 516–17
Djamileh (Bizet), 330
Dodds, J., 518
Dodecaphony, 418
Dogon, 63
Dohnanyi, E., 393
Dominant chord, 17
Dominant key, 172
Domino, F., 528
Dona nobis, 204–5
Donatello, 78
Don Carlos (Verdi), 332
Don Giovanni (Mozart), 177, 205
Donizetti, G., 331
Don Juan (Byron), 243
Donno, 67
Don Quixote (Strauss), 302, 303
Dorsey, T., 522
Dot, 10
Double bass, 31, 33
Double Concerto in A Minor (Brahms), 271
Double Quartet for Strings (Zwilich), 503
Double reed, 35
Down-beat, 20
Drone, 54
Druckman, J., 495
Drum, 61
Drumroll (Symphony no. 103) (Haydn), 186
Drums, 41, 66, 68, 72
Dudevant, A., 263
Dufay, G., 94, 96
Dumas, A., 263, 333
Dumbarton Oaks Concerto in E-flat (Stravinsky), 388
Dunbar, P. L., 461
Dundun, 67
Duos, 45
Duple meter, 19
Durand, A., 436
Duration, 4, 9–10, 14
Durey, L., 380
Dvořák, A., 45, 48, 315, 318–24, 326–27, 354, 454
Dying Slave, The (Michelangelo), 86
Dylan, B., 515, 531, 532, 534
Dynamics, 11
    of classical music, 195
    notation of, 11
    of romantic, 360
    of twentieth-century, 431

E

Early Sunday Morning (Hopper), 446
Easter Sunday, 135
Ecstasy of St. Theresa, 109, 114
Edgar (Puccini), 340

Edge blown, 35
1812 Overture (Tchaikovsky), 286
Eighth note, 9
Ein Deutsches Requiem (Brahms), 271, 356–60
"Ein' Feste Burg Ist Unser Gott" (Luther), 134
Einstein on the Beach (Glass), 496
El amor brujo (de Falla), 314
Eldridge, R., 515
Electoral Court, 125
Electric Band, 527
Electric jazz, 526–27
Electronic, 494–95
Electronic instruments, 30, 44
Electronic Studies I and II (Stockhausen), 494
Elegy (Blake), 403
Elements
    musical, 13–22
    in non-western music, 53–54
    of style of Beethoven, 222–31
Elijah (Mendelssohn), 279, 354
Ellington, E. (Duke), 520–21
Emerson, R. W., 437
Emerson, Lake, and Palmer, 533
Encyclopédia, 165
End blown, 38
Endless melody, 350
English horn, 35, 36, 38
English Suites (Bach), 150
Engravings (Debussy), 377
Ensembles, 44–49, 103, 431
Episodes, 145
Erlkönig (Schubert), 30, 256–60
Eroica (Beethoven), 222
Esoteric music, 63
Essay on Musical Esthetics, 175
Estampes (Debussy), 377
Este, R., 480
Este palace, 101
Esterhazy, P. A., 185, 186, 187
Esther (Handel), 125
Ethnic music, 52
Études, 262
Eugene Onegin (Tchaikovsky), 285
Euphonium, 40
Eurydice, 119
Eve, 85
"Ev'ry Valley" (Handel), 13, 14
Ewe drum orchestra, 67–68, 69
Experimenters, 467–68
Exposition, 144, 172–73, 178–80, 183, 188
Expressionism, 417–20, 478

F

Fabian, 529
Fabulous Thunderbirds, 534
Facsimile (Bernstein), 498
Fair Maid of Perth, The (Bizet), 330
Fallen Woman, The (Verdi), 332, 333–39
Fall of an Avalanche in the Grisons, The (Turner), 247
False recapitulation, 273
Falstaff (Verdi), 332

Fancy Free (Bernstein), 498
Fanfare for the Common Man (Copland), 464
Fantaisie in F Minor (Chopin), 263
Fantasia, 102, 144, 263
Fantasiestücke (Fantasy Pieces) (Schumann), 261
Farewell (Symphony no. 45) (Haydn), 186
Fauré, G., 45, 356, 375
Faust (Gounod), 329
Faust et Heline (Boulanger), 381
Fauves, 365
Fearful Symmetries (Adams), 497
Felix, N., 35
Fermata, 21
Feste Romane (Respighi), 314
Festivals (Debussy), 377
Fetes (Debussy), 377
Fidelio (Beethoven), 219, 222
Fifth String Quartet (Bartók), 394, 395
Fifth Symphony (Shostakovitch), 412
Figured bass, 117
Fillmore East and Fillmore West, 531
Fine, V., 468
Fingal's Cave (The Hebrides) (Mendelssohn), 278, 279, 283
Fingerboard, 31
Finger holes, 35
Firebird, The (Stravinsky), 387
Fitzgerald, E., 513, 518
Five, Russian, 309, 387
Five Piano Pieces (Schoenberg), 421
Flageolets, 72
Flags, 10
Flat, 8
Florence, 78–79, 81
Flute, 35, 36, 38, 68, 72
Flying Dutchman, The (Wagner), 348
Folk music, 52, 53, 55–72
Folk-rock, 531, 532
Fontane di Roma (Respighi), 314
Force of Destiny, The (Verdi), 332
Form, 26
Formal innovations, of romantic, 360
Formal structures, of classical, 195
Forte, 11
Fortissimo, 11
Foster, S., 437, 450, 451
Fountains (Ravel), 380
Fountains of Rome, The (Respighi), 314
4'33" (Cage), 493
Four-movement plan of sonata, 172
Four Seasons, The (Vivaldi), 154–57, 159–60, 191
Four Sections, The (Reich), 497
Four Temperaments, The (Hindemith), 411
"Fourth of July" (Montes de Oca), 435
Fragonard, J.-H., 165, 169
Franck, C., 375
Franck, J., 184
Franklin, A., 515, 530, 531
Franklin, B., 448
Free jazz, 525–26
Freeshooter, The (Weber), 347
French opera, 329–30
French Revolution, 164–66, 219, 242

TWENTIETH CENTURY

MUSICAL EVENTS	DATES	COMPOSERS
	1900	Jean Sibelius (1865–1957)
		Erik Satie (1866–1925)
		Ralph Vaughan Williams (1872–1958)
German expressionism, represented chiefly by Schoenberg and Berg, developed before World War I		Arnold Schoenberg (1874–1951)
		Charles Ives (1874–1954)
		Maurice Ravel (1875–1937)
		Manuel de Falla (1876–1946)
		Ottorino Respighi (1879–1936)
		Béla Bartók (1881–1945)
		Zoltán Kodály (1882–1967)
Stravinsky's *The Rite of Spring* (1913)		Igor Stravinsky (1882–1971)
Schoenberg announces his method of composing with twelve tones (1922)		Anton von Webern (1883–1945)
		Charles T. Griffes (1884–1920)
First performance of Gershwin's *Rhapsody in Blue* (1924)		Alban Berg (1885–1935)
American jazz influences composers in the 1920s	**1925**	Wallingford Riegger (1885–1961)
N.Y. Philharmonic Orchestra first broadcast over radio (1928)		Edgard Varèse (1885–1965)
		Sergei Prokofiev (1891–1953)
		Darius Milhaud (1892–1974)
		Lili Boulanger (1893–1918)
		Paul Hindemith (1895–1963)
First performance of Ives's Second Piano Sonata (1939)		Virgil Thomson (b. 1896)
Many European composers emigrate to the United States during the 1930s and early 1940s, including Schoenberg, Stravinsky, Hindemith, and Bartók		Roger Sessions (1896–1985)
		Henry Cowell (1897–1965)
		George Gershwin (1898–1937)
		Roy Harris (1898–1979)
		Aaron Copland (1900–1990)
Copland's *Appalachian Spring* choreographed by Martha Graham (1944)		Ruth Crawford Seeger (1901–1953)
		Miriam Gideon (b. 1906)
Early experiments in electronic music; development of *musique concrète* in Paris (1948)		Elizabeth Lutyens (1906–1983)
		Dimitri Shostakovich (1906–1975)
Introduction of long-playing records (1948)		Olivier Messiaen (1908–1992)
American experiments in electronic music at Columbia	**1950**	Elliott Carter (b. 1908)
University (1952)		Howard Swanson (1907–1978)
		Samuel Barber (1910–1981)
		William Schuman (1910–1992)
John Cage develops chance music in the 1950s		Gian Carlo Menotti (b. 1911)
Stockhausen's *Gesang der Junglinge* (1956)		John Cage (1912–1992)
Boulez's *Improvisations sur Mallarmê* (1958)		
Terry Riley's *In C,* first major minimalist work (1964)		
John Corigliano's *Tournaments Overture* (1965)		
Druckman's *Animus* Series (1966)		Hugo Weisgall (b. 1912)
Rochberg's Third Symphony, using technique of collage (1968)		Benjamin Britten (1913–1976)
Leonard Bernstein's *Mass* is opening work at Kennedy Center		Milton Babbitt (b. 1916)
in Washington, D.C. (1972)		Ulysses Kay (b. 1917)
		George Rochberg (b. 1918)
		Leonard Bernstein (1918–1990)
Milton Babbitt's *Phonemena* (1974)		Lukas Foss (b. 1922)
Dominick Argento's *From the Diary of Virginia Woolf* wins	**1975**	
Pulitzer Prize (1975)		György Ligeti (b. 1923)
Philip Glass's *Einstein on the Beach* (opera) (1975)		Pierre Boulez (b. 1925)
Krzysztof Penderecki's *Paradise Lost* (opera) (1976)		Gunther Schuller (b. 1925)
Miriam Gideon's *Songs of Youth and Madness* (1977)		Karlheinz Stockhausen (b. 1928)
Ex-Beatle John Lennon murdered (1980)	**1980**	Jacob Druckman (b. 1928)
Digital recordings become widely marketed (1980)		George Crumb (b. 1929)
One-hundredth anniversary of Metropolitan Opera House,		Terry Riley (b. 1935)
New York (1983)		Steve Reich (b. 1936)
Introduction of compact discs (CDs) (1983)		LaMonte Young (b. 1935)
Michael Tippett's *The Mask of Time* (oratorio) (1984)		Philip Glass (b. 1937)
Peter Maxwell Davies's *Third Symphony* (1985)		John Corigliano (b. 1938)
Live Aid concert for Ethiopian famine relief (1985)		Ellen Taafe Zwillich (b. 1939)
Pianist Vladimir Horowitz returns to Russia for a recital (1986)		John Adams (b. 1947)
John Adams's *Nixon in China* (1987)		
Pianist Vladmir Horowitz dies (1990)	**1990**	Wynton Marsalis (b. 1961)
Leonard Bernstein dies (1990)		
Dancer Martha Graham dies (1991)		

CULTURAL EVENTS ARTISTS AND WRITERS	DATES	WORLD EVENTS POLITICAL LEADERS

MIDDLE AGES AND RENAISSANCE

CULTURAL EVENTS	DATES	WORLD EVENTS
Gothic cathedrals begun (St. Denis, Paris, 1144; Chartres, 1145)	**1100**	
	1150	
	1200	Magna Carta signed by King John (1215)
	1250	Marco Polo leaves for Cathay (1271)
Dante's *Divine Comedy* (1307)	**1300**	Hundred Years' War begins (1337)
Chaucer's *Canterbury Tales* (1386)	**1350**	
Botticelli (1444–1510)	**1400**	Battle of Agincourt (1415)
Gutenberg Bible (1456)	**1450**	Fall of Constantinople (1453)
Michelangelo (1475–1564)		Columbus discovers America (1492)
Raphael (1483–1520)		
St. Peter's begun in Rome (1506)	**1500**	Henry VIII King of England (1509)
		Martin Luther's ninety-five theses (1517)
		Council of Trent (1545–1563)
	1550	Elizabeth I Queen of England (1558)
		Spanish Armada defeated (1588)

BAROQUE

CULTURAL EVENTS	DATES	WORLD EVENTS
El Greco (1541–1614)		
William Shakespeare (1564–1616)		
Caravaggio (1573–1610)		
Peter Paul Rubens (1577–1640)		
Francesco Borromini (1599–1667)	**1600**	Jamestown settled (1607)
Cervantes, part I of *Don Quixote* (1605)		Thirty Years' War begins (1618)
Rembrandt van Rijn (1606–1669)		Mayflower Compact (1620)
Giovanni Lorenzo Bernini's *Ecstasy of St. Theresa* (1644)		Louis XIV King of France (1643)
Samuel Pepys's *Diary* (1660)	**1650**	Restoration of Charles II in England (1660)
John Milton's *Paradise Lost* (1667)		Reign of Peter the Great begins (1682)
Christopher Wren begins St. Paul's Cathedral (1675)		Salem witchcraft trials (1692)
Isaac Newton's *Principia Mathematica* (1687)	**1700**	War of the Spanish Succession begins (1702)
		Reign of Louis XV begins (1715)
Jonathan Swift's *Gulliver's Travels* (1726)		Age of Enlightened Despots (1740–1796)

CLASSICAL

CULTURAL EVENTS	DATES	WORLD EVENTS
Francisco Goya (1746–1828)		
Jacques Louis David (1748–1825)		
Pompeii rediscovered (1748)	**1750**	Franklin's discoveries in electricity (1752)
Voltaire's *Candide* (1759)		Seven Years' War; French and Indian War (1756)
William Wordsworth (1770–1850)		Beginnings of the Industrial Revolution (ca. 1770)
J.M.W. Turner (1775–1851)		American Declaration of Independence (1776)
Immanuel Kant's *Critique of Pure Reason* (1781)		French Revolution begins (1789)
Thomas Malthus's *Essay on Population* (1798)		Bill of Rights (1791)
Eugene Delacroix (1798–1863)		Eli Whitney's cotton gin (1793)
Goethe's *Faust, Part I* (1808)	**1800**	Louisiana Purchase (1803)
Jane Austen's *Pride and Prejudice* (1813)		Battle of Waterloo (1815)

ROMANTIC

CULTURAL EVENTS	DATES	WORLD EVENTS
Edgar Allan Poe (1809–1849)		
Goya's *Witches' Sabbath* (1815)		
Herman Melville (1818–1891)		Monroe Doctrine (1823)
Shelley's *Prometheus Unbound* (1820)	**1825**	Erie Canal opened (1825)
Victor Hugo's *Hernani* (1830)		July Revolution in France (1830)
Claude Monet (1840–1926)		Invention of telegraph (1832)
Ralph Waldo Emerson's *Essays* (1841)		Queen Victoria's reign begins (1837)
Alexander Dumas's *Count of Monte Cristo* (1845)		California Gold Rush; revolutions in Europe (1848)
Karl Marx's *Communist Manifesto* (1848)		
Harriet Beecher Stowe's *Uncle Tom's Cabin* (1852)	**1850**	Opening of Japan to the West (1853)
Vincent van Gogh (1853–1890)		American Civil War begins (1861)
Charles Darwin's *Origin of Species* (1859)		Emancipation Proclamation (1863)
Leo Tolstoy's *War and Peace* (1865)		Civil War ends; Lincoln assassinated (1865)
Karl Marx's *Das Kapital* (1867)		Franco-Prussian War begins (1870)
Henri Matisse (1869–1954)	**1875**	Invention of telephone, internal combustion engine (1876)
Pablo Picasso (1881–1973)		Irish Insurrection (1880)
Friedrich Nietzsche's *Thus Spake Zarathustra* (1883)		Wilhelm II, last Kaiser of Germany, crowned (1888)
Mark Twain's *Huckleberry Finn* (1883)		Nicholas II, last Czar of Russia, crowned (1894)
Brooklyn Bridge built (1883)		Dreyfus Affair (1894–1905)
Eiffel Tower completed (1889)		Spanish-American War (1898)
		Boer War (1899)